everything in past tense.

WITHDRAWN
UTSA LIBRARIES

AGING AND
MENTAL DISORDERS

AGING AND MENTAL DISORDERS

Psychological Approaches to Assessment and Treatment

STEVEN H. ZARIT
Andrus Gerontology Center
University of Southern California

With a Chapter by Robert M. Tager

THE FREE PRESS
A Division of Macmillan Publishing Co., Inc.
NEW YORK

Collier Macmillan Publishers
LONDON

The Free Press
A *Division of Macmillan Publishing Co., Inc.*
866 Third Avenue, New York, N.Y. 10022

Collier Macmillan Canada, Ltd.

Library of Congress Catalog Card Number: 79–6768

Printed in the United States of America

printing number

1   2   3   4   5   6   7   8   9   10

Library of Congress Cataloging in Publication Data

Zarit, Steven H
    Aging and mental disorders.

    Bibliography: p.
    Includes index.
    1. Geriatric psychiatry.   I. Title.
RC451.4.A5Z37   618.97'689   79–6768
ISBN 0–02–935850–7

For My Parents

Contents

Acknowledgments

I HAVE ALWAYS FELT that authors are excessively modest in their acknowledgments, but my experience in working on this book during the past two years has taught me to appreciate the substantial contributions of other people. In citing those who have been most helpful to me during this period, I recognize how indebted I am to each of them.

This project was initially suggested to me by Ron Chambers, Senior Editor of The Free Press. Without his enthusiasm and support I would still be working on the first chapter. I received help in developing the concept and plans for this book from Patricia Alpaugh, who was to be coauthor, but unfortunately had to withdraw from the project. The framework and scope of the book owes much to her.

I have been fortunate in the last few years to have worked with several exceptional students in the Leonard Davis School of Gerontology and the Department of Psychology of the University of Southern California. Through their own struggles they have challenged me and helped me broaden my horizons. I would especially like to mention those with whom I have worked closest: Julie Bach-Peterson, Gary Baffa, Mariette Baldwin, Francoise Becker, Karen Berger, Deborah Cherry, Nan Corby, Dolores Gallagher, Becky Guider, Nan Kramer, Diane Oeffler, Kathleen Peters, Christine Piatt, Karen Reever, Richard Southern, Lynne Steinman, Judy Weston, and Anita Woods. I am particularly grateful to Kenneth Cole for his assistance in the research for this book.

Most of the clinical examples that appear here have been drawn from work done at the Andrus Older Adult Center, an outreach program of the Andrus Gerontology Center of the University of Southern California. As supervisor of the adult counseling program there, I had the best clinical staff of anyone who has ever worked with the aged. They are a heterogeneous group, including older persons trained as peer counselors and students from several disciplines—gerontology, psychology, and social work. Moreover, they have been unequaled in enthusiasm, innovative thinking, their caring for older persons, and their appreciation of California champagne, and they deserve special mention: Julie Bach-Peterson, Nancy Bopp, Sara Cornwell, Jack Donahue, Joanne Henkelman, Magdalena Malagon, Chris Piatt, Vic Stone, Milton Tepper, Kate Wilber, Anita Woods, and Helen Zimnavoda. Susan Fong was an invaluable consultant for us.

My colleagues at the Andrus Gerontology Center have created a challenging atmosphere, which has provided me the motivation and skills to undertake this book. I would like to acknowledge several people who have been particularly helpful: Judy Aklonis, William C. Albert, James E. Birren, David Peterson, K. Warner Schaie, Larry Thompson, and Robert Wiswell. Linda Oku always makes the Center a better place to work. I am indebted to Margaret Hartford, first director of the Leonard Davis School of Gerontology, whose enthusiasm and interest helped me through some difficult times. The staff of the Leonard Davis School has contributed in many ways to this book, particularly Pauline Abbott and Loweta Mack. Much of the preparation of the manuscript was done by Joanne Henkelman, supertypist and gerontologist.

I have had many stimulating conversations in the past few years with Robert M. Tager, who is medical director of Casa Colina Hospital in Pomona, California. His contribution is evident not only in the chapter on physical assessment that he wrote for this book, but throughout.

In the final preparations of the manuscript, Michael Sander of The Free Press provided considerable assistance. Wendy Loucks gave much needed help with the index.

I am grateful for the support and consideration given by my family and friends, and especially want to mention Penny, Benjy, and Megan, who create a bright spot in the California smog.

My education and career has been most strongly influenced by Robert L. Kahn of the University of Chicago. He gave me the concepts and tools necessary to be a researcher and clinician. The ideas in this book that are of lasting value are his.

PART I

Basic Processes
of Aging

CHAPTER 1

Mental Health and Aging:
An Overview

OLD AGE HAS BEEN THE NEGLECTED PHASE of the human life cycle in the behavior sciences, including the mental health professions of social work, psychiatric nursing, clinical psychology, and psychiatry. Little attention has been paid to developmental processes past adolescence and to the creation of effective treatments for older persons. As a result, the field of geriatric practice in mental health is an emerging one, attempting simultaneously to refute some of the myths and misconceptions that people hold about old age and to develop positive concepts for assessment and treatment.

There exists a considerable challenge in clinical practice with older persons. Instances of poor assessment and treatment are unfortunately all too common, and potentially treatable problems are sometimes ignored. Older persons, for example, are rarely evaluated for reversible causes of dementia, or what are sometimes referred to as acute brain syndromes. These disorders, which cause severe behavior problems, can in many instances be treated effectively. Too often, however, individuals with such problems are labeled as hopelessly senile. Another difficulty that sometimes goes untreated is depression. Older depressed persons will be regarded as too old to change, so no treatment is undertaken to alter this potentially reversible situation. Another area where there is considerable misunderstanding is sexual functioning. Someone over 60 who complains of sexual problems is likely to be told by professionals and friends alike that he or she is too old to think about that, even though highly effective therapies for sexual difficulties exist.

These are just a few of the common problems encountered in clinical work with older persons. In most communities there are still relatively few practitioners in any health or mental health discipline with the training and expertise to qualify them for working with the aged. Many writers have regarded this lack of knowledge of aging as the result of an age bias in society (see, for example, Butler 1969). Providing education and training in the field of aging is an important step toward correcting misapprehensions about old age and for implementing practices that enhance rather than diminish the potential of older persons. This step alone will contribute a major advance in the care of the aged. But beyond the problems of age bias, there also needs to be much more research into the causes and treatment of mental disorders in old age, in order to develop more successful approaches in those areas where effective therapies do not exist. The practitioner who enters this field thus encounters a paradoxical situation: there is considerable knowledge that, if applied, will lead to substantially better mental health practice, but at the same time there are areas where much has yet to be learned about the problems of the aged. The challenge of gerontologic practice is to combine enthusiasm and interest in working with the aged with an understanding and knowledge in several areas, including the biological and behavior sciences and the social factors and policies that affect older persons.

Plan of the Book

This book provides an introduction to clinical practice and to the issues in clinical research for the behavioral and emotional problems of the aged. In order to provide effective clinical services to older persons, it is important to have knowledge in three broad areas: (1) information about the aging process and its impact on behavior; (2) a basic understanding of current mental health concepts and procedures, including diagnosis and treatment; and (3) knowledge of the specific clinical issues involved in working with older persons. Experienced clinicians with little training in aging, whether social workers, psychologists, psychiatric nurses, psychiatrists, or workers in another field, need to have an understanding of what occurs normally as we grow older, and to be aware of clinical procedures for assessment or treatment that are specific to working with the aged. Students, depending on what formal course work and clinical experience they have received, may already be knowledgeable about aging or clinical practice, but may want to broaden their perspective and integrate an applied approach with the growing body of research findings on the aging process. For persons who have worked extensively with the aged, it is hoped that the attempt undertaken here to define and systematize the fields of clinical practice and research will contribute to their professional development.

Because of the widespread misunderstanding of what occurs with old age, it is critical for the professional working with older persons to have information about the aging process. This will dispel some of the myths and prejudices about old age, and at the same time prevent us from going too far in the opposite direction by painting an excessively optimistic picture of old age. While age prejudice contributes to the problems experienced by older persons, it is also important not to lose sight of the kinds of impairment that can occur as one grows older. Chapters 2, 3, and 4 review the biological, psychological, and social changes that occur with aging, providing a balanced view of both the potentials and problems involved in growing old.

A professional working with older persons should be able to make careful assessments, using procedures suitable for the aged that clearly identify presenting problems and lead to an appropriate treatment plan. It is important to understand basic principles of assessment as well as specific issues that are critical in practice with the aged, such as the differential diagnosis between depression and senile dementia. Knowledge of the etiology and course of various disorders in later life is also necessary, and will aid in the tasks of diagnosis and developing treatment plans. Chapters 5 through 9 discuss theoretical models of psychopathology in the elderly and suggest procedures for assessment. Because of the importance of physical problems in both causing and exacerbating psychological disorders of the elderly, information to aid persons without extensive health training in making physical assessments is presented in Chapter 7.

In Chapters 10 through 14, therapeutic interventions with the elderly are discussed, including a general model of treatment, procedures of individual, group, and family therapy, working with brain-injured persons, and sex therapy. These chapters present both general principles of treatment and specific applications to older persons.

A major intention of this book is to connect new developments in the mainstreams of psychology and psychiatry to the field of aging. Research in gerontology has often proceeded without a theoretical framework and without consideration of work on nonaging populations. As a result, advances in other disciplines are often integrated slowly into the field of aging. This book thus surveys not only the gerontological literature, but those areas of potential application to clinical practice with older persons. In Chapter 3, for example, research on personality and aging is considered in the light of recently developed models of personality, while in Chapter 8 new developments in the conceptualization and treatment of depression generated with young patients are presented. It is emphasized throughout that both a general knowledge of mental health concepts and practices and specific information about the special needs of aging persons are necessary for providing responsible and effective mental health services.

A significant assumption that underlies this integration of current clinical perspectives with issues in aging is that working with older persons in an effective and responsible manner is sometimes similar to and sometimes different from treatment with the young. Depending on the client's presenting problem, economic and social circumstances, and health, a clinician would proceed in some cases as with younger individuals, but at other times special knowledge and skills are necessary. Clinical practice with older persons involves more than just applying what one has learned generally about the etiology and treatment of mental disorders, but the aged are not so different from the young that one can ignore the principles of effective practice learned with other age groups.

In approaching issues of assessment and treatment, this book presents a distinct theoretical perspective. Behavioral and cognitive approaches are emphasized, while other schools of thought are described only briefly. The decision to focus in depth on behavioral and cognitive perspectives, rather than to provide a general overview of all the major clinical approaches, was based on the premise that the direct and problem-oriented style of behavioral and cognitive therapies represents the most effective way of working with older persons. The choice of behavioral methods may be surprising to some people. Old age and the difficulties associated with growing older are typically perceived principally as medical problems. Important physiological changes do occur as we age, and must be taken into account in understanding the mental disorders of older persons and in choosing appropriate interventions. But a medical perspective has its limits. The psychological disorders of older persons are generally associated with certain habits or thoughts, and tend to be more frequent in specific contexts. Even in cases of senile dementia or other physiological disorders, behavior problems are more frequent in particular situations, and also vary depending on the affected person's past habits and beliefs. By focusing on specific habits, thoughts, or social interactions, the clinician can have a more direct impact on what is immediately troubling the individual.

This direct approach is also more appealing to many older persons, who conceptualize the problems they are having as specific to their current situation and circumstances. Furthermore, since their problems often do involve how they interact with others and other social circumstances, such as experiencing a loss in income, it is important to help them with those problem situations in at least part of one's treatment. To cite an example, a mother may be depressed because she feels her children take advantage of her, asking her continually to do favors for them such as baby-sitting or borrowing money. She will benefit from a direct approach that clarifies what she feels is her proper role in the situation and teaches her to assert her own needs with her children.

Behavioral and cognitive approaches stress making empirical observations and doing outcome research, both of which have particular relevance to working with older persons. Because of all the biases and myths about aging, persons working with the elderly need to be good observers of behavior and to have a solid understanding of empirical research, in order to avoid being influenced in their clinical judgments by social stereotypes. Clinical approaches that emphasize intrapsychic processes place the practitioner in the position of having to guess or intuit what the person must be feeling; while this activity can have its benefits, there is the risk of bringing into it too much of one's own emotions and perspectives. Basing clinical interventions squarely on what is observable or reported by clients minimizes the possibility of misconstruing or mislabeling what is going on.

The empirical orientation of behavioral and cognitive approaches also facilitates conducting outcome studies. While the issue of evaluation research is important to the mental health field as a whole, it is of special value in treatment with older persons (Kahn and Zarit 1974). Because of tendencies to see the aged as impaired or as needing to be taken care of, programs sometimes create a self-fulfilling prophecy that reinforces the impairments and dependencies of their older clients while undermining areas of independence. It is only through active systematic observations of our impact on older clients that we can learn whether we are having beneficial or detrimental effects, and thus improve our procedures.

The role of the empirically oriented clinician has been described best by Mahoney (1974), who writes:

> Our knowledge of effective therapeutic procedures will grow only if we take an active role in its harvest. The age-old dichotomy of "clinician" versus "researcher" should be buried with many other bifurcations which currently polarize our search for knowledge. The most effective therapist is one who is in close touch with the "data" and who sensitively adjusts therapeutic strategies to the ebb and flow of relevant feedback. (p. 270)

It is through this sort of empirical approach that the capacities of older persons to benefit from various treatments can be assessed.

Defining Aging

When we talk about how people change as they age, we usually imply a unitary process that brings about those changes. Aging is often thought of as an internal biological determinant that gradually alters appearance, physical capacity, and behavior. That type of simple conceptualization, however, is misleading. Aging can be more accurately defined as occurring at three levels: biological aging, psychological aging, and sociological aging (Birren 1959). Biological aging refers to those changes in the structure and functions of body organs and systems that occur over time.

Because the most notable changes as people grow older are in their outward appearance, biological aging is most often assumed to play a primary role in causing changes in behavior. Biological factors are of considerable importance, but cannot explain many major changes in behavior over the adult years. Psychological aging refers to changes in behavior due to increased experience, changes in one's perception of one's self, or in reaction to biological changes. Sociological aging includes changes in norms, expectations, social status, and social roles available to persons over the course of the life cycle. Clearly, if others' reactions to a person change with chronological age, then one's behavior is also likely to change.

These three processes of aging undoubtedly interact to some extent, but also may act independently of one another in given situations. Take, for example, the issue of cautiousness in behavior. In general, most research has indicated more caution among the elderly (see Chapter 3). One could suggest that increased caution is due to biological factors, such as the slower conductance of electrical nerve impulses or the increasing probability of sensory loss as persons grow older. Psychological changes, however, may also account for increased caution. As persons gain in experience they may become more aware of the possible mistakes and pitfalls involved in any venture. In appraising more thoroughly what risks might be involved, they show caution in their performance, or display what in some situations might be called "wisdom." At a sociological level, one could argue that the aged are expected to be careful and not to make rash or foolish mistakes. Part of the social role of being old may involve learning to be cautious. Research in gerontology has only recently begun to use the types of multivariate design that can estimate the relative contributions and interactions among the various causes of change. We can, at present, just speculate on the relation of changes in behavior to these three aspects of aging.

These three types of aging are commonly confused with one another. As an example, we typically define the period of old age as beginning at age 65. This choice is based on social convention, principally the use of 65 for retirement age by the Social Security Administration. Yet when most people discuss old age, they imply that it is a stage of life with common, underlying biological features. Persons at 65 differ considerably from one another in the extent of biological age changes that have occurred in various organs and functions (see Chapter 2 for a more complete discussion). Furthermore, a reductionist emphasis of biological factors leads people to overlook the actual determinants of behavior, such as incentives, reinforcements, and social expectations, that exert considerable influence over behavior and emotions at any age.

A distinction has recently been proposed between the young-old, persons between the ages of 55 and 75, and the old-old, those individuals over 75 (Neugarten 1975). The category of the young-old is seen as the result of a combination of factors, including early retirement, economic prosperity, and better health care. These social changes have produced a group of active and energetic older persons who differ considerably from the social stereotypes of old age. In contrast, at the advanced ages of the old-old, persons are more likely to have the infirmities generally considered part of old age. Although this distinction has its uses, one should be cautious about viewing these periods as biologically determined stages of life. While persons at age 75 have more chronic illnesses and other problems that limit their functioning than they have at 60, there is still considerable individual variation on biological indicators. The concepts of young-old and old-old indicate the probability of whether a person will be functioning well or will have suffered decrements. But unlike chronological age in children, where one can say with a high degree of certainty that a child will walk or talk within a given period of time, one's age does not correspond to specific, universal developmental changes in later life.

Health status is often more important than age as a determinant of functioning. While senility, for example, is considered a disease of old age, persons can develop presenile dementias, with brain atrophy that is similar to senile dementia but that occurs before age 65. In most respects the behaviors and the need for assistance of persons with presenile dementia will be similar to persons over 65 with senile brain disease. The similarities are due to the presence of a comparable illness, and not to age. At the same time many persons continue to function well to advanced ages. One client seen by the author was an 80-year-old man who was president of a prosperous company. He went to his office daily, was directly involved in company operations, and was only slightly less physically fit than the author. While chronologically he could be described as old-old he had more in common with successful businessmen in their late middle years than with someone who might be regarded as old. Chronological age and health status are correlated to some extent, with chronic ailments and physical limitations occurring more frequently in the old. Nevertheless, exceptions to a general pattern of decline are found so often that it is misleading to talk about a stage of old age, in which most persons manifest certain patterns of behavior or other universally shared characteristics.

The Emerging Field of Mental Health and Aging

There has been increasing attention to the aging process and the problems of older persons in recent years. Over the past decade numerous courses have been developed in colleges and universities dealing with various aspects of aging, and the concerns of older persons have received somewhat more exposure in the media, although the overall level of programs or articles about old age is still low. One reason for this increased interest is a shift in the age of the population. As more persons survive to old age, the proportion of persons who are old is increasing. In the mental health field, however, concern with the problems of the aged has been slow in developing. While the prevalence of psychiatric problems among the old is high, the amount of services provided to them is lower than for any other age group, except young children.

PROPORTION OF AGED IN THE POPULATION

Both the number of persons over 65 and the proportion of aged to the rest of the population have risen dramatically in this century (see Figure 1.1). In 1900 approximately 4 percent of the population of the United States, or 3 million people, were over 65. The most recent census in 1970 showed 10 percent, or approximately 22 million persons, over 65 (Bouvier, Atlee, and McVeigh 1975). Projections for the future show a continuing increase in the proportion of old persons in the population. This increase will be gradual until the year 2010, when there will be a sharp increase in the number of old as the post-World War II baby boom cohort begins to reach 65.

By 2010, between 13 and 15 percent of the population will be over 65. Barring major changes in longevity, the current trends toward zero population growth will result eventually in a population with 16 percent over age 65 (Bouvier, Atlee, and McVeigh 1975). The number of persons living to advanced ages is also increasing. In 1900 only 29 percent of the aged were over 75, while currently 38 percent are past 75 (Bouvier, Atlee, and McVeigh 1975).

Several factors have contributed to this shift in the age distribution of the population. The primary causes are drops in the birth rate and decreases in mortality, particularly among infants and children. Because of the increasing control of infectious diseases and other health problems, more persons live to old age. There have not, however, been major changes in the human life span. Although life expectancy at birth has increased considerably in this century, from 50 years for a person born in 1900, to 71 years for someone born in 1970, most of this change is due to the control of infant mortality and childhood diseases. Life expectancy for persons reaching age 65 has not changed as dramatically. In 1900 a person who turned 65 could expect to live another 11.9 years, while in 1970 life expectancy was 15.3 (Bouvier, Atlee, and McVeigh 1975). Thus, while the human life span is not much longer, more persons survive to old age, accounting for the increase in the proportion of aged persons in the population.

When the aged were only a small proportion of the population, the need for specialized training in and services for the elderly was limited. As the number of older persons has grown, knowledge about working with the aged is of greater importance.

FIGURE 1.1. **Population in the United States over and under 65 years old, 1880 through 1970 and projected to 2000.**

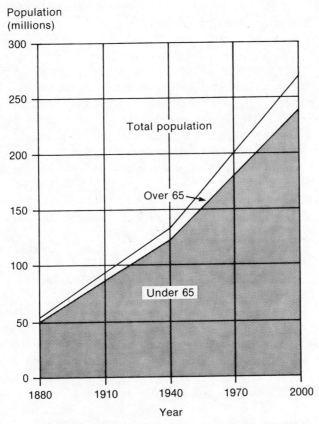

Source: Leon Bouvier, Elinore Atlee, and Frank McVeigh, "The Elderly in America," *Population Bulletin* 30, no. 3 (Population Reference Bureau, Washington, D.C., 1975). Reprinted by permission. Data from The Commission on Population Growth and the American Future, *Demographic and Social Aspects of Population Growth* (Washington, D.C.: Government Printing Office, 1972), pp. 52–53.

PREVALENCE OF PSYCHIATRIC DISORDERS

Precise estimates of the incidence and prevalence of psychiatric disorders among the elderly are difficult to make. Because of the lack of agreement on what criteria should be used for denoting impairment, the various community surveys that have been made often differ considerably in procedures for estimating disorders and in the rates of mental health problems they report. Many types of indicator have been used, including observer-rated or self-reported symptoms, diagnoses made by trained clinicians, functional impairments in daily activities, and various combinations of these criteria. In mental health surveys summarized by Kramer, Taube, and Redick (1973), the prevalence of disorders among the elderly range from 45 per 1,000 persons to 308 per 1,000. Based on these studies, they estimate that no less than 2 percent and perhaps as high as 20 percent of aged persons are in need of mental health services.

In perhaps the most carefully conducted survey of older persons, Kay, Beamish, and Roth (1964a; 1964b) interviewed samples of older community residents and institutionalized aged persons in the English city of Newcastle-upon-Tyne. The institutional samples were drawn from mental hospitals, geriatric wards, and old age homes. Using explicit criteria for classifying persons into various diagnostic categories, they found an overall rate of psychiatric disorders of 26 percent. Table 1.1 shows the percentage of cases in each diagnostic category. For the organic brain syndromes, cases were classified as severe or mild. Severe impairment was rated when there was disorganization of personality and impairment in everyday life activities. Mild organic brain syndrome was marked by the presence of some memory loss but few other changes. Of note is that the total number of persons living at home in each diagnostic category, including severe arteriosclerotic or senile dementia, is greater than for institutionalized persons.

While the overall rate of impairment found in Newcastle-upon-Tyne is thus high, it is not clear whether older persons have more psychiatric disorders than other age groups. In some instances criteria for mental health have included biases that exaggerate the impairment of the aged. In the Stirling County study (Leighton et al. 1963), for example, a rise in the prevalence of disorder was reported from ages 20 to 60. Ratings of symptoms and the extent of impairment due to symptoms was highest among the persons in their 60s. There were no differences, however, in the prevalence of psychoses (excluding those caused by senile brain disease), neuroses, or personality disorders in the age groups studied. The major reason for the reported increase in symptoms and impairment was that older persons were more likely to report psychophysiological complaints, such as gastrointestinal symptoms, musculoskeletal disorders including arthritis, cardiovascular symptoms, headaches, skin reactions, and other problems. The authors considered these problems as possibly caused by emotional factors, a conjecture that is certainly open to question. The reported increase in symptomatology may be due to poorer physical health, rather than to psychological problems.

In other epidemiological surveys age has not consistently emerged as a causal factor. In a review of several studies, Dohrenwend and Dohrenwend (1969) report that the highest rates of pathology were not found consistently in a particular age group. They noted 5 studies in which the

TABLE 1.1. Prevalence rates of cases with psychiatric disorder among subjects living at home (percent)

	MALES (N = 115)		FEMALES (N = 194)		TOTAL (N = 309)	
1. Organic brain syndromes:						
Severe	6.1		4.1		4.9	
Mild	6.1	12.2 ± 3.0 [a]	4.6	8.8 ± 2.0	5.2	10.0 ± 1.7
(a) Senile:						
Severe	0.0		2.1		1.3	
Mild	2.6	2.6	3.1	5.2	2.9	4.2
(b) Arteriosclerotic:						
Severe	5.2		1.0		2.6	
Mild	3.5	8.7	0.0	1.0	1.3	3.9
(c) Other:						
Severe	0.9		1.0		1.0	
Mild	0.0	0.9	1.5	2.6	1.0	1.9
2. Functional disorders		25.2 ± 4.1		34.0 ± 3.4		30.7 ± 2.6
(a) Schizophrenia, chronic	0.9		1.0		1.0	
Late paraphrenia	0.0		0.0		0.0	
Paranoid states	0.0	0.9	1.5	2.6	1.0	1.9
(b) Affective disorders and neuroses:						
Moderate/severe	12.2		8.8		10.0	
Mild	8.7	20.9	20.6	29.4	16.2	26.2
(c) Other		3.5		2.1		2.6
3. All disorders		37.4 ± 4.5		42.8 ± 3.6		40.7 ± 2.8

Source: W. D. K. Kay, P. Beamish, and M. Roth, "Old Age Mental Disorders in Newcastle upon Tyne," part 1, *British Journal of Psychiatry* 10 (1964): 146–158.
[a] The symbol ± indicates the standard error.

greatest amount of pathology was found in adolescence, 12 surveys that reported a peak in the middle years, and 7 that indicated a maximum rate of psychopathology in old age. They ascertained further that there was no consistent relation between age and the prevalence of psychoses (excluding those caused by senile brain disease), neuroses, or personality disorders. Despite the different types of assessment made in the various studies they reviewed, they did find consistent associations between psychopathology and social class. Because of the measurement problems in epidemiological studies of mental disorders, no conclusive statements can be made at this time concerning the relation of impairment and age. Nonetheless, the absence of consistent findings suggests that the number of persons with functional psychiatric disorder does not rise substantially with age. It does appear that mental health problems affect a substantial number of older persons, but the aged do not seem to have a special vulnerability to mental disorders, as is sometimes assumed. These findings suggest that age per se cannot be considered a barrier to treatment, since it is not consistently found to be the cause of psychiatric problems.

Use of Psychiatric Facilities by the Aged

Despite the extent of psychiatric impairment among the aged, older persons receive fewer mental health services than any other age group, except young children. In a major review of the rates of admission and of total services offered in psychiatric facilities, Kramer, Taube, and Redick (1973) show that only a small proportion of aged persons receive community psychiatric care. In outpatient clinics 10 percent of clients are between 45 and 54, 4 percent between 55 and 64, and only 2 percent are over 65. That contrasts with census figures that show 10 percent of the population are over 65. The rate of service to the elderly in community mental health centers is similarly low, with only 4 percent of clients over 65. Among partial hospitalization programs, 2.6 percent of patients are past 65. Surveys of psychiatrists in private practice have found that less than 4 percent of all patients in treatment are over 65 (Butler and Sulliman 1963; Marmor 1975).

In contrast to the low rates of community care, older persons represent a higher proportion of persons treated in state and county inpatient psychiatric hospitals. Figure 1.2 shows the number of psychiatric care episodes for various types of facility. As can be seen, the proportion of persons in outpatient settings declines with age, while the number in state and county mental hospitals increases (Kramer, Taube, and Redick 1973).

There is some indication that the large percentage of older institutionalized patients is due to past rather than current practices. The number of older persons being admitted for the first time to state and county

FIGURE 1.2. Number of patient care episodes per 100,000 population in psychiatric facilities by type of facility and age, United States, 1966.

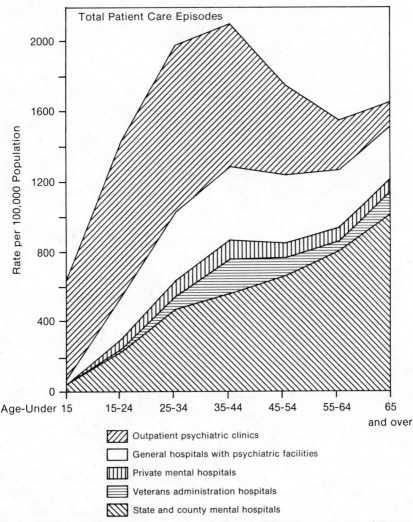

Source: M. Kramer, C. A. Taube, and R. W. Redick, "Patterns of Use of Psychiatric Facilities by the Aged: Past, Present, and Future." In C. Eisdorfer and M. P. Lawton, eds., *Psychology of Adult Development and Aging* (Washington, D.C.: American Psychological Association, 1973). Copyright © 1973 by the American Psychological Association. Reprinted by permission.

institutions dropped markedly during the 1960s (Kramer, Taube, and Redick 1973). This decline suggests that the large proportion of older persons still institutionalized in mental hospitals represents primarily chronic patients who have grown old in hospital. At the same time, the drop in first admissions indicates that older persons with psychiatric problems are more likely to be sent to nursing homes than to psychiatric facilities (Kramer, Taube, and Redick 1973). Estimates on the percentage of nursing home patients with psychiatric disorders reflects this trend. In a review of existing studies, Pfeiffer (1977) suggests that as many as 80 percent of nursing home patients may have mental health problems. While state and county facilities have rarely been models of progressive treatment, this shift to placing older persons in nursing homes represents a step backward. Nursing homes have personnel with little or no training in mental health, and patients with psychiatric problems are rarely seen on a regular basis by a trained mental health professional, whether social worker, psychiatric nurse, psychologist, or psychiatrist.

Commenting on these trends in mental health care, Kahn (1975) has argued they represent an exclusion of the aged from recent advances in treatment. Whereas mental health practices before World War II generally involved custodial treatment, the postwar community mental health movement includes an emphasis on brief, active treatment and limited use of hospitalization. The aged person with a problem, however, is typically not seen in an outpatient facility or as a new admission to short-term inpatient units where active treatment is given. Rather, as custodial care in mental health facilities has been phased out, aged patients have been diverted into nursing homes.

The extensive use of custodial instead of active treatment for aged psychiatric patients would be justified if, indeed, the majority of older persons had problems that could not be managed in any other way, or that did not respond to treatment. As noted in the surveys of mental disorders reviewed above, however, the most prevalent problems of older persons involve neuroses, especially depression. Furthermore, as Kay, Beamish, and Roth (1964a) report, even those persons with severe psychiatric disorders are often residing in community settings, suggesting that custodial care is not always needed even for these problems.

In summary, the number of older persons in the population has been growing, and there is general agreement on a substantial need for mental health services. At the same time, older persons represent only a small percentage of those receiving various outpatient services, and they have increasingly been excluded from acute psychiatric inpatient services. Thus, while interest and concern for the aged with behavioral disorders has increased in recent years, the development and expansion of services is still at a formative stage.

Factors Affecting the Care of Older Persons

Several factors have contributed to this gap between the need for psychiatric services for the elderly and actual provision of those services.

Principal among them are the negative beliefs held by persons about old age, attitudes of older persons themselves about mental health, and the lack of training programs for professionals to work with the aged.

ATTITUDES ABOUT AGING

Both laypersons and many mental health professionals view the later years as something to avoid, if at all possible. By putting old age out of our minds, perhaps we hope that it will go away, or that at least we will not "catch it." In general, the aged are viewed as uninteresting and having little to contribute to others. To cite an example of the prevailing age biases, it was found in one recent national opinion survey that the aged were not thought by the general public to be bright or alert, open-minded or adaptable, sexually active or good at getting things done (Harris and Associates 1975).

There is also a tendency for younger persons to exaggerate the problems experienced by the old. The aged are considered by persons under 65 to be in poorer health, to have more money problems, to be lonelier, and to be more frequently the target of street crime than is actually reported by older respondents (Harris and Associates 1975). When comparing what problems young and old consider personally serious, however, the aged are more likely to mention fear of crime, concern with poor health, and loneliness. These problems, then, are of importance to many older persons, but their prevalence is exaggerated by those under 65.

One manifestation of these negative beliefs is the feeling that it is of more value to treat younger persons, because they have their whole lives ahead of them, while an older person is likely to die soon. Certainly a person of 20 is likely to have more years ahead of him than someone who has turned 65. But as noted earlier, a person of 65 can expect to live for another 15 years. Persons who live to be 90 have one-third of their lives ahead of them at 60.

CAN THE OLD BE HELPED BY PSYCHOLOGICAL TREATMENT?

A reason often given for not treating older persons with psychological disorders is that they cannot be helped. In the mental health field this idea can be traced to Freud, who cautioned his followers not to waste their time on the aged, because their defenses were too rigid. As Lawton and Gottesman (1974) note, however, one cannot remain rigid and still adapt to all the biological and social changes that occur with aging.

There is no doubt in the minds of clinicians who have worked with older persons that they can respond to psychological treatment. The question in the heading above should be asked in a more specific way: which aged, compared to which group of young, will or will not respond favorably to therapy?

Some of the pessimism about treating the aged has come from a confusion between chronic mental problems and disorders of old age. Much of the early research and practice with aged persons was in state mental hospitals, where the population consisted largely of chronic patients who grew old in the hospital. Reporting on mental health problems of the old, these studies made no differentiation between lifelong problems and those originating in old age. The administrative practices of many institutions furthered this confusion. Upon reaching 65 an inmate would be transferred to a geriatric ward and considered a geriatric case, no matter what problem brought him to the institution in the first place. The lack of success in rehabilitating these persons with lifelong problems has been interpreted by some as evidence that the aged cannot be helped (Kahn and Zarit 1974).

Another reason for this therapeutic nihilism is the mistaken impression that complaints of psychological distress in the elderly are due to aging, and therefore nothing can be done for them. As will be seen in subsequent chapters, the aging process undoubtedly has an influence on behaviors. In particular, there is probably some relation to the two most common mental health problems of later life: the organic brain syndromes and depression. In both cases it has been suggested that the aging process makes the person more vulnerable (in some unidentified ways) to developing either a degenerative brain disease or an affective disorder. As noted earlier, however, most older persons do not manifest the behavior impairment characteristic of senile dementia. While there are currently no effective therapeutic procedures to arrest or retard senile brain disease, it affects only 5 to 10 percent of older individuals. Moreover, as will be discussed in Chapter 14, significant gains can be made through counseling of persons with brain disease and, more important, by working with those persons who are caring for them. In terms of the affective disorders, poor health and other losses are typically reported by older persons in the period of time preceding a depressive episode. These precipitating events are also associated with depression at younger ages (Paykel 1975). Whether or not biological changes have made the older person more vulnerable to depression, depressed feelings are usually manifested in appropriate situational contexts; that is, many older persons have good reason to be depressed. Furthermore, the relation of aging to a greater vulnerability to affective disorders is undoubtedly complex. Many older persons who are struggling with difficult situations, such as limited incomes, poor housing, a greater vulnerability to street crime, or social isolation, do not become depressed. When asking if the aged can respond to psychotherapy, one might wonder how the young would react to similar environmental deprivations as affect some elderly.

The issues of whether the elderly benefit from psychological treatment and which elderly show the best responses are empirical questions that have not been evaluated. As in other areas of mental health, there is a critical need for more and better-designed evaluation studies to assess the effects of various interventions. But it can no longer be maintained a priori that the aged are unable to respond to treatment.

ATTITUDES OF THE AGED TOWARD MENTAL HEALTH SERVICES

One reason for the low number of older persons served in mental health facilities is the attitudes of the aged themselves about treatment. Among the ideas they express spontaneously are that one has to be crazy to go to a psychiatrist or other professional, or that just talking about one's problems will not do any good. Many people in today's cohort of old believe it is a sign of weakness to go to others for help with personal problems. They are concerned that they will be shamed or stigmatized in the eyes of others by seeking mental health services.

This reluctance to go for help can be exaggerated by those working with the aged. In senior centers where this author has given talks or been involved in service programs, program directors have sometimes cautioned that the participants are reluctant to become involved in counseling or even to discuss mental health issues. The response of the older participants is generally much more positive than predicted. Their acceptance is even greater when talks are given by older persons who have been trained as peer counselors (see also Alpaugh and Hickey-Haney 1978).

LACK OF TRAINED PROFESSIONALS

Another factor contributing to the limited mental health services available is the small number of professionals who have received training in aging. In a survey of graduate training programs in various disciplines, Birren and Renner (1980) report that with only a couple of exceptions, aging has not been incorporated in the curricula of graduate education. Training in geriatrics is extremely limited in medical schools. In a national survey, only 15 of the 96 responding medical schools taught geriatrics in a special course, and in all cases this course was an elective. Among the other schools, 66 stated that work in geriatrics was available on an elective basis during the clinical training that students receive in their third and fourth years (Akpom and Mayer 1978).

A survey of graduate and professional schools in the state of California indicates a paucity of material on aging in most curricula (Birren and Hirschfield 1977). The course offerings and requirements of 8 disciplines were studied: Adult Education; Dentistry; Law; Medicine; Social Work; Nursing; Public Administration; and Counselor Education. Of the 93 graduate programs in these fields that were surveyed, 56 reported no faculty member with a knowledge of aging, and 70 indicated that none of the required courses included content on aging. For those programs in which theses or dissertations were written, only 2 master's and 1 doctoral paper done between 1971 and 1976 had a gerontological topic.

A national survey of graduate programs in psychology indicated a similar lack of training in aging (Storandt 1977). Approximately 60 percent of the 191 departments that responded to the inquiry stated there were currently no graduate courses offered on the psychology of aging. Sixteen departments had a specialization in aging and development, and another 11 were forming new programs. There was similarly only a small amount of clinical or research activity reported by those departments with a clinical psychology program. Dissertations, clinical training, or other specialized activities with a focus on aging had taken place in 11 percent of the departments, and usually had involved only 1 or 2 students in each program.

The limited training in the field of aging has led to a gap between the number of personnel in mental health fields with a specialization in gerontology and projected estimates of how many people are needed to provide services. Surveys of various mental health professions have indicated that in the entire country there are 20 psychiatrists, 50 psychiatric nurses, and 100 clinical psychologists with special training in aging who are working with older persons (Storandt, cited in Birren and Sloane 1977). If the need for service of the older population is considered as 10 percent of the existing populace, it has been estimated that the following personnel would be required in the next ten years: 1,000 psychiatrists, 2,000 clinical psychologists, 4,000 psychiatric social workers, 4,000 psychiatric nurses, and 18,000 paraprofessionals (Birren and Sloane 1977). Given the magnitude of training that number of people, it is likely that deficiencies in the number of mental health personnel with a specialization in aging will persist for some time, even as the proportion of older persons in the community increases.

Summary

The study of mental disorders of old age is an emerging field. On the one hand is the need to shed the many myths and misconceptions that are held about the aging process. On the other, the development of practice skills with the aged depends on applying what is appropriate from assessment and treatment procedures developed with younger persons, and learning special techniques that are necessary for the unique circumstances of older persons.

The importance of developing sound clinical skills for aging persons is underscored by shifts in the age of the general population. While older persons once constituted a small percentage, their proportion of the total population has been increasing steadily. Despite this increase, mental health services have made only a limited response, and provide fewer ser-vices to the aged than to any other group. Professional and graduate education has also not given much attention to the aging process, and there are relatively few programs at present in which one can gain spe-cialized knowledge and experience in working with older persons. The need for innovative programs and for people to develop and staff them can only increase in the coming years.

CHAPTER 2

Biological and Psychological Processes of Aging

THROUGHOUT HUMAN HISTORY, concern about aging and the inevitability of death has held a central place in the writings of philosophers and theologians, as well as in popular stories and myths. Many cultures encompass folk tales about earlier periods in their history or about distant places where persons live to very advanced ages (Birren and Clayton 1975). Stories of fountains of youth, of elixirs that prolong youth and life, as well as more serious treatises on aging and death, are an important part of our cultural heritage. Despite this historic interest in aging, systematic study of the aging process began relatively recently. Reviewing the origins of gerontology, Birren and Clayton (1975) report that the first significant cluster of scientific publications appeared in the 1920s and 1930s. Because of its recent origins, scientific gerontology has often been concerned with evaluating the sweeping and sometimes oversimplified theories of aging derived from historic and current social thought. To cite one example, during the last 20 years there has been extensive debate over whether it is best to remain active or to disengage from social involvements when older, with proponents on both sides approaching the argument with ideological zeal and limited empirical evidence. There is, however, now emerging a large body of research studies on both biological and psychological changes with aging, which, though still limited in many respects, permits a more careful analysis of the various theories and myths of aging, and also the development of new propositions that are soundly based on empirical evidence.

In this chapter various biological and psychological theories of aging will be reviewed. From a biological perspective, processes of change will be examined at both the cellular and systems levels, with special attention to changes in the brain, in functional health, and in the senses. Psychological processes in the later years will then be examined, with a specific focus on the cognitive abilities of intelligence, learning, memory, and reaction time, and on the methodology of studying the aging process. Theories of personality and aging will be reviewed in Chapter 3.

Biological Theories of Aging

The most prevalent view of the aging process is that we experience a gradual decline in functioning that begins relatively early in life and continues to a period of senescence and death. This conceptualization is based in part on mortality curves, which plot the incidence of deaths in the population at various ages. Despite changes in life expectancy since the early 1800s, when these curves were first drawn, the slopes of the curves have remained about the same. As shown in Figure 2.1, there is a logarithmic increase in the risk of dying with each advancing decade of life (Strehler 1977). To account for this pattern, it has been proposed that persons become progressively weaker as they age and, consequently, stressors of smaller and smaller magnitude can bring about death. Aging is therefore seen as a constantly accelerating process of decline.

When moving from study of the population as a whole to the individual level, the pattern of change in organisms as they age appears to be more complex. While declines occur, there are also long periods of stability, restitutive qualities through which small amounts of biological change can be tolerated without affecting functioning, and periods of accelerated decline, such as those caused by illnesses. Furthermore, considerable individual variation has been found in the timing and occurrence of age changes. An understanding of the complexity and variability of the processes of aging is important in order to differentiate normal from altered functioning in later life, and to identify adaptive capacities of older persons for facilitating treatment of psychological dysfunctions.

Several distinct but potentially overlapping theories have emerged to try to explain why aging occurs (Marx 1974a; 1974b; Daniel 1977; Finch 1977; Hayflick 1977; Strehler 1977; Shock 1977). Genetic models propose inherited controls over the length of the life span, over cell mitosis, and perhaps also in the emergence of specific processes that lead to age-related declines. A wear-and-tear theory holds that accumulated damage to various cell structures leads to a running down of various functions necessary to sustain life. From another perspective, it is thought aging may be due to alterations of the body's autoimmune systems. Those processes that

FIGURE 2.1. Gompertz plots of mortality behavior of a number of species and of humans in different environments. A, male rats; B, male humans (Egypt); C, male human, white (U.S.), North Central Division, 1949–1951; D, male human; E, female human, white, North Central Division, 1949–1951; F, *Drosophila melanogaster.*

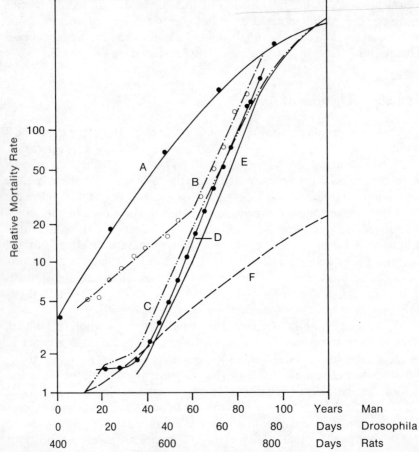

Source: B. Strehler, *Time, Cells and Aging,* 2d ed. (New York: Academic Press, 1977). Copyright © 1977 by the Academic Press. Reprinted by permission.

repel infections and other foreign intrusions in the body may begin at some point to attack and weaken or destroy healthy cell structures. A homeostasis model suggests that, with increasing age, organisms have difficulty in maintaining a steady state in various functions such as body temperature and blood glucose level, and in returning to a steady state following stress. Other research suggests a more critical role for the stress response. From this perspective, the organism's ability to function under stressful conditions is considered the principal change with aging.

GENETIC CONTROL OF AGING

There is increasing evidence that the human life span, and at least some aspects of the aging process, are under the control of genetic mechanisms. For one thing, the life span within a given species has fixed limits (Jarvik 1975; Hayflick 1977a; 1977b). Despite variations among members of a species, the life spans of members are more similar to one another than to those of other species. The fixed, seemingly programmed span of human life can be illustrated by the fact that it has been estimated that if cures were available for the 3 major causes of death—heart disease, renal disease, and malignancies—life expectancies would increase by only 5 years (Hayflick 1977a). Second, among humans there are sex differences in life expectancy, with women averaging from 2 to 7 years greater longevity than men. These estimates vary slightly from one society to another, but are manifested even where social roles and expectations for women are similar to those of men (Woods, Harootyan, and Birren 1976). Women also display fewer negative changes over time on a battery of cognitive tests (Jarvik 1975). These findings suggest a greater hardiness among women that is probably related to genetic differences between women and men. Another factor indicating genetic influences on aging is that some of the diseases of later life, such as arteriosclerosis and Alzheimer's-type senile dementia, run in families (Jarvik 1975; Busse 1973).

The probability that life span, and therefore, to some extent, the aging process, is programmed by genetic material is supported by the research of Hayflick (1977a; 1977b). He has found that normal, somatic cells of vertebrates can undergo only a finite number of divisions before the cells die. Cultures of human embryo lung cells, for example, are capable of approximately 50 divisions before dying. Cells taken from adult donors undergo fewer divisions, with the actual number of doublings inversely correlated with the donor's age. Experiments in which normal cells are serially transplanted from one laboratory animal to another have demonstrated similar results. Even when placed in younger, healthy animals, the transplanted cells will die after the usual number of doublings (Daniel 1972; Denny 1975). In fact, the only cells found to have an apparently unlimited capacity for division are cancer cells. Based on these findings, Hayflick (1977b) proposes that the number of divisions of which cells are capable of has been genetically programmed. He also suggests that the number of doublings of which cells are capable may be roughly proportionate to the life span of a given species, though evidence for this proposition is still limited.

CHANGES IN CELL STRUCTURE WITH AGE

Although cells have a limited capacity for doubling, declines in cell functioning and cell death usually occur before that limit is reached. This "premature" death of the organism may be due to several factors, including the accumulation of damage to cell structures, increasing difficulties in regulating physiological functions, or altered responses to stress. It has been proposed that cell dysfunction and death occur either through the accumulation of "noise," that is, damage to DNA or RNA within the cells that leads to accumulated errors in protein synthesis, or because of cell shutdown, where the genetic information for synthesis of certain proteins runs out (Comfort 1970; Marx 1974a). There can be many sources of damage to this genetic coding material and to other cell matter, including radiation, chemical, mechanical, or thermal imbalances, or viral and other infections (Timiras 1972; Sokoloff 1975). While there is some indication that cells can repair damaged DNA or RNA, it may be that damage begins to accumulate too rapidly for repair, or that certain types of this genetic coding material cannot be restored to proper functioning if damaged.

Another source of change at the cellular level is an accumulation of waste materials. The free radicals, which occur as by-products of metabolic processes of cells and can also come from environmental sources, are capable of damaging DNA and other cell structures. Control of free radicals in cell cultures through the use of Vitamin E has been shown to increase the number of doublings of which those cells are capable before cell death. This finding further points to the importance of DNA and RNA damage in relation to the aging process (Marx 1974a).

Within higher organisms there is a redundancy of genetic coding material; that is, more material is present than is actually necessary for maintaining adequate levels of protein synthesis. Accumulation of errors in the genetic material or loss of some of that material may lead to a gradual loss of reserve or redundancy within cells, until functioning is severely compromised (Marx 1974a). This lack of redundancy may be related to the reduced capacity of aging organisms to respond to environmental stresses, or to lowered resistance to various diseases (Barrows 1971). In a study of the production of enzymes of the liver, for example, young mice who were exposed to cold showed a linear increase of enzyme activity, while among older mice there was a delayed period before enzyme activity reached levels shown by young animals (Finch, Foster, and Mirsky 1969). There may similarly be a decreased resistance to radiation and to other stresses (Upton 1977). Aging may therefore result in a lowered rate of synthesis of proteins or in imperfectly produced proteins, with the effects of this change being particularly pronounced under stress (Denny 1975). As only certain proteins appear to have age-related decrements, the types of disease and other stress to which the aging organism is vulnerable may be determined by its genetic program that provides for varying rates of synthesis of different proteins (Barrows 1971).

PHYSIOLOGICAL CORRELATES OF AGING

The ways in which the changes in cell function and protein synthesis described above are manifested at complex levels are not precisely known. Physiological functioning, however, does not consistently correlate with chronological age. Unlike infancy and childhood, the adult years are not characterized by a series of specific physiological events at particular ages, with the exception of menopause, nor are there a series of sequential stages that mark the decline from maturity to death (Timiras 1972). Certain characteristics, including blood suger level under fasting conditions, blood pH, or total blood volume, show no changes even to advanced ages. Other functions, such as the level of serum cholesterol in the blood, increase gradually into the middle years and then show a decrease. More commonly, many body functions begin to show a linear decrease at around age 30, which continues for the rest of the life span. Two qualifications of this trend are important. First, with increasing age there is also greater variability from one person to another. In considering such functions as renal blood flow or glucose tolerance, scores of younger individuals cluster closely together. Among aged subjects, some manifest large differences compared to younger individuals, others have relatively smaller degrees of change, while a few continue to function at levels comparable with those of younger persons (Shock 1968; 1977; Tobin 1977). The effects of aging on these functions, then, differ from individual to individual. Second, the rate of average decline in physiological capacities varies from one function to another, as illustrated in Figure 2.2. As noted above, functions such as fasting blood glucose show no apparent change with age. On the other hand, basal metabolic rate and total body water have been found to change gradually on the average, with the extent of change reaching 18 to 20 percent by age 90. The average differences between young and old in functions such as renal blood flow and maximum breathing capacity is somewhat larger, with the aged having approximately 60 percent of the capacity found in 30-year-olds.

Two additional factors affect these findings. First, measurements have generally been made of healthy individuals, in order to separate the effects of specific diseases from purely age-related changes (Tobin 1977). This distinction between aging and disease may be somewhat artificial since, as noted earlier, one of the principal effects of aging at the cellular level may be to make the individual more vulnerable to certain diseases. This increased risk of illness suggests that somewhat greater changes in physiological capacities than described above can be expected to occur. On the other hand, it has been proposed that some of the changes that have been attributed to age, particularly in muscles and in the cardiovascular system, may be the result of hypokinetic disease, or a lack of physical condi-

FIGURE 2.2. Estimated linear age decrements for different physiologic functions: fasting blood glucose, basal metabolic rate, total body water, resting cardiac output, renal blood flow, maximum breathing capacity. The average value for 30-year-old subjects is taken as 100 percent for each function, and linear decrements with increasing age are plotted as percent of the mean value at age 30.

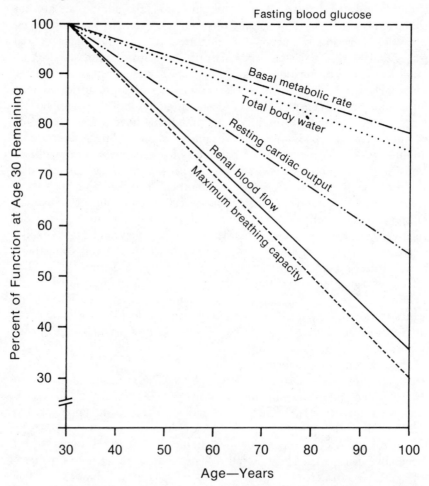

Source: N. W. Shock, "Biologic Concepts of Aging," in A. Simon and L. J. Epstein, eds., Aging in Modern Society (Washington, D.C.: American Psychiatric Association, 1968). Copyright © 1968 by the American Psychiatric Association. Reprinted by permission.

tioning (De Vries 1975). People tend to lead increasingly sedentary lives as they age. The results of inactivity can be striking, even in the young. When well-conditioned young men, for example, are placed on a regimen of enforced bed rest for 3 weeks, they show many of the physiological changes that characterize the aging, particularly in the cardiovascular system. Evidence for the importance of hypokinetic disease comes from the success of conditioning programs for older persons. Engaging in vigorous exercise has resulted in improvements in characteristics that are usually described as changing with age, including the respiratory system, percentage of body fat, physical work capacity, and systolic and diastolic blood pressure (De Vries 1970; 1975).

Another major characteristic of physiological change with age is that it takes longer for a system to readjust to normal functioning following introduction of a stimulus. With intravenous injection of glucose, for example, blood sugar returns to normal resting rates more slowly in the aged than in the young. Similar evidence of slower responses to stressors is found in the acidity of the blood, pulse rate, and blood pressure. These findings suggest that there is a loss of reserve capacity of some physiological systems with aging, and that the capacity to respond to stresses is reduced (Shock 1968; Upton 1977). Other factors, such as decreased neural or hormonal regulation or poorer coordination of normal brain interactions, have been proposed as major aspects of aging that decrease the organism's adaptation (Upton 1977; Marx 1974b).

In general, physiological characteristics in old age are marked by a high degree of individual variability. While there is generally a decline, some functions decline more than others, some individuals show levels of functioning at or close to those of young persons, and some changes may be reversible to some extent through a conditioning program. At the same time, the risk of age-related illnesses increases and there is a slowing in the rate at which many body functions return to normal following stress. The effects of aging can perhaps best be summarized as leading to an increased risk of decline, both in the absence of disease states and because of greater vulnerability to certain diseases. The extent of actual changes found in older persons, however, varies considerably among individuals. Thus there is probably no clear physiological stage of senescence, but as persons grow older, they manifest gradual and varying degrees of deviation from normal levels of functioning.

CHRONIC DISEASES IN LATER LIFE

This increased risk of decline is reflected in the high prevalence of chronic health problems among the aged. It has been estimated that 85 percent of the older population have one or more chronic conditions (Wilder 1971). Heart disease and hypertension are widespread among persons over 65. Surveys indicate that one-half of all persons over 65 have definite signs of heart disease, while another 25 to 30 percent have various abnormalities suggesting possible heart disease (Keller 1975). Similarly, hypertension affects many older persons, particularly the black elderly. Twenty-five percent of white men and 47 percent of white women are hypertensive, compared with 53 percent and 64 percent respectively for black men and women (Keller 1975). Other common problems in the later years include gastrointestinal disorders (ulcers, digestive problems, and constipation), rheumatism, and arthritis. Chronic disorders such as diabetes, asthma, and hay fever are manifested by many older persons, but do not increase in prevalence past age 45 (Kimmel 1974). Some chronic diseases are also affected by social class. Visual problems, atherosclerosis, cardiovascular disease, high blood pressure, and lung disease are found more frequently among persons from lower socioeconomic levels (Cole 1974; Kimmel 1974).

These figures on the prevalence of health problems raise two related issues: what constitutes normal functioning in the aged, and to what extent are these chronic difficulties actually disabling. Because of the changing distribution of scores in measurements of physiological functioning with age, many older persons have indicators of functions such as glucose tolerance that would be considered pathological if found in the young. Whether these scores actually represent pathology, or if the normal range of function shifts somewhat with age, has not been determined. It can be said, however, that many older persons do have incipient health problems, and that many health indicators involving the heart, blood pressure, and blood sugar levels fall in questionable but not clearly impaired ranges (Tobin 1977).

At the same time, despite the presence of clear or suspected pathologies, most older persons are not impaired or are only minimally impaired in their daily functioning, including such activities as work and household tasks.

Approximately 63 percent of persons over 65 have no difficulties in carrying out major activities, while another 20 percent have minimal problems in their functioning (Wilder 1973; Bouvier, Atlee, and McVeigh 1975). Only 4 to 5 percent of older persons live in total care institutions, such as nursing homes (Bouvier, Atlee, and McVeigh 1975), and another 5 percent of community residents are restricted to their homes because of chronic disabilities (Cole 1974). Thus, despite the presence of potentially disabling conditions, most older persons experience few or no limitations of activity.

Sensory Changes in the Aged

One area of prominent change is in the senses. The occurrence of severe visual and hearing problems increases markedly with age, and there are similar decrements in other sensory abilities. Using legal blindness as a criteria, incidence rises from 250 cases per 100,000 during the ages 40 to 64, to 500 cases per 100,000 between 65 and 69, and 1,450 cases per 100,000 for persons over 69 (Fozard et al. 1977). The major causes of blindness in later life include glaucoma, cataracts, macular disease, and diabetes. It has been estimated that the incidence of glaucoma among persons over 65 is between 5 and 13 percent. Similarly, visually impairing cataracts are found in 9 percent of persons in their 60s and in 36 percent of persons in their 80s (Fozard et al. 1977). In addition to the increasing number of persons with visual losses, most persons experience some decline in vision that is related to physiological changes in the eyes, such as the increased yellowing, opacity, and flatness of the lens. Changes in vision include reduced visual acuity, poorer accommodation to low levels of illumination, loss of sensitivity to colors, especially those at the blue end of the color spectrum, increased sensitivity to glare, reduced peripheral visual fields, and an increased area of blind spot (Fozard et al. 1977; Botwinick 1978). Corrective lenses and the use of greater levels of illumination can compensate somewhat for these changes, but for many it is not possible to restore visual functioning to the levels of younger persons.

The most frequent change in hearing is presbycusis, a progressive, bilateral loss of hearing for high tones. Precise estimates of the prevalence of hearing loss are more difficult to obtain than for visual problems. Vision incorporates the standard of legal blindness, but no similar criterion exists for describing degree of hearing loss. It has been estimated, however, that approximately 13 percent of the aged show presbycusis in an advanced state, with this disorder somewhat more prominent among men (Corso 1977). These changes affect both the absolute thresholds for perceiving speech and the ability to discriminate among tones. Hearing losses lead to problems in understanding speech, particularly if the stimulus is not clear, as when words overlap or are interrupted (Corso 1977). The perception of degraded speech, that is, where sentences are interrupted, spoken faster than normal rate, presented in conditions of unfavorable acoustics, or in other ways distorted, has been found to decline after age 40, with a sharp decrement shown by persons in their 60s. There is, however, no apparent loss of abilities to perceive undistorted speech (Bergman et al. 1976), barring physical failings that might impair these abilities.

Changes in the other senses have been studied less extensively than vision or hearing. While there is some conflicting evidence, it has been estimated that there are losses in taste and smell, which affects degree of pleasure experienced in eating (Engen 1977; Schiffman 1977). Some older persons, perhaps as many as 25 percent, also experience a decreased sensitivity to touch and to vibrations, and there is a loss of the ability to respond to extreme temperatures (Kenshalo 1977).

These sensory changes can critically affect the relationship of an individual to his environment. Visual and hearing losses, in particular, make the carrying out of everyday activities increasingly difficult and can lead to feelings of isolation or alienation from others or the environment.

Simulations of the experience of many older persons, involving, for example, the construction of glasses that create the effects of the aging eye, demonstrate dramatically the nature of these losses (Pastalan, Mautz, and Merrill 1973). The relation of these changes to the psychological disorders of the elderly will be explored in later chapters.

Aging and the Brain

The brain is the most critical site in the body where age changes may be manifested. It is widely thought that older persons suffer changes in the brain that significantly impair their functioning, including memory, judgment, and personality. All but the most vigorous older persons are sometimes regarded as a bit senile by family, friends, and even physicians. But like other myths about aging, true senile dementia is found in only a small proportion of persons over 65.

The term "senile dementia," which has been adopted in the most recent revision of the Diagnostic and Statistical Manual of the American Psychiatric Association (1978) to replace the category of chronic organic brain syndrome, refers to any condition of intellectual deterioration caused by diffuse cerebral damage. As such, dementia is not a disease, but a descriptive category used to classify persons with similar cognitive deficits and other behavioral symptoms. The foremost symptom is severe memory loss, involving the inability to retain new information.

It has generally been estimated that 5 percent of those over 65 have mental impairments associated with diffuse brain damage (Busse 1973). As noted in Chapter 1, Kay, Beamish, and Roth (1964a; 1964b) found a prevalence of 5 percent of community elderly with major cognitive deficits indicative of senile brain disease, and another 5 percent with mild intellectual impairments suggesting the possible presence of dementia. In a recent reassessment of the data from the Newcastle-upon-Tyne survey, Kay (1977) reports that the rate of dementia rises with age, affecting 2.4 percent of 65-year-olds and 22 percent of 80-year-olds.

All persons have some changes in brain structure as they age. In humans, brain weight shows a marked decline with increasing age; it has been felt that this decline is due to a progressive loss of neurons, since these cells do not undergo mitosis. Estimates generally are that between 20 and 44 percent of brain cells are lost during the human life span, depending on the part of the brain and method of measure (Sokoloff 1975; Brody and Vijayashankar 1977), although some recent evidence suggests that cell loss may actually be much smaller (Meier-Ruge et al. 1975). In addition to cell loss, other changes with aging include increasing amounts of lipofuscin within cells, and the formation of neurofibrillary tangles and neuritic (senile) plaques (Terry and Wisniewski 1975). In most persons these changes are present only in small amounts.

These changes in brain weight and brain structure have important implications for behavior and for the regulation of various physiological processes, such as stress reactions. But senile behavior is generally found when there is a more rapid deterioration in the brain. The major causes of this accelerated decline are development of neurofibrillary tangles and senile plaques in large numbers throughout the brain, or cell death brought about by arteriosclerotic disease. These brain disorders are described more fully in Chapter 6

Aging and Behavior

It has long been assumed that aging has an effect on behavior, but the changes that are described have varied considerably among cultures and among historical periods. Old age has been perceived as making persons foolish or wise, sad or content, childish or no longer ruled by passion and impulse. These contradictions may actually all be correct, reflecting the variety of changes possible in old age. A lifetime is the accumulating of experiences that make us continually unique—more different each day from any other person in what we have perceived and felt. In evaluating how, in fact, persons do change, two factors must be kept in mind: methodological problems often get in the way of making a straightforward assessment of the effects of aging, and there may be more than one "normal" pattern of growing old.

EFFECTS OF COHORT ON BEHAVIOR

When contrasting young and old, it is often tempting to conclude that any differences are the result of age. We often ignore another likely source of difference: generation or cohort. The period in which a person is born has a profound impact in shaping his or her beliefs, values, mores, and life style. What people learn, and even how they learn, changes over time, so that each subsequent generation may have quite different formative experiences from the last. These early influences also continue to be manifested in different ways over the course of the life span.

In trying to disentangle the effects of cohort from age, Schaie (1967) makes the distinction between age differences and age changes. A comparison between young and old on an intelligence test, for example, reflects age differences that may be due to the effects of the aging process or to other variables, including differences between generations in initial level of abilities, greater familiarity and ease with being tested among the younger age group, who are typically college students, or historical events unique to that testing period. Age changes, that is, those aspects of development related to the aging process, can only be estimated by following the same persons over time. To control for the possibility that historical events might affect how a particular cohort changes with age, Schaie recommends a "cross-sequential" design, where several cohorts are followed over time. To look at the relation of aging to intelligence, ideally one would select persons of different ages at the outset of the research, for example, groups of 35-, 45-, and 55-year-olds, and study these panels for several years. If initial differences in scores among the 3 age groups are due in part to cohort factors, then these differences will continue to be manifested at each testing interval. On the other hand, one can determine if there are actually age changes in intelligence by comparing the changes manifested by all 3 cohorts during the same age interval, for example, from ages 55 to 65. If persons in all 3 cohorts decline during late middle age, that is evidence of an age change.

This type of research has drawbacks. It is time consuming and expensive to conduct. In particular, it is subject to high dropout rates and the mortality of some subjects. The resulting longitudinal panels, therefore, are likely to represent atypical groups of older persons, quite possibly the most advantaged. Given these problems with both cross-sectional and sequential studies, it is difficult to determine precisely what differences in behavior are related to the aging process, and which are due to other factors, especially generational differences. In time it may be possible to conduct truly experimental research in the field of aging, involving manipulation of the underlying physiological mechanisms that are proposed to be affecting behavior (Birren and Renner 1977). At present, however, interpretations of research findings need to be sensitive both to the potentially powerful effects of generational influences on all aspects of behavior in cross-sectional studies and to the biases in a longitudinal sample.

What Is "Normal" in Old Age?

Another consideration is that there may be no typical pattern of change in old age. In the study of mental development in childhood, there has been a careful charting of normative changes, so that behaviors at a particular age can largely be anticipated. The existence of well-documented norms also facilitates identification of abnormal patterns of development. In research on the relation of aging to behavior, there has often been a similar emphasis on discovery of the average or typical pattern shown in old age. This goal, however, has been elusive, partly because of some incorrect assumptions about the effects of aging.

In the search for a "typical pattern" of behavior in old age, there has often been an implicit assumption that the process of psychological change involves a long, gradual decline, beginning somewhere in a person's 30s or 40s and continuing until death. This model includes several suppositions about behavior in later life, including that all functions are likely to be declining, that all aged individuals share similar characteristics to some extent, and that the postmature period is one in which decrements, rather than growth and other positive change, are emphasized. These types of expectation have sometimes led to self-fulfilling prophecies of decline among persons dealing with the aged, and among older persons themselves.

This model of a gradual and unitary process of decline represents an oversimplified statement on behavioral changes with age. As with biological aging, psychological processes show a complex and sometimes highly individualized pattern of change. It is probably accurate to state that, with advancing age, more and more persons come to experience decline in psychological functioning (Botwinick 1978). However, the ages at which declines are manifested and the extent of change may vary considerably from one person to another.

The principal behavioral feature of the old may be the large range of abilities found among them. Most research has shown a pattern of increasing statistical variance in the scores of the aged on psychological measures, when compared with the young. That is, older persons are more different from one another than are the young. This should not be surprising when one considers the complex factors that affect human abilities, including genetic endowment, opportunities for learning, and motivation. As people have different experiences during the adult years, so is the opportunity for growth and development of various abilities likely to vary, even into old age, when some persons continue to show increments on such functions as intelligence (Schaie and Labouvie-Vief 1974; Schaie 1975).

Relation of Physiological Changes to Behavior

Many people assume that the aging process results in gradual changes in behavior, just as we have a few more wrinkles and gray hairs with each passing year. There is no question that persons change over time, especially in our complex and rapid-paced society. But there is some evidence to suggest that mild, age-related declines in physiological variables have little or no impact on behavior. Persons are able to tolerate some degrees of impairment without any marked effect, but behavior changes are found if the decrement exceeds a certain limit.

Two important studies suggest this type of discontinuous model of behavior changes. In the human aging study conducted by the National Institutes of Health (Birren et al. 1963), a sample of community-residing older men was divided into those who were free of disease processes and those with minimal, but asymptomatic, signs of diseases, principally arteriosclerosis or hypertension. Among the optimally healthy there was slightly elevated blood pressure, but physiological indicators of cerebral function, such as cerebral blood flow and the oxygen supply to the brain, were comparable to that found in younger persons. Scores on various psychometric measures, including tests of intelligence and memory, were also high and did not correlate either with the various measures of physiological function or with chronological age. For subjects with signs of arteriosclerosis, however, there was evidence of reduced cerebral blood flow and altered metabolic processes. Scores on most psychometric tests were also significantly lower than those within the intact group, with performance showing correlations with some of the physiological indicators, including vital capacity of the lungs and cerebral oxygen consumption, and with chronological age (Birren et al. 1963). Thus the presence of specific altered physiological states was found to be related to behavior dysfunctions, while in the absence of those states there were no associations between physiological and psychological indicators.

The results of the Duke longitudinal study on the relation of blood pressure to intelligence also suggest a pattern of discontinuous changes. Blood pressure, on the average, has been found to rise with age. In its effect on behavior, moderately elevated pressure (125–185 mm Hg systolic pressure) is related to stability of intellectual abilities from the sixth to seventh decades of life, while higher values are associated with declining test scores, particularly on the performance battery of the Wechsler Adult Intelligence Scale (WAIS) (Wilkie and Eisdorfer 1971; 1973).

Other findings suggest a similar pattern: that mild variations in physiological and psychophysiological indicators from the norms of adulthood are not related to altered behavior. In considering electrical activity in the brain, for example, evidence of diffuse slowing in brain waves is seen in increasing numbers of persons at advancing ages, especially past age 75. In an organically impaired sample this type of slowing is related to both reduced cerebral blood flow and intellectual deterioration. In healthy aged, however, slowing in brain waves is not associated with intellectual impairment (Marsh and Thompson 1977). The extensive differences in functioning between persons with dementia and those who are not affected also suggests a discontinuous model of change.

One possible explanation for this pattern of discontinuous change may be the capacity of persons to compensate for mild changes in functioning. There can be continued growth in one area while other functions are declining somewhat. In other instances, as age-related decrements in physiological functioning are manifested, individuals may be able to adjust to some extent by drawing upon experience and prior learning to perform activities in more efficient ways. Compensatory behaviors may also have a major impact in the presence of debilitating diseases. While persons with senile brain diseases, for example, generally show marked behavioral alterations, some manifest very little impairment, despite the presence of extensive brain damage (Blessed, Tomlinson, and Roth 1968).

This pattern of discontinuous change contrasts sharply with developmental patterns in childhood, when biological maturation, chronological age, and psychological development are correlated. In later life, age cannot be viewed as a reliable indicator of functioning, or as suggesting a typical or average pattern of response. Age 65, 70, or some other age are not likely to be critical markers, and do not indicate the onset of a stage of senescence. Those critical markers are likely to be encountered with the occurrence of major illnesses, which become increasingly probable with advancing age, but which vary in time of onset from one person to another.

It should be noted that this discontinuous model of aging has been based principally on the relation of certain physical variables to psychological measures. Whether this pattern will be found when studying other behavioral measures, or when more sophisticated means of evaluating the relation of physiological and psychological processes are available, remains to be determined. Physiological variables other than cerebral blood flow or electrical activity also need more attention. Increased knowledge of such factors as hormone levels, especially in response to stressful situations, may lead to a revision of this model of physiological-behavioral interaction. Given our current knowledge, however, changes in behavior brought about when there is significant physiological impairment are much more apparent than those gradual and variable changes found in the absence of a severe decrement.

A related issue is whether decrements in function result at all from aging, or if the principal causes of changes are illnesses, sensory decrements, and other pathological conditions. One clear effect of aging is in creating a predisposition to various ailments that lead to psychological decrements, such as vascular changes that result in reduced cerebral blood flow. At the same time, consideration of such psychophysiological measures as electroencephalograms (EEGs) suggests that an illness model cannot account sufficiently for all the changes found in older persons (Marsh and Thompson 1977). It may be that illnesses have the most dramatic impact on behavior, but that other, more subtle changes in functioning may occur in healthy individuals (Thompson and Marsh 1973). The popular stereotype of aging reflects the condition of the ill and impaired elderly, but as we begin to learn more about the process of aging in healthy older persons, we are likely to be impressed with their continuing competence in most areas of functioning.

AGING AND COGNITIVE FUNCTIONS: INTELLIGENCE

The research findings on age changes in cognitive functioning reflect these patterns: there are increasing differences among persons at advancing ages, and the older one gets, the more probable it becomes that declines in some areas will be experienced. These findings are demonstrated most clearly in the area of intelligence, which has been studied extensively with both cross-sectional and longitudinal methods.

Findings from these two methods of study have resulted in quite different pictures of the expected change in intelligence. Cross-sectional studies have consistently reported lower scores among older subjects. Poorer performance was manifested both on tests involving verbal information that rely on prior learning, such as the verbal subtests of the WAIS, and on those tests requiring novel or unusual responses, for example, the performance subtests on the WAIS or the Raven's Progressive Matrices (Botwinick 1977). Following 3 cohorts, however, Schaie and Labouvie-Vief (1974) found that younger subjects had initially higher scores on a battery of tests, the Primary Mental Abilities (PMA), but in following each cohort over time, there was no decrease in scores on subtests involving verbal abilities, at least until the decade of the 70s. The initial variations among the 3 groups appeared due to cohort differences. Each succeeding generation scored higher initially on the PMA, and these differences were stable over time. These findings are shown in Figure 2.3. On the left side of the figure cross-sectional gradients are plotted,

FIGURE 2.3.   Cross-sectional and longitudinal age gradients for the space test from the primary mental abilities. The 2 graphs on the left depict changes over 2 different 7-year time periods for 2 different samples of subjects. The graphs on the right provide comparable cross-sectional and longitudinal gradients for a single sample followed over a 14-year period.

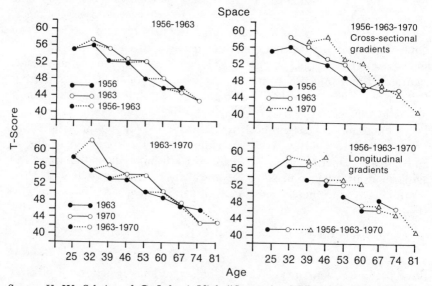

Source: K. W. Schaie and G. Labouie-Vief, "Generational Versus Ontogenetic Components of Change in Adult Cognitive Behavior: A Fourteen Year Cross-Sequential Study," *Developmental Psychology* 10 (1974): 305–320. Copyright © 1974 by the American Psychological Association. Reprinted by permission.

which indicate a decline in intelligence, while on the right side scores of the 3 cohorts are plotted over time, and show a stability in achievement as persons grow older. Other longitudinal studies have also indicated greater stability of intelligence scores than expected, with no or small amounts of decline in verbal abilities before age 70, and a relatively greater but not catastrophic loss after 70. Declines are reported on procedures involving novel responses (e.g., the performance subtests of the WAIS), but less than in cross-sectional research (Wilkie and Eisdorfer 1973; Eisdorfer and Wilkie 1973; Blum, Clark, and Jarvik 1973).

These findings have been criticized for the methodological difficulties inherent in longitudinal research, including the high dropout rate at successive testings and the likelihood that some subjects from the panel will die between test intervals (Horn and Donaldson 1976; Botwinick 1977). Persons who have dropped out or died are considered more likely to have shown a declining pattern of scores than those subjects who return for successive testing sessions. Several studies have identified what has come to be called "terminal decline," that is, a drop in scores on various cognitive tests preceding a person's death (Riegel and Riegel 1972; Blum, Clark, and Jarvik 1973; Lieberman 1968). In the longitudinal study of aging twins, Jarvik and her associates (Blum, Clark, and Jarvik 1973; Jarvik 1975) noted a pattern of change on subtests of the WAIS, which they termed "critical loss." Among persons who showed 2 or 3 of the following changes in scores during a 5-year period—a drop in vocabulary, a 2 percent drop in block design, or a 10 percent loss in digit symbol—almost three-quarters did not survive to the next 5-year test interval. Most persons not manifesting this critical loss were still alive at the next test period. Only limited information was presented about health factors that may have been involved, but the two groups, survivors and nonsurvivors, were similar in age (Jarvik 1975).

In a study conducted by Lieberman (1968), there was an attempt to differentiate terminal decline from specific illnesses. Lieberman tested residents of an old age home with a battery of cognitive tests, including the Bender-Gestalt figure-copying test and the Draw-a-Person test. Testing occurred at 3- or 4-week intervals and all subjects were tested at least 5 times. Of 25 subjects, 8 died within 3 months of the final testing, while 17 were alive a year after the final test sessions. The 2 groups (those who lived and those who died) did not differ in their initial level of performance on these tests, but persons who later died manifested declining test scores during the course of the study. Among persons who survived a year beyond the final testing, some individuals had serious illnesses that required treatment in the hospital or infirmary, but they recovered and had not shown a pattern of declining test performance preceding the illness. Based on these findings, Lieberman suggests that at advanced ages there is a generalized physiological decline that precedes death, and that this decline is reflected in poorer test performance. As suggested by the biological theories of aging, the organism may run out of genetic program or accumulate too many errors in cell functions to continue a viable existence.

Two other factors that are causes of deteriorating cognitive perform- ance were noted earlier in the chapter. These were the presence of even minimal signs of arteriosclerosis (Birren et al. 1963) and high blood pressure (Wilkie and Eisdorfer 1973). Follow-ups of both of those study samples, the NIH human aging subjects and the Duke longitudinal panel, indicate that impaired persons with minimal arteriosclerosis and those with high blood pressure did show a higher death rate in the next decade compared to subjects with normal functioning (Wilkie and Eisdorfer 1973; Granick and Patterson 1972). These factors are un- doubtedly related to the phenomenon of terminal decline reported in other studies.

Both positions on changes in intelligence, supporting either stability or change, are therefore correct. In the absence of major illnesses and/or a decline preceding one's death, there is considerable stability. At the same time, the older one becomes, the more likely it is that there will be some changes. Declines are most likely to be manifested in tests involving novel stimuli or problem-solving situations, and as the consequence of specific disease states, including arteriosclerosis, hypertension, and possibly a process of terminal decline before death. There are, however, many individuals in their 70s and even 80s whose performance on a wide range of psychological tests is at or near levels found in the young (Jarvik 1975; Schaie 1975). The effects of time may therefore be in increasing the risk that declines in intelligence will occur, either because of change in the central nervous system or other physiological changes. Rather than one pattern of test scores characterizing the aging population, individuals are likely to show varying degrees of change from earlier functioning, with some manifesting only minimal decline, while others have relatively extensive losses.

CHANGES IN OTHER COGNITIVE FUNCTIONS

Two of the most common assumptions about cognitive functioning in the later years is that the old are slow and forgetful. As with intelli- gence, however, the pattern of change is actually more complex.

Reaction Time. Reaction time is, perhaps the one ability that most closely approximates a pattern of gradual decline with aging. A slowing in reaction time is, according to Birren (1974), a principle manifestation of neurological aging, and is related to a slowing in the conductance of of electrical impulses in the central nervous system. In comparing reaction time of various parts of the body, for example, jaw, hand, and foot, it has been found that the old are slower than the young on all 3 measures, and that their scores did not differ depending on the site tested (Birren and Botwinick 1955). Since the length of the peripheral nervous system paths varied considerably among jaw, hand, and foot, these findings suggest that the peripheral neural pathways are not related to age differences in reaction time. Slowing is, instead, due principally to changes in the central nervous system.

Complexity of task has also been related to slowing in the aged. Older persons have longer reaction times both on simple tasks, involving no choice, and when a choice has to be made. The extent of slowing, however, increases disproportionately compared to the young as the complexity of task increases (Botwinick 1978). Both optimally healthy and impaired older persons show slowing, with changes more pronounced in the latter (Birren et al. 1963). This slowing process may begin at a relatively early age. Performance, for example, on the Digit Symbol test of the WAIS, which depends to a great extent on speed, begins to decline at around age 20 (Honzik and Macfarlane 1973).

Although slower on the average in their reaction time, older persons also have a greater variance of scores than the young; scores of the young tend to cluster around the mean, while those of aging persons can differ considerably from one another (Schonfield 1974). This means that while older persons are usually slower than the young, a few persons do perform at very high levels characteristic of the young, and others show only small differences from performance levels typical of the young.

This slowing in reaction time is related to one other factor: training. Botwinick and Thompson (1968) compared young and old persons on reaction time, dividing the young into athletic and nonathletic. There were significant differences in performance between the old and both groups of young, but the difference was much smaller with the nonathletes. In a similar vein, Woodruff (1975) attempted to demonstrate the trainability of the old. Noting the association between reaction time and a slowing of the dominant alpha frequency in the EEGs of the aged, she used biofeedback procedures to teach older persons to increase their alpha frequency. This manipulation was associated with improvements in reaction time. These studies do not counter the evidence that slowing is principally related to changes in the central nervous system. Rather, they indicate how the rate of change may be modified to some extent.

The implications of changes in reaction time are not clear. It has been proposed that decreased reaction time may account to some degree for the higher rate of accidents among the old (Birren 1974), although in some situations a slowness in responding could prevent a mishap. Birren (1974) has also suggested that the speed of mental operations is inherently involved with various kinds of intellectual task, such as those involving complex problem solving, creativity, or retrieval of information from stored memories. Findings on the relation of reaction time to intellectual performance, however, have been inconsistent (Botwinick 1978). Thus, slowing in reaction time is present to some extent in most older persons, and is accentuated by disease, but its relation to more complex cognitive and social behaviors remains to be explored more fully.

Memory and Age. The most common assumption about older persons is that their memories are beginning to fail. While memory deficits are prominent in persons with dementia, the extent of changes in healthy older persons has probably been exaggerated both by the elderly and by those who associate with them, including relatives and professionals. One aspect of this tendency to exaggerate memory problems is the discrepancy reported in several studies between memory complaints and actual memory functioning. Complaints about memory problems are quite common; for example, one-half of persons over 60 in a community sample (Lowenthal, Berkman, and associates 1967) and two-thirds of a sample of older psychiatric patients (Kahn et al. 1975) stated they had memory difficulties. These complaints, however, have not correlated with scores on objective tests of memory performance (Lowenthal, Berkman, and associates 1967; Kahn et al. 1975; Gurland et al. 1976; Perlmutter 1978). The most frequent complaint is that of poor recent memory, but Kahn and his associates (1975) found that persons who complained of forgetting recent events performed as well on tests of recent memory as on measures of remote memory.

Two related factors probably contribute to this discrepancy between complaints and performance. First, the types of problem reported by older persons are primarily commonplace events, such as forgetting someone's name, forgetting what they went to the store for, or forgetting where they put something in the house. Because of the stereotypes about aging, older persons may take these everyday incidents, which would be ignored in the young, as indicating a pathological decline in memory (Kahn et al. 1975). Second, while complaints do not correlate with memory performance, significant associations have been found with measures of depression (Kahn et al. 1975; Gurland et al. 1976). Dividing their sample into persons with intact brain function and those with evidence of chronic organic brain syndrome, Kahn and associates (1975) report that depression was significantly correlated with memory complaints in both groups (see Figure 2.4). Thus in the organically impaired, who have actual pathologic disturbances of memory, complaints about memory were related to affective status. Memory complaints, then, and possibly other self-perceptions of cognitive performance, are affected by stereotypic age expectations and the tendency for depressed persons to underestimate their abilities (Beck 1967).

While the extent of memory impairment in the aged is exaggerated, some aspects of memory are likely to change with age. Memory processes can be considered as involving primary or short-term memory, and secon-

FIGURE 2.4. Relation of memory complaint and memory performance (combined performance on memory tests) according to level of depression (Hamilton Scale) and presence of altered brain function (combining Face-Hand test and mental status questionnaire).

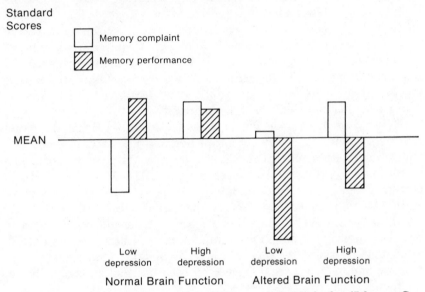

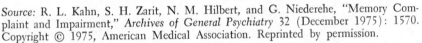

Source: R. L. Kahn, S. H. Zarit, N. M. Hilbert, and G. Niederehe, "Memory Complaint and Impairment," *Archives of General Psychiatry* 32 (December 1975): 1570. Copyright © 1975, American Medical Association. Reprinted by permission.

dary or long-term memory. Primary memory refers to the storage capacity for information that is consciously and actively being processed at a given time. When told a phone number, for example, most persons can usually retain that number for a brief period of time. The capacity of primary memory, that is, the amount of information that can be held for active processing at any given time, appears to be stable with increasing age, so long as no reorganization of the material is required (Craik 1977). A task such as digit span forward from the Wechsler Memory Scale (Wechsler 1945) does not decline with age (D.A. Walsh 1975), but digit span backwards, which requires reorganizing the stimuli, has been found to be somewhat poorer among the old. Even when there is brain damage due to alcoholism or dementia, the capacity of primary memory appears unimpaired (Talland 1965; Zarit et al. 1978).

Secondary memory involves a transfer or fixing of material from primary memory into a storage system, and the later retrieval of that information. One's attention can then be directed away from the original material, but it remains accessible at a later, appropriate time. Age differences have been reported in both the acquisition of new material and its later retrieval (Craik 1977). These processes have been studied by comparing the performance on learned items under conditions of recall and recognition. Recall tests ask subjects to produce spontaneously the material previously learned, while tests of recognition provide several choices, including the material that was previously presented. While the aged consistently do more poorly on recall tasks, tests of recognition have had contradictory results. Some studies have indicated equivalent performance to the young on recognition (Schonfield 1965), suggesting that the aged may have decrements in the retrieval of information. Other studies have reported decrements in both recognition and recall, compared with the young (Gordon and Clark 1974; Perlmutter 1978).

This apparent contradiction may be due to the fact that the recall-recognition comparison may not adequately test differences in acquisition and retrieval. Recognition depends less on retrieval processes than does recall, but to be successful at a recognition task, one does not have to acquire as much information in the first place as would be necessary for recall (McNulty and Caird 1966). Students who have taken multiple-choice and essay exams know they have to prepare differently for each, studying the material more thoroughly for essays, where they must recall, rather than recognize, the correct answer. Therefore, it cannot be assumed that the finding of no age difference on some recognition tasks indicates a retrieval deficit.

Other research suggests that the major difference in memory between young and old is at the point of acquisition. Most studies have focused only on recall after a delay in the presentation of the original material. If persons are tested for how much they learned initially, and then evaluated for later recall, it has generally been found that older subjects differ most from the young at the point of acquisition. They do not lose more information than the young over time (see Botwinick 1978 and Craik 1977 for reviews). There are a few exceptions to this pattern, but long-term follow-ups of how well information is retained are generally lacking.

Age differences in the recall of material from secondary memory may be related, in part, to the paucity of information-processing strategies that the elderly employ, such as organizing the material into meaningful units or categories, or using mediators. The old have been found generally to use poorer strategies for organizing new information (Heron and Craik 1964; Mandler 1967; Craik and Masani 1967). Instruction in organizing strategies has resulted in improved memory function, particularly in persons having low verbal skills (Taub 1968; Hultsch 1969; 1971). Similarly, the aged have been reported to use few mediational techniques in acquiring new information (Hulicka and Grossman 1967; Canestrari 1968). Performance on a paired-associates learning task has been found to improve when the aged are instructed in the use of either verbal or visual mediators, compared to persons receiving no specific instructions (Canestrari 1968). The use of visual mediators has also been related to improved memory for word-list tasks, and for associating names with faces (Zarit, Gallagher, and Kramer, in press).

Another factor affecting memory performance is the familiarity of the material. While there are marked differences between old and young in the recall of nonsense syllables, older persons show a relative improvement when tested with meaningful material, though still performing at somewhat lower levels than the young (Botwinick 1978; Walsh 1975). These findings suggest, on the one hand, that the old are less willing to devote energy to apparently meaningless tasks. In one study (Hulicka 1967) there was an attrition rate of 80 percent of elderly subjects, who refused to continue a paired-associates learning task when one part of the pair consisted of a word and one part of letters (e.g., "insane—TL"). On the other hand, it has been suggested that the aged may be less able to process new information at deeper levels, that is, to attribute meaning to new material through articulation and association with prior learned material (Walsh 1975). The results of attempts to improve performance by encouraging meaningful coding of material have had contradictory results, some showing no effects with semantic orienting (Walsh 1975; Eysenck 1974) and others report improvements (Zelinski, Walsh, and Thompson 1976).

Older persons also display relatively greater deficits in performance than the young on learning and memory tests under 2 specific conditions: when there is time pressure to respond (Canestrari 1963) and with the introduction of distractions, such as in a dichotomous listening task involving playing different stimuli in each ear (Craik 1977). People troubled by occasional forgetfulness can benefit from directions to take their time and to eliminate potential distractions when they want to learn new information.

Comparisons of secondary memory in the aged usually involve relatively brief periods of time from 10-minute delays to a day or two. Older persons who complain of poor memory are generally concerned with longer time spans. They typically report that they can remember events from the remote past, but have difficulties with more recent memories (Kahn et al. 1975). This complaint suggests either that new material is not acquired as efficiently as in the past, or that there are problems with retrieval, both of which are consistent with the findings discussed above. Precise evaluations of the extent of this problem are difficult to make. Those "old memories" that persons report are often highly significant events, such as weddings, births of children, or other specific incidents in their early lives. To compare recall of these significant events with more recent happenings, which have less personal importance, may be misleading. Commonplace clinical examinations of recent and remote memory often make the error of comparing events that are not equivalent in their significance, for example, by asking the questions: "What did you have for breakfast?" and "When did you get married?" The equivalent question to the latter would be: "What did you eat for breakfast the day you got married?"

When past learning, such as of historical events or personal information, has been compared with performance on relatively abstract tests of memory (e.g., items on the Wechsler Memory Scale), past memories were relatively more intact (Botwinick 1967; 1978). When attempts have been made to test persons on relatively equivalent material (e.g., asking about a past political event and one that happened recently), older persons performed well on both recent and remote measures, even when they complained of problems with recent memory (Kahn et al. 1975). This type of complaint about recent, as compared to remote, memory may be related in part to stereotypes about aging, and in part to difficulty in acquiring some types of new information that are not personally meaningful.

There is some evidence that older persons may have more frequent occurrences of what has been termed the "tip of the tongue" phenomenon (Brown and McNeill 1966). This involves being unable to recall a name or a word when we have the feeling we know it. In a series of studies (Camp, Lachman, and Lachman 1977; Throneberry, Lachman, and Lachman 1977), old and younger subjects were examined for the tip of the tongue experience on a test of world knowledge from several sources, including newspaper headlines, the movies, the Bible, and mythology. It was found that older persons were more likely than the young to have this feeling of knowing a name they could not recall at that moment. The older subjects, however, actually knew more names on the test, so the proportion of tip of the tongue experiences to their total knowledge was not greater than in the young. Furthermore, when given a multiple-choice test on items they felt they knew, older subjects gave correct responses as frequently as the young. These findings suggest that while older persons may have more tip of the tongue experiences for old memories, these occur in proportion to their greater knowledge base, and the information can be retrieved as efficiently as in the young when appropriate cues are given.

Unlike intelligence, changes in memory have not been studied in relation to specific health conditions, with the exception of senile dementia. As in the case of intelligence, it would be expected that changes in memory are likely to be most pronounced in the presence of various disease states, especially those affecting the central nervous system. There is also a paucity of longitudinal data on changes in memory performance by old and young subjects. There needs, therefore, to be a delineation of factors that lead to changes in memory performance in old age, and a careful assessment of memory that clearly distinguishes complaints from actual performance. Making a distinction between meaningful and non-meaningful tests is also useful.

Furthermore, one critical point has not been established—how these various assessment tools actually relate to the everyday occurrences of forgetting that concern older persons. Aspects of memory measured in a laboratory, such as recall of word pairs, may not be related to forgetting in commonplace situations. Behavioral observations of older persons that begin to delineate the links between cognitive tests and everyday functioning would greatly enhance our understanding of the later years.

Summary

The processes of aging, both at biological and psychological levels, suggest several recurring themes, foremost of which is the increased variability of humans from one another as they age. Both in physiological indicators such as glucose tolerance and in psychological measures involving reaction time, intelligence, or other characteristics, some older persons manifest large degrees of decline in comparison to the young, while others show only small or even negligible differences from the young. There may also be a decreased resistance to stress, as evidenced in the slowing of physiological responses of older organisms to such factors as cold temperatures, and in the considerable impact on psychological functioning of illness. As persons age, there is an increasing likelihood that both biological and psychological decrements will occur, but predictions about any given individual or about normative functioning are difficult to obtain, because of the variations in performance found in the old. Thus, general statements about how the aged remember or about intelligence in old age need to be qualified to take into account individual differences Another critical factor is the type of test material. The aged typically perform better on simpler or familiar types of tasks than on tests involving novel responses, unfamiliar activities, or increasing levels of complexity.

The extent of decline in psychological dimensions such as memory or reaction time is accentuated by some of the chronic ailments that often occur in later life, particularly when the central nervous system is affected. Among the healthy aged, however, physiological changes may not affect behavior to a great extent until some threshold is passed, thereby moving physiological indicators into a pathological range.

One's conceptualization of these processes of aging is ultimately related to the development of various intervention strategies. If the aged are viewed as all experiencing a slow, gradual decline, there is likely to be a lack of specificity in response to the psychological and social problems found in later life. Since growing old is inevitable, this view may also lead to a preponderance of custodial and reactive strategies. Aging is more accurately described as bringing about an increased risk of deleterious changes. This individualized approach can facilitate the development both of treatment programs that are in response to specific decrements found in a particular person, and of preventive strategies, such as the control of hypertension, that would reduce the risk of decline in some persons.

CHAPTER 3

Personality and Aging

PERHAPS THE MOST INTERESTING and least understood question about the aging process is how we change over the course of the years in our thinking, feeling, and experiencing of events. We wonder whether those characteristics that we deem the most important aspects of our selves will be affected by the passage of time, worrying that we may lose what we value the highest or that we will become someone we do not like. Or we consider how those problems and traits we do not like in ourselves will fare over time, whether we will finally overcome habits we feel are limiting or unattractive, or if our faults may become like our noses, even more pronounced over the years. We worry about how our appearance will change and whether that will drive others away from us. And we wonder whether we might become rigid and irritable, or if somewhere along the way we might acquire the wisdom and serenity that some philosophers have promised as the outcome of a good life.

Because personality is a global concept involving what is unique or characteristic of a particular individual, it has been difficult to define in ways that lend themselves readily to measurement and to the empirical validation of theory. Early personality theory stressed the importance of one or a few traits or instincts, which were used to explain all the actions and emotions of an individual. According to Mischel (1977):

> We have theories of personality built on a few body types, or on a handful of factors, or on simple conditioning and environmental contingencies, or on the vicissitudes of one or more favorite motives—sex, aggression, competence, achievement, dissonance, self-realization—or on a humanism that correctly emphasizes the humanity of people but too easily loses sight of (or perhaps interest in?) its antecedents. (p. 252)

This process, according to Mischel, stretches each explanatory concept to the breaking point, and has not led to an incremental development of theory in the field of personality. One instead has several different view-points, with few positions complementary to one another. Evidence contrary to major tenets of each theory can also be cited. Thus dynamic theorists do not assess adequately the impact and influence of environmental events, while a behaviorist who stresses environmental determinism has few concepts to explain why two persons in similar situations respond in different ways. This lack of development of basic concepts in the field of personality has complicated the study of changes with age, an enterprise that is complex even under the best circumstances, where variables are easy to define and make operational. As a result, a coherent literature on personality and aging has been slow to emerge.

In this chapter a framework for the study of personality and aging will be presented, drawn particularly from the work of Walter Mischel (1968; 1976; 1977) and of D. Bem and Allen (1974), and from the methodological considerations discussed by Schaie and his associates (Schaie and Labouvie-Vief 1974; Schaie and Marquette 1972; Schaie and Parham 1976; Schaie and Gribbin 1975a). Using that framework, studies of personality and aging will be reviewed, with a discussion of their implications for clinical practice.

Rather than reducing behavior to the result of some internal state, whether motive, "dynamics," or trait, it is important to recognize that specific actions often reflect situational contingencies, and could not be predicted by focusing only on the person. The attempt to reason backwards from behavior to motives is fraught with dangers. Under some conditions, the response of the person in a given situation will have more to do with the situation than with the person.

Concepts of Personality

According to Mischel (1976; 1977), personality concepts will help us to explain some of the behaviors of persons some of the time.

In the development of personality research there were repeated attempts to show the predictive values of traits such as achievement or dependency, or of characteristics with a hypothesized instinctual basis, such as aggression, to the behavior of persons across several situations. While measurement of a trait was often highly predictive of behavior in the situation in which it was first measured, there was often little consistency in behaviors across situations. Where traits have been assessed across situations or over time, the highest correlations that have been obtained usually do not exceed 0.30, and thus account for only 9 percent of the variability of behavior.

This inconsistency in behaviors across situations has important practical consequences. It has been found, for example, that the best predictor of posthospital adjustment of psychiatric patients is the setting into which the person is placed, such as whether there are jobs or family support available. In-hospital behaviors, including psychological tests, which are often used in discharge planning, actually have little relation to outcome (Fairweather et al. 1969). Similar observations suggest that the role of environmental variables is a powerful determinant of behavior (Mischel 1976).

While some researchers have proposed that the lack of consistency in behaviors of persons across situations is due to poor measurement of traits, Mischel (1976) argues that one would logically expect consistencies in behaviors to be low. The fact that an individual acts differently across situations indicates the ability to discriminate changes from one situation to another. This variability is adaptive, enabling the individual to respond to the unique characteristics of a situation. In contrast, someone with a high degree of inflexibility in responses would be likely to act inappropriately or ineffectively in many circumstances.

While we are often flexible in responding to various situations, we also perceive ourselves as recognizably similar over time and from one situation to another (Kimmel 1974). When personality traits are rated from global scales, rather than inferred from behaviors, there is a high degree of stability in the ratings over time (Mischel 1976). This is the case whether the ratings are done by the person or by others, and there is often a high correlation between self-ratings and the assessments of others. Thus, persons see themselves and are seen by others as consistent and recognizable across situations and over time, but their behaviors in a specific situation can usually be predicted better from the situational context than from the presence of a particular trait.

In discussing this inability to predict behavior from traits, D. Bem and Allen (1974) suggest that the error is due to the type of assumptions made about the nature of individual differences. They propose that most research has been guided by a "nomothetic" assumption "that a particular trait dimension or set of trait dimensions is universally applicable to all persons and that individual differences are to be identified with different locations on those dimensions" (D. Bem and Allen 1974, pp. 308–309). As an example of this type of research, they cite the Hartshorne and May (1928) study of honesty in children, which proposed that behavior in various situations could be predicted from the rankings of children on an honesty-dishonesty dimension. The researchers found instead that the behavior of individuals varied considerably across the situations in which they were observed. Instead of a nomothetic approach, D. Bem and Allen propose viewing personality from an idiographic perspective. In particular, they suggest that traits may not be related to one another in the same way from one person to another, and that traits may not have the same relevancy for each person. According to D. Bem and Allen, persons have some characteristics that they see as pertinent to themselves and in which they are consistent. Other traits, however, have lesser importance, and it is in behaviors reflecting those traits that we are inconsistent from one situation to the next. Furthermore, persons differ in what traits they are consistent in. In reinterpreting the Hartshorne and May findings, D. Bem and Allen (1974) propose that honesty was a dimension on which some of the children showed consistency and others did not, and that this factor is the critical one for predicting behavior in a particular situation, not what the child scored on the abstract trait "honesty."

To test their theory, D. Bem and Allen assessed undergraduates on several traits, including friendliness and conscientiousness. For each trait persons rated their overall level and also their variability from one situation to another in the expression of that characteristic. For example, concerning friendliness, subjects were asked: "In general, how friendly and outgoing are you?" and "How much do you vary from one situation to another in how friendly and outgoing you are?" (D. Bem and Allen 1974, p. 312). Two behavioral measures of these traits were obtained, the first assessing the traits of friendliness and conscientiousness in various situations, and the second asking friends and relatives of subjects to rate them on a global measure of each trait and on subjects' behaviors in specific situations. The results indicated that persons who rated themselves as consistent in a trait were more likely to report acting consistently across several situations. There was also higher agreement between the ratings of other judges and that of subjects, and among the various other judges with each other, when the subject saw himself as consistent in that trait. In contrast, if the person said he was not consistent, he reported variable behavior and other judges often did not agree with one another in their ratings. As an example, mothers' and fathers' reports of friendliness in the subjects only correlated with one another at the .28 level for subjects who were low in consistency for friendliness, but there was an association of .75 between mothers' and fathers' ratings for those high in consistency. It should also be pointed out that self-ratings of the amount of friendliness were not correlated with the extent of variability across situations. Some persons who saw themselves as very friendly might show more variability in different settings than others who rated themselves lower on the friendliness dimension.

The implication of this research for a model of personality is that persons are consistent in their behaviors across situations only for those traits and characteristics that are pertinent to them. In order to understand or predict the behavior of any individual, one must assess the characteristics for which the person perceives himself to be consistent and inconsistent. In considering personality in old age, it has been proposed that several traits, including dependency (Goldfarb 1969) and cautiousness (Botwinick 1978), become more prominent in late life, but the importance and predictive value of any of these traits across situations would vary from one person to another. Similarly, one would predict that traits on which the person sees himself as consistent follow a different pattern from those characteristics rated as inconsistent. It is important, then, to learn what characteristics are pertinent to a particular individual, and whether those dimensions have changed in old age.

Methodological Considerations in the Study of Personality and Aging

As was discussed in Chapter 2, the study of age changes in cognitive abilities is often confounded with differences in the levels of abilities between cohorts. Thus, an age difference in intelligence between a 70-year-old and a 40-year-old may be the result of maturation or may be due to generational differences in such factors as early childhood nutrition, socialization, and education. In considering personality development there are several possible patterns of change that must be considered (Schaie and Parham 1976). First, some traits may be strongly influenced by hereditary factors or shaped by the environment in early childhood, and remain relatively constant over the life span. Second, some traits may be influenced and modified by social events that occur at specific points during the life cycle, including marriage, parenthood, career changes, and, in later life, the losses that become increasingly prevalent. Third, there may be traits that are modified in response to social and cultural changes. In addition, as the D. Bem and Allen (1974) analysis suggests, which traits are affected by environmental events, social change, or even by early childhood influences may vary from one individual to another.

Most of the research on personality and aging has been cross-sectional, raising the possibility that the findings of age differences reflect a generational effect, rather than age changes. In a few exceptions there have been longitudinal studies of single cohorts, but the results may be unique to that generation or may confound age changes with the effects of historical events (Schaie and Parham 1976). To make a more accurate estimate of the effects of aging, cohort, and social and cultural events on personality, Schaie and Parham propose using a cross-sequential, time-sequential research design, in which several cohorts are followed longitudinally. This method makes it possible to estimate the effects of cohort differences by seeing if initial age differences between cohorts remain stable or change over time. Thus if 65- and 70-year-olds differ in ratings of dependency at an initial testing, the finding at a 5-year follow-up that the 65-year-olds turned 70 now have dependency ratings similar to the 70-year-olds at the first testing suggests an age change. If the results showed that the ratings in dependency did not change over time, that would suggest the importance of cohort. Similarly, one can contrast the findings of two or more cohorts making the transition from 65 to 70. Comparable patterns of change in two generations from 65 to 70 indicate the effects of developmental processes, while different patterns suggest that unique historical events that occurred in one or both 5-year periods had important, and differing, effects on personality of the two cohorts.

Schaie and Parham (1976) applied this method of analysis to persons who were evaluated at successive 7-year intervals and who ranged in age from 22 to 71 at the time of initial measurement. Using a factor analysis of questionnaire data, they obtained 13 factors similar to dimensions of the 16 Personality Factor (PF) scale (Cattell 1957), and also 6 attitudinal measures. They found cohort differences in 9 of their 13 factors and 4 of the attitudinal measures. Age changes were apparent for only 2 factors, excitability and universal political concern, both of which increased with age. Schaie and Parham also investigated time changes by comparing the original 1963 sample to a new cross-sectional sample drawn in 1970, and performing an analysis of variance on the personality scores, with age and time of measurement as independent variables. Time of measurement was significantly related to several dimensions, including developing a practical, down-to-earth style, decreased positive interest in financial support and universal political concern, and increases in conservatism and group dependency. These time changes are presumably the result of the cultural and political climate of that era.

This research has two major implications for the study of personality and aging. First, it is apparent from the findings that a major source of differences between young and old in psychological traits is due to cohort membership rather than changes with age. Second, there was evidence of considerable change over time in many of these dimensions for all age groups. The results emphasize the importance of social and cultural influences. In fact, the authors suggest little evidence of characteristics that have a lifelong stability because of the effects of biological factors or early childhood socialization (Schaie and Parham 1976). These findings indicate that in evaluating personality in older persons it is important to consider the influence of cohort and social change on behavior, as well as developmental changes.

In addition to the effects of cohort and social change, differences between men and women must be considered in the study of personality and aging. Scaie and Parham (1976) suggest the possibility of varying patterns of development for men and women at different points in the life cycle. Futhermore, in some characteristics sex differences may be more pronounced than either cohort effects or developmental changes. In a cross-sectional comparison of four cohorts—adolescents, young adults, middle-aged, and persons within one or two years of retirement—Lowenthal, Thurnher, and Chiriboga (1975) report that sex differences were often larger than age differences. In particular, they found that men had a stronger and more positive self-image than women at all stages, while women reported more of both positive and negative affective experiences over a recent time period. Another difference was in the nature of friendships formed. Men emphasized shared interests and activities as the basis for making friends, while women stressed shared affect and reciprocity in the relationship. Women also appeared more satisfied than men with the friends they had and with their own capacity for friendship.

A Model of Personality and Aging

In studying personality, Mischel (1976; 1977) identifies three relevant perspectives: (1) how environmental conditions produce an effect on persons; (2) person variables that mediate the effects of the environment on an individual; and (3) the interaction of the person and environment. While not exhaustive of the possible ways of viewing the person, these three dimensions have critical theoretical and empirical links to behavior, and an examination of each contributes to an understanding of personality changes in aging.

ENVIRONMENTAL CONDITIONS

As was discussed earlier in this chapter, the impact of the environment on behavior is considerable, warranting its inclusion in a theory of personality. Mischel (1976) notes six dimensions of human environments relevant for the study of personality. How these dimensions might affect older persons is discussed below.

1. *Ecological.* Ecological factors include climate and geographic qualities, architecture, and the physical uses of space. Physical factors such as how hot or crowded a room is or the arrangement of furniture have a marked effect on behavior. E. P. Friedman (1966), for example, has reported that social relationships among residents in an old age home were more readily formed when rooms were in greater proximity. In an experimental project, Lawton, Liebowitz, and Charon (1970) found that providing private rooms around a common social area for brain syndrome patients resulted in increased movement of patients but decreased staff-patient interactions. Among the community elderly there is some indication that proximity influences friendships, with persons selecting friends from residents living nearer to them (Lawton and Simon 1968).

2. *Behavioral Settings.* This dimension refers to the number of settings, such as grocery store, bank, or church, in which interactions may occur. In rating the daily activities of older persons in two communities, one in Kansas and the other in Yorkshire, England, Barker and Barker (1968) reported few differences between residents of the two communities,

but both samples of aged residents differed from younger adults in significant ways. In particular, they interacted in fewer behavioral settings, were less likely to have a central role in their interpersonal interactions, and spent less time within each behavior setting. This type of direct observation provides information on how the environments of older persons are restricted and have lost some of their complexity.

There has been some speculation about the value of complex, stimulating environments for the old. In early childhood, of course, an environment that is rich in stimulation from persons and inanimate objects is considered more conducive to intellectual development (see White 1969). A few researchers have considered this dimension for the elderly. Lowenthal, Thurnher, and Chiriboga (1975) report, for example, that the ablest persons in their sample of individuals approaching retirement often reported there were few challenges or stimulating situations in their present lives, compared to the past. In a cross-sequential study that looked at factors related to the maintenance of intellectual abilities, Schaie and Gribbin (1975b) found that persons who improved in scores on an intelligence battery (Thurstone's Primary Mental Abilities) reported a more complex environment. Whether their surroundings had a stimulating effect on intellectual functions or some common factor such as vitality accounted both for cognitive gains and for being in a complex environment could not be determined. These findings of an association of environment and cognitive abilities suggest the value of further inquiries of this sort.

3. *Organizational.* According to Mischel (1976), this dimension includes the size, type of staff, and organizational structure of various community institutions. Organizational structure can have a profound impact on behavior. An example is provided by the famous mock-prison experiment of Haney, Banks, and Zimbardo (1973). In this study students participated in a simulated prison. Subjects were carefully screened so as to exclude anyone showing evidence of antisocial behavior. Within one week many of the "guards" were exhibiting brutal and harassing behaviors toward the "prisoners." According to the authors, these behaviors could not be accounted for by traits such as a lack of empathy among those students assigned to be guards. Rather, the roles and authority structure in this situation brought out antisocial behaviors.

In his classic monograph, *Asylums*, Goffman (1961) has identified some of the structural features of settings that have important consequences for behavior. In particular he noted that in total institutions (which he defines as any setting where an inmate spends 24 hours a day and is under the control of a single authority and set of rules) the potential for constant surveillance and control of behavior makes it possible to extract a much higher degree of conformity to rules and standards of behavior than in everyday settings. Five features of total institutions affect the extent of control over individual behavior. First, there is a hierarchical authority structure, with inmates at the lowest rung. As a result, the staff potentially has total control over inmates, including the power to adjudicate any disputes between inmates and staff. Thus in a disagreement between staff and inmate, such as over food or dress or any other facet of life, it is probable that the inmate will be considered at fault and punished or reprimanded. The second feature of total institutions is that they often take control of personal habits. In extreme cases, activities such as urinating or defecation are regulated. In virtually all total institutions there is some control of activities, such as eating at certain times or being out of one's room or bed by a particular time. According to Goffman (1961), these types of rule make it difficult and frustrating for inmates to satisfy personal needs in an efficient way.

A third feature of total institutions is that inmates are often made to feel humiliated and mortified. In particular they often have to engage in behaviors that are considered typical of children or others in society who have low status. For example, mental patients are sometimes provided only spoons to eat with, or have to ask for matches to light a cigarette. Similarly, in many nursing homes residents are not allowed to close their doors for privacy. There may also be direct punishments of inmates, such as beatings or the punitive use of drugs. Fourth, the nature of the setting often makes it impossible for the person who is humiliated to engage in face-saving behavior. If an inmate who has been punished acts sullenly, his sullenness may become the focus of attention and possible further punishment by the staff. Other defensive tactics the inmates may use so that they do not have to acknowledge the authority of the institution, including apathy, withdrawal, or anger, may similarly come under attack. A fifth factor is that status within the total institution is solely defined by one's place in the institution's hierarchy; one's status on the outside world counts for little. A person who was a physician, for example, will go through the same initiation procedures in a prison as someone who was an unskilled laborer.

These qualities of total institutions are particularly relevant to nursing homes and hospitals in which only a small proportion of older persons reside. Some of these factors, however, may also come into play in other settings that do not involve 24-hour surveillance, for example, in schools or government agencies. One important question is whether the aged are viewed and treated differently by personnel in various organizations because of their age. They may be accorded a lower status, or there may be a greater tendency for others to dismiss their complaints and needs, rather than to question the organization's actions or procedures.

4. *Characteristics of Inhabitants.* The age, sex, abilities, and status of persons with whom we regularly interact at work or around the home can affect both our behavior and self-concept. A major issue in the geronto-

logical literature is the value of age-segregated housing, which is discussed in Chapter 4. One imaginative project describes the potential benefits of age integration in specific settings (Kahana and Kahana 1970). Old persons who were admitted to a state mental hospital were randomly assigned to one of three units: (1) a demonstration ward for aged patients; (2) an ordinary geriatric ward; and (3) a unit of adult patients. Improvements in cognitive and social functioning were greatest on the adult unit and in the geriatric demonstration ward. On the adult unit, the care and attention that aged patients received from younger residents appeared to have a stimulating and beneficial impact comparable to that of the highly funded demonstration ward.

Two important features characterize communities of the old. First, because of their greater longevity, women outnumber men in the older population. There are only 72 men to every 100 women among persons over 65, and the proportion of women in the population rises with advancing age (Bouvier, Atlee, and McVeigh 1975). As men typically participate in social programs less than women, women vastly outnumber men in many social settings. This situation affects the potential for heterosexual sexual outlets for older women and limits the variety and type of social interactions that are possible. A second factor in communities of older persons is that in age-segregated housing there will be increasing numbers of persons with serious health problems and disabilities. That type of situation raises the possibility for developing mutual self-help programs, such as typified by the cooperative arrangements developed by the Council for Jewish Elderly in Chicago (Glasscote, Gudeman, and Miles 1977). On the other hand, a community with a large number of disabled persons may be a limiting or depressing environment for some older persons.

5. *Perceived Social Climate.* This dimension includes the nature and intensity of social interactions. It is likely that perceived qualities of the environment or of other persons in a setting, such as whether they are seen as positive or negative, will affect mood and behavior. As other aspects of the environment change as we age, it follows that our perception of the social climate also changes.

6. *Functional Properties.* Functional properties of a setting include the incentives, reinforcements, and punishments for various behaviors, that is, what actions are encouraged, discouraged, or actively punished. Both Hoyer (1973) and Labouvie-Vief (1976) have proposed that there are typically fewer incentives and expectations for competent behavior in the elderly. The absence of rewards for positive behaviors may be one reason for the high prevalence of depression in old age (see Chapter 8).

Person Variables

Person variables are those characteristics of the individual that both mediate the effects of the environment and also help actively to shape the environment. While environmental conditions have a powerful influence on behavior, there are in all but the most extreme situations variations in the ways people respond to similar settings. Furthermore, individuals undoubtedly exercise some self-selection of environment, choosing settings that are conducive to their values, goals, temperament, or some other characteristic (Mischel 1976; 1977). As discussed earlier, those person variables most salient to an individual are likely to be related to consistent behavior across situations, while other characteristics may predict the person's actions in only one or two particular settings.

Among the person variables that either have been studied or have some relevance for later life are competencies, cognitive style, sex-role behaviors such as aggressiveness and passivity, wisdom, and self-concept. This list represents a less than comprehensive agenda of characteristics that we might want to survey. But given the limited attention to personality and the poor conceptualization of many studies, a more complete review is not possible at the present time.

Although often overlooked by personality theories, the competencies of a person to understand incoming stimuli and follow through effectively with appropriate actions is an important dimension. Intellectual competencies in the aged have been studied extensively, as was discussed in Chapter 2, with many functions showing little change at least until advanced age. Other behavioral and social competencies, such as the ability to initiate and maintain social conversations or to perform various complex tasks effectively, have received little attention.

Cognitive style refers to the ways persons organize and interpret incoming stimuli. Two related measures of cognitive style have received considerable attention over the past two decades. Based on a series of laboratory studies, Witkin and his associates (Witkin et al. 1962) have proposed that persons are either field-dependent or -independent in the ways they respond to stimuli. One of his measures, the rod-and-frame test, can be used to illustrate the meaning of this characteristic. The task involves trying to adjust the rod in a darkened room so that it is vertical to the ground. Because the room is dark, the person must rely on an internal sense of the vertical, rather than the usual environmental cues. Persons who can solve this and similar problems are called field-independent, that is, they are able to make responses based on internal judgments and to avoid distracting environmental influences. Field-dependent persons, in contrast, are more likely swayed in their performance by environmental cues.

The second measure, locus of control, was developed by Rotter (1966) to assess whether an individual feels he has control over events and the ability to obtain reinforcement from the environment. Perceived control over events may be an important dimension for affecting how persons respond to stressful situations and for maintaining a more positive self-concept.

Studies of these cognitive style variables indicate they are stable during the adult years, although little research has been conducted on their predictive value in old age (Kimmel 1974). Looking at their relation to functioning in the later years, Kuypers (1972) reported that subjects with an internal locus of control were more active and better adapted to their environments than were externally oriented persons. Internal locus of control, however, was associated with higher intelligence, so it cannot be determined whether intelligence or locus of control was more important for good adaptation.

One measure of cognitive style that has received considerable attention in the aging literature is rigidity. Despite the widespread assumption that persons grow more rigid in their behaviors as they age, there is inconsistent evidence of greater rigidity. Based on a factor analytic study of 18 measures of rigidity, Chown (1961) identified 5 principal components. Age and intelligence, however, accounted for more of the variance in the 18 measures than did the rigidity factors. Because age and intelligence were also correlated, it was not possible to determine if aging or low intelligence was the principal determinant of these rigidities.

In a cross-sequential study of rigidity, Schaie and Labouvie-Vief (1974) were able to make a clearer assessment of the relation of age and rigidity (see Figure 3.1). Their study included persons from several cohorts who

FIGURE 3.1. Cross-sectional and longitudinal age gradients for personality-perceptual rigidity.

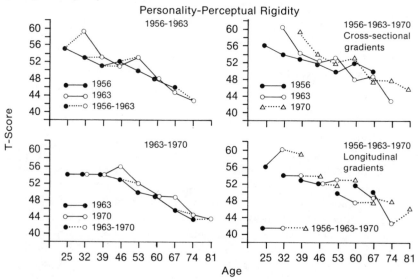

Source: K. W. Schaie and G. Labouvie-Vief, "Generational Versus Ontogenetic Components of Change in Adult Cognitive Behavior: A Fourteen Year Cross-Sequential Study," *Developmental Psychology* 10 (1974): 305–320. Copyright © 1974 by the American Psychological Association. Reprinted by permission.

ranged in age from the 20s to the 70s and who were tested three times at 7-year intervals. The measure of rigidity used was the Test of Behavioral Rigidity, which factors into three dimensions. These factors are: (1) motor-cognitive rigidity, that is, the ability to shift from one activity to another; (2) personality-perceptual rigidity, which measures self-reports of persons' abilities to adjust to new surroundings and to change habits and thought patterns; and (3) psychomotor speed, including copying familiar words and writing synonyms and antonyms of familiar words. Using first a cross-sectional analysis of the data (comparing the scores of persons of different ages), they found more rigid behavior among older subjects on all 3 measures. When plotting the longitudinal findings, however, the relation of age to rigidity was markedly altered. For psychomotor speed there was a decline in scores over a 14-year period for the three oldest cohorts (aged 53, 60, and 67 at the start of the study). On the dimension of motor-cognitive rigidity, only the oldest group had an age decrement. For personal-perceptual rigidity, the three oldest cohorts showed increased rigidity. These changes were particularly pronounced between the first and second test sessions, while in the next 7-year period the changes were more gradual and the scores of the oldest cohort indicated less rigidity.

These findings have two implications. First, the extent of age decrement in a dimension such as rigidity is likely to be exaggerated by cross-sectional comparisons. While some change was apparent among the oldest groups, these decrements were considerably smaller than when cohort differences were not controlled. Second, while rigidity is often discussed as a unitary dimension, there are several components of rigidity. As the findings of Schaie and Labouvie-Vief (1974) indicate, the pattern of changes may vary from one type of rigidity to another.

Another measure that has received considerable attention in the aging literature is cautiousness. There is some evidence that older persons are more cautious than the young, at least in certain situations. Cautiousness has been measured in several ways, including the types of error subjects make on various tests and risk taking in hypothetical situations. As with the research on rigidity, these forms of measuring cautiousness are not necessarily related, and there may be more than one dimension of cautious behavior.

Cautiousness in performance on tests is indicated by the types of error made. When a test involves giving a right or wrong answer, persons can make either an error of commission, that is, give the wrong answer, or an error of omission, by not responding to the item. It has generally been found that the aged make more errors of omission than the young (see Botwinick 1978 for a review). Thus the aged appear to be willing to guess on answers only when there is a high degree of certainty of being correct. A similar cautiousness appears in hearing. In an experiment conducted by Rees and Botwinick (1971), old and young were presented a series of sounds that had been determined from prior testing to be within their hearing range. Subjects were instructed to indicate whether or not a sound was played. Old persons responded correctly when no sound was played, but reported more frequently than the young that no sound was played when there was actually a faint sound. Their underreporting of these sounds suggests that when there is a degree of uncertainty in a situation, older persons are more likely to choose not to make a response. This study also suggests how mild hearing losses can become disabling, if persons are reluctant to guess at what they might have heard.

Modifying cautiousness in responding has been found to be related to improved test performance. Using the Primary Mental Abilities test (PMA), which is a measure of intelligence, Birkhill and Schaie (1975) gave sets of instructions to subjects that either encouraged or discouraged guessing. Test scores were significantly better for subjects who were encouraged to guess.

Cautiousness in hypothetical life situations has been evaluated by asking persons to give advice to someone else, for example, on whether or not to take a new job (Wallach and Kogan 1961). Subjects were asked to consider the amount of risk involved (whether there were high or low chances of succeeding) and to determine what probabilities for success there should be before they would advise making the change. Older persons differed from the young principally in that more advised not making any change, even when there was a high certainty of success. This type of behavior is similar to making errors of omission. If persons who advised taking no risk whatsoever are excluded from the analysis, the remaining older subjects were found to counsel the same degree of risk taking as did younger persons. Surprisingly, when older persons are asked to evaluate risk taking in hypothetical situations involving older persons, they were more willing to recommend taking a chance than when they were advising a young person (Botwinick 1978). Cautiousness, then, may only apply in certain situations, and may not consistently affect the decisions that the aged make about their own lives.

While it is generally assumed that aging brings about psychological decrements, there are also some positive expectations, including that persons who learn from their experiences will acquire a measure of wisdom. This quality has received surprisingly little attention in the literature. One reason is the difficulty in defining wisdom. In a series of studies, Clayton and Birren (in press) found that subjects could nominate other individuals who they felt were wise, but factor analysis of qualities they attributed to wisdom failed to indicate stable dimensions. It may be that, more than other aspects of personality, wisdom depends on the relation of one's actions to a particular situation or context. Clayton and Birren (in press) also investigated the ages of persons who subjects nominated as "wise." These persons were generally 10 to 15 years older than the subjects, with some convergence on the period of late middle age (the 50s). The oldest subjects tended to see someone a little younger than themselves as wise. Thus, persons who are generally attributed the quality of wisdom in this culture are more likely to be middle-aged than old.

One area that has received considerable attention in gerontological writings is sex-role behavior. In one of the first modern psychological treatises on old age, Swiss analyst Carl Jung (1933) proposed that differences between men and women become smaller during middle and old age. He wrote:

> We might compare masculinity and femininity to a particular store of substances of which, in the first half of life, unequal use is made. A man consumes his large supply of masculine substance and has left over only the smaller amount of feminine substance, which he must now put to use. It is the other way round with a woman; she allows her unused supply of masculinity to become more active. (p. 107)

From a functional perspective it would also appear that some convergence of sex-role behavior is adaptive in old age. Married persons who have specialized in carrying out various tasks required to maintain a household (e.g., the woman cooks while the man makes repairs) can anticipate a period of time when one of the partners becomes physically disabled or dies, leaving the other to sustain all activities. There has been speculation that widowhood is more difficult for men because they often have little experience in carrying out household tasks such as cooking and laundry. Women, on the other hand, have a higher probability of being widowed, and would seem better prepared if they can maintain a wider range of activities than those typically ascribed as "feminine."

To investigate the sex-role concepts of older men and women, Neugarten and Gutmann (1968) used responses of healthy community residents to a specially drawn picture showing a family scene with an older couple in apparent conversation. Following the method of the Thematic Apperception Test, subjects were asked to tell a story about the picture. Stories were rated for the roles that each character was seen playing. Among the younger respondents in the study (aged 40–55), both the older man and older woman were typically described in ways consistent with society's sex-role expectations. The old man in the picture was seen as dominant and powerful in the family interaction. The old woman was characterized as playing a subordinate role. In contrast, older subjects (55–70) saw the older woman as having a dominant influence and described the old man as somewhat passive and uninvolved in family interactions. The extent to which these stories parallel shifts in actual behavior is not known.

Sex-role behaviors of older persons have been explored further by Cherry and Zarit (1978) using S. Bem's (1975) concept of androgyny.

Sex-role androgyny is defined as seeing one's self as having both masculine and feminine qualities. Using adjectives that have been rated as more typically masculine or feminine, S. Bem has constructed a scale for the measurement of androgyny. Subjects are asked to indicate which adjectives apply to them. Based on their responses, it is possible to classify persons into one of 4 types: (1) masculine; (2) feminine; (3) androgynous; and (4) undifferentiated, describing oneself as low in both masculine and feminine qualities. S. Bem (1975) has proposed that androgynous persons are more likely to be better adapted than either masculine or feminine individuals, because they would be able to make more flexible responses to situations that demanded actions that are not stereotypically masculine or feminine. For example, one would predict that an androgynous woman would have less difficulty dealing with a stereotypically masculine situation, such as making car repairs, than would a woman who saw herself as high in feminine qualities.

In a cross-sectional study of sex-role androgyny, Cherry and Zarit (1978) raised 2 questions. First, following the work of Neugarten and Gutmann, are older women more likely to see themselves as androgynous than are younger women? Second, would androgynous women perform better than feminine women on tasks that are typically considered masculine, such as tests of spatial orientation and arithmetic, and in their perceived competency in various real-life situations, such as getting the car fixed? Contrary to expectations, there were no differences in the number of old and young women who were rated as androgynous on the Bem scale. Furthermore, androgyny was not related to better cognitive performance or greater perceived competency in typical masculine activities for either young or old subjects. One positive finding was that women who endorsed more masculine adjectives as typical of themselves reported lower levels of anxiety and depression than women with low masculinity scores. These results are consistent with reports that suggest that women who see themselves in stereotypically feminine ways are likely to experience more conflict and distress (Broverman et al. 1972).

One other recent study has explored age differences in assertiveness, a characteristic that is usually perceived as masculine (Baffa and Zarit 1977). Young and old women were shown one of several videotapes of a dialogue adapted from an assertion-training book. In this dialogue a customer returns a pair of defective shoes to a store clerk who is at first unwilling to give the customer a refund (Smith 1975). The parts of customer and clerk were played variously by two young actresses and two older actresses, so that one of four tapes could be shown to subjects: (1) younger persons playing both roles; (2) a young customer and an old clerk; (3) an old customer and a young clerk; and (4) older actresses playing both roles. Each subject saw only one of the videotapes and was asked to rate the asserter (customer) and the clerk on three dimensions of the Osgood Semantic Differential: activity, potency, and evaluation. In addition, subjects completed a self-rating scale of assertiveness. It was anticipated that older women would be seen more negatively when taking assertive actions, but there were no differences in the ratings of the asserter when played by a young or an old actress. Furthermore, there were no differences between young and old subjects in their ratings of assertive actresses, with both groups rating the assertive behavior in positive ways. The older women in the sample, however, described themselves as less assertive than did the young.

These studies provide inconsistent evidence of a convergence of sex-role behavior in later life. While stories from a projective test suggest that older women are seen as dominant and older men as passive, other findings indicate that sex-role androgyny is as frequent in young as in old women, and that younger women describe themselves as more assertive. Since all these studies are cross-sectional, the potential for confounding age, cohort, and social-cultural effects is great, particularly for a concept such as sex role, which has been undergoing considerable change in recent years.

Self-concept, or the ways in which individuals typically see themselves, is another dimension that has received a lot of attention. Ratings of self-concept appear to be relatively stable over time, at least during the adult years (see Kimmel 1974 and Mischel 1976 for brief reviews). One study that indicates a high degree of stability and also the influence of cohort differences on personality variables was conducted by Woodruff and Birren (1972). University undergraduates who were given the California Test of Personality in 1944 were retested 25 years later on that measure. In addition, a new sample of undergraduates from the same university was gathered. A longitudinal comparison of the cohort that was tested in 1944 and 1969 showed little evidence of change. There were, however, marked cohort differences, with the responses of the older group indicating higher self- and social adjustment in both their 1944 and 1969 scores, compared with the undergraduates who were tested in 1969. One additional finding was of greater differences between the scores of men and women in the older cohort than in the younger one.

Whether this stability of self-concept is shown into old age is not known. One study (Schwartz and Kleemeier 1965) suggests that illness may have a dramatic effect on self-descriptions. Young and old subjects were asked to describe themselves on the Osgood Semantic Differential. Each age group included 25 persons in good health and 25 with significant health problems. Differences in responses were found between healthy and ill subjects, but not between young and old, when controlling for health. This study suggests the importance of health status for personality and behavior in the aged. Changes in personality in later life may be related more to the development of chronic health problems than to a generalized effect of aging. All too often, however, research on personality and other behavioral problems has not incorporated health as a variable.

As this review indicates, the research on person variables in old age is somewhat limited. Most research is cross-sectional and many of the findings on various characteristics are contradictory, with one study suggesting an age decrement and another reporting no age differences (see Schein 1968 and Neugarten 1977 for reviews). One major reason for this confusion, as suggested earlier, is that we are only consistent in our actions on a few characteristics. Which person variables have this saliency varies from one individual to another. The importance of person variables, however, is considerable. While environmental conditions often influence behavior, the individual's expectations, cognitive set, and values are critical in choosing the settings in which he will interact in the first place. Furthermore, person variables account for the varied responses of individuals to similar environmental conditions or to treatments, and also play a major part in how individuals assess their behaviors. It is hoped that cogent understanding of how these person variables change with age will emerge in the next few years.

INTERACTION OF THE PERSON AND ENVIRONMENT

The relation of the individual to his environment is at the crux of understanding personality and behavior. Considerable attention has been paid to what factors in persons or in their environments are associated with successful aging. Knowledge of what constitutes good or poor mixes of person and environmental variables could make possible advances in the prevention of mental health problems of the aged.

One approach to the question of adaptation in later life has been to develop personality types based on interview data and the results of projective tests. In a study of 87 men over the age of 55, Reichard, Livson, and Peterson (1962) classified subjects into five groups: (1) mature; (2) rocking chair; (3) armored; (4) angry; and (5) self-haters. They reported that adaptation in old age was an outgrowth of earlier personality style. They also noted a trend for the oldest subjects to report less anxiety, depression, and other maladaptive behavior patterns.

Neugarten, Havighurst, and Tobin (1968) reported similarly that adaptation of older persons was related to personality type and not to age. They classified subjects into four types: integrated, passive-dependent, armored, and unintegrated. Integrated persons were those who had a complex inner life and a high degree of competency in everyday activities. The passive-dependent persons principally looked to others for satisfying their emotional needs. Those considered armored were high achievers, who strove to exercise control over the environment and their own impulses. The last type, unintegrated, had poor emotional control and low intellectual competency. While integrated persons generally manifested the best adaptation, some passive-dependent and armored persons also had a good adjustment. They concluded that there was no discontinuity in personality with age, but rather that the interaction of persons with their environment is mediated by long-established habits.

There is evidence from one longitudinal study that these global personality types are generally stable over time. Returning after 40 years to a group of persons who were first interviewed when they were 30 years of age, Maas and Kuypers (1974) report a high degree of consistency over time in personality type. The one exception was a group of women who at age 30 were depressed and disorganized, but who blossomed in middle age, usually through the dissolution of unhappy marriages and embarking on careers.

These formulations of personality types consider salient personality characteristics such as proposed by D. Bem and Allen. The dimensions used in these studies, however, are rather sweeping. Mischel (1976) cautions that broad characterizations of personality are often misleading, because of the effects of particular situations on behavior, and because persons themselves may have other traits that moderate the expression of these global dimensions. These concepts also tend to be defined in a circular way. The judgment that someone is integrated or unintegrated, for example, depends in part on assessing that person's behavior in various situations, and therefore would be expected to be related to adaptation. Future research in this area needs to look for salient dimensions of personality, as in the studies cited above, but using more specific and better-defined personality constructs.

Developmental theorists have also focused on the unique qualities of particular periods in life. These stage models propose that adaptation at a given period in the life cycle depends in part on prior experiences and in part on how the person responds to the particular demands or challenges inherent in that stage of life. While stage approaches have generally dealt only with the childhood years, several intresting frameworks for viewing adulthood and aging have been proposed. The best-known model of adult personality is Erik Erikson's (1963). Other contributions have been made by Buhler (1961), Frenkel-Brunswick (1968), Gould (1975), Kuhlen (1968), Levinson et al. (1973), and Peck (1968).

The crux of this approach is that there are unique qualities in each stage of life that affect behavior. In childhood there are clear stages of development that coincide with biological maturation. During adulthood, however, biological changes are more gradual and do not set off clearly demarcated stages of life (Timiras 1972). Developmental changes have instead been seen as related to two factors, mastery of life tasks and the inherent value of change. Most attention has focused on identifying psychosocial tasks in various stages of adulthood.

Erikson's (1963) psychosocial tasks of adulthood are well known: intimacy versus isolation in young adulthood; generativity versus stagnation in the middle years; and integrity versus despair in old age. The successful mastery of issues at each stage is seen as necessary for progressing to the next stage.

In a major theoretical work, Daniel Levinson and his associates (1973) propose somewhat different steps. They divide the adult years into a series of six stages: (1) leaving one's family of origin; (2) getting into the adult world; (3) settling down; (4) become one's own person; (5) a mid-life transition; and (6) a restabilizing period in middle adulthood. Like Erikson, they stress that the psychological task at each stage builds on how prior conflicts were handled by the individual. As an example, they argue that persons at midlife face reevaluating what they have accomplished in their lives in the light of deeply held feelings of what they would have liked to become. Successful accomplishment of this reevaluation allows the person to direct his energies in middle adulthood toward pursuing personally relevant objectives. An unsuccessful person might, in contrast, continue to fight old battles or give up in resignation over past failures.

The notion of an inherent process of change in adulthood is implicit in many developmental theories as well as in the work of humanistic psychologists like Maslow (1968) and Rogers (1951). Although Levinson and associates cite psychodynamic issues as leading to successive changes, they also assume that the continued development of the person requires changes made at periodic intervals. Without that process of reassessment, they feel persons stagnate and do not reach their full potential. Their vision of adulthood is one of an alternation of stable and transitional periods, and suggests an inherent process of change linked to life experiences and the passage of time.

The developmental tasks of old age have been described as centering on issues of loss: loss of one's own abilities, social losses, and the nearness of one's own death (Jung 1933; Buhler 1961; Butler 1963; Kuhlen 1968). Adaptation to loss is the crucial process facing older persons; debate has focused on whether the individual should try to maintain external activities and involvements in the face of declining powers and resources, or become increasingly preoccupied with introspection, leaving the major role in life activities to younger persons.

In his book *Modern Man in Search of a Soul*, Jung (1933) first proposed what he saw as an inevitable process of turning inward during the second half of the life cycle. He stated that in middle age it becomes imperative for the individual to deal psychologically with the increasing probability of one's own death. In order to do so successfully, that is, not to become paralyzed by anxiety or despair, Jung suggests that we must turn away to some extent from worldly pursuits, and develop philosophical or religious perspectives on our own life and death. To fail to do so leaves a person preoccupied with fears of death. According to Jung:

> Aging people should know that their lives are not mounting and unfolding, but that an inexorable inner process forces the contraction of life. For a young person it is almost a sin—and certainly a danger—to be too much occupied with himself. After having lavished its light upon the world, the sun withdraws its rays in order to illumine itself. Instead of doing likewise, many old people prefer to be hypochondriacs, niggards, doctrinaires, applauders of the past or eternal adolescents—all lamentable substitutes for the illumination of the self, but inevitable consequences of the delusion that the second half of life must be governed by the principles of the first. (p. 109)

This theme of turning inward is implicit in Erikson's (1963) concepts of integrity and despair. Erikson proposes that the last period of life involves taking stock psychologically of one's life and accomplishments. He suggests that the individual who feels he has lived his life well and has done the best he could develops a sense of integrity and makes a good adjustment to old age. In contrast, persons who dwell on past errors or missed opportunities feel despair in later life at their inability to rectify these mistakes.

Identifying a similar process, Butler (1963) has stated that some older persons undertake a process of life review, in which they make an assessment and summing up of their life activities. He does not, however, feel that life review is a universal process, nor that its outcome is always positive. As with Erikson's dichotomy of integrity and despair, Butler states that the life review can lead to feelings of depression in some persons.

In a series of studies of healthy community residents, Neugarten (Neugarten and associates 1964; Neugarten 1977) found evidence to support the idea that older persons were turning inward and away from active life involvements. In their perceptions of the environment, 40 year olds saw their surroundings as rewarding risk taking and bold actions, and viewed themselves as able to take advantage of these opportunities. Persons in their 60s, however, perceived themselves as conforming to the demands of an increasingly complex and dangerous world. In their responses to the projective test, the Thematic Apperception Test, and in interview data, older subjects indicated more preoccupation with internal thought processes and less interest in feelings and activities of others. There is some indication that these age differences are found in other cultures (see Neugarten 1973 for a review).

The theme of turning inward was developed in detail by Cumming and Henry (1961). Based on cross-sectional data drawn from a sample of healthy, community-dwelling residents of Kansas City, they proposed that, starting in late middle age, there was a mutual process of disengagement between the individual and society, with persons gradually cutting down their activities and social involvements. This process was seen as adaptive. Disengagement made it possible for persons to exit gracefully from their social roles before it became necessary to do so because of failing health or other decrements in functioning.

The theory of disengagement provoked a heated controversy in the field of gerontology, one that still forms the basis of most discussions of adaptation in later life. Two counterpositions were advanced: the activity theory and the continuity theory. According to proponents of the activity theory, good adaptation in later life is associated with maintaining a high level of activity. In contrast, the continuity theory proposes that one's level of activity in old age reflects a continuation of patterns of life style developed earlier in life. While there may be some decrease in activity overall with advancing age, neither high nor low activity per se is associated with better adaptation (Maddox 1968; Neugarten, Havighurst, and Tobin 1968).

Numerous studies have been made on the relation of life satisfaction or well-being to activity level. In their original study of disengagement, Cumming and Henry (1961) reported higher life satisfaction among disengaged than among active persons. Most subsequent research, however, has found a positive association of activity and well-being (see Larson 1978 for a review).

There are two problems that complicate these findings. First, probably the best predictor of morale or well-being in the aged is health, rather than activity (Larson 1978). Since one's level of involvement depends to a great extent on functional health, low activity and low life satisfaction may both be the result of poor health. In contrast to the original proposal of Cumming and Henry (1961) that disengagement precedes poor health, some researchers have found that a pattern of disengagement develops as the consequence of poor health (Maas and Kuypers 1974; Lowenthal and Boler 1965; Lowenthal 1968).

A more critical problem in these studies has to do with the conceptualization of adaptation. Most researchers have focused on indices of life satisfaction or morale, but for several reasons these may not be good measures of adaptation. First, they are inappropriate when assessing an institutionalized sample or any group of aged persons in which there are likely to be persons with senile dementia. Brain-damaged older persons tend to deny any problems or difficulties, with denial more pervasive when there is greater brain impairment (Zarit and Kahn 1974). As a consequence, an older person with senile dementia may report greater life satisfaction or higher morale as the consequence of increasing brain pathology, and not because he possesses a certain trait, is active or inactive, or has participated in a particular treatment program. Among the non-brain-damaged elderly, measures of well-being or life satisfaction may also reflect a tendency to deny problems. Since the various scales that have been used have generally not included a correction factor for social desirability, it is likely that responses reflect the concern of some older persons to give the "right" answers or to portray themselves in a positive light in the researcher's eyes. Since today's cohort of elderly are on the average less educated and less sophisticated about research than younger persons, one should not minimize the effects of this type of response bias on any rating scale.

The most critical limitation of measures of well-being or life satisfaction is that the significance of the scores is ambiguous, and it is by no means certain that a person reporting more positive affect is better adapted than someone else reporting less. In measures of mood that have been developed with clinical samples, the scores of groups of anxious or depressed patients, for example, have been found to differ in some statistical sense from those of nonpatient samples. A person whose scores improve on such a measure thereby moves from a range in which one's affect is usually dysfunctional to a condition more typical of the general population, and generally not associated with impaired functioning. In contrast, the fluctuations of morale of a nonpatient sample does not necessarily have a similar relation to adaptation. Differences in morale scores in nonclinical samples have not been validated as indicating different levels of adaptation, and, in fact, higher morale may not consistently be associated with better adaptation. According to Lowenthal and Chiriboga (1973), persons who were judged by trained observers as more complex, creative individuals reported greater levels of negative affect than "simple" persons, who made few demands on their environment and were judged as less resourceful and less well-adapted.

Alternative ways of looking at the quality of a person's adaptation would be to focus on self-descriptions and patterns of activities in which the person engages. In studies of outcome in psychotherapy, Rogers and Dymond (1954) found that with successful treatment there was a decrease in the discrepancy between descriptions of how one saw oneself and how one would like to be. A similar notion could be applied to a person's activities. One could determine what it is a person currently does and what it is he would like to be doing. It seems plausible that persons with a greater discrepancy between what they are doing and what they would like to be doing would describe themselves (and would be described by others) as more poorly adapted to their current situation than those with smaller discrepancies. Certainly assessing individuals this way would yield richer findings than merely finding out if they are active or disengaged.

This type of approach has also been suggested by Flanagan (1978). Based on the responses of national surveys of three cohorts of 30, 50, and 70 year olds, he identified 15 areas or components that are related to the quality of life. Among the areas are such things as material comforts, health and personal safety, relationships to family and friends, creative expression, and recreational activities. Flanagan also asked his sample how well their needs were met in these 15 components. His results are reported in Table 3.1. The oldest cohort reported their needs for community and political participation were better met than did the young, but they also indicated finding fewer available opportunities for learning and, as might be expected, work. There were also some important sex differences. The needs of older women for a close relationship with a husband were not being met, reflecting the high rate of widowhood and limited opportunities to form new attachments. On the other hand, other social needs, such as relationships to friends, were better met in older women than older men. Older men, in contrast to both older women and younger men, were more dissatisfied with opportunities for creative expression and recreational activities. Coupled with their lack of satisfaction with work activities, these findings suggest that many older men may feel unfulfilled in important areas of their lives.

Much of the confusion in the debates over disengagement versus activity may be due to viewing older persons as a group, rather than trying to differentiate the impact of health on activities. A 70 year old who still has similar vigor and health as he had at age 40 has quite different capabilities from another person who has chronic and debilitating ailments. Good adaptation for the first person may indeed involve continuity of activities and life style. For the second, however, trying to maintain all one's previous involvements and responsibilities would be a frustrating experience. The implication for developmental theory is that all older persons should not be viewed as going through a similar process at that stage of life, but that we face a critical challenge when major losses occur. How we respond to those losses, including our own dying, is the last major developmental task in our lives.

There can be considerable practical gain in working with older persons by focusing on adaptation to losses. When an individual is faced with losses, some degree of turning inward may be inevitable. Of course, too much disengagement may also be harmful. In the rehabilitation of persons with physical disabilities, there is often a fine line between setting goals that are too high or too low. If nothing is expected or demanded of a person following an illness, he may make himself a helpless invalid and miss out on his potential for continuing satisfying activities. On the other hand, the expectation that one can always make oneself as good as new can lead to intense frustrations.

The role of expectations in responding to physical disabilities is illustrated in the following example. Mr. O. was a 68-year-old man who had suffered 2 strokes that left him partially paralyzed on his left side, and also with reduced visual fields. He was not given rehabilitation following the strokes, and spent 2 years after hospitalization without leaving his apartment, because he could not negotiate the stairs. He was then involved in a day-care program for the elderly that included physical therapy. He was first taught to get up and down the stairs so he could attend the program. Once he was able to attend, he set as a goal for himself that he would dance again. He worked very hard at the physical therapy program and showed some rapid improvement in the first few months. After that he apparently reached a plateau and improved very little. As he still needed a 3-pronged cane for assistance in walking, he was increasingly frustrated and depressed because he could not achieve his goal of being able to dance again. He became preoccupied with somatic problems and finally had to be hospitalized briefly. At that point, many of his gains in functional abilities were lost. This example shows how encouraging someone to be as active as he was before the onset of his disability can be motivating at some points but damaging at others. The encouragement to Mr. O to become more active helped produce some improvements in functional abilities, but the failure to help him modify his goals in the face of unremitting disabilities led eventually to increased problems.

In adapting to the decrements that can occur in aging, the best course is neither to deny completely the impact of changes in one's functional abilities nor to give up. Robert Butler (1975) has perhaps summarized this attitude best. He writes:

> The old must clarify and find use for what they have attained in a lifetime of learning and adapting; they must conserve strength and resources where necessary and adjust creatively to those changes and losses that occur as part of the aging experience. The elderly have the potential for qualities of human reflection and observation which can only come from having lived an entire life span. There is a lifetime accumulation of personality and experience which is available to be used and enjoyed. (p. 2)

This perspective suggests neither activity nor disengagement. Rather, Butler implies both continued activities in those areas of functioning in which the person can still engage and some measure of increased introspection to discover what is useful and meaningful from one's own experiences. This turning inward, moreover, does not mean that the elderly should be encouraged to sit in rocking chairs and dwell on the past. Butler stresses the creative use of the past. As examples, this may involve presenting the oral traditions of one's family to new generations or the use of skills one learned when young.

The relation of person variables to environmental conditions warrants more careful attention for the aged. There is a need to move away from the simple-minded prescription of activities, no matter how dull or unstimulating to a given individual, as a cure for any of the psychological distresses of old age. Activities need to be stimulating and meaningful to

TABLE 3.1 Percentages of a sample of 1,000 30-year-olds, 1,000 50-year-olds, and 1,000 70-year-olds reporting each of the 15 components as important or very important to their quality of life [a] and percentages (in parentheses) of the same sample reporting their needs as well met or very well met for each component [b]

Component	Male			Female		
	30 yrs.	50 yrs.	70 yrs.	30 yrs.	50 yrs.	70 yrs.
Physical and Material Well-Being						
A. *Material comforts*—things like a desirable home, good food, possessions, conveniences, an increasing income, and security for the future.	80 (74)	87 (72)	87 (77)	75 (76)	84 (68)	84 (73)
B. *Health and personal safety*—to be physically fit and vigorous, to be free from anxiety and distress, and to avoid bodily harm.	98 (86)	96 (84)	96 (84)	98 (86)	97 (82)	96 (79)
Relations with Other People						
C. *Relationships with your parents, brothers, sisters, and other relatives*—things like communicating, visiting, understanding, doing things, and helping and being helped by them.	68 (81)	64 (71)	62 (71)	83 (81)	76 (71)	78 (68)
D. *Having and raising children*—this involves being a parent and helping, teaching, and caring for your children.	84 (80)	84 (84)	82 (82)	93 (83)	92 (87)	88 (84)
E. *Close relationship with a husband/wife/a person of the opposite sex.*	90 (84)	91 (82)	84 (86)	94 (81)	81 (72)	42 (69)
F. *Close friends*—sharing activities, interests, and views; being accepted, visiting, giving and receiving help, love, trust, support, guidance.	71 (81)	77 (81)	75 (82)	79 (82)	81 (79)	89 (77)
Social, Community, and Civic Activities						
G. *Helping and encouraging others*—this includes adults or children other than relatives or close friends. These can be your own efforts or efforts as a member of some church, club, or volunteer group.	60 (61)	72 (72)	67 (72)	71 (62)	77 (73)	81 (73)
H. *Participation in activities relating to local and national government and public affairs.*	47 (54)	63 (60)	67 (63)	42 (54)	59 (61)	59 (60)

Personal Development and Fulfillment

I. Learning, attending school, improving your understanding, or getting additional knowledge.	87 (58)	68 (64)	50 (72)	81 (50)	68 (56)	60 (64)
J. Understanding yourself and knowing your assets and limitations, knowing what life is all about and making decisions on major life activities. For some people, this includes religious or spiritual experiences. For others, it is an attitude toward life or a philosophy.	84 (74)	84 (75)	80 (76)	92 (71)	90 (74)	88 (78)
K. Work in a job or at home that is interesting, rewarding, worthwhile.	91 (79)	90 (76)	56 (76)	89 (79)	86 (68)	60 (78)
L. Expressing yourself in a creative manner in music, art, writing, photography, practical activities, or in leisure-time activities.	48 (60)	42 (68)	39 (73)	53 (57)	56 (68)	58 (69)

Recreation

M. Socializing—meeting other people, doing things with them, and giving or attending parties.	48 (73)	47 (74)	55 (74)	53 (74)	50 (70)	63 (72)
N. Reading, listening to music, or observing sporting events or entertainment.	56 (71)	46 (72)	54 (80)	53 (70)	56 (75)	65 (80)
O. Participation in active recreation—such as sports, traveling and sightseeing, playing games or cards, singing, dancing, playing an instrument, acting, and other such activities.	59 (64)	55 (60)	50 (64)	50 (63)	53 (59)	52 (63)

Source: J. C. Flanagan, Identifying Opportunities for Improving the Quality of Life of Older Age Groups (Palo Alto, Calif.: American Institutes for Research, 1979). Reprinted by permission.

a "At this time in your life, how important to you is _____?"

b For 50- and 70-year-olds, the question read, "How well are your needs and wants being met in this regard?" For the 30-year-olds, the question read, "How satisfied are you with your status in this respect?"

the individual. There is nothing more distressing than to see a group of bored senior citizens going through the motions of an activities program someone else has deemed good for them. At the same time, the ability of the aged, especially those with decrements in functioning, to use their pasts creatively demands changes in our environments, habits, and attitudes toward the elderly so that there are more meaningful ways for them to participate in our communities. If there is a best way to age, it is to be able to hold onto what has been most important about one's self and one's experiences, while accommodating to those changes that are necessary. And because of the wide range of differences in goals, expectations, and experiences found among persons, the path toward successful aging will vary from one individual to another.

Summary

The study of personality can be conceptualized into three levels of analysis: environmental conditions; person variables; and the interaction of the person and his environment. In research on personality and aging, one must disentangle age changes from the effects of generation differences, social and historical changes, and sex differences. Overall, there is only limited evidence on changes in personality with age. These changes do not appear dramatic, especially when longitudinal or cross-sequential research designs are used. On dimensions such as rigidity, which are typically considered to increase with age, the amount of decrement is small when measured cross-sequentially. Findings on other person variables also indicate only small changes. In considering what factors are related to successful aging, it was concluded that some decrease in activities and involvements is likely in the later years, especially when there is diminished health and vigor. Both an attitude of giving up and pushing oneself to be as active as previously can lead to poor functioning.

CHAPTER 4

Social Problems and Social Policy

WHILE MANY OF THE PROBLEMS of old age are brought about by biological decrements, social forces have a critical influence on the lives of the elderly. There is probably some truth to the old adage that money does not buy happiness, but living on meagre incomes, as many elderly do, is stressful and inhibits their options for shaping their lives. Other factors that have an impact on the lives of older persons include the availability and quality of health care and the opportunity to engage in satisfying social interactions, whether with family and friends or in community organizations. Furthermore, social programs such as Social Security or Medicare, which purport to give assistance to the elderly, often fall short of their goals in critical ways. In evaluating the behavior problems of older persons, it is important to know how these factors affect their lives, and to be familiar with both the strengths and limitations of the social programs and other resources that are available.

Income and Aging

The distribution of income among older Americans is characterized by great extremes. Although many of the richest persons in the country are old, large numbers of aged individuals are found living near or at federal poverty levels.

The effects of public policies over the past half century, including principally the Social Security Act of 1935 and the Supplementary Security Income (SSI) program established in 1974, have been to improve to some extent the situation of many of the poorest among the old. Until Congress passed the Social Security Bill, aid to the indigent elderly was governed by customs that had their roots in the English Poor Law, which stressed the obligation of relatives to take care of aged persons and of local governments to provide some minimal assistance (Albert and Zarit 1977). The studies of the Advisory Council to the Commission on Economic Security, which was established by President Roosevelt in 1934, indicated the extent to which these customs failed to ensure adequate resources for the elderly. Based on surveys of several states, between 23 and 65 percent of the elderly were found to have less than $300 in annual income and less than $5,000 in property. Many of these persons had no income at all. In Connecticut in 1932, for example, more than one-third of all aged persons were without any income (Albert and Zarit 1977).

The inclusion of the vast majority of working persons into the Social Security System, approximately 90 percent of the current work force, or into the separate pension program operated for federal employees who do not participate in Social Security, has provided an important source of income to most older persons. The effect has been to reduce the number of very poor elderly. In contrast to the severe level of poverty found in the 1930s, 28 percent of persons over 65 were below the federal poverty level in 1966. This figure dropped to 16 percent in the early 1970s (Schulz 1976). Poverty among the elderly, however, is still more prevalent than in the general population, 11 percent of whom fall below federal markers (see Figure 4.1).

Since these figures were calculated, there has probably been further reduction in the number of older persons living in poverty. The Supplementary Security Income program, which was established in 1974, provides payments of up to $208.20 for single persons and $312.30 for married persons (as of May 1980). Someone with no income or with income from other sources that is less than those levels, and who has less than $3,000 in other assets, is eligible to receive a supplementary check up to those amounts. In addition, 43 states and the District of Columbia add a further supplement to SSI payments (Schulz 1976). In California, for example, an older person with no other sources of income would receive monthly payments through SSI of $356.00.

The SSI program was designed in part to remove from the aged poor the stigma associated with receiving welfare. This program, however, has had mixed results. Prior to 1974, older poor persons were eligible in most states for Old Age Assistance and other benefits through Public Aid programs. In states where welfare payments were low or not available, many elderly who enrolled in SSI received a sudden increase in income. In many urban states, however, the effect of this program was to decrease benefits. Older persons who previously received such assistance as rent subsidies through Public Aid lost those benefits when they were transferred from state programs to the federal SSI. Furthermore, some persons in

FIGURE 4.1. Median income of persons (excludes persons without any income) by age, sex, and race, 1973.

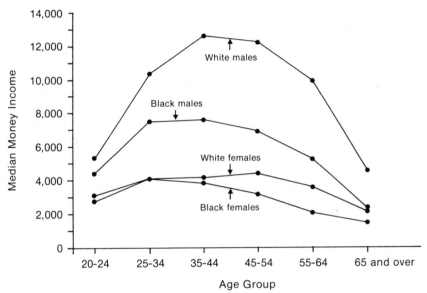

Source: J. H. Schulz, "Income Distribution and the Aging." In R. H. Binstock and E. Shanes, eds., *Handbook of Aging and the Social Sciences* (New York: Van Nostrand Reinhold, 1976). Data from U.S. Bureau of the Census, Consumer Income. Current Population Reports, Series P–60. no. 97 (Washington: Government Printing Office, 1975), Table 53.

need still are not eligible. One group are those older persons with a small amount of assets but limited income. Many older persons prefer to live with a lower income rather than take the steps to become eligible for SSI, such as spending their remaining savings or cashing in small insurance policies. In addition, some older persons who are eligible for SSI have not applied for it, either because of ignorance or a misunderstanding of the program, or because they see it as welfare and are unwilling to accept that. Even though administered through the Social Security Administration, subsidies are not provided automatically to persons below the income floors. Thus older persons who do not know of the program or who are distrustful of government agencies do not receive SSI payments.

While the number of older persons in severe poverty has decreased, income problems continue to be a major source of concern for many elderly. Rather than instances of extreme impoverishment, the more common occurrence is relative poverty. Many individuals experience a major drop of income during later life. It has been estimated that one needs approximately 75 percent of preretirement income to maintain the same standard of living after retirement (Atchley 1977). As shown in Figure 4.1, however, median family income for persons over 65 is approximately 50 percent of that of all households. In a major survey of retirement it was estimated that persons had a 56 percent decline in income after retiring (Streib and Schneider 1971). Those who do not have any sources of income other than Social Security are at the worst disadvantage. Depending on their level of previous earnings, recipients of Social Security get between 24 and 36 percent of their former income (Schulz 1976). Given these figures, it is not surprising that one study found the gap between young and old in overall economic status as measured by income, employment, and education actually widened between 1950 and 1970 (Palmore and Whittington 1971).

The extent of the disadvantage in income is greater among particular subgroups of the population. The largest amount of poverty in old age is found among members of minority groups and women. Among the black aged, for example, approximately 36 percent fall below the federal poverty level, compared to 30 percent of all blacks and 14 percent of aged whites (Figure 4.1.) Among older women, the number of poor is also substantial. Twenty-five percent of widows, 31 percent of divorced women, 54 percent of women separated from husbands, and 22 percent of women who never married fall below federal poverty levels (Schulz 1976). These figures contrast sharply with that of older women who are currently married, only 8 percent of whom are living in poverty. Women in minority groups are perhaps the most disadvantaged in income during old age. It has been estimated that 96 percent of older black women are poor (Atchley 1977).

The greater poverty among women and ethnic minorities is related to several factors. First, Social Security benefits are based on prior earnings. Since minorities and women tend to have held lower-paying jobs, their subsequent benefits are less than a white man's. Second, persons in lower-income jobs are less likely to be covered by private pensions that could supplement Social Security. Third, certain types of job, such as domestic work, were only recently included in the Social Security program, so that many persons who are now retired and who did that type of work do not receive Social Security. Finally, older women who are divorced or whose husbands have died receive reduced benefits from Social Security. Many private pension funds similarly have reduced survivors' benefits, or pay nothing after the recipient's death.

While older persons theoretically can supplement what they receive from Social Security from other sources, these opportunities are, in fact, limited. The major ways of adding to one's income are through prior investments, continued employment, and participation in private pension funds. One prevailing expectation is that it is the person's responsibility to save and invest a percentage of income for old age (Albert and Zarit 1977). The intention of the Social Security Act was, in part, to supplement these savings, rather than to provide a guaranteed income. Nonetheless, the number of persons who receive substantial amounts of income from stocks or other investments, including savings dividends, is quite small. Atchley (1977) reports that most retired persons have liquid assets of $2,000 or less, and therefore derive very little income from those investments. One major asset of the aged is in property. About 60 percent of retired couples and 30 percent of single retired persons own their own homes (Atchley 1977). Many older persons, however, are unwilling to sell their houses as a means of providing income. Furthermore, until 1978, when Congress passed a tax exemption on capital gains from the sale of a house, the profits were heavily taxed.

Continued employment is another possible means of supplementing income. During this century, however, the number of older persons who are employed has been dropping steadily. In 1900 approximately two-thirds of older men worked for a living, compared to one in four who currently work (Bouvier, Atlee, and McVeigh 1975). Most older women do not work, although the percentage who were employed increased slightly between 1940 and 1970. Among women aged 65 through 69, for example, there was a jump in the number employed from 9.5 percent to 17.2 percent during that time period. Estimates from 1975, however, indicate a drop in the number of employed older women (Bouvier, Atlee, and McVeigh 1975). Altogether, approximately one-sixth of older persons derive income from employment (Atchley 1977).

There are a number of obstacles for older persons seeking work. Foremost is the attitudes of employers. A Department of Labor survey, for example, indicated a substantial number of employers did not favor hiring older workers (Bouvier, Atlee, and McVeigh 1975). Another factor is that persons under age 72 earning more than $5,000 per year from employment will lose some Social Security. For every $2 in wages above $5,000, $1 is deducted from an individual's Social Security benefits. A person receiving an average Social Security payment of $300/month who earned the maximum $5,000 would thereby have an income of $8,600/year. No deductions in Social Security benefits are made for income from other sources, such as dividends.

According to U.S. Census Bureau surveys, approximately 5 percent of men between the ages of 65 and 75 and between 5 to 7 percent of women are looking for work but cannot find it (Bouvier, Atlee, and McVeigh 1975). It is not known how many other older persons might seek employment, especially part-time work, if it were more readily available. Apart from the question of whether or not it is psychologically desirable to continue working past age 65, many older persons would benefit from the additional income.

A third possible source of income for older persons is private pension funds established by employers. While many workers have been covered by private pensions, only a small number of today's aged receive benefits. It has been estimated that as few as 1 in 10 workers who may have been enrolled in a pension plan actually collect any money. One reason for this discrepancy is that there have often been complicated rules covering the vesting process, or how a person becomes eligible to receive a pension. Until passage of the Employee Retirement Income Security Act in 1974, a worker often had to have 30 years or more of continuous service with the same company to become vested in the pension. Persons who changed jobs or, in some cases, were laid off from work for brief periods of time did not qualify for pensions. In other cases, an older worker who became disabled or who was laid off before retirement age, but who had the needed years of continuous service, still did not receive payment if the pension plan stipulated that he had to work to a certain age. There were also specific episodes of abuse, where workers were fired shortly before becoming eligible for a pension (Albert and Zarit 1977).

The Employee Retirement Income Security Act of 1974 was designed to correct many of these inequities in private pensions. It established uniform procedures for vesting and for financing pension funds so that workers could receive payments even if the company went out of business (see Albert and Zarit 1977 and Atchley 1977 for reviews of provisions of this law). These reforms, however, are not retroactive and will not be fully implemented until 1981. Thus there has been no impact on persons who are currently retired and who must continue to look to Social Security for their major support.

One additional note on the financial status of the elderly is that the relative decline in income found in old age actually begins around age 45. Most workers past age 45 continue to experience a rise in income, but in recent years the trend has been for younger workers to receive higher starting salaries than the older workers had. As a result, median family income shows a relative decline after age 45 compared to younger age groups (Schulz 1976). Thus, in addition to the drop of income experienced at retirement, many older persons had been receiving relatively less income for a long period of time before retirement.

Despite their relative loss in income, older persons do not consistently perceive it as inadequate. In surveys of the elderly, many persons near or at poverty levels report satisfaction with the amount of money they have, although occasionally persons whose income has been reduced but is nonetheless substantial indicate considerable dissatisfaction (Streib 1976). These findings may reflect the reluctance of many poor persons to say anything derogatory to someone in an authority position, out of fear their benefits will be cut off. It also suggests, however, that there will not be strong political pressure from the elderly themselves to provide better incomes to the poorest among them.

Medical Expenses and Medical Care

MEDICARE AND THE ECONOMICS OF HEALTH CARE

The passage of the Medicare program in 1965 as amendments to the Social Security law was designed to protect older persons from undue financial burdens from medical costs. Despite the intent of this program, the cost of medical care to the aged has been rising. This increase is due to the coinsurance and deductible requirements of the Medicare program, the number of services not included in the insurance coverage, and the rising cost of health care in general. Thus in 1966 older persons had to pay an average of $178 a year in medical expenses out of their own pockets, while in 1974 the figure was $478, more than before Medicare was passed (Albert and Zarit 1977). The extent of coverage has also been decreasing since Medicare was implemented. In 1967 Medicare covered approximately 46 percent of the medical expenses of the elderly, while in 1976 only 38 percent was paid (Albert and Zarit 1977).

Medicare consists of two programs, Plan A, which provides basic hospitalization insurance and is received automatically by all persons who are eligible for Social Security, and Plan B, which is a voluntary plan for some outpatient services. Fees of $6.30 a month for Plan B are deducted from one's Social Security payments. The coverage for hospital care under Plan A is extensive, although there are ceilings on the benefits that will be paid. As of 1979, Plan A provided full coverage for the first 60 days of treatment in hospitals, including regular nursing services, inpatient drugs, equipment, and other expenses, except for a deductible of $160. If a person is discharged within 60 days and does not require hospitalization for the succeeding 60 days, this period of full coverage is renewed. For persons requiring hospital stays longer than 60 days, there is a coinsurance period of 30 days during which they must pay $28 a day, with Medicare covering the remaining amount. After 90 days of consecutive stay there is an additional "lifetime reserve" of 60 days, in which the insured pays $46 a day. Given these deductible and coinsurance requirements, the cost to the beneficiary for hospitalization of 150 days amounts to $3,760.

In addition to acute hospital coverage, some other services are available. A person who has been hospitalized for at least 3 days in an acute facility is eligible for care in a nursing or convalescent home at no cost for 20 days. For an additional 80 days there is a required coinsurance payment of $18 per day. Following discharge from a hospital or nursing home, an individual can receive up to 100 visits for home health care from a nurse or other qualified personnel, though the procedures for qualifying and the types of service reimbursed are limiting factors. Inpatient psychiatric care is covered for a maximum of 190 days over one's lifetime.

As in Plan A, Plan B provides coverage for particular expenses after payment of an annual deductible of $60. Included under Plan B are doctor's fees, office drugs or supplies, emergency room fees, and other benefits. There is a coinsurance payment for all covered services. The amount that the insured must pay is approximately 20 percent, varying somewhat if the physician accepts payment directly from Medicare or bills the patient. Not covered are numerous common problems of the elderly, including sight, hearing, dental, feet, and any out-of-hospital prescriptions.

The effects of these requirements and other Medicare regulations is that the coverage for preventive and outpatient services that might deter certain chronic conditions or deteriorative processes is much more limited than for inpatient care. Furthermore, home health services, while theoretically available, receive reimbursement only when particular, and often changing, requirements are met. To receive home health care one needs to have been hospitalized for at least 3 days and to need home treatment for the same condition that caused the hospitalization. But there are some exceptions. In a recent case, two sisters who were living together were denied home health care, even though there was apparent need. The older one, who was arthritic and diabetic, had not been hospitalized and was denied services, even though on some days she could not move from bed. The younger sister was hospitalized briefly because of increasing behavior problems, but services were denied to her because her disability, senile dementia, was excluded from coverage by the local insurance carrier. To cite another example of the inconsistencies of coverage, it is possible for a diabetic to receive visiting nurses to inject insulin, but someone to fill the syringe of a blind diabetic is not reimbursed. Often a service involving a small expense, such as a homemaker, which might be instrumental in preventing institutionalization, will not be covered because the complicated eligibility rules are not met, but that same person would be insured for nursing home care for the same functional problems. Furthermore, when Medicare coverage runs out and persons use up their own assets, payment for long-term care will be provided by Medicaid—the joint federal-state program for medical care for the poor of all ages. Programs such as day care or holiday relief hospitalizations are not consistently covered by either Medicare or Medicaid.

Even some inpatient services may be denied to older persons. While physical rehabilitation programs are useful to restore functioning to persons who have had strokes, head or back injuries, or fractures, Medicare does not consistently insure these services, even though these programs would have been available to the individual under private insurance programs for persons under 65, such as Blue Cross. In California, for example, a physician who wants an older person to participate in a physical rehabilitation program must document that the patient is neither too sick nor too well, a provision that effectively eliminates some patients who might otherwise benefit. As a result, they often have to go to a nursing home, where rehabilitation services are typically quite limited. Furthermore, particular categories of patients are often excluded. Again in California, virtually no individuals with hip fractures can receive rehabilitation services (Albert and Zarit 1977). Since Medicare is operated by local insurance carriers, the types of coverage and exclusion vary somewhat from state to state or even within states where there is more than one carrier.

Another facet of Medicare is that it provides a disproportionate amount of assistance to persons who are well-off. In one study of Medicare payments described by Mechanic (1978), persons with incomes over $15,000 a year received twice the amount for physicians' services as did persons with less than $5,000 annual income. Similarly, whites receive 30 percent more for inpatient care and 60 percent more for physicians' care than do elderly blacks. Major reasons for this discrepancy are the coinsurance and deductible provisions of Medicare, which place a heavier burden for out-of-pocket expenses on the poor elderly. While the poorest group is eligible for enrollment in state Medicaid programs, it is often the persons just above poverty levels who have the greatest burden. They are not eligible for Medicaid, while coinsurance and deductibles take a larger percentage of their incomes than for other elderly who are better off economically.

A further difficulty older persons face is that Medicare regulations are always in a state of flux. In fact, Congress can amend Medicare policies every year. The result is a certain amount of confusion both among professionals working with the aged and among older persons themselves, who must deal with a bewildering variety of regulations. Because of the complexity of requirement, decisions on eligibility or payments may even vary within a local area. In an introductory text in gerontology, Atchley (1977) makes this observation: "Because Medicare regulations are constantly changing, it is not possible to include much detail about the program. This situation represents a minor headache to authors writing books in gerontology and a major headache to older persons who are never quite sure what is covered or for how long." (p. 115, n. 2). Medical costs have clearly not ceased to be a problem for many elderly despite the passage of Medicare, and the confusing policies and high out-of-pocket expenses result in placing the greatest burden on the poorest among the old.

QUALITY OF CARE: How DOCTORS VIEW THE ELDERLY

At the same time medical expenses have been increasing, many older persons complain about deficiencies in the medical care they receive. It is common, especially in big cities, to see crowded physicians' waiting rooms filled with older persons who sometimes wait an hour or more to see a hurried and impatient doctor. The typical complaints of the elderly are that the doctor takes no time to explain things, or hurriedly dismisses their problems. Many physicians undoubtedly provide excellent care, both from the perspective of medical skills and their manner of relating to patients, but the frequency with which older persons express dissatisfaction indicates that there are some problems in the delivery of health care to the aged.

In his discussion of contemporary medical care, David Mechanic (1978) emphasizes that there is considerable dissatisfaction among patients. From the outset he stresses that patients' complaints do not necessarily reflect the technical competence of the physician. Dissatisfaction indicates that the patient's expectations have not been met in some significant way, whether involving medical care or other aspects of the doctor-patient interaction. Physicians are trained in medical skills, but often in their daily practice they pay little attention to providing support, reassurance, or education to the patient, or to spending sufficient time with the patient to understand his situation. These qualities, however, may actually have some relation to good medical care. Mechanic (1978) reviews studies of patient compliance with complex medical regimens that indicate the general adherence to treatment plans is low, except where the patients have been offered encouragement, support, and instruction by the physician and where aspects of the regimen have been modified to fit into the patient's daily routine. Another factor involved in compliance is how physicians give instructions to patients (Davis 1968; Svarstad 1976; Mechanic 1978). Doctors may dismiss complaints about the side effects of medications, the results of prior treatment, or general complaints about a treatment plan. In order to gain compliance, however, these types of feedback from patients need to be acknowledged. Doctors may also perceive their instructions as the only scientifically correct approach, and become impatient with the questions and complaints of their "untrained" patients. The instruction process, however, represents a complex social interaction in which scientific findings about human behavior also need to be applied.

In addition to these general considerations of doctor-patient interactions, there are specific features of the medical problems of older persons that complicate medical care. According to Mechanic (1978), physicians are trained principally in the treatment of acute conditions that have clear, distinct symptoms. When a disease is present with typical patterns and a straightforward treatment, the doctor can see himself as providing a tangible service. Many physical disorders, however, have indistinct, vague, or fluctuating symptoms that do not consistently respond to treatment. Because the elderly tend to have more chronic than acute health problems (see Chapter 2), their complaints are less likely to fit into an organized pattern. Physicians sometimes use the same approach in these situations as with acute conditions, seeking to cure what in many cases has no direct treatment. They vacillate between active treatment and blaming the patient or the patient's age or some other characteristic for his not getting well, or, occasionally, denying that a problem exists at all. Medical students often view older persons as "crocks" who complain about their ailments but do not have anything wrong with them. Their problems are real, although they may not fit the categories of easily diagnosed or treated disorders. An alternative approach is to try to establish rapport with one's patients more fully and help them to accept certain chronic conditions.

The person with a chronic ailment also may have difficulties in relationships with other individuals. In addition to one's own discomfort, chronic problems can exhaust the resources of others. Furthermore, the behavior of the chronically ill will not confirm expectations that people have about someone who is sick. As originally formulated by Parsons (1951), four major features of the "sick role" are: (1) inability to overcome one's problem without help; (2) an exemption from normal social obligations such as work or other responsibilities while one is ill; (3) motivation to try to get well; and (4) the responsibility to seek medical help and to cooperate with it. It is generally believed that persons become ill because of chance or other circumstances beyond their control. Thus a sick person who cannot fulfill normal role requirements and who make demands for care on others is not reprimanded for this behavior (Mechanic 1978). On the other hand, if the individual fails to meet the requirements of being sick, he can be perceived by others as deviant or bad. Persons who fabricate symptoms to get out of responsibilities or who fail to take necessary therapeutic actions are typically disapproved of by others, including physicians and family members. Among the aged, those with chronic problems fail to meet the expectations for illness behavior in another way—they do not get well. Rather than experiencing an alleviation of symptoms, their complaints remain relatively constant or may even increase in severity. They may become increasingly displeased with their medical care, especially if little gain results and there are unpleasant side effects to medications. This persistence of illness behavior upsets the expectations of others and can lead to a lack of understanding or support of the person.

Chronic problems are often accompanied by feelings of loss, which further complicates interpersonal relationships. As an example, an 84-year-old woman was brought into a clinic by her daughter-in-law for an evaluation. The patient had suffered a major impairment in vision as the result of cataracts with macular degeneration, and also had a severe hearing loss. She was very depressed and complained she had had to give up many of the social and recreational activities she previously enjoyed. Her daughter-in-law showed a distinct impatience with her complaints, insisting that if she only had the will, she could overcome her problems. She further stated she would do anything to help her mother-in-law, but rejected some simple suggestions. This impatience with someone affected by chronic impairments is fairly common. There is some indication from studies of family relationships that most intergenerational conflicts occur when an aged parent is ill and must depend on children for assistance (Troll, Miller, and Atchley 1979).

Hearing problems, which are prevalent in the elderly (see Chapter 2), have a particularly disturbing effect on relationships. In addition to the obvious communication problems, there is often a misunderstanding of what hearing aids can do. Persons with hearing losses who have been fitted with hearing aids sometimes do not wear those devices or complain about the discomfort caused by the way the aid amplifies sound. Family members will despair that they cannot get the person to wear the aid, and are bewildered about the complaints that it does not work adequately or that the person still has difficulty hearing. What is not generally known is that these complaints about the inadequacies of the devices are justified. Two basic problems are that some hearing disorders cannot be corrected with aids, and that many hearing aids are not fitted well. The types of evaluation of hearing losses made by audiologists do not correspond to the manufacturers' descriptions of their products. Thus, a person with a hearing loss for a certain range of tones may be fitted with an aid that is appropriate for a different type of problem. Even when aids are well-matched to a person, there are technical problems with the devices, so that sound is not reproduced faithfully. Hearing aids typically have a brassy tone, uneven amplification of tones, and an excessive amplification of background noise. A person with an aid will often have considerable difficulty listening to conversations in a crowded room because other voices or noises are not filtered out ("How to Buy a Hearing Aid" 1976). Since these problems are not typically known, the person fitted with a hearing aid who continues to have problems is often blamed by others for not getting better.

In many other chronic conditions, symptoms are often not alleviated by treatment, or there are side effects or other difficulties associated with treatment. As a result, the person does not get better but may come to be viewed as a problem patient or hypochondriac, and the sympathy and support given to someone who is sick will gradually be withdrawn.

There is, obviously, some point when complaints about poor health can become excessive, or when a person obstinately refuses to follow even the best-explained medical regimen. A more complete discussion of hypochondriasis will be found in Chapter 9. On the other hand, many complaints are not exaggerations. The management of chronic disabilities is an area in which much more needs to be learned in order to facilitate the best adaptation of the person and the acceptance of continuing difficulties by family members, physicians, and others. Because health problems are common in the old, improving the management of chronic illness can have a significant impact on how aging persons live.

Housing and Housing Preferences

Along with income and medical care, housing is an important aspect of the material needs of individuals. It is commonly thought that many aged persons live in old age homes or nursing homes, or in the planned, middle-income retirement communities that have been developed throughout the country, but only a small number actually live in those types of specialized housing. Most housing surveys indicate that approximately 4 to 5 percent live in an institutional environment where nursing services and other personal care are provided (Atchley 1977). Another 1 percent lives in congregate housing, as typified by a retirement hotel in which residents receive meals and often some other housekeeping services, but otherwise maintain their independence. Similarly, the number of persons living in planned retirement communities is small.

The most typical pattern is for older persons to live in homes that they own, either in rural areas or in older, urban neighborhoods. Because of population trends for younger persons to migrate from the country and small towns to the cities and for younger city dwellers to move to the suburbs, there are greater proportions of older persons in rural areas and in cities (Hendricks and Hendricks 1977). It has been estimated that as many as 70 percent of the aged own their own homes (Riley et al. 1968). In many cases, however, the housing has deteriorated, either because the residents cannot afford repairs or are unable to provide the upkeep. In addition, older urban residents often find that the neighborhoods in which they have lived for 20 years or more have begun deteriorating, but they are unable or unwilling to move to a better area.

Despite these tendencies for older persons to live in somewhat deteriorated housing, overwhelming numbers report satisfaction with their current residence. Summarizing several surveys of housing preferences of the elderly, Lawton and Nahemow (1973) report that most have a high degree of satisfaction with their housing and do not want to move. There are exceptions, of course. Older residents of an urban slum, for example, often indicate a strong desire to move to a better neighborhood. Even when living in very undesirable circumstances, however, some older persons prefer their old house and neighborhood to other alternatives. One couple in Los Angeles continued to live in their neighborhood of 30 years, despite the fact that it had deteriorated considerably. When asked if they had though of moving, the woman said that her husband, who had senile dementia, could go out for walks and find his way around. She was afraid that he would not be able to do so in a new environment. Many older persons may live in less-than-desirable situations because of that preference for old neighborhoods and for what is familiar to them.

Very little is known about the factors in a neighborhood that are related to good functioning among older residents. While the availability of services and easy access to food stores and other retail businesses is often considered important, a person in good health who drives or has access to adequate public transportation may function well whether or not services are close. For someone with limited means or limited mobility, however, easy access to services is essential. Thus the most important consideration may be the match between the person's abilities and characteristics of the neighborhood environment, rather than the presence or absence of certain environmental qualities.

One dimension of the neighborhood environment that has been found to have practical significance is the density of the population of older persons. In a survey of neighborhoods in Cleveland, Rosow (1967) reported that older persons had more friends and greater amounts of social interaction when they lived in neighborhoods with a high concentration of aged. Furthermore, in areas with a higher density neighbors often were available to provide assistance for older persons who became ill, if there were no family members who could help. Some aged persons, however, did not function as well in high-density neighborhoods. In particular, those who led an isolated life style reported lower morale if they lived in a place with a high concentration of older persons than did similar persons living in a low-density area. This group of loners had only low contact with neighbors, whether living in a low- or high-density area. Thus the concentration of older persons in a neighborhood increases the extent of socialization for many, though not all, individuals.

Related to the issue of population density is the debate over the value of age-integrated versus age-segregated housing. While Rosow's findings point to potential gains when large numbers of older persons live in close proximity, it should be remembered that the people he studied were living in age-integrated neighborhoods, rather than specially constructed senior housing. Many other factors may affect the formation of friendships in buildings and communities of only aged persons. It is therefore unwarranted to assume that older persons would have even more friends in senior housing than in the types of neighborhood Rosow described, with high concentrations of older persons. The arguments over whether age-integrated or age-segregated housing is better are based more on emotions that on solid and demonstrated facts. Critics of age-segregated communities usually state that it is wrong to separate older persons from the rest of society. They sometimes also point to the values expressed in some retirement developments, where safety, quiet, and order are emphasized (see Curtin 1972; Jacobs 1974). Among proponents of age-segregated housing, on the other hand, there is often an air of knowing what is best for older persons. They imply that if people would only go along in a rational manner with planned housing, many of the problems of the aged would be eliminated.

Older persons themselves have a mixed response to the prospects of living in age-segregated housing. In surveys reviewed by Lawton and Nahemow (1973), about 30 percent of community-living older persons indicated a preference for age-segregated housing. In contrast, most persons living in age-segregated housing indicated satisfaction with that type of residence, and only 9 percent reported a preference for a different type of housing. The opportunity to be around their peers undoubtedly influenced their choice in the first place. It should be noted that there are tendencies throughout the adult years for persons to live in communities where they can associate with others of similar ages. The growth of planned developments for older persons may be only one manifestation of this trend, rather than an attempt to isolate the aged from the rest of us.

Types of age-segregated communities may vary considerably. Planned retirement communities are typically available only for middle-class persons or the well-to-do, although some working-class persons have retired to mobile home parks. The latter may offer excellent facilities and opportunities for interaction, but in some cases the housing and other community resources are substandard. For the person with the financial means to choose his or her preferred housing, both age-segregated and age-integrated communities are available. Persons with limited incomes typically have less of a range of choices of where they can live, and it is for them that subsidized senior citizen housing is developed. In general, the results of several relocation studies of healthy individuals who moved from age-integrated neighborhoods into special housing for the elderly indicate benefits from the move. Furthermore, in contrast to relocation studies of the impaired elderly (see Chapter 10), there is no evidence of increased mortality or other adverse effects when moving from one type of community housing to an age-segregated project (Wittels and Botwinick 1974).

Probably the best-known and best researched project is the Victoria Plaza housing development in San Antonio, Texas (Carp 1966; 1975). When contrasted with a matched group of older community residents who did not move into age-segregated housing, it was found that persons living in Victoria Plaza reported more happiness, more optimism, and seemed to have an overall better adjustment both at 1-year and 8-year follow-ups. The levels of activity and social participation were also higher for residents of Victoria Plaza at the 1-year follow-up. In reviewing these studies, however, Lawton and Nahemow (1973) caution that the considerable attention focused on Victoria Plaza, and the fact that all the residents whom Carp studied moved in at the same time, may have led to the development of an esprit de corps among residents that is different from more typical housing projects. While they feel there are often benefits for aged persons when moving to this type of housing, they suggest the gains may be more modest than found in Victoria Plaza.

Age-segregated housing has also been reported to have unfavorable effects. By removing older persons from familiar neighborhoods, they no longer had access to settings in which informal interactions occurred and that offered more opportunities for diversities in one's life style (Sussman and Steinberg 1970, cited in Montgomery 1972).

Two other factors must be considered in evaluating age-segregated housing. First, with respect to subsidized housing such as Victoria Plaza, comparisons of in-movers with those who continue to reside in the community may measure something other than the response to an age-segregated environment. If the communities the older persons are leaving are dangerous and deteriorating, then the gains they express may be related to relieving the fears associated with living in an undesirable area. In other words, many of these persons might have shown similar gains if they were moved from inner-city housing to a comfortable and safe suburban apartment in an age-integrated building. The problems of housing for the elderly with limited means involve income as much as the structure of the community (see Rosow 1967). Second, when considering whether older persons want to live in age-integrated or -segregated subsidized housing, a preference for living among their age peers may reflect their awareness of contemporary social problems, rather than a strong desire for age segregation. Age-integrated buildings can be difficult places for an older person to live because of the high crime rates among economically disadvantaged youths. Age-segregated buildings offer more security. For practical reasons, then, older individuals may be more satisfied in age-segregated buildings.

The issue of what type of housing is best for the elderly thus depends both on the alternatives that are actually available as well as the needs, preferences, and ability of the particular older person who is being considered for a specific residence. If our cities were safe and if the aged had the financial resources to choose whatever housing they preferred, it is not known how many would continue to live in familiar, urban neighborhoods and how many would opt for a planned community with special social and recreational activities. Furthermore, little is known about how type of housing and type of community may contribute to supporting the older person with physical or mental impairments. What can be concluded is that older pesons should not be told to move to a particular type of housing because it would be good for them. We should not make authoritative statements about what housing is best, or ignore the preferences of older persons themselves for one type of housing or another.

Fear of Crime

As indicated in the discussion of housing, older persons are often concerned about crime and fearful of being victims of crime. In surveys of community residents, fear of crime is one of the most frequent problems mentioned (see Bild and Havighurst 1976). At the same time, surveys indicate that young persons are more likely to be the victims of most crimes, with the exception of purse and wallet snatchings (Antunes et al. 1977). While police crime statistics are not always a good indicator of the total amount of criminal activities, there is no reason to expect that the elderly would underreport crimes against them more than any other group. One is thus left with the paradox that older persons are quite fearful of crimes, but are not often victims of crime.

In an attempt to account for this discrepancy between fear of crime and the actual number of incidents involving older victims, Antunes and his associates (Antunes et al. 1977) reviewed the pattern and types of crime committed against the elderly, which are shown in Table 4.1. When compared to the young, older persons are less likely to be the victims in crimes of violence such as assult and rape. The most frequent crimes committed against older persons are robbery and personal larceny, such as purse snatching. These crimes, which can be termed "predatory," are directed as frequently toward the old as toward the young. They also tend to be committed on the street, rather than in or near the person's home. The assailant is typically a youth who acts alone and who is unarmed. When violent crimes do involve the elderly, these occur in or near the home, rather than on the street. Thus while the total amount of crime against the elderly is lower than for other age groups, certain types of crime do occur frequently. The older person's fears of going out alone, and particularly fears of young males on the streets, are justified by the high rates of predatory crimes. Furthermore, older persons are more easily victimized, as indicated by the fact that many of these crimes are committed by unarmed persons acting alone.

The fears of the elderly do therefore have some basis in fact. The high rates of crime, especially in urban areas, are part of a larger social problem that affects all persons, including the aged. But the special vulnerability of the aged to predatory crimes could be taken into account in preventive programs. Community education programs often stress not going out, especially at night, and placing secure locks in one's apartment or home. These measures, however, may actually increase the isolation and fears of older persons. Taking a different approach, Antunes and his associates (1977) make two suggestions that could make the elderly less attractive victims. First, as has been done with cab drivers and other groups who have been targets of robberies, there could be a campaign for the elderly not to carry more than a small amount of cash at a given time. By

TABLE 4.1. Distribution of victims by crime category and age of victim

Age of Victim	12–16	17–20	21–26	27–32	33–39	40–49	50–64	65+
Type of Crime								
Assault	74.8	73.3	70.8	72.2	71.4	65.6	50.2	28.1
Robbery	17.4	15.7	16.9	16.3	19.2	22.3	27.0	39.1
Personal larceny	5.0	7.2	7.3	9.2	7.1	10.9	21.9	31.3
Rape	2.8	3.8	5.0	2.3	2.3	1.2	.9	1.5
Violent crime (rape and assault combined)	77.6	77.1	75.8	74.5	73.7	66.8	51.1	29.6
Predatory crime (robbery and personal larceny combined)	22.4	22.9	24.2	25.5	26.3	33.2	48.9	70.4
(N)	(1155)	(973)	(1075)	(567)	(369)	(463)	(473)	(236)

Source: G. E. Antunes, F. L. Cook, T. D. Cook, and W. G. Skogan, "Patterns of Personal Crime against the Elderly: Findings from a National Survey," *The Gerontologist* 17 (1977): 321–327. Copyright © 1977 by the Gerontological Society. Reprinted by permission.

making predatory crimes less profitable, these acts could be deterred. Second, a buddy system or escort service might be developed so that older persons are not out alone as much, particularly those persons who could be more easily victimized because of limited mobility. Lone assailants might be less likely to commit a crime if others are around.

Social Roles and Social Status

A prominent characteristic of the later years is the likelihood that the individual will experience losses of various kinds. There is an increasing chance of illness and of the chronic impairments that often accompany the ailments of the old. The person may experience some changes in psychological abilities, often in tandem with, but sometimes independent of, changes in health status. Losses in social roles and social status can occur, such as through retirement, or the death of a spouse or other family members or friends. While changes in status at earlier times in the life cycle are accompanied by new role expectations that take the place of activities that one gives up, the transition into old age involves the loss of formal roles with no increase of responsibilities, privileges, or activities (Rosow 1974).

Social Status and Aging

In a major synthesis of sociological research on aging, Irving Rosow (1974) identifies 7 sources or determinants of social status and argues that there are losses in each of these areas as we age. These determinants of status are: property, possessing strategic knowledge, productivity, mutual dependence among generations, tradition and religion, the kinship network, and community life. With property, for example, Rosow contrasts contemporary society with agrarian cultures. In the latter, persons tend to accumulate property as they age and can use their wealth when they are old to control the young and to wield influence in the community. In our society the young are able to accumulate wealth and possessions without assistance from their parents. Similarly, the old in our society have little of the special knowledge valued by others. In many simpler societies aged persons possess information about farming or other technologies and of cultural traditions. In a fast-changing society, however, knowledge is rapidly outmoded and the older person is often at a disadvantage when compared with someone with recent training in a technical area. In terms of productivity and contributions to the economy, the older worker is also disadvantaged. Because of the increasing prevalence of health problems with age, the productivity of older persons is lower than that of other adults. Since there is an excess of labor, especially for unskilled and semiskilled work, the potential contribution of the old through work is not valued highly. Another contrast with simpler societies is the amount of material aid the aged can give to younger generations. Where there are limited resources, it is necessary for the generations of a family to live together or in close proximity and to help one another. With the increasing wealth in Western society, however, it has become possible for young persons to set up independent households, often as soon as they obtain a first job or while going to college. They require less direct assistance from their parents or grandparents and therefore there is less mutual dependence between generations. Even in Japan, where there has always been a strong family tradition, the recent prosperity has made it possible for many young couples to set up households independent of their families. Rosow notes similar losses or declines as persons age for the other determinants of status.

In a critique of Rosow's approach, Neugarten and Hagestad (1976) argue that the aged have not lost status compared to their position in American society 100 years ago. While it may be that the "good old days" were not really so good, that should not obscure the major point made by Rosow that many individuals experience a decline in social status in their life. This decline is linked to other features in the social life of the aged. In particular, Rosow (1974) has suggested that there is a lack of clearly defined roles for older persons because of their low status in the community. Riley and her associates (1969) made the similar observation that the low social standing of the old leads to a certain amount of ambiguity about what are socially desired involvements or behaviors. Describing the transition to old age, they write: "To the extent that some new roles fail to present goals that are valued by society, there can be no clear expectations of constructive performance, facilities and resources for training are likely to be in short supply, and rewards tend to become minimal or even negative" (p. 963). In other words, because of the lack of defined roles, it is more difficult for the aged to replace lost involvements.

This lack of clearly defined roles and involvements has a gradual, rather than sudden, effect on most older persons. As described below, reactions to specific social changes such as retirement are varied, with many persons reporting a positive outcome. It can also be assumed that individuals often enlarge their informal roles as a way of accommodating to the loss of formal ones (Neugarten and Hagestad 1976). Nonetheless, for many persons being old is associated neither with any increased status or privilege, nor with the provision of any clear place and obligations in the social order.

RETIREMENT

It is widely assumed by the public that retirement is a stressful and sometimes tragic event for older persons. Retirement, however, usually does not have adverse effects, except when the person is not able to replace work with other involvements. Many persons look forward to retirement. Puner (1974) makes this point with a fictional retirement speech: "I'll be brief. The working conditions here are terrible. I haven't liked a day of it. I'm glad I'm out of it!" In discussing attitudes toward work, Puner also quotes Abraham Lincoln: " 'My father taught me to work, but not to love it. I never did like to work and I don't deny it. I'd rather read, tell stories, crack jokes, talk, laugh—anything but work' " (p. 164). While it is typically emphasized that the retired have trouble filling their time with meaningful activities, the other side of the issue is that many individuals do not enjoy various aspects of their work and welcome its absence.

As these comments indicate, one important variable affecting adjustment to retirement is the type of work experience the person is leaving. Those in working-class jobs are more likely to have positive attitudes about retirement than individuals with higher education and managerial or professional jobs (Atchley 1977). Their major concern in looking forward to retirement is financial and, as described earlier, this apprehension is realistic. The principal dissatisfaction with retirement, in fact, is over income (Sheppard 1976).

The experience of retirement has not been found to be accompanied by sudden changes in well-being, mental health, or physical health, despite expectations and personal anecdotes to the contrary. Most research has indicated that there are few changes in these dimensions of functioning following retirement (Lowenthal, Berkman, and associates 1967; Streib and Schneider 1971; Sheppard 1976). In one major study one-third of the respondents indicated that retirement was better than they expected, while only a negligible number said it was worse (Streib and Schneider 1971). The expectation that retirement leads to poor health may result from the fact that many persons are forced to retire because of health problems. Approximately one-half of all persons who retire do not do so voluntarily. While approximately one-third of these persons are affected by mandatory regulations, the remaining individuals leave their jobs either because of poor health or because their jobs are eliminated (Atchley 1977). Thus at least some retirees were in poor health before their retirement.

Many people experience a honeymoon period immediately after retiring during which they fill their lives with long-put-off activities and otherwise enjoy their leisure (Atchley 1977). This honeymoon usually comes to an end and the individual must make a more permanent adjustment to being retired. Health plays a critical role in this long-term adaptation. Individuals who are dissatisfied with their retirement are more likely to be in poorer health (Shanas et al. 1968). For persons in good health, both satisfaction and some ambivalence are expressed. Most persons say they are pleased with being retired, yet at the same time indicate that they would like more meaningful, challenging, or involving activities. Overall, then, the significance of work to the individual, income, health status, and the availability of meaningful alternatives all emerge as critical to one's adjustment to retirement. Many people willingly give up the drudgery or routine of their jobs, but it is frequently difficult to find satisfying alternatives. It should be noted that for some persons work is probably the most preferred type of involvement, and it is on these individuals that mandatory retirement falls the hardest.

Volunteer roles are sometimes suggested as an alternative to work. Based on the limited research available on volunteerism in later life, the effects of these involvements are not straightforward. One comparison of volunteers with older persons who were working found that those with jobs reported greater personal satisfaction (Carp 1968a). In the research of Heymann and Sabol (1977), however, volunteers had more satisfaction with their positions than did older persons participating in a special jobs program. In that study the volunteers surveyed were in an organization largely directed by volunteers and in which there was considerable opportunity to assume responsibilities and to advance within the organization. This kind of volunteer role may be a special case. Typical volunteer positions offer only limited involvement and little opportunity to take on responsible activities. Furthermore, one's need for more income undoubtedly affects the potential value of volunteering. Persons from predominantly middle-class backgrounds, such as in the Heymann and Sabol study, may be more willing to forgo payment for activities when they are presented with stimulating volunteer positions.

The creation of meaningful volunteer roles is an important challenge for using the abilities of older persons. One program has trained older persons in counseling skills so they can function as peer counselors under professional supervision (Becker and Zarit 1978; Alpaugh and Hickey-Haney 1978). While outcome studies of their effectiveness have not been made, these peer counselors add an important dimension to the university-based counseling program in which they are involved. Older clients who feel a young student cannot help them can be assigned to an age peer as therapist or cotherapist. Furthermore, the presence of older peer counselors gives student trainees a positive model of old age and leads to more awareness of what it is like to grow older. A similar program that has received wide attention and that builds on the experience and skills of older persons is "Foster Grandparents" (Nash 1968; Saltz 1971).

One important consequence of retirement is that it can upset the balance in a marital relationship. This is particularly the case in those families where the husband has worked outside the house while the wife has principally done the housework. Older women frequently make jokes about having husbands underfoot after retirement, and some express more direct feelings of anxiety concerning how they will manage after their husbands retire. Problems often occur after the honeymoon period that follows retirement. Subsequently many husbands find substitute activities that maintain some role separation in the household.

MARITAL AND FAMILY RELATIONSHIPS

Marriage and family ties are the major source of support and satisfaction for many older persons. Changes in that support prove the most difficult stress for an individual to overcome. Losses in family involvements, of course, can occur through death or estrangement. Among these, widowhood has received the most attention. Other changes, such as the death of a child or family conflict, also can have a major impact on the individual.

Marital relationships of older persons are generally characterized by a high level of satisfaction. While many middle-aged persons report dissatisfaction with their marriages, older persons report as much contentment as at any other period of marriage, except perhaps among newlyweds (see reviews by Lowenthal and Robinson 1976 and Kimmel 1974). It is not known whether this is because unsatisfying marriages have been dissolved through divorce or separation, or if couples enter a new phase in their relationship. In one study conducted by Stinnett, Carter, and Montgomery (1972) older couples placed a high degree of value of companionship and honest expression. Similarly, love tends to be defined more in those terms by older persons than by the young (Reedy and Birren 1978). Among older couples having marital problems, it was reported that their spouses often held different values and philosophies or had different interests (Stinnett, Carter, and Montgomery 1972). The quality of marital relationships is viewed somewhat differently by men than by women. Older men generally express more satisfaction with their marriages than do women (Lowenthal, Thurnher, and Chiriboga 1975; Troll, Miller, and Atchley 1979). Men look to their wives principally to care for their needs, while married women express the desire for more companionship and resent their husband's dependence on them. These differences are found in both middle-aged and older couples.

Other family relationships can be described in a similar way: there is frequent contact and support between older persons and their relatives, especially children, and also areas of discord. Interactions with children are often the most important relationship for older persons. Among the current generation of elderly, the overwhelming majority who were ever married have one or more children (Troll, Miller, and Atchley 1979), and they interact frequently.

Far from demonstrating the disappearance of the nuclear family, family ties between older persons and their adult children are generally fairly

TABLE 4.2. Family contacts of older men and women, excluding those who share a home with children (percentage distribution)

FAMILY CONTACTS	DENMARK			BRITAIN			UNITED STATES		
	Men	Women	All	Men	Women	All	Men	Women	All
Saw child during the previous week	63	63	63	63	63	63	63	63	63
No contact with child, but saw a sibling or other relative during last week	5	5	5	7	5	6	7	9	8
Have no children, but saw sibling or other relative during last week	6	10	9	15	25	21	12	17	14
No family contacts during last week	24	21	22	19	13	15	21	14	18
Have neither children, siblings, nor relatives	2	1	2	7	8	8	—	1	1
Total	100	100	100	100	100	100	100	100	100
N =	935	1,086	2,021	692	1,006	1,698	878	1,008	1,886

Source: E. Shanas, P. Townsend, D. Wedderburn, H. Friis, P. Milhøj, and J. Stehouwer, Old People in Three Industrial Societies (New York: Atherton, 1968), p. 201. Copyright © 1968 by the Atherton Press. Reprinted by permission of the authors.

strong (see Table 4.2). Surveys of older persons both in the United States and in European countries indicate that most older persons live within easy traveling distance of children (Shanas et al. 1968; Lowenthal and Robinson 1976). Children of aged parents usually maintain regular contact with their parents, both through visits and phone calls. It is more the exception, and perhaps therefore all the more tragic, for there to be a complete break in the relationship between parents and children. Furthermore, when persons need help of various kinds, it is most likely to come from their children. Daughters typically provide assistance to their parents, but if there are no daughters, then sons often give similar aid. Persons who have no children turn first to siblings for help, and then to friends and neighbors (Shanas et al. 1968; Rosow 1967). It should also be noted that many aged parents continue to assist their adult children financially and in other ways (see Table 4.3).

Most of the research on family relationships has emphasized the frequency of contacts and the presence of mutual help patterns. There has been little investigation, however, of the quality of the relationships. In

TABLE 4.3. Proportion, by age group, of older men and women giving help to and receiving help from children

AGE AND HELP PATTERNS	DENMARK		BRITAIN		UNITED STATES	
	Men	*Women*	*Men*	*Women*	*Men*	*Women*
Gave help to children						
65–69	21	27	56	60	66	66
70–74	28	29	42	50	62	57
75 and over	24	27	34	37	47	55
Received help from children						
65–69	12	18	55	60	60	72
70–74	19	16	50	60	57	72
75 and over	23	32	54	75	66	79
Received regular money help						
65–69	1	3	3	5	1	5
70–74	1	3	3	8	1	8
75 and over	2	4	2	4	2	7
Received occasional money gifts						
65–69	3	6	12	23	21	39
70–74	3	8	17	25	23	43
75 and over	4	10	14	28	31	48

Source: E. Shanas, P. Townsend, D. Wedderburn, H. Friis, P. Milhøj, and J. Stehouwer, *Old People in Three Industrial Societies* (New York: Atherton, 1968), p. 214. Copyright © 1968 by the Atherton Press. Reprinted by permission of the authors.

one of the few exceptions, Bengtson and Cutler (1976) focused on patterns of affection in three-generation families. They found that all generations felt a high degree of affection, understanding, and trust of each other. There was, however, some asymmetry in how the relationships were perceived by each generation. The oldest group reported more subjective affection in their relationship with their middle-aged children. The middle-aged, in turn, described themselves as providing and also receiving more help from their parents than was reported by the oldest group. According to Bengtson and Cutler, these findings suggest that parents and adult children have somewhat different stakes in their relationships with each other: the parents focusing on emotional aspects while children are concerned with giving and/or receiving assistance.

One important area where more research is needed is how the illness of an aged parent affects parent-child relationships (Lowenthal and Robinson 1976). Some writers (Kimmel 1974) have talked about a role reversal in this phase of family life, suggesting that issues of dependency and authority become critical. In clinical settings several patterns can be observed. Some people give up virtually all independent activities and decision making and request or demand to be cared for by their children. Other parents may refuse stubbornly to turn over any authority to their children and will frustrate every therapeutic plan that is put forward, whether it involves taking medication, having a housekeeper provide some assistance, or any other measure. There needs to be more attention to these situations, as well as investigations into the best ways of helping families resolve the dilemmas they face when caring for aging parents. It should also be noted that illness of an adult child, while occurring less frequently, will also have a marked impact on the intergenerational relationship.

While family ties do not diminish as much as most people expect, family responsibilities lessen. When one's last child leaves the house, it undoubtedly alters the behavior of both father and mother. This "empty nest" period of family life is considered anecdotally to be a very difficult time, though systematic research has failed to reveal clear-cut patterns of reaction. Rather, it appears that couples and individuals who are having difficulties during the empty nest period had similar problems before that time (Lowenthal and Chiriboga 1972).

Grandparenthood offers the opportunity for new family responsibilities and relationships for many persons. Being a grandparent is often a very satisfying experience. It has been described as having all the pleasures of raising children, with none of the responsibilities (Neugarten and Weinstein 1968; Alberts 1977). But while pleasurable, being a grandparent is not considered an important involvement for most older persons. In many cultures grandparents play a major role in raising grandchildren. This type of involvement appears to be declining here (Neugarten and Weinstein 1968). While for many people this absence of responsibility is welcome, there are undoubtedly some persons, both men and women, who want to continue the type of family interaction they had when raising their own children. In the case of work roles, some persons prefer working to any of the other alternatives. One finds the same situation with family involvements. Some individuals would undoubtedly do better in old age if living in a culture where a high degree of continued family involvement was the expectation rather than the exception. Neugarten and Weinstein (1968) also report a trend of younger grandparents in their sample to have less frequent contacts with grandchildren, often, though not always, due to the geographic distance between households. Thus for some, grandparenting is a very limited involvement.

Divorce is less frequent among older couples than in other age groups, but it has been estimated that there are 10,000 divorces each year among persons over 65 (Troll, Miller, and Atchley 1979). Little is known about the effects of divorce in late life, except for isolated clinical examples that highlight the suffering or loneliness of some divorced persons. These instances may or may not be generalizable to all newly divorced older persons.

Overall, the effects of changes in family structure and responsibilities in later life can be described in similar terms as retirement. Most people do not have catastrophic reactions to the empty nest, to grandparenthood, or to any other phenomenon of family life. Many find both the empty nest period and grandparenting satisfying experiences. Someone whose family life has special significance, however, may not be able to find other roles or involvements that can substitute for family interactions. In a few cases, long-standing family problems are resolved by breaking most or all ties between parents and children.

Widowhood, of course, can have a dramatic effect on one's life. Reactions to widowhood are described in more detail in Chapter 9. For many persons it results in withdrawing from the couple-oriented activities in which they had previously engaged (Streib 1976; Lopata 1973). The effects, however, vary somewhat by class and ethnic background (Troll, Miller, and Atchley 1979). Middle-class women experience a loss of status, especially if they are left without sufficient income or had a major involvement in their husband's life. Working-class women, on the other hand, experience greater social isolation. Race or ethnic group also affect how widowhood is experienced. Working-class black women report less distress when widowed than their white counterparts, perhaps because they have traditionally played a more dominant role in the family (Troll, Miller, and Atchley 1979).

Widowhood is principally a problem of older women and not of men. Women have a greater life expectancy than men and generally marry men who are older than they. Differences in life expectancy in this society are about 7 years, and the mean difference in age between a husband and wife is 4 years. Given these figures, women could be expected to outlive their husbands by an average of 11 years. In 1970 there were 6 million widows (Bouvier, Atlee, and McVeigh 1975). Only 18 percent of aged men, compared to 55 percent of women, are widowed. Related to their greater life expectancy, women also tend to be in better health than their husbands. One result is that women frequently care for ailing husbands. Lopata (1973) found that 46 percent of widows had provided care to their husbands before their death.

Because of the proportion of older men to women in the population, the loss of a spouse has different consequences for each sex. A man whose wife dies is likely to remarry. He has as potential marriage partners both the women his own age and younger women, since marriage to the latter is socially acceptable. In contrast, women who want to remarry find that there are few men their own age or older who are not married, and may not consider it appropriate to marry someone younger.

In addition to marriage, there are fewer opportunities for women than for men for other kinds of interaction in old age with someone of the opposite sex. One needs only to go to any program for senior citizens to see that the women greatly outnumber men. A woman who has previously formed close relationships with men but not women faces particular problems in the later years. One woman who sought counseling, for example, had worked until her retirement in a men's clothing store, and thoroughly enjoyed her contact both with male customers and with the other employees, who were primarily men. Forced to retire because of a mandatory age requirement, she had no interest in going to senior centers to be around other women when she had not enjoyed their companionship throughout her adult years. This example points out that the diversity of friendships and involvements available to the young are not so for older persons, and for older women in particular.

While men who are widowed are likely to remarry, the loss of a spouse can sometimes have a major impact on their social relationships. For many men, their only confidants are their wives, and in many marriages the wife also makes the social and family arrangements. Women, in contrast, typically name another woman as a confidant (Lowenthal and Robinson 1976). Thus the loss of a spouse is more likely to disrupt one's network of supporting relationships in the case of a man whose wife dies, than for the opposite.

Summary

As Rosow (1974) has described, the later years involve a loss of roles and for many persons a decrease in social status. While not typically followed by behavior disturbances that require professional attention, these losses add up for some people, so that they do not feel as fulfilled or satisfied with their lives as they had. For others, new informal roles take the place of prior responsibilities. The old should not be described either as happy or unhappy in their retirement. Reactions to these losses depend on the meaning of the loss to the individual, and the opportunities for other involvements.

PART II

Psychopathology and Assessment

CHAPTER 5

Psychopathology and Behavioral Assessment

OLDER PERSONS MAY MANIFEST many types of psychological disorder, ranging from the minimally impairing to those problems that severely alter the person's competencies. Three cases illustrate the diversity of presenting symptoms of the aged. Miss A. is a quiet, retired professional, aged 68, who came to an outpatient clinic because of loneliness. She felt isolated from other persons and had few activities or interests that stimulated her or utilized her talents. Mrs. C., also 68, wanted someone to intercede with her landlord, whom she claimed had been causing her apartment to shake and to be filled with unpleasant smells. She was currently sleeping in the bus station and reported that she had had similar problems in the last 4 places she had lived. Mr. K., a 60-year-old retired engineer, complained of memory problems. He had retired early from his job after developing Parkinson's disease. Although he had little functional impairment from his illness, he spent his days engaging in few activities. He stated that he watched daytime television programs, and was then unable to remember what had just happened. He also said he did not pay much attention to what he was watching.

The professional has to make similar decisions for each of these cases. First, it must be determined whether a problem is present that warrants treatment. Loneliness, for example, is experienced by most persons at some times in their lives, and the question can be raised whether special mental health treatment is necessary. If, on the other hand, we should provide psychological treatment to someone who is lonely, then how much loneliness should be present before we make an intervention? Second, it is necessary to clarify and delineate what type of problem or problems a client manifests so that the most appropriate treatments can be used.

Presumably the feelings of persecution reported by the second client re-present a different sort of phenomenon from either loneliness or the subjective complaints of poor memory, and should be treated with proce-dures specific to that kind of disorder.

The ways in which the practitioner deals with these basic circum-stances are influenced by two factors: (1) one's concepts concerning the nature of psychopathology; and (2) the means of assessment used to determine whether a problem is present. Our conceptual framework or model of psychopathology is critical because it influences whether we perceive that a person has a problem. How we formulate that problem also influences our judgment about whether treatment is likely to be effective and what type of treatment to use.

To cite an example of how concepts of psychopathology affect these decisions, 2 extreme positions can be contrasted: the "aging as pathology" and "aging as social pathology" models of dysfunction. Briefly, the "aging as pathology" model views the aging process as leading inevitably to deterioration of basic physiological and psychological functions. This per-spective considers the behavioral or emotional problems of an older person as a normal concomitant of the aging process. A corollary to this position is that since no effective means exist for slowing or reversing the phe-nomena of biological aging, custodial care is the most appropriate in-tervention. While stated in an extreme form, this model is held implicitly both by many of the lay public and by professionals who interact with the aged, and results in an excessive use of custodial and other inappro-priate treatments (Kahn 1975). In contrast, the "aging as social pathology" model suggests that the problems of the aged derive from the age dis-crimination and economic disadvantages to which older persons are sub-jected. Some professionals, for example, have claimed that the intellectual deficits associated with senile dementia are produced not by an underlying brain pathology but because of a lack of social stimulation and of relevant social involvements for older persons. Someone working within this frame-work would not be concerned with the issue of differential diagnosis of organic and functional conditions, but would treat all complaints of the aged as manifestations of the losses of status and role that often accom-pany aging in our society. While these models represent extreme views, they serve to illustrate how our ideas about the nature of psychopathology in the aged influence clinical decisions.

The means of assessment we use are also dictated by our beliefs about the nature of psychopathology. If one views the brain disorders of later life as distinct in their etiology from other types of behavioral problem, then it is necessary to develop procedures for making differential diagnoses. Someone, however, who feels that all problems of the aged are rooted in altered brain functioning would not be concerned with that type of assess-ment. To cite another example, the methods of evaluation are quite different if depression is seen as the result of an underlying and unconscious conflict or as the consequence of poor social and other behavioral skills necessary for obtaining positive reinforcements from the environment.

Our knowledge of the causes of and cures for mental disorders of persons of any age is often quite limited. This is particularly the case when considering the problems of older persons, which have only recently been studied in systematic ways. At the present time there is no agreed-upon and empirically based framework for conceptualizing the psychopathologies of old age. In the present chapter several models of psychopathology and their application to the problems of old age will be reviewed. From these models a framework will be proposed for the psychological assessment of older persons. The evaluation of brain disorders and physical assessment are discussed in subsequent chapters.

Models of Psychopathology

THE MEDICAL MODEL

The medical model is the most widely held conceptualization of psychopathology. The very terms used to refer to problems in behaviors or emotions are derived from this model. Thus we speak of mental health or illness and, as in medical care, have emphasized one-to-one treatment between doctor and patient as the preferred means of therapy.

The medical model was developed in the nineteenth century to extend the growing field of scientific medicine and research to mental disorders. Prior to that time, different conceptualizations were held. In the middle ages it was believed that mental disorders were the result of possession by demons or witchcraft. During the Age of Enlightenment, mental patients were seen as having been exposed to morally corrupting influences (Nathan and Harris 1975). The development of large state mental hospitals in the nineteenth century was in part motivated by the notion that mental disabilities might be cured by moving the individual to a healthful, rural environment. As a medical orientation developed in the mid- to late 1800s, major discoveries of the causes of mental disorders were expected that would be similar to the advances in the care of infectious diseases.

The medical model implies that various mental and emotional disturbances are due to structural damage to body organs, especially the brain, or to altered physiological processes, such as in disorders of metabolism or endocrine function. Just as the symptoms of fever, headache, and mild nausea are often caused by a viral agent, it is hypothesized that mental symptoms are also due to an underlying illness. This assumption has influenced both assessment and treatment. There have been repeated attempts to group symptoms into disease entities. The Diagnostic and

Statistical Manual of the American Psychiatric Association, or DSM III (1978), is one outcome of this process. The focus of treatment has often been on curing the hypothesized disease entity, rather than responding to the presenting symptoms.

Psychoanalytic models of diagnosis and treatment form an important variant of the medical model. Rather than viewing the causes of disorders as medical illnesses, however, psychodynamic theories stress the importance of early psychological experiences as the roots of symptoms manifested in adulthood. Similar to the medical model, psychoanalytic writers have emphasized that symptoms reflect an underlying illness, and that one must treat the deep-seated conflict that lies at the core of the symptoms (Nathan and Harris 1975).

Development of the medical model for the diagnosis and treatment of mental disorders has led to several major advances. Among these are a general humanization of care for persons with mental problems, the identification and treatment of specific disorders that have an organic basis, such as the mental symptoms associated with syphilis, and the development of psychotropic drugs that can assist substantially in the treatment of particular problems. The recent discovery of the relation of manic-depressive psychoses to imbalances in the salt lithium carbonate made it possible to attenuate the drastic mood swings that characterize this disorder (Foster, Gershell, and Goldfarb 1977).

In terms of older persons, the medical model provides an appropriate framework for conceptualizing some common psychiatric problems. Principle among these are the brain disorders, which are caused by structural damage or by various physiological disturbances that lead to altered brain functioning. Similarly, the study of stress reactions of the elderly may lead to major advances in treatment of mental disorders. It has been proposed, for example, that older persons have altered or impaired responses to stress (Marx 1974a). The development of ways of bolstering or augmenting stress reactions of the aged can provide important steps in the prevention of some mental disorders.

The medical model also has critical problems that limit its extension to all psychological disorders, including those of the elderly. First, at a very basic level, it provides an inaccurate conceptualization for the majority of psychological disturbances. Most emotional or behavioral problems do not result from similar etiological factors as do physical illnesses, such as tissue damage, viruses, or organ dysfunction. It would appear, rather, that mental disorders are related to continuous adverse or stressful influences that individuals are exposed to over long periods of time, and to persons and other environmental influences in an individual's life (Zax and Cowen 1976). Second, it has not been possible to develop a reliable diagnostic system based on the medical model. There has been no agreement on what symptoms are necessary for the diagnosis of hypothesized underlying disorders for many types of mental problem. It is not clear, for example, how much depressed affect a patient must have before one can make a diagnosis of one of the affective disorders, and attempts to obtain reliabilities in diagnosis have often failed. Furthermore, many of the diagnostic labels commonly used are not related to specific treatment procedures and have limited predictive value (Nathan and Harris 1975). A further assumption that similar symptoms reflect a single underlying etiology can also be questioned. In elderly patients, for example, paranoid delusions and hallucinations may be indicators of several distinct problems, including acute or chronic organic brain syndromes, chronic paranoid schizophrenia, a hearing disorder, or a response to increasing social isolation (Berger and Zarit 1978).

The medical model also makes assumptions about the process of treatment, but procedures that are effective in dealing with acute medical problems are not appropriate for most behavior disorders. This viewpoint has been elaborated by Thoresen and his associates (in press), who write:

> A person experiencing bacterial pneumonia can be given powerful antibiotics. These drugs will usually be effective regardless of the person's knowledge of their mechanisms of action. Further, these drugs do not require the person's active involvement other than to comply to the prescribed regime for taking the medication. . . . A change in behavior can seldom be achieved by means of an automatic effect produced by any treatment technique. Instead, meaningful change which is maintained requires persons to possess a variety of skills for assessing and managing a myriad of environmental and cognitive events. . . .

Thus the treatment of psychological disorders involves the active attempts of clients or patients to change some aspects of their behaviors or thoughts, and represents a different sort of process from the usual exchange between doctor and patient.

A major problem of the medical and psychodynamic models of psychopathology is their emphasis that disordered behaviors emanate from within the individual. This assumption has two important consequences. First, by looking for the cause of maladaptive behaviors or emotions within the individual, one can miss critical interpersonal and other environmental events that have a profound influence on dysfunctional behaviors (Rimm and Masters 1974; McLemore and Benjamin 1979). A person who complains of depression, for example, may receive attention from her spouse only when she talks of feeling sad or upset, while at other times he will interact little with her. Over the years there has been impressive evidence of the influence of environmental factors on all sorts of behavioral and affective responses. Even for persons with organic disorders, that is, problems that derive from structural damage to the brain, the environment continues to influence actions and feelings. Any conceptual model of psychopathology must systematically incorporate these environmental factors into its diagnostic and treatment procedures.

Another consequence of viewing disordered behavior as due principally to an internal psychological or medical defect is that behaviors and emotions are not evaluated for their own sake, but only for how they might be signs of a more basic illness. As a result, assessment takes the form of trying to fit a patient's observable actions or statements to a hypothesized syndrome or disease. Once a diagnosis is made, however tentative, there is a tendency to look for confirming signs of pathology in everything a person says or does. Because any behavior can sometimes reflect pathology within this framework, it is difficult to find agreement on consistent diagnostic criteria.

A study by Rosenhan (1972) illustrates how difficult it is to differentiate normal from abnormal behavior using this illness model. Persons who were functioning adequately in their everyday lives presented themselves for admission to various mental hospitals, including both public and private institutions. These "pseudopatients" were instructed to state to the admitting unit that they were hearing voices that whispered to them the words "empty," "hollow," and "thud." Rosenhan characterized the symptom as indicating "existential psychosis," of which no recorded cases have ever been presented. Despite the vagueness of the symptoms, all the pseudopatients were admitted to inpatient units. Upon admission they dropped all pretext of having symptoms, but were still not discovered by the staffs, although in some instances other patients felt they were reporters or investigators. In retrospect, Rosenhan (1972) argues that the reason these pseudopatients were not discovered is the vagueness of the diagnostic labels used. Because mental patients are presumed to have some disease inside of them that affects their behavior in nonspecific ways, anything they do or say can be interpreted as pathological. As examples of this process, the pseudopatients observed that such normal actions as writing and standing in line early for lunch were noted by staff as signs of inner conflicts. In any disagreements between patient and staff the patient was typically regarded as wrong, because he was "mentally ill." Even straightforward requests for information or directions would sometimes be ignored by hospital personnel. If a patient then became angry over not receiving an answer, his response would be taken as indicating a mental problem. Thus the diagnostic labels that are used lead to a self-fulfilling prophecy, where normal and appropriate behaviors are misperceived as signs of mental illness.

Another problem is the tendency to perceive mental illness as a global impairment, affecting everything the person does, rather than as related to specific contexts or actions. Except for those with the most profound disorders, persons with behavior problems are capable of functioning in a competent fashion in many situations. In other words, a person with a mental disorder is not generally deviant in everything he says or does, but problems may be pronounced at particular times or in certain situations. This theme is emphasized in the movie *King of Hearts,* which shows the mental patients in a small French town during World War I living in relative harmony, while 2 competing armies slaughter one another. While this is a romantic view, it does make the valid point that having a mental illness does not mean a person is incapable of exercising judgment or of functioning adequately all the time or in all circumstances.

Aging as Illness—A Variant of the Medical Model

An overreliance on the medical model can lead to similar problems in the aged. There is a tendency to see any problem of older persons as due to a vaguely defined internal disorder—the aging process. Aging is incorrectly perceived by many persons as involving a gradual deterioration in functioning in all areas. Thus, whenever an older person does anything that is strange, out of the ordinary, or disturbing to others, this "misbehavior" may be perceived as due to old age. Just as the ordinary actions of the pseudopatients were seen as signs of mental illness, behaviors of the old are sometimes inappropriately labeled "senile" or "senescent."

As an example of this inappropriate labeling, a 73-year-old client of a geriatric day-treatment program was brought up for evaluation at a staff conference. Two members of the staff insisted Miss G. was senile, because she was unable to knit and because one member of the staff observed her become flustered at the bank when she was unable to find her checkbook in her purse. While these behaviors can certainly be manifested by persons with organic brain disease, they are also shown by normally functioning individuals. Miss G. was, in fact, tested for the presence of characteristics associated with senile brain disease, including persistent forgetfulness, and was found to have no noticeable memory or learning problems. The complaints of the staff made sense, however, in another way. Miss G. had never knit in her life and, moreover, had severely restricted vision in both eyes because of cataracts and glaucoma that undoubtedly made it difficult for her to learn to knit. Furthermore, she was a difficult person to get along with, often interfering with the staff when they interacted with other clients, or suggesting she knew how to manage the program better than the staff did. She had worked her whole life in preschool education and had extensive experience in an activities-oriented program. The staff members were obviously quite upset because of her interference, but because she was old they attributed the problem to "senility" and "old age."

Many other examples can be given to illustrate this tendency to view the behaviors of the old as being derived from a vaguely defined inner pathological state called "old age." Older persons are often viewed by physicians as "crocks," and even the most appropriate complaints or requests for information are dismissed as due to the person's age. In the legal systems of various states, someone can be denied legal rights over property or person solely on the criterion of being old, without any test of competency. Thus the medical model creates the expectation that anything a person with a mental problem does is a sign of that "illness," particularly for older persons whose problems are perceived as due to an inner pathological state of "old age."

To what extent is the process of biological aging implicated in the development of behavioral problems of the aged? The answer cannot be estimated with a great deal of certainty, but it is likely that the biological changes that accompany the normal aging process contribute in varying degrees to the onset of behavioral and affective symptoms. The most direct relation is between somatic illness and psychiatric symptoms. As people grow older, there is an increased prevalence of a variety of chronic illnesses, which directly or indirectly affect mental functioning. As an example of an illness with a direct impact on behavior, the senile brain diseases become increasingly prevalent at advanced ages (Kay 1972). Many other chronic illnesses affect psychological functioning in indirect ways. Diseases such as diabetes, arthritis, or cardiovascular disease often place limitations on an individual's mobility or the performance of particular activities. These restrictions, coupled with the distress involved in many chronic ailments, can have a great impact on the person's mental state. As will be discussed in Chapter 8, illnesses are a major precipitant of depression in the elderly.

It has also been proposed that the aging process involves changes in an organism's ability to respond to stress. In studies of young persons the occurrence of stressful life events is associated with higher rates of somatic illness (Rahe 1974) and with greater psychiatric symptomatology, especially depression (Paykel 1975). A stress model of aging would predict that the aged are even more vulnerable to the effects of stressful life events than are the young. There is, however, no empirical evidence for evaluating this hypothesis. In looking at the impact of life events on psychological functioning, Neugarten (1972) has proposed that the aged may, in fact, be better able than younger persons to adapt to various stresses. She has suggested that life events such as widowhood or retirement need to be viewed from a developmental perspective as "on-time" or "off-time" in the life cycle. An on-time event is one that occurs at an expected or average time. The consequence of its being on-time is that the individual is likely to have made some preparation for the event and to receive greater support from his social network. Using widowhood as an example, Neugarten would argue that an older woman is more likely than a younger one to have anticipated becoming a widow. She may have made more preparations for that event and would be more likely to know other widows from whom she could draw support.

Another critical variable in adaptation to stress is the magnitude of the stressful events. In studies of adaptation to illness, it has been found that older persons with mild to moderate degrees of cardiovascular or cerebrovascular disease react differently from younger patients. While the young who are affected to the same extent are likely to deny their illness, older persons were generally depressed. Among those persons whose physical deterioration was more severe, however, older patients were likely to have greater psychological impairments, particularly in the manifestation of extensive denial of illness (Goodman 1972; Zarit and Kahn 1974). Similarly, Lowenthal and her associates (Lowenthal, Berkmen, and associates 1967) reported that life events such as illness, retirement, or widowhood were not related to psychopathology when only one such event has occurred in the recent past. When cumulative stresses were experienced, there was an association with impaired psychological functioning.

One further point about the relation of stress and aging should be considered. In studies of humans, chronological age is used as an index of aging. As was discussed in Chapter 2, individuals vary in the rate and extent to which biological changes associated with aging occur. Thus, rather than assuming all 65-year-olds or all 75-year-olds have similar reactions to stressful events, it is more likely that aged persons will have varied reactions to stresses, depending upon how much age decrements are present for each individual. We often make too many assumptions about a person's functioning based on chronological age, when the critical variable is actually the presence or absence of specific age changes in the various physiological systems of the body.

Aging, then, cannot be assumed to have a straightforward relation to psychopathology. Chronological age has considerable social significance, but does not necessarily indicate the presence of an underlying illness or impairment that compromises psychological functioning. Similarly, stressful events may have a greater impact on the aged than on the young, but the effects of these events may be tempered by the amount of anticipatory socialization that has preceded their occurrence as well as by the severity of the stressor. It is tempting but often incorrect to assume that mental disturbances of the aged are due to old age.

Overall, the medical model for psychopathology has its uses and limitations for the problems of the elderly. It serves to call attention to disorders that have an organic basis, and focuses on somatic therapies, such as medications that sometimes have major benefits for persons with mental problems. In the absence of a clear-cut medical diagnosis, however, the tendency to view the person's problem as derived from some hypothetical internal disorder leads to an inability to differentiate normal from abnormal behavior. Because of the tendency to view old persons as impaired due to their age, excessive use of the medical model and its variants reinforces the likelihood that one will blame a problem on something inside the person and miss those factors in the individual's environment that are influencing or controlling the disturbed behavior.

A Behavioral Model

A behavioral model proposes that problem or maladaptive behaviors are governed by similar principles of learning as are other actions. Rather than looking for a hypothesized underlying etiology, as in the medical model, a behavioral approach focuses on the specific maladaptive actions, thoughts, or emotions, and the contexts in which they occur. Treatment is conceived as providing new learning that competes with the maladaptive behaviors and/or manipulating stimulus cues or reinforcers that are related to the specific problems. From this perspective assessment involves clarifying the presenting problem, obtaining a social history that focuses on the origins of the problem behavior, and identifying relationships in the person's current environment that may be controlling or reinforcing the maladaptive behaviors.

Behavioral theories suggest several ways in which maladaptive mental disorders can develop. First, prior stressful experiences may have led to the association of anxiety or other inhibiting emotional reactions with specific actions. Because of this prior conditioning, the person's performance in certain situations is impaired. Second, an individual's earlier learning of some habit or skill may have been deficient or may not have taken place at all. There is often little direct socialization, for example, of the skills necessary for maintaining an intimate relationship. A person may have learned very little about how to reach compromises, or may have been taught specific habits that actually interfere with maintaining the relationship. Perhaps the best example of where the absence of prior learning or faulty learning affects behavior involves sexual dysfunction. Treatment programs such as those developed by Masters and Johnson (1970) emphasize teaching new habits that promote successful sexual functioning and replace the dysfunctional habits that had been learned earlier. Third, particular environmental stimuli may have come to be associated with maladaptive responses, and serve as cues that release those responses. As an example, many smokers have come to associate drinking coffee with having a cigarette. In trying to stop smoking, the person may feel the strongest urge to have a cigarette when drinking coffee or engaging in other behaviors that have become associated with smoking. Fourth, maladaptive behaviors may be currently reinforced. A person who is depressed may receive attention when complaining of his problems, but may not have much involvement with others on other occasions.

In recent years this direct behavioral approach has been extended to include cognitive dimensions. The major problem for some persons may not involve how well they function in various situations, but how they evaluate their performance. Two persons could carry out identical tasks, one judging his performance as adequate while the other sees his functioning as impaired. Feelings of depression have been linked to this kind of inaccurate evaluation of one's own performance. Similarly, certain beliefs that the person learned previously may lead to dysfunctional behaviors (Ellis 1962; Mahoney 1974). An individual who believes she must please everyone she comes in contact with may make excessive efforts to be liked and feel crushed if she does not receive approval from some persons. Thus beliefs about oneself, about others, and about the nature of social relationships may be intervening variables between perceptions and problem behaviors or emotional distress.

Another cognitive factor that has received attention recently is the person's problem-solving strategies. When faced with a task, people engage in an inner monologue. This inner voice plans for undertaking that task and monitors one's progress. These ways we have of talking to ourselves can be effective or ineffective for solving the problem at hand. Hyperactive children have been found to use few or inadequate strategies in approaching learning problems. Programs that teach these children to guide their actions with appropriate verbal comments have resulted in improved performance on cognitive tasks and in behavior (see Meichenbaum 1977). The person's inner monologue may therefore be an important mediator of behavior.

One advantage of a behavioral approach is that by focusing on the specific problems presented by clients and the contexts in which they occur, it is often possible to identify what factors in the person's environment are influencing them. These can then be manipulated to lead to improvement in the presenting symptoms.

Unlike the medical model, there is less difficulty in differentiating normal from abnormal behavior from a behavioral perspective. In the medical model the professional uses relatively unreliable criteria to determine if symptoms suggest an internal conflict or disorder. In contrast, a behavioral approach is not concerned with whether an illness is present. The focus is placed instead on the perception of problems in functioning by the individual or by persons closely associated with the client. The issue of what does and what does not constitute a problem is clarified, because the problem is defined as that for which the person seeks treatment. When a person is brought to treatment by others, the process of determining whether his behavior is a problem that warrants treatment is more complex. The process of assessment involves determining how each of the involved persons contributes to the problem situation. One may then formulate a treatment plan that includes all the relevant individuals, i.e., those persons who contribute to or participate in the problem. Ways of making this type of assessment are discussed later in the chapter.

A behavioral assessment may also indicate functional links between the problems presented by a patient and other behaviors. Depressed persons, for example, generally report their low spirits as the principal problem, but recent work has found that depression is related to certain dysfunctional thoughts that lead to overly negative evaluations of one's self (Beck 1976), and to the failure to engage in activities that one finds pleasurable (Lewinsohn, Biglan, and Zeiss 1976). This process of identifying functional associations among thoughts, behaviors, and mood represents a different process from inferring a disease from overt symptoms.

This type of approach contrasts sharply with the psychodynamic by identifying dimensions in the person's immediate situation, rather than the distant past, that trigger or reinforce problem behaviors and affect. While it has been argued that treatment will be ineffective if it focuses only on presenting symptoms and leaves the core of the problem unresolved, there is little empirical evidence of phenomena such as symptom substitution that are predicted by psychodynamic theorists (Rimm and Masters 1974).

The focus of a behavioral model is on the specific problems presented by clients, rather than on trying to infer a single etiology or syndrome of which those symptoms are a sign. Treatment proceeds by dealing with problems one at a time with an appropriate intervention, rather than by taking a global approach through which it is hoped that some of the exchanges between client and psychotherapist will generalize to everyday situations. There is also more stress on giving clients tasks to perform or homework, since psychological problems are conceived as related to specific environmental contexts.

A behavioral approach, then, investigates the context in which problem behaviors occur, and identifies those factors in the immediate environment or in the person's prior learning that can lead to changing the problem behavior. Behavioral methods can be used in a complementary fashion to the medical model. In cases where an organic basis for a disorder can be ruled out, then a behavioral assessment would be the next step in diagnosis. When an organic disorder is present, however, the first step would be to employ whatever relevant medical interventions are necessary. As a subsidiary aspect of treatment for organic disorders, behavioral assessment may be useful for identifying ways of modifying specific problem behaviors.

OTHER MODELS

Four other models of psychopathology have relevance for viewing problems of the aged.

Legal. Legal criteria are important because they set broad guidelines for how practice in the mental health field may be conducted. While specific guidelines may vary somewhat from one state to another, persons are usually judged as requiring care if they are a danger to themselves or to others. This criterion thus applies only to the most severely disturbed patients. In situations where someone refuses treatment or denies problems that others complain about, that person can be compelled to accept help only if it is demonstrated in the manner prescribed by state law that he requires involuntary treatment.

In most cases, treatment must involve the active consent of the individual. This principle is particularly important in dealing with the aged. Persons other than the aged individual, such as neighbors or children, often seek treatment on his behalf. In many of these situations the older person has some problems, such as a limited ability to care for a household or declining interest in social activities. But unless these abilities for self-care are so severely reduced that the individual meets legal criteria for needing treatment, interventions cannot be made without consent. All too often older persons are relocated or other major changes made in their lives without their active approval. While it is upsetting to professionals and families to see persons refuse treatment that could help them substantially, anyone who functions within the broad legal definition of competency has the right to make that decision.

Humanistic. Another model of psychopathology is drawn from humanistic psychology. This approach stresses that the individual has a natural tendency to strive for growth and development, or what has been called self-actualization. (Rogers 1951; Maslow 1968). Clients often have an ideal view of how they would like to be functioning. Neurotic behavior has been found to be associated with a discrepancy between how the person would like to be and how he sees himself as actually functioning (Rogers and Dymond 1954). This discrepancy is often a key to identifying problems and goals for treatment. Some older clients have difficulty imagining how they would like their lives to be different; meaningful treatment objectives can be set by helping them to articulate their ideas. Another major contribution of this model is its emphasis on the worth and dignity of the individual. Accent is placed on seeing the world from the client's perspective. The therapist does not play an authority figure but, instead, shows genuine emotions during treatment seessions, especially warmth and nonpossessive caring.

While this approach has made many positive contributions, there is a tendency similar to the medical model to confuse normal and abnormal behavior. Because the goal of treatment is often stated as helping the person achieve optimal functioning, everything short of optimal functioning can be viewed as a problem. An almost romantic quality exists in the writings of many humanistic therapists that posits striving for a conflict-free, higher order of consciousness.

As in the case of the medical model, this type of formulation makes it difficult for therapists to distinguish between problem behaviors and those that do not require treatment. Because most people are not functioning at what might be called their potentials, either in interpersonal relationships, in work, or in other areas, there is always some room for further growth and improvement. That type of situation, however, is conceptually different from the person who experiences significant degrees of emotional distress and whose abilities to carry out basic, everyday activities are impaired to some extent. Clients do not have to be helped to their full potential in order to provide relief from major symptoms and life stresses.

Psychotherapy can also produce feelings of dependency in clients. Most people know someone who has been in and out of psychological treatment for several years and, though functioning adequately in many ways, feels the need for ongoing assistance. This tendency for dependencies to develop is exacerbated in some older persons. It is important, therefore, that there be clearly stated goals for therapy, and attempts not be made to solve every problem the person has. Delimited objectives minimize the risks of undermining the client's independence.

It can be argued that all psychotherapy involves some value judgment about how to function effectively. The humanistic model stresses worthwhile human aspirations, but, despite its client-centered orientation, the specific goals that are frequently stated, such as having complete honesty in relationships with others or insight into one's motives, are not shared universally. Furthermore, individuals function competently and effectively in many life situations without having personal insight. There is also increasing evidence that positive changes can occur in therapy without insight into one's motives (Rimm and Masters 1974). Thus while insight and personal growth are often desirable outcomes, they are not necessary conditions for a person to function competently.

Statistical. A statistical model of psychopathology also has some relevance for evaluating problems of the aged. In this approach problems are conceptualized as those behaviors or other events that deviate significantly from accepted community norms. The advantage of this approach over the medical model is that it makes the criteria for diagnosis of a problem consistent with how the problem is actually conceptualized. We judge behavior such as transvestitism maladaptive in our society because it is statistically rare, although in some cultures such activities are actually encouraged in some individuals. The statistical approach recognizes that unusual behaviors are likely to have unpleasant social consequences for individuals. Persons who dress, speak, or otherwise act in unusual ways are going to be avoided or attacked by others, depending on the situation. Their difference from others becomes a problem in functioning by adversely affecting social interactions.

The disadvantage of this approach is that there are no criteria for distinguishing nonconformity and social protest from problems that are harmful to the person or to others, or that the person wants to change.

Homosexuality is a good example. While statistically deviant and often psychologically threatening to heterosexuals, homosexual behavior has not been found to be related to reduced competency or to poor psychological functioning, as has often been assumed. Once considered a "mental illness," homosexuality has recently been removed by the American Psychiatric Association from its list of disorders. If someone with a history of homosexual relationships requests help to increase his or her sexual feelings toward the opposite sex, that would be a valid basis for starting treatment, but without that active interest in treatment by the client, there can be no compulsion to make him abandon his homosexual orientation or to give up any other socially deviant but harmless actions. Thus behavior that differs from community norms may or may not be properly identified as a problem, depending on whether it affects the person's overall competency and whether the individual perceives it as a problem.

A statistical model of normal behavior has additional problems when applied to the aged. There is generally no agreement on what normal behavior is for older persons. Criteria of adequate functioning during the adult years often include competency in a work role, in interpersonal relationships, and sexually (Schaie and Schaie 1977). In old age, however, there is often little opportunity for or encouragement of any of those activities. Furthermore, as discussed in Chapter 3, no consensus exists on whether it is better to stay active or to disengage from activities as one grows older. Perhaps the best formulation of what is normal in old age is that there are increasing differences among individuals over the adult life span. These differences are due both to exposures to varying life experiences and to the differential rates at which biological aging processes affect each individual. What is normal in old age is an increased variability of functioning among persons.

One other drawback of this statistical approach is that many behaviors that are judged by others as bizarre or eccentric may actually be appropriate for that person's generation or culture. Because of the rapid pace of social change, many personal habits and behaviors that were acceptable 50 or 60 years ago are no longer encouraged. Furthermore, many elderly persons have a different cultural background from younger professionals. They are more likely to have been born in a foreign country, in a rural area, or a small town, while today's professionals are most likely American-born and from an urban or suburban area. A strict statistical approach to evaluating persons would obscure differences between problems that actually impair the person's ability to function effectively and those eccentricities that have no harmful consequences.

Social Deprivations.   A fourth model of psychopathology is that social deprivations lead to disordered behavior. It has been proposed, for example, that factors such as the high stress of urban life or social class are associated with a greater incidence of psychopathology at all ages (see

Hollingshead and Redlich 1958; Srole et al. 1975). Particular emphasis is often placed on social isolation and loneliness as causes of mental disorders in the elderly. It a series of studies Lowenthal and her associates (Lowenthal 1964; 1965; Lowenthal, Berkman, and associates 1967; Lowenthal and Chiriboga 1973) found that extreme isolation in old age was associated with poor adaptation in some persons but not others. Individuals who had a lifelong history of social isolation often did well in old age, while those who had only marginal social ties during the adult years had serious problems in adjustment during old age, when their few social contacts were lost. Furthermore, among persons who have had major stresses or losses, such as widowhood or retirement, the presence of a confidant reduces the amount of distress that is experienced (Lowenthal and Haven 1968). Perlin and Butler (1963) report comparable findings. Older men whose life styles could be characterized as having always been isolated often adapt well to old age. In analyzing these findings they speculate that the social expectations for maintaining intimate relationships are removed in the later years, and these men were perhaps no longer experiencing themselves as deviant or different from others in their cohort who were now also socially isolated.

Social isolation and psychopathology in the aged may both be the consequence of a more basic problem. Many chronic physical illnesses result in limitations in mobility and thereby also affect one's social interactions. In these instances both the illness and the resulting social isolation undoubtedly contribute to the development of behavioral problems.

Many authors have pointed out the effects of social deprivations on the quality of life of older persons. In a moving book on the problems of the aged, Curtin (1972) quotes one older women who describes old age as similar to a prison term, with no time off for good behavior. Despite the deprivations to which the elderly are exposed, however, many continue to function effectively. The relation of social deprivations to poor functioning is a complex one that depends on several factors, including the type and amount of stress, the person's prior history, and current social and psychological resources (Lowenthal and Chiriboga 1973). Stressors, like social isolation or other negative life experiences, can be described as creating the context in which maladaptive behaviors may develop in an older person, but should not be viewed as the sole determinant.

Assessment of Psychological Disorders

Assessment of elderly patients is the critical key in the development of effective mental health programs for the aged. Careless or uninformed diagnosis can lead to inadequate treatment of various problems. Persons with senile dementia may be considered as depressed, and vice versa. Or a person's problems may be attributed to age, without any attempt to find an environmental determinant. Assessments can also provide important information about the most effective ways of treating a particular client.

The assessment of psychopathology has traditionally emphasized identifying underlying syndromes suggested by the presenting symptoms. Classifying systems such as the DSM III are useful for outlining broad groups of disorders, such as psychotic versus neurotic or grouping together psychological problems in which mood is a factor. The DSM III also provides an overview of the variety of mental disorders. It is important, therefore, to have a good working knowledge of traditional diagnostic categories. This information can be found in texts on psychopathology (Nathan and Harris 1975; Zax and Cowan 1976).

In the criticisms of the medical model cited earlier, it was noted that current classifying systems of mental illness, such as the DSM III, use labels that are of little use in planning treatment. Most schools of psychotherapy do not differentiate their techniques to any great extent according to the psychiatric label. Dynamic therapists, for example, generally stress uncovering unconscious material, whatever the type of presenting problem, although some variations in approach for different disorders are described. The labels themselves, however, carry little information that is specific for treatment.

An alternative method for assessing psychological disorders is to get descriptions of the person's problems in as specific detail as possible. This should include the frequency of problem behaviors, in what circumstances they occur, and current reinforcers of behavior. By identifying the particular contexts in which problem behaviors are manifested, one can develop hypotheses concerning environmental or person variables that are associated with the problem behavior, and then intervene to change some aspects of the person-environment interaction.

The Functional Assessment of Older Persons

A thorough method of behavioral assessment that identifies factors relevant to treatment has been developed by Kanfer and Saslow (1965; 1976). While not specifically developed for older persons, this method of assessment provides a useful outline for gathering observations of the aged. In particular, it emphasizes the contexts in which problem behaviors occur. This approach identifies modifiable aspects of the situation, rather than attributing a patient's difficulties to old age, or to a characterological deficit about which nothing specific can be done.

In their system of functional behavioral analysis of psychiatric problems, Kanfer and Saslow suggest seven major areas: (1) analysis of the

FIGURE 5.1. Functional behavioral analysis of problems.

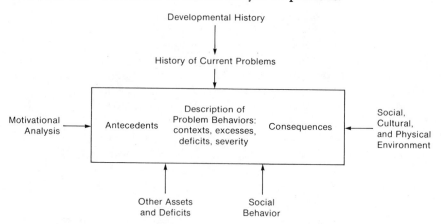

problem situation; (2) identifying antecedents and consequences of the problem behavior; (3) the individual's other assets and deficits; (4) an analysis of social relationships; (5) motivational analysis; (6) the relation of the patient to his social, cultural, and physical environment; and (7) a developmental history (see Figure 5.1). Each area will be discussed in some detail.

1. *Analysis of the Problem Situation.* The presenting problems of clients should be described as fully and specifically as possible. When one is confronted with difficult patients, there is a tendency to apply global labels to their problems. Calling patients hostile, aggressive, or confused, or describing them as passive or dependent personalities both presumes that the problems in functioning are determined by some internal state, and phrases the problem in terms that do not suggest treatment potential. Instead of labeling them, it is more useful to describe what it was that the patient did that made one feel he was hostile, dependent, or confused. The first step in a functional behavioral analysis is to describe fully what the problem behaviors are, considering for each problem its frequency, intensity, duration, and the situations in which it occurs.

Problems can be further classified as excesses or deficits of behaviors. This distinction calls attention to the fact that most maladaptive behaviors are normal actions that occur either too often or not enough, or at inappropriate times or situations. This process also serves to set clear and operational targets for treatment. As an example, the label "depression" includes persons with widely varying symptoms. Two common problems, however, are an excess of negative statements about one's self and deficits in social skill. One would determine the extent to which these specific aspects of depressive disorders are present in an individual case, and then develop a treatment plan that variously involves decreasing negative self-evaluations or increasing the person's level of social skills. Both approaches have been found to be related to significant reductions in reported depressed affect (see Beck 1976; Lewinsohn, Biglan, and Zeiss 1976). This type of assessment makes it possible to develop treatment goals and procedures that are specific to an individual, rather than based on abstract and somewhat arbitrary constructs such as depression or other classifications.

Problems involving excesses in behavior are usually readily apparent to observers, but deficits are sometimes harder to distinguish. To use the example of a depressed patient again, complaints of dysphoria are an obvious excessive behavior. It may not be noticed, however, that the person also has deficits in social skills that inhibit normal social functioning. In hospitals and nursing homes, the "good" patient who keeps to himself and is not troublesome sometimes surprises the staff with a sudden outburst or other disruption. In retrospect, it can be seen that his quiet, withdrawn, and nondemanding ways, which the staff labeled as "good," were actually deficits in behavior that led to increasing tension or frustration in his interactions with the environment. One should thus consider if there are some things a patient should be doing that he is not.

In describing the presenting problems, the severity of the maladaptive behaviors should also be considered. Gurland (1980) proposed five dimensions of severity: (1) the degree of distress subjectively experienced by the person; (2) the extent of impairment in performance of usual activities; (3) danger to one's self; (4) danger to others; and (5) the amount of burden on others.

One's estimate of severity is critical for clarifying several situations. First, persons with mild, transient problems may not warrant treatment. The danger of creating a dependency on a therapist or social agency can be greater in some cases than the risk involved in allowing persons to work out mild problems on their own. Second, some severe problems require prompt and intensive interventions. Particularly where a person's life or the lives of others are endangered, prompt actions, including legal steps if the person does not accept treatment voluntarily, are necessary. Third, where there is no clear danger and the person refuses treatment, the decision of the professional on what to do is more difficult. Despite the frustration or pain they cause to family members or others, some people may deny they have a problem. While they cannot be treated involuntarily, one can offer help and assistance to family members, so that they may become more effective in managing their interactions with these persons.

2. *Analysis of Antecedents and Consequences of the Problem Behavior.* Analysis of antecedents and consequences involves determining what happens immediately before the problem behavior and what are its main consequences or effects. Problems often occur only in specific situations or in

response to particular events, and can be considered under the control of those stimuli. Lewinsohn and his associates (Lewinsohn et al. 1978) classify antecedents of problem behavior or emotions into four types: (1) social settings (e.g., thinking pessimistic thoughts mainly when alone or with someone who is perceived as successful); (2) physical circumstances (e.g., being in the kitchen as an antecedent to between-meal snacks); (3) the behavior of others (e.g., reacting to mild criticism); and (4) one's own thoughts and feelings (e.g., feeling anxious or pessimistic before initiating a conversation).

By determining what factors are associated with the manifestation of problem behaviors, it is possible to pinpoint interventions to specific situations. People often report their problems as global, that is, affecting everything they feel or do, but this type of analysis highlights their more difficult interactions. Depressed persons, for example, typically say they feel depressed most of the time, but they can learn to identify specific antecedents of depression—those circumstances in which they feel more depressed. One man, for example, became depressed and anxious whenever he went for a doctor's appointment. These visits triggered feelings of helplessness, and also resentment at the doctor's authoritarian manner. By identifying an increase in depressive symptoms in this situation, it is possible to make an intervention in how the person thinks about the physical examination and how he interacts with the doctor, so that his thoughts and actions do not lead to depressive emotions. Even unusual and disturbing behaviors are under the control of specific environmental events. A person in a nursing home, for example, may exhibit bizarre behavior at times, with disturbances following interactions with particular staff members. One can then determine what occurs in those interactions that may be triggering the problem behavior. As opposed to labeling someone as confused or agitated, this approach leads to a direct intervention that will alter the problem behavior.

The consequences of a behavioral problem include factors that reinforce the problem. One consequence of paranoid behavior in the elderly is that it evokes a lot of attention. If an older person calls a family member and states that someone has broken into her apartment, it is likely to bring about a rapid and concerned response. Some common consequences of problem behaviors are increased interaction with others, receipt of other positive, tangible rewards, or allowing the person to avoid unpleasant situations. It is critical to identify these reinforcers of problem behavior, so that the treatment plan can include provision of these same reinforcements for appropriate behavior. For example, if a husband pays attention to his wife only when she cries, psychotherapy will not be successful until he interacts with her under other circumstances.

3. *Other Assets and Deficits in Functioning.*   In addition to focusing on the problem behavior, one can determine what other positive qualities

the patient has, and what deficits are present in other areas of functioning. The consequences of problem behaviors are often illuminated by considering other deficits. When evaluating a person, it is possible to ask, "What would be different if you did not have this problem?" It sometimes becomes apparent that the individual has few skills or resources for becoming involved in satisfying activities. Because of these behavioral deficits, the person may actually have no other alternative than to continue behaving in the same ways, and no incentive to change. For persons with deficits in behavioral and social skills, effective treatment involves teaching those skills so that one's desired goals can be achieved through appropriate behaviors (See Meichenbaum 1976; Lewinsohn, Biglan, and Zeiss 1976).

Identifying behavioral assets also provides important information for developing a treatment plan. Many persons with severe behavioral problems in one area can function effectively in other parts of their daily life. One 65-year-old man, for example, who became depressed over health and family problems, had many interests and abilities, including regular exercise, active concertgoing, and many good friends. Because he was depressed, he had neglected some of these activities. When encouraged to resume them as part of the therapy, his mood improved rapidly. Identification of these areas of competence made it possible to increase their occurrence and thereby diminish the frequency with which problem behaviors were manifested. Knowledge of these assets in functioning can also be important to the therapy process in reducing negative self-evaluations made by clients and helping them place their current problems in a broader perspective, so that they do not come to see themselves as overly impaired or ill.

4. *Analysis of Social Relationships.* There should be a consideration of the person's social network, especially those persons who have an influence over or are affected by the problem behavior. It is then possible to determine the extent to which these persons should be involved in the treatment process.

An important aspect of the client's social relationships is identification of who has gotten the person to come for help, whether it is the individual himself or some other person. This issue is crucial in determining the focus of the treatment. In instances where family members or some other persons were principally responsible for an older person coming to treatment, one can raise the question of "Whose problem is it?" In many situations the older person will concur with those who brought him that he indeed has some difficulties in functioning and wants help. In some instances, however, determination of who has the problem is more complicated. When other persons complain about an older individual's behavior, but the "patient" does not view it as a problem, it is evaluated whether the actions in question raise any danger to the older person or to others. Persons will sometimes ask that an individual be treated for idiosyncratic actions that have no dangerous impact but are annoying. Older persons who keep many pets, whose yards are not maintained up to community standards, or who engage in mildly bizarre behaviors such as talking to themselves or believing in supernatural happenings may come to the attention of community service agencies because of complaints by neighbors or relatives. So long as they are able to take care of themselves and their homes meet minimal health standards, they cannot be judged as needing treatment. It is crucial not to label someone as mentally ill, solely because his actions violate acceptable middle-class standards of behavior. Somewhat disheveled or dirty households are not sufficient to warrant an intervention, unless it is desired by the person himself.

In situations where an individual's actions are disturbing to others, it can be pointed out that continuing these behaviors may have some bad consequences. One woman, for example, would stand outside her apartment, waving a Bible at neighbors and passersby in order to drive away the devil. Apart from annoying her neighbors, she was otherwise functioning well and had no problems in self-care. As part of a supportive treatment program for her, it was explained that the Bible waving might be misinterpreted by others, who would then try to have her hospitalized. She was encouraged instead to wave the Bible at persons from behind her door, a change she welcomed because she agreed that the Bible was powerful enough to work even through doors. While not directly treating her fears, this intervention prevented her situation from becoming worse.

Some brief counseling with neighbors may also be critical in situations like these. Their annoyances are often well justified, but there are sometimes ways of helping them to understand the situation so that they are less upset, or to allay some of their fears about what the "crazy person" might do. At the least, it is important to explain why the person is not being hospitalized. When family members are involved, some sessions with the older person and the family members can be useful to help work out a better understanding of the older person's behavior and to correct some of the family's misconceptions.

An important focus of the assessment should be the client's ideas about social relationships. An older person may feel that her children are taking advantage of her by asking her frequently to baby-sit for her grandchildren, but she does not want to tell them directly because she believes they should anticipate her needs. Or children may feel some actions of their parents, such as carrying on a romance, are inappropriate. People's ideas about social relationships that lead to passive or unassertive behavior are often associated with feelings of depression or helplessness. The most frequently encountered idea is that others should anticipate one's needs, without the person himself having to make them known. In some instances a client will have expectations about social relationships that are unrealistic or cannot possibly be fulfilled, given the usual patterns social interactions take in the culture. One woman, for example, wanted to be included in every detail of her 30-year-old married son's life, an expectation that led to considerable conflict with her son and daughter-in-law. It was important to have her modify her ideas about social interactions in order to help her relate in more gratifying ways with her son.

5. *Motivational Analysis.* There should be a consideration of those persons, events, activities, or objects that are reinforcers for the patient, and also those events that are experienced as aversive or that the person avoids. This information will be useful in developing a behavioral therapy program for the patient.

A related consideration is the person's motivation for treatment. It should be determined what goals the person has for himself, and what he feels will be different about his life if he reaches those objectives. Through this approach it may be discovered that the individual does not really want to change but would like others to change in their reactions to him. Sometimes, too, a person is actually satisfied with his behavior but wants to change to please others or because of an abstract notion of what one is supposed to be like. An older person may come to treatment complaining of inactivity, for example, but will actually prefer leading a leisurely life. She may feel that she has to get active and involved with people or some terrible thing will happen. Some older persons incorrectly assume that senility is brought about by inactivity. When encountering this situation, it is appropriate to reformulate the problem as acceptance of what the person is already doing, rather than attempt to make any changes.

An important question to ask in an assessment is why a person decided to seek treatment at this time. When clients have been convinced to come by someone else, their motivation may not be high, making it necessary to engage their interest in working on their problems. It is probably better not to treat an unmotivated person with mild difficulties, than to create a situation in which he does not get better and may conclude that nothing can help. In some instances there may have been some change in a patient's circumstances that made him decide to come for help at this time. Identifying what has changed may help clarify the treatment goals. If a woman who has been depressed for some time seeks help because a close friend has recently moved away, a goal of treatment may be to help her develop a new relationship, or turn to other friends she relied on in the past.

6. *Analysis of the Social-Cultural-Physical Environment.* This assessment involves determining how well persons fit in with the expected norms for behavior and for the carrying out of tasks in their current environments. While the goal of treatment should not be to make persons adjust to their surroundings when they are unhappy about them, it is sometimes appropriate to help someone establish a better balance between personal needs and the demands of the environment. Some older persons

may be expected by others to fulfill demands for competence of role behavior that they can no longer meet or no longer want to meet. The wife of a retired man, for example, was concerned because he watched more television and was not as active as he had been in the past. He stated, however, that he had enough activities to keep him busy and he enjoyed taking things a little easier. More commonly, the aged receive little encouragement or expectation for competent behavior. They may even be expected to be passive and incompetent, leaving them feeling inadequate or depressed. It may be important to help some people to establish their own standards for how they want to act and to develop strategies for responding to the negative expectations of others.

A major area of concern for the aged is the ability to perform self-care activities. Being able to bathe, dress, shop, and cook enable a person to maintain an independent living arrangement. Major deficits in self-care result in the need for some form of assistance, either informally through family or neighbors or with the intervention of a social service agency. Assessment of these activities is discussed more fully in Chapter 7.

7. *Developmental Analysis.* A developmental history should be obtained on patients for 2 major reasons: to provide information about the person's usual functioning in the past, and for a history of the circumstances under which the particular problem or problems for which the person seeks treatment have developed. In dealing with the aged a developmental history is particularly useful. It gives the clinician an idea of what resources and abilities persons previously had, and how they handled stressful situations. Sometimes reminding persons of these abilities helps them spontaneously to use coping strategies that were effective for them in the past.

In obtaining a history of the presenting problem, it is important to identify any changes in the person's environment that were associated with altered behavior. Changes in health status and their consequences for the person's behavior and self-concept are also often pertinent. The history of the problem is different from the investigation of antecedents and consequences of problem behavior. The former is concerned with when the problem behaviors were first manifested and what the circumstances were, while the latter looks at specific occurrences of the problem and what happened immediately before and after.

From a developmental perspective it is possible to encounter three types of problem in the aged. First, some problems will have their origins in earlier periods of life. Persons with schizophrenic disorders, for example, often function at only marginal levels throughout their lives and have periodic episodes of disturbed behavior. Similarly, persons with affective disorders may have had similar episodes earlier in life. The importance of this information is that those treatments that were most effective in the past are likely to have a positive effect on the current episode. If a depressed person responded well to electroconvulsive therapy or to a particular medication, that can be tried again. Similarly, a positive response to a particular style of psychotherapy indicates that the person may show improvements now with the same treatment. Furthermore, these past experiences of improvements can be used to reassure patients that they will get better this time. This reassurance is particularly effective with severely depressed persons, and can be used to counter feelings of hopelessness and suicidal thoughts.

A second type of problem in the aged arises when behaviors of an individual that were adaptive earlier in the life cycle are no longer effective for obtaining personal goals or for sustaining a satisfying lifestyle. A person who works in a somewhat compulsive way, for example, may function well on the job that demands meticulous attention to detail. Upon retirement, however, that person's compulsive habits may no longer serve any purpose, and as a result he may begin manifesting some undesirable behaviors, such as excessive worrying or engaging in somewhat meaningless, repetitive actions that do not provide the satisfaction inherent in working.

A third type of problem in the aged occurs as a result of sudden changes in the person's environment, especially the occurrence of major losses. The person reacts to the losses by developing maladaptive behavior. Losses are associated with many of the behavioral disorders that first appear in old age, especially depression.

The history of the person's present problems also provides important information for making a differential diagnosis, for example, between senile dementia and depression or between acute as opposed to chronic brain disorders. The differing courses of those disorders are discussed in Chapter 6.

A Note on Psychological Testing

The use of psychological tests of personality with the aged has only a limited value. Most procedures that are commonly used have not been standardized for older persons or have only been used with impaired groups of elderly. Much of the literature on the Rorschach test, for example, looks at the responses of the institutionalized elderly, and then generalizes to suggest that these findings represent the way older persons respond to this test. Another limitation of most psychological tests is the assumption that they can be interpreted to reveal an underlying or true problem that is not apparent from direct observations of behavior or discussions with clients. Behaviors, including test-taking responses, are often specific to a situation and may not reliably predict an underlying trait or dynamic (Goldfried and Kent 1972). Tests have also been perceived as an objective way of making major decisions about patients but, because of their limited validity, they are usually no more "objective" than any other type of information (Bersoff 1973). One further consideration is that the diagnostic interpretations of most psychological tests do not suggest appropriate treatments. In contrast to the functional behavioral analysis described above, which identifies relevant variables in the environment that are influencing problem behaviors, testing suggests vague diagnostic formulations but not differential treatment strategies.

The collection of systematic samples of behavior such as occurs in a test situation has many potential and valuable uses. These include conducting research on the effectiveness of treatments and developing more systematic ways to diagnose problems. Two reliable and structured interview procedures for mental health problems of the elderly are available—the OARs scale (Pfeiffer 1975b) and the CARE instrument (Gurland et al. 1976). The CARE in particular allows for a more systematic and objective approach to the diagnosis of behavioral problems in the elderly. As both instruments are lengthy, however, their practical applications are limited. Overall, then, while formal testing has some potential benefits, especially in the areas of program evaluation and outcome studies, existing tests either have limited value or are too cumbersome to apply in most clinical settings.

Summary

Psychopathology in later life can be viewed from several conceptual frameworks, including a medical approach, legal and social criteria, and a behavioral model. Each theoretical system contains assumptions about why disordered behavior occurs and has implications both for assessment and treatment. The usefulness of a particular model can be judged by whether dimensions relevant for treatment are identified. A medical approach is warranted in many cases because the older persons' problems are caused by or related to the effects of an illness. The majority of disorders in old age, however, have no obvious physiological correlates, and a behavioral analysis, which focuses on such factors as the frequency of occurrence and the antecedents and consequences of problem behaviors, is more likely to indicate treatable aspects of the situation. A behavioral method of assessment locates problems in the immediate situational contexts in which they occur, as well as evaluating the person's current social and psychological functioning and developmental history. A functional behavioral analysis is also appropriate in organic disorders to clarify what aspects of the person's situation or action are potentially modifiable.

CHAPTER 6

Brain Disorders
in Old Age:
Causes and Assessment

THE BRAIN DISORDERS OF OLD AGE present the greatest challenge for clinical practitioners in making correct assessments and providing creative treatments. While the majority of persons over 65 do not have a brain impairment, as many as one-half of older patients seen in inpatient and out-patient facilities are diagnosed as having an organic disorder (Kramer, Taube and Redick 1973; Pfeiffer 1977). Moreover, some practitioners mistakenly assume that nothing can be done for organically impaired older persons, and overlook potentially treatable conditions. Disorders such as Alzheimer's-type senile dementia cannot currently be slowed or reversed through medical means, but other conditions can often be treated.

According to Engel and Romano (1959), two basic processes can lead to the dysfunction of any body organ: failure of metabolic processes to maintain the functioning of the organ, or the death of a sufficient number of organ cells to impair functioning permanently. These two processes are actually interrelated, since prolonged metabolic insufficiencies will lead to cell death in the affected organ. Senile dementia describes cases where extensive cell death and other structural changes in the brain have occurred. As discussed in Chapter 2, the principal causes of dementia are vascular disease and an Alzheimer's-type deterioration. In contrast, acute brain syndrome or delirium refers to conditions where metabolic processes have been altered, leading to a state of "cerebral insufficiency" (Engel and Romano 1959). Changes in the amounts of oxygen, glucose, amino acids, proteins, and possibly other substances can impair metabolic processes. If

135

this imbalance is prolonged, it will cause diffuse brain damage. On the other hand, correcting the imbalance in time can restore the person's functioning to prior levels.

The differential diagnosis of senile dementia from treatable illness is the most important skill in clinical practice with the aged. While medical assessments are frequently desirable, nonphysicians can learn to identify potential cases in which the impairment can be reversed, as well as to differentiate dementia from normal changes in old age. In this chapter the etiology and assessment of these two types of brain disorder are described. Treatment approaches for persons with organic brain impairments are presented in Chapter 13.

Acute Brain Disorders

There is some confusion of the terms used to refer to acute brain syndromes. Delirium, confusional state, toxic psychosis, infective-exhaustive psychosis, pseudodementia, reversible dementia, and acute brain syndrome are all used somewhat indiscriminately and interchangeably (Lipowski 1967). Engel and Romano (1959) suggest that the usual distinction between acute and chronic brain syndrome is not entirely accurate because particular causes of cerebral insufficiency, such as pernicious anemia and myxedema, can develop slowly. Their gradual development is more characteristic of chronic than acute disorder. Butler and Lewis (1977) propose the terms "reversible" and "irreversible" brain syndromes to replace those of acute and chronic. They stress that there has not been sufficient attention to identifying potentially reversible organic conditions in the elderly. These terms, however, are also imprecise, because in some instances an acute disorder is not reversible, for example, when caused by a rapidly growing tumor. Similarly, following a cerebral vascular accident there are likely to be both reversible and irreversible changes in behavior. In some instances acute reactions are the result of a terminal disease process, and thus are not reversible. Both Engel and Romano (1959) and Lipowski (1967) prefer "delirium" to other terms, as a more precise description of the behavioral changes that occur with cerebral insufficiencies. Lipowski (1967) also notes that "acute brain syndrome" is not widely used outside of the field of psychiatry, but that most physicians in other specialties are familiar with the concept of delirium. The recent revision of the Diagnostic and Statistical Manual of the American Psychiatric Association (1978) has also replaced "acute brain syndrome" with the term "delirium." It should be noted, however, that some reversible conditions may not be marked by clear and prominent symptoms of delirium. Rather, the patient may be withdrawn or lethargic.

Many common problems can bring about delirium in an aged person. Among the etiological factors noted by Lipowski (1967) are the toxic effects of drugs or alcohol; hepatic encephalopathy; uremia; pulmonary insufficiency; infections; head trauma; metabolic disorders including endocrinopathies, excesses or deficiencies of minerals, electrolytes, or water, or deficiencies in nicotinic acid, thiamine, vitamin B_{12}, or folic acid; brain tumors; cerebrovascular and cardiovascular diseases. An acute brain syndrome can also occur during the healing process from a bone fracture (Kral 1975).

Another cause of an acute reaction is malnutrition. Cases are frequently reported of older persons living alone in the community who are discovered by social agencies in disordered and dirty conditions with no food in the house. They often manifest bizarre behavior of various kinds, including paranoid delusions. In many instances one finds a history of depression. The affected person may have suffered some loss, such as the death of a spouse, became depressed, and subsequently experienced a loss of appetite. This situation continued until deficiencies developed in important nutrients and the person's mental functioning and self-care abilities became markedly disturbed.

In addition to these physiological causes, environmental factors are associated with delirium, including sensory deprivation, social isolation, immobilization, relocation to an unfamiliar environment, sleep deprivation, and other stressful environmental events (Lipowski 1967; Kahn and Miller 1978). Relocation to a hospital, even for a brief stay, occasionally results in markedly altered behavior in some older persons. These behavior problems tend to be especially prominent at dusk or in the evening, and it has been speculated that the dimmed light at those times of day reduces the environmental cues available to persons. Losses and other stressful events can also sometimes lead to an acute reaction. In one case a woman responded to the death of her husband with delusions, hallucinations, and other disorganized behaviors typical of delirium. This disturbance lasted about 3 weeks, after which the woman returned to her previous level of functioning.

These etiological factors can lead to delirium in persons of any age; periods of delirium and other altered behavior commonly occur among children who run a high fever. The aged, however, may be particularly vulnerable to these acute disorders. Because of changes in metabolic processes due to aging or disease, the older person may more readily develop a cerebral insufficiency than a younger person. As an example, drugs are metabolized and removed from the bloodstream more slowly on the average by older persons. Thus the levels of medication in an older person's blood are likely to build up to toxic levels faster than in a young individual. As older persons are also more likely to have multiple prescriptions, there is more chance for a toxic drug interaction to occur. Another factor leading to greater vulnerability to an acute brain syndrome is the presence of cerebral damage due to any cause (Lipowski 1967). In one study of a series of 21 consecutive patients undergoing cataract surgery, 17 manifested some symptoms of delirium in the week following surgery, and all had some minimal signs of cerebral dysfunction before the surgery (Linn et al. 1953). Persons with dementia due to vascular diseases or Alzheimer's disease may be the most vulnerable to an acute brain syndrome. In actual practice, however, their behavioral disorders are likely to be attributed to senility, and little attempt made to discover reversible problems. Lipowski (1967) also notes that the presence of more than one factor that could possibly lead to delirium increases the likelihood that it will actually occur.

Senile Dementia

The term "Alzheimer's-type dementia" has been applied to a condition of brain impairment characterized by the widespread development of senile plaques, neurofibrillary tangles, and granulovacular changes. Alzheimer's Disease has historically been considered a rare "presenile" dementia that affects persons between the ages of 40 and 55 and results in considerable intellectual deterioration. In contrast, brain impairment in old age was felt either to be a normal outcome of the aging process or the result of arteriosclerotic changes that restricted blood flow to the brain. Pathological studies indicated, however, that many persons with senile dementia had changes that were similar to those found in presenile Alzheimer's Disease (Terry and Wisniewski 1975; 1977). It has been estimated that approximately 65 percent of cases of senile dementia are of this type (Terry and Wisniewski 1977; Tomlinson and Henderson 1976).

As was noted in Chapter 2, most older persons have evidence of small amounts of the abnormal structures of senile plaques, neurofibrillary tangles, and granulovacular changes found in Alzheimer's Disease. Neurofibrillary tangles, for example, are typically present only in the hippocampus and amygduloid nucleus, while the amount of plaques present in the cerebral cortex is small in about 90 percent of aged persons (Tomlinson and Henderson 1976). In some persons, however, these brain changes develop in large numbers throughout brain matter. Mental impairment results because these abnormal structures disrupt normal cell functioning and are associated with the dissolution of large numbers of neurons.

Senile plaques are degenerated cell structures located at synapses between cells. They may affect the conductance of nerve impulses across cells. The neurofibrillary tangles are found within brain neurons. These masses of tangled fibers partially displace normal cell structures in the cytoplasm and may interfere with cell metabolism or the transfer of substances from the neuron body to the axons or dendrites (Tomlinson and Henderson 1976). With an Alzheimer's-type dementia there is also diffuse brain atrophy, especially in the frontal and temporal lobes. Arteriosclerosis or artherosclerosis are usually not present in the Alzheimer's patient. Cerebral blood flow, however, is reduced somewhat, possibly due to the lowered nutritional needs of the brain resulting from the loss of cells, rather than to circulatory problems (Terry and Wisniewski 1977).

The causes of the development of these changes throughout the brain are not known. Because of the increased prevalence of this disorder with age, it has been speculated that these Alzheimer's-type changes might eventually be widespread in all persons, if they did not die first of other causes. On the other hand, many persons in their 80s and 90s have been found in postmortem examinations to have few of these abnormalities (Kay 1977; Tomlinson and Henderson 1976). Other theories posit specific factors that set off these changes. Possible causes have included a genetic disorder, a slow-acting virus, metabolic dysfunctions, or metallic poisoning, perhaps involving zinc or aluminum (Terry and Wisniewski 1975; Busse 1973). Focusing on neurofibrillary tangles, Terry and Wisniewski (1977) state that identification of the cause depends in part on whether the fibers are made up of new protein or of protein that is normally present in the brain. New protein may be synthesized through the activation of a dormant gene, by the introduction of new genetic material through mutation, or by a slow-acting virus that brings new genetic material into cells. In a rarer form of dementia, Jakob-Creutzfeldt's Disease, a viral agent has been identified. Experimental studies have also shown the transmission of Alzheimer's-type characteristics by the introduction of material from an affected cell into a normal one. It is not clear, however, whether those findings point to a virus or are merely artifacts of the experimental situation (Crapper and de Boni 1978). Protein found normally in the brain may also contribute to neurofibrillary tangles and other Alzheimer's-type changes if abnormal oxidation or the presence of high concentrations of metals like aluminum, which have been reported in some studies, cause the misassembly of new molecules.

Although not typically present in cases of Alzheimer's-type dementia, arteriosclerosis and atherosclerosis are the second major cause of dementia. Vascular disease accounts for between 10 and 20 percent of cases (Terry and Wisniewski 1977; Tomlinson and Henderson 1976). This disorder is marked by a reduced blood flow to and in the brain, causing damage of brain cells (Sathananthan and Gershon 1975). Hypertension can also contribute to the cerebral damage. Tomlinson and Henderson (1976) note that while the majority of cases of dementia have clear features of either the vascular or Alzheimer's-type, some persons show evidence of both types of change.

Vascular disease can take several forms, including: (1) major ischemic lesions caused by narrowing of the carotid, anterior, or middle cerebral arteries; (2) the development of tiny multiple infarcts throughout the cerebral cortex; and (3) diffuse subcortical ischemia (Terry and Wisniewski 1977). Mental impairment is most likely to appear if, in addition to many small lesions, there are also one or more large areas of infarction. The presence of multiple tiny lesions in certain critical parts of the brain, however, may also cause substantial impairment, although the effects of the location of lesions needs further study (Tomlinson and Henderson 1976).

Dementia can also be caused by degenerative neurological disorders other than the Alzheimer's-type, including Pick's Disease and, as mentioned before, Jakob-Creutzfeldt's Disease. These illnesses are relatively rare. Additional factors that lead to dementia are normal pressure hydrocephalus, chronic alcoholism, anoxia such as can occur during a heart attack or in surgery, and untreated hypothyroidism. Many conditions that cause acute brain disorders also can lead to dementia if proper treatment is not received.

Assessment of Brain Disorders

The assessment of a possible organic problem involves three steps: (1) determining whether or not a problem is present; (2) if there is an organic disorder, evaluating what type of problem it is; and (3) assessing the severity of the problem. Deciding whether an organic problem is present is perhaps the most obvious, and also the most neglected, step in assessment. As has been mentioned previously, many persons assume, without making a careful assessment, that the disorders of the elderly are due to senile deterioration. Professionals may be influenced by older persons themselves, who often complain of poor memory and other problems that could possibly have an organic basis, and by the complaints of relatives or friends of aged patients, who may mention stereotypic age changes that they have noticed in the patient.

A careful assessment of patients is necessary because many of the behaviors that supposedly characterize organic problems occur to some extent in persons with normal brain functioning. Forgetfulness is a good example of a behavior that is frequent with no brain damage. While many persons take forgetfulness as primary evidence of organic brain dysfunction, the issue is not whether someone is forgetful, but the extent and persistence of the problem. Since all persons are forgetful to some extent, one's assessment must be guided by some standards of how much forgetfulness is likely to indicate an organic problem. Similarly, many of the other diagnostic criteria for an organic brain syndrome are vague and do not differentiate normal from abnormal behaviors. Some common criteria are poor judgment, confusion, and emotional flatness or lability. Like memory problems, poor judgment can occur without any brain impairment, and it can safely be asserted that there are many persons with very poor judgment who do not have a senile or any other brain disorder.

Confusion, on the other hand, is often used in a vague, imprecise way, and does not differentiate adequately between normal and brain-impaired behavior. An older person who gets lost in a big hospital complex can be labeled as "confused," but getting lost is not necessarily a sign of organic dysfunction. Sometimes the confusion label is applied when the observer does not understand the patient's behavior. One 67-year-old hospital patient was described as confused when she repeatedly took her clothes from her bureau drawers and then put them back again. The hospital staff considered her organically impaired because of this behavior, but no actual organic deficit was present. Rather her actions were part of her compulsive and ruminating style, and were related to preoccupations over where she would go when she left the hospital. Confusion is also used to describe persons who do not know what time it is, what place they are in, or who the people around them are. As will be discussed below, a more careful description of these behaviors than "confusion" is necessary to assist in the differential diagnosis of acute from chronic conditions. All in all, "confusion" is one of the most misused and confusing terms, and is an inadequate concept for differentiating altered from normal behavior. The last criterion, emotional flatness or lability, is also vague and can be mainfested by persons with a variety of problems other than organic brain syndrome.

Because of the overlap in behaviors between persons with normal and with impaired brain function, assessments must be based on some guidelines and standards, rather than on casual observations or the complaints of patients and their families. It is not the content of complaints or problems that is critical, but the onset, extent, pattern, and duration that are essential for the diagnosis of a brain disorder.

CHARACTERISTICS OF ACUTE BRAIN SYNDROME

When there is some question of central nervous system impairment, an assessment of the person should be made for the presence of an acute disorder, as opposed to dementia. These conditions are frequently mistaken for one another, or identified as other disorders. Because of the occurrence of florid mental changes in some persons with delirium, they may be labeled as schizophrenic, and consequently do not receive treatment for what is upsetting central nervous system functioning. Similarly, since there are sometimes severe intellectual deficits in persons with an acute reaction, they are often treated as if they are senile.

Assessment for possible reversible brain disorders involves consideration of three factors: (1) the presence of connotative or metaphorical language changes; (2) the occurrence of delusions and hallucinations; and (3) the onset of the symptoms. Connotative responses can be brought out through the use of a standard mental status test, such as the one shown

FIGURE 6.1. Mental status questionnaire.

---

1. Where are you now? (What place is this? What is the name of this place? What kind of place is it? These questions are asked, if necessary.)

2. Where is it located? (address, approximately)

3. What is the date today? Day?

4. Month?

5. Year?

6. How old are you?

7. When were you born? Month?

8. Year of birth?

9. Who is the president of the United States?

10. Who was president before him?

Additional questions:

Have you ever been in another (place with same name)?

Who am I?

What do I do? (What is my job called?)

Have you ever seen me before?

Where were you last night?

Source: R. L. Kahn, A. I. Goldfarb, M. Pollack, and R. Peck, "Brief Objective Measures for the Determination of Mental Status in the Aged," *American Journal of Psychiatry* 117 (1960): 326–328.

in Figure 6.1. A patient who is asked these mental status questions can give three possible responses. He can answer correctly, suggesting intact brain functioning. He may respond that he does not know or give a wrong answer, which is often indicative of dementia. Or the person may respond to connotative, rather than denotative, aspects of the question. As an example, when asked where he is, a hospital patient may respond by saying "Huntington Hotel" rather than "Huntington Hospital." This error is not perceptual, because the patient can usually read the name of the hospital if, for example, he is shown the bedsheets. He will persist in stating that he is in a hotel, and may even suggest that the sheets got there by mistake (Weinstein and Kahn 1955; Kahn and Miller 1978). Some common disorientations of place include stating one is in a resort, a restaurant, at home (when in the hospital), or in a cemetery. Sometimes the person will maintain he is in the correct and incorrect place at the same time. One patient, for example, stated she was in her apartment, which is also called "Mount Sinai Hospital" (Weinstein and Kahn 1955).

These types of symbolic answer suggest the presence of an acute disorder. They are rarely given by persons with other psychiatric disorders and do not usually occur in persons with dementia, except in cases of terminal decline or when the person has an acute disorder superimposed on a chronic condition.

Other questions on the mental status examination in Figure 6.1 bring out these symbolic responses. When asked "Where were you last night?" some patients will fabricate a journey, stating they went on a cruise or were in jail or at home (when they were not), or at some place other than the hospital. Another question asks if the person has ever been in another hospital with the same name: "Have you ever been in another Huntington hospital?" Called "reduplication of place," patients may locate a hospital they say has the same name in another part of town, often closer to their homes. One patient, for example, stated she had been in another Resthaven Nursing Home several blocks away and gave an address that was on the same block as her home. Reduplication can also occur for time or person. When the interviewer asks "Who am I?" and "What is my job called?," patients will sometimes identify him as someone else or give an occupation that does not fit the context, such as insurance salesman.

As these responses suggest, one common theme in connotative answers is a denial of illness (Weinstein and Kahn 1955). When asked directly about their health, such as "What is your main trouble?," patients will often deny having any problems or difficulties. This will be the case even when the person has an obvious deficit, such as a hemiparesis following a stroke. One or more of these symbolic responses on a mental status examination suggests the need for a thorough evaluation for an acute disorder.

In addition to these changes in language patterns, other mental symptoms are frequently found in persons with a delirium. Hallucinations or delusions can occur, especially involving feelings of persecution or other paranoid ideation. As with denial of illness, these paranoid thoughts place the cause of the person's problem outside himself (Weinstein and Kahn 1955). It has been estimated that between 38 and 100 percent of all persons with an acute brain syndrome have some delusions or hallucinations (Lipowski 1967; Simon and Cahan 1963). Other mental changes include difficulties in carrying out simple cognitive tasks, such as digit span or serial subtraction, and a varying degree of impairment in memory. It should be noted, however, that some persons with an acute disorder can perform at a high level on standard tests for brain damage, such as the Wechsler Adult Intelligence Scale (WAIS) (Kahn and Miller 1978). Another symptom is that patients may assert themselves sexually in inappropriate situations, for example, crawling into bed with another patient. This behavior is often shown by men for whom sexual adequacy was a concern prior to their illness (Weinstein and Kahn 1955).

One important feature for distinguishing an acute condition from dementia is that the history of these disorders differ considerably from one another (Gurland, 1980). Persons with delirium will display fluctuations in the pattern or severity of cognitive symptoms over a period of a few hours to a few days. Symptoms tend to be most pronounced at night (Lipowski 1967). There is also recent and sudden onset in most cases. In contrast, persons with dementia will have a history of gradual and progressive impairment of intellectual abilities. An individual may, however, have a history of both progressive impairment and a recent sudden onset of behavioral disturbances, indicating the possibility of an acute brain syndrome in someone with chronic damage. Gurland (1980) also notes that the course of the disorder also distinguishes delirium from normal aging and from other psychiatric problems. The history of a healthy older person is likely to be one of barely perceptible changes over a period of several years. In contrast, if a person describes episodes of symptoms that last a few months and are followed by symptom-free intervals, that suggests an affective disorder. Persons who had a dramatic illness in early adulthood, with some residual impairment over the course of their life, may have a schizophrenic disorder. It should be noted, however, that individuals with prior histories of other psychiatric problems can also develop an acute brain reaction, and if they currently present fluctuating symptoms, disorientation, or other signs consistent with delirium, a careful evaluation should be made.

Both Lipowski (1967) and Engel and Romano (1959) suggest the importance of diffuse slowing of EEG waves for making a differential diagnosis of an acute brain syndrome. This type of change is not shown by persons with functional psychiatric disorders, such as depression or schizophrenia. In the aged, however, about 20 percent of persons over 75 show some diffuse slowing. Furthermore, diffuse slowing is also usually present in persons with pronounced chronic brain syndrome (Thompson and Marsh 1977; Wang 1969).

In the early stages of delirium, symptoms may be mild and transient. A person will report difficulties concentrating or thinking, mild feelings of depression, anxiety, or fatigue, or may manifest irritability, restlessness, or apathy (Lipowski 1967; Engel and Romano 1959). Disorientation and other mental changes will emerge as the disorder develops. In some individuals, however, the principal manifestation is apathy or a withdrawal from activities. Because of the absence of more dramatic symptoms, their acute brain syndrome might go unrecognized (Lipowski 1967).

There are no precise estimates of the number of older persons affected by acute brain disorders. In a comprehensive screening ward for psychogeriatric patients, Simon and Cahan (1963) reported that over half of all persons admitted had evidence of either delirium or simultaneous acute and chronic disturbances. Butler and Lewis (1977) quote one survey of a general hospital that indicated 13 percent of patients had an acute brain syndrome and 33 percent had both an acute disturbance and chronic brain dysfunction. In a relatively young (mean age = 51.1 years) sample of patients who had open heart surgery, 13 percent developed symptoms of delirium postoperatively (Gilberstadt and Sako 1967). As mentioned earlier, the majority of aged persons having cataracts removed had behavioral disturbances in the week following surgery, including increased psychomotor activity, paranoid delusions, hallucinations, somatic complaints, and disorientations. In all but 4 cases these behavioral problems subsided within 1 week of surgery. In the other 4 patients, medical complications had occurred that presumably also prolonged the acute brain syndrome (Linn et al. 1953).

It is likely that many acute brain syndromes go unrecognized. Especially in hospitals and nursing homes, the symptoms are often regarded as signs of senility. Persons may either be ignored or medicated, with no active attempt to treat the cause of the delirium. While medications such as the phenothiazines sometimes control the behavioral problems that accompany an acute brain syndrome, high levels of these medications can become toxic. Patients in hospitals and nursing homes who develop behavior problems often are placed on a relatively high dosage of one of the phenothiazines. When the behavioral problems do not improve or get worse, the dosage is increased. If increases in medication are associated with further behavioral disturbance, it is likely that the drugs have reached toxic levels and are contributing to the delirium.

In nursing homes in particular there is often little medical effort to uncover acute and potentially reversible conditions affecting brain functioning. Many of the more severely impaired persons in nursing homes have both acute and chronic brain syndromes, and treatment of the acute condition could result in improved functioning. In one study of nursing home patients, reductions in medication and elimination of interacting drugs resulted in improvements in functioning in as many as two-thirds of patients in the facilities in which the project took place (Cheung 1977).

When a person is identified as having a possible acute brain syndrome, a thorough medical evaluation is important. Libow (1977) describes the appropriate medical tests, which are shown in Table 6.1. Sometimes the precipitant of the problem is apparent from the history provided by relatives or medical records. Drugs are a common cause in the elderly, and any behavioral changes that follow the onset of a new medication suggest a possible toxic reaction to that drug. Sudden changes in one's environment, such as moving or the deaths of significant others, can also be followed by an acute reaction. Persons with dementia, as noted earlier, are particularly susceptible to developing delirium. The successful management of persons with chronic brain impairment depends on the correct identification and treatment of any acute disturbances.

TABLE 6.1. Laboratory tests for the investigation of chronic organic brain syndrome

---

1. Basic tests
    a. Complete blood count
    b. Erythrocyte sedimentation rate
    c. Serum Na^+, K^+, Cl^-, BUN, Sugar (SMA-6)
    d. Serum Ca^{2+}, PO_4, liver function tests (SMA-12)
    e. Serum B_{12} and folate
    f. Serologic test for syphilis (VDRL, etc.)
    g. Thyroid function test (i.e., total serum T_4 concentration, T_3 resin up-take, serum-free T_4 and T_3, or PBI)
    h. Chest x-ray
    i. Electrocardiogram
2. Elective tests: Where specifically indicated
    a. Skull x-ray
    b. Spinal tap with examination of CSF (in the absence of papilledema or other evidence of increased intracranial pressure, such as erosion of the dorsum sellae, etc.)
    c. Brain scan
    d. Electroencephalogram (EEG)
    e. Computerized axial transverse tomography (CAT; EMI scanner, etc.)
    f. Isotope cisternography
    g. Cerebral angiography [a]

Source: L. S. Libow, "Senile Dementia and 'Pseudosenility': Clinical Diagnosis," in C. Eisdorfer and R. O. Friedel, eds., Cognitive and Emotional Disturbances in the Elderly. Copyright © 1977 by Year Book Medical Publishers, Inc., Chicago. Reprinted by permission.

[a] The pneumoencephalogram is intentionally omitted because of its morbidity, especially in the elderly, and because the CAT scan has essentially excluded its need.

In general, once the causal factor is removed, the symptoms of an acute brain syndrome subside in from 1 to 4 weeks. Sometimes there are dramatic improvements in patients. One 77-year-old woman was first interviewed on a Friday afternoon. She had been hospitalized for a broken leg but subsequently fell and broke a hip during rehabilitation efforts. She was an active woman who was uncomfortable with her long confinement. Current plans included at least 1 more month of inpatient treatment. On examination she showed a reduplication for place (stating she had been in another hospital with the same name that was 2 blocks away) and was disoriented for time. She had a marked cognitive impairment, as indicated by poor performance on digit span, paired-associates learning, and recall of historical facts. Either her confinement or the fracture may have led to this acute reaction. She was not taking any medication at that time. The following Monday afternoon she was examined again. That morning the social service staff had worked out a plan with her son to allow her to return home more quickly than anticipated, and she was informed she would be leaving the hospital at the end of the week. On examination she was no longer disoriented and performed at high levels on the cognitive tests. Kahn and Schlesinger (1951) also report on a man whose disorientation disappeared when he went home from the hospital.

As these examples suggest, dramatic and rapid improvements can be expected in many persons with delirium. While in most cases the changes will require a longer period of time, many persons can be observed to return to their prior levels of functioning. This is also true of those who develop an acute reaction on top of existing chronic impairment. The correct identification and treatment of acute brain disorders can markedly minimize the extent of impairment found among older persons.

Assessment of Senile Dementia

The most consistent sign of senile dementia is intellectual impairment. With mild diffuse damage, this will be noted principally in the inability to acquire new information. In terms of the model of memory presented in Chapter 2, there is a deficit in secondary but not primary memory. A person with dementia will be able to repeat correctly a string of digits, but will recall little or no information from stimuli that exceed the capacity of primary memory, such as a one-paragraph story (Zarit, Miller, and Kahn 1978). When the extent of brain damage is great, there will be a generalized impairment that affects most cognitive abilities. Other behavioral changes may, but do not necessarily, occur. Among the more common reactions are paranoid thoughts, denial of memory loss and related problems, withdrawal and apathy, irritability, and depression. Often there is a change in the pattern of adaptation to dementia as the impairment progresses. Depression and paranoid delusions are more common in persons with mild intellectual impairments, while denial and withdrawal are manifested typically with more severe brain dysfunction (Zarit and Kahn 1975). As was discussed earlier in the chapter, standard diagnostic signs such as confusion or poor judgment are too vague for making reliable assessments.

The assessment of brain damage cannot proceed according to some textbook criteria, since there is considerable individual variation in the manifestation of symptoms. According to Kahn and Miller (1978), organic brain dysfunction is a complex "psycho-bio-social" phenomenon. Biological factors such as the sites and amount of brain damage, and whether it is acute or chronic, affect behavior. In addition, psychological and social factors influence the type and extent of impairments.

Consider, for example, the important distinction between focal and diffuse brain impairment. Focal refers to damage at particular and circumscribed sites in the brain. This type of damage can be caused by several factors, including head traumas (e.g., gunshot wounds), tumors, or a cerebrovascular accident. Focal brain damage is associated with limited deficits in functioning. Often only specific abilities are impaired, while other cognitive functions are intact or mildly altered. With many types of focal damage, such as old head injuries, the condition is static and no further deterioration of function would be anticipated. Focal conditions, therefore, differ considerably from the type of impairment in cases of dementia, where there is diffuse, progressive brain damage and global deficits in performance.

The social and psychological factors that affect the behavior of persons with senile dementia are of considerable interest. It is often thought there is a one-to-one correspondence between brain damage and behavior, but the degree of association is not that high. Rather, the brain damage creates the potential for altered behaviors, but the extent and ways it is manifested depends in part on other characteristics of the person and his environment.

In research on the relation to behavior of changes in brain structure in cases of dementia, such as estimates of the number of senile plaques, moderate correlations have been found. Based on early studies (Rothschild 1937; 1942), it was considered that senile brain damage, especially the presence of senile plaques, was not associated with behavioral disorders in the elderly. Recent research, however, which has used more sophisticated microscopic analysis of brain impairment, has found significant associations between the extent of brain damage and behavioral problems, especially intellectual impairment (Blessed, Tomlinson, and Roth 1968; Corsellis 1962). Using a quantitative measure of the number of plaques per unit area in samples of brain tissue taken from the frontal, occipital, temporal, and parietal lobes, Roth, Tomlinson, and Blessed (1967) reported a correlation of .63 of plaque count and impairment scores based on a mental status measure. Somewhat lower relations were found between plaque counts and measures of behavioral impairment. Furthermore, patients with other psychiatric diagnoses, including depression, could be differentiated from dementia patients at postmortem examination on the basis of plaque counts. The plaque counts of functional patients were more similar to those of nonpsychiatric patients than to persons with brain impairment. The latter always had more extensive cerebral damage (Blessed, Tomlinson, and Roth 1968).

These reports have also stressed that a number of cases were exceptions to this pattern. In the research of the British investigators (Corsellis 1962; Blessed, Tomlinson, and Roth 1968; Tomlinson and Henderson 1976), there were noted some persons with massive cerebral damage who showed only limited behavioral changes and, conversely, individuals with minimal brain impairment but extensive behavioral deficits typical of dementia. According to Kahn and Miller (1978), these discrepancies are probably not due to errors in measurement. Rather, on theoretical grounds one would expect only moderate correlations between the extent of brain damage and behavior change, because other factors also affect behavior. Among the influences on behavior they cite are: education, work, personality, energy level, characteristic patterns of adaptation, physical mobility, attitudes, motivation, and the degree of sophistication of the test. They also present clinical examples of well-educated persons who can compensate well for a brain pathology and who show esoteric patterns of impairment. In the case of one 71-year-old attorney, for example, his only symptom was difficulty reading speeches to chapters of a social organization.

Since behavior does not always reflect the amount of brain damage, the problems of making an evaluation of whether brain damage is present is complicated. No one psychological test will always correspond accurately to the underlying brain structure, because of the intervening psychological and social dimensions. Kahn and Miller (1978) argue that in choosing assessment measures one must consider both the validity of the instruments, that is, to what extent they reflect brain impairment, and the types of error in misdiagnosis that occur.

Two possible errors can be made in assessing a person for dementia: false positives, where a person scores in an impaired range on the tests but does not have an underlying brain pathology; and false negatives, where test scores fall in the normal range, despite the presence of considerable brain damage. To decide on appropriate assessment measures, we must consider what type of error can be better tolerated, comparing the implications of failing to make a diagnosis when dementia is present with those of diagnosing it when there is no brain dysfunction.

In contrast to cases of delirium for which early detection can lead to effective treatment, determining that someone has senile dementia has no specific therapeutic implications. Effective treatments do not exist to reverse or retard the course of the Alzheimer's-type degenerative processes that are the major cause of dementia in the aged (see Eisdorfer and Stotsky 1977 for a review of pharmacological and other treatments). When dementia is associated with vascular disease, effective management may reduce the rate of further damage but will not reverse existing cognitive impairments. There are likewise no specific psychosocial strategies that should be applied in every case involving a diagnosis of dementia. Families, for example, are sometimes routinely advised they should make plans to place an aged dementia patient in a long-term care facility, even though many persons with severe impairments can be maintained in the community without undue burden on family members (Reever, Bach-Peterson, and Zarit 1979). There is some limited predictive value in the diagnosis, mainly in terms of the expectation of shortened life expectancy. It is also sometimes important to inform families that the dementia patient is not malingering, or that pressing him to do mental tasks will not regenerate brain cells. In contrast to these small advantages, making a diagnosis of dementia can have some negative consequences. It sometimes leads to pessimistic attitudes about treatment, so that potentially reversible conditions such as depression do not receive attention. In other words, if we make a large number of false positive diagnoses, we may fail to treat persons for whom gains are possible, but there are no major negative effects in making false negative errors in assessment.

The usual neuropsychological approaches to assessment of brain damage have a limited usefulness in cases of dementia, because of their tendency to give false positive results. Tests such as the WAIS, the Halstead-Reitan battery, and the Graham-Kendall Memory for Designs test are strongly related to past achievements and experiences, especially education. It is difficult to estimate to what extent a particular score or pattern of scores is related to cerebral damage or to past learning. Despite their widespread use in clinical settings, some of these procedures have been found to have poor discriminating ability between functional psychiatric and organic disorders (see Kahn and Miller 1978 and Gurland 1973 for reviews). Even such widely used procedures as digit span, the Graham-Kendall Memory for Designs, the Bender-Gestalt, the Benton Visual Retention, and Trailmaking fail to distinguish.

In the case of the WAIS, scales regarded as signs of brain damage do not differentiate well in the aged. A distinction is usually made between "Hold" tests, which represent information acquired in the past, and "Don't Hold" tests that involve new learning. It is generally considered that the "Don't Hold" tests are susceptible to age and brain damage, but research has shown that the tests best differentiating organically impaired patients from a control group are Information, Comprehension, Arithmetic, Picture Completion, and Object Assembly (Botwinick and Birren 1951). The first 3 of those scales are "Hold" tests, and also are reported not to decline with age. In a recent review Schaie and Schaie (1977) found different patterns of test scores on the WAIS for aging and organic disorders.

Other drawbacks of typical neuropsychological procedures are that they are time consuming, can only be administered to cooperative and motivated patients, and sometimes have been validated only on young samples (Kahn and Miller 1978). Some tests, such as the Halstead-Reitan battery, have been validated principally on highly educated individuals; their usefulness with other groups has not been determined.

A few tests have been found to be sensitive to the effects of senile dementia. Among the most useful are the New Word Learning and Retention test (Inglis 1970) and the Paired-Associates Learning test (Caird, Sanderson, and Inglis 1962). As with other complex tasks, however, education, motivation, and the effects of the specific testing situation can affect scores on these procedures. In research conducted by the author in which the Paired-Associates Learning test was used, it was necessary to present the word pairs both visually and verbally in order to distinguish elderly depressives from persons with chronic brain syndromes. Without the added stimulus of the visual presentation, the test produced considerable anxiety in most patients and was failed by approximately 80 percent of persons screened.

THE MENTAL STATUS EXAMINATION

As an alternative to the neuropsychological battery, both Kahn and Miller (1978) and Gurland (1980) suggest the use of standardized clinical measures for making a differential diagnosis of dementia. Mental status examinations, such as shown in Figure 6.1, have the advantage of being brief and easy to administer. While false negative results are somewhat more likely with these procedures, their simple nature reduces (though it does not eliminate) the chance of false positive tests. Furthermore, as described earlier, mental status tests are good screening devices for changes typical of acute reactions. Similar measures have been developed by Pfeiffer (1975a), Jacobs et al. (1977), and Folstein, Folstein, and McHugh (1975).

Mental status examinations have been found to have high validity in the diagnosis of dementia, using various criteria. There has been repeated evidence that errors on mental status procedures agree with the diagnoses made by psychiatrists (Kahn et al. 1960; Irving, Robinson, and McAdam 1970; Gurland, 1980). Errors on a mental status examination also differentiate dementia from other disorders, especially depression. While depressed persons often give the impression of intellectual impairment, with their slow and reluctant performance on tests and complaints about poor memory, factor analytic studies have indicated that depression and senile dementia can be reliably differentiated on the basis of performance on cognitive tests (Gurland et al. 1976). Patients with dementia were found to show impairment on 3 factors of cognitive performance, including orientation and memory deficits, such as knowing one's year of birth and the name of the interviewer. In contrast, depressed persons had higher scores on dimensions of anxiety, depression, and somatic complaints, while showing no cognitive impairments. While some persons with dementia are sometimes also depressed, the presence of an intellectual impairment on these measures usually indicates brain damage.

Other studies have supported the validity of a mental status examination as indicating diffuse brain dysfunction. It has been found, for example, that errors on the mental status questionnaire are associated with the course of the illness, with mortality rates higher among persons giving more incorrect responses (Goldfarb, Fisch, and Gerber, 1966). Errors have also been found to correlate highly with other measures of brain impairment, including more extensive batteries of tests involving learning and memory (Zarit, Miller, and Kahn 1978), electroencephalographic examination (Irving, Robinson, and McAdam 1970), and computerized axial tomography of the brain (Kasniak, Garron, and Fox 1975). As noted earlier, Blessed, Tomlinson, and Roth (1968) found that results of a mental status-type examination correlated more strongly with the amount of cerebral damage than did other behavioral or cognitive measures.

In contrast to the symbolic answers typical of patients with acute brain syndromes, persons with dementia will typically make simpler errors on a mental status examination. They will not know where they are or will not remember the name of the hospital, but usually will not confuse it with a different type of setting, such as a resort or hotel. They will not be able to recall correctly the date, their birth date or age, or the names of recent presidents, or will answer incorrectly (e.g., stating it is June when the month is actually February).

The extent of intellectual impairment present can be estimated from the total of errors made on the numbered items on the mental status questionnaire. No or 1 errors indicate normal functioning; 2 to 5 errors suggest mild impairment; 5 to 7 errors are associated with moderate impairment of abilities; and persons making more than 7 errors usually have severe impairments (Kahn et al. 1960; Zarit, Miller, and Kahn 1978).

It has sometimes been suggested that an older person will miss answers on the mental status examination because of poor motivation or because information such as the date has not recently been available or of interest. These qualifications usually are not borne out by clinical experience. As discussed above, depressed persons and others with low motivation but no cognitive deficit are able to answer these orientation and information items correctly on the mental status questionnaire. Similarly, while it is common for a person to be off by a few days on the day of the month, one is unlikely to identify the month or year incorrectly. If there is some question that incorrect answers are due to the patient's not having been exposed to the correct information, this can be tested by giving that individual the actual date and month or other items and determining if he can retain that information. Persons with dementia will have a persistent memory deficit and, except in mild cases, will not be able to acquire the information necessary for correct responses.

The course of symptoms may also be used to clarify diagnosis. A history of gradual deterioration is consistent with dementia. In contrast, depression tends to be episodic, while the effects of normal aging are minimal changes that are barely noticeable from year to year. In acute brain reactions, onset is typically sudden.

Another procedure that has been useful in identifying the presence of diffuse brain damage is the Face-Hand test, which is shown in Figure 6.2. Developed by Bender and his associates (Bender 1952; Fink, Green, and Bender 1952), this procedure measures a person's ability to detect stimuli

FIGURE 6.2. Face-Hand test.

Instructions: 1. With eyes closed: "Please close your eyes. I am going to touch you and I want you to show me where I touched you." On trials 1 to 4, if person makes an omission, ask, "Anywhere else?"

2. With eyes open: "Now open your eyes. I am going to touch you again. Pay close attention and show me where I touched you."
(Test is to be terminated after either trial 4, 8, 12, or 16, whenever the person has completed the previous 4 trials correctly.)

Circle omissions: Indicate displacements

1. Right cheek — left hand
2. Left cheek — right hand
3. Right cheek — right hand
4. Left cheek — left hand
   Right cheek — left cheek
   Right hand — left hand
5. Right cheek — left hand
6. Left cheek — right hand
7. Right cheek — right hand
8. Left cheek — left hand
9. Right cheek — left hand
10. Left cheek — right hand
11. Right cheek — right hand
12. Left cheek — left hand
    Right cheek — left cheek
    Right hand — left hand
13. Right cheek — left hand
14. Left cheek — right hand
15. Right cheek — right hand
16. Left cheek — left hand

Scoring: A positive result is indicated if the subject continues to make errors on the 5th trial or after.

Source: R. L. Kahn, A. I. Goldfarb, M. Pollack, and R. Peck, "Brief Objective Measures for the Determination of Mental Status in the Aged," *American Journal of Psychiatry* 117 (1960): 326–328.

that are applied simultaneously to the hand and cheek. There are test trials, which involve stimulating the cheek and hand simultaneously, and learning trials, in which first both cheeks and then both hands are touched. Errors after the first 4 test trials and 2 learning trials suggest the presence of diffuse brain damage and can indicate either chronic or acute problems. Typical errors are to omit the hand or to displace the more distant stimulus (hand) to a proximal site, such as to shoulder or cheek. An example of a displacement error would be to state one had been touched on both cheeks when cheek and hand were touched. Errors usually are bilateral, with omissions or displacements made for stimuli to both sides of the body. If a person makes only unilateral errors, for example, omitting those stimuli applied to the right hand, this may indicate focal damage to areas of the brain that process sensory information. Bilateral errors on the Face-Hand test past the fourth trial have been found to be associated with intellectual impairment on a battery of tests of learning and memory. When used jointly with the mental status questionnaire, more cases of persons with intellectual impairment were correctly identified (Zarit, Miller, and Kahn 1978). Errors on only one of these procedures (mental status questionnaire or Face-Hand test) were found to be associated with mild intellectual deficits, while positive scores for organic brain syndrome on both tests were related to marked impairment in performance on other cognitive tests.

There has been little attention to identifying the cause of senile dementia on the basis of test scores or pattern of errors. One study reports significantly poorer performance on several cognitive tests for persons with Alzheimer's Disease, compared to subjects diagnosed as having brain damage of vascular origin (Perez et al. 1975). It has also been suggested that fluctuations in performance tend to be somewhat greater and depression more frequent in persons with a vascular dementia. Because vascular disease often affects the circulation of blood to other organs as well as to the brain, persons with that disorder are in poorer health overall than individuals with Alzheimer's Disease.

It should be noted that where test results are ambiguous and do not clearly indicate the presence of chronic diffuse impairment, it is likely that other indicators are also inconclusive, including clinical judgments and procedures such as the EEG or computerized tomography (Gurland 1973). Since brain structure does change in varied amounts with normal aging, and since mild diffuse impairment does not differ much from normal brain status, early detection of the senile brain diseases is at best problematic. Further research in this area is warranted, since early detection would be an issue if treatment procedures for these diseases can be developed.

CASE EXAMPLES

The following cases illustrate the use of the mental status questionnaire and the Face-Hand test in clinical situations.

Mr. B. was brought to a counseling program by his wife, who was concerned that he had given up many of his activities. He had retired 2 years earlier because of increasing difficulties in running his business. One of his biggest problems was forgetfulness, which had gradually worsened over the past 4 years. Mr. B. reported feeling content to stay home, doing very little other than watching television. He did not appear depressed, and reported no depressed feelings or other problems typical of depression. Mental status testing indicated that he made 5 errors and also had persistent omissions on the Face-Hand test through the first 8 trials.

The extent of errors on these 2 tests clearly suggests the presence of senile dementia. Because of his wife's concern about his lack of activities, they were advised to increase somewhat the things they did together such as taking walks. His wife also wanted him to join a social group, but as he had never done something like that before and expressed no interest in it, it was suggested that she not pursue that course unless he changed his mind. Because of his cognitive deficit, he might have had problems in making the adjustment to a totally new situation such as a social group. In this case the presence of marked cognitive impairment and Mr. B.'s own reluctance to be more active indicated that his wife should not overtax him with demands for increased participation, but some amount of activity might be mildly beneficial to him and reassuring to her.

In another case, the reports of memory loss were not verified with testing. Mrs. A. was a 74-year-old woman brought to a counseling center by her sister. Both Mrs. A. and her sister reported that the client had memory problems. Since her retirement nearly 10 years earlier, Mrs. A. had had few activities to occupy her time, and had been restless and depressed over her situation. She reported spending most of her day worrying over her financial situation, including such things as whether she had paid bills and if her checkbook calculations were accurate. She would frequently ask her sister questions about these matters. Her sister, in turn, spent her days painting. She resented these interruptions and preferred to be left alone to do her work. Her only interactions with her sister came when Mrs. A. requested assistance.

On examination Mrs. A. made no errors on the mental status or Face-Hand tests. She did appear depressed and anxious, and confirmed this impression. She also reported trouble sleeping, especially waking during the night. From this evidence it was concluded that Mrs. A had no apparent brain impairment, but that she was depressed and had virtually no activities in which she was involved. A treatment program for depression was developed, which increased her activities slightly and reduced her feelings of depression. Follow-up indicated no evidence of intellectual deterioration typical of senile dementia.

It is not always possible to make a clear determination of whether dementia is present, as the following case indicates. Mrs. M. was brought to a counseling program by her daughter. Both mother and daughter reported that Mrs. M. was increasingly forgetful. Mrs. M. said she forgot where she put things, and was forgetful when handling money matters. She also described herself as pessimistic. She had gradually given up activities and did not see anything that could potentially engage her interest. She complained about feeling depressed. Her son, with whom she was close, had recently moved away, and while she said she tried to view this situation philosophically, she was quite sad about it. Testing revealed 1 mental status error (she did not know the date) and an atypical pattern on the Face-Hand test, on which she made 1 omission repeatedly on each block of 4 trials. Following the first 4 trials, persons who continue to make errors usually do so on most or all trials in each group of 4. Because of this atypical response, she was retested 2 weeks later, with similar results.

It was decided to provide treatment for depression, since there was no clear evidence of senile dementia and because Mrs. M. was noticeably depressed. Discussions began about her negative attitudes and also tried to identify pleasant activities in which she would be interested in participating. Within the first weeks of treatment, however, there were some notable incidents of forgetfulness, including being unable to recall having gone to a doctor's appointment 3 days earlier and getting lost while driving the car. While this type of forgetfulness can happen in persons without brain impairment, these incidents raised the possibility that some deterioration might be present. As Mrs. M. was depressed, however, it was decided to continue treatment as originally planned to try to reduce her feelings of depression, and to provide follow-up to determine if her cognitive symptoms worsened. The testing in this case yielded ambiguous results, but the implications for treatment would have been the same, whatever the findings. Her subsequent involvement in a volunteer program led to her reporting less depression.

The EEG and CT Scan

Direct measures of brain activity, such as EEG recordings or computerized axial tomography, also do not provide unequivocal evidence for the presence or absence of significant amounts of brain damage. Concerning the EEG, abnormal brain wave patterns are consistently found among persons with moderate to severe intellectual impairments (Wang 1969; Marsh and Thompson 1977). These abnormalities include slowing of the dominant alpha frequency and diffuse slowing in the delta and theta range. Alpha slowing is also common among the healthy aged, however, and the relation to intellectual impairment is not a straightforward one. Slowing of Alpha frequency is not necessarily related to poorer intellectual performance in a healthy sample, though it may predict subsequent changes. Wang (1969) reports that persons with slower dominant alpha frequency differed little from others on intellectual tests during an initial testing session but, when followed over a 3½ year period, were more likely to manifest a decline in intellectual abilities. Similarly, while diffuse slowing is common among brain-impaired samples, approximately 20 percent of normal elderly show this pattern after age 75 (Marsh and Thompson 1977), and the significance of these changes is not known.

Another common abnormality in the EEG records of the aged is focal disturbances, especially as indicated by slow delta or theta activity. These types of focal sign are typical of persons with cerebrovascular insufficiencies or with tumors. According to Wang (1969), however, focal slowing may be present in healthy older persons for several years without the appearance of clinical symptoms. As Marsh and Thompson (1977) point out, this lack of correspondence between EEG activity and intellectual performance in the community aged may be due to measurement errors. It may also be possible, as with other physiological indicators, that small amounts of abnormalities can be present without leading to altered functioning. In the diagnosis of senile dementia, then, the EEG reliably indicates the presence of severe abnormalities, but in the healthy aged, evidence of slowing of brain waves and of focal disturbances may not have any clinical significance. As with psychological testing, small deviations from normal functioning may be due either to transient conditions or to the onset of a pathological process, but these two possibilities cannot as yet be differentiated on the basis of an EEG evaluation.

Computerized axial tomography, sometimes referred to as CT scan, CAT scan, or EMI scan, provides a nonintrusive way for assessing brain structure and is useful in the diagnosis of those illnesses, including senile brain disease, that cause alterations in anatomic structures. In contrast to usual X-ray procedures, the CT scan is capable of differentiating tissue structures with differing densities. In order to construct a picture of the brain, a narrow X-ray beam scans the head, taking multiple pictures that are then reconstructed by a computer to show anatomic structure (Aita 1977b). Brain pathologies will be indicated by deviations from normal anatomic structure, such as hemisphere asymmetry or differences in density of brain tissue (Aita 1977a). In the aged the effects of Alzheimer's Disease and other degenerative illnesses will be manifested in enlargement of the ventricles and widening of the cortical sulci (Caird 1977). In most though not all patients, the extent of cerebral atrophy as determined by CT scan has correlated with behavioral measures of dementia in persons with moderate to severe impairment (Caird 1977; Kasniak, Garron, and Fox 1975; Fox, Topel, and Huckman 1975). Because there is some enlargement of the ventricles with normal aging, however, it is often difficult to differentiate normal from pathological changes in the early stages of a degenerative disease. Even in middle-aged persons, some mild degree of cortical atrophy may have no diagnostic significance (Wells and Duncan 1977). Some cases have been reported where either there is marked intellectual impairment and no signs of atrophy on the CT scan, or atrophy with no intellectual impairment. The finding of no atrophy in someone with intellectual impairment suggests the possibility of a reversible condition due to metabolic disturbances, pernicious anemia, or some other factor (Caird 1977). In the opposite condition of atrophy but no intellectual impairment, obstructive or normal pressure hydrocephalus should be considered.

Disorders Mimicking Dementia

There are several conditions that may mimic the symptoms of senile dementia. Some authors have posited the existence of a syndrome of pseudodementia (Kiloh 1961; Post 1975). Patients are described as manifesting symptoms that resemble dementia, including cognitive impairments and apathy, but that reflect a depressive reaction rather than an underlying brain pathology. Case reports have emphasized the return of complete mental functioning. Unfortunately, the limited descriptions in these reports do not include test findings of an actual cognitive deficit. Problems in memory and other deficits are described impressionistically. Furthermore, it has not been evaluated if these cases of pseudodementia represent acute brain reactions that remit spontaneously. The phenomenon of pseudosenility may exist, but additional documentation is needed.

It is sometimes difficult to differentiate between someone with an extreme, retarded psychotic depression and senile dementia. In the former, however, there is usually evidence of a sudden onset, and possibly similar episodes earlier in life. The extent of cognitive impairment is mild in most cases of depression (A. S. Friedman 1964; Hilbert, Niederehe, and Kahn 1976). Depressed persons will generally not make errors on mental status tests.

Another disorder that mimics senile dementia is vertebralbasilar insufficiency, which is brought about by the constriction of the vertebral-basilar artery system. Typical symptoms include vertigo, dizziness, intermittent ataxia, and memory impairment. Recent surgical procedures have been found effective in removing obstructions in these arteries. Impressions of improved intellectual performance have also been reported (Woods, Birren, and Zarit 1978).

Persons with a limited educational background and intelligence present special problems for making an assessment. Their performance on any cognitive test, including mental status, can fall into an impaired range without reflecting a diffuse degenerative process. When dealing with a person who has little or no formal education, mild impairments are likely to reflect a lifelong pattern and may not be signs of dementia.

Clinical Issues in Evaluation

In testing for possible senile dementia, it is important first to put the patient at ease and to begin by asking some general questions about concerns or problems. As some rapport builds between interviewer and patient, the tests can be introduced. The mental status examination can be presented as a test of memory. The response to this test is almost always favorable. Persons with good mental functioning who do well on the test usually do not resent having to answer simple questions. When someone does object to the testing, that person can be assured that this procedure is performed with all patients and is necessary to rule out any major problems. Persons with pathological memory deficits who cannot answer the mental status questions correctly typically do not show concern over their errors. On occasion a person with a mild deficit will become upset at not getting one of the answers, but that individual can be reassured so that testing can continue. Catastrophic reactions to this test are rare, except in aphasic patients. The Face-Hand test is similarly nonthreatening and almost always elicits patients' cooperation. Persons making errors are rarely aware of them, even when the test is done with eyes open.

The outcome of senile dementia is a gradual process of deterioration that culminates in the individual's death. In an early study by Roth (1955), hospitalized patients with diagnoses of arteriosclerotic brain disease or senile psychosis (Alzheimer's-type dementia) were followed for a 2-year period, during which 73 percent of those with arteriosclerotic disorders and 82 percent with senile psychosis died. Since hospitalization in Britain is typically provided for only the most severe cases, the course of these illnesses is probably more than 2 years. Another estimate is that Alzheimer's Disease halves the life expectancy of affected persons (Gurland 1980). Based on clinical experience, individuals generally come for outpatient mental health services from between 2 and 4 years after the first onset of symptoms, but a 10-year history of progressive deterioration is not uncommon.

The pattern of increasing decrements in abilities that is typically described in the literature includes increasing intellectual impairment and, finally, inability to perform self-care activities (see Gurland 1980 for a review). These findings are based principally on institutionalized samples. Since institutional care often results in some impairment in self-maintenance activities such as dressing and bathing (Kahn and Zarit 1974; Epstein and Simon 1968), it is not clear how much of this pattern of decrement is due to the illness or to the treatment. Increasing problems in self-care are likely with progressive brain damage, but some community residents do not lose these abilities until immediately preceding their death.

Because the dementias reflect disease processes of an organ (the brain), there is a tendency to view persons with these disorders as more similar to one another than they actually are. The single common characteristic of individuals with brain disease is intellectual impairment. In other areas of functioning, such as self-care, interpersonal behaviors, and changes in adaptation, performance is much more variable. Some persons with severe intellectual impairment are able to maintain self-care activities at a high level, while other individuals with only a small deficit may show gross behavioral disturbances. There is, generally, too much of a tendency to see everything the brain-damaged person does as determined by the disease state. As with persons with intact brain functioning, the behaviors of persons with senile dementia reflect characteristic responses of the affected individual and the effects of those who interact with him. The process of functional assessment described in the preceding chapter provides a systematic way of understanding and treating the problems of persons with senile dementia, as well as those with normal brain function.

Summary

The assessment of brain disorders in the elderly is probably the most important clinical task facing the practitioner. It is an area filled with many myths and misconceptions, but accurate evaluations are possible and do make significant contributions. The identification of acute brain disorders is essential in order that proper medical treatment can be assured. With senile dementia, on the other hand, all other potentially reversible conditions should be ruled out first before a diagnosis is made. Finding cognitive impairments indicative of senile dementia should not lead to a pessimism about treatment, since an analysis of person-environment interactions can sometimes identify effective interventions. Treatment approaches to persons with brain disorders and their families are discussed in Chapter 13.

CHAPTER 7

Physical Assessment

Robert M. Tager

As WITH PSYCHOPATHOLOGY ASSESSMENT, physical assessment can be viewed using several different models. The most common is the medical model based on the diagnosis and treatment of disease processes. A statistical model is also sometimes used in evaluating how an individual varies from an established norm. A functional model is based on an individual's competency in self-management and with regard to family and the community.

An example of application of the medical model in the assessment process is the physical examination performed by a physician. This examination is designed to to detect disease processes at the earliest possible time so that appropriate treatment can be instituted. Perhaps the best example of the statistical model is in the area of exercise, where an individual's performance of a specific task can be compared with the performance of a group of similar individuals on the same task. An example of the functional model of assessment is to be found in the field of rehabilitation medicine. Rehabilitation professionals emphasize the assessment and restoration of function of the individual rather than the specific treatment of disease or comparison with other individuals.

It is the latter model that will be emphasized in this chapter. This model allows the professional to evaluate factors related to an older individual's ability to function independently in the community or in variously structured environments. This method of assessment can also lead directly to referrals for specific services. Disease entities will also be

Dr. Tager is Medical Director, Casa Colina Rehabilitation Center, Pomona, California, and Clinical Associate Professor, Leonard Davis School of Gerontology, University of Southern California.

considered in the framework of how they affect the function of the individual.

The medical, statistical, and functional models of assessment are not mutually exclusive; they all play a significant role in the physical and emotional assessment and health care of the older adult. Such assessments may lead to intervention or assistance in the areas of prevention, maintenance, or restoration of health and function. The philosophies of traditional medicine and current concepts of health are both important in the assessment process, and the individual client or patient will gain the most benefit when the professional applies those concepts that are most pertinent to that individual's physical condition, emotional status, and belief system.

Comprehensive Assessment Procedures

There are many different reasons to assess the function of an older person: to make a diagnosis and render appropriate treatment; to determine if there is a specific loss of function and then make an appropriate referral; and perhaps the most important for those working with the elderly in a longitudinal way, to determine if a change has occurred. If psychologists, social workers, nurses, or other professionals are able formally or informally to assess the physical function of their client or patient at one point in time, and then periodically reassess, they will be able to determine if there has been improvement or decline.

In the discussions that follow, the goal is to describe major aspects of the medical and functional models, so that the professional can gain a knowledge of physical assessment that can be applied during interview situations, treatment procedures, or in review of written records. The approach can also be used informally by observing the older individual during conversation or while participating in an activity.

The specific factors that will be reviewed that affect assessment are the patient's social history, mental status, symptoms and diseases, basic self-care functions and needs, mobility, and communication. These different aspects of health status can be conceived of as involving a cycle. Symptoms and disease lead to a disruption of capacities for independent living, proceeding in turn to required appropriate efforts for the restoration of those functions.

Although physical assessment is stressed, certain behavioral and emotional factors are so closely integrated with physical function that they cannot and should not be separated; these will be discussed in the appropriate places. Emphasis will also be placed on what the observer sees and hears. The observer can see appearance and behavior. It is possible to observe visually both common changes that occur in age that do not indicate specific, known pathological processes, and changes that are indicative of pathological alteration. The observer can hear symptoms and feelings. Much useful information is revealed not only by the content of speech, but by the characteristics of speech as well.

In the presentations on visual and auditory observations, every attempt is made to minimize the use of technical medical terms. In pursuing that interest, more descriptive and fewer labeling terms can be used. The statement that a patient cannot recognize faces is generally more vivid than saying that he exhibited prosopagnosia. Similarly, when listening to patients' accounts of symptoms, it is possible to describe them directly without categorizing them with medical terms. For example, the statement, "Mr. M. must sit up at night because he cannot breathe when he lies down," gives more information about what Mr. M. is experiencing than to note that he has orthopnea. Another benefit of good descriptions is that they allow people of many different fields to understand the same communications about patients.

THE PATIENT'S HISTORY

The first step in an assessment is to consider the historical background of the individual. Such information could be obtained directly from the person, from family, or from written records. In addition to determining the previous level of function and of health, it is extremely important to find out information regarding the individual's personal characteristics. Past behavior will determine or contribute significantly to current behavior. Similarly, attitude and motivation that is currently observed may well relate to the past. Educational background and employment history can also give significant information about the individual and ways of relating to him. A person's belief system is also pertinent and too often ignored. An example of the latter is that of an elderly women who was an excellent candidate for rehabilitation following a stroke, but who was extremely hesitant about entering the program. Further investigation revealed that the clothing suggestions for female rehabilitation patients included slacks, and she was raised with a belief that it was immoral for a woman to wear slacks. This having been discovered, the problem was solved by a discussion of available options, and a successful rehabilitation program followed.

WHAT YOU SEE: APPEARANCE AND BEHAVIOR

There are a number of physical changes commonly observed in the elderly population. These are described in detail in various textbooks on geriatrics (e.g., Brocklehurst 1973; Rossman 1971). Most are related to degenerative changes that occur gradually rather than being caused by specific, treatable disease processes. Two of the most common are the graying of hair due to decrease in pigment production and the wrinkling of skin due to loss of elasticity. Hair loss is common, especially baldness in males. The shortening of stature frequently seen in the aging is contributed to by narrowing of the intervertebral discs, and the bent-forward posture, kyphosis, by degenerative changes in the vertebra. There is a loss of subcutaneous fat, often producing a notable drooping of the face, upper arms, abdomen, and breasts.

Edentulessness, or lack of teeth, is frequent, and it is hoped that preventive measures in dentistry will decrease its incidence. An often-mentioned finding is the so-called "arcus senilis," which is a whitish arc or ring commonly seen in older people over the outer border of the iris. There has been some controversy as to its significance, but it causes no loss of function. The name of the condition itself leaves much to be desired.

A number of definitely pathological changes can also be seen. One of the most dramatic changes is observed following a stroke where one side of the body has a weakness or paralysis. The lower half of the face on the affected side droops and there may be some difficulty in handling saliva on that side. The arm is usually more paralyzed than the leg and often tends to a flexed position, whereas the leg tends to straighten and be brought forward in a circular motion in gait (circumduction) rather than a straightforward swingthrough. Another disorder of the central nervous system, Parkinsonism, typically results in a lack of facial expression, a flexed or bent-forward posture, a rhythmic tremor of the hands at rest, and a shuffling gait. Individuals so affected may also have difficulty initiating movements, including beginning the first steps of walking.

Disorders of other organ systems usually do not produce such obvious changes, but there are some notable exceptions. Congestive heart failure may result in shortness of breath, an inability to lie flat comfortably, and a swelling of the ankles. Some types of kidney disease may also produce swelling of the ankles. Emphysema can produce a barrel-shaped chest, a ruddy complexion, and visible difficulty breathing. Other changes in skin color, such as the pallor of anemia or yellow of jaundice, can be seen. The important thing for the nonphysician health care professional is not to make a diagnosis but to be able to observe changes in appearance either from a norm or over time, and to be able to communicate the existence of that change to others.

The aids or appliances used by a person also provide information regarding degrees of physical function. Many can be seen readily, while others are discovered by conversation or interviews. Glasses, of course, give some indication of impaired vision, especially if they are quite thick. Hearing aids are fairly common appliances used by elderly people, and those who are dependent on them are at a significant disadvantage when the aid is lost or is not functioning properly. A third appliance, which is sometimes noticeable and frequently present, is dentures.

There are numerous gait aids, including several types of crutch, but the most common that are used by elderly people are canes and pick-up walkers. A pick-up walker provides a stable base of support for a person who has the use of both upper extremities, but it is a bulky piece of equipment. The most convenient cane is the simple straight cane, but for individuals who need a broader base of support there are several four-pointed canes with varying broadness of base. A wheelchair is an obvious appliance and the most subject to architectural barriers.

It is necessary that all appliances be properly selected and fitted and that the user be adequately trained in their use. If these factors are not assured, the individual will not gain the maximum degree of function intended and will be subject to the risk of injury. One of the commonest examples of this is for a person who questionably needs a cane to buy one without measurement or be given one that is too long and then use it in the wrong hand for his condition.

Behavior can, of course, be observed visually to obtain significant information regarding both physical and emotional status. Some common changes that are not necessarily linked to a specific pathological process needing treatment ("normal") are a mild slowing of movement, a slowing of reaction times, and a greater need for support in some situations. Observing a person get into and out of a chair can give information regarding speed of movement, strength, and balance. If the observer has seen this action performed by the same individual for a number of times previously, a comparison can be made and change, if any, can be noted.

Emotions are most readily mirrored in the face except in a person with Parkinsonism, where facial expression is flattened. Happiness, sadness, serenity, anxiety, joy, depression, well-being, and pain can all be seen, evaluated, interpreted, discussed, and compared from time to time. An excellent source of photographs depicting facial expressions of emotions is to be found in the book *Family of Man* (Steichen 1955).

Other observable evidences of emotion include the slowing of movement and slumped posture of depression and the quick, sometimes jerking movements of anxiety. Frequent changes of position and tremulousness may also indicate anxiety in an individual in whom there is no organic movement disorder. There are other, often more subtle observations that can be made, and the professional's skill will increase with experience and validation of conclusions by additional information or by the observations of others.

The observation of clothing and the manner in which one is dressed can give more than socioeconomic information. The usually neatly dressed person who begins to look unkempt may be becoming depressed or developing a physical illness. Inappropriate dressing by type of clothing or the way in which it is used may indicate organic brain dysfunction. It must always be remembered that most observations do not lead to definite conclusions by themselves, but they may indicate a trend or a need for further investigation.

What You Hear: Symptoms and Feelings

Both the characteristics and the content of speech can provide information about an individual. Feelings may be expressed directly or may be detectable through speech characteristics. Intonation and volume can give clues regarding mood. Speech that is well modulated and of normal volume can easily be contrasted with speech that is monotonous and of low intensity. The latter could be indicative of depression or perhaps hypothyroidism. This is an example of similar observations possibly resulting from different causes. Rate of speech can also be a helpful observation, with excessively rapid speech being common in anxiety states and the manic phase of manic-depression, but it can also indicate hyperthyroidism or use of stimulant drugs.

Hesitancy in speech might reflect uncertainty or lack of confidence. It can also result from organic causes. Sometimes a tremor can be detectable or slurring can be heard. Both of these would more likely be of organic cause, but tremulousness of speech could also be caused by anxiety. People who have a stroke affecting the dominant (usually left) side of the brain may acquire aphasia. Aphasia can take many forms, but usually has some component affecting both speech production and auditory comprehension.

The content of speech may reflect emotions, emotional symptoms, or physical symptoms. Anxiety or depression may be stated as such or may be expressed by talk about worries and concerns. Symptoms of sadness or loneliness should be looked for, especially in the older person living alone or in isolation. It is important to heed the topics emphasized, but it is equally, or more, important to attend to topics that a person is hesitant to bring up or discuss. An older person who avoids talking about or minimizes the loss of a friend may well be experiencing intense emotions.

One of the more common complaints expressed by older persons is loss of memory. This can be very distressing but, as noted in previous chapters, complaints of memory loss may often be related to depression. Not long ago an elderly woman came to my office complaining of a very distressful loss of memory. She was on time, was very neatly dressed, and related her history unhesitatingly, including dates, without any reference to notes. After she had recounted her history of memory loss and her past medical history, she became more relaxed and began to talk more conversationally. She expressed sympathy for her husband, who was severely disabled with arthritis and who needed much care from her. When asked if that was a burden on her, she said that it was not. Further discussion revealed that her husband's care had caused her to stop her previously active social life and to see her friends less and less. Memory testing revealed normal memory. Her problem was reactive depression, and she responded very well to counseling and arrangements for intermittent care for her husband at home so that she could again see her friends.

The above case illustrates the common complaint of memory loss, the topic that was not readily brought up, and the initial denial that the husband's illness was a burden. The example also shows the value of some extra time spent to make a correct assessment and provide appropriate intervention.

Another example where thorough observations helped clarify the initial complaint is that of an apparently depressed elderly man. His family related that he had been losing interest in his usual activities and had been keeping more to himself. His clothing was somewhat unkempt and he sat with a slumped posture. His speech was slow and he had a short attention span. A neurological examination revealed several abnormalities, including an unsteady gait and asymmetrical reflexes. Appropriate tests were performed and a chronic subdural hematoma, apparently due to a forgotten bump on the head, was found and neurosurgically removed. The collection of blood pressing on the brain and causing increased intracranial pressure caused the picture that looked very much like depression.

COMMON PHYSICAL SYMPTOMS AND THEIR SIGNIFICANCE

A number of common physical symptoms in the aged should be noted, since these may indicate conditions that are curable or correctable. Two of the most common areas of complaint are vision and hearing. Difficulty seeing nearby objects or printed material, presbyopia or farsightedness, is a very common condition and can be corrected by glasses. A progressive loss of vision regardless of distance signifies a more serious condition, but 2 of the more common pathological conditions, cataracts and glaucoma, are often correctable. Diabetes can also lead to loss of vision caused by retinal disease, but the first 2 are more common.

Impaired hearing presents a major problem and early detection may well prevent future hardship. Correct diagnosis, treatment if necessary, and properly selected hearing aids are essential to maintain function. Decreased hearing, of course, impairs communication, and this has many ramifications. Social interaction with family and friends is more difficult and community activities can be limited and less rewarding. Shopping can become troublesome and driving less safe. In the family situation, paranoid ideation can develop, with the older individual thinking that the conversations that he can't hear are about him. It is also more difficult for family members to relate readily to their hearing-impaired older relative. Thus early detection and corrective action can prevent the development of severe problems for both the older person and his family.

Constipation is also a frequently mentioned symptom. Constipation can have either a physical or emotional cause. Depression is the primary emotional correlate but, as in some earlier examples, one should not jump to a conclusion without consideration of alternative causes, and should seek consultation or make a referral when indicated. There are many physiological causes of constipation, the most easily corrected of which is inactivity. A diet lacking sufficient fiber (roughage) can also cause constipation and can be corrected by appropriate nutritional supplement. Disease entities such as hypothyroid disease and certain gastrointestinal diseases can also cause constipation. A person who has chronically taken laxatives and then stops them may develop constipation due to a dependency that has been developed. Extremely close monitoring of bowel function for the older person who is immobilized is critical, since fecal impaction can develop if the problem is not attended to.

Pain is one of the most frequent complaints of all ages and a common cause of medical office visits. Headache, abdominal pain, back pain, and pain in the lower extremities are the usual locations. It is possible for a complaint of pain to be a means of getting attention, such as in a situation where it is not acceptable or appropriate to complain about loneliness, but the professional should not overlook the possibility that there can be an underlying disease process present. It is important to remember that even chronic complainers get sick from time to time. Any person with any acute or severe pain should have the benefit of medical evaluation.

There are a number of symptoms that might be grouped under the topic of well-being or lack of well-being. Loss of appetite, fatigue, and insomnia fall in this category. Loss of appetite or anorexia is one of the cardinal signs of depression but, as with other symptoms that can have an emotional etiology, physical causes should not be ruled out without reason. From the organic point of view, difficulty swallowing may be the basis of the problem. Persons who have had several strokes or extensive cerebrovascular disease are particularly prone to swallowing difficulty (dysphagia). Some older individuals develop an impairment of taste and/or smell and this can lead to decreased appetite. One must also consider the availability of palatable and nutritious foods, the individual's preferences, and ethnic or national background. Poor dental health or improperly fitting dentures can also decrease appetite. Finally, certain drugs in excess, such as digitalis or tranquilizers, can cause appetite loss.

Fatigue may be of either emotional or physiological cause, or both. Just prior to the obvious onset of an illness, during its process, and following its conclusion, fatigue is a common symptom in both the young and the elderly. In the elderly, however, the symptom of fatigue may be more pronounced and prolonged. Physical exertion of a degree and duration to which the individual is not accustomed can also cause fatigue. A similar feeling can result from the overuse of tranquilizers, or from excessive use of hypnotics to sleep. The primary emotional cause of fatigue is depression, and reversal of the depression through counseling or medications may resolve the fatigue.

Older individuals not uncommonly complain of the inability to sleep, or insomnia. There are many possible causes, some of the most common being behavioral. For one thing, older persons generally need less sleep than the young, but they may have limited activities and interests and boredom can ensue. If the older person tends to nap during the day, there will likely be difficulty sleeping at night. Pain, minor illnesses, and other discomforts can also interfere with sleep, as can anxiety or fear. The injudicious use of hypnotics, tranquilizers, caffeine, and alcohol can also do much to disturb sleep pattern. Insomnia and its treatment are discussed in Chapter 9.

There are numerous other physical symptoms, a more complete listing of which can be found in textbooks on geriatrics (e.g., Brocklehust 1973; Rossman 1971). Two additional ones that will be covered here are losses of consciousness and difficulty breathing. Fainting, or syncopy, can be caused by irregular heart rate, slowed heart rate, or reflex lowering of blood pressure, such as after straining. Cerebrovascular insufficiency to the brainstem can also result in loss of consciousness. There are also less common causes such as convulsions and low blood sugar. A common warning sign prior to fainting is a sensation of lightheadedness or the spinning-around sensation of vertigo.

Like fainting, shortness of breath or dyspnea can have a number of different causes. Chronic lung disease such as emphysema can cause marked and progressive breathing difficulty; in individuals so affected, an acute infection can cause marked decompensation of breathing. Cigarette smoking can also worsen the symptoms and hasten the disease process. Congestive heart failure causes difficulty breathing, especially in the lying-down position, as well as swelling (edema) of the ankles. Anemia can cause rapid and sometimes difficult breathing because of the decrease in the blood's oxygen-carring capacity due to the low hemoglobin. Obesity can also bring on dyspnea due to the pressure of the large abdomen on the diaphragm, thereby reducing the ability of the lungs to expand.

Neurological Disorders

Neurological diseases also affect the elderly population. The most common of these is stroke. In considering the effects of any neurological disease there can be a logical progression in assessing patients. One should first consider the mental status of the individual, including state of consciousness, orientation, degree of cooperation, and memory function.

Communication abilities are evaluated with respect to one's capacity both to perceive and understand information through auditory, visual, and sometimes tactile senses, and to express information by speech, writing, or drawing and gestures. The next area to assess is that of the cranial nerves, which includes all of the functions about the face and neck. This is followed by consideration of the motor abilities of gait, posture, muscle tone, strength, and coordination. The sensory system evaluation includes the perception of sharp versus dull touch and proprioception, or the sensation of position in space. There are many other functions of the sensory system; these will not be detailed here, but can be found in the nervous system section of textbooks for many different health care fields. In a neurological examination these are followed by an assessment of the reflexes, which are important to diagnosis but are not usually pertinent with respect to functional capacity.

Stroke provides an example of a disorder where many aspects of nervous system function are involved. Especially in the case of an individual who has had multiple strokes, the mental status may be impaired, sometimes with some degree of disorientation and/or memory loss. Opposite the side of brain damage, there may be a loss of vision to half of each visual field (homonomous hemianopia), which renders the individual unable to see people or objects to that side. The lower portion of the face opposite the brain damage is often weak or paralyzed, sometimes causing a drooling of saliva on that side. In a person who has a stroke involving the dominant (usually left) side of the brain with a right-sided paralysis, there is frequently disordered communication in the form of aphasia. With involvement of the nondominant side (usually right) of the brain and left-sided paralysis, there is not uncommonly a denial of the paralysis and lack of awareness of the left side of the body. The paralysis following stroke often affects both the upper and lower extremities, but with the upper usually more involved than the lower.

Gait is characterized by a flexed position of the involved upper extremity and a straightening of the lower extremity, with increased muscular tone causing a circular motion on bringing that extremity forward in gait and perhaps necessitating the use of equipment such as a cane and sometimes a short leg brace. Sensation may be impaired in the involved extremities, further impairing function and necessitating additional retraining. Reflexes are also usually abnormal but, as mentioned, generally do not cause additional dysfunction; however, exceptions do exist. The example of stroke will be used again since it is a relatively common disorder of elderly people and it exemplifies the problems of losses of function in mental status, communication, and in both motor and sensory capacities. Stroke will also supply a model for describing the rehabilitation process, which can then be applied to many different disabilities that are less pervasive in nature.

Assessing Functional Status for Independent Living

For the functional areas, especially mobility and self-care, assessments can be quantified by the amount of assistance from another person that is necessary to accomplish the activity. *Independent* means that the person needs no physical, verbal, or visual assistance. *Supervised* means that the individual needs only verbal or visual assistance for functioning, and *stand-by assistance* means that he also occasionally needs a small degree of physical assistance. *Minimal assistance* indicates that the person usually needs a small amount of physical assistance but can initiate and follow through most of the activity with this amount of assistance. *Moderate assistance* signifies that the person needs assistance throughout the activity but usually can initiate or carry out part of the activity. *Maximal assistance* means that the individual attempts to help but is unable to initiate or carry out significant parts of the task. The lowest level is where there is no function, total care is needed for that activity, and the individual can be described as being *dependent* in that task.

The above terms are not absolutely defined, but they are descriptive and do give an indication of function that can be applied to decisions regarding independent living. The assessment is not only pertinent to the level of function of the involved person but to the ability of the family member or members who might be rendering care. Although, for simplicity and clarity, much of the emphasis in describing function is in the description of motor tasks, it must be remembered that sensory function is extremely important in functional capacity and that certain types of loss of sensation can disable a person with moderately good strength. In this section the functions will be discussed, and subsequently the restoration of impaired functions through the disciplines of rehabilitation will be covered.

First, a person's basic functions and needs must be considered. The presence or absence of independent bowel and bladder management can mean the difference between independent or semi-independent living and institutionalization. Many families, already stressed by illness or disabilities of an older family member but still able to care for him, are no longer able to do so when he is incontinent of bowel or bladder. Incontinence can be due to disease of the genitourinary or gastrointestinal systems, or it can be due to nervous system disease. Some people with chronic brain syndromes or with multiple strokes lose control of their bladders and occasionally of bowel. Especially when the change has been acute, it is sometimes possible to use retraining techniques.

Eating and feeding are, of course, critical factors. If swallowing mechanisms are intact, it is easier to assist with eating than to supply help with bowel and bladder dysfunction. Eating skills can be rated by the system described above, such as maximal, moderate, minimal, or other grade of assistance needed. Thus a person who needs minimal assistance with feeding may only need selected foods that are easier to eat, cutting of meat, and perhaps a few other simple forms of assistance that could be supplied by an elderly spouse without more than a small amount of training or instruction. Feeding is also a part of self-care but is noted here because of its intimate relationship to the basic function of swallowing.

Skin management is another basic function and one of great importance. Skin cleanliness and especially avoidance of pressure areas is imperative. Bed sores, or decubitus ulcers, are a severe complication for a person with impaired mobility and may result in institutionalization for treatment. Although any immobilized individual may develop this complication, the elderly are at greater risk. Diabetics also need more attentive skin care since ulcerations can occur in the skin of the legs or feet.

Other factors related to the ability to live independently are the existence of pain and the necessity of medication for pain or illness. Pain can significantly limit function, especially for activities that aggravate the pain, but also in a general fashion when the pain is severe. Continued and unremitting pain can also lead to anxiety and depression.

A disease requiring injectable medications may make a significant difference in independent living. Diabetics usually inject their own insulin, but if an impairment such as weakness, paralysis, or impaired cognitive function make this impossible, there is a problem unless a family member can help. The necessity of injectable pain medication and sometimes of injectable antibiotics may require, at least temporarily, institutionalization.

Mobility is another major issue to be assessed in evaluating an older person's ability to function, and factors range from bed mobility to community activities. Mobility is best understood by dividing it into component functions. The lowest level is bed mobility, that is, the ability to turn side to side and to turn over in bed, to be able to sit up in bed, and to get the legs off the side of the bed. A person may be independent in these actions, may require varying degrees of assistance, or may be completely dependent on others. The next step in mobility that needs to be evaluated is transfers, that is, the ability to get up, down, or move from one sitting surface to another. After a person has his legs off the side of the bed and is sitting steadily, there are several alternatives. He can rise in preparation for walking, transfer to a wheelchair, or transfer to a bedside chair or commode. Transfers can be made with or without equipment. Common aids are straight cane, quadraped cane, and pick-up walker. Transfers also may require varying amounts of assistance from another person. It is thus possible, by observing transfers, to grade the degree of function present. This in turn can be used to assess what the individual may need in order to live independently. Some of the important types of transfer to consider are those to and from bed, toilet, bath, shower, and car. A number of different disorders that can affect the elderly can impair transfers, including arthritis, stroke, and peripheral nerve and vascular disease and their complications.

For those individuals confined to a wheelchair or who need a wheelchair for part of their mobility function, special problems are involved. First there is the matter of training to use the chair to the best advantage and maximum safety. For independence with a wheelchair, an individual must be able to transfer into and out of it, to manipulate its features, such as brakes, and to be able to propel it. Various dysfunctions of strength or coordination could impair mobility, but there are many for which adequate compensation can be achieved through training and properly designed equipment. The next matter to be attended to with regard to maximum independence in the home environment is that of architectural barriers. Doorways must be wide enough to allow access and areas where turns are necessary must be broad enough. Stairs provide a problem; ramps are sometimes a solution for small flights of stairs. The person dependent on a wheelchair also must contend with a number of problems in the community, including lack of access to public transportation and architectural barriers in public buildings, restaurants, and theaters. Fortunately, in some areas the latter is a decreasing problem as modifications are made and new structures are built without barriers.

In assessing ambulation, the degree of assistance needed can give a good indication of function; the amount of equipment required gives an indication of degree of independence. Generally the less equipment needed, the more mobile an individual will be. The very bulk and weight of various pieces of equipment can limit what a person can do. The easiest ambulation is, of course, on level surfaces. Stairs and environmental surfaces such as ramps, curbs, grass, and thick carpets may present problems to an individual. Depending on a person's ability to negotiate such surfaces and to climb stairs, additional training, equipment, or modifications may be necessary to assure maximum function. We tend to take for granted our ability to walk from a hard surface to a pile carpet, but to the older person with weakness and impaired sensation this might be a formidable task, since balance and equilibrium reactions may not function normally in that situation. This is an example of the type of information that could be obtained from direct observation or from interview or conversation. The ability to ambulate at least short distances, such as from bed to bathroom and back, is another factor that can mean the difference between independent living and the need for ongoing assistance. Degree of endurance is also of great importance for mobility.

Another major factor to assess from the functional point of view is that of self-care abilities and the activities of daily living. Feeding ability can be reconsidered here since, in addition to its relationship to the basic functions of eating and swallowing, feeding is one of the primary elements of self-care. This function is assessed with respect to one's ability to manage the food on the plate, such as cutting, to get the food on a utensil, and to get it to and in the mouth.

Self-care skills and activities of daily living increase in task complexity. Grooming and hygiene skills are not only pertinent to independent living but, like feeding, are related to personal dignity. Grooming refers to such skills as combing one's hair, shaving, and trimming nails. Hygiene refers to washing one's face, brushing teeth, cleaning nails, and other tasks related to cleanliness and health.

Bathing requires the additional skills of getting in and out of the tub or shower safely as well as the skill of washing. Toileting, as bathing, requires special transfer techniques as well as safety precautions. It is also important that the individual be assessed for the need for adaptive equipment, such as a raised toilet seat or wall-grab bars for safety. Dressing is another self-care skill that requires many subskills. The donning of shirt, pants, socks, and shoes by a person with limited function or endurance can be a formidable task. Some older people have specific diseases or disorders that adversely affect such functions, and others have diffuse impairments caused by degenerative diseases and chronic illnesses.

One of the higher levels of activity of daily living is that of home management. This encompasses a broad spectrum of activities requiring many skills. Home management includes the making of one's bed, housecleaning, and kitchen activities, including the preparing of meals. Obviously, mobility skills are involved as well as cognitive and manipulative skills. The historical background will indicate just how important each of these elements is to an individual's independent living. There is a significant difference between the person living alone and one living with a spouse who can assist. After the degree of function and necessary help are assessed, alternative arrangements such as external help through home health agencies may contribute to more effective community living.

Communication skills must also be evaluated from various points of view. The spectrum ranges from the expressing of basic needs to intellectual or social conversation, and from the ability to use a telephone in an emergency to communicating while shopping and using public transportation. The scope of communication skills includes basic functions and needs, family living, socialization, and community living. As mentioned earlier, most communication occurs through the auditory, visual, and sometimes tactile senses, and through the abilities to speak, write and draw, and gesture. Communication may be impaired by diseases affecting hearing, vision, or tactile sensation, or affecting the structure or function of speech or writing. Abilities may also be affected by disorders of the central nervous system, such as occur with stroke, that can impair the processes of understanding and expressing information. An individual who has had a stroke affecting the dominant cerebral hemisphere (usually left) often acquires some degree of aphasia.

TABLE 7.1. **Factors involved in qualitative and quantitative assessment of functional capacity with respect to independent living in the community**

Historical background, including physical and emotional status and belief system	Communication
	Emotional stability and adjustment
	Social adjustment and environment, including significant other, family, sexuality, etc.
Current health status and limitations	
Diet and nutrition	
Mental status	Recreation and leisure activities
Basic functions and needs	Transportation
Mobility	Financial and occupational status
Self-care	Housing and architectural barriers

Emotional stability, social adjustment, and other factors may have a significant direct or indirect effect on physical functional capacity. These will not be detailed in this chapter but, in actual practice, any separation of emotional and physical factors makes it difficult to obtain a total picture of the individual's function.

Three other dimensions that contribute to the ability of an individual to live independently or to the degree of dependence also should be considered. The first is the type and availability of transportation. Type of transportation is relevant to individuals who need equipment such as walkers and wheelchairs. Availability becomes an issue for carrying out many routine activities, such as shopping, doctors' appointments, socialization, and leisure activities. The second factor is adequate financial status. The third dimension is availability of housing and freedom from architectural barriers.

Evaluation of diet and nutrition should be included in an assessment and in some settings can be done by a clinical nutritionist or dietitian. Nutritional intervention can be performed during hospitalization and appropriate recommendations and referrals made for the time of discharge.

Table 7.1 outlines the factors involved in qualitative and quantitative assessment of functional capacity with respect to independent living in the community. Not all of the dimensions are absolutely necessary for survival, but the concept of independent living should include a significant element of quality of life and, as such, all of these areas should be considered. The factors are not in any order of importance and the impact of each may vary from person to person, depending on the circumstances. For instance, a high level of self-care skills would not be as critical for the individual with an able-bodied, supportive spouse as it would be for the person living alone. Transportation and financial status might be more important to the person on a special diet than to one on a regular diet.

The factors outlined in Table 7.1 can be used by the professional as a checklist of things to consider in a thorough assessment of function and potential. They form the nucleus for the development of an assessment procedure that is specially designed for a specific purpose. The list can also be used to evaluate the completeness of other assessment procedures. It should be remembered that various purposes may need more or less formalized assessment protocols. A professional at a senior activities center may find that informal observation of status and change in the participants suits the situation best. Information collected for research purposes, on the other hand, would have to be formalized and structured. A clinical record might include some elements from either end of the spectrum.

Stress and Aging

Although specific disease entities are described in detail in various textbooks, one of the significant health factors in aging has not yet achieved common inclusion: that of stress in aging. The topic of stress has become a major issue in health care and affects people of all ages. Although older people are often not subject to the same causes of stress as the younger population, such as competitive employment, they en-counter many additional stress-producing factors, especially in the area of loss. In order to be able to understand stress in aging and to assess its effects on the older individual, it is necessary to understand some basic concepts of stress and its physical and emotional consequences.

Much of our current knowledge of stress is derived from the work of Selye (1974) and of researchers stimulated by some of Selye's early find-ings. Basically, stress is a response to a change. The impact of particular stressful events depends both on their magnitude and on the individual's reaction. The same stimulus induces greater or lesser stress response in different individuals, depending on their reactivity to that stimulus. We all have in common certain physiological responses to stressful stimuli, and these share adaptive properties with the so-called "fight or flight" response. When a person or animal is confronted with a dangerous situation, the responses are adaptive and can be life saving. Unfortunately, we offer the same responses to many stimuli that are not truly life threatening. If these are very frequent, intense, or prolonged, they can produce physiological and anatomical harm. There also can be significant emotional consequences. Enjoyable and exciting situations have a similar effect of increasing arousal. Thus one's goal is stress management, rather than elimination of all arousing events.

An example of a life-threatening situation in which a stress response is beneficial is that of a person's stepping off a curb to cross the street only to notice that a car is coming toward him at a high speed and the driver does not see him. Certain factors come rapidly into play. The individual orients to the car coming toward him with marked focusing of attention. His muscles tense in preparation for some evasive action. Blood pressure rises, pulse rate quickens, and respiratory rate increases. These factors contribute to increased cerebral circulation and increased blood oxygenation, thus aiding brain and muscle function for evasive action. The hands and feet become cool and a tightness develops in the abdominal region as blood is shunted away from the periphery and bowel region toward increasing cerebral and muscular function. The cumulative result is that the individual is then able to assess the situation quickly, take evasive action, and avoid a tragedy. When the danger is past, the various physiological changes return to baseline levels and, usually, no significant harm has been done.

The stress responses are nonspecific and also may occur in other situations. Even positively looked-upon changes such as family get-togethers and marriages produce a stress response. An older person who has experienced loss of a loved one, difficulty maintaining housing and who is experiencing some loss of functional capabilities may have a rather prolonged stress response, including tightness of muscles producing aches and pains, elevation of blood pressure leading to hypertension, or other factors that cause gastrointestinal malfunction. Such disorders may be temporary or may lead to more serious consequences.

It is vital that the professional be aware of stress-producing events, or stressors, as they are sometimes called, in an individual's life. In older people such stressors are often related to either real or perceived losses. As noted in previous chapters, some of the more common losses include the death of family members or friends, loss of financial status, loss of social status, and loss of certain functional capacities. Even when a loss is only perceived and not real, such as the earlier example of the woman who had a complaint of memory loss, a stress response can occur.

It is as important for the professional to recognize stress and its effects as it is to recognize the existence of disease. Early recognition of stress-producing factors and stress responses can result in intervention that could prevent disease or dysfunction from occurring. Counseling, certain types of exercise, and relaxation training can be effective interventions. Many colleges, universities, hospitals, and community agencies are beginning to offer programs on stress management for professionals and for the public.

The relation of stress as a contributing factor to many commonly occurring diseases should also be noted. Perhaps the most important is that of hypertension, which is a major risk factor for stroke and coronary artery disease. Stress plays a role in arthritis and in various gastrointestinal disorders. Stress has also been linked to cancer and may play a significant role in the function of the immune system. Frequent emotional consequences of stress are depression, anxiety, anger, and fear.

Restoration of Function

Function can be disrupted by disease and injury, with the resultant dysfunction dependent on such things as rate of onset and severity. Even after acute medical treatment, a number of diseases and injuries can lead to permanent disabilities, such as stroke resulting in paralysis of one side of the body or the amputation of a limb due to peripheral vascular disease. Injuries that can cause permanent disabilities include those of the brain and spinal cord as well as traumatic amputation. Certain orthopedic problems such as hip fracture or total hip replacement may cause temporary disability. Other temporary disabilities may come as an aftereffect of severe illness or major surgery. The field of medical rehabilitation is designed to restore function to disabled individuals through a comprehensive, interdisciplinary approach. Specialized disciplines work as an interdisciplinary team in order to restore function. Although each has a specific area of function, the essence of the rehabilitation process is an integrated teamwork approach. Each team member performs an evaluation and begins specific treatment. The team then meets at regular intervals to compare their findings and discuss a coordinated approach to the problems identified. Some complex cases may need most or even all of the rehabilitation disciplines, while other cases may require only a few or possibly even 1 specified discipline.

In a comprehensive medical rehabilitation center, the medical evaluation and management and team leadership is assumed by the rehabilitation physician. Basic functions and needs, certain educational tasks, and general care are primarily in the province of rehabilitation nursing but, as with all disciplines, there is some overlap. Diet and nutrition are evaluated by a dietitian or clinical nutritionist and appropriate counseling is done. Mental status is evaluated in detail by a clinical psychologist in addition to the physician's assessment during the medical examination. Emotional stability and adjustment are also evaluated and treated by the psychologist. Mobility is generally in the province of physical therapy, as are the problems of improving functional strength and endurance. Self-care skills and activities of daily living are considered in occupational therapy. Communication skills are evaluated and treated by the speech pathologist. Social adjustment and family relationships are evaluated by the social worker and appropriate individual or conjoint counseling is done. Financial counseling may be included, as well as referrals to community agencies for services such as transportation. Recreation and leisure activities are attended to by the recreational therapist. Housing and architectural barriers often need to be assessed in different aspects by various members of the team, including occupational therapist and social worker.

The process of assessment can best be described through use of a compiled example. The case that follows illustrates an extensive need for a variety of services and also provides an outline of the approach for assessing function. Many individuals may need only 1 or 2 such services in order to regain independence.

At age 68, Mr. H., a retired small businessman, was active in community affairs and with his hobby of woodworking. He had high blood pressure that was well controlled on medication and had had diabetes for several years, which was controlled with insulin. Mr. H. was accustomed to being independent and in charge of things, and this was acceptable to his wife of 45 years. Mr. H. believed that any reduction of his independent status would be a sign of weakness. He was generally even tempered but would become angry when he was hindered from completing a task he had set out to do. He had never engaged in much physical exercise but was now taking a daily one-half mile walk around his block with Mrs. H.

Mrs. H. was active with her church group and had frequent visitors. She was in good health but had only moderate physical strength. She prepared well-balanced meals for both of them, including the special diet required for Mr. H. because of his diabetes and high blood pressure. They had 2 children, both of whom were married and living out of state, but who visited at holiday times.

One morning Mrs. H. entered her husband's workshop and found him sitting on a chair and unable to speak. The right side of his face drooped and he was unable to move his right arm or leg. He did not seem to see her when she approached him from his right but could see her when she moved to his left side. He made a few attempts to speak but was unsuccessful. Mrs. H. called their physician, who arranged for ambulance transportation to the hospital. Detailed examination and testing revealed that Mr. H. had sustained a stroke due to the occlusion of an artery supplying the left side of his brain. After receiving acute care including that necessary to prevent complications and reaching a stabilized condition, Mr. H. was transferred to a comprehensive medical rehabilitation center.

Mr. H.'s medical records were reviewed by the rehabilitation physician, he was examined, and his wife was informed of the results. She was also interviewed by a social worker who obtained further background information and answered questions about the facility. Mrs. H. found that she would be part of the rehabilitation process, that the staff would work closely with her, and that she would receive training necessary to help in her husband's care when he returned home. She would also receive counseling to aid her in coping skills and help her adapt to this change in their life situation. Mr. H. had a urinary catheter and had become constipated because of his illness and inactivity. These problems were attended to by the rehabilitation nursing staff, which also kept close watch on skin condition, both because of his impaired mobility and his diabetes. They monitored his blood pressure and regularly checked his urine for sugar. As Mr. H. progressed in the program, they taught him how to inject his insulin with his left hand and taught his wife how to draw up the proper amount in the syringe.

Mr. H. began to regain some communication ability, and his function was carefully evaluated by the speech pathologist, who aided him in improving general communication abilities. She informed Mrs. H. and the rehabilitation team members about how best to communicate with Mr. H. Speech therapy was also used to improve the volume and clarity of his speech.

As communication abilities improved, a psychologist evaluated Mr. H.'s mental status and cognitive skills and helped him to adapt to the frustrations of his disability and his feelings of a lack of being in control. The psychologist also helped Mr. H. direct his anger in a more productive manner rather than diffusely taking out frustrations on the staff or on his wife.

A dietitian assessed Mr. H.'s nutritional status, through both interview and laboratory reports for the record period. The diet he had been using at home was reevaluated according to current needs and his wife was counseled on how best to apply this diet after Mr. H. was discharged home.

The physical therapist gradually helped Mr. H. improve his bed mobility and transfers, and eventually he progressed to the point where he was ambulating, first with a broad-based 4-pointed cane and maximum assistance, and ultimately with a straight cane with his wife standing by. The occupational therapist worked on teaching Mr. H. to use his nondominant hand while he was also working to improve function in the weak right hand. He was taught to feed himself, to dress himself, and to perform the basic activities of daily living. He was also given exercises and training that would lead him back to being able to work on his woodworking hobby, at least to a limited degree.

The recreational therapist helped Mr. H. to reach some self-fulfillment during his leisure time. His leisure activities were geared to those he had previously enjoyed, adapted to his disability. Transportation and financial status were discussed with Mrs. H. and also with her husband and appropriate community agency referrals were made. An occupational therapist went out to the house to evaluate the existence of architectural barriers and to make recommendations for safety.

During this course of events, the rehabilitation team met weekly to discuss the problems that Mr. H. was experiencing, to compare ideas on solving these problems, and to plan the treatment approach for the forthcoming week. After about a month of this treatment Mr. H. was able to return home with his wife at a semi-independent level, with plans to return for out-patient treatment in order further to increase his strength, mobility, self-care, and communication skills.

The rehabilitation process would be similar in a modified form with a patient who had an amputation, a spinal cord injury, or severe arthritis. It can be seen how almost any physical disability, with its concomitant emotional and social factors, can be approached by this general process. The functions needed for independent living by the severe arthritic, the stroke patient, or the postcancer surgery patient are essentially the same. The approaches may be significantly different to restore various functions but, as indicated in the example, there are a number of disciplines of specially trained individuals who work to restore functional capacity in the various areas.

Structured Assessment Measures

The emphasis in this chapter has been on making detailed observations of patients' symptoms and functioning. Over the past 15 years there have been developed a number of different methods of physical assessment that systematically measure many of the areas of functioning described above. While differing from one another in purpose and in amount of detail, these various measures generally have in common elements of mobility and self-care. Some add such categories as communication, psychological function, social interactions, health status, and social adjustment. Structured measures are often useful to someone beginning in the field because they provide a comprehensive list of areas that should be explored. They are also effective research measures for documenting changes in abilities over time.

One of the most widely used methods is an index of activities of daily living (Katz et al. 1963), which was designed to study the results of treatment and prognosis in chronically ill and elderly persons. The activities of daily living that are considered are bathing, toileting, transfer (such as in and out of bed or chair), continence, and feeding. Another method (Gauger et al. 1964) is based on levels of subsistence. The method is designed to evaluate elderly persons by their abilities and requirements for care, including activities of daily living, medical factors, and social factors. One of the more popular measures has been the Barthel Index (Mahoney and Barthel 1965). This method is designed to evaluate the ability of patients with neuromuscular or musculoskeletal disorders to care for themselves. The assessment is based on the amount of time and amount of physical assistance needed to carry out various tasks. The tasks are in the areas of mobility and self-care and are generally quite basic in nature. The person who scores 100, which is maximum, on the Index is described as being "continent, feeds himself, dresses himself, gets up out of bed and chairs, bathes himself, walks at least a block, and can ascend and descend stairs" (p. 62). This does not mean that he is able to live alone; he may not be able to cook, keep house, and meet the public, but he manages without attendant care.

Lawton (1971) has proposed assessment procedures to aid in diagnosis and selection of proper treatment for elderly people. This assessment is also based on function and is largely grounded in physical health and self-care or activities of daily living function, but significant attention is also paid to social behavior and to the important areas of attitude, morale, and life satisfaction. Another method (Gurel, Linn, and Linn 1972) was designed to evaluate institutionalized geriatric patients and is based on behaviors relevant to chronically ill adults. Both physical and mental factors are evaluated and a physical and mental impairment-of-function evaluation (PAMIE) scale is described. A detailed questionnaire (Pfeiffer 1975b), the OARS multidimensional functional assessment questionnaire, was developed to assist in designing appropriate service programs for individuals and communities. In addition to self-care assessment, the method includes assessment of mental health and social and economic problems. The close interrelationship among physical, mental, and social function is emphasized by Linn (1976), and self-assessment of health is also discussed. The interrelationship between mental and physical illness is also emphasized by Anderson (1976) as necessary for accurate diagnosis of the elderly. He addresses the problems of clinical assessment and diagnosis in aging and also considers the problem of multiple pathology.

Various assessment methodologies can be used to measure outcomes and quality of care. One of the more recent methods (Granger and Greer 1976) partially utilizes a refinement of the Barthel Index. Additional indices of function were developed to assess medical rehabilitation outcomes. The quality of stroke rehabilitation (Anderson 1978) has been investigated by assessing patient outcomes. Program evaluation of medical rehabilitation has become an important issue with regard to the documenting of effectiveness. Some of the previously mentioned assessment procedures could be applied to this need, and some (Carey and Posavac 1978) were designed for that specific purpose. Another method (Breckenridge 1978), which emphasizes the functional status, has been computerized so that participating facilities can compare results.

The fields of medical rehabilitation and gerontology have many similarities and face many common problems. Both fields are concerned with preventing dysfunction, maintaining function, and restoring losses of function in their clients or patients. Both fields are concerned with the whole individual rather than fragmenting him or her into one or several component parts. Both fields also share a common goal of maintaining or restoring their clients or patients to as maximum a degree of independence as possible. In addition, both fields have a need to assess function in order to deliver service appropriately and to evaluate the results of that service.

Summary

Approaches to physical assessment for nonmedical personnel have been presented. Because of the interaction of physical and behavioral disorders in later life, some systematic observations about health status usually are warranted. Emphasis has been placed on making careful observations of symptoms and functioning of patients, rather than on the use of medical terminology. These observations can be used in deciding when to make referrals for medical treatment or rehabilitation. The value of a functional approach to assessment also lies in identifying the abilities of the person and pinpointing problems related to independent living, so that appropriate interventions can be made. Comprehensive assessments are a useful way of focusing on the cycle of disease, dysfunction, and restoration of abilities that many older persons experience. A number of structured measures of physical assessment are available, which can serve as guides in patient evaluations or as research tools.

CHAPTER 8

Depression

MRS. V. IS A 72-YEAR-OLD WOMAN who came to a counseling center because she wanted help to arrange for her funeral. She had surgery 1 year ago for a bowel obstruction, but until recently her doctor had not informed her that it was malignant and that her condition was terminal. She is upset over being treated that way. She is now too weak from chemotherapy to continue working, and also feels abandoned by friends who do not call her. Her other major concern is her daughter, from whom she has been estranged for several years. She wonders what her life has meant.

Mrs. A. is a 64-year-old woman who reports being depressed for the past 2 years since she lost her job. She describes herself as a sinner, but could explain only vaguely how she had sinned. She feels she is bad because she no longer cleans her apartment well, no longer goes to church daily (she does go on Sunday), and is a burden to her husband. She says she does not sleep at all and has no appetite or taste. She also complained of memory problems, but testing indicated no impairment. She had similar depressive episodes in the past, the last one being 14 years ago, when she was treated with electroconvulsive therapy (ECT).

Mr. Y, a 73-year-old man, was severely depressed over his wife's condition. He had been caring for her at home for the last 4 years until recently, when it became too difficult and he had to place her in a nursing home. He is upset, however, over the care she is receiving and says they treat people like animals there. He visits her every day, spending the whole day. He is also fearful that her children (from a previous marriage) will move her to a nursing home close to where they live in a town several hundred miles away. He was downcast and tearful throughout the interview.

While the life circumstances of these persons vary considerably from one to another, the outcome for each has been similar: feelings of hopelessness, despair, and that nothing in their lives makes sense or matters anymore. Depression is, in fact, the most prevalent psychiatric disorder of the later years. This is not surprising, given the increasing likelihood that persons will experience losses and other stresses as they age. Physiological changes, such as the decreased responsiveness to stress, may also make older persons more vulnerable to recurrent feelings of depression. Yet, at the same time, the rate of recovery from depression is high, both when active treatment is given, and because even severe depressive episodes appear to run their course over time.

In this chapter the incidence and prevalence of depression in later life will be reviewed, and various theories of the etiology and course of depressive disorders will be presented. These theories include biochemical approaches, the relation of depression to life changes, and behavioral and cognitive theories of depression. There have been recent advances in understanding and treating depression with persons under age 60. Investigations of depression in the aged, in contrast, have been limited in scope and carried out with little theoretical orientation. There is some risk in applying models of depression developed with younger persons to the problems of the elderly, because it is not at all certain whether depression in old age represents phenomena similar to or different from affective disorders earlier in life. On the other hand, applying these new developments in the theory and treatment of depression to elderly persons extends the range and sophistication of interventions available to the practitioner, and also serves to highlight critical issues in the treatment of aged persons that need to be explored further.

The Depressive Disorders: Basic Characteristics

The affective disorders are first and foremost disturbances of mood. In addition to depressed mood, other characteristics are often found in varying degrees in clinical cases. In summarizing the literature on depression, Lewinsohn, Biglan, and Zeiss (1976) propose 5 classes of symptoms as important in the diagnosis of a depressive disorder. These include: dysphoria (feelings of sadness, apathy, and boredom); behavioral deficits, such as minimal social participation and decreased activities; behavioral excesses, especially complaints about one's life situation, guilt feelings, or doubts about one's own abilities; somatic symptoms, such as headaches, sleep problems, and poor appetite; and what are termed "cognitive" manifestations, that is, persistently low feelings of self-esteem and sense of failure, self-blame, and hopelessness. These categories of symptoms that characterize depression are shown in Table 8.1.

Most practitioners and researchers would agree that these various

TABLE 8.1. Symptoms of depression

DYSPHORIA	BEHAVIORAL DEFICITS	BEHAVIORAL EXCESSES	SOMATIC SYMPTOMS	"COGNITIVE" MANIFESTATIONS
Feelings dominated by sadness and blueness. Loss of gratification—"I no longer enjoy the things I used to." Professes to have little or no feeling. Feels constantly fatigued—"Everything is an effort." Loss of interest in food, drink, sex, etc. Feeling of apathy and boredom.	Minimal social participation—"I do not like being with people." Sits alone quietly, stays in bed much of time, does not communicate with others, does not enter into activities with others. Inability to do ordinary work. Decreased sexual activity. Psychomotor retardation. Speech slow, volume of speech decreased, monotone speech, whispering. Gait and general behavior retarded. Does not attend to grooming; neglect of personal appearance. Lack of mirth response.	Complaints about: material problems—money, job, housing; material loss—money, property; the demands of others; noise; memory, inability to concentrate, confusion; lack of affection from others—"No one cares about me"; being lonely. Expresses feelings of guilt and concern about: making up wrongs to others; suffering caused to others; not assuming responsibilities; welfare of family and friends; indecisiveness—"I can't make up my mind anymore"; crying, weepy, screaming; suicidal behavior—"I wish I were dead"; "I want to kill myself."	Headaches. Sleep disturbances: Restless sleep, waking during night, complete wakefulness, early morning awakening. Fatigue—"I get tired for no reason." Gastrointestinal—indigestion, constipation, weight loss. Dizzy spells. Loss of libido. Tachycardia. Chest sensations. Generalized pain. Urinary disturbances.	Low self-evaluation: Feelings of failure, inadequacy, helplessness, and powerlessness. Negative expectation—"Things will always be bad for me." Self-blame and self-criticism—"People would despise me if they knew me."

Source: P. M. Lewinsohn, A. Biglan, and A. M. Zeiss, "Behavioral Treatment of Depression." In P. O. Davidson, ed., *The Behavioral Management of Anxiety, Depression and Pain* (New York: Brunner/Mazel, 1976). Reprinted by permission.

symptoms are present to some extent in cases of depression. There are no widely accepted criteria, however, for determining the necessary number and severity of these symptoms to constitute a depressive disorder, or even if depression can be qualitatively distinguished from normal mood states. The term "depression" is actually used in 2 different ways: as a construct to indicate an underlying pathology, and to describe specific behavioral events, such as crying, inactivity, or reports of feeling unhappy, worthless, or dejected (Lewinsohn, Biglan, and Zeiss 1976). According to Lewinsohn and his associates, the construct "depression" implies a consistent set of internal events and behaviors, but such consistency in descriptions of depression is lacking. There is no reliability in the diagnosis of depression, and no single, homogeneous set of symptoms that characterize it. It is also not clear how the construct "depression" differs from normal mood swings and grief following losses, all of which are often characterized by similar features of dysphoria and somatic symptoms such as poor appetite and insomnia (Klerman 1971; Lewinsohn, Biglan, and Zeiss 1976). It remains to be determined if there is some boundary between normal and abnormal mood states, that is, whether these represent similar or qualitatively different phenomena.

The descriptive nosology of depression includes three pairs of terms: unipolar-bipolar, reactive-endogenous, and neurotic-psychotic. Of these concepts, only the first distinction has a clearly documented empirical basis. Bipolar disorders involve distinct manic and depressed states. The manic phase lasts at least 1 or 2 weeks and is characterized by hyperactivity, push of speech, grandiose delusions, decreased sleep, flight of ideas, and distractibility. The depressed state in bipolar disorders persists for a minimum of 2 weeks and is marked by feelings of sadness, diminished activity, loss of interest in activities, somatic symptoms (loss of appetite, insomnia, loss of energy), and sometimes suicidal ideation. The differentiation of bipolar from unipolar disorders is important since the former have been found to be responsive to a large extent to treatment with lithium carbonate (Prange 1975; Fieve and Dunner 1975), including cases involving the aged (Foster, Gershell, and Goldfarb 1977).

The other descriptive terms, neurotic-psychotic and reactive-endogenous, refer to unipolar disorders and are less well defined. The concepts of endogenous and psychotic depression overlap to some extent, indicating a more severe disturbance than neurotic or reactive depressions (Paykel 1975). Both psychotic and endogenous depressions are also considered as more likely to have biological components, especially as evidence accumulates of the effectiveness of somatic therapies with these more severe states (Klerman 1971). In contrast, reactive and neurotic depressions are viewed as related to stresses and/or to characteristic personality styles or habits. There are differences, however, between the concepts of endogenous and psychotic. "Psychotic" refers to the presence of delusions or other marked distortions of reality and, from a psychoanalytic perspective, the degree of ego regression. "Endogenous" need not include a thought disorder. It is, instead, considered to be characterized by four features: (1) severe depressive affect and somatic symptoms; (2) lack of a recent precipitating event; (3) a stable, nonneurotic, or obsessive premorbid personality; and (4) an autonomous quality where the depression runs its course without apparent relation to the environment (Klerman 1971). Factor analytic and cluster analysis studies have yielded groupings that resemble the construct of endogenous, or in one case contain features of both endogenous and psychotic, depression. Patients with these characteristics are also somewhat more likely to benefit from antidepressant drugs or ECT, while persons classified as "reactive" improve as fast without medication as when treated with it (Prange 1975; Klerman 1971).

It is not clear at this time how many other clusters or groupings there are, or if endogenous depressions differ qualitatively or only in degree from these other clusters (Klerman 1971). The classification of endogenous depression has also varied from one study to another, with relatively low reliability in making the diagnosis and limited predictive value for recovery. Thus these terms should be viewed as hypothetical constructs rather than categories of illness. There is a need for further clarification of these concepts.

LATE LIFE DEPRESSIONS

A related issue is whether depressions in later life represent the same or different phenomena from those in earlier years. There are unfortunately only a few studies that compare depressive symptomatology in the adult years and old age. Older depressed patients have been clinically described as manifesting an atypical pattern, with apathy, listlessness, and a quiet attitude of self-deprecation emphasized more than in the young (Epstein 1976). Excessive feelings of guilt or repressed anger are less frequently observed, although there has been some controversy on that point. Pfeiffer and Busse (1973) find that guilt is not often present in depression, particularly in the aged. In contrast, Butler and Lewis (1977) emphasize that guilt may be an important motivating factor at any point in the life cycle, including among older persons, who may seek forgiveness for past actions. Somatic complaints, such as insomnia, loss of appetite, other gastrointestinal problems, and headaches, also tend to be emphasized more by older depressed patients when compared with younger patient samples (Gurland 1976; Zung 1967), while feelings of dysphoria or sadness are reported less (Zung 1967). Another prominent somatic complaint is that of recent memory loss, which has not, however, been found to be related to actual cognitive impairment (Kahn et al. 1975). Among nonpatient samples of the aged there are similar patterns of symptoms. Older subjects report somatic complaints more often than the young, but indicate feelings of depression less frequently (Zung and Green 1972; Blumenthal 1975).

Since somatic illnesses increase with age, it is not clear if somatic symptoms in either clinical or nonclinical samples represent correlates of depression or of actual health problems. Instances of masked depression or depressive equivalents have also been reported, where the principal manifestations of an affective disturbance are in somatic or other complaints, but the person denies depressive feelings (Beck 1967). Both actual and masked depressions can also occur in the context of physical illnesses (Epstein 1976). Thus, distinguishing between somatic concerns that are related to physical illnesses and those indicating an affective disorder is a complicated task. Behavioral observations of older patients may help make this differentiation. Signs of apathy, listlessness, or a sad demeanor, for example, suggest that somatic complaints may be related to unexpressed feelings of depression. This distinction is critical, since somatic symptoms that are signs of depression are likely to respond to treatment for depression, even in persons having concomitant physical illnesses (Epstein 1976). These limited studies, then, suggest that depression does take somewhat different patterns in the aged than in younger persons.

Comparisons of young and old persons with depressive disorders usually have not taken into account another important factor: whether the symptoms of persons whose disorders are manifested for the first time in late life differ from those of individuals who have had repeated depressive episodes beginning in early or middle adulthood. While it is generally expected that persons with clinically significant degrees of depression are likely to have repeated episodes, there have been few attempts to clarify how those episodes might vary over time in terms of precipitants, symptoms, or even response to treatment. Based on clinical observations, it can be suggested that persons with repeated depressive episodes are likely to respond again to those treatments that worked best in the past. Thus one important distinction between an old person with the first onset of depression and one who had earlier episodes is that for the latter a careful history should suggest an appropriate treatment plan, whether medications, ECT, psychotherapy, or some combination of these interventions.

Another issue is how a patient's age at first onset of a significant depressive episode affects treatment. It is widely considered that the younger a person with a psychopathologic disorder, the greater the probability of success in treatment. There is, however, some empirical evidence to suggest that is not the case for elderly depressives. Roth (1955), for example, found no correlation between patient's age and recovery from depression. Post (1962) has similarly reported recovery levels that appear comparable to younger age groups. In one study older depressed inpatients were divided into those with early onset and persons with onset of depressive symptoms after age 60 (Kay, Roth, and Hopkins 1955). The 2 groups did not differ in their performance on intellectual tests or in presenting symptoms. They did vary, however, in prognosis. Those with later onset had, overall, a better recovery, and were significantly less likely to be readmitted to the hospital in the 20-month follow-up period. There is clearly a need, however, for more investigations comparing the onset, course, and treatment of depressive disorders in the aged and young, in order to determine the implications of such factors as age at first onset, current age, differences in symptoms between young and old, and history of prior treatment.

INCIDENCE AND PREVALENCE OF DEPRESSION

Because of the lack of clear criteria for what constitutes depression in general, and depression in old age in particular, estimating the actual incidence and prevalence of depressive disorders in the later years is a formidable task. Three criteria have been used: hospital admissions, psychiatric diagnosis of community samples, and comparisons of symptoms between young and old in community and hospitalized samples. Each of these indicators has some limitations.

Using psychiatric admissions may underestimate the incidence and prevalence of depressive disorders in old age. Admission rates are affected by the judgment of professionals that hospitalization is warranted and likely to be of benefit. There is some evidence of reluctance to admit both very young (under 21) and old (over 65) persons to inpatient services (Gurland 1976). Since the passing of Medicare this tendency has increased, with older psychiatric patients more likely to be placed in nursing homes than in mental hospitals (Epstein and Simon 1968; Kramer, Taube, and Redick 1973).

Psychiatric diagnoses that are made on community samples may also underrepresent the extent of depression in old age. As the patient's age influences the decision to hospitalize, it also affects how a diagnosis is reached. In a cross-national survey of mental disorders, it has been found that American psychiatrists diagnose depression less frequently than the British. Among younger patients the Americans were more likely to make a diagnosis of schizophrenia, while for those over age 60, organic brain syndrome was diagnosed more frequently (Copeland et al. 1974). Depression may, in fact, be viewed by many physicians and mental health professionals as a normal concomitant of aging. Thus an older person manifesting symptoms that would be treated in the young may not be identified as requiring treatment (Gurland 1973).

Ratings of symptoms in undiagnosed community samples may also be somewhat misleading for 2 reasons. First, it is not clear how the transient mood states that are likely to be reported on various symptom checklists are related to the more severe and persistent affective disorders (Gurland 1976). Second, as noted earlier, there is an increased prevalence of somatic symptoms in the old that may reflect health problems in some persons, and not depression.

Because of these difficulties in estimating the actual incidence and prevalence of affective disorders, there is some variation in figures, depending on where and how the studies have been conducted. In general, however, the rates of depression reported in the aged are high, whatever the criteria employed, though perhaps not as high as in earlier periods of life. In considering hospital admissions, the diagnosis of depression is made more frequently in younger persons. A diagnosis of neurotic depression is most often made for patients under 45; psychotic depression is more frequently diagnosed in persons aged 45 to 64 at time of admission (Gurland 1976). Thus, compared with younger age groups, older persons (over 65) are diagnosed as depressed less frequently. On the other hand, when considering only geriatric admissions (persons over the age of 60 or 65), depression is the most frequent diagnosis, with estimates ranging between 21 and 54 percent of all geriatric admissions (Peak 1973; Vickers 1976). When looking only at first admissions to hospital, depression is the most commonly made diagnosis of elderly patients (Pfeiffer and Busse 1973). Based on a comprehensive screening of patients to an inpatient unit in Britain, Roth (1955) reported that over half of all admissions past the age of 60 had a diagnosis of affective psychosis (including manic depression), with 66 percent of these cases being first admissions. The proportion of cases diagnosed as affective was somewhat lower if only patients over 70 were considered. In hospitalized samples, then, admissions for affective disorders are more frequent among persons under 60, but among geriatric admissions, depression is the most common diagnosis.

Surveys of nonpatient populations of older persons also indicate findings of a high prevalence of depressive symptoms. When community samples are judged by trained raters, the diagnosis of depressive disorders is made more often in persons under the age of 60, but it is estimated that between 2 and 10 percent of the elderly are sufficiently depressed to warrant a clinical diagnosis (Gurland 1976). When considering the prevalence of depressive symptoms, including somatic complaints, persons over 65 have been found to manifest greater amounts than younger individuals (Gurland 1976). Depression is, in fact, the most common complaint among otherwise healthy community residents, with respondents indicating they have more frequent and more disruptive episodes than earlier in life (Perlin and Butler 1963; Busse 1970). The prevalence of depressive symptoms is even higher in persons with chronic health problems. Among cardiac patients, for example, approximately 50 percent manifested significant degrees of depressive symptoms (Dovenmuehle and Verwoerdt 1962). Depression can also be a significant problem in persons with senile dementia (Kahn et al. 1975).

Depression and depressive symptoms, then, represent the most prevalent psychiatric disorder in old age. Comparisons with younger age groups suggest that the diagnosis of depression is more likely to be made for persons before 60 or 65, but that levels of symptoms reported by the old are high.

These estimates of prevalence must be viewed as tentative, until clearer criteria for assessing depressive symptoms and disorders are developed. Of particular importance for the elderly is clarification of the relation of transitory depressed states, which may increase with age, to the depressive disorders. For the practitioner, this means developing criteria to distinguish ephemeral conditions that improve rapidly from more persistent disorders that warrant intervention.

Theories of Depression *# How Dep. affects longevity.*

Given this high prevalence of depression in later life, 2 critical questions are: Why do the aged become depressed as frequently as they do? Is their depression of a different quality or type from that in younger persons? There are speculations that depression may be related to senescent changes in the organism, such as in brain structure or function or in the body's ability to respond to stressful events. Depression in the elderly has also been linked to social and psychological changes of the later years, such as the increased rolelessness and losses that are experienced and the lack of opportunities to compensate for these changes. In the following sections the relation of depression to various aspects of functioning will be examined, including: senile brain damage; biochemical processes; life stresses; and personality and behavioral processes.

DEPRESSION AND THE SENILE BRAIN DISORDERS

Before the pioneering work of such British psychiatrists as Sir Martin Roth and Felix Post, it was widely considered that most behavioral problems in later life were manifestations of senile brain degeneration. There is now, however, a clear indication that depression and senile brain disease represent distinct processes.

The principal evidence for this differentiation is drawn from test performance, outcome data, and postmortem studies. Cognitive testing has indicated major differences between older depressed patients and others with senile dementia. The former show significantly better performance on tasks involving information and orientation, and on intelligence tests such as the Raven's Progressive Matrices (Roth and Hopkins 1953;

Gurland et al. 1976). In following hospitalized psychiatric patients over the age of 60, there are also major differences in outcome. Roth (1955; Kay, Roth, and Hopkins 1955) reported that persons with a diagnosis of an affective disorder had a considerably better outcome than patients with signs of organic brain disease. At 6 months following admission, a majority of persons with affective disorders had been discharged and only a few (10 percent) had died. In contrast, patients classified as having either senile psychosis or arteriosclerotic psychosis had a much higher incidence of deaths (58 percent and 34 percent, respectively), and those who survived the 6-month period tended to remain within the hospital. These differences in outcome were maintained over a 2-year follow-up period. By that time two-thirds of the affective patients had been discharged from the hospital, and only 6 percent required readmission.

Following depressed patients for a longer, 6-year period, Post (1962) reported similar findings. Depressed older persons had relatively low mortality rates and did not develop organic brain disease in greater numbers than would be expected in the population at large. The prognosis is markedly different for persons with principally affective or with organic symptoms.

Postmortem examinations of psychiatric patients have also revealed qualitative differences between persons classified as functional before their deaths and those diagnosed as having senile dementia. The latter showed extensive evidence of brain deterioration, including the presence of senile plaques and neurofibrillary tangles. Among functional patients, including those with affective disorders, few or no such senile changes were evident, and these subjects did not differ from hospital patients with no psychiatric disorders in the extent of brain pathology found in the postmortem examinations (Corsellis 1962; Blessed, Tomlinson, and Roth 1968).

This distinction between organic and functional disorders in the elderly is sometimes more difficult to make in actual practice. Persons with either of these disorders often give the impression of having cognitive deficits, particularly in memory, but there is consistent evidence that depressed persons are capable of better intellectual performance than those with senile dementia. The impression of poor performance in the depressed often results from their complaints about poor memory and other intellectual deficits. As discussed in Chapter 2, complaints of poor memory are more likely to indicate depression and not a major memory loss, although some organically impaired persons do complain about poor memory. The presence of cognitive impairment in older depressed persons is not borne out by testing (Kahn et al. 1975; Gurland et al. 1976). Their performance usually falls within normal levels, and they can be distinguished from persons with organic deficits on the basis of simple cognitive and orientation tasks, such as discussed in Chapter 6.

It should also be noted, as mentioned earlier, that a patient may both be depressed and have an organic deficit. The issue of differential diagnosis is usually treated as a matter of "either-or"—either the person is depressed or has senile dementia. In fact, depressive symptoms often accompany organic disorders, especially in the earlier stages of senile brain disease, when the person affected is likely to have some awareness of his or her problems. As the disorder progresses, however, there is more likely to be denial of all difficulties, including depression and memory problems (Kahn et al. 1975; Zarit and Kahn 1975). In some instances depression may be the first symptom of a brain disease, including senile dementia, tumors, or other disorders, even when other neurological signs are not present. As indicated above, however, most instances of depression in the aged are independent of brain impairment.

When depression does occur as a concomitant of an organic process, treatment of the feelings of depression can result in important gains for the person, even when the organic disorder cannot be reversed. Improvements in mood, activity level, and motivation can result in better interpersonal relationships and a better overall accommodation to one's disorder.

BIOLOGICAL AND GENETIC THEORIES

Speculations about the biological origins of depression have been prevalent since the earliest descriptions of this disorder. Theories of body humors, which dominated Western medical thinking from the time of Hippocrates to the eighteenth century, proposed that depression resulted from an imbalance of body fluids. The depressed person was said to have an excess of black bile, and treatment involved removal of this excess through bleeding, purgation, and sweating. Good food, exercise, and regular sleep and bowel movements were also emphasized to reestablish a normal balance of body humors (Diethelm 1975).

Contemporary research into the biochemical correlates of depression has been prompted in part by the serendipitous discovery of mood-altering drugs (Baldessarini 1975). These include lithium salts, which attenuate mood swings in manic-depressive disorders, and reserpine, which has been found to produce depression in about 20 percent of the cases when used in the treatment of hypertension (Lipton 1976). The success of the tricyclic medications and electroconvulsive therapy (ECT) in treating severe depression has also added evidence for potential biochemical factors.

In the search for critical variables, major attention has been given to a group of chemicals referred to as neurotransmitters, which facilitate the transfer of electrical impulses across the gap or "synapse" from one nerve cell to the next. The neuronal synapse is considered a particularly vulnerable point. Drugs or specific metabolic problems can affect the transmission of impulses without altering cell structure or other cell processes (Baldessarini 1975). It has been hypothesized that alterations in the synthesis, storage, release, or utilization of the neurotransmitters may be related to depression (Lipton 1976).

Two groups of neurotransmitters, the catecholamines and the indoleamines, have been the principal subjects of investigation, although there are likely to be many other chemicals affecting the conductance of neural impulses and possibly altering mood (Baldessarini 1975). The catecholamine norepinephrine, which facilitates the transmission across the neural synapse at particular sites in the brain, is the end product of a series of chemical changes that begin within the cell body and then progress down the axon (Lipton 1976). An amino acid, tyrosine, is hydroxylated to form DOPA by the enzyme tyrosine hydroxylase (TOH). DOPA is then modified first to form dopamine and then norepinephrine, which is stored in the axon. When a nerve impulse travels down the axon, norepinephrine is released into the synapse. Some of the chemical is absorbed by a receptor in the postsynaptic cell and leads to the transmission of the impulse across that neuron. Of the remaining norepinephrine that was discharged, some is washed away in the bloodstream and some is reabsorbed by the presynaptic neuron and can be reutilized. On uptake the norepinephrine may be deactivated by monoamineoxidase (MAO) (Lipton 1976). This process is illustrated in Figure 8.1. Another chain of reactions involving the indoleamines leads to the production of serotonin at other receptor sites.

Based on animal research, it has been proposed that norepinephrine and serotonin have antagonistic effects (Baldessarini 1975). Norepinephrine is seen as principally facilitating or enhancing various behaviors, especially appetitive behaviors such as hunger or sex. When norepinephrine levels are lowered through the use of drugs, laboratory animals have demonstrated lower levels of motor activity, including decreases in exploratory behavior and in the escape response when electric shocks are given. Painful shocks have been found in themselves to be related to decreases in catecholamines. Under some conditions shocked animals display "helpless" behavior, that is, they do not try to escape from subsequent aversive stimuli, even when it is possible to do so (Weiss, Glazer, and Pohorecky 1974). In these laboratory analogues, however, catecholamine levels soon return to normal. The relation of these transitory stress reactions to affective disorders in humans must therefore be regarded as tentative.

Lower levels of catecholamines are also associated with decreases in self-stimulating behavior in animals who have electrodes implanted in the so-called pleasure center of the brain, located in the lateral hypothalamus and portions of the limbic system (Baldessarini 1975). These findings suggest that the catecholamines may be related to the experience of reinforcers, involving both biologic needs such as hunger or sex and

FIGURE 8.1.   Metabolism and function of a typical monoamine-operated synapse. Very similar events occur at dopamine- or serotonin-containing nerve-terminals. NE: norepinephrine; MAO: monoamineoxidase; COMT: cate-chol-*O*-methyl-transferase; AMe: S-adenosylmethionine.

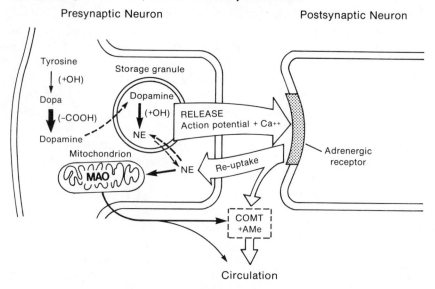

Source: R. J. Baldessarini, "Psychopharmacology of the Amphetamines," *Pediatrics* 49 (1972): 694–701. Copyright © 1972 by the American Academy of Pediatrics. Reprinted by permission.

possibly also social rewards (Akiskal and McKinney 1973). One other important function of the catecholamines may be in modifying the activity of the hypothalamus in ways that affect the release of hormones by the pituitary (Baldessarini 1975).

High levels of serotonin, on the other hand, have been found to produce sedation and a diminished responsiveness to stimulation. When serotonin is lowered, animals manifest increased excitation, higher sexual and aggressive behavior, slower habituation to stimuli, and lowered seizure and pain thresholds (Baldessarini 1975).

Although these descriptions derived from laboratory experiments suggest antagonistic effects of norepinephrine and serotonin, it is not likely that depression is associated in a straightforward way with high levels of one substance and low levels of the other. Some drugs, for example, that block either norepinephrine or serotonin synthesis do not produce depression, or result in depression in only some individuals (Lipton 1976). Thus only 20 percent of persons given reserpine, which lowers norepinephrine levels, develop depression. There is also some evidence that depression may represent a condition of overarousal, rather than a metabolically depressed state (Lipton 1976). In addition, if depression is related to altered metabolism of the catecholamines and/or the indoleamines, it is not apparent why depressive disorders are self-limiting and episodic.

Other hypotheses have suggested that affective disturbances are related to the balance of levels of catecholamines and indoleamines, rather than absolute levels of either group of amines. According to the "permissive biogenic amine hypothesis" of Prange and his associates (Prange 1975), deficiencies in the synthesis of the indoleamines permit the development of affective disorders, but do not cause them. If, in the context of lowered levels of indoleamines, catecholamine production is also altered, then a depressive disorder would follow. Another approach suggests there is a loss of synchronization in the synthesis of the neurotransmitters. In animal studies it has been found that factors that lower norepinephrine levels lead to increased amounts of TOH, which is earlier in the chain of synthesis, and this increase leads to greater production of norepinephrine. Mood-elevating drugs seem, paradoxically, to lower TOH activity. These kinds of interaction suggest that imbalances in the activities of chemicals at various points in the synthesis of norepinephrine and serotonin may lead to affective disturbances (Lipton 1976). There is also some evidence that the activities of the thyroid and pituitary may be associated with the onset of and recovery from depression. The hypothalamic releasing hormone, for example, may affect mood by increasing the sensitivity of neuron receptors to the neurotransmitters (Lipton 1976).

Why the prevalence of depression increases with age can only be surmised at this time. Levels of MAO, which destroys norepinephrine at neuron ends, are higher in the aged. This increased MAO activity may cause lower levels of amines to be present at synapses (Lipton 1976). It has also been speculated that changes in thyroid and pituitary functions with age are related to the high prevalence of depression. Their role in mediating autonomic responses to stress may be impaired or diminished. In addition, increased levels of stress, including isolation, which alter levels of the biogenic amines in laboratory animals (Lipton 1976), may contribute to the greater vulnerability of the aged.

The importance of biological factors in affective disorders is supported by the findings of genetic predispositions in both manic depression and unipolar depression. Relatives of patients with affective disorders have been found to show consistently higher rates of these problems themselves, compared with the general population. The incidence of disturbances in relatives is higher for bipolar than for unipolar disorders (Cadoret and Winokur 1976). Similarly, the degree of risk in relatives is higher if the onset of the affective disorder is before age 50 (Mendlewicz 1976). Risk in probands of patients with unipolar depression is estimated at between 15 and 20 percent if onset is before 50, and between 8 and 9 percent with late onset. Looking at this change in risk with age, Mendlewicz (1976) proposes 2 explanations. First, it is possible that there are 2 (or more) types of depressive disorder, one that occurs in early life and has a relatively greater genetic factor, and one that occurs later and is influenced less by genetic dispositions. Second, there may be a continuum of depressive disorders, with genetic factors contributing less than other variables in later life. It should be noted that the rate of disorders in relatives of patients, particularly for neurotic depressions, is considerably lower than if entirely determined by genetic factors (Paykel 1974; 1975).

The potential of biochemical research for improving treatment of depression is great. At present, medications or ECT are virtually the only effective treatments for the most severe cases of depression, preventing long and disabling hospitalizations. Further breakthroughs in understanding the factors that affect various mood states should increase our ability to respond quickly and effectively to the distress experienced by persons with affective disorders. At the same time, there must be some caution not to place too much emphasis on biochemical factors or on an illness model of depression. Findings of biological correlates of depression do not imply causation. Stresses or habitual patterns of behaving may lead to alterations in the ways in which one's body is mobilized to respond to stress or in the balance of the various amines and their precursors. Biological vulnerabilities, personality, and stresses may all influence the development of depression, with the amount contributed by each of these factors varying from one person to another. There may, therefore, be several pathways leading to a common end state of altered physiological responses and depressed behavior (Akiskal and McKinney 1973). Another caution is that biochemical studies, while increasingly sophisticated in their technology, have virtually ignored the wide range of individual differences among patients in the manifestation of depression. Furthermore, the samples that have been used are not always described in adequate ways, making it difficult to compare subjects from different studies. Biochemical research in depression offers the potential of major discoveries concerning the nature and treatment of affective disorders, but the practical significance is still limited at this stage of development in the field.

LIFE CHANGES AND DEPRESSION

Early theoretical studies of depression emphasized its similarity to an exaggerated style of mourning, and suggested the influence of deaths of parents and other traumatic childhood separations in increasing a person's vulnerability to depression in later life (Freud 1950). Young children who experience abrupt separations from their mothers manifest depressed affect and are characterized by low levels of activity and poor eating (Bowlby 1973). The relation of childhood losses to depression in the adult years is still controversial, although a majority of studies do suggest higher rates of depression among persons who experience the death of a parent during childhood and adolescence (Heinicke 1973). Whether this vulnerability remains in old age, or if other etiological factors become more prominent, remains to be determined.

Recent life events are also prominently associated with the onset of depression (Paykel 1974; 1975; Goodwin and Bunney 1973). Life changes have been investigated principally through the use of various inventories that contain events commonly encountered during the adult years (e.g., birth of a child, changing jobs, moving to a new community). High rates of life changes have been found in several studies to be related to an increased risk of physical illness (Rahe 1972), and to depression (Paykel 1975).

It has been proposed that persons with a predisposition to depression may show a heightened sensitivity or vulnerability to stress, and thus may be reacting differently to relatively commonplace life events than other individuals would. Studies of life changes, however, consistently report that the amount of changes experienced by depressed persons before the onset of the disorder is greater than those experienced by other persons, including normal community residents, other psychiatric patients, and persons hospitalized with medical illnesses (Paykel et al. 1969; Brown et al. 1973; Sethi 1964; Levi et al. 1966; Jacobs, Prusoff, and Paykel 1974; Paykel 1975). In geriatric patients, precipitating stresses were found more frequently among depressed patients than among those with late life paranoid disorders (Kay et al. 1976).

When the total life changes are divided into desirable and undesirable events, depressed patients report having experienced significantly more undesirable events in the recent past than controls, with no differences in the incidence of favorable changes (Paykel 1974). Depressed persons also had experienced more exits of others from their lives, due to various reasons, than did controls. There is, however, no single category of events (e.g., employment, health, family, marital, legal) that consistently predicts depression (Paykel 1974). The amount of undesirable change caused by a life event, rather than the specific nature of that event, may be the critical factor involved.

Life events have also been found to be precipitants in both endogenous and reactive depressions. As discussed earlier in this chapter, the concept of endogenous depression involves in part the lack of precipitating events. It has been suggested, however, that because persons labeled as endogenous are more severely depressed than are reactive cases, clinical interviews at the time of initial contact with them do not necessarily elicit accurate information about precipitants (Goodwin and Bunney 1973). Interviewing severely depressed persons is a formidable task because of their lethargy, slowness, and lack of motivation to respond. Studies that follow endogenous patients over time can gather more complete information as the patient's mood improves. Using this approach, nearly all depressed patients report life stresses, with no distinction between supposedly endogenous and reactive cases (Leff, Roatch, and Bunney 1970; Goodwin and Bunney 1973). Thus severity, rather than the absence of precipitants, may be the most important characteristic of endogenous depressions, with life changes involved in the majority of instances of depressive disorders.

In old age the undesirable life changes that precipitate depression may principally involve losses and illness. Based on clinical interviews, Post (1962) found that losses or the threat of losses preceded the onset of depression in about two-thirds of the cases in a consecutive series of patients. Where illness has been specifically considered as a precipitant, however, its role appears relatively more important. In a clinically heterogeneous sample of persons over age 50, Rubenstein, Zaidi, and Kahn (1976) found a relation between higher life changes and greater symptoms of depression, but the highest levels of depression were found when one of the precipitating factors was illness. Kay, Roth, and Hopkins (1955) suggest that illness is a somewhat more prominent factor among depressed patients with late life onset than in older patients with a prior history of depression.

The treatment of depression may also vary when illness is a precipitant. Looking at the relation of life changes to morale, Lowenthal and Haven (1968) report that persons who experienced retirement or widowhood and who had a confidant had higher morale following these losses than did persons with no confidant. The presence of a confidant, however, did not affect morale when the life change was an illness.

In addition to these more obvious kinds of stress, the absence of life changes may also be experienced as stressful. In comparing persons approaching retirement with individuals at earlier stages of the life cycle, Lowenthal, Thurnher, and Chiriboga (1975) report that the preretirees had experienced the fewest recent life changes, and furthermore regretted the absence of changes in their lives. Their subjective boredom with the static quality in their lives may be another stress of later life over which persons have little control.

Seligman (1975) has developed an intriguing model of the relation of depression to life changes. Based on evidence mainly from animal research, he characterizes depression as "learned helplessness." When exposed to uncontrollable stress, such as random electric shocks, animals become inactive and withdrawn. Seligman suggests that these animals have learned that there is no possible control over the aversive stimuli, and thus make no efforts to escape even after it becomes possible. He believes that a similar process is critical for depression in humans, that in reaction to uncontrollable stress we feel helpless to affect the environment.

Seligman's research has been criticized on the basis that these stress responses may be specific to certain types of aversive stimuli, such as electric shock, and not to other environmental stresses (Weiss, Glazer, and Pohorecky 1974). On the other hand, depressed humans have generally experienced many recent life stresses, and often perceive themselves as having little control over their lives. The relation between helplessness and depression warrants further study, and may be particularly relevant in the old, when major life events such as deaths, changes in health, and retirement are things over which persons have little or no control.

There are few studies that compare the relation of life changes to depression in young and old. One could argue that the aged are more vulnerable to the effects of losses. They may not be able to compensate well, because of limited opportunities for new involvement (Rosow 1974), or a limited physiological capacity to respond. From a psychological perspective, losses that occur in rapid succession may keep a person in a perpetual state of grieving. The general dysphoria of many older persons may be related to a prolonged mourning process (Kastenbaum 1973).

In summary, life changes often play a critical role as precipitants of depressive disorders in both young and old, with illness being a prominent factor in the later years. The relation of life stresses to depression indicates that there is a strong basis in reality for persons' complaints of distress.

Assessment of precipitating events can uncover information that is critical for treatment. Often a first step is to help patients gain some control over the events that they report as preceding their depression. Someone distressed over financial problems, for example, may be able to take some concrete steps to improve his situation, such as applying for SSI or finding a job. By helping depressed persons with their practical problems, the therapist reduces the ongoing stress they are experiencing.

Another consideration is that when a person has suffered an irreversible loss, there may be an appropriate period of grieving and mourning before he can take positive steps to make an adjustment. With the death of a spouse, we have expectations of a distinct period of mourning. It is likely that reactions to other losses are similar, though the person may receive less understanding and support than does the newly widowed. Friends and relatives may be prodding the person who had the loss to "make the best of it" or to "get involved" before he is able to accept that loss. Of course, some people appear to get stuck in the mourning process, and even after a reasonable length of time remain unable to make any adjustments. There are undoubtedly situations in which clinicians should encourage the expression of grief, but there is also a point after which further focus on the depressive feelings is not productive.

Some persons will move fairly rapidly toward making an adjustment to a loss. It has sometimes been stressed that persons who do not have an adequate period to mourn for any loss will have the most difficult time in the long run, because of their unexpressed feelings. Observations of people responding to losses suggest that those who make a fast adjustment usually do as well, and sometimes better, than individuals who grieve longer. They need to be supported as they move to overcome their loss, rather than be impeded by a therapist who feels they have not expressed their feelings sufficiently. Other clients will dwell excessively on their losses. At that point the therapist needs to take an active, directing role to move the person toward appropriate goals that will diminish feelings of depression.

Behavioral and Cognitive Theories

Behavioral theories of depression have emphasized the context in which depressive behaviors are manifested, that is, the antecedents and consequences of these behaviors. In a theoretical paper, Ferster (1973) describes depression as involving a reduction in the frequency of behaviors emitted by the person that are positively reinforced by others. In other words, the actions of a depressed person are not capable of eliciting the same degrees of attention, interest, caring, and other positive sources of gratification as those of nondepressed individuals. This situation is often reflected in clinical encounters. At first a therapist may show considerable interest and empathy, but as the depressive complaints, slowness in speech, and other manifestations of dysphoria persist, he becomes increasingly impatient, less interested, and perhaps even angry with the patient. Thus the kinds of behavior emitted by the depressed person do not hold the attention or elicit rewards from others. This lack of positive gratifications leads to feelings of sadness and worthlessness, and to a low output of behaviors.

Lewinsohn, Biglan, and Zeiss (1976) propose 3 reasons why persons might develop this behavioral deficit in eliciting positive rewards. First, the frequency of behaviors that are likely to be positively reinforced can decrease if the schedule of reinforcements that the person is receiving is too lean. In other words, where there is an initial lack of responsiveness from those individuals who are important to the patient, he may attenuate appropriate behaviors that are capable of eliciting positive feedback. One often observes this situation in marriages where, over time, the positive comments and attention of one of the partners decreases. The other person, in turn, reacts by decreasing those behaviors that previously drew positive comments and attention. As the rewards that he or she previously received diminish, that person begins to have feelings of worthlessness or sadness.

A second factor leading to this behavioral deficit occurs when the reinforcements that a person receives are not contingent on his or her behavior, which is similar to what was discussed earlier as learned helplessness. The third factor identified by Lewinsohn and his associates are sudden changes in the environment, which alter environmental cues that had elicited behaviors that led to positive rewards. For example, one's spouse is likely to be a person toward whom many behaviors are directed that are potentially rewarded. In addition, a husband or wife may serve as the stimulus for eliciting other positively rewarded behaviors, such as in going out together to social events or entertainment. When one's spouse dies, those behaviors directed toward the spouse will, of course, terminate. Additionally, behaviors directed toward other persons that occurred in the presence of one's spouse may also decrease. As is known from the literature on widowhood (e.g., Lopata 1973; Silverman 1977), the surviving spouse lacks both the caring and attention of his or her partner, and withdraws from many of the pleasurable social activities in which the 2 of them had participated. The widow or widower does not feel like going out alone, because he or she is used to doing those things with the other. Thus various life changes, particularly negative ones, can lead to low activity levels and to dysphoria by reducing the environmental cues for behavior that receives positive reinforcement.

This formulation suggests why depression develops, but does not account for 2 critical factors: why do only some persons become depressed following a loss while others do not, and how is depressive behavior maintained in the environment for long periods of time beyond the actual loss (Lewinsohn, Biglan, and Zeiss 1976)? These questions can be addressed by considering 3 issues: reinforcement of depressed behaviors; differences in social skills between depressed and nondepressed persons; and differences in cognitive style between those who become depressed and those who do not.

It is likely that most persons who are depressed are positively reinforced for their behaviors, thereby strengthening the depressive symptoms. When persons complain of sadness or talk about their life difficulties, it is probable that friends or relatives will initially pay attention to them. As the complaints persist over time, however, some persons will no longer be willing to listen. It is likely, though, that the depressed person will be able to find some other individual to attend to his complaints. Another possibility is that friends or relatives begin to attend to the depressed person's complaints only some of the time. By providing attention or reinforcement at variable intervals, they may actually be strengthening the habits involved. Behaviors that are learned with a schedule of variable-interval reinforcements have proven in laboratory situations to be the most difficult to extinguish (Rimm and Masters 1974). As attention to the depressed person becomes intermittent, another factor may come into play. Those around him may attend only to the most severe complaints (e.g., I feel there is no use to living). Thus they may inadvertently shape his behavior by reinforcing only the more extreme manifestations of depression.

There are other, obvious ways in which persons can be rewarded for depressed mood or behavior. Because of their depression, they may get help in performing tasks that have been their responsibility, such as household chores or aspects of their work. They may be able to avoid unpleasant or anxiety-producing situations, stating they do not feel well enough to undertake various activities. Finally, other persons may modify their own behavior in ways to accommodate the depressed person's moods. When depressed and acting helpless, the person may paradoxically find he has considerable control over the behavior of others, who try to make allowances or to be solicitous or especially considerate in order to cheer him up.

Because of the possibility of these secondary gains, the assessment of a depressed person must include what rewards the person gets from his symptoms. Even in clear-cut cases of reactive depression, where the onset of symptoms follows particular environmental changes, reinforcements affect the frequency and severity of symptoms. It is necessary to identify reinforcers so that a treatment plan will not be undermined by continued rewarding of the depressive behavior. Additionally, those reinforcers that apparently maintain the depression can be provided contingently to depressed behaviors. To give an oversimplified example, if a wife has been attending to her depressed husband only when he complains of his various problems, she needs to begin to give him attention and affection for making specific positive behaviors. It should also be noted that a sudden withholding of secondary gains without replacing them in a more appropriate way can lead to increased manifestations of depression, as the person tries to reestablish those sources of reward.

A second factor related to the development and persistence of depressive behaviors is that the person who stays depressed following life changes may have fewer social skills initially than persons who do not become depressed, or who are depressed only for brief periods (Lewinsohn, Biglan, and Zeiss 1976). Being more skillful in social situations increases the likelihood that other people will respond positively to oneself. In studies conducted by Lewinsohn and his associates (Lewinsohn, Biglan, and Zeiss 1976), it has been found that persons who obtain the highest rates of positive reinforcement from others are active, respond quickly to others, are relatively insensitive in a group to an aversive person, use a high proportion of opportunities to react to the statements of others, give more positive reinforcements to others, and direct behaviors evenly to all members of a group. Their research has indicated that depressed persons, on the average, manifest fewer of these social skills that elicit positive reinforcements from others. These persons are, perhaps, more vulnerable to life changes that alter the amount of positive reinforcements they receive, because they have fewer skills for developing new sources of stimulation and reward. Lewinsohn, Biglan, and Zeiss do note, however, that not all depressed persons lack social skills and, among those who do, the types of deficit vary from one person to another.

Another factor accounting for differences in reaction to life changes is the individual's cognitive style. Persons who are depressed have been described as having an exaggerated way of conceptualizing their experiences that leads to overestimation of both good and bad events. One of of the leading proponents of cognitive theories of depression is the psychiatrist Aaron Beck. Beck (1967; 1976) has described what he calls the depressive triad, in which the person views himself, his environment, and his future in an exaggerated negative way. These depressive thoughts intervene between events and one's emotional response. The evaluation of an event or one's own actions in an overly negative way leads to feelings of despondency, hopelessness, or worthlessness. A woman, for example, whose husband has left her may feel appropriately sad or disappointed, but if she sees it as the end of the world or views her future as hopeless, she will become increasingly inactive and despondent. Beck views depressive thoughts as latent in most persons, but able to be brought to the fore during a stressful period. These pessimistic or negative evaluations of actions and events have been described in several studies. In a classic experiment, Beck (1967) had depressed and nondepressed persons participate in a ring toss game. Depressed persons initially predicted they would have lower scores than the others, and after the game rated their performance as significantly worse than nondepressed subjects, but their actual scores did not differ from those of other participants. Depressed persons also differ from the nondepressed in rating everyday events. In one study depressed patients were asked to judge the impact on their lives of the 42 items that comprise the Holmes and Rahe (1967) life change inventory (Schless et al. 1974). Both before and after treatment, depressed persons rated the events as having significantly more impact than did nondepressed controls. Thus there is evidence that their exaggerated cognitive style persists even when their affective status is within normal ranges.

A related perspective is that of Kahn (Kahn and Fink 1958; Kahn et al. 1975), who proposes that depressed persons tend to perceive events in stereotyped and clichéd ways. The statements described by Beck are seen from this viewpoint as manifestations of a highly stereotyped way of conceptualizing experiences. Depressed persons express themselves in dramatic and oversimplified ways, making statements such as "I'm the worst person in the world" or "Everything about my life is terrible." Following treatment, the exaggerated language often persists, but in the opposite way. The person now sees the world through rose-colored glasses (Kahn and Fink 1958).

This tendency to perceive events in oversimplified ways is related to poor adaptation. The person categorizes events as either perfect and beautiful or disappointing. Since everyday events are usually more complex than that, involving a mixture of satisfying and disappointing elements, a person who can only conceptualize experiences in extremes will either gloss over flaws or become excessively distressed when an activity is not perfect. To cite an example, eating in a restaurant is an event that many people find satisfying. While some restaurants may be consistently excellent and others are terrible, most fall somewhere in between. A typical meal may be good overall, but with some minor flaws in service or the quality of a few dishes. Someone who reacts by exaggerating these flaws will not get any satisfaction from the meal or the evening out, but will dwell on the disappointing aspects of the experience. When this type of extreme reaction to environmental events and to one's own actions occurs over time, the person becomes increasingly despondent.

The tendency to view one's self in an exaggerated, negative way may increase with age. Some persons may come to view themselves in terms of the negative stereotypes about old age, and to be overly pessimistic about their abilities and self-worth. There is some evidence that stereotypes of aging affect older persons' perceptions of their performance. As discussed earlier, persons who are depressed rated their memory as significantly worse than nondepressed subjects, even though their performance on objective memory tests was no worse (Kahn et al. 1975). These results are similar to Beck's ring toss game, where depressed persons viewed themselves more negatively than others even though there was no objective evidence of poorer performance. In this instance, however, their self-evaluations reflected a prominent stereotype about aging, that one's memory begins to fail. Other negative expectations about aging may lead to similarly distorted perceptions of one's abilities, with these self-assessments related to poor morale.

Lewinsohn and his associates have integrated the cognitive and behavioral perspectives on depression in their development of the Pleasant Events Schedule, an instrument used for assessment and treatment of affective disorders (Lewinsohn and Libet 1972). The schedule consists of 320 events and activities selected from the universe of potentially pleasant events. Events most often associated with mood are listed in Table 8.2. Two ratings are made by subjects: how pleasant they perceive each activity to be and how often they have engaged in that activity during the past month. Depressed persons have been found to differ in their responses from nondepressed in 2 ways. They report having engaged in fewer pleasant activities, and they indicate that they find fewer activities potentially enjoyable (Lewinsohn, Biglan, and Zeiss 1976). In other words, the depressed person is both doing fewer things that are rewarding, and cognitively has a more restricted range of activities that are perceived as leading to personal satisfaction. Often the person indicates that he might do some of these activities, but that would not

TABLE 8.2. Activities most frequently associated with mood

1. Laughing (IA)	26. Planning or organizing something (E)
2. Being relaxed (IA)	27. Going to a restaurant
3. Being with happy people (S)	28. Expressing my love to someone (S)
4. Eating good meals	29. Petting, necking (S)
5. Thinking about something good in the future (IA)	30. Being with someone I love (S)
6. Having people show interest in what you have said (S)	31. Seeing good things happens to my family or friends (IA)
7. Thinking about people I like (IA)	32. Complimenting or praising someone (S)
8. Seeing beautiful scenery (IA)	22. Having coffee, tea, a coke, etc., with friends (S)
9. Breathing clean air (IA)	34. Meeting someone new of the same sex (S)
10. Being with friends (S)	35. Driving skillfully (E)
11. Having peace and quiet (IA)	36. Saying something clearly (E)
12. Being noticed as sexually attractive (S)	37. Being with animals
13. Kissing (S)	38. Being popular at a gathering (S)
14. Watching people (S)	39. Having a lively talk (S)
15. Having a frank and open conversation (S)	40. Feeling the presence of the Lord in my life (IA)
16. Sitting in the sun (IA)	41. Planning trips or vacations (E)
17. Wearing clean clothes (IA)	42. Listening to the radio (S)
18. Having spare time (IA)	43. Learning to do something new (E)
19. Doing a project in my own way (E)	44. Seeing old friends (S)
20. Sleeping soundly at night (IA)	45. Watching wild animals (IA)
21. Listening to music (IA)	46. Doing a job well (E)
22. Having sexual relations with a partner of the opposite sex (S)	47. Being asked for my help or advice (S)
23. Smiling at people (IA, S)	48. Amusing people (S)
24. Being told I am loved (S)	49. Being complimented or told I have done well (E, S)
25. Reading stories, novels, poems or plays (E)	

Source: P. M. Lewinsohn, A. Biglan, and A. M. Zeiss, "Behavioral Treatment of Depression." In P. O. Davidson, ed., *The Behavioral Management of Anxiety, Depression and Pain* (New York: Brunner/Mazel, 1976).
Key: Types of activities: S = social interactions; IA = affects incompatible with being depressed; E = activities leading to feelings of adequacy or competence.

make any difference in how he felt. The exaggerated quality of the depressed person's reactions are evident in these responses. These activities may not be perceived as pleasurable because the person feels worthless and undeserving of pleasant activities. Everyday, commonplace events that others find satisfying are seen as not satisfying or perfect enough to contribute to his well-being. Paradoxically, there is often a concurrent feeling of needing to be perfect, so the person cannot see gaining pleasure from events that are not perfect and grand. Thus the exaggerated thoughts of depressed persons, which Beck, Kahn, and others have noted, are likely to be related to patterns of activities. Potentially enjoyable events are not engaged in and are not even perceived as enjoyable.

Lewinsohn and MacPhillamy (1974) have investigated the responses of older persons to the Pleasant Events Schedule. Their findings show that the nondepressed aged rate events as potentially enjoyable to the same extent as do younger persons. In contrast to the young, however, they engage in fewer activities that they perceive as potentially enjoyable. The reasons for this difference are not clear, perhaps being related to lower activities levels, lessened opportunities for engaging in activities, or the effects of chronic health impairments. This lower rate of engaging in rewarding activities does suggest why transient feelings of depression are prevalent in the aged, and why older persons are vulnerable to depressive episodes. By participating in fewer potentially rewarding activities, the older person is experiencing fewer daily satisfactions. In the event of encountering further losses, he is likely to have even fewer pleasant activities.

Lewinsohn's treatment approach has been to utilize both cognitive and behavioral procedures, based on assessments made with the Pleasant Events Schedule and other evaluations (Lewinsohn, Biglan, and Zeiss 1976; Lewinsohn et al. 1978). It has been found that engaging in activities that the person sees as pleasurable but has not been doing results in improvements in mood. One aspect of the treatment, then, is to increase, through encouragement and other incentives, the amount of activities that the person finds pleasant. Second, where the individual perceives few events as potentially pleasant, cognitive interventions are made that help the person to see potential gains from more activities, and to learn to associate positive feelings with engaging in those activities. Often a patient will follow through on a homework task set by the therapist, but will come back to the next session stating that engaging in that particular activity did not make any difference. The person may, in fact, be somewhat less depressed, but is unable to make the connection between feeling different and engaging in activities. In that situation, the therapist needs to point out the difference, and to help train the person to recognize and associate positive feelings in various situations. These cognitive interventions are similar to the types of procedure Beck (1976) describes in the treatment of depression.

Another aspect of treatment from Lewinsohn's model is to increase a person's social skills to correct for specific deficits. This may be done through role-playing and modeling, and with assertion training procedures (see also Gambrill and Richey 1976; Lange and Jakubowski 1976).

A common response to someone who is depressed is to tell that person to get active or involved. That advice often does not work, and is not the type of intervention proposed by Lewinsohn. Lewinsohn's research suggests that it is not just any activity that is desirable, but those that the person finds satisfying. Telling a person to become more involved also presumes that he has the ability to obtain rewards in a social situation. As has been discussed, some persons do not have the skills to engage success- fully in certain activities and must be trained first in social or other behaviors.

Beck (1976) also emphasizes direct training to change the person's cognitions and behaviors. Using techniques related to Ellis's Rational Emotive Therapy (Ellis 1962), he describes a process of challenging and pointing out to the person ways in which his thoughts are incorrect and irrational. Through extensive repetition, he attempts to modify these thoughts so that the person dose not take commonplace events as indicating lack of worth or ability.

The first step in the cognitive therapy of depression is to identify negative thoughts, or what are called "automatic thoughts" (Beck, Rush, and Kovacs, unpublished). Patients are taught to become aware of thoughts they had immediately before feeling sad. This can be demon- strated in the therapy sessions by asking patients to evaluate themselves and the therapist. Someone may describe himself, for example, as boring or worthless, or may draw incorrect inferences about a situation, such as feeling worthless because the therapist sees him as just another patient. When these automatic thoughts have been identified and related to specific contexts in the person's everyday life, the therapist can train the patient to provide alternative interpretations of events. In the example cited above, it is true that the therapist views the person as just another patient, but it does not follow that that makes the individual worthless. Someone else, who thinks that the problems she is having in her marriage mean that she is unlovable, can be helped to examine that situation and develop different explanations. Instead of feeling unloved or worthless, it is more realistic to think that "Even though he and I are not getting along right now, I have many good qualities." By substituting this thought, encounters with her husband will not lead to her feeling depressed, and it will then be possible to try out new ways of interacting so that she gets more from the relationship.

Both Beck and Lewinsohn use procedures that involve having clients monitor and record their mood in everyday activities. This charting is used to identify behaviors, situations, or thoughts that are antecedents to or consequences of feeling depressed. If a person feels more depressed in certain situations, new behaviors can be planned so that he functions more effectively at those times or reduces the number of unpleasant activities in a given day. Negative thoughts that lead to depressive feelings can also be identified this way, and the person taught to counter these ideas with more balanced ways of looking at himself or the situation. Charting also serves to demonstrate how the person's mood improves as he makes specific changes, such as increasing pleasant activities or challenging automatic thoughts. An example of how activities can be related to mood is shown in Figure 8.2.

Lewinsohn and Beck also emphasize the use of schedules to plan out activities in advance for a given day or week. This planning is used to decrease engaging in activities the person finds unpleasant and to increase activities that are pleasant or involve mastery. Working out schedules can reveal negative thoughts that would impede engaging in activities, such as if someone feels that trying to change will only make things worse. (The procedures of these 2 treatment approaches for depression are described in manuals and are available through the senior authors: Peter Lewinsohn, Department of Psychology, University of Oregon; Aaron Beck, Psychiatry Department, University of Pennsylvania. Lewinsohn and his associates have also prepared a self-help book that contains many valuable exercises for treatment of depression [Lewinsohn et al. 1978]).

A major emphasis in both the behavioral and cognitive approaches is using the therapy sessions to plan for changes in how the person acts in specific everyday situations. Depression is viewed as related to particular thoughts and actions, and the treatment involves direct modification of these established habits. The issue of generalizing from therapy to daily life is central. It is through changing the person-environment interactions that depressive emotions will be reduced

The following cases illustrate behavioral and cognitive elements in depression in 2 older persons. Miss F. was a 69-year-old woman who had never married and retired 4 years earlier. She had previously had few activities outside her work, and had lived with her parents until their deaths about 15 years ago. She reported feeling depressed and lonely since her retirement. She said that when she retired she had wanted to get involved in a variety of activities, but currently the only things she did were go to a senior nutrition site for lunch, and do occasional volunteer work there. She wanted to make friends, but had trouble making conversation, especially with men.

The treatment involved identifying activities she found pleasurable. She had purchased an organ but had not played it, and as a first step she was encouraged to practice it. Her mood gradually improved, and she took on more activities. Attempts to get her more involved with others focused on increasing her conversational skills, although she progressed more slowly in this area. Follow-up after a year indicated she was generally less depressed than before, although she had occasional periods in which she was sad, usually related to her inability to form new relationships. For Miss F., a behavioral approach of increasing pleasant activities and some social skills training reduced but did not eliminate her feelings of depression.

In contrast to Miss F., Mrs. B. reported many examples of negative,

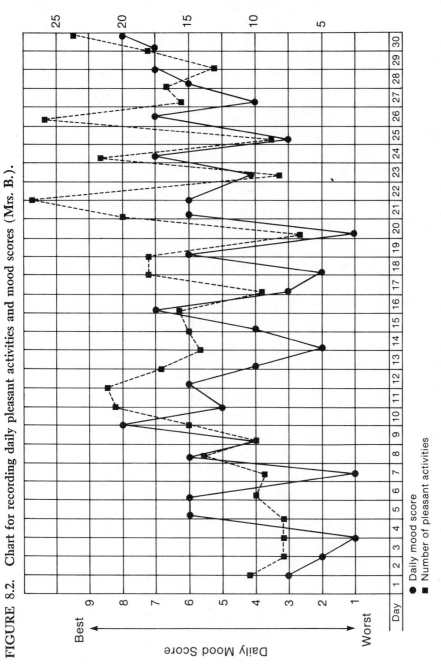

FIGURE 8.2. Chart for recording daily pleasant activities and mood scores (Mrs. B.).

● Daily mood score
■ Number of pleasant activities

Source: P. M. Lewinsohn, R. F. Munoz, M. A. Youngren, and A. M. Zeiss, Control Your Depression (Englewood Cliffs, N.J.: Prentice-Hall, 1978), p. 152. Copyright © 1978. Reprinted by permission of Prentice-Hall, Inc., Englewood Cliffs, N.J.

211

self-defeating thoughts, and the treatment approach was largely cognitive. Mrs. B. was a 74-year-old widow who was moderately active, but often came away from activities feeling more depressed than when she started. As an example, if she did not get a response from someone at a senior center when she initiated a conversation, she concluded that no one would ever be her friend. While engaging in an activity she enjoyed, she would begin thinking of unpleasant things, including that she did not deserve to have any pleasant experiences, and she would come away from the activities feeling sad. Counseling involved identifying these automatic negative thoughts, and helping her to substitute more positive self-statements. Mrs. B. responded immediately to the idea that her depression was the result of pessimistic thoughts, and she showed a rapid improvement. Some behavioral tasks were also included. Something that bothered her was that she left many tasks undone. She was encouraged between sessions to finish one of them, which she did, and this example was used both as a sign that she could complete things and an indication to tackle tasks one at a time, rather than feeling overwhelmed by them.

The cognitive and behavioral models propose links between a person's thoughts and everyday behaviors that affect mood. These approaches suggest direct interventions to alter those aspects of behavior or cognitions that are associated with feelings of depression. Persons are encouraged to undertake various activities, and at the same time to develop more differentiated ways of perceiving themselves and evaluating their performance.

Summary

Depression is the most prevalent psychological disorder of the later years. Both among clinically identified cases and in symptoms reported by community samples, depression is found more often than other problems. This is potentially a positive situation, since most depressed persons are likely to experience some short-term symptomatic relief with treatment. On the other hand, despite its importance, there are many critical issues about depression and its treatment in the aged that have not been addressed. These include whether depression is one or several disorders, whether late life depression represents a process similar to or different from affective disorders at earlier stages of life, whether treatment should be the same as at earlier ages, and how clinical diagnoses relate to the transitory feelings of loneliness and depression often reported by the elderly. There needs, in addition, to be further clarification of the relative roles of biological correlates found in some cases of depression and of psychosocial stresses.

Despite these uncertainties, there are some useful guidelines for assessment and treatment of an older, depressed patient. The most critical step is to conduct an individualized assessment. Depression at this time is too broad and vague a concept to have much specificity for treatment. Several issues should be considered in the assessment. Based on the patient's history, it should be determined if there has been a pattern of manic-depressive psychosis or of repeated episodes of depression in the past. Treatment for manic-depressive psychosis is highly specific, involving the use of lithium carbonate. Recurrent depressive episodes are likely to respond to treatments that were effective in prior instances. Both the severity of the depressive symptoms and the extent to which the persons can report precipitating events should be determined. With greater severity and where few or no precipitants are reported, medications should be considered for part of the treatment plan. Where the depression is reactive, the meaning of the changes to the person may lead to the development of an effective course of treatment, and in some cases to concrete interventions that help offset some negative life changes. With reactive depressions in the elderly, straightforward support and encouragement will also be effective. Another area for assessment is the extent to which the person manifests the behavioral and cognitive problems found to be associated with recurrent depressions, including a lack of social skills, low engagement in potentially pleasant activities, secondary gains of the symptoms, and a negative self-concept that affects the person's evaluations of everyday behaviors. A treatment program should be developed reflecting the specific problems and deficits that are present.

From the limited studies available, the elderly depressed patient does appear to have a relatively good prognosis. Depressive symptoms are usually found to be independent of the senile brain diseases, so that effective treatment is likely to return many persons to adequate levels of functioning. Even in the person for whom the precipitating event was a brain disease or other illness, treatment of the depressive component can result in improvements of the person's behavior and also that of his or her family.

CHAPTER 9

Functional
Psychiatric Problems

THE TYPES OF PSYCHOPATHOLOGY manifested by older persons are probably more varied than at any other period in the life cycle. While depressive symptoms are most frequently observed, a range of disorders can be seen, from the continuation of lifelong symptoms of chronic psychosis to types of paranoid state that do not appear to have equivalents in the earlier years of adulthood. Disorders that receive attention among the young can have a high prevalance in old age, as in the case of suicides, or can present a difficult, unyielding symptomatology, as with hypochondriasis. This chapter will review the etiology and treatment of several disorders of the later years, including paranoid states, hypochrondriasis, suicide, sleep disorders, alcoholism, and schizophrenia. The concerns of the dying and bereaved will also be discussed. While not typically considered psychiatric problems, the reactions of dying and bereaved persons are of interest to the gerontological practitioner because of the frequency with which death touches the lives of the elderly. In reviewing these various disorders, attention will be given to the specific contexts of old age in which symptoms are manifested. It should be noted that the types of problem to be discussed are usually considered as "functional," that is, having no identified organic basis. In Chapter 13 the treatment of persons with organic brain syndromes will be presented.

The diagnostic categories used in this chapter are based on traditional classification schemes. These syndromes cannot, however, be viewed as illnesses or as necessarily having one underlying etiology. Paranoid symptoms, as discussed below, can occur for several apparently distinct reasons. Similarly, it is not known if hypochondriasis represents one or several types of problem, and there has even been debate whether excessive health complaints should be considered a psychiatric disorder. Placing 2 persons in the same category, then, runs the risk of overlooking major differences between them. Moreover, these classifications have not been developed on a basis of responses to treatment. Treatment might, in fact, be radically different for 2 persons with the same diagnostic label. These categories, therefore, must be viewed as tentative, and in all cases a functional behavioral analysis of clinical patients, such as described in Chapter 5, is recommended.

Late Life Paranoid States

Paranoid states occur less frequently than depression in the later years, but often have a greater impact. Delusions about intruders, thefts, or reports of imaginary plots or voices are likely to be highly disturbing to a person's relatives, friends, and to those community agencies involved in the problem. Someone manifesting paranoid symptoms violates conventions about the nature of reality, and will be labeled as mentally ill, often with little effort to understand or treat the problem. In contrast to depressive symptoms, which are often ignored, paranoid reactions sometimes evoke a prompt but negative intervention. Because of the disturbing nature of the symptoms, steps may be taken to relocate the paranoid person to a protected setting, without an evaluation of his or her ability to continue to provide self-care. In other circumstances the person may merely be labeled by community agencies as "crazy" or a crank, and be avoided or placed on a referral carousel from one agency to another. Even though their symptoms are highly disturbing to others, paranoid persons do respond well to treatment (Pfeiffer 1977).

There are few estimates available of the actual incidence and prevalence of paranoid disorders in old age. Based on several series of inpatient admissions, Roth and his associates (Roth 1955; Kay and Roth 1961; Kay 1963) report that 10 percent had predominantly paranoid symptomatology. Fish (1960) presents similar figures. Of inpatient admissions to psychiatric hospitals, 41 of 264 (16 percent) persons over the age of 60 had paranoid symptoms, with 34 (12 percent) having probable onset after age 60. No estimates are available on the prevalence of paranoid behavior in community elderly or outpatient clinics. It is likely, however, that any such surveys would underreport the actual numbers, since paranoid persons do not generally present themselves for treatment and are wary about cooperating with community investigators or outreach workers.

There appear to be 4 possibly distinct etiological factors for paranoid disorders in the later years. First, paranoid ideation may represent the continuation of a long-term chronic psychosis that originated in early or middle adulthood. While there are few studies of how this type of symptomatology changes over time, it is likely that treatment would proceed in a similar way as in earlier periods of life. One complicating factor, however, is that prior psychiatric treatment may have created certain problems. Persons who were hospitalized for long periods of time may have severe behavioral deficits associated with institutional life, in addition to their thought disorder (Wing and Brown 1970; Ochberg, Zarcone, and Hamburg 1972). As a consequence, they may need relatively more assistance in taking an active role to meet everyday demands, such as those involving housing, meals, work, and management of social interactions. The paranoid person with prior psychiatric contacts may also be more suspicious of any attempts at treatment, especially when previous hospitalizations involved unpleasant, painful experiences.

Second, paranoid behavior may accompany either acute brain reactions or senile dementia, including those disorders brought about by toxic levels of medication (Pfeiffer and Busse 1973; J. Young 1972). Persons with brain disorders are a sizable percentage of the total of paranoid patients. Following persons over a period, Post (1966) confirmed the presence of an organic disorder in 13 of 61 patients with late life paranoid states. In a somewhat larger series of patients for whom less diagnostic information was available, he reports that 33 of 93 paranoid patients had suspected or actual organic pathologies. A somewhat lower estimate of cerebral dysfunction in paranoid patients was made by Kay and Roth (1961). There is no evidence, however, that all late life paranoid disturbances have their origins in senile brain disease. Where symptoms of brain dysfunction are initially absent, late life paranoia is not associated either with cognitive deterioration or shortened life span (Tanna 1974; Kay and Roth 1961).

The frequency with which paranoid behaviors accompany altered cerebral function suggests the importance of making an evaluation for organic causes in paranoid patients. With an acute origin, both the symptoms and underlying causal factor may be reversible. With senile dementia, whether vascular or Alzheimer's-type, the course of the paranoid symptoms is likely to be different from that in persons with no brain damage. In cases of dementia the paranoid behavior often appears to serve an adaptive function, helping the individual explain his gaps in memory. He may, for example, accuse others of misplacing or stealing some items when he cannot remember where he placed these things. As the extent of cerebral dysfunction increases, however, the paranoid thoughts will become infrequent or abate altogether. With severe dementia the person can no longer remember well enough to be concerned with the gaps in his memory.

In managing someone who is making these accusations, the mental health professional and the family should take a supportive role. It will not be possible to reason away the accusations or to win the argument over whether or not something was stolen. These symptoms need to be viewed as the individual's way of accounting for increased forgetfulness. Instead of arguing, one should express concern over the person's difficulties and try to engage him in other activities and topics of conversation. Informing the family that the paranoid accusations will decrease in time is also helpful. These approaches are discussed more fully in Chapter 13.

Two other major factors in the etiology of late life paranoid states are social isolation and sensory losses. The prior social adjustment of many paranoid patients has often been poor. They led somewhat isolated lives, had few or no successful intimate relationships, and had a poor sexual adjustment (Kay et al. 1976; Post 1966; 1968; 1973). They are likely to be living alone, to be female, to have few close relatives, and, if they had children, to maintain only limited contact with them. They are often in good physical health. Their adjustment to work and other social demands may have been good, with their histories mainly indicating problems in relationships (Post 1968). The actual onset of the paranoid symptoms often follows a period in which the person experiences an increasing sense of social isolation. This isolation can be brought on by discrete stressful events, such as deaths, physical illness, or family disagreements. In evaluating the role of precipitants, Kay and his associates (1976) found that stressful events were reported by paranoid patients less often than in cases of late life affective disorders, but 50 percent of persons with paranoid states had experienced major life changes prior to onset of their problem. Post (1966) also reports a high frequency of stresses prior to onset.

Persons with paranoid ideation have also often had sensory losses, especially of hearing. Hearing impairments are found significantly more frequently in paranoid patients than in other older persons (Cooper et al. 1974). Deafness was usually severe, bilateral, and had its origin by middle age. Optimum visual acuity has also been found to be poorer in persons with paranoid disorders, compared with depressed patients (Cooper and Porter 1976).

When paranoid ideation is manifested for the first time in later life, it is usually described as more circumscribed than cases of paranoid schizophrenia (Pfeiffer 1977; Kay et al. 1976; Tanna 1974). According to Tanna (p. 466), "The clinical picture consists of delusions and hallucinations, but usually without thought disorders, gross affective, volitional or psychomotor symptoms, or characteristic personality deterioration." Delusions are sometimes "encapsulated," that is, focused on one particular topic, like an imaginery intruder. When more pervasive, the delusions often have an understandable basis. They may be related to the specific deficits in sensory functions or to other aspects of a person's situation (Pfeiffer 1977). Someone with a hearing loss thus may complain that others are talking about him. Only a minority of patients exhibit the more bizarre

imagery or other symptoms that are characteristic of paranoid schizophrenia, such as feelings of being controlled by others, of participation in
the thoughts of others, or of passivity (Pfeiffer 1977; Tanna 1974).

Post (1966) identifies 3 patterns of symptoms in later life paranoid
states. In the first there are auditory hallucinations and false beliefs of persecution. The second pattern is characterized by understandable delusions.
These include feelings of being observed or having one's conversations
taped, or feeling that odors, gasses, or other unpleasant substances are
directed at the individual. Evidence of "first-rank" symptoms of schizophrenia are seen in the third pattern, including hearing voices that discuss
the patient and his activities in the third person, bizarre and fantastic
delusions, and feelings of passivity. Post (1966) suggests that the etiology
of the paranoid state—whether due to organic causes, social isolation, or
sensory losses—is not related to the symptom pattern. In contrast, Cooper,
Garside, and Kay (1976) found differences when comparing deaf and non-
deaf patients with paranoid disorders. They reported fewer predisposing
personality factors among the deaf paranoid patient, including less sus-
piciousness, hostility, and emotional coldness.

It is not clear how etiology affects treatment. Post (1966) suggests
similar approaches to patients, whether the premorbid history involves
social isolation or hearing loss. He reported no difference in outcome when
comparing these etiotogical factors, and also when contrasting persons
with different symptom patterns. Pfeiffer (1977), however, notes than any
correction of sensory losses has a beneficial impact on the psychological
symptoms.

It is not known how late life paranoid states are related to paranoid
schizophrenia. According to Post (1966), the poor premorbid history of
some patients suggests they were borderline schizophrenics before the
manifestation of paranoid symptoms. Because of differences in symptoms,
however, late life paranoid states are usually considered as distinct from
paranoid schizophrenia (Kay et al. 1976; Tanna 1974). Prognosis is also
better with late onset. According to Retterstöl (1968), 81 percent of
patients with late onset of symptoms had a favorable outcome, compared to 23 percent of persons with chronic psychosis.

One additional diagnostic consideration should be noted. In some instances paranoid ideation is present in a person who also manifests significant signs of depression. In those cases, antidepressant medication and
possibly other methods of treatment for depression appear effective
(J. Young 1972).

Paranoid symptoms often have obvious functions. First, the thoughts
of being persecuted have developed in circumstances of isolation, when a
person has a heightened sense of vulnerability. His feelings of weakness
may then be accounted for in the malevolence of others (Berger and Zarit
1978). Second, the paranoid ideation may fill in for stimuli that are not

present, either because of sensory isolation or deafness (Pfeiffer and Busse 1973). Not hearing speech clearly, especially in a group situation, the deaf person may conclude that others are talking about him, or may distort those bits of speech that are partially perceived. Similarly, voices and intruders may provide some social stimulation to the isolated older person. A patient seen by the author had complained of hearing voices, which had become increasingly threatening. Following treatment, which involved both supportive counseling and medication, she stated that she knew she had made up these voices, because she missed the sounds of human conversation. One common symptom pattern is that of an imaginary companion who often visits and is sometimes malevolent, threatening the person or stealing small objects. The complaints made about stealing by persons with senile dementia who manifest paranoid ideation also serve to fill in for the things they cannot remember.

One other important aspect of paranoid disorders is that there are often striking consequences to this behavior. A person who is socially isolated and who calls the police to complain about an intruder usually receives some prompt, stimulating attention. Complaints to one's children about threats, intruders, or similar problems also are likely to bring about a decisive response, at least when initially made. Sometimes paranoid persons can be observed bouncing from one social agency to another. They are initially responded to with interest, especially where their complaints have a plausible basis. As their symptoms persist, however, their relationship with agency personnel will deteriorate and they will move to another place seeking help. It is likely, then, that paranoid behavior is shaped to some extent by environmental response, functioning to obtain desired reinforcers for a period of time.

There are few systematic studies of treatment of paranoid states in the elderly. Three general approaches, however, can be suggested. These involve the use of medications, development of a supportive relationship, and provisions of attention and other reinforcers contingent on appropriate behavior.

The use of phenothiazines has been reported to eliminate or diminish paranoid behavior in the elderly (Fracchia, Sheppard, and Merlis 1973; Whitehead 1975). Post (1966), for example, reports that in a series of 71 patients, 43 had complete remissions, 22 were somewhat improved, and only 6 were unchanged. These improvements were sustained during a follow-up period that ranged between 1 and 3 years. Phenothiazines, however, sometimes result in adverse side effects, some of which can be irreversible (Kennedy 1975). In addition, Pfeiffer (1977) notes that many paranoid persons are suspicious of the medication and do not follow through with proper dosage.

The development of a supportive relationship is critical both as an adjunct to medications, and as a general approach in responding to the paranoid complaints. Post (1973), for example, emphasizes uncritical acceptance of the patient. He expresses regret at what the person has had to endure, and presents medications as helping the person resist the onslaughts against him. In general, it is not very useful to take a "reality orientation" approach to paranoid symptoms. This has undoubtedly been tried already and has not worked. There can, instead, be acceptance of the symptoms, with the therapist directing comments to the feelings of anger, helplessness, vulnerability, or pain that are indicated by the paranoid ideation. Family members can also be encouraged to take this reflective approach, and not to argue over the reality of the patient's perceptions.

Beck (1976) also proposes that the therapist not attack the delusion directly. Instead, he suggests helping the client learn to cope with the problem by exploring the consequences of his actions. In one case where a man had made accusations against his wife, the therapist responded by saying he had no information about whether the accusations were correct, but asked what would happen if the patient continued to accuse her. The patient replied he did not care. The therapist then pointed out that she might leave him. In considering this consequence, the man stopped his accusations. As a result, his relationship with his wife improved.

Third, there must be careful consideration by the therapist of the potentially rewarding consequences of paranoid behavior, and the development of alternative ways of providing those reinforcements. The following example illustrates how social reinforcements might be used. When initially involved in a senior day-care program, an 82-year-old woman talked virtually only of her fears of being poisoned in her apartment. Apart from the day-care program, she had few social contacts and recently became even more isolated as the result of the death of one brother and the illness of another. The staff's approach was to listen politely and without excessive comments to her complaints. In turn, they responded actively to any other topics initiated by the client, and spontaneously began discussions about some matter, such as her appearance. Over a few months the amount of time she spent complaining about being poisoned diminished, while her appearance and ability to maintain a social conversation improved greatly.

Whatever the basic approach, care must be taken not to reinforce inadvertently the paranoid symptoms. The possibility that there are other reinforcers besides attention should be considered. One further caveat is that there should be some investigation to determine if the complaints have a basis in reality. There are too many instances of estates being plundered and of other forms of mistreatment of the elderly to assume, de facto, that the complaints are delusional.

Coordinating psychopharmacological and psychotherapeutic treatments will sometimes present problems when these are not being handled by the same person. Clients may want to continue talking about their troubles to the mental health worker, but will be unwilling to see a psychiatrist or other physician for medication. Sometimes they will specifically refuse to see a psychiatrist, but will go to a physician; in other instances they will block any attempt at medical intervention. Conflicts about medication can endanger the tenuous trust established between worker and patient. These problems are likely to be greatest in situations where medical and nonmedical personnel do not work as a team.

Many paranoid persons can continue to function effectively in community settings (Berger and Zarit 1978). There usually is no impairment in self-care activities, or danger to self or others. The principal problem in maintaining a person in the community is likely to be the discomfort the symptoms produce in others, such as family members, neighbors, or the personnel of various social agencies. If treatment results only in diminished symptomatology, rather than complete remission, it may be critical to work with those persons who interact with the client to ensure their tolerance and understanding of the problem. For family members, in particular, it should be pointed out that institutionalization will not cure the disorder, but is likely to have other negative effects.

Because of the limited research available, few studies consider the long-term prognosis. While there is agreement that paranoid disorders do not affect mortality, some studies suggest a relatively favorable outcome (Post 1966; Retterstöl 1968), while others indicate poor prospects for improvement (Tanna 1974). Most reports do indicate, however, that a majority of persons respond at least to some extent to treatment, with a resultant diminishing of the presenting symptoms.

Hypochondriasis

As with paranoid delusions, hypochondriasis is a notable problem among the elderly and has a disturbing impact on others. The complaints typically made by hypochondriacs are rather commonplace, involving pains of various sorts, especially of muscles or bones, or symptoms of the digestive system. It is the persistence of hypochondriacal patients that is most frustrating. They do not respond to reassurance or to calm explanations, and show only short-lived improvements with placebo treatment. They also resolutely resist any suggestions that their complaints have a psychological origin and are not related to health problems. Even direct angry confrontations do not usually have any impact.

The persistence of hypochondriacal symptoms is readily apparent in a case history of a 70-year-old woman reported by Earley and von Mering (1969). This woman, whom they considered typical of the chronic hypochondriacal outpatients with whom they had contact, had been seen in the clinics of a university medical school for an 18-year period. During that time she made 548 visits to the clinic, an average of 33 per year, including as many as 12 visits per year to specialty clinics of various sorts. During this period she was seen by over 226 physicians and 42 medical students, who made 164 diagnoses. She had extensive physical examinations, including 138 laboratory tests, of which 91 were called negative and 7 positive. The results of 40 others could not be determined from the charts. According to the authors, her chart included one notation that "she feels doctors don't know how sick she is. They tell her nothing is wrong with her—and this after all the above visits" (Earley and von Mering 1969, p. 136).

There are, unfortunately, few systematic studies of the etiology, prevalence, or treatment of hypochondriacal complaints. Estimates of prevalence would be difficult to make, since these patients are usually seen by family doctors or in medical clinics and are not consistently referred for psychiatric treatment. Much of the existing literature is concerned with the taxonomy of hypochondriasis. A major issue is whether it is a psychiatric disease entity, warranting a classification of its own, or whether these exaggerated complaints are secondary to other psychiatric disorders. There has, in contrast, been little consideration of how these symptoms develop, function, and are reinforced by the present environment. It is commonly assumed that many elderly persons are hypochondriacs, but while chronic illnesses and reports of somatic illnesses are found to increase with age, it is not known whether the prevalence of hypochondriasis also rises in the later years.

Hypochondriacal behavior can be considered to have 2 features. First, the person perceives himself to be ill and is preoccupied with his own health when there is no objective indication of an organic problem. Second, reassurance and information about the person's health status are ineffective in reducing these concerns (Goldstein and Birnbom 1976). A clear distinction between objective and exaggerated health complaints may not always be possible, especially in the elderly. Because of the prevalence of chronic health problems in old age, many complaints do, in fact, have an organic basis, but they may be exaggerated, or there can be an excessive preoccupation with them.

Some authors have divided hypochondriasis into primary and secondary syndromes (Pilowsky 1970; Goldstein and Birnbom 1976). Primary hypochondriasis is the situation in which the principal symptoms involve somatic complaints and no other psychiatric diagnosis would be possible. Secondary hypochondriasis includes those patients who manifest significant degrees of depression or anxiety in addition to their health concerns. In comparing persons classified as primary or secondary hypochondriacs, Pilowsky (1970) reports some differences in their background and symptoms. Persons termed primary had a longer duration of symptoms and made more complaints involving the musculoskeletal system and skin, hair, and appearance. Those classified as secondary were more likely to have made a past suicide attempt. Male patients considered secondary reported more problems in sexual adjustment. Of the total sample, about half of the secondary cases had depressive symptomatology, while the remaining patients were described as anxious. Persons in both categories had displayed obsessional and anxious patterns of behavior in the past, including some hypochondriacal symptoms. There were no major differences between these 2 groups in age, sex, family background, marital status, or work history.

Alarcón (1964), in contrast, suggests a depressive component in all cases of hypochondriasis. In a series of 152 depressed inpatients over the age of 60, he reported that 63 percent had hypochondriacal symptoms. In one-third of all cases the hypochondriacal symptoms preceded the depression. For one-quarter of the cases hypochondriasis was the dominant symptom, with depression apparent only on direct questioning of patients. He described these patients as not looking depressed. They often smiled and appeared in control except when talking about their ailments. In some instances depressive symptoms were observed to emerge at a later point in time than at hospitalization.

Because of differences in the selection and description of patients by Pilowsky and Alarcón, it is difficult to evaluate if those persons termed primary hypochondriacs by the former are similar to these cases where depression has been masked by hypochrondriac complaints. Whether hypochronriasis consists of 2 (or more) syndromes, as suggested by Pilowsky, or if there are similar etiologies in all cases remains to be determined.

Some other symptom patterns are also reported. Goldstein and Birnbom (1976) classify 4 patients as having primary hypochondriasis, when in each case the onset of symptoms accompanied the acute stress of actual or anticipated relocation. With treatment, the symptoms subsided within 2 months. This pattern suggests there needs to be a distinction between hypochondriasis as a reaction to stress, perhaps analogous to reactive depressions, and as a more persistent pattern of behavior. Other types of hypochondriacal reaction include the presence of illness complaints in persons with senile dementia (A. C. Walsh 1976) and the occurrence of single delusional symptoms, which is sometimes termed monosymtomatic hypochondriacal psychosis (Riding and Munro 1975). These delusions include such things as feeling that one's body is emitting a bad smell, perceiving a part of the body to be infested with bugs or worms, and complaining that the shape of one's face or other body parts is abnormal. Riding and Munro suggest that the occurrence of this type of delusional complaint is extremely rare.

Attempts to determine the etiology of hypochondriacal symptoms have focused alternately on how people learn to express feelings of distress and on the secondary gains or reinforcements for these behaviors. Citing studies that show the response to pain varying across ethnic groups, Mechanic (1972) proposes that hypochondriasis represents a type of vocabulary of stress. Many persons consider somatic complaints more desirable to report than emotional distress. The latter is often viewed as a sign of weakness, and would produce negative reactions among persons close to the patient. Mechanic also notes that hypochondriacal complaints involve such things as headaches, digestive problems, or musculoskeletal symptoms, which occur frequently in the general population, especially in persons under stress. Given the high prevalence of these symptoms in the first place, he proposes that their occurrence when a person is under stress or in other ways emotionally aroused can become attributed to an illness. He suggests this attribution may be due to several factors, including chance, prior experiences, cultural learning, or the secondary gains associated with being ill. When the person has no other language to express distress, or experiences a significant relief of tension, these symptoms can become enduring.

Some studies report that hypochondriacal patients have limited social and educational backgrounds, suggesting they have had few opportunities to learn varied means of expressing and dealing with distress. In a report on the self-perceptions of health status by community residents, Maddox (1964) found that persons who were consistently more pessimistic about their health than indicated by objective assessments were more likely to be women, to be from lower socioeconomic groups, to be less socially active, to report receiving little positive appreciation and encouragement from others, and to feel that they were criticized a lot. Pilowsky (1970) similarly notes that hypochondriacal problems were more common among the lower middle class or semiskilled workers.

The preponderance of women noted by Maddox among community residents has not been found consistently in psychiatric samples. Both Pilowsky (1970) and Alarcón (1964) report approximately equal numbers of men and women manifesting hypochondriacal complaints, while Goldstein and Birnbom (1976) treated predominantly female patients.

Based on clinical observations, hypochondriacal patients often have few interests other than their health concerns. If asked what would be different about their lives if they did not have this problem, they do not have positive ideas or can indicate only in a vague way what they would be doing. Their health complaints thus do not appear to keep them from engaging in more attractive relationships and activities. They sometimes have histories of marginal adjustments both to work and in their interpersonal relationships that suggest they possess few behavioral skills

For a person with limited alternatives, the secondary gains involved in hypochondriasis can serve as a more satisfying and involving way of life. Being ill removes the necessity of fulfilling some obligations, especially those the person has had difficulty with. On the other hand, illness may serve as a way of explaining personal failures or the inability to achieve a more satisfying way of life (Busse 1976). Moreover, the many clinic visits, the rituals surrounding patient care in large medical complexes, and the attention of physicians may give the person feelings of satisfaction and importance he did not have before the onset of this problem. The long waits often endured in clinics may even be rewarding, serving as a forum where these chronic outpatients can socialize with other patients or with receptionists or other staff (Earley and von Mering 1969).

This view of hypochondriasis as shaped and rewarded through attention and other positive consequences also suggests why it can be a persistent problem. Because of the possibility that an illness actually is present, physicians must be thorough in investigating a person's health complaints. The distinction between actual and exaggerated complaints is made even more difficult in older persons who do have chronic ailments. If one physician becomes convinced that the ailments are hypochondriacal, the patient can readily find another doctor who will initially treat the complaints as illness. If a physician suggests the problem is psychological, the person may develop new symptoms or turn to another doctor who will search for a new drug or other treatment to cure the disorder. There is, in other words, a limitless supply of reinforcement for hypochondriacal symptoms. Because of the ease of gaining these rewards and the amount of attention he or she has received, a hypochondriacal patient will not respond to simple admonitions that the symptoms are not real.

There have been virtually no systematic studies of treatment of hypochondriasis and few reports of treatment outcomes. Pilowsky (1970) suggests the use of antidepressant medications and/or ECT with secondary hypochondriasis and minor tranquilizers for primary hypochondriasis. According to his figures, however, many patients in both groups received both types of medication. In comparing outcome, men classified as primary had the least improvement. Women in the primary group and persons judged as having secondary hypochondriasis reported marked reductions in symptoms.

Goldstein and Birnbom (1976) also based their treatment plans on whether patients were classified as manifesting primary or secondary hypochondriasis, although, as noted earlier, their 4 primary cases appeared to have had a more recent onset of symptoms than those persons in Pilowsky's (1970) study. All 4 were treated on an outpatient basis, with no medications. They were seen for a 20-minute weekly interview and received a 5-minute phone call between sessions. For each subsequent session they were given a nonthreatening task to accomplish, and were praised at the start of that interview for showing the strength to complete the task. Within 2 months treatment was judged to be a success in all 4 cases, and was terminated.

A more intensive program of treatment was employed for the 16 cases of secondary hypochondriasis. Treatment included hospitalization for between 5 and 7 weeks. ECT was used for 6 patients and the rest received antidepressant medications, sometimes in conjunction with tranquilizers. Nine patients were involved in family therapy. After discharge, 8 patients continued in a day-care program. Hospitalization was considered critical in order to stop problematic interactions in the family. While on the ward, the staff ignored the somatic complaints, encouraged performance of activities, and tried to reduce opportunities for secondary gains for the hypochondriacal symptoms. All the patients showed improvement, but at a slower rate than hospitalized persons with other psychiatric disorders. The family therapy was used to restore a balance among family members following recent stresses, usually involving changes in residence. The authors considered treatment successful in 8 of the 16 cases, all of whom received both family therapy and day-care follow-up. They also caution that treatment, even in successful cases, proceeds slowly.

Because of the small numbers of patients and lack of adequate control groups in these studies, the findings must be regarded as tentative. The value of various medications and psychotherapy approaches requires more careful study. Some further suggestions for treatment can be made at this time, but these must also be viewed as tentative. Assessment of hypochondriacal patients should include their social skills, other resources, and sources of reinforcement for symptoms in addition to physician visits. Where a person is deficient in eliciting reinforcements from others, a systematic effort can be undertaken to shape these skills. This type of program can include modeling and assertion training, similar to the model used by Lewinsohn and his associates (Lewinsohn, Biglan, and Zeiss 1976; Lewinsohn et al. 1978) for treatment of depression. The therapist can ignore hypochondriacal complaints while attending to positive behavior, including such things as the person's appearance. As in the Goldstein and Birnbom (1976) study, simple home tasks can be used to build up confidence and skills. For this type of treatment to succeed, a client must agree to participate and not to seek medical help for his or her complaints for a given period of time. It is necessary to make this stipulation part of an explicit contract with the client, in order that treatment not be undermined by discussions of medical care, and symptoms not reinforced. Before psychological treatment is begun, there must, of course, be adequate verification that these symptoms are exaggerations, and there should be careful monitoring of the person's health status so that proper medical treatment is given, should an organic problem develop. In addition, where family members are reinforcing problem behaviors or can be useful in the development of new skills, they can be involved in treatment. This step is likely to be critical. In many instances spouses and other family members show an ambivalence toward the hypochondriacal patient, demanding more independence but, at the same time, encouraging dependent behaviors in both subtle and some direct ways. They are also often reluctant to make any changes in their usual habits out of anger, frustration, or a desire to remain in control. They will therefore undermine changes in the patient's behavior, unless they are involved in the treatment.

Suicide

Suicides of older persons represent a disproportionate amount of successful suicides among the population as a whole, and constitute a major problem for the mental health of the elderly. There have been consistent reports of high rates of successful suicides among persons over 65. While the suicide rate for the population as a whole was 11.6 per 100,000 persons in 1970, it was 36.9 per 100,000 for persons over 65 (*Vital Statistics* 1974). Among all persons who committed suicide in 1970, 31.5 percent were over 65. This increased potential for suicide is accounted for mainly by the large number of suicides among older white men. Looking at the rates of suicides at different ages, Pfeiffer (1977) notes a steady increase at each succeeding age level. The rate of suicide among white males aged 15 to19 is 9.4 per 100,000, while among men 65 to 69 it is 37.4 per 100,000. A peak is reached at age 80–84, where the suicide rate is 51.4 per 100,000. Among white women and nonwhites, suicide rates are lower at all ages, and are generally somewhat lower after 65 than in middle age. Women make more suicide attempts than men, but men of any age are more likely to complete the act (Pokorny 1968). Similar increases with age in suicides of men are found in virtually all Western countries (Weiss 1968).

One further aspect of this problem is that older persons are more likely to be serious in their suicide attempts and more likely to be successful. Thus the proportion of successful suicides to suicide attempts is higher among the old than the young (Gardner, Bahn, and Mack 1964). Based on figures from several studies, Pfeiffer (1977) suggests that the ratio of attempted to successful suicides among younger persons is 7 to 1. Among the aged, however, the ratio is 2 to 1. In other words, half of all elderly persons attempting suicide are successful. These figures may actually be low. It is likely that the number of "passive suicides," such as when someone stops eating or fails to maintain a therapeutic drug regimen, is underestimated.

One reason for this high completion rate is that the older suicide is not as likely as someone younger to intend that his actions have an impact on another person. When the suicide is not principally directed at affecting someone, the attempt is likely to be more dangerous (Dorpat and Boswell 1963; Rubenstein, Moses, and Lidz 1958).

Persons attempting suicide are often depressed before the attempt.

Various studies suggest that between 30 and 50 percent of persons who commit suicide were depressed (Murphy and Robins 1968). This may be especially true for the aged. The rate of suicide among older depressed persons may be as much as twice that in younger individuals who are depressed (Gardner, Bahn, and Mack 1964; Weiss 1968). The more severely depressed a person is, the more likely that a suicide attempt will be either serious or successful. Many depressed persons, of course, are not suicidal. It has been suggested that the key symptom suggesting suicidal risk is the feeling of hopelessness (Beck, Kovacs, and Weissman 1975). Hopelessness or pessimism in a person who does not otherwise appear depressed may also indicate a risk of suicide. Agitation and a history of compulsiveness also have been reported as related to suicide risk in depressed patients (Wolff 1969).

Among older men, who have the highest rates of suicide, feelings of depression may not always be directly reported. In a comparison of persons of all ages who attempted suicide, it was found that women were more depressed than men (Beck, Lester, and Kovacs 1973). Older men who subsequently commit suicide often express feelings of depression principally through somatic complaints, or with apathy and withdrawal from activities. Thus while feelings of depression and hopelessness are associated with suicide, some older men who have suicidal intentions may not express these feelings in direct ways.

Other psychiatric symptoms have been found to increase the risk of suicide. Among older persons these include alcoholism and acute or chronic brain dysfunction, especially when the person is depressed about his condition (Murphy and Robins 1968; Resnik and Cantor 1970; Sainsbury 1962). The risk of suicide has also been found to be greater in persons who are single, widowed, or divorced, or when there has been a recent loss or death (Resnik and Cantor 1970; Weiss 1968). Another important factor is the presence of a serious physical illness. Comparisons of young and old persons who have committed suicide indicate that physical illnesses have contributed to the suicide more frequently in the aged (Weiss 1968). In addition, economic circumstances may be an important variable for older men. Among younger persons, those from a higher socioeconomic level have higher rates of suicide. Among the aged, persons from lower social classes have a higher rate, and there is some indication that recent economic difficulties and a prior, irregular work history increase the probability of a suicide attempt (Weiss 1968; Gardner, Bahn, and Mack 1964). Thus several dimensions are clearly associated with an increased probability of suicide in old age. The risk is greatest among older men, in persons who are depressed or have other psychiatric problems, when there is a weak social support system, if recent losses have occurred, where there are financial problems, and in the presence of a serious physical illness. A 14-item scale that evaluates these risk factors has been developed by Tuckman and Youngman (1968) and is shown in Table 9.1.

TABLE 9.1. Suicide rates [a] measured by high- and low-risk categories of risk-related factors among 1,112 attempted suicides

Factor	High-Risk Category	Suicide Rate	Low-Risk Category	Suicide Rate
Age	45 years and older	40.5	Under age 45	6.9
Sex	Male	33.8	Female	5.3
Race	White	16.7	Nonwhite	9.0
Marital status [b]	Separated, divorced, widowed	41.9	Single, married	12.4
Employment status [b]	Unemployed, retired	24.8	Employed [c]	16.3
Living arrangements	Alone	71.4	With others	11.1
Health	Poor (acute or chronic condition in the 6-month period preceding the attempt)	18.0	Good [c]	13.8
Mental condition	Nervous or mental disorder, mood or behavioral symptoms including alcoholism	17.6	Presumably normal, including brief situational reactions [c]	11.7
Method	Hanging, firearms, jumping, drowning	45.5	Cutting, or piercing, gas or carbon monoxide, poison, combination of methods, other	13.1
Potential consequences of method	Likely to be fatal [d]	31.5	Harmless, illness-producing	6.0
Police description of attempted suicide's condition	Unconscious, semiconscious	16.3	Presumably normal, disturbed, drinking, physically ill, other	13.0
Suicide note	Yes	22.5	No [c]	13.7
Previous attempt or threat	Yes	22.6	No [c]	13.3
Disposition	Admitted to psychiatric evaluation center	21.0	Discharged to self or relative; referred to doctor, clergyman, or social agency; other disposition	11.6

Source: J. Tuckman and W. F. Youngman, "Assessment of Suicide Risk in Attempted Suicides," in H. L. P Resnik, ed., *Suicidal Behavior: Diagnosis and Management* (Boston: Little, Brown, 1968). Copyright © 1968 by Little, Brown and Company, Inc. Reprinted by permission. [a] While mental health statistics generally use rates per 100,000 population, it was more appropriate to use per 1,000 population because of the small size of the sample. [b] Does not include housewives and students. [c] Includes cases for which information on this factor was not given in the police report. [d] Several criteria used in estimating whether the method used was likely to be fatal.

These social and psychiatric factors indicate a potential for suicide, but do not predict whether there is any danger in an individual case. Several studies suggest two principal factors related to increased risk in a given individual: prior suicide attempts and talking about suicide (Gardner, Bahn, and Mack 1964; Pokorny 1968; Tuckman and Youngman 1968; Murphy and Robins 1968). It is sometimes considered that people who attempted suicide but did not succeed were making a gesture to alert others to their needs or to get back at someone with whom they were angry or disappointed. While some suicide attempts are clearly this type of gesture, in most cases the attempt reflects an ambivalence: there is a genuine wish to die, but at the same time the person wants to live (Stengel 1968). There are no obvious distinguishing features between persons attempting and those completing suicide. The failure of a suicide may reflect chance circumstances rather than a deliberate attempt to bungle it or to have it discovered. Since virtually any method of suicide can fail, an incomplete suicide should not be taken to indicate the person did not want to die. The possibility of future attempts must, therefore, be considered as high. In fact, as many as one-third of all successful suicides made a prior attempt (Murphy and Robins 1968).

Communicating an intent to commit suicide is another important indicator. While it is sometimes assumed that persons who talk about suicide will not follow through, it has been found that prior communications are important. Between 60 and 80 percent of persons who commit suicide talked about it prior to the attempt. Among those who talk about suicide, between 2 and 10 percent go on to attempt it (Pokorny 1968; Murphy and Robins 1968). The intent may be communicated in several ways. In a study of 134 cases of successful suicide, Robins and associates (1959) reported 4 principal methods of communication: (1) a direct statement of intent to commit suicide, shown by 41 percent of the sample; (2) statements that one is tired of living or would be better off dead, found in 24 percent; (3) indicating a desire to die, shown by 22 percent; and (4) discussions of methods of committing suicide, found in 18 percent. In addition, there may be indirect communications of suicidal intent, such as putting one's affairs in order, making funeral arrangements, and making statements about not seeing family or friends again.

It is often considered that suicidal communications are intended to have a desired impact on others, as a cry for help, or as a manipulation. In some instances the statements are made for other reasons, including a warning to others to prepare for the person's death, as a taunt, or because the person is preoccupied with suicidal ideation (Murphy and Robins 1968). Whatever the motive of the statement, however, there is a chance that the person will follow through. When someone communicates suicidal intent, one's intervention should be prompt. If there is imminent danger that the person will make an attempt, a brief hospitalization is appropriate. When it appears that the person is only considering suicide and has no immediate, definite plans, outpatient treatment can be used.

Assessing the potential for suicide in an older client involves 2 steps. First, if any of the risk factors described above are present, for example, if persons are depressed or have experienced some recent financial reverses, they should be asked directly if they have been considering suicide. The question can be phrased to inquire if they have been thinking about dying or about ending their life. While it is sometimes feared that an inquiry about suicide will implant the idea in someone who has not been considering it, this has not been found to be the case (Pokorny 1968; Murphy and Robins 1968). Second, there should be an assessment of the suicidal plan of persons who are thinking of ending their life. An inquiry can be made to determine if the person has made specific plans, and what the details and timing of the plans are (Shneidman and Farberow 1968). In general, there is more risk when any of these factors are involved: the person has a specific plan for suicide, has the means to carry it out, and has a time framework in mind for the attempt. The suicidal patient can also be asked what reasons he has for not doing it, as a way of determining the immediate risk of suicidal action.

Resnik and Cantor (1970) suggest that treatment of the suicidal older person involves 3 aspects. First, there should be the establishment of trust between client and therapist through expressions of sincerity, warmth, and concern. Second, the therapist should take actions to overcome the major problem facing the patient. In cases of depression this may involve arranging for medications in addition to psychotherapy, and helping the person to deal with the life situations that led to feelings of despair. Sometimes telling a person that depression is a self-limiting influence is helpful (Mintz 1968). If there is an active medical problem, the client should also be evaluated for depressive feelings, as medications are often effective in reducing the behavioral correlates of illnesses (Epstein 1976). Third, it is suggested that others become involved with the patient, in order to provide him with continued support. This step is particularly important in those cases where the motive for suicide develops from interpersonal conflict or feelings of isolation or alienation. Working only with the patient in that situation ignores the major problem that provoked suicidal feelings (Shneidman and Farberow 1968). It is also recommended that the therapist not lapse into a hopeless or casual attitude about the suicide (Mintz 1968). Persons in treatment who committed suicide often had therapists who responded in those ways. While treatment of suicidal patients usually is performed in individual sessions, group psychotherapy appears to have a beneficial effect (Farberow 1968).

In working with suicidal patients, Beck and his associates (Beck 1976; Beck, Kovacs, and Weissman 1975; Kovacs, Beck, and Weissman 1975) suggest focusing on feelings of hopelessness, rather than on the details of the suicidal action. Among the common expressions of hopelessness are statements like: "There is no point in living"; "I am feeling so miserable that the only thing I can do is escape from it all"; "I am a burden to my family"; "I won't ever be able to get what I want from life" (Beck, Rush, and Kovacs, unpublished). Their approach involves convincing the client that hopelessness is the result of illogical thinking, overgeneralizations, or erroneous assumptions. The therapist then provides alternative interpretations of the person's current life situation and future prospects. Patients can also be shown they have choices other than suicide. As an example, Beck (1976) presents the case of a woman who threatened suicide because of the breakup of her marriage. She stated she could not live without her husband. In this instance the therapist pointed out that she was happy before she got married, was popular with men, and that the marriage had not been a successful one. Through this approach the patient became aware that she was not losing as much as she had considered, and that she could manage without her husband.

Beck and his associates (Beck, Rush, and Kovacs 1976) note other reasons for suicide in addition to exaggerated feelings of hopelessness. In some cases there is a basis in reality for the hopelessness, such as living in severe economic deprivation. Social interventions are appropriate when stressful environmental conditions can be altered. Another major reason for suicidal thoughts is to manipulate or get back at someone else. One approach is to identify the interpersonal behaviors that have led up to this extreme reaction. The patient can then be taught alternative ways of interacting that demonstrate he can be effective in relationships without attempting suicide.

Identifying alternatives to hopelessness in the aged presents a special challenge, since the therapist might readily agree with an old, ill client that the future has few prospects. This type of pessimism is never justified. The therapist, instead, must consider other possible interpretations of the person's current situation and provide a positive role that the person might play in the future. Kübler-Ross (1975), for example, describes a severely depressed person who had a terminal illness. This woman complained that she had made all the wrong decisions in her life, recited a history of failures, and stated that her life had come to nothing. Kübler-Ross responded by asking the woman to tell what she learned from her experiences, so that it might be of benefit to others. This request led to the woman's becoming involved both with the hospital staff and other patients, and serving a positive role on the hospital ward. She later stated that these months were the best period in her life. Butler (1977) has suggested other positive roles that older persons may play, including having a knowledge of the past, possessing certain skills in crafts or other activities, taking on the role of an "elder" who has special insights into human affairs, and leaving behind a legacy. In the case of someone who realistically has few alternative because of physical impairment, the therapist can explore how the person would like to live out his life and if there are any tasks or other unfinished business he wants to accomplish.

There has been considerable philosophical debate in recent years on the rights of persons to terminate their own lives. If a person's life can only be maintained by artificial means, some states now have procedures to allow for withdrawing of the life-support system and for the refusal of treatments that would only prolong life minimally. In the elderly, it is critical to differentiate these terminal conditions from other situations. Treatment of an older, suicidal patient should be as vigorous as for a younger person for 2 reasons. First, these feelings of despair are likely to be transitory. With treatment, the person will be able to find sources of satisfaction and meaning in life. Second, under the various ethical and legal codes governing mental health professionals, there is responsibility for preventing the suicides of one's patients. It can be argued philosophically that persons do, in fact, have the right to end their lives. In legal codes covering practice, however, professionals cannot allow passive or active attempts at suicide.

Insomnia

Sleep disorders are a prevalent phenomenon of modern life. Most persons experience periodic difficulties in sleeping, due to stresses, anxiety, excitement, or somatic ailments. A considerable number of persons experience more persistent problems. Surveys of community residents have indicated that almost 1 in 3 persons complain of insomnia (Karacan et al. 1973). In old age, it has been estimated that at least 50 percent suffer from insomnia (Feinberg and Carlson 1968; Kahn and Fisher 1969).

There are actually several types of sleeping disorder, which can be present individually or in various combinations. Commonly reported problems include: taking a long time to fall asleep, frequent awakenings during the night, with a long latency in getting back to sleep; increased frequency of dreaming; lighter sleeping; and waking early (Amin 1976). The prevalence of sleep problems among the aged may be due to several factors, including changes in sleep patterns with advancing age and the occurrence of depression and other psychiatric disturbances that affect sleep.

Several changes in the sleep cycle have been noted in comparisons of young and old persons. Older persons have been reported to take longer to fall asleep and to wake more often during the night (Amin 1976; Kahn and Fisher 1969; Feinberg, Koresko, and Heller 1967; Feinberg 1976). The total amount of time spent sleeping during the night is less, especially at advanced ages. There are also changes in the pattern of the sleep cycle.

Researchers have identified 5 phases of sleep, characterized by different types of electrical activity in the brain. These include 4 stages ranging from light (stage I) to deep sleep (stage IV), the latter of which is accompanied by a pattern of electrical activity consisting of long, slow waves called delta waves. A fifth phase, REM sleep, is characterized by rapid eye movements, fluctuations in blood pressure, and erections in males. Most dreaming takes place during REM sleep. Stage IV sleep and delta wave activity have been reported to decrease with age (Kahn and Fisher 1969; Agnew, Webb, and Williams 1967). At very advanced ages there is less than 50 percent of Stage IV sleep than typically found in the young. Decreases are also reported in the amount of REM sleep. While young and old spend similar amounts of time in REM sleep, negative correlations have been reported between age and REM sleep in aged samples (Kahn and Fisher 1969; Feinberg, Koresko, and Heller 1967). Decreases in REM sleep have also been reported to be related to the overall health and vigor of older persons (Kahn and Fisher 1969).

Whether these changes in sleep are due principally to aspects of the aging process or to other factors is not clear. While subjects in sleep research are often described as "normal," little descriptive data is presented. Some of the samples have included institutionalized persons, who may have a higher incidence of sleep disorders and of brain pathologies that affect sleep. Some may be depressed, which is also related to sleep problems. The extent of changes in sleep patterns in older persons and the correlates of those changes need further clarification.

The sleep patterns found in depression are similar to those reported as concomitant with aging. Persons who are depressed typically spend less time in stages III and IV, and show less delta wave activity (Hawkins and Mendels 1966; Mendels and Chernik 1975). Among depressed persons over 50, the changes in delta wave activity are even more pronounced. REM sleep, however, is more variable. Some studies report lowered REM sleep in depressed patients while others note normal or elevated amounts of REM sleep. These differences may be due to the effect of antidepressant medications, rather than altered mood (Mendels and Chernik 1975). As depressed patients improve, their sleep patterns usually return to normal, although some persons continue to experience problems.

Other common causes of sleep disorders include drug dependence, neurological dysfunctions (e.g., sleep apnea and nocturnal myoclonus), and insomnia not clearly related to distress or psychiatric symptoms (Borkovec 1977).

An important consideration in responding to patients is that complaints of insomnia have an uncertain relation to changes in the sleep cycle. It has been reported, for example, that persons with insomnia report far more time spent awake than actually occurs, based on laboratory observations (Monroe 1968; Carskadon et al. 1976). In fact, observations of good and poor sleepers indicate considerable overlap between the groups in all phases of sleep. Thus, the extent of sleep problems are somewhat exaggerated. The implications of specific changes in the sleep cycle for everyday functioning are also not known. In the extreme, sleep deprivation or interruptions of REM sleep can produce marked behavioral alterations, including hallucinations and disorientation. Persons who are deprived of REM sleep or stage IV sleep will subsequently increase the amount of time spent in those phases, as if to make up for the deprivation (Mendels and Chernik 1975; Luce and Segal 1969). But the relation to behavior of spontaneous changes in total amount of time spent asleep, total REM sleep, or total stage IV sleep has not been determined.

Although there are, unfortunately, no systematic investigations of treatments for insomnia in old age, some tentative suggestions can be made for dealing with sleep complaints or sleeping problems. First, there should be an assessment to rule out somatic illness and drug dependencies. Sleeping medications have a limited effectiveness, especially when used habitually, and can contribute to sleep problems. Hypnotic drugs, which are commonly prescribed for insomnia, suppress the amount of REM sleep. If the drug is stopped, there occurs REM rebound, or an increase in the amount of time dreaming and also of night wakings. Because withdrawal from the drug results in worse sleeping problems, many persons find it difficult to discontinue these medications (Kales and Kales 1970). Both the hypnotics and most other sleeping medications (flurazepam hydrochloride [dalmane] is an exception) lose their effectiveness with constant use, usually within 2 weeks (Amin 1976; Kales and Kales 1970). As tolerance to these drugs is established, there can be increased sleeplessness and attempts to remedy that with higher dosages. Because dependencies are built up by chronic users, these persons should be withdrawn carefully in a medically guided program to control the possibilities of complications during this period (Amin 1976).

A second consideration is that persons with sleep disorders should be evaluated for depression. When depressed affect is present, treatment can focus primarily on the depressive problem. The symptomatic treatment of insomnia with tranquilizing or hypnotic drugs will have only a temporary impact on the sleep disturbance, while in some instances increasing the extent of depression. In more serious cases of depression the patient can be assured that the sleeping problem is only temporary and will diminish along with the depression. Use of tricyclic medications usually results in decreased complaints of insomnia, but the effects of these substances on the sleep cycle have not been fully evaluated (Mendels and Chernik 1975).

In some cases sleep disorders may take the form of a "depressive equivalent." A person may be excessively preoccupied with the mechanics of sleeping, while denying other problems. When persons have experienced losses or other stresses, and/or they have significantly altered their life style as the result of sleeping problems, it is likely that the complaints about sleeping are masking a more basic difficulty. Like hypochondriacs, these persons are likely to lack insight into their problems. Treatment approaches can include attempts to overcome behavioral deficits and lowered activity levels, and the use of paradoxical suggestions (Haley 1976). The following case is an example of this type of problem.

Mrs. J. was an 83-year-old woman who complained of chronic insomnia for most of her adult life. For the past 20 years she had been dependent on sleeping pills. Her sleeping problems had become worse during the past 3 months. This change was associated with her failing the examination to renew her driver's license. She subsequently passed the examination but her sleep continued to be poor. She reported going to bed at around 10 or 11 P.M., and awakening at around 2 or 3 A.M. If she did not take sleeping pills she could not get back to sleep.

Mrs. J. reported that she no longer had any interests, did not get along with people, and that most of her friends were dead. She had no health problems. She felt that if she could get a good night's sleep, her feelings of nervousness and depression would diminish.

In this example there is both a history of habitual use of sleeping medications, which were probably aggravating the sleep problem, and few other interests or activities to involve the patient. While she felt depressed, Mrs. J. insisted that all of her problems were the result of not being able to sleep. What she wanted most was a new medication or some other quick procedure that would help her sleep better.

Sleep disorders may also be present independent of other somatic or psychological disturbances. Older persons complaining of insomnia may be noting the effects of age changes in sleep. In some individuals the development of poor sleep habits or of anxiety specifically around the sleeping situation may lead to insomnia. Treatment, therefore, can consist in varying degrees of helping persons to accommodate to changing patterns of sleep in later life and to correcting those habits that inhibit sleep.

The treatment of chronic insomnia involves the use of several types of technique. According to Thoresen and his associates (Thoresen et al., in press), insomnia should not be viewed as an illness that can be cured with a single technique, whether a drug or a behavioral approach such as biofeedback or deep-muscle relaxation. Rather than focusing just on the symptom, one needs to assess the habits and ideas persons have concerning sleep, and also how daytime activities may contribute to the problem.

Five major areas of intervention are described: changes in cognitions; deep-muscle relaxation; mental relaxation; behaviors related to sleeping; and difficulties in daily activities (Coates and Thoresen 1977; Thoresen et al., in press). Problem thoughts associated with insomnia include the general, pessimistic, or self-deprecating statement, such as "My situation is hopeless," as well as specific thoughts when lying awake, such as "I'll never get to sleep." These pessimistic thoughts are identified and the person encouraged to substitute more positive thoughts that will lower anxiety and facilitate sleep. As an example, the person who is lying awake in bed can say to himself: "If I don't fall asleep right away, then I can lie here and relax and fall asleep very soon" (Coates and Thoresen 1977). Deep-muscle relaxation, described in Chapter 11, can be used both before going to sleep and during the day to lower tension and anxiety. Studies have consistently indicated that this procedure is effective in reducing sleep problems (Borkovec 1977). Mental relaxation involves having the person identify pleasant scenes and images and focus on those when in bed, rather than on anxiety-producing thoughts.

Specific behaviors the person engages in before going to bed or while in bed can also influence sleep problems. Coates and Thoreson (1977) recommend several good sleep habits for reducing insomnia: (1) going to bed only when sleepy rather than at a particular time; (2) using the bed only for sleep (or sex) and not other activities, such as reading or watching television; (3) getting out of bed and going to another room if one cannot fall asleep; (4) getting up at the same time every morning; and (5) not taking naps. Kales and Kales (1970) also recommend some behavioral steps, including exercise during the day but not before bedtime, because the latter will arouse the individual, and engaging in relaxing, rather than complex or challenging mental activities, before going to bed. The daily activities that Coates and Thoresen (1977) discuss as having an impact on sleep are: (1) learning how to relax and deal with tension-producing events; (2) thinking positively about one's self; and (3) thinking positively about the world. These approaches are particularly appropriate when someone experiences considerable anxiety or depression during the day.

Death and Dying

A life-threatening illness can occur at any point in the life cycle, not just in old age. With the control of infectious diseases and the drop in the mortality of women in childbirth, however, it has become increasingly likely that a person will live to and die during old age. Because of that, the practitioner working with older persons will encounter individuals who have life-threatening illnesses, and must be able to respond to their concerns and those of their families.

The major issue facing the practitioner is that death is a taboo subject. It is probably easier to engage persons in a conversation about sex or other emotional topics than it is to discuss death. This situation has the effect of isolating from others those persons with life-threatening illnesses.

Medical personnel may inform the patient only indirectly about his condition or, in some cases, not even tell the person that his illness is terminal. At the same time, families may not know what to say or do for the dying person. Unable to face the tragic implication of the illness, they may try to maintain in their own minds that everything will be all right, that the condition will remit with the next treatment. Or they may want to protect the dying person from knowledge of his condition, so as not to upset him unduly. Yet from interviews with patients, it appears that they usually guess their conditions from the behavior of both medical personnel and family members (Kübler-Ross 1968). This situation of avoidance leads to what has been described as the "drama of mutual pretense" (Glaser and Strauss 1965). Everyone knows the person has a life-threatening illness, including the patient, but they create routines that function to deny to one another that death is probable. Medical personnel continue to do their jobs in the same ways, even when further treatment will not have an effect, and family members talk about the future and try to maintain an optimistic attitude. The patient also joins in this mutual deception. The consequences of this avoidance can be to create feelings of isolation in the dying person and to impede a positive sharing of feelings among family members.

There are 2 assumptions about why this avoidance occurs. First, a person's own fears about death may make it difficult for him to talk about dying with a terminally ill individual. These fears may be general, that is, the person has a horror of considering death, or they may be specific to the situation. It has often been noted, for example, that physicians and other medical personnel view their purpose as curing the person, and some may feel guilty or responsible when a patient dies. Similarly, family members may feel guilty about real or imagined events that might have made the situation different, such as blaming themselves for not insisting that the person go to a physician at an earlier point in time. Second, it is assumed that the prospects of death for the person who is ill will be too frightening to discuss. In fact, many persons with life-threatening illnesses need to talk about their condition, to make realistic plans before they die, and to settle some unfinished business, both practical or in an emotional sense (Kübler-Ross 1968).

From her work with terminally ill patients, Kübler-Ross (1968; 1975) describes 5 stages that dying persons go through. It is not known how many persons with life-threatening illnesses actually progress through these stages, or if there is a natural progression through the stages, as Kübler-Ross implies. The stages, however, describe typical patterns of reactions, and are useful concepts for giving others an understanding of the dying person. The stages are: denial, anger, bargaining, depression, and acceptance. As Kübler-Ross (1968) points out, the reactions of anger, bargaining for more time, and depression are appropriate responses to one's approaching death. Rather than arguing with the patient to cheer up, it is more helpful to accept these feelings and to give the person a chance to discuss his situation.

As death nears, the person may want the companionship of only one or a few others, and will sometimes sit quietly for long periods of time. The family members often have difficulty accepting this withdrawal. They want the patient to hold on to life. At that point, they need to be helped to see that the best they can do is accept the dying person's response, that death will be made easier by letting go rather than through continuing struggle.

Acceptance is seen in a positive way, not as resignation. It is the sense of having put one's affairs in order and of having lived the best one could. The person feels prepared for death and is often at peace.

Weisman (1972) proposes a concept similar to acceptance, that of the "appropriate death." He defines an appropriate death as one where the circumstances are consistent with the dying person's life style and wishes. To give persons this control over their own fate, they must be allowed to decide on major issues of care, such as the use of pain medications, or whether they are to remain in the hospital, go home, or to a hospice. They also need the opportunity to resolve any personal conflicts or fulfill some remaining wishes or desires.

There are several important interventions that can be made with hospital personnel, the families of dying persons, and the dying persons themselves in order to alleviate some of the pain of this loss. First, where patients and their families have not been given adequate information to assess the patient's medical condition, they should be supported in their right to obtain the information. A person who does not want to know his condition should not be pressed with the facts, but in many cases patients have legitimate questions that go unanswered. In particular, patients need to know the risks and chances involved in any further treatment. Where the only course available is painful treatment that has little probability for success, patients should have the choice to assess whether they want further treatment. It is usually assumed that everyone wants to pursue every possible source of cure in a life-threatening illness, but as the chances of remissions dim, at least some persons appear to prefer to terminate treatment.

A second important intervention is to allow the terminally ill person the opportunity to talk about his situation. This may involve being available to the person as a confidant, listening in a supportive way, or helping the person to reach closure on psychological concerns or such practical matters as wills or business affairs. This role may also involve bringing family members into the situation. When the family has been avoiding facing the issue of the person's impending death, their visits to the patient can serve as an irritant. They will try to cheer him up or talk about the future, but not about the important loss that is occurring. While it is not necessary to dwell upon issues of dying, some sharing of concerns and feelings by family members with the patient usually appears to be beneficial.

Third, family members often need support at this time. They may be facing problems in getting financial affairs in order or in negotiating with the health bureaucracy. Or they may be having psychological difficulty with the impending loss. As noted above, family members often maintain their denial that anything is wrong and try to have the patient hold onto life when that is no longer possible. They need to be able to explore their feelings in a supportive atmosphere. There is a critical line between helping persons to know they have done what they can in communicating their feelings to the dying person or in settling old problems, and pushing the person too much, so that there is an unnecessary dwelling on depressive feelings. Because talking about death openly was so strongly avoided in the past, some current writings imply that going in the opposite direction with total and complete emotional honesty is the only healthy response. In all cases a therapist should only go as far as family members indicate they want to go in exploring feelings. The major task, then, is to give family members the chance to talk about this issue in a supportive atmosphere, and to allow them to proceed at their own pace.

It has been suggested that the reactions of family members to a life-threatening illness in one of them depends in part on the way that person functioned within the social structure of the family (Peterson 1980). To cite 2 extreme examples, one would expect family members to react differently if the dying person had principally managed instrumental functions, such as finances or making decisions, or if that individual provided emotional support and was a confidant for other family members. The type of involvement of the dying person with the rest of the family can offer some clues to the intervention needed. If, for example, the person perceived by others in the family as strong is ill, that individual may need permission to communicate feelings of weakness or other emotional reactions. The type of relationship of each person with the dying individual is important, because it is within the context of those relationships that some resolution of feelings about one another or of long-standing problems may take place. To extend Weisman's concept of an appropriate death, the ways in which persons work out their relationship with one another and the problems they have in doing so will depend on how they have interacted in the past. For counselors to intervene in helpful ways, they would need to evaluate these family issues.

Grief and Mourning

While we sometimes speak of a person dying from a broken heart, this is usually taken as metaphor. There is, however, a factual basis for this belief. The loss of a loved one, particularly a spouse, is a highly stressful event that has been found to be associated with an increased incidence of physical and mental symptoms and a higher rate of mortality among the recently bereaved, when compared to matched groups of nonbereaved (Rees and Lutkins 1967; Young, Benjamin, and Wallis 1963). These persons do not, of course, die from a broken heart, but it can be speculated that the stresses resulting from their loss and the subsequent problems in readjustment make them more vulnerable to a variety of disease processes (see Rahe 1972).

Being widowed is not usually considered a psychiatric problem, but does represent a stress with major consequences for the individual. Widowhood is often found to be accompanied by severe symptoms of psychological distress. The time immediately after the death of one's spouse is typically experienced as a period of numbness or shock (Parkes 1970; Shneidman 1976). In some cases the bereaved person will carry on with the funeral arrangements and other matters, appearing brave in the eyes of friends or relatives. In other instances, however, this initial shock leads to a general numbing of reactions and unresponsiveness. The person at that point in time may be highly suggestible and may later have amnesia regarding this period. Within about 1 week, symptoms of distress emerge more clearly (Parkes 1970). The most prominent manifestations are depression, sleep problems, and frequent crying (Clayton, Halikes, and Maurice 1971). Other reactions, though seen less frequently, may be highly disturbing both to bereaved persons and to those around them. These problems include pain attacks, difficulties concentrating, complaints of poor memory, irritability, anger, guilt feelings, anorexia, weight loss, hallucinatory experiences, and multiple somatic symptoms (Clayton, Halikes, and Maurice 1971; Parkes 1970). The period of most intense grief lasts from 1 to 3 months, and is sometimes accompanied by an intense preoccupation with the deceased. This preoccupation may involve dwelling on those places or objects that the bereaved person associates with his or her spouse. It may also be comprised of what Parkes (1970) calls a perceptual set for the lost person. The bereaved person has a tendency to pay attention to those stimuli in the environment that suggest the deceased, sometimes creating the illusion that the person is present. There may be hallucinatory experiences where the widow believes she has seen her husband. The feeling that one's lost spouse is present, especially in the first months following death, is very common.

While acute symptoms usually subside within a few months, the effects of the death continue to be felt for a longer period. There continue to be differences between widows and persons not widowed, particularly in psychological and somatic complaints, for 18 months and possibly longer after the loss (Parkes 1970).

Feelings of guilt, anger, and suicidal ideation can be prominent during the bereavement period. Thoughts of suicide have been reported in only 1 percent of a large sample of recently widowed men and women (Clayton, Halikes, and Maurice 1971). While statistically infrequent, the possibility of suicide should be carefully evaluated in working with the bereaved person. Guilt and angry feelings are more common. Guilt is more likely to be expressed in terms of the deceased person's illness, that the survivor should have gotten him to the hospital sooner, or taken other steps that might have changed the course of the illness (Clayton, Halikes, and Maurice 1971). Expressions of regret over not having said or done things with one's spouse while he or she was alive are somewhat less frequent. Anger will be directed either at the deceased, for having abandoned the person, or at others who have in some ways failed to support the widow. One common area of complaint involves the physician's handling of the spouse's illness, particularly that he did not discuss the seriousness of the illness and did not let the survivor know when death was imminent (Clayton, Halikes, and Maurice 1971). Physicians who were seen as having a beneficial effect had taken time to talk to the widow, offered reassurance, or made some other gesture to indicate their concern, such as sending flowers or paying a visit to the funeral home or widow's home.

Parkes (1970), in examining expressions of anger toward physicians, clergy, and family members, suggests that by their intensity they must be considered as part of the bereavement reaction, but while angry feelings can become exaggerated during this period of acute grief, it should not be overlooked that anger is often an appropriate reaction to the circumstances faced by a widow. Because of their own fears of death or the lack of socializing experiences in dealing with the bereaved, many persons are uncomfortable around a recently widowed person. These can include family members, friends, lawyers, physicians, and personnel in those state and private organizations through which the widowed person must rearrange his or her financial affairs. These individuals may try to avoid the recently widowed, offer innocuous advice, or get impatient when the widow does not bounce back quickly. If he or she recovers quickly, they may imply that the normal period of grief is not being observed. This difficulty of others in dealing with death and bereavement can only increase the sense of isolation of the newly widowed, and lead to feelings of resentment and anger.

Some studies show widows engaging in increased use of physicians for treatment of the physical and mental symptoms of bereavement, while others suggest little physician involvement. Looking at the medical records of young women who were widowed, Parkes (1964) compared the period since the spouse's death to that preceding the bereavement period. The number of consultations for both physical symptoms and psychological symptoms was found to be much greater during the bereavement period. In contrast, Clayton, Halikes, and Maurice (1971) found that a majority of widows and widowers in their sample used sleeping or other psycho-active medications during the first month of bereavement, but few called or saw their physicians during that time. Based on a 30-month follow-up, Maddison and Viola (1968) report that only a minority (15 percent) of widows consulted with their physicians concerning psychological symptoms and none saw a psychiatrist, even though the level of psychological distress experienced was high.

There have been few studies that have systematically explored the relation of the person's age when his or her spouse dies with subsequent adjustment. As noted in Chapter 4, because women have a life expectancy 7 years greater than men's, and since women tend to marry men who are older than themselves, a majority of married women will become widows in the later years. Based on 1974 figures, 52.4 percent of women over the age of 65 are widows, compared to 14.4 percent of men (Butler and Lewis 1977). It has been suggested that adjustment to widowhood might actually be better among older persons. Neugarten (1970) has viewed widowhood and other similar events from a life-span perspective. She proposes that events can be "on-time" or "off-time," depending on when they occur. Widowhood would be considered on-time in later life, because there will have been greater opportunity for anticipatory socialization. The widowed person will know others with similar experiences who can offer support and practical advice. Family responsibility, especially the care of children, will also have lessened. On the other hand, the death of a spouse in old age may be more difficult to overcome. Because of the greater longevity of women, widowers have a good opportunity to remarry either younger women or women of their own age. For widows, however, the opportunities for finding a mate, or even socially sanctioned sexual outlets, are restricted. While there are more older women than men, men marry more frequently. It has been estimated that 35,000 older men marry each year, compared to 16,000 older women (Butler and Lewis 1977). In addition, older widows and widowers alike may experience other losses in their social network, as friends or relatives, or in some cases even their children, also die. Thus while in some ways there is potentially greater support for an older person who is widowed, the loss may have a more profound impact.

A majority of current studies of widows have focused only on the younger widow, in some cases under 65, and in a few projects under 45. One study compared patterns of bereavement in persons over and under 65, with few differences found at approximately 1 month after the death (Clayton, Halikes, and Maurice 1971). Further investigation is needed to clarify if there are different manifestations of grief and different treatment issues in young and old widowed persons.

Sex differences in adjustment to widowhood have been consistently reported. While it was noted above that widowers are more likely than widows to remarry, the loss of their wife has catastrophic effects on some older men. The risk of mortality following the death of a spouse has been found to be greater in men than women (Young, Benjamin, and Wallis 1963; Rees and Lutkins 1967). Men also often face more adjustment problems (Berardo 1970). They may not be able to manage household routines, such as cooking, shopping, and laundry. If they depended on their wives for managing social affairs, they may find themselves cut off from friends and even other family members. In some other respects, however, the loss of a spouse has a greater impact on widows. Current cohorts of older women tended to work intermittently during their married lives, or not at all. The jobs they held also were likely to be low paying and to involve few skills. As a consequence, they are not likely to have accumulated much in their own Social Security account and in private pensions. In addition, in the past many private pensions paid little or no money for survivor's benefits (Albert and Zarit 1977). The older woman who wants to return to work to supplement her income faces a limited job market because of age discrimination and because she may not have acquired many work skills during her married life. While 1 in 4 men over 65 work, only 1 in 10 elderly women are employed (Albert and Zarit 1977). Another difficulty is that the unattached woman often feels out of place in social gatherings. It is considered unusual for women to go to social events unescorted. With the problems of urban crime, many older women become virtual prisoners in their homes at night. In some social situations the widow is viewed as an oddity who does not fit into the couples-oriented event, or may even be perceived as a threat who might steal other women's husbands. One common complaint is the inability to make new friends. Given these considerations, it is not surprising that widows report loneliness as their worst problem (Lopata 1973).

Counseling the recently bereaved person can have major beneficial effects. Treatment is likely to involve 3 facets: providing a supportive relationship, giving information about what the widow or widower is experiencing, and problem solving. A supportive relationship will reduce the feelings of distress and loneliness following a death. Having a confidant has been found important in improving morale in widowed persons (Lowenthal and Haven 1968). Professional counseling can augment the widow's existing friendships, or take the place of a confidant when none is present. Second, it is useful to help bereaved persons put their experiences into a broader perspective. Some may view their behavior, such as feeling the presence of their deceased spouse, as abnormal. Explaining that this is a normal reaction is often helpful. Others may wonder when it is appropriate to resume activities, and can be helped to decide, based on their own needs, how to proceed. They can similarly be helped to place their feelings of guilt, anger, or abandonment in a broader perspective. If persons have the feeling they did not do enough for their spouse, they can be helped to see both what they did give and that most people share this feeling of not having done enough. If they feel relieved that their spouse has died after a debilitating illness, they can be helped not to feel guilty for this feeling. The counselor can point out that their feelings do not represent a betrayal of their spouse, and often reflect appropriate concern that one's spouse not suffer too long.

Widowed persons may also need help with tangible problems, especially involving finances and housing. In addition, when other family relationships, such as between a mother and her children, have become complicated by the death, family sessions may help reestablish positive feelings and support.

It is sometimes considered that the best treatment involves helping the widow to grieve. It is presumed that if there is not sufficient mourning following the death, the feelings will linger and impair the person's subsequent functioning. Parkes (1970) does report that women who showed less distress in early phases of widowhood had a poorer adjustment after 1 year. His sample, however, was small and highly selective. It is likely that some persons can adjust well to their loss without excessive expressions of grief. If the spouse was ill for a long time before death, they may have mourned beforehand, or feel relieved of the burden of care. Their mourning may also be briefer if the relationship was not a good one. There is no evidence of norms for the amount of mourning that is healthy. If a bereaved person does want to discuss the loss, or begins to reconstruct his or her life soon after the death of a spouse, that individual should not be pushed by a therapist into expressions of grief. The possibility of unexpressed feelings can be tentatively explored, but if the individual does not want to proceed in that direction, that decision must be respected.

In recent years widows' programs have been established that are run by widows themselves. The groups offer an opportunity for sharing feelings of grief and loss with persons who have gone through the same thing. They are also helpful in the practical problems of reconstructing one's life following the death of a husband (Silverman 1977). There are, unfortunately, no reports of similar programs for widowers.

There is some evidence that suggests that the value of widows groups may be in creating an alternative social world to couple-oriented activities. Barrett (1978) compared the effects of 3 types of therapy group for widows: a self-help group; one in which the development of confidant relationships was emphasized; and a group modeled on women's consciousness raising. Results in these groups were contrasted to a waiting list. Participation was not limited to recent widows, and the average duration of being widowed was over 4 years. The findings indicated significant changes over time on the various outcome measures used, but no overall difference between the treatment groups and the waiting list. Follow-ups indicated, however, that these changes were maintained over time, and that there was a surprisingly high rate of contact among group members after completion of the treatment. In other words, a major effect of widows groups may be in forming new social relationships.

Other Disorders

Two major psychiatric problems, alcoholism and schizophrenia, are manifested by many older persons. In the case of alcohol abuse, the prevalence in old age has often been underestimated. With schizophrenia, there continues to be a controversy over whether new cases develop for the first time after age 60. Nonetheless, persons who develop schizophrenic disorders earlier in the life span often continue to have problems in functioning into old age, and represent the majority of cases in some geriatric mental health services.

ALCOHOLISM

It is sometimes believed that alcoholic problems have their widest prevalence in middle age between years 35 and 50. Some writers have suggested that at advanced ages there is a burning-out phenomenon, during which the alcoholic gradually reduces his consumption. Several studies, however, suggest a high prevalence of alcoholic problems among the community elderly and for in- and outpatient psychiatric samples.

Based on community surveys, it has been estimated that between 2 and 10 percent of the elderly are alcoholics, with the figures higher for widowed persons or those having medical problems (Schuckit 1977). One household survey indicated that the highest rate of alcohol problems was found in the 45- to 54-year age group, with a prevalence of 23 cases per 1,000. In the 65- to 75-year group, however, the rate was 22 cases per 1,000. Among widowers, it was estimated that 105 per 1,000 had drinking problems (Bailey, Haberman, and Alksne 1965). In research that focuses on consecutive admissions to psychiatric units, the figures are even higher. Gaitz and Baer (1971) report that 44 of 100 consecutive admissions to a geriatric treatment unit had alcohol problems. Restricting their sample to those persons who had a first psychiatric admission after age 60, Simon, Epstein, and Reynolds (1968) found that 28 percent of all patients in a geriatric screening ward had a serious drinking problem. For 23 percent of the total sample, alcohol abuse was the major disorder causing hospitalization. In one survey of persons over 65 at a community mental health center, 17 percent were alcoholics (Zimberg 1975).

In addition to its prevalence in the aged, especially among widowers, alcoholism may have more deleterious effects on older persons than on the young. Studies of alcohol ingestion in animals indicate that older organisms have more behavioral impairment, metabolize the alcohol more slowly, have greater changes in brain chemistry, and display greater toxicity. Limited research on humans indicates similar findings (see Wood 1978 for a review). Furthermore, alcohol can cause impairments in those organs that are most vulnerable to the effects of aging: the liver, lungs, heart, gastrointestinal tract, and brain.

An important dimension in the assessment of older alcoholics is whether drinking problems were of recent origin or long standing. It has been suggested that the older alcoholic usually begins drinking heavily in middle age (Schuckit 1977). Gaitz and Baer (1971) found that only 5 of their 44 admissions for alcoholism had an onset in old age. On the other hand, the high prevalence noted in elderly widowers suggests that many persons begin drinking heavily later in life, following stressful events. One comparison of alcoholics with early and late life onset confirms this impression. Rosin and Glatt (1971) report that those older patients with a long history of alcoholism presented a clinical picture of personality disorders, including neurotic, self-indulgent, and egocentric behaviors. Among persons with late onset who began drinking heavily in middle age or later, illnesses or other stresses associated with old age appeared to be the precipitants. For 15 of the approximately 34 persons with late onset, the precipitant was bereavement; for another 10 persons, alcoholism developed after retirement; and in 6 individuals the alcohol problem appeared to begin following the development of an Alzheimer's-type dementia. Thus there may be different factors related to alcoholism depending on whether onset was in early, mid-, or late adulthood.

Three clinical groups of elderly alcoholics have been described (Gaitz and Baer 1971; Simon, Epstein, and Reynolds 1968). These are: alcoholics with no accompanying chronic organic brain damage; alcoholics with chronic brain disease caused by the alcohol; and those with brain damage due to arteriosclerotic or Alzheimer's-type dementia. The extent of cognitive and personality disturbance is greater when chronic brain damage is present. The mortality rate is also higher, 37 percent compared to 12 percent at a 30-month follow-up (Gaitz and Baer 1971). In comparisons of alcoholics with brain damage to patients with dementia but no alcohol problem, the former were judged to have fewer personality and behavioral problems, based on a standardized psychiatric examination. The two groups did not differ in their cognitive functioning. Those in the alcoholic group who died during the follow-up period, however, were considerably younger than senile dementia patients, 65.7 years compared to 74.1 years. One other major difference between these 2 groups was that the family members of persons with dementia and no alcoholism held significantly more positive attitudes toward the patient, despite the presence of more disturbed behavior (Gaitz and Baer 1971). Thus a major implication of alcoholism in elderly persons is that it places a greater strain on family relationships than do other disorders.

The importance of screening for alcoholic problems among older persons is that these patients are often mistaken as having disorders associated with age or chronic illness (Rosin and Glatt 1971). Many of the symptoms they present, including social isolation, falls, malnutrition, general physical decline, and chronic brain damage, are found in elderly persons with no alcohol problems. It has also been noted that many physicians are reluctant to diagnose an alcohol problem (Zimberg 1975). There is some preliminary evidence, however, that elderly alcoholics who had a late onset of drinking respond well to treatment. Schuckit (1977), for example, reports that 73 percent of elderly alcoholics with onset of drinking in middle age successfully completed a treatment program. Among younger alcoholics the completion rate was 40 percent. Zimberg (1975) also reports that treatment with elderly alcoholics who had a late onset of drinking is often successful and rapid. His treatment consisted of the use of antidepressant medications and the development of a supportive, socializing relationship. This approach is consistent with the evidence cited above that the late onset of alcoholism often follows stressful events, much like a reactive depression. He further notes that in contrast to younger alcoholics or those elderly persons who evidenced early onset of drinking, treatment usually did not involve either medication with antibuse or involvement in Alcoholics Anonymous.

The following case illustrates the type of rapid response to treatment that Zimberg describes. Mrs. K. was a 66-year-old woman with a 5-year history of excessive drinking. She was brought to a gerontology counseling service by her son and daughter-in-law, with whom she lived. They were concerned because she did little during the day except sit and sip wine. She also engaged in some behaviors that the daughter-in-law found embarrassing, such as walking outside and picking up rocks, and being unable to follow through on simple household tasks that she was asked to do. Her drinking had apparently coincided with or just preceded her retirement. Her husband had died 2 years before that event. After her retirement she gradually began curtailing activities, and following her move from her home town to her son's house she gave up virtually all outside interests. She stated the one thing she enjoyed was the wine. On examination she showed a moderate degree of cognitive impairment in a mental status examination.

In the initial treatment session a contract was made with her to try to give up the wine. She was to substitute punch for it, because she liked to have a sweet drink to sip during the day. She was encouraged to try to find enjoyment from other activities. Her son, who would drink as much as a 6-pack of beer a day, also agreed to give that up. The following week the family members said she had been able stop drinking. At that point efforts were made to involve her in activities and to cope with some of the problems in the family relationships. After 6 weeks the son and daughter-in-law felt her mood, attention, and other behaviors had improved considerably. Mrs. K. was also satisfied and the treatment was terminated. Follow-up 2 years later indicated that neither the drinking nor relationship problems had returned.

This case is remarkable for the rapid improvement. It also raises the issue that late life drinking problems are reactive, rather than chronic, disorders that will respond to treatment similar to that for reactive depressions. More systematic study of elderly alcoholics is needed, however, to determine the optimal treatment approaches both for those persons with late life onset and individuals with a longer history of alcoholism. Greater attention to alcohol problems is warranted, both because of the potential health problems and other complications that can result, and because the prospects for treatment of many elderly alcoholics appear favorable.

SCHIZOPHRENIA

There is a long-standing controversy over whether schizophrenic disorders can occur in late life. Some authors have regarded older persons manifesting pervasive paranoid symptoms as affected by a schizophrenic disorder. Others have emphasized differences between paranoid patients with early or late onset, particularly the better prognosis of the latter (Kay et al. 1976; Tanna 1974). Excluding persons with paranoid symptoms, only a few cases of schizophrenia with an apparent late life origin can be found in the literature (see Post 1980 for a review).

Few new cases seem to emerge in old age. On the other hand, many persons who developed schizophrenic disorders early in life continue to manifest problems in old age. Schizophrenia has been described both as a chronic problem with little likelihood of remission and as becoming gradually more muted in its manifestations as the person ages, but few systematic studies have been made of how symptoms change over time. Based on a review of the available research, Post (1980) presents evidence that suggests 3 possible courses of schizophrenic disorders that originated in earlier life. First, some adults hospitalized for schizophrenia suffer only that single episode, and function adequately afterwards. The onset of the psychosis is sudden, and in other respects the case histories suggest a reactive problem. In the other 2 groups of patients the onset of symptoms is more insidious. One group has an apparent decrease in symptomatology over time, although continuing to manifest lower levels of social functioning than would be expected in the adult population. In the other group, consisting of approximately one-third of cases on whom records are available, there is no major change in symptoms or functioning with advancing age. Because the sample of patients in the studies that Post reviewed often experienced repeated and sometimes long-term hospitalizations, it cannot be determined if the patterns of symptoms are due to the natural course of the disorder or to the effects of institutionalization.

The treatment of elderly schizophrenics is likely to constitute a major problem for a geriatric service. Because schizophrenics coming for treatment have the most intractable symptoms, i.e., they have not improved with time or prior treatment, the issues they present will be difficult and time consuming. It is probable that maintenance on phenothiazines will have some benefits, but there are no systematic studies available on the use of these medications with elderly schizophrenics or on the value of other treatment approaches. One must also consider that persons who spent many years hospitalized in mental institutions will have developed few of the social skills necessary for functioning independently in the community. Their problems will be due less to the "illness" and more to a syndrome of social inadequacy that was induced by the institution.

Both Macmillan (1958) and Whitehead (1970) describe programs in England that reintegrate elderly schizophrenics into community settings, and minimize inpatient time. These programs emphasize the availability of community services and continuity of care between hospital and outpatient settings, including such things as day care and interventions with family members to help them cope with their relatives. The success of these English programs, however, has not been duplicated in this country. Long-term populations of schizophrenics have been discharged from mental hospitals during the past decade, but were largely placed into nursing homes. While done in the name of better treatment, this shift has actually had the opposite effect. Patients find themselves in a similar institutional environment, but with even less availability of psychiatric treatment, except for medications (Kahn 1975).

Elderly schizophrenics, then, present a special problem for geriatric services. They have chronic mental symptoms and have in the past often received only inadequate, custodial care, but their problems are not, in a strict sense, geriatric disorders. Using resources for their care takes away from what is available for the treatment of persons with actual geriatric problems, and with a better prognosis. A program combining the use of medications and community supports, however, appears effective in reducing the need for continuing institutionalization of these patients.

OTHER MENTAL HEALTH PROBLEMS

As in the case of those problems that have already been discussed, there is little evidence of how various other mental health disorders change over time. There is some question, in particular, about whether anxiety states and obsessive-compulsion disorders continue to be manifested in old age. While some authors consider that anxiety represents a problem of older persons, others do not distinguish between anxiety and depression in their conceptualization or treatment. Based on clinical impressions, the occurrence of simple phobic reactions appears negligible in later life. The extent to which other anxiety states occur, independent of depression, and whether different treatment is appropriate, remain to be clarified.

Similarly, the incidence of obsessive-compulsive disorders in later life is not known. It has been suggested that these and other neurotic symptom patterns abate with age (Meyer 1974). In some cases, however, persons who are depressed or who have hypochondriacal symptoms present a history of obsessive thinking or compulsive behaviors before the onset of their current problem. It is not known, then, to what extent neurotic symptoms in adulthood continue, are diminished with the passage of time, or shift in focus with advancing age. In part, this lack of information reflects the imprecision in the current diagnostic categories and diagnostic system. The development of more reliable diagnostic procedures in general will lead to better descriptions of the types of problem occurring in old age, and, in turn, to more systematic treatment approaches.

Summary

The types of psychological problem presented by an elderly population are varied, ranging from situational disturbances after the death of a spouse to problems that are often more persistent and upsetting, like paranoid or hypochondriacal complaints. At this point in time, our understanding of many of these problems is limited. There has not been adequate identification or description of persons with these disorders. There have also been only limited studies of their treatment. How psychological symptoms change over the course of the life span has not received sufficient attention. In reports of outcome, the limited evidence available is often contradictory. Some authors, for example, are pessimistic about improvements in older paranoid patients, while others suggest there can be considerable success. Because of our limited knowledge, treatment approaches must be conservative. The practitioner should be cautious so that clients do not become overly dependent, or intensive treatment serve to create some new difficulties. At the same time there is a need for a measure of creativity in working with older patients, both in making more systematic and precise evaluations and in developing treatment approaches.

PART III

Treatment of Behavioral Problems in Old Age

CHAPTER 10

Principles of Treatment: A Model of Community Care

AGE IS GENERALLY CONSIDERED to be a barrier to the effective treatment of psychological problems. The old are variously seen as not capable of responding to therapies, or not sufficiently interesting to highly trained therapists, or not worth the time to a therapist who might otherwise work with the young, who have their whole lives ahead of them. This pessimistic attitude is unjustified. The problems of the aged, even those considered the most intractable, often respond to treatment. In fact, the possibilities in treatment are not dissimilar to those with the young. With the effective delivery of services, the independence and competencies of many older persons can be maintained or even enhanced. For those persons with chronic or deteriorating conditions, active treatment can mitigate some of the adverse psychological consequences of the disorder, allowing patients and their families to adapt in the best possible way to the illness or disability.

In their survey of innovative mental health programs for the aged, Glasscote, Gudeman, and Miles (1977) suggest that treatment can be categorized according to 3 dimensions: (1) supportive services for physical maintenance of the individual, including housing; (2) clinical services; and (3) life-enhancing and preventive services. Examples of each treatment dimension are shown in Table 10.1. A comprehensive approach to the treatment of older persons involves attention to these various types of service. Individuals having personal or family adjustment problems or who are experiencing an acute crisis can receive traditional clinical services, including individual, family, and group psychotherapy. But the problems

TABLE 10.1. Comprehensive services for the aged

Accommodation

Services intended to help people continue living in their own homes, including
meals on wheels, chore services, telephone links, visits from social work-
ers, nurses, and physicians, and "friendly visits" from neighbors or other
volunteers.
Communal housing
Special housing, including congregate housing
Halfway houses
Board-and-care (or personal-care or sheltered-care) facilities
Intermediate-care-level nursing homes
Skilled-level nursing homes

Clinical Services

Therapeutic day programs
General hospital psychiatric units (or treatment on the regular wards of general
hospitals that do not have separate psychiatric units)
Community mental health centers and other facilities having outpatient mental
health services

Preventive, Supportive, and Life-Enhancing Programs

Nutrition programs
Social day programs
Peer support groups
Adult education programs
Legal aid
Transportation service
Programs providing opportunities to serve as volunteers
Outreach

Source: R. M. Glasscote, J. E. Gudeman, and D. G. Miles, *Creative Mental Health
Services for the Elderly* (Washington, D.C.: Joint Information Service, 1978). Reprinted by permission.

of many older persons are in part the result of social circumstances or
physical illness, so that successful interventions may involve such things
as arranging for economic supports, helping to coordinate different aspects
of medical care, finding home services for those with physical impairments, or developing an informal support network, consisting of neighbors
and friends of the patient, to call or drop by at regular times to see that
everything is all right. A model of mental health services for the elderly
that stresses the psychotherapeutic relationship of patient to professional,
to the exclusion of other interventions, will not be effective for the majority of older persons with behavioral problems. Professionals who are
not willing to leave their offices at times, to work as part of a treatment
team, or to talk to personnel of other agencies to coordinate services
should not work with the elderly.

This chapter will present a community-oriented model of mental health services for older persons that stresses the integration of clinical and supportive services. Subsequent chapters describe various approaches to providing clinical and preventive services, including individual psychotherapy, various group approaches, family treatment, and interventions for sexual problems and in cases of brain disorders.

The Paradox in Aging Services

Like members of ethnic minorities or women, the aged have held a disadvantaged position in society, which has been reflected in the mental health field. As described in Chapter 1, few older persons have actually received mental health services, even from agencies such as community mental health centers, which are mandated to serve all persons in their catchment area. Even as mental health programs have become more open to the needs of minorities and other special groups, a smaller percentage of older persons have been receiving such services. Since 1946 there has been a drop of 71 percent in the number of older persons admitted for the first time to an inpatient psychiatric service, with similar decreases in the use of outpatient services (Kahn 1975). At the same time, the number of older persons in nursing homes has increased sharply, rising by almost one-half million between 1960 and 1970 (Redick 1974). During that period the proportion of all persons receiving institutional care of some sort has risen from 4 to 5 percent of the total of persons over 65. Between 1963 and 1973, the number of nursing homes increased 96 percent, and the number of beds 268 percent (Department of Health, Education, and Welfare 1975). In addition, as state mental hospitals have "deinstitutionalized" long-term patients, many older, chronic schizophrenics have been transferred to nursing homes. Thus older persons now found among nursing home populations include those with geriatric mental disorders who are no longer being served in the state mental health systems and those with chronic mental disabilities.

This situation has created an interesting paradox: we are simultaneously doing too little and too much in responding to the mental health needs of older persons. The pattern of doing too little is evident—services are either not provided or sometimes not available. At the same time, the one type of facility that has been used increasingly by the aged, including those with mental health problems, is the nursing home. Institutionalization in a nursing home, however, usually represents an intervention that is more intensive than needed and that has unfortunate, negative consequences. This paradox reflects the prevailing custodial philosophy of care of the aged. Believing that not much can be done, mental health planners and service personnel have offered few imaginative programs to ameliorate or prevent the major mental health problems of the elderly. Many problems that would respond to treatment, if attention were given to them at an early point, become unmanageable if not treated. They strain the resources and patience of a person's family, and create feelings of hopelessness in the person (Macmillan 1958). At that crisis point the person or family are told there is nothing that can be done and institutional care is recommended. Because of the lack of ameliorative, community-based services, there is, ironically, an overuse of more intensive, long-term institutional care. Thus the prevailing pessimism creates a self-fulfilling prophecy: by treating the elderly as capable of responding only to custodial care, we have increased substantially the number of chronically institutionalized older persons.

The Custodial Model: Limits and Implications

Custodialism as a philosophy of care is not likely to be explicitly advanced by many persons in the field of aging, but it is nonetheless widely prevalent in all varieties of programs. At its core is an emphasis on adjustment and accommodation, rather than involving the person actively in treatment to set and work toward goals. Professionals view themselves as having to make decisions about what is best for their older clients, who are then encouraged to follow these imposed plans, and labeled as deviant, childish, confused, or senile when they do not. Because of the physical impairments, low social status, and low education of many older persons, it is relatively easy for professionals to fall into a pattern of deciding they know what is best for their clients. Placed in a dependent situation, older persons are not actively engaged in working toward solutions of their problems. In addition, their dependent position leads to the generalization that they must be helped in all areas of their lives, not only those situations in which they are having difficulties.

Custodial philosophies are most likely to be encountered in those settings providing long-term care, such as nursing and convalescent homes and, to a lesser extent, various kinds of retirement hotel, especially those with a greater degree of regimentation. Because of their visibility to the community and care-givers, these institutions have an impact on all types of service offered to the elderly. They establish an expectation that eventually all elderly will need this type of care. Those expectations affect the delivery of other types of service, because even the best-functioning older persons come to be viewed as requiring someone to take care of them. The belief that most elderly cannot make decisions and cannot function independently is, of course, incorrect. But assumptions about the necessity of long-term care for many older persons, that such care is inevitable and that it is the best alternative, are also incorrect.

Because custodial approaches have become so deeply ingrained in our treatment of the aged, it is often overlooked that the ways we provide care actually produce many of the disabilities that we say require custodial care in the first place. The following sections review some of the problems created by the custodial approaches in long-term care settings. By under- standing the process through which overcaring leads to disabilities, it will be possible to develop active treatment approaches, and to diminish our reliance on institutional care.

Nursing Home Care

The are several problems with the use of nursing homes for treatment of the various health and mental problems of the aged. Numerous exposés in recent years (see Townsend 1971; Mendelsohn 1974) have made many persons aware of the glaring deficiencies in some long-term care settings. Instances of brutal treatment, negligence, overmedication, unclean facili- ties, poor food, and reprisals against patients who complain have occurred far too often (Subcommittee on Long-Term Care 1974). More subtle abuses have included excessive bills, charging patients for services or medications that are not delivered, and providing kickbacks to physicians, pharmacists, or other persons in exchange for the right to provide services to patients. Conditions of this kind are deplorable, but there are more basic problems with the concept of long-term institutional care.

The first problem with the use of nursing homes for treatment of the physical and mental disorders of the aged is that the relocation of an older person from community to an institutional setting is stressful. The concern with problems of relocation developed from some serendipitous findings. Following the closing of an old-age home and relocation of its residents to nursing homes, Aldrich and Mendkoff (1963) compared the death rate among former residents in the first year after the move with the expected mortality of residents calculated from records covering the previous 10 years. They found the death rate in the year after relocation was sub- stantially higher than the expected mortality for residents of all ages. During that year 32 percent died, compared to an average of 19 percent for the preceding 10-year period. In a study with major impact and com- parable findings, Blenkner and her associates (Blenker 1967) looked at the impact of social services on older persons. Individuals coming to a family service center were randomly assigned into one of 3 treatment groups: intensive, intermediate, and minimal. The minimal program con- sisted of information and referral, while the intensive service included the active involvement of both a nurse and a social worker; the intermediate fell somewhere in between in amount of professional involvement. After a 6-month period it was found that the intensive treatment group had 4 times the death rate as those assigned for minimal treatment, while those in the intermediate program had about twice the risk of dying. The reason for this variance is that case workers providing intensive treatment often felt it necessary to place the person in an institutional setting. The increased death rate was found principally among those relocated older persons.

What is remarkable about this study is that the assignment to treatment groups was random. That means that persons in the minimal group were likely to have been experiencing the same types of health, social, and psychological problem as those in the intensive treatment group. The former did manage to cope with their difficulties in a community setting. In contrast, the involvement of professionals led to the provision of what has to be considered too much service. Relocation to a protected setting was too often judged to be warranted, and did not lead to a better amelioration of problems. Rather, this type of intervention had an unintended negative consequence for some relocated individuals.

The number of persons involved in the Blenkner study were small, but subsequent research on relocation has shown consistently that there is an increased risk in health and mortality, especially when the move is from community to institution (see Lieberman 1974 for a review of relocation studies). Relocation of the elderly from one community setting to another does not seem to have a deleterious outcome (Wittels and Botwinick 1974), while studies of relocation from one institutional setting to another have had contradictory findings, some indicating an increased risk of mortality (Killian 1970) and others showing no differences (Borup, Gallego, and Heffernan 1979). One recent trend in gerontological research has been to try to alter the risks involved in relocation by preparing the individual more extensively for the move, or in some other ways increasing the person's perceived control over the relocation (Schulz and Brenner 1977). While commendable, these programs have not as yet demonstrated reduced risks under controlled experimental conditions. Moreover, they ignore the most direct solution—developing alternatives for institutional care.

In addition to increased risk of mortality, institutional settings also have a deleterious impact on independent functioning. Upon encountering a severely deteriorated, bedridden patient, it is often difficult to imagine what types of treatment other than custodial might have been possible. It should be considered, however, that the physical and mental deficits of some nursing home patients have been brought about by institutional care, rather than by illnesses or age. In assessing the behavior of older persons, Kahn (1975; 1977) has proposed the concept of excess disabilities, that is, difficulties in functioning that exceed what would be expected based on the person's physical condition alone. Two persons, for example, may have suffered cerebrovascular accidents (strokes) that caused similar amounts of brain damage, but one individual is able to learn to perform a variety of activities again, such as dressing and walking with the assistance of a cane, while the other remains nearly totally incapacitated. Similarly, in comparing 2 persons with senile dementia, one may manifest an excessive amount of cognitive impairment by withdrawing and refusing to respond to tasks he is capable of performing. Excess disabilities can develop because of the response of an individual to illness. Persons who adapt to a cerebrovascular accident by denying they are ill or by passively withdrawing from their surroundings have been found to show greater amounts of impairment than persons who have similar degrees of brain damage but who acknowledge their illness more directly (Zarit and Kahn 1974). Excess disabilities can also develop because of the responses by others to a person's impairment. Where an environment encourages and reinforces independent behavior, that behavior is likely to be relearned and maintained. If an environment discourages independence, however, functional abilities are likely to deteriorate.

Patterns of care within nursing homes appear to lead to the manifestation of excess disabilities, through the provision of too much assistance. Staffs often perform functions of which the person is capable, for example, dressing or feeding patients, or wheeling ambulatory patients around in chairs. Many of the individuals given help in daily activities can initially perform these actions with little or no assistance. By providing help, however, the nursing staff will undermine the person's independence in 3 ways. First, these actions decrease the individual's confidence in himself to carry out a given activity. Second, some persons may become psychologically dependent on the assistance, looking for help when it is not needed. Third, the person's physical ability to carry out many actions can deteriorate if he or she does not exercise the muscles involved. This phenomenon has also been described as hypokinetic disease (de Vries 1975), where disuse leads to the atrophy of muscles and to a decreased functional capacity of the individual.

The pressures to provide too much care are strongly ingrained within nursing homes. The function of the long-term care facility is often conceived as one of providing care and assistance. Some authors even propose as an important criterion for judging the quality of a facility the amount of tender loving care (TLC) that is given (Homburger and Bonner 1964). In perceiving one's role as caring, however, the staff, from good intentions, may take over too many activities from the patients, especially those individuals who are having some difficulties performing an activity or who do not perform a given activity particularly well, such as dressing or even feeding themselves. The nursing home staff may also take over functions because it is easier than to allow patients to take their time. Some homes insist that all residents be dressed by a certain time. To reach this goal the staff will go through the rooms, getting everyone dressed. This will have an especially adverse effect on those individuals who can dress themselves, but who do so slowly, and thus would not finish within the staff's timelines unless assisted. In some facilities patients are lined up in a row at meals and fed in an assembly-line manner, in order that the meal be finished on schedule and with no undue mess. Individuals who could feed themselves slowly, and with an occasional spill, are often fed this way.

Nursing homes sometimes provide too much caring out of a sense of self-protection. In an effort to avoid the displeasure of state regulating bodies and of patients' families, the staff will take no chances that patients would do anything that is risky or might potentially be discomforting. A person who walks unsteadily will be encouraged to sit in a wheel chair to avoid a chance of falling. Someone who feeds himself in a halting way will be fed, so that visitors will not see food stains on his clothes. A person having trouble dressing herself will be dressed by the staff, so that her family can feel she is being well cared for. This pressure for too much care is deeply ingrained, even when a facility maintains a rehabilitation program. In one long-term care institution visited by the author, the physical therapy provided to patients was boasted of by the administration as an example of the high quality care in that facility. Patients receiving physical therapy, however, were not allowed to practice their walking when back on the nursing floors. The 2 or 3 hours of training they received weekly was not sufficient to restore their functional capacity. Because the pressure not to take any risks with patients is great, especially those risks that could lead to the displeasure of relatives or official regulatory agencies, patients are restricted in certain activities. As a consequence, many lose functional abilities that they had, in full or in part, when they entered the institution.

A study by Epstein and Simon (1968) demonstrates the extent of impairment in self-care activities of nursing home patients. They compared the outcomes at 1 year of 2 equivalent samples of psychiatrically impaired older persons. The first, evaluated before 1965, was sent to state mental hospitals for treatment; the second was seen after 1965, when changes in state policy mandated sending the mentally impaired elderly to nursing homes. The study compared only those older persons with no history of psychiatric illness before age 60. While in many respects the 2 samples were comparable, it was judged at the initial evaluation that more of the persons sent to state mental hospitals showed evidence of simultaneous acute and chronic brain syndromes. The outcome at 1 year indicated a somewhat higher death rate among those sent to state mental hospitals (39 percent, compared to 25 percent) and similar discharge rates (25 percent from state mental hospitals; 21 percent from nursing homes). On tests of orientation, those still in state mental hospitals performed better than nursing home patients. In areas of self-care, however, there were great differences, with the mental hospital patients performing much better in areas such as toileting, bathing, grooming, and dressing. This

difference in self-care was shown even by patients who were no longer institutionalized, with those who had been in nursing homes performing more
poorly. In discussing their findings, Epstein and Simon (1968) note that
independence was fostered in the state mental hospitals because of staff
unavailability. Since the staff was not around to provide help, those persons who could manage their own self-care activities continued to do so
without any interference. While the 2 samples in this study were not
strictly comparable in terms of initial diagnosis, the outcome does suggest
the impact of nursing home care on self-maintenance activities, particularly how providing too much care undermines independent functioning.

The custodial philosophy of nursing homes leads to excess disabilities
in another way. In these settings there is very often no active treatment
of reversible psychiatric problems, such as delirium (acute brain syndromes)
or depression. In particular, while a considerable number of long-term care
residents can be observed manifesting various symptoms of depression,
very few are being treated with antidepressant medications (Glasscote
et al. 1976). The psychoactive medications used most commonly are tranquilizers to control behavior, but these can lead to toxic reactions and
other undesirable side effects.

The issue of excess disabilities is a unique problem for facilities serving
the aged. In addition, nursing homes have many of the same problems
that result from a regulated, institutional life as do other 24-hour care
settings, such as mental hospitals and prisons. According to many authors,
residents of these facilities are often suffering from a syndrome of institutionalism, that is, behavioral problems that derive from the nature of
the setting, but that are independent of whatever difficulties the person
had before entering (Ochberg, Zarcone, and Hamburg 1972; Macmillan
1958; Wing and Brown 1970). In mental hospitals, for example, the extent
of difficulties due to institutionalism are often greater than would be
caused by the behavioral problems that brought the person there in the
first place. The effects of institutionalization have been described by
Lieberman (1969) as

> poor adjustment, depression and unhappiness, intellectual ineffectiveness
> . . . , negative self-image, feelings of personal insignificance and impotency,
> and a view of the self as old. Residents tend to be docile, submissive, show
> a low range of interest and activities, and to live in the past rather than
> the future. They are withdrawn and unresponsive in relationship to
> others. (p. 331)

These problems derive from the nature of total care settings, as discussed
in Chapter 3.

As a result of being frustrated in their desire to maintain control over
decision making and aspects of personal care, individuals in institutions
lose their ability to cope in nonregulated setting. According to Ochberg,

Zarcone, and Hamburg (1972), "The institution sacrifices maintenance of the individual's coping mechanisms for the needs of the institution. Institutionalism then begins as a process of adaptation, but one that goes awry and untimately leads to maladaptation, especially a decrease in task orientation and an increase in the tendency to play the 'sick' role" (p. 92). The behaviors of persons in nursing homes need to be viewed in this context.

ALTERNATIVES TO NURSING HOMES: WITHIN-INSTITUTIONAL EFFORTS

There have been 2 basic approaches in attempts to ameliorate the problems of long-term care settings. The first stresses the need for reform of current facilities; the second emphasizes that many persons currently in long-term care could be maintained community settings if supportive services were available. Attempts to reform current practices in long-term care are well intended but fail to deal with the basic problems of custodialism and overcaring. But more important, these efforts to improve the quality of long-term care have had only a limited impact.

A variety of services have been tried in order to offset the negative effects of institutional life. These interventions have ranged from minimal, such as increased use of student volunteers, to sophisticated and intensive milieu-therapy programs (Gottesman 1973; McGinity and Stotsky 1967; Stotsky 1967.) Among the interventions offered have been activity and recreational programs (R. W. Davis 1967; Herman 1968; Jones 1972; Srour, Finnegan, and Delcioppo 1966); group psychotherapy (Saul and Saul 1974); physical therapy (Morrison 1969); music or art therapy (Shapiro 1969; Wagner and Lerner 1968); and behavior modification programs (Libb and Clements 1969; Filer and O'Connel 1964). In-service training programs have also been used (Penchansky and Taubenhaus 1965), and are required at periodic intervals in some states.

Where measurements have been made on the outcomes of these various interventions, the results are usually encouraging. Most studies report improvements in patient functioning following the development of a new program. There are, however, some problems in these studies that call into question the effectiveness of this approach. These problems include poor measurements, lack of adequate control groups, confusion about objectives, and inability to maintain positive findings over time. Measurements often consist of nonspecific characteristics, such as "improved self-concept," "better morale," "increased socialization," "increased group interaction," or "activity and conversations increased" (Kahn and Zarit 1974). "Morale" is a good example of the problems inherent in nonspecific measurements. Most interventions claim either explicitly or implicitly that they raise morale. Morale, however, is a global concept, and not necessarily related to the specific behavioral objectives of most intervention programs. It is quite conceivable that the programs will improve morale, but not have any impact on the person's functioning. In fact, it would seem that virtually any intervention would be able to improve morale or other nonspecific measures. This may be due to a "Hawthorne" effect, where any change in a boring environment is found to result in improvements in behavior (Lieberman 1969). Whether change of a few points on a morale scale is important for overall well-being, and whether that is really a goal of the patients themselves, have not been given adequate consideration.

As discussed in Chapter 3, morale or life satisfaction scales have another major drawback that is especially critical in an institutional population. Persons with senile dementia have a tendency to manifest denial as cognitive impairment increases. Thus a person may report higher life satisfaction while deteriorating in a more basic way (Kahn and Zarit 1974; Zarit and Kahn 1975).

Vague or global measures may also hide other types of deterioration. Jones (1972), for example, reported an increase of social interaction through the introduction of recreation therapy, but also noted more expressions of hostility, conflict, and mistrust among patients involved in the program. One particularly well-designed project reported a small amount of improvement in the experimental group relative to control subjects, but also observed that they had a higher death rate over the course of the intervention (Brody et al. 1971; Kleban, Brody, and Lawton 1971). Other studies have indicated the reinforcement of undesirable behaviors (Davison 1969). These findings suggest that where only general indicators of morale or life satisfaction have been employed, it cannot be assumed that other aspects of functioning have also improved.

The lack of adequate control groups is an obvious problem in many studies of intrainstitutional interventions. A similar problem exists when only cooperative or responsive patients are selected for inclusion in a program. Under those circumstances, persons most likely to improve become the experimental group, often with little or no information given about what percentage of persons were not selected or what kinds of problem those persons had.

Intervention programs are also often unclear about their objectives. It is usually not specified whether the intervention is to increase independence, leading to eventual discharge, or to improve adjustment to the facility, although these goals have quite different implications for treatment. In adult, hospitalized samples of psychiatric patients, ratings of improvement in behavior on the ward, which are often used to indicate readiness for discharge, have not been found to be related to adjustment following discharge (Forsyth and Fairweather 1961). Persons who are considered good patients are often unassertive, willing to follow staff directives and routines, and never any bother. This type of person is likely to have the hardest transition to an unstructured, noninstitutional setting. The extent to which these characteristics are shaped or reinforced by a treatment program decreases the likelihood of an eventual successful discharge. Some research suggests that these good patients may not even do well within the institution over the long run; persons who make the best adjustment to institutional life have instead been found to be aggressive and self-centered (Aldrich and Mendkoff 1963; Gottesman 1965; Kleban and Brody 1972; Turner, Tobin, and Lieberman 1972).

The objectives of intrainstitutional programs also do not distinguish between the person's functional deficiencies that may have led to institutionalization and the effects of institutional care on behavior. Treating features of a nursing home patient's behavior, such as apathy or withdrawal, with an activity or socializing program is actually placing the patient in a classic double-bind. In the particular program the patients are encouraged to behave as they did in the outside world, but back on their floors they once again become part of the institutional hierarchy in which they have little control over decisions affecting the most personal aspects of their lives. Exhortations to patients for greater openness and awareness of feelings are similarly naïve. Honest expressions of feelings are not likely to be accepted by many staff or administrative personnel, who retain ultimate control over patients. This type of double-bind may account for the increase in hostile and angry behavior reported by Jones (1972). Programs that emphasize a therapeutic milieu are probably more effective in countering the negative effects of institutional life, but 2 considerations must be taken into account. First, these programs become, in effect, treatments for the effects of institutionalization, rather than for problems that brought a person there initially; second, staff or administrative resistance to a truly noninstitutional environment may be so great as to undermine these efforts in important ways (Cohen and Kraft 1968; Kelman 1962). It is more convenient and efficient for an institution to have set routines and a hierarchical authority structure that denies patients status and control over personal habits and routines.

An additional problem with intrainstitutional interventions is that the mild positive benefits have been found to be short-lived, with behaviors declining after completion of a program (Pappas, Page, and Baker 1958; Cosin et al. 1958), or without the leaders' presence. This was the case even when the staff was trained to maintain the behavioral gains (Penchansky and Taubenhaus 1965).

These efforts to offset the negative effects of institutional care would be considered the best that could be done, if institutionalization were inevitable. Many persons do believe that patients are in nursing homes because no other treatment is possible. For many patients, perhaps the majority of those who reside in long-term care settings, institutionalization and its consequences might have been prevented in the first place.

OVERUSE OF LONG-TERM CARE

The potential of many persons currently in long-term care settings to function at a more independent level has been documented in many ways. First, as discussed above, at least some of the impairments manifested by persons in nursing facilities are due to the effects of the institution, not to illness or old age. By preventing institutionalization, some of the deterioration could be avoided. Second, it is often assumed that the amount of care provided in nursing homes at either the skilled nursing level or in health-related care is too extensive to be available in any other type of setting. The actual need for care, however, is far less than imagined. In an observational study conducted in several nursing homes, it was found that only 2 percent of patient time was involved, on the average, in receiving nursing services. The major amount of time was spent in passive activities or no activity (56 percent), while 7.6 percent of patient time was in interactions with staff and 6.1 percent in other psychosocial activity (Gottesman and Boureston 1974). Furthermore, evaluations of the current population of nursing home patients have indicated that between 40 and 80 percent do not require the care provided in an institutional setting, but are there because few or no alternative community services can be arranged (Kistin and Morris 1972; Tobin, Hammerman, and Rector 1972).

It is often assumed that older persons are placed in institutional settings because their families do not want to be involved in their care. Placement in an institution does seem to occur when there is a breakdown in the social support network of the older person. Lowenthal and her associates (1967) report that institutionalization occurred in a majority of cases when the care-giving person became physically, emotionally, or financially exhausted from providing care. Placement was not associated with a worsening of the older person's condition. They also found many persons residing in the community with levels of physical and mental impairment as great as those individuals requiring institutionalization. The person's support system, and not physical or mental illness, is thus the critical factor leading to institutionalization.

This situation suggests that assistance to family members or other caretakers can help to prevent institutionalization. The usual dilemma faced by service providers is to choose between meeting the needs of families who have become overburdened in providing assistance, and the needs of the individual who often prefers to remain and would function better in a familiar setting (Kahn and Zarit 1974). Assistance and support to the family before the situation becomes overwhelming can enable them to continue to provide care for longer periods of time. Macmillan (1958), for example, stressed the importance of an early intervention with family members or other caretakers in order to avoid unnecessary institutionalization. He noted that after families have been overstressed, they are reluctant to accept any solution except removal of the older person from the community. Providing help before that point is reached enables the family to gain confidence that their needs, as well as those of the older client, will be taken into account. It also treats the main problem leading to institutionalization: a breakdown in social supports.

Alternative Programs: Maximizing Independent Functioning

This review of the consequences of custodialism suggests several conclusions. Most important, many older persons who reside in long-term care settings might be cared for in other, less intrusive ways. If institutionalization can be prevented in the first place, the negative consequences can be avoided. Second, the effects of custodialism have been to increase the demands for long-term care while providing little effective treatment. It is a wasteful system that fails to recognize treatable problems and produces new disabilities as a consequence of the types of intervention used.

PRINCIPLES FOR POSITIVE TREATMENT

Four principles are critical for the effective treatment of the mental health and related concerns of the elderly. First, there needs to be an emphasis on community care and the development of programs that create viable alternatives to institutionalization. Second, coordination of community-based programs is crucial in order to ensure effective delivery of services. Third, services need to be provided according to the principle of minimum intervention (Kahn 1975), which, by limiting professional involvement, will support the continued competencies of older persons. Fourth, there must be a vigorous treatment of reversible problems, such as depression and delirium. The overriding goal of these strategies is to support those areas of independent functioning that the person retains, despite some degree of physical and mental disability. The success of services for the aged need to be measured against this goal.

Community-oriented services can have 2 major effects. First, some of the difficulties experienced by older persons and their families that currently lead to institutionalization can be treated through a variety of outpatient and home services. Second, community care can be preventive —dealing with problems at an earlier stage, before they are likely to become intransigent.

COMPREHENSIVE SERVICES

The types of service in a community-oriented program should be comprehensive, ranging from minimal aids to extensive interventions. Among the programs to be included would be: phone reassurance; home visits by volunteers; in-home services, including health aides, visiting nurses, and housekeeping; outpatient programs of occupational and physical therapy; individual and family psychotherapy; a day-treatment program; and brief, time-limited inpatient hospitalization.

One important feature of a community-oriented program is home visits by assessment teams. By seeing clients in their own home, more accurate evaluations can be made of their capacities to remain in that setting (Macmillan 1958; Glasscote, Gudeman, and Miles 1977).

An example of a comprehensive mental health program is that established by Duncan Macmillan (1958; 1967) at Mapperly Hospital in Nottingham, England. By emphasizing community treatment, Macmillan (1958) found that only a small percentage of persons required continual long-term care. In one year, for example, 439 persons were admitted for inpatient treatment, but by the end of the year only 49 were still in the hospital. Similar programs in Britain and the United States have been effective in reducing the use of long-term institutional care (Perlin and Kahn, 1968; Whitehead 1970). Recent innovative programs have created some new options in services and living arrangements for the elderly, including a variety of preventive and outreach services that are shaped to the needs of the particular community (Glasscote, Gudeman, and Miles 1977).

COORDINATION OF SERVICES

Coordination of services is an important feature of this type of program. In many American cities a wide range of services exist on paper, but there is little actual attempt to coordinate them. Obstacles include differences in eligibility requirements among agencies, differences in philosophies and treatment approaches between staffs of different agencies, and the lack of someone to follow up clients to ensure that services are actually delivered. Persons are sometimes subjected to assessments by every agency they go to, but with little or no actual service provided. They may make several visits to a single or a few agencies to determine eligibility (Federal Council an Aging 1975). They are sometimes placed on a referral circuit, eventually ending up back at the agency that first saw them. The impact of this situation is often that needed services cannot be arranged in a community setting.

A study by Blenkner, Bloom, and Nielson (1971) illustrates this problem. Persons referred to a community agency for protective services were assigned either to a control group, which received the usual services of the agency, or to a demonstration project with experienced caseworkers who were directed to maintain persons in their own homes. At a 1-year follow-up there were few differences between the experimental and control groups, except that *more persons* in the experimental group had been institutionalized. After 5 years the experimental group had higher rates of both institutionalization and mortality. How can these apparently paradoxical findings be accounted for? In the experimental group the caseworkers had a greater involvement with their clients, and undoubtedly felt that some actions must be taken when problems or crises developed. When trying to arrange for help, however, they had to coordinate the services of various community agencies, a process that proved to be very difficult. Given the uncertainties of arranging for community services, especially in any crisis situation, the caseworkers turned to institutional settings as the only available source of treatment. Similar problems of coordination have been reported by other programs that attempted to prevent institutionalization (Gaitz and Hacker 1970).

Funding for various outpatient and home services is a critical problem. Recent changes in HEW regulations have made more money available for home-delivered services, but the amount provided is small and has not stimulated the widespread development of accessible, reliable services (Glasscote, Gudeman, and Miles 1977). Even inpatient treatment that can restore independent functioning in some instances is not adequately covered by Medicare.

In California, for example, Medicare does not consistently provide reimbursement for rehabilitation for physical disabilities. In the instance of hip fractures, where many patients can secure marked benefits from a therapy program, virtually all cases have been disallowed in recent years. The consequence is to foster unnecessary disabilities. Two cases suggest the magnitude of the problem. In the first, a woman with a variety of problems, including transportation and depression, was referred to a counseling program. She had been confined to a wheelchair for 6 years following a hip fracture. She could not receive rehabilitation services at the time of her fracture because Medicare did not cover them. Inquiries in the community to try to arrange for some home-delivered services for her revealed that in the past 6 years she had become quite well known to the various community agencies. She was considered by them to be a pest, making demands that they could not meet. Yet her basic problem, which led to all her subsequent requests for help, would have been treatable if she had received proper care. In the second case, a woman who suffered a hip fracture spent 6 months bedridden in a nursing home. She was then placed in a hospital rehabilitation program and discharged within 3 weeks *to her own home.* Medicare, however, disallowed payment for the treatment. Thus, even when improvements can be clearly documented, funding is not necessarily available.

With other disabilities, there is similarly an inconsistency in funding (see Chapter 4). By creating these funding patterns, Medicare and other programs increase the number of persons with physical disabilities, and consequently the stress on the patient, on his family, and on other community agencies.

Another consideration in coordinating services is the lack of discharge planning by acute hospitals. Following a major accident or illness, there are many adjustment problems that are likely to be encountered when returning home. These problems range from mild apprehension on the part of the patient or spouse to the need for actual structural modification, such as the installation of bars and ramps for a person with impaired walking. One survey of aftercare planning indicates almost no help given for the physical, financial, mental, vocational, or other adjustment problems faced by persons on their return home (Bidwell, Berner, and Meier 1972). One way of dealing with this situation has been to use convalescent facilities for brief admissions, but in most nursing homes there will be no active intervention to deal with the specific problems the person will encounter in returning to the community. Treatment is "rest" rather than rehabilitation, which does not prepare the patient for the transition to home.

In order to be effective, critical services must be coordinated. In Macmillan's program in England, he was faced initially with the difficulty that the law required hospital and community care services to be provided by different staffs. Discharge plans formulated by one team would often be ignored or not followed through by another, and it was difficult to move a person smoothly from inpatient to community settings. Through a change in the law, he arranged for staff to have double appointments in both hospital and community care, so that the same team would follow a person through all service levels. In this country a similar change in public policies is needed to allow for comprehensive coordinated care.

Other innovations can be used for coordinating services. In a program developed as part of a community mental health center, Perlin and Kahn (1968) included the coordinated team approach developed by Macmillan. In addition, for those services they could not provide, they initiated a practice of sharing the salary of a staff person with another agency. This person, working part-time in both agencies, was used to coordinate referrals. Under this arrangement referred persons were more likely to follow through in contacting the other agency, and the appropriate service was more likely to be provided.

The current emphasis on coordination of services by Area Agencies on Aging have been, in contrast, far more limited. Their major role has often been to develop information and referral systems that do not guarantee that services will actually be delivered. In some instances persons are referred from one information and referral service to another. There is also some preliminary evidence that callers to an information and referral service may not be those with the most pressing needs for assistance (Bersani 1978).

One implication of providing coordinated services is that the staff's roles in a geriatric program cannot be strictly defined. The uses of psychotherapy provide a good example. Individual and family counseling can often have a favorable impact on various problem situations faced by older persons, but in many instances there may be problems that go beyond usual therapeutic processes. A client who is depressed may be concerned about money and may be eligible for SSI, which would relieve some of his financial difficulties. Because this is not psychotherapy in any strict sense, many workers would consider it a waste of their time and training to help make these arrangements. To maximize an effective coordination of services, however, it is probably better for the psychotherapist to help with straightforward social interventions, and to turn the person over to another member of the treatment team only if the person's problem requires an extensive intervention or particular technical knowledge. On the other hand, many older clients may not perceive the potential benefits of counseling, or may be unwilling to request counseling because of its negative connotations. When given assistance with other matters, like physical or housing problems, they may spontaneously engage the staff person in a counseling process. When a program is organized in this practical way, clients will neither have an unnecessary label attached to their concerns, nor will they feel shuffled around from one person to another, and the trust established in working on other difficulties can facilitate the counseling.

Minimum Intervention

The third important feature of a positive system of care is that services be provided according to the principle of minimum intervention (Kahn 1975). When the goal of a program is to maximize the independent functioning of clients, there must be consideration not to undermine their independence by providing too much assistance. According to Kahn (1975), minimum intervention is

> least disruptive of usual functioning in the usual setting. Thus, it would be more sensible to provide care in the home or in the day-care center than in the hospital; in the storefront rather than in the clinic. . . . Minimal intervention is a positive concept and must be differentiated from neglect. It must also be differentiated from "maximal-minimal" intervention, in which the person is removed from his community and then placed in an institution that provides no psychological or social compensatory measures. (p. 29)

In working with persons with behavior disorders in general, and with the elderly in particular, there is a tendency to want to help solve all the client's problems—the dilemma that has brought him into the service agency and any other difficulties he is having, including the types of everyday stress that most people experience. To give an example, many older persons in urban areas find that the neighborhoods in which they live have deteriorated over the years, and they possess neither the money nor the desire to relocate to another area. A depressed older person coming into a service agency in that type of neighborhood may complain, among other things, of a fear of being mugged. In that situation, many persons would begin helping the client to relocate to a safer environment, perhaps a protected one such as a retirement hotel or a health-related facility. This step, however, should not be taken except at the explicit direction of the client because of the risks involved in relocation, and because it removes an important area of personal control—the choice over residence —from the older person. While an unfortunate consequence of urban life, threats of crime have become a part of everyday existence of many persons. Many professionals do not consider that the risks of intervening may often be worse than maintaining the status quo.

The principle of minimum intervention addresses a critical issue: it is important *not to do* what the helping person has been trained to think is best for the older client. In many situations, doing what would be best would have the effect of increasing the stress and dependence of the older client. In Blenkner's research, as discussed above, the desires of caseworkers to ensure that persons' needs were being met during crisis situations led to higher rates of institutionalization and mortality. What is best has to be redefined to include a consideration of which type of intervention will address the client's presenting problems while also supporting continued independence.

From an older person's perspective, minimum intervention is likely to be experienced as least disruptive. By trying to maximize functioning in familiar and comfortable settings, some of the negative effects of serious psychological disorders can be attenuated. This is particularly true in the case of the brain disorders. While it is usually considered that institutionalization eventually becomes necessary, the experience from several English programs that emphasize community care is that only a small percentage of cases need continual long-term care. The majority can be maintained in the community through a variety of home or outpatient services, including intermittent and brief hospitalizations. Behavioral problems caused by the brain disorder appear to be minimized in the person's home or other familiar setting. The following example illustrates the dramatic improvements possible when moving a brain-damaged patient from hospital to home.

While in the hospital, the man had a mild stroke and thereafter rarely spoke and was incontinent. At the end of two weeks the nurse accompanied him home. "He walked in, looked at the open fire, and said, 'Oh, isn't this nice?' He saw the cat and said, 'Oh, there is Whiskey,' and took the cat on his lap. He sought out the toilet when he needed it. He was a completely different man in the afternoon from what he had been in the morning." (Glasscote, Gudeman, and Miles 1977, p. 140)

The nurse who made these observations added that even those persons with the most severe organic impairments "will tell you about their pictures and ornaments within their home, which is their little kingdom where they can find their way around. In a big hospital ward they are absolutely lost and seem more demented than when in their own home" (Glasscote, Gudeman, and Miles 1977, p. 140).

In many situations, implementing the principle of minimum intervention involves playing an educational role with the families of older clients. Families will sometimes request interventions that are not needed or that, if implemented, would lead to greater dependency and only limited improvement. This problem is often seen when there are isolated mental symptoms, such as encapsulated paranoid ideation. Many of these symptoms have little actual impact, doing no harm either to the person or to those around him. A person may insist, for example, that a light shines in on him at night. The symptom upsets his spouse because of its delusional nature, that is, the event has not occurred. The man, however, states he has no problem and rejects treatment. The treatment with the least risk involved would be to counsel her to accept the symptom without arguing or disputing it, because it is not in fact damaging. Whether the person acknowledges that it is a delusion or persists in it is not likely to affect his overall functioning, or necessarily to lead to other delusional thoughts. There are times, of course, when delusions and other thought disturbances require active treatment, such as when there is an underlying medical problem or if the symptom is being reinforced.

The following example indicates both where an active intervention is needed and when it is best to advise the family to accommodate to unusual behaviors. A 77-year-old woman was hospitalized because of paranoid ideations that were extremely disturbing to her and to the family. Her principal delusion was that her sister-in-law was attempting to poison or kill her. She was treated with phenothiazines and counseling and discharged after a brief hospitalization. On discharge she manifested no unusual behaviors, except she insisted that the year was 1 year earlier, 1975 rather than 1976. She continued to do well on subsequent visits, but the family was concerned that they could not get her to acknowledge the correct year. As there was no harm in her behavior, the family was encouraged not to argue and to ignore this problem. Thus, if it is determined that an isolated problem behavior is not harmful, not being reinforced, and not part of a larger medical or behavior problem, there is more to be gained by not actively treating it. This approach minimizes placing the person in a dependent or sick role.

With more pervasive symptoms, there are also likely to be instances where, on balance, an active attempt at treatment will create additional difficulties and change the presenting problem only minimally. A person with senile dementia, for example, may deny having memory problems. This denial often upsets a spouse, who feels her efforts in providing help or in reminding the person of appointments or other matters are not appreciated. She may feel that if her husband would only acknowledge a memory loss, he would be more helpful to her, both in how he asked for information and in not asking so often. Changing his denial would be quite difficult, as he may literally not be able to remember that he cannot remember. Instead, the spouse can be helped to view repeated requests for information differently: as an annoying consequence of the memory loss, but not representing anything more serious.

Professionals often find themselves involved in treating personal idiosyncrasies or eccentricities that have no negative consequences for the individual. A person may have habits that are bizarre or strange, but before attempting to change them in any way, it must be carefully assessed if these behaviors have any important consequences. In many instances mental health workers compare the living situations of the elderly against an abstract, middle-class standard. An older person may keep too many cats in an apartment or have a messy, somewhat dirty home. This situation may be undesirable to the worker, but not necessarily to the person or to those surrounding her. Other personal idiosyncrasies also have no negative effects. Someone may prefer a relatively isolate life. Encouraging that individual to join a senior center and to become involved in group activities is inappropriate. Viewing someone as impaired because of his or her social isolation represents a value judgment. Isolation does not always represent a threat to well-being (Lowenthal 1964).

Persons providing various types of service and treatment for the aged face a dilemma of knowing precisely how much to intervene and when to restrain themselves. There are 2 types of error in this situation—doing too little or doing too much. The most prevalent errors in the past have involved making too strong an intervention. On the other hand, in guiding one's actions according to the principle of minimum intervention, care should be taken not to overlook a situation that does constitute a danger to the older person or to those around him. There are times when prompt interventions are necessary or where inattention to a problem constitutes a risk. Imminent risk of suicidal behavior or an acute organic brain syndrome, for example, demand that intercessions be made. If there is any sudden change in a person's behavior or other indications of an acute medical problem, a proper evaluation should be arranged. In most circumstances, however, there is not likely to be a clear delineation of risk. A person may be unsteady in his walking, for example, with a danger of falling. Most workers are likely to be guided by the principle that it is most important to avoid this danger, but restraining the person's activities in any way will create other problems. There must be a balancing of any risk against the potential losses involved in taking away areas of independent functioning.

Several factors are included in deciding how much risk to take with an older client. First, there should be some assessment of the probability of a particular danger, such as a fall or leaving the gas on. If the danger is minimal, that is, something that might happen but has not occurred, or has occurred infrequently, then some risk should be taken. Second, if there is a likelihood that the person will endanger himself in some way, the worker should have a frank discussion with him about the risk involved and about the limitations that avoiding any danger would incur. The client should decide whether to continue to take these risks in all cases, except where there is obvious and severe cognitive impairment that affects his understanding of the situation. The mental health worker should not presume to know what is best for the person, or that the client does not fully understand the risk. Taking away responsibilities will produce unnecessary dependencies, and will reduce the client's feelings of competency. A therapist may have to intervene actively with other family members, if they are being overprotective, in order to support a client's choices. In situations where there is moderate or severe cognitive impairment, the family's opinion must be given more weight, although it is precisely here that overprotective responses may have the most negative consequences and lead to the greatest losses in functioning. The dangers of too much care must therefore be presented convincingly to the family. Legal considerations are also important, since major decisions cannot be made for an individual unless guardianship or other kinds of responsibility have been assigned by the courts.

Similar issues may arise when the presenting problems have been adequately resolved, but the therapist perceives that there are other difficulties with which the person requires assistance. Many of these may be long-standing habits. Before pressing for treatment, the therapist must consider if these difficulties really constitute a major problem for that individual. It is often lost sight of by psychotherapists that the normal condition of most persons is to have some areas of personal limitation and some self-defeating habits. If there is no imminent distress resulting from the person's behavior, and if the person has no strong interest in working on those problems, stopping therapy is likely to provide the greater benefit. If treatment were continued, further dependencies would be built up. Alexander (1964), in discussing psychoanalytic techniques, notes that a dependency relationship is often developed in the process of inducing transference, but there is little attention to helping the person recover independence as treatment proceeds. Thus, even as some of the presenting problems are resolved, other difficulties are created because of the treatment. This issue is likely to arise, whatever the method of psychotherapy, and especially with aged clients, where the social stereotype suggests a dependent condition. Prolonged treatment, therefore, has the disadvantage of undermining aspects of independent functioning.

TREATMENT OF REVERSIBLE CONDITIONS

The fourth principle of effective care is that there must be vigorous treatment for those reversible conditions that affect the elderly. In particular, the outcome of treatment in cases of both depression and delirium is generally good. Unfortunately, adequate screening is often lacking, and many professionals are not even knowledgeable about these conditions. This assessment is especially important in persons with a history of senile dementia, where any behavioral disturbance is likely to be dismissed as senility, but may, in fact, be due to a transient condition. Such common occurrences as toxic reactions to medications, including anesthetics, acute infections, and other somatic ailments can produce major behavioral problems and a crisis for caretakers who are assisting the older person (see Chapters 6 and 13). Effective treatment involves providing relief to the caretaker, giving information that this condition is temporary, and, most important, tracking down and treating the cause of the acute dysfunction. By treating these reversible problems, the extent of mental disabilities in an aged population can be markedly reduced.

OTHER CONSIDERATIONS IN TREATMENT

Potential Service. An important aspect of comprehensive services for the elderly lies in reassuring clients that more extensive assistance will be available when needed. Many older persons or their families make requests for help in anticipation of future needs. If it is guaranteed that services will be available, many persons will, paradoxically, never use them (Kahn 1975). This phenomenon of "potential service" can be seen with respect to admissions to congregate-living and health-related facilities. Older persons often make the decision to relocate to a health-related facility because of the feeling that they might need help at some future time, and want to assure that it will be available (Zarit 1978). If they are told that a room will be held for them for when they need it, they may decide they can continue in the community for a while longer.

In one innovative program, Brody and Cole (1971) offered persons on the waiting list for admission to a geriatric facility the choice of a "deferred admission status." When their names reached the top of the list they would not be admitted, but would keep their position on the waiting list, thus guaranteeing prompt admission if they required it. After 14 months, 70 percent of the deferred admission applicants were still living at home, and only 22 percent had required admission.

Similar guarantees of potential service can be offered to families or other persons who are providing assistance to the older person. Macmillan (1958), for example, developed a program of "holiday relief," in which he would hospitalize a person briefly so that the family could take a vacation. This type of respite program now exists in several English communities (Glasscote, Gudenman, and Miles 1977). Other types of guarantee to the family that the agency will assume more responsibility in the future may have the paradoxical effect of increasing the family's willingness to provide care. They feel assured that if they do become overburdened in the future, there will be effective help.

Involvement of Families in Treatment. In discussing the treatment of psychological problems in children, Haley (1976) stresses the importance of bringing in all the members of the family, even those who are only peripherally related to the presenting problem, such as siblings or grandparents. Involving all relevant family members at some point in the treatment is also essential for older persons. In some situations the real problem is the concern of the family about the older person, rather than the older person's functioning. In other cases, the most effective way of working with the person's problem may be in helping the family develop new responses to it. In the instance of paranoid behavior, it would be important for family members not to reinforce its manifestations inadvertently. With senile dementia, the most effective response in many situations is to provide information and support to the person's spouse or children. Another benefit is that involvement of other family members offers them reassurance that the problem is being taken care of.

Dependent Clients. Interventions that stress maintaining independent abilities may be resisted by some clients who prefer to have many of their needs taken care of. Persons with lifelong dependency needs may, in fact, adapt well to the later years, when it is considered socially appropriate to express those behaviors. In some situations the desire to be taken care of may undermine continued independence. A person who is receiving retraining for daily activities, for example, relearning how to dress following an illness, may make repeated requests for help from staff or family members. Meeting those demands in a community setting can have the same impact on functional abilities as the overcaring found in nursing homes. In working with dependent persons, encouragements to take more responsibility should be coupled with discussions of the consequences of giving up activities, so that the individuals themselves can choose their course of action.

Families may also require counseling in order to learn not to overprotect an older relative. Family members or other caretakers who foster "sick-role" behavior or other unnecessary dependence in a person should be made aware of the potential consequences of their actions and helped to formulate other responses with which they are comfortable.

Uses of Inpatient Care. In emphasizing the prevention of institutionalization, it is recognized that there are situations where inpatient care is both necessary and desirable. When there is acute illness, of course, treatment should be prompt, including hospitalization when appropriate. With more chronic problems of the sort typically manifested by nursing home patients, there are 2 considerations: to what extent community-based comprehensive services are available, and what must be done where those services are not present. With a system of comprehensive care, there are likely to be circumstances during which institutional care for chronic problems is desirable, for example, to relieve temporarily the burden of care being borne by the family, or to deal with a crisis situation. Continuity of care between inpatient and outpatient services would make it possible to move the person back into the community once the crisis is resolved. This type of short-term admission, or even repeated admissions, may have considerable benefits. It has been found, for example, that intermittent inpatient care can reduce dramatically the number of inpatient days for persons who otherwise would be sent to long-term care, while having a positive impact on family members (Robertson, Griffiths, and Cosin 1977; MacDonnell, McKenzie, and Cheetham 1968; Glasscote, Gudeman, and Miles 1977). This program has been effective both for physical disabilities and for the behavior problems associated with senile dementia.

Our current concept of institutional care for chronic health and mental health problems of the aged is that of a receptacle that receives and holds persons no longer able to function in the community. Under an optimal system of services, however, institutional care can function on a revolving-door basis, involving short-term treatment and the ability to reintegrate the person into the community service network. The usual criteria for judging the quality of nursing home services include patient-staff ratio, physical facilities, and the like, but a better index would be the extent to which persons can be effectively placed back in the community (Kahn and Zarit 1974).

Another alternative is the development of congregate-housing arrangements that accommodate the needs of the impaired elderly. The original proposals for congregate living suggested the provision of various social and health services to residents as they became needed, but most programs have offered few services except meals (Glasscote, Gudeman, and Miles 1977). When a resident develops increasing physical or mental limitations, he or she is usually transferred to a health-related or skilled nursing facility. Sometimes even minimal impairments result in transfers. In California, for example, state regulations prohibit congregate sites from housing persons with certain disabilities, such as having to use a walker. From an administrative perspective, creating special facilities for different levels of care is more convenient both for staff and for state regulators. The impact on residents, however, has not been considered. Many persons in congregate settings, even where continuity of care is offered in other buildings on the same campus, are quite fearful about having to move to a different level of care. For those persons with cerebral insufficiencies of any degree, relocations are likely to increase the extent of disorientation and of other behavioral problems. One's goal, instead, must be to minimize unnecessary relocations. More flexible programs could enable even severely impaired persons to continue at a congregate site. Nursing or other supportive services could be brought in, with few of the adverse effects of a total-care setting. Examples of successful programs of this type that do not have an institutional atmosphere or unduly invade the privacy of the older person are described by Glasscote, Gudeman, and Miles (1977).

This ideal system unfortunately does not exist in most communities. No alternative to long-term institutional care is currently available to many persons. When such is the situation, it is the responsibility of the professional to provide assistance to families if they must institutionalize someone, and to deal with feelings of guilt or other concerns. The family should not be burdened with the information that this type of placement would not likely be necessary if additional community resources were available. At the same time, the worker should be sure that every possible alternative has been explored.

In making this type of placement, there should still be an emphasis on maximizing the older person's role in reaching a decision to relocate and in the choice of a setting. Many facilities routinely allow prospective residents to visit, to see the room they will have, and to become acquainted with the staff. The preferences of one's client may not always appear the most rational, but should nonetheless be supported.

Relocating nursing home residents back to community settings is often a difficult proposition, due to the problems in delivery and coordination of in-home and outpatient services. For persons who have been improperly placed or whose conditions have improved, the involvement of a worker or of family members can overcome some of the obstacles of the relocation. As a more comprehensive, community-oriented system of care develops, there will likely be some pressure for massive discharges of nursing home patients to less restrictive, less expensive facilities. Currently in some states there is continual reevaluation of residents, with persons shifted out of the facilities when they do not meet certain criteria for long-term care. Few incentives are given, however, for long-term care settings to plan effectively for this type of move, so that the end result is that individuals are dumped abruptly back into the community or into a board-and-care setting. Furthermore, many persons, once settled into a long-term care setting, resent the uncertainties created by this shifting around. Even highly structured plans to rehabilitate and relocate persons run into considerable resistance from residents who do not want to be moved. (Kelman 1962). Rather than emptying our current long-term care facilities, there must instead be an emphasis on building up alternative services, so that unnecessary institutionalization can be prevented in future cohorts of aged persons.

Summary

Our system of care for the physically or mentally disabled older person has been shaped by an implicit philosophy of custodialism. Preventive, outpatient, or in-home services are not consistently available, and arranging for these types of assistance involves dealing with an often chaotic system of competing agencies and complex regulations. The result is that many community-living older persons are not given effective assistance, with the most impaired turning to the only consistently available service: the long-term care facility.

The proper treatment of mental health and related problems in the aged requires the development of a comprehensive and community-oriented system of care. Services need to be coordinated, to avoid shifting the person around needlessly from one agency to another or from one residence to another. They also must be applied according to the principle of minimum intervention, so as to decrease the chance of undermining the remaining competencies of an older client. Where they have been tried, comprehensive programs have greatly reduced the need for long-term institutional care, and appear to provide a better quality of service that leaves in the clients' own hands as much control as possible over their lives.

CHAPTER 11

Individual Treatment: Supportive, Behavioral, and Cognitive Approaches

DESPITE THE WIDESPREAD APPLICATION of psychological treatment for a variety of emotional and human relationship problems, there are few case examples in the literature describing treatment with the aged, and virtually no systematic outcome studies of the impact of psychotherapy in an aged sample. Beginning with the pioneering work of Goldfarb (Goldfarb and Turner 1953; Goldfarb and Sheps 1954), there have been periodic attempts to develop a more extensive treatment literature. These have included a variety of approaches, such as Goldfarb's psychodynamic therapy, existential treatment (Moustakas 1977), a systems approach (Haley 1974), behavioral techniques (Hoyer 1973; Richards and Thorpe 1978), and somatic approaches involving massage, relaxation, and other exercises (Gelba 1976; Ellwell 1977). A recent review by Eisdorfer and Stotsky (1977) describes the varied procedures that have been used in treatment of the aged. These efforts, however, have remained fragmentary, and an extensive and thorough body of information about treatment comparable to that of other special groups, such as children or adolescents, has not emerged. The practitioner or student interested in gaining skills with the elderly is faced with a smorgasbord of techniques, but no detailed guidelines on the efficacy of various modes of treatment.

The model of psychotherapy presented in this chapter has been developed from 3 sources: findings concerning core qualities inherent in most psychological treatments; recent advances in direct treatment methods of younger persons that use behavioral and cognitive techniques; and the

282

experience of the author in providing and supervising psychotherapy with older clients. Before discussing the specific treatment procedures, basic assumptions about psychotherapy will be explored. It will be considered whether psychological treatment is generally a useful approach with older persons. This question has by no means been settled, despite the growing interest among professionals and universities in the problems of the aged. Another major issue is whether successful psychotherapy with the aged involves procedures similar to or different from those used with the young. In the absence of controlled outcome studies, clinical experience must provide guidelines about modification in technique. Finally, the theoretical basis of a behavioral and cognitive approach to psychotherapy will be discussed, including its applications to problems of the aged and advantages over other techniques.

Issues in the Psychotherapy of Older Persons

IS PSYCHOTHERAPY GENERALLY HELPFUL IN THE AGED?

Psychological treatment involves the interaction of 2 or more individuals, with the goal of relieving or restructuring problems of one of them, the client. The specific process of treatment has been made operational in various ways. Therapy may be characterized by acceptance of the client by the therapist (Rogers 1951). In other approaches the therapist systematically applies instructions, explanations, or other communications that will lead to improvement in the client. These communications can involve insight, as in the dynamic psychotherapies, the use of directives to disrupt and change problematic sequences of behavior, as in a systems approach, or the application of principles of learning, such as characterizes behavioral treatments. At the core of each approach is the assumption that the client's problems and distress will improve as the result of the interactions. Treatments also differ in varying degrees from normal human interactions. Persons who are having problems, for example, have often been given advice on how to respond more effectively to their situation, but that advice has not been sufficient to relieve their distress. Thus the therapist is assumed to bring some special knowledge or technique to the interaction that will help the client to overcome his or her problem more quickly and more effectively than if no treatment were given.

Whether psychotherapy is generally effective with the aged is both an ideological and empirical issue. On ideological grounds, the profound influence of Freud and the psychoanalytic movement in the development of psychotherapy has inadvertently contributed to a lack of interest in treating older persons. Freud's view that only the young were suitable candidates for psychoanalysis has been adopted by many therapists, including those employing nonanalytic techniques. The aged have been considered variously as too rigid for treatment, lacking in insight, or uninteresting clients. Articles written from a gerontological perspective usually begin with a vigorous denial of these negative qualities. There has been little consideration of this issue, however, on empirical grounds. One obvious test would be to evaluate the response to treatment of groups of young and old. While this comparison is fraught with methodological difficulties, such as matching initial symptoms of young and old clients and equating the treatment, it could indicate the extent to which gains are possible among the aged.

At a different level, the question of whether the elderly can benefit from psychological treatment implies that the old consist of a category of persons who share in some essential characteristics supposedly derived from the process of aging. As has been discussed in previous chapters, nothing is farther from the truth. The aged are a diverse group. There are individuals who manifest little or no change as they grow older, or may even gain in important qualities, such as in their knowledge of the world, practical matters, interpersonal relationships, or what might be termed "wisdom." The category "aged" also includes persons who have suffered distinct psychological deficits as the results of illnesses, especially those affecting the central nervous system. The old, moreover, live a variety of life styles and have had varied life experiences. Some persons possess limited educations or narrow and rigid outlooks on life. Other older persons have always expanded their perspectives by becoming involved in novel and challenging situations. Those experiencing major psychiatric problems also cannot be grouped together. Among a typical client sample would be individuals who functioned effectively most of their lives and possess many adaptive skills, persons who have experienced occasional or periodic life problems and neurotic symptoms, and some with more severe chronic problems and deficits in interpersonal and/or intellectual skills. The question, then, should not be whether the aged can be treated at all, but rather which group of old are we considering for treatment, and what kind of treatment? Instead of classing the aged as a group, a therapist must consider both the background and presenting problems of clients on an individual basis to determine the appropriateness of treatment.

PSYCHOTHERAPY WITH THE AGED: DIFFERENCES FROM YOUNGER PERSONS

A related issue is whether psychotherapy with the aged is different from that with younger adults, or if it should be considered only as an extension of existing approaches to an older clientele. As implied above, the aged are likely to present a variety of problems for treatment, some unique to old age and some resembling problems found earlier in life..

Among the disorders more commonly presented by older clients are adjustments to losses and dealing with death. In turn, the therapist is more likely to provide information and to be an advocate for aged clients.

As has been discussed in previous chapters, there is an increased probability as we age that we will experience losses in health, social position, and among persons who are closest to us. Losses can, of course, occur at any age, but there are more losses in old age, and they have different implications. Issues of loss have sometimes been discussed in the psychological treatment of younger persons, but have not played a prominent part in conceptualizations of the process of psychotherapy. The younger person who experiences these types of loss is often encouraged to work through them. This model holds that a cathartic expression of grief will help restore normal functioning. In working with the aged on similar issues, however, it is sometimes presumed that older persons cannot move from expressions of grief to active restitution. In contrast to the young adult, an older person often cannot replace concretely what has been lost. For example, the death of a child is a tragic event for parents, but a young couple is usually able to have other children. Similarly, with the death of a spouse, a young man or woman will have many opportunities for meaningful heterosexual relationships, while for older women who lose their husbands there will be little or no opportunity for developing new relationships with men. In terms of such social experiences as the loss of one's job, a young person has ample opportunities for finding new work, including such means as job retraining or returning to school. An older person who seeks work has a much more restricted range of jobs that are likely to be available, because of age discrimination. Thus the young often find it possible to replace to a great extent what has been lost. Among the aged (as well as those younger persons who incur physical handicaps through accidents or illnesses) the losses are more likely to be permanent and irreversible. A model of treatment that presumes that the person's abilities to seek active involvements will be restored through expressions of grief is thus inappropriate in the aged. The losses may often represent relatively permanent restrictions in the person's involvements and activities.

The fact that the losses the aged experience are sometimes irreversible has contributed to the therapeutic pessimism surrounding treatment of older persons. We share too readily our clients' despair over the fact that their lives will never be the same again. It is possible, however, to accommodate to major losses in positive ways, even though the means are not usually available for replacing the persons or things that have been lost. As with younger persons who have had losses, a first step is often for the counselor to listen in supportive ways to expressions of grief, and to learn through this process the unique meaning of the loss to the older person. How long this expression lasts undoubtedly varies depending on the individual and the meaning of the loss to that person. It should not be assumed that there is a "normal" grief period that the person must go through. At some point, however, a counselor should shift from expressions of grief to what Butler (1977) has described as the process of restitution.

Restitution can involve several features. There can be an attempt to place the specific events into a broader, perhaps philosophical perspective. The counselor can encourage clients to take more active control over their own actions and in giving meaning to their experiences. Seligman (1975) has observed in laboratory animals that the experience of uncontrollable events leads to passive and withdrawn behavior (see Chapter 8). Because most losses involve similarly uncontrollable events, it can be hypothesized that procedures that help persons regain a sense of mastery in their lives will be beneficial. For some clients this process can involve philosophical discussions of the meaning of life, or explorations into religious or ethical values. For others it may include considerations of the future, of how they would like to live out their lives. Some persons may benefit from learning new behavioral skills to offset some aspects of a loss. A widow, for example, may need to take over activities previously performed by the spouse, or may want to learn skills for developing new social and/or sexual relationships. Other issues that may arise include settling unfinished business with family and friends.

Another aspect of the losses the aged experience is that older persons have adapted to stressful situations in the past. In contrast to the young person experiencing losses, an older individual will have had major life stresses prior to the present incident and may have developed particular coping skills. By helping clients to reassert those coping abilities the counselor both supports their continued independence and contributes to feelings of competency.

Older persons may also be concerned with their own deaths. Among both the healthy aged and the ill, one often observes an active process of coming to terms with death. This interest can be both with practical matters, such as planning a will, and with one's feelings about death, one's hopes and fears and the meaning one gives to death and life. Contrary to what is generally expected, it is not necessarily a depressing experience to explore these concerns. A constructive therapy process can be effective in helping persons cope more effectively with their impending death, whether it is imminent or not expected to occur for several years.

As in dealing with other losses, helping clients gain a sense of control over the circumstances of their deaths has beneficial effects. Persons are often afraid not of dying, but of how they will die, whether in pain or lonely or as a burden to their families (Kübler-Ross 1968). They can be helped to express these concerns and to make specific plans so that the events they are afraid of will not happen. These plans include such things as estate planning, making a living will so that one's life will not be needlessly prolonged, and identifying support services such as hospices.

These practical concerns are sometimes overlooked or regarded as defenses against more basic fears of death, but attention to concrete matters related to dying is helpful to some people.

The following example indicates the benefits of dealing with practical matters. A 74-year-old man was referred by a legal services program that he had contacted concerning arranging a guardianship for his wife. He was a very anxious, tearful man who had an advanced case of lung cancer. During the interview he would periodically stand up and pace about the room. He described his concerns about his wife, who had senile dementia and depended on him for many household tasks, including cooking, cleaning, shopping, and managing finances. He had to go into the hospital for treatments and did not know how she could care for herself. His wife, however, would not acknowledge her limitations and had rejected his suggestions about moving to a nursing home. To plan for his wife's care, the counselor encouraged him to bring his son, who was being named guardian, to the next session. During that session the therapist and the client's son worked out an arrangement for providing some in-home services, and having the son check in on his mother at regular intervals. The client was visibly relieved by this plan, since he could leave his wife where she wanted to be and could feel her needs would be met. Though he died soon after, subsequent follow-up found that his wife was able to continue in her own home with the help of the supportive arrangements worked out.

The prospect of dying can also lead to an introspective process through which the person tries to cope with his impending death. Butler (1963) has suggested that many older persons engage in a process of active reminiscence or life review, in which they take stock of or sum up their achievements and failures. For someone to whom fears of death are a major problem, initiating a life review can be helpful. Butler (1963) cautions, however, that the outcome of this process is not always beneficial. He has observed persons who have become more depressed and isolated as an apparent consequence of reminiscing. It also should not be assumed that a fear of death is the central feature of all psychological disorders of the aged. Many problems are not or are only tangentially related to fears of death, and can be dealt with effectively by focusing on the person's immediate life circumstances.

Because of the prominent role of losses in the psychological disorders of older persons, psychotherapy tends to be focused on specific, concrete issues. Pfeiffer and Busse (1973), for example, suggest that the aged respond better to treatment when there are specific goals and the therapist plays a more active role than with the young. There are times when therapists serve as an advocate for clients. They provide information about opportunities for older persons and social programs for which they may be eligible, and also intervene directly to arrange for social services for those clients who cannot do so themselves.

The importance of providing information to older clients is illustrated by the following case. A 64-year-old woman came to a counseling center depressed over many circumstances in her life, including having recently been fired from her job and having little money to live on. While there were many interesting "dynamics" about why she was depressed, her counselor gave immediate attention to her most pressing problem—her finances. She was given the names of employment agencies that specialized in placing older persons, though she was also told that there were few jobs available. She was able, however, to find a job quickly (in fact, she had 2 job offers), and her whole outlook brightened. Her other problems, which had seemed forbidding, became more manageable. She terminated treatment after 2 months, and occasional follow-up visits indicated she continued to function well.

Because of the confusing array of social service programs with varying regulations and eligibilities, the therapist must at times find out what clients are eligible for and intervene with social agencies to coordinate services. Making a referral is often not sufficient, because on arriving at the service agency the client may discover that he or she does not meet the eligibility requirements, or the agency does not provide the needed service, or the agency no longer provides the service or has gone out of business entirely.

The provision of even simple services can often be difficult. In one instance it took a 3-month period and several hours of involvement by staff to arrange for a client to receive the special glasses she needed following cataract surgery. Because this women was on Medicaid, private optical companies would not fill the prescription, stating that they were often reimbursed less than cost of their work. It was only through an intensive effort that it was possible to obtain the glasses. While this situation is an extreme one, clients often face similar dilemmas in trying to obtain services.

As this example indicates, an organization will have policies that exclude persons who need the services they provide, or will put roadblocks in the way of clients, especially those regarded as difficult or problem persons. The direct intervention of a mental health worker can sometimes influence an organization to provide the necessary assistance. Social changes that led to a truly comprehensive system of medical and social services would, of course, be the best solution to these problems.

Another factor often affects the course of individual treatment in the aged. Older persons on the average will have had less prior exposure to and information about psychotherapy than the young. Except for certain elite groups, today's cohort of older persons has perceived psychological treatment either as something reserved for persons with severe problems, or as ineffective because it involves talking rather than actions. When seeking help for emotional or behavioral problems, they may also view treatment as similar to medical care. This expectation about the nature of psychological treatment can lead to major misunderstandings between clients and therapists (Orne and Wender 1968). In receiving medical treatment, for example, patients are expected to be relatively passive. The treatment is usually rapid and does not involve the patient's emotions or feelings about treatment, or about the physician. One's symptoms result from some specific cause such as a disease, injury, or organ malfunction, and the doctor's task is to treat this cause and make the patient well. In contrast, clients in virtually all schools of psychotherapy are expected to be active in their own treatment. The therapist functions as a facilitator but the major changes are made by the client. Moreover, one's symptoms do not stem from an underlying "disease" in most cases, and thus treatment does not involve a straightforward approach to cure the illness, or to remove some foreign or toxic element from one's body. The client's problems are, rather, an integral part of his or her thoughts, feelings, and behaviors.

In order to deal with possible differences between client and therapist in anticipations about psychotherapy, Orne and Wender (1968) propose conducting a socializing interview, consisting of between one-half hour and several sessions, to acquaint clients with what will be occurring during psychotherapy. The purpose of these interviews is to clarify the roles of patient and therapist, and to provide a rationale for why psychotherapy is likely to be effective. Beck (1976) also stresses the importance of achieving a consensus between patient and therapist on the problems to be treated, the goals of therapy, and how those goals will be reached. In presenting a problem-solving approach to therapy, he states to patients:

> One of the goals of therapy is to help you learn new ways of approaching problems. Then, as problems come up, you can apply the formulas that you have already learned. For instance, in learning arithmetic you simply learned the fundamental rules. It was not necessary to learn every possible addition and subtraction. Once you had learned the operations, you could apply them to any arithmetic problem. (p. 230)

Beck also provides his clients with a brief article that provides a rationale for why people have problems and describes the treatment process.

By preparing clients adequately for what will occur during therapy, their initial apprehensions and resistance can be reduced. Orne and Wender (1968), for example, report that persons who had previously failed in treatment often progress rapidly when given an introductory explanation of the basis of treatment. They also cite a study (Hoehn-Saric et al. 1964) that suggests that treatment is more rapid with clients who are given an initial explanation of the therapy process than with a control group who receive no anticipatory socialization. In the aged, where the extent of information about and understanding of psychotherapy techniques is probably more limited than in any other age group, this type of anticipatory socialization may be a critical aspect of treatment.

Psychotherapy of the aged also shares many qualities with treatment of the young. The principal concerns of older clients usually involve interpersonal problems or their own feelings of distress. While the social context of these problems is often different than that of the middle-aged or young adult, the types of intervention and course of treatment are similar. To cite an example, the marital problems of older persons often involve the same failures in communication and lack of assertiveness about personal needs that characterize many younger couples. The age of a client thus has a relation to the course of psychotherapy in varying degrees, with some persons presenting problems specifically associated with the aging experience, such as losses and decrements in health, while others are similar to other adults in their problems and responses to treatment.

USE OF A BEHAVIORAL AND COGNITIVE APPROACH

Behavioral and cognitive methods of psychotherapy are based on .the premise that in the absence of physiological disturbances, mental disorders are the result of specific habits or thoughts of the client and are precipitated and reinforced by particular environmental events. The process of treatment involves identifying problem behaviors and situations and developing interventions appropriate for each particular problem. Psychiatric disorders are viewed as the outcome of many dysfunctional habits and thoughts, rather than as the result of a global deficit or illness. Someone who is depressed, for example, may engage in few enjoyable activities, may be troubled by insomnia, and may hold negative beliefs about himself and his abilities; different techniques would be used for each of these deficits.

Many practitioners emphasize only the interpersonal relationship between client and therapist as the primary focus of treatment. That aspect of psychotherapy is important, but must be placed in perspective. Feelings of honesty, trust, and emotional warmth facilitate treatment. On the other hand, the development of a successful relationship between client and therapist is not sufficient in itself in many cases to reach the treatment goals. While the interaction of client and therapist contains elements that are similar to many important life experiences, it is also different in many respects from other relationships and situations. Focusing only on what happens in the psychotherapy session assumes that there is some global deficit within the person that accounts for his difficulties in functioning, and that can somehow be modified by the therapeutic relationship. A behavioral perspective maintains instead that a person's problems involve how he acts, thinks, and feels in particular situations. A problem-oriented approach that emphasizes applying learning from the psychotherapy sessions directly into those situations has a better chance of success, since it treats the times and circumstances during which the person experiences difficulties and feelings of distress.

A behavioral approach also contrasts with psychodynamic therapies, which view symptoms as signs of an underlying conflict or intrapsychic problem. As an example of dynamic therapy, a woman experiencing distress and disappointments in her relationships with her children would be treated through exploration of her unconscious wishes and fears, and perhaps by a review of her relationships with her own parents. This type of therapy, however, fails to take advantage of the factors in the person's immediate situation that stimulate or reinforce the problem behavior and can be treated directly. In the above example, a problem-oriented approach would explore the antecedents and consequences of the client's interactions with her children, and also her ideas about the situation, especially any distorted or exaggerated thoughts. Treatment might involve training her to interact in more effective ways with her children or to evaluate her interactions in a different, more positive way. Sometimes a client does not present a single, discrete problem, but has several difficulties that are interconnected in varying degrees. A woman, for example, may present feelings of helplessness and depression, but when she tries to act in more competent ways, her husband avoids her or disapproves of the behavior. A treatment program would involve both the presenting problem of feelings of helplessness in specific situations, and the fact that the woman is punished or ignored for acting in assertive ways.

We frequently assume that psychotherapy must uncover the roots of a problem in order for meaningful change to occur. Insight or awareness, however, are not necessary conditions for change. Furthermore, most problems are only partly rooted in a person's past. Sometimes individuals have difficulties in situations because they have not had adequate preparation or socialization. A simpler society would offer clearer role models and less variation in the possible life styles one might lead. But in a complex society there are many roles one can play, and a person may not have had prior experiences that prepared him or her to function well in particular circumstances. In areas of adult behavior such as dating, sexuality, relationship skills, and parenting, direct training has helped overcome anxiety and dysfunctional habits. There is probably even less positive socialization and planning for old age, so that we might expect many problems of the aged to be related to not knowing how to act effectively, rather than to some prior trauma or conflict. It is also likely that persons who face markedly changed circumstances in later life find that old habits and attitudes that were effective when they were younger no longer result in an adequate impact on the environment. The situation of retired men illustrates this point. They have often been pictured as unable to adjust to the lack of structure and assigned tasks. Their usual ways of acting have been disrupted. Rather than being rooted only in the past, their problems involve making a new adjustment to circumstances for which they have only limited preparation.

The issue of symptom substitution has often been raised as a criticism of problem-oriented therapies. The concept of symptom substitution is that if presenting symptoms are treated without dealing with the underlying disorder, or without uncovering the circumstances in which the problem was first manifested, then basic conflicts will produce other symptoms. In a recent review, however, Rimm and Masters (1974) point out that there is no empirical evidence for symptom substitution in studies of problem-oriented therapies. They note that some clients may present one problem, but as treatment progresses other areas of difficulty are uncovered. This situation is conceptually different from symptom substitution and can be dealt with by a problem-oriented model.

Another criticism of problem-oriented therapies is that they provide symptom relief but do not change the person's characteristic habits, defenses, or conflicts that brought about the problem in the first place. Underlying this assumption is the fact that most schools of psychotherapy actually use an illness model that views problems in functioning as coming from a deficit or blockage within the person. Focusing only on covert phenomena can cause the therapist to miss major factors contributing to a problem, such as a lack of incentive in the environment for competency, or the person's not having learned effective interpersonal skills for particular situations. Furthermore, the attempt to treat the personality of a client rather than the presenting problems causes confusion in the goals of treatment. We create an expectation that our client will be conflict-free if therapy is successful. Since everyday life involves a certain degree of conflict or disappointment, therapy can become an open-ended process that goes on forever unless there are clearly stated goals against which progress can be measured.

The distinction that treatment programs must make is not between symptom relief versus substantive change, but between the extent of the difficulties the person is having and what he or she wants help for right now. Two hypothetical persons can be contrasted, both having many behavioral problems, but one wanting help with only a few specific things, while the other desires more substantial changes. The first person could reach those specific objectives without working on all his other problems, and while he would still face many dilemmas, he would have the positive sense of having made progress in one area. His life is not made over, but it is better in some small way, which is an appropriate goal for that individual.

The use of behavioral approaches with older persons is based on their effectiveness with the young, and on the belief that the straightforward approach seems well suited to many of the problems of the aged. Furthermore, behavior therapists have emphasized empirical studies of treatment. A strong empirical tradition means that effective forms of therapy will be identified and separated from methods that have little value, and that failures will not be ascribed to some global characteristics, such as personality traits or the client's age.

An Outline of Counseling Procedures

The specific therapy procedures for working with older persons involve engaging clients in a supportive relationship and using behavioral and cognitive interventions for targeted problems. The feeling of support, that the therapist is on the client's side, is a prerequisite for effective treatment, and plays a prominent role in therapy with older persons. Behavioral and cognitive approaches provide methods for altering the more persistent and distressing problems of clients.

SUPPORTIVE COUNSELING

The term "supportive counselor" is generally used in a vague way, referring neither to specific styles of intervention nor to precise treatment objectives. There are, however, specific procedures and goals that might appropriately be called "supportive" and have many potential applications for older clients. As used here, "supportive counseling" refers to techniques that provide encouragement, reassurance, and positive regard to an older client.

There are 2 major reasons for creating a supportive relationship with one's clients. Giving support and encouragement is sufficient to lead to major improvements in some clients. Many individuals who experience a loss or some other stressful event benefit from having a close, caring relationship, and they rapidly resume the coping patterns they used before the loss. Some depressed older persons, including individuals who have been depressed for over a year, improve quickly with a few therapy sessions that emphasize reassurances and their own positive qualities.

The second purpose of a supportive relationship is to create an atmosphere in which changes can take place. Without some trust and liking between client and therapist, the most technically skillful practitioner will be limited in effectiveness.

Truax and Carkhuff (1967) have described 3 core qualities as necessary for effective counseling: empathy, nonpossessive warmth, and genuineness. Empathy is a response that indicates at a feeling level an understanding of the client's concerns. Warmth and genuineness refer to the ways in which the counselor's comments are made. Communication of both warmth and genuineness can help the client feel accepted by the counselor. As clients sense the acceptance of their counselors, they may begin to experience more positive regard for themselves.

Acceptance of the client, however, does not mean that the counselor must accept or approve of the problem behaviors that brought the client into counseling in the first place. Instead, acceptance is seen as facilitation of the client's own problem-solving abilities. It is often possible, for example, for counselors to reformulate the presenting problem from a broader perspective, taking into account the positive qualities of the person. By bringing into the counseling process an acknowledgment of the person's strengths, and by phrasing the problem in relation to those strengths, the counselor will help the client to tolerate and cope more effectively in his or her current situation. Clients who complain of feelings of worthlessness can be responded to empathically to communicate acceptance and understanding of their situation, and also, as the counseling relationship develops, to provide feedback in a supportive way about their positive qualities and abilities. This feedback should be genuine to be effective. A counselor who praises a client without giving it much thought may find that the client has experienced these statements as an empty reassurance that things will be better, such as has already been offered by friends and relatives. A therapist who has begun to understand the unique qualities of a particular client through empathic responses can provide encouragement or reassurance in a way that makes sense within the client's own perspective, and that leads to increased positive regard. By the end of the initial therapy session, the counselor should be able to begin to give some genuine, positive feedback to clients, enlarging this process somewhat in subsequent sessions.

The following example indicates how a basically supportive approach can facilitate change in an older person. Mr. G. was a 70-year-old man whose wife had died 3 months earlier. He reported feeling very lonely and seeing his wife everywhere. They had been constant companions for the past 10 years, which he described as "sunshine." He also felt guilty over not making her take care of her health problems, especially that she continued to smoke (she died of a heart attack). He was managing to care for himself, but worried what would happen to him in the future. The counselor allowed Mr. G. to express his feelings about his loss, responding in an accepting and empathic way. She also provided reassurances about his feelings of guilt and his seeing his wife everywhere, explaining that these were common reactions, and pointing out that he had done the best he could while she was alive. He improved quickly and after 5 sessions he terminated treatment, stating he had made plans to get involved in more activities.

It should be pointed out that assurances to the client about guilt feelings or some other troubling thought are not effective unless the client first feels understood. Showing empathy, which involves looking at the situation from the patient's perspective, makes it possible for the therapist to rephrase the problem or point out things the client has ignored about his situation in a way that fits the person's own experiences. If not done in this manner, reassurances become little more than stating that "Everything will be all right."

A supportive approach can be used in a crisis situation. A 71-year-old woman, Mrs. R., was brought to a counseling center by her husband and son. She had been increasingly withdrawn over the past few weeks, and was described currently as virtually doing nothing during the day. Mrs. R. had a very sad expression, sobbed during the interview, and was initially unresponsive to questions. She stated in whispers that things were too horrible to talk about. The therapist challenged her at first, asking what could be so horrible that caused her to feel this bad. She gradually revealed that she was preoccupied with the thought that she would kill her husband while he slept. The therapist explained that people often had bad thoughts, but that did not mean they would actually do what they thought about. He questioned her about her past and pointed out she had always been a good person and would therefore not do something like that now, and thinking about it did not make her bad. By the end of the session she no longer felt she would harm her husband. Though still depressed, her demeanor had brightened and she agreed to continue treatment. Within a month she was functioning normally and resumed her usual activities.

The development of trust in the therapy relationship through a supportive approach can be important in working with severely disturbed patients. Mrs. K. was a 68-year-old woman who had been living in the bus station. She carried all her possessions in a sack, and stated that she had had to move 5 times in recent years because people broke into her apartment, smeared "brown stuff" over her things, made crazy noises, and caused her bed to shake. She felt people from Social Security were doing all these things. These problems had occurred for the past 5 years. There was no history of prior psychiatric treatment. The counselor accepted Mrs. K.'s stories uncritically, empathizing with the distress that she felt and offering to be her ally in finding a safe place. After a few sessions Mrs. K. expressed confidence in her counselor and found for herself a new apartment with which she was satisfied. She refused, however, to see a physician for medications. After that point she dropped in occasionally, reported periodic increases in symptoms, but managed to care for herself adequately. In this case, as in other instances of working with paranoid persons, the client developed feelings of trust quite slowly but, once formed, these positive feelings create_ _xt in which she was willing to work on specific problems. T_ _an involve self-care, as in this case, or psychologically _s developing better relationship skills or more _ _ng other people.

One use of em_ _y the nature of the individual's di_ _ent only a portion of their prob_ _eeling the way they are. Empathic r_ _guish more clearly what aspects of their curre_ _thering them.

Gendlin _as emphasized a directed process that he calls

"focusing" to help clients define and clarify their problem, and to facilitate their own problem-solving efforts. This procedure is particularly useful for clients who are unable to identify their concerns or who have difficulty staying on one issue. Gendlin describes this type of client as "being in a stew." He tries to say something useful to himself in order to understand or talk himself out of the problem, but this talking either helps just a little or makes the client feel more stuck and distraught with his problem.

The process of focusing involves stopping this private monologue and substituting a method for making one's problems more manageable. First, clients are instructed to relax and be silent, not talking to themselves for about 30 seconds. During this time they are encouraged to get a bodily sense of their problem, and to let words emerge from those feelings. By letting the words emerge from this bodily sense, they can discover the actual significance of the problem to them. In contrast, the words of one's internal monologue often represent a mixture of one's hopes and fears, and thoughts of what one should do or feel, that leave the person with vague feelings of malaise. Focusing is different from getting in touch with one's feelings, which can be exacerbating in a depressed or highly anxious person. It is, rather, an experiencing of the whole situation that the person faces, allowing to emerge from that sensing a clarification of what is frightening or concerning the individual.

As the person begins to find the right words to go with the experiencing of the whole situation, there is often a sensation both of sharpened, clarified feelings and of relief. Sometimes, however, in trying to put these sensations into words the feelings may be lost, and the client must again try to focus without words on the situation. A series of steps for training clients to focus effectively is shown in Table 11.1.

To demonstrate how focusing can be used, a woman may complain of feeling distressed because of the ways she is treated by her children, but she cannot be specific about what is bothering her. She may say initially that she is upset that her daughters do not call her frequently. Through focusing on the whole problem, it may be discovered that she is not concerned that she is being neglected but that her feeling is one of helplessness. As she explores it further it becomes apparent to her that she fears most that in the event of an emergency her daughters will not be aware of what has happened to her. The treatment, then, may involve developing an intervention that will increase her feelings of security in some way, for example, by having her approach her daughters specifically about that concern, or by setting up some other mechanism for providing herself with reassurance that she will be taken care of. The counselor thereby starts with the general complaint of being upset with one's children and, through the use of focusing, clarifies more specifically what it is about the relationships that is upsetting by helping to bring out the whole sense of the problem situation.

TABLE 11.1. Steps in focusing

Explain that this manual consists of a set of instructions in thinking which has been found to be helpful to people. It isn't meant to be a test, and no one will ask you what you have thought about. You will be asked whether you have found this method of thinking helpful.

After a pause, try to break in gently with the next instruction.

This is going to be just to yourself. What I will ask you to do will be silent, just to yourself. Take a moment just to relax ...... (5 seconds). All right now, just to yourself. Inside you, I would like you to pay attention to a very special part of you .... Pay attention *to that part where* you usually feel sad, glad, or scared .... (5 seconds). Pay attention to that area in you and see how you are now.

See what comes to you when you ask yourself, "How am I now?" "How do I feel?" "What is the main thing for me right now?" Let it come, in whatever way it comes to you, and see how it is.

30 seconds or less

If, among the things that you have just thought of, there was a major personal problem which felt important, continue with it. Otherwise, select a meaningful personal problem to think about. Make sure you have chosen some personal problems of real importance in your life. Choose the thing which seems most meaningful to you .... (10 seconds).

Of course, there are many parts to that one thing you are thinking about—too many to *think* of each one alone. But, you can *feel* all of these things together. Pay attention there where you usually feel things, and in there you can get a sense of what *all of the problem* feels like. Let yourself feel *all of that.*

30 seconds or less

As you pay attention to the whole feeling of it, you may find that one special feeling comes up. Let yourself pay attention to that one feeling.

1 minute

Keep following one feeling. Don't let it be *just* words or pictures—wait and let words or pictures come from the feeling.

1 minute

If this one feeling changes, or moves, let it do that. Whatever it does, follow the feeling and pay attention to it.

1 minute

Now, take what is fresh, or new, in the feel of it *now* ...... and go very easy. Just as you feel it, try to find some new words or pictures to capture what your present feeling is all about. There doesn't have to be anything that you didn't know before. New words are best, but old words might fit just as well. As long as you now find words or pictures to say what is fresh to you now.

1 minute

If the words or pictures that you now have make some fresh difference, see what that is. Let the words or pictures change until they feel just right in capturing your feeling.

1 minute

Now I will give you a little while to use in any way you want to, and then we will stop.

Source: E. T. Gendlin, J. Beebe III, J. Cassens, M. Klein, and M. Oberlander, "Focusing Ability in Psychotherapy, Personality, and Creativity," in J. Shlien, ed., *Research in Psychotherapy III* (Washington: American Psychological Association, 1968). Copyright © 1968 by the American Psychological Association. Reprinted by permission.

As the above discussion indicates, the use of empathy and focusing also helps clients decide upon goals. They can discover what it is they are currently doing that they dislike or do not want to do, and what they prefer to do. There is a tendency to recommend getting active and involved as a solution to all the problems of the aged, but this type of advice often rings hollow to the client, who has been told all this before by friends or children or by himself. Setting the goal of therapy as getting more involved or starting a new activity should come only after a clarification of what the client feels is currently missing in his life, that it is part of his sense of the problem, so that the activity proposed by the counselor will be seen by the client as related to his specific needs.

For many older clients, especially those troubled with transient feelings of depression or loneliness, this type of supportive approach will lead in a few sessions to the formulation of goals. At that point the client is able to transfer the experience from the counseling session into his other life situations, feeling more effective and/or taking some new directions in those activities. Others, however, do not respond sufficiently and need more than just a supportive approach. Creating a positive relationship with these clients facilitates their cooperation with other types of intervention, such as the behavioral and cognitive methods described below.

Behavioral and Cognitive Interventions

A behavioral approach to treatment assumes either that maladaptive behaviors and emotional responses have been learned, or that the individual has a deficit in some behavioral skill because of a lack of or maladaptive learning (Rimm and Masters 1974; Mahoney 1974). Through the principles of learning, these problem behaviors can be modified. In recent years there has been an attempt to integrate behavioral and cognitive approaches by treating thoughts and feelings as covert behaviors that are also subject to similar principles of learning. Positive reinforcement, for example, may increase the frequency of covert as well as overt events. While some assumptions of this integrated model are only weakly supported by empirical evidence, it does appear a more promising approach than concentrating solely on either actions, thoughts, or feelings (Mahoney 1974).

There are some features shared by all the procedures discussed below. First, the goals of treatment are broken down into a series of specific tasks, and are typically arranged according to degree of difficulty. Clients begin with easier steps and then move toward more difficult behaviors. Second, the client records his activities, thoughts, and/or feelings that are related to the treatment goals to provide baseline information and objective evidence of change. Third, therapy involves working on one problem at a time, rather than jumping back and forth between concerns.

Finally, the rationale of treatment is explained to clients. They are active in setting goals and their compliance is based in part on their understanding of how each step in treatment helps move them closer to their objectives.

Behavior therapy rests on 2 related models of learning—classical and operant conditioning. In classical conditioning, a neutral stimulus or cue comes to be associated through learning with an emotional reaction. To cite a simple example, a person may have learned to feel anxious while speaking in front of a group. To deal with this problem, one can undergo a reconditioning process, learning to associate a different emotion with public speaking. The technique of systematic desensitization does precisely that, teaching the person new associations and behaviors in the anxiety-provoking situation. In contrast, an operant conditioning model emphasizes that the frequency of behaviors is associated with the amount and type of reinforcements or punishments contingent on these behaviors. An operant approach to behavior problems involves finding incentives (reinforcements) for desired behaviors and, in some cases, punishments for undesired behaviors. Behaviors are broken down into a series of small steps, so that persons can move to their goals gradually. It is further assumed that the effective shaping and reinforcement of behavior patterns will create responses that are incompatible with the anxiety the person may have experienced previously in a given situation. Assertion training combines aspects of classical and operant conditioning, sometimes shaping new behaviors through training, modeling, and reinforcement, and sometimes helping persons manage anxiety in particular situations by pairing the anxiety-producing cues with relaxation or with other behavioral responses that inhibit anxiety.

At a more general level, a behavioral approach to treatment includes attention to specific, observable, and/or definable problems. If a person reports feeling depressed, one determines how often and in what situations these feelings occur. There would be attention to the consequences (reinforcements) both of feeling and not feeling depressed. Treatment would similarly be organized in a series of operational steps leading to new behavioral and emotional responses.

Relaxation and Desensitization. The most widely researched behavioral technique has been that of systematic desensitization. Developed by Wolpe (1958), systematic desensitization involves training the client to experience a state of deep muscle relaxation through tensing and relaxing various muscle groups. When a state of relaxation has been induced, the person is instructed to imagine the anxiety-producing situation in a series of steps or "hierarchy," beginning with scenes that evoke little anxiety and progressing to more difficult situations. Someone with a fear of flying, for example, would begin by imagining a scene associated with only a small amount of anxiety, such as driving to the airport. After repeated pairings of that scene with a relaxed state, the person will be able to envision it with no experience of anxiety. The therapist would then present another scene in the hierarchy, such as driving up to the airline terminal, which would again be paired repeatedly with relaxation until it produced little or no anxiety. Desensitization can occur either through the use of imagery or in the actual situation. For some persons, imagery does not produce feelings of anxiety similar to the actual situation, and desensitization can take place only through participation in the latter.

Desensitization is appropriate as treatment for particular kinds of problem, especially when a client presents one or a few phobias. Feldman and DiScipio (1972) cite the use of desensitization with someone hospitalized with Parkinson's Disease to reduce a fear of falling so that the patient could participate in physical therapy. In general, however, older persons do not frequently report fears or anxiety associated with specific situations. As a result, there may be few opportunities for the use of systematic desensitization.

One portion of systematic desensitization, relaxation training, does have potentially wider application with older clients. It can be beneficial in the treatment of certain problems, including insomnia, hypertension, other psychosomatic disorders, or as an adjunct to other treatments (Rimm and Masters 1974; Paul and Bernstein 1976; Fedoravicius 1977). Relaxation has also been used as part of a program in treating chronic pain (Fordyce et al. 1973; Beers and Karoly 1979).

When beginning treatment with highly anxious or depressed clients, training in relaxation can give them some immediate relief. Lewinsohn et al. (1978) report that depressed persons generally respond favorably to the relaxation training. In addition, the client can be taught to relax himself when in difficult or stressful situations. In a treatment session clients would be taught to bring the feelings of relaxation under voluntary control by pairing relaxation with cue words such as "calm" or "relax" (Paul and Bernstein 1976). They can say the word subvocally while relaxed, repeating this word several times while exhaling. This self-induced relaxation can then be used as an adjunct to other forms of treatment, such as assertion training. When the person is trying new behavior either in a session or *in vivo* and begins to feel anxious, he could say the cue word while exhaling a deep breath, thus relieving some of the tension that is inhibiting performance. A client who had difficulty meeting persons, for example, could be taught ways of initiating conversation with persons he meets in various social settings, such as a senior nutrition program or recreational centers. If he experienced anxiety before or while starting the conversation, the use of the cue word would help relieve that tension. Another use of relaxation is with patients with multiple and exaggerated somatic complaints. In these cases, relaxation is an adjunct to shaping more effective interpersonal behaviors (Fedoravicius 1977).

In training clients to use the relaxation techniques (the training can be conducted with groups or on an individual basis), the counselor should see that they are in comfortable chairs, have loosened their clothing, and that there are no bright lights or distracting noises. The nature of relaxation should be explained to clients, and it should be ascertained whether they have any problems such as arthritis or back or neck injuries that would make the tensing of specific muscle groups painful (Rimm and Masters 1974). Any painful parts of the exercise should be eliminated. Before the training is begun, the therapist should ask clients to indicate how much anxiety they are feeling. Using what Wolpe (1958) has described as subjective units of distress, or SUDs level, the therapist asks clients to describe their current feelings of tension or anxiety on a scale from 1 to 10; 1 indicates feeling completely relaxed and 10 represents the most tension they ever feel.

The therapist can then instruct the clients to close their eyes and to begin the first part of the exercise. To gain maximum benefit, muscles should be tensed for periods of about 10 seconds, with about 15 seconds of relaxation in between. Tension should be concentrated in the part of the person's body being focused on by the exercise, with other muscles kept relaxed. The trainer can remind clients of this during the exercise. While instructing clients to tense and relax their muscles, the therapist should also instruct them to focus on the feelings of tension or of relaxation, helping them to identify the differences between these states so that they can monitor their own subjective tension more effectively. Training can be combined with biofeedback equipment, especially for clients who have difficulty experiencing subjective differences between tension and relaxation.

During the last part of the relaxation exercises, the therapist can check the clients' current level of SUDs by asking them to raise a finger when the therapist says the number that indicates how much anxiety they are feeling. The therapist would then begin counting slowly from 1 to 10. This procedure can serve to check whether clients have actually benefited from the training. It may take more than one presentation of the relaxation exercises before some older clients are capable of experiencing a decrease in SUDs level or of sufficiently discriminating feelings of anxiety from calm. Until the client experiences a subjective decrease in tension with this procedure, it will not be a useful part of the treatment.

At the end of the exercise, the therapist can instruct clients to let a pleasant scene come to mind, focusing on that image while maintaining the relaxation in their muscles. The training is ended by telling clients that the therapist will begin counting backwards from 10 to 1, and that when 1 is reached, they should open their eyes. Steps in a relaxation exercise are shown in Table 11.2.

As mentioned above, one aspect of relaxation involves teaching clients to discriminate better between feelings of anxiety and relaxation. The

TABLE 11.2.   Steps in training of progressive relaxation

1. Tense and relax hands
2. Tense and relax biceps
3. Tense and relax triceps
4. Pull shoulders back and relax; push shoulders forward and relax
5. Turn head slowly to the extreme right and relax; repeat to left
6. Move head forward to the chest and relax
7. Mouth: open as wide as possible and relax; purse lips in a pout and relax
8. Eyes: Open as wide as possible and relax; close as hard as possible and relax
9. Take a deep breath, hold, and then slowly exhale

Additional exercises can be done for other muscle groups

Source: D. C. Rimm and J. C. Masters, *Behavior Therapy: Techniques and Empirical Findings* (New York: Academic Press, 1974). Reprinted by permission.

benefit of this part of training is to help individuals monitor their own behaviors and to identify more specifically those situations in which they are experiencing greater difficulties. One way of explaining this kind of discrimination to older clients is to demonstrate that individuals tend to feel tension in different parts of the body, that some persons may feel tension in their abdomen, while others experience it in their back, neck, legs, or some other site. A particular client may then be able to identify where he feels tension. This information can be used both to help clients discriminate between feelings of tension and calm, and to modify the relaxation procedure to focus more on those muscle groups where the most tension is reported. Commercial tapes of relaxation exercises are available and can be used during therapy sessions or for practicing relaxation at home.

It has been reported that vigorous exercises have a relaxing effect similar to tranquilizing drugs, and possibly also to relaxation training (de Vries 1975). For some individuals, a medically supervised program of aerobic exercise would be an alternative to deep muscle relaxation. Exercise might, in fact, be very useful for those older persons who are engaging in a low level of activity at the outset of treatment.

One further aspect of relaxation is that it can be taught in groups. Training in relaxation during the first or second session of groups for older persons has been observed by the author to help reduce anxiety over being in a group, and also to give some members a feeling of progress in dealing with their problems.

Operant Procedures. Perhaps most commonly associated with behavior therapy in the public's mind, operant conditioning has not been given much attention in treating the problems of the aged. This approach, however, has considerable potential for dealing with maladaptive patterns of functioning that are encountered in older persons. In particular, because of the many social changes that are associated in this culture with growing older, the environment may no longer provide external supports for positive, adaptive behaviors (Hoyer 1973). Persons who received attention, praise, material rewards, or other reinforcements for performing the social roles of worker, spouse, parent, or friend may find these incentives decreasing as they grow older. This lack of positive incentives can lead to a diminished output of behaviors, and perhaps also to feelings of dysphoria or anxiety. Alternatively, some individuals may exaggerate behaviors in an attempt to continue to receive desired reinforcers. Someone, for example, who has experienced a decline in social interactions may find that aggressive or demanding behaviors result at least initially in attention and other responses on the part of friends or family members. Other maladaptive behaviors, such as passive or incompetent actions, may actually be rewarded by some persons who interact with the aged. Nursing home staffs, for example, typically define a "good" patient as one who does what is told and causes no trouble. Passive and withdrawn behaviors, which characterize many nursing home patients, must be considered as shaped to some extent by these reinforcement contingencies. Thus an operant approach to the behavior of the aged provides a framework both for assessing what reinforcers may be supporting problem behaviors and of procedures for altering these maladaptive responses.

The basic principle of operant techniques is that a behavior is more likely to be repeated if followed by positive consequences (Krasner 1974). While many behaviors have no apparent overt reinforcers, they may be maintained through self-reinforcement, that is, the individual appraises the behaviors in a positive way, or because they were reinforced in the past. The method of operant therapy is to provide reinforcers for positive, adaptive behaviors, while identifying and in some cases removing the incentives for maladaptive actions.

The first step of operant therapy is the assessment of target behaviors. It is important to determine precisely what the maladaptive behaviors are, how often they occur, and in what situations. This assessment can lead to discovering the functional relationship between the problem behaviors and reinforcers. Second, the person's other adaptive behaviors are assessed. Many psychotherapists focus exclusively on maladaptive behavior. Clients, however, will possess many adaptive behavior patterns. These may occur infrequently but, through the use of reinforcers, can be increased to compete with the maladaptive behavior. The focus of treatment, then, can be to increase the frequency of desired behaviors, especially those actions that the person already manifests (Rimm and Masters 1974). Third, it is important to discover reinforcers that are appropriate to the individual client, that is, reinforcers that will effectively lead to increases in the frequency of targeted behaviors. The extent to which various events have reinforcing properties varies among individuals. For that reason, the clinician must determine what reinforcers are effective for a specific client. In making this assessment, 4 types of reinforcer can be considered: (1) material reinforcers (e.g., food, money); (2) social reinforcers, including praise, facial expressions, physical nearness to another, and physical contact; (3) activity reinforcers, i.e., the person engages in a desirable action after completing the targeted behavior; and (4) negative reinforcers, which involve the removal of an aversive or noxious stimulus contingent upon engaging in the targeted behavior (Rimm and Masters 1974). As discussed in Chapter 8, Lewinsohn and his associates (Lewinsohn, Biglan, and Zeiss 1976; Lewinsohn et al. 1978) have compiled a useful assessment tool, a list of over 300 pleasant events that are potentially reinforcing. Events that appear to be reinforcing maladaptive behaviors are likely to be effective for shaping more positive approaches and should be considered in the treatment plan. A person whose maladaptive behavior is reinforced by attention, for example, can be given attention contingent on more appropriate actions.

Two steps are critical in an operant approach: shaping alternative behaviors and providing adaptive ways of obtaining desired reinforcements. Individuals who manifest maladaptive behavior are frequently punished for that behavior. While punishment often does reduce the frequency of a behavior, it may not be effective in eliminating it because the person who is punished may not have other appropriate ways to obtain reinforcements. Rimm and Masters (1974) comment that they have often encountered children who are punished contingently for maladaptive behaviors, but are not taught alternative ways of behaving. A similar situation can be envisioned among the aged. An older person who desires attention and involvement with others may be punished for inappropriate responses, but will not be helped to make appropriate social responses.

Similarly, when maladaptive behaviors are being maintained by certain reinforcers, putting the person on an extinction schedule that removes the reinforcements may not be effective without simultaneously providing those reinforcers contingent on appropriate behavior. To cite an example, if a suicidal patient receives considerable attention contingent on suicidal threats, the sudden removal of that reinforcement might lead the person to increase the magnitude of the problem behavior, even going so far as to make an actual suicide attempt. Similarly, a depressed person who obtains desirable gains, such as getting out of unpleasant household tasks, contingent on depressive statements may increase the magnitude of complaints if the reinforcers are suddenly removed.

Because the reinforcers of a client's behavior are often provided by other persons, operant therapy involves careful assessment of the social network. Despite the intervention of a therapist, problem behaviors may be continued to be reinforced by significant persons with whom the client interacts. As an example, it may be reinforcing for a husband to provide "help" to his depressed wife. As she starts to improve, he may sabotage the treatment by continuing to reinforce her maladaptive behaviors, or by developing problem behaviors of his own.

Another feature of operant techniques is having the client chart the occurrence of the desired behavior. This record keeping has 2 purposes. First, it provides objective evidence to the therapist of the extent to which the goals of treatment are being met. Second, in seeing their behavior gradually improve in the direction of a desired goal, clients may experience feelings of success that generalize to other areas of behavior (Rimm and Masters 1974).

Some maladaptive behaviors will result in sudden, dramatic consequences for the individual. Certain types of sexual deviance, for example, have a high probability of leading to arrest or severe social disapprobation. In those instances, aversive techniques should be considered as a method of reducing the problem behaviors or thoughts at the outset of treatment, until positive, competing behaviors can be shaped.

A major application of operant conditioning has been the use of pleasant events to increase activities and diminish feelings of dysphoria, a technique developed by Peter Lewinsohn and his associates (Lewinsohn, Biglan, and Zeiss 1976) and described in Chapter 8. The following case indicates the effects of reinforcing events. Mrs. T. was a 63-year-old woman who stated that her major problem was spending too much time with her husband, who had retired 2 years earlier. He did not help her around the house, and disapproved if she went out on her own. She had felt increasingly depressed, and for the last 2 weeks had been crying a lot. She cried throughout the initial interview, and also reported having no appetite. She felt her husband was not willing to come for marital counseling.

As Mrs. T. was engaging in few enjoyable activities, she and her counselor drew up a list of things she might want to do. She rejected her own initial idea of wanting to get a job, and instead focused on social activities that were more enjoyable to her. At first she did not see the connection between activities and her mood, but after attending a discussion group she stated, "I hate to admit it, but I enjoyed it." She began attending classes and engaging in several other activities. Her feelings of depression decreased, and she was able to take a real estate licensing exam, despite her husband's disapproval. In this case, engaging in events that the client perceived as enjoyable was associated with an overall increase in activities and lessened depression.

Operant reinforcement can also be used to modify other behaviors besides activity level, by pairing reinforcers (including activities) with the desired actions. In Chapter 9 a case was presented that involved reinforcing appropriate social comments when dealing with a woman with paranoid delusions. Some other applications include programs to lose weight (Jeffrey and Katz 1977) and to stop smoking (Thoresen 1977).

Operant techniques have been used widely in institutional settings. Token economies have been developed that reward residents for desired behaviors with chips or scrip that can be exchanged for goods in a canteen or for participation in desirable activities, such as attendance at a movie (Ayllon and Azrin 1968; Rimm and Masters 1974). These types of program have been implemented with older persons (see Richards and Thorpe 1978 for a review). As with other treatments, however, token economies must be used for the best interests of the individual, and not of the institution or staff.

In general, operant procedures should support the independence of the individual. A program of operant conditioning could be valuable for hospitalized persons or in rehabilitation settings to shape behaviors, such as dressing or other self-care activities, that are necessary to maximize independent functioning. There is a danger, however, that these procedures would be used to control problem behavior without supporting positive or independent activity. Where the operant program principally reinforces adjustment to the setting, it would be serving the institution and not the residents. Thus the goals of a token economy or other operant approaches in an institutional setting must be carefully considered.

Assertion Training. Assertion training represents the application of procedures of operant and classical conditioning to a variety of problems and situations. Training procedures may also include techniques of cognitive therapy, which are described later in this chapter. The focus of assertion training is the development of behavioral responses that increase personal competency and effectiveness in interpersonal situations. Assertiveness involves the open, direct expression of feelings and preferences (Rimm and Masters 1974; Lange and Jakubowski 1976). It is differentiated from unassertive behavior, where the person inhibits statements about feelings or preferences, and also from aggression, which involves attempts to dominate another. As with the conditioning therapies, a theoretical principle of assertion training is that acting in a competent, effective way is incompatible with feelings of distress, and therefore creates a new emotional response in a situation in which the person previously felt uncomfortable.

Assertion training has come to have two features: practicing assertive behaviors and learning assertive beliefs that facilitate assertion. Both aspects of assertion training are relevant for the behavioral problems of older persons, who may not have adequate or efficient coping skills for a number of reasons. First, as persons age and retire from their major life activities, such as work or maintaining a family and household, there may be few other places available for them to gain reinforcement of competent behavior. Thus some older persons appear once to have acted in assertive ways in a variety of situations but, because of age-related experiences, no longer behave assertively. Second, many older persons present histories of never having acted assertively. For some areas of functioning, such as in developing new friendships, they never learned appropriate ways of introducing oneself, or of starting and maintaining conversations. One man, for example, came to counseling several months after the death of his wife. His goal was to court and marry another woman, but in his approaches to women he alternated between being excessively shy and aggressive. When asked by the therapist about his relationship to his wife he said she was the only woman he had dated, and they married when he was 19. In other words, he had little experience with the courtship skills necessary to develop a relationship.

A third reason for the lack of effective coping skills among older persons is that changes in cultural mores have outmoded some of the beliefs they learned earlier in life. In dealing with physicians, many older persons feel it is important to respect their authority and judgment, and that it is wrong or even disloyal to question the decisions of one's doctor. The physician's role in society has changed somewhat, however, with more emphasis placed on medical than on relationship skills. This is reflected in the frequent complaints of older persons that doctors do not listen to them, or will not answer questions, or fail to offer them the kind of understanding they received from family doctors in the past. When their relationship with doctors is a troubling problem, training in assertive skills may help them to become more effective patients. They could be taught ways, for example, of asking all the questions they want answered and in persisting if the physician does not respond directly. This approach helps them deal with feelings of powerlessness and frustration with regard to their medical care. Similarly, in their ideas about intergenerational relationships, some older persons were socialized to believe that children should anticipate their parents' needs. They feel that direct requests to their children for help should not be necessary. Their children, however, may not be aware that their parents are expecting them to anticipate certain needs, or may resent having to anticipate these needs. The older person then feels hurt or neglected bcause a child failed to do something for the parent.

Older persons may also hold other unassertive beliefs similar to those involving doctor-patient and parent-child relationships. When today's cohort of aged persons were young, it was considered impolite to be direct with others about one's own feelings or preferences. As an example, many people feel it is improper to ask a guest at one's home to leave, no matter how late it has become. The hosts may use a number of indirect communications, such as yawning or letting the conversation drop off, but will feel they cannot directly ask the person to go. If the guest does not pick up these vague signals, the hosts may become increasingly frustrated and angry at him. Thus, by trying to be polite, they may become upset at their friends, thereby undermining the friendship they tried to maintain with an unassertive politeness.

Another reason for unassertive beliefs in the aged is the negative stereotypes about old age. These beliefs cause some persons to feel that they are not important enough to express their preferences. Having the sense of not being useful or valued, they may feel they would be imposing on others by being assertive. It should be noted that unassertive beliefs are not a problem in and of themselves, but should be focused on in treatment only to the extent that they inhibit more effective responses, or contribute to maladaptive behaviors.

In describing the techniques of assertion training, 3 major aspects can be identified: (1) assessing the situations for which assertion training is appropriate; (2) learning new behaviors within therapy session and through the use of homework assignments; and (3) developing a set of assertive beliefs, if the individual feels it is wrong or inappropriate to express one's needs in a direct, assertive way. When identifying the situations in which assertion training may be appropriate for an individual, the therapist should break each problem down into a series of discrete behavioral steps. As in desensitization and operant training, the shaping of new responses begins with simple and nonthreatening behaviors, and progresses to more complex and difficult actions.

Assertion training uses several techniques within therapy sessions to shape new behavioral patterns. Principal among these are behavioral rehearsals, in which the individual carries out a new behavioral response in conjunction with the therapist, and modeling, where the therapist takes the assertive role and demonstrates possible responses. The method of successive approximations is used for teaching persons new actions through behavioral rehearsal. With each rehearsal the client is praised for what is done well, and encouraged to make the behavior match the model or desired goal more closely. Though some older persons are initially uncomfortable with this kind of role-playing, they will gradually overcome their inhibitions.

Attention should be given to both the verbal and nonverbal aspects of behavior. A client, for example, who wants to be able to meet new persons can practice ways of initiating conversations with strangers. With each trial he would receive feedback about his tone of voice, the words he uses, and nonverbal behavior such as posture, gestures, and eye contact. The goal of this process is to have the person engage in the desired behavior in a somewhat more assertive or stronger way than might be necessary. If the client then becomes somewhat anxious and inhibited when trying out this new behavior in a real situation, his actions may not be as forceful as when practiced but, because of the overtraining, they may nonetheless be effective. For some persons who feel inhibited even in the therapist's office, directions to exaggerate the desired behavior may be helpful. If, for example, an individual can begin to shout the questions he wants to ask his physician, he would then be able to learn to repeat this behavior in strong but nonaggressive ways.

When teaching new assertive behaviors, the therapist should pay attention to the individual's mood. If the client is so anxious about attempting a particular behavior that it inhibits the training, the therapist might use relaxation techniques, or possibly, if the individual's anxiety level is extremely high, desensitize him or her to the situation. Another way of responding when the situation being rehearsed provokes high anxiety is to start the training with a simpler behavior and problem.

It is also important to focus on the client's feelings while engaging in the assertive behavior and immediately afterward. The therapist wants to build the client's confidence so that he can be effective and not feel overly anxious when engaging in this new behavior. It can be pointed out to clients that they do not feel fear or anxiety while engaging in the assertive behavior in the training session, and can therefore function well in the outside world.

Another facet of assertion training is that clients receive homework assignments to practice specific behaviors learned during the therapy sessions. It is necessary at first to choose assignments that have a high probability of success, so that the individual will immediately be rewarded for acting in these new ways. Later on, when the individual is both more effective and better able to tolerate failures, more difficult tasks can be attempted.

When clients carry out homework assignments, it is important to inquire how they felt while doing the task and immediately afterward. Some clients, particularly depressed individuals, will do homework tasks and then report no difference in how they feel. They may even seem somewhat improved to the therapist, but deny that their actions made a difference. In such a case clients must be trained to monitor their moods more closely during and immediately after the homework tasks, in order to learn to differentiate from other moods the positive feelings that result. Some depressed clients may consistently underestimate and undervalue their own performance. With these individuals, a more intensive effort to identify and change negative cognitions (such as described in the following sections) may be warranted.

Discussions of assertive rights are also a major aspect of treatment (Alberti and Emmons 1974; Smith 1975; Lange and Jakubowski 1976). A summary of these rights is shown in Table 11.3. Discussions of assertive rights are a stimulating way to present the idea of assertion. In addition, the therapist may want to help clients distinguish assertive from aggressive or nonassertive behavior (Lange and Jakubowski 1976). Many persons, for example, confuse politeness and a lack of assertion, and feel they cannot

TABLE 11.3   Personal rights: An assertive belief system

1. We all have the right to respect from other people.
2. We all have the right to have needs and to have these needs be as important as other people's needs. Moreover, we have the right to ask (not demand) that other people respond to our needs and to decide whether we will take care of other people's needs.
3. We all have the right to have feelings—and to express these feelings in ways which do not violate the dignity of other people (e.g., the right to feel tired, happy, depressed, sexy, angry, lonesome, silly).
4. We all have the right to decide whether we will meet other people's expectations or whether we will act in ways which fit us, as long as we act in ways which do not violate other people's rights.
5. We all have the right to form our own opinions and to express these opinions.

Source: A. J. Lange and P. Jakubowski, *Responsible Assertive Behavior* (Champaign, Ill.: Research Press Co., 1976). Reprinted by permission.

refuse another person's requests, because that is not polite. Lange and Jakubowski suggest several ways of distinguishing real politeness from a lack of assertion. One way is for the person to note how he feels about acceding to the request. He may feel anxious, for example, about lending his car at a time when he actually needs it, or to someone he thinks is a bad driver. Another indicator to help an individual distinguish politeness from a lack of assertion is if he wants to remind the person about situations in the past when doing a favor caused some discomfort. He may have lent his friend a book that was not returned or came back with rumpled, torn pages. If he is acceding to a new request to borrow a book because of a lack of assertion, he may want to remind the person of what happened last time. A person may also accede to a request as part of a hidden bargain. He will not want to lend his car out, for example, but feels if he does, then he can call upon his friend for a different favor. It is a common complaint of some persons that they always do favors for friends or relatives but never get anything in return. They often give their favors, however, with a specific hidden bargain in mind, or feel more generally that they cannot refuse a request, no matter how many times the other person has disappointed them. By becoming aware of these covert messages, individuals will learn to distinguish politeness from situations in which they feel they are being taken advantage of.

In developing assertive beliefs it is important to demonstrate to clients that not acting assertively is more likely to endanger a friendship than are assertive responses. In the above examples the person who unwillingly accedes to requests from friends may become angry at them for asking, or for not reciprocating a hidden bargain. If he has lent something to a friend, he may worry about its being returned or damaged. As a consequence of acting unassertively, then, the person may harbor some anger or resentment at his friend that affects the relationship. There is often more damage to the friendship than if a request was refused.

When first learning assertion techniques, some people complain they lead to a self-centered way of acting. They would suggest that the above examples imply it is wrong to be polite or do favors for others. That is a misunderstanding of assertion training. The techniques are not used to manipulate or take advantage of others, but to make persons more effective in recognizing and stating their own preferences. There will be many situations in which they want to do favors or otherwise be helpful to others, but they will know it is also their right to refuse a request.

There are no systematic studies of assertion training in old age. Corby (1975) discusses some of the issues in running assertion groups for older community residents. Older women have also been found to describe themselves as less assertive than young women (Baffa and Zarit 1977). In clinical cases, older persons have been able to learn assertion skills for a variety of situations that troubled them, such as in family and social relationships, or in dealing with such various groups as business people, professionals, landlords, tenants, or bureaucrats. This training has been associated with an increased sense of competence and reduced feelings of distress.

The following case is an example of how a discussion of assertive rights and assertion training was used with an older client. Mrs. H. was a widow of 3 months who was living with her 35-year-old son. She had gone through a period of mourning and was now most concerned with her relationship with her son and her sister. Her son worked intermittently and contributed little to the financial support or care of the household. She did most things for him, and also was reluctant to leave him alone at night. She described him as "a little retarded" and did not know how much she had to help him. Her sister tended to dominate her, and Mrs. H. had trouble expressing what she wanted from her sister.

The treatment plan involved clarifying what assistance Mrs. H. thought appropriate to give her son, in other words, what her rights were. She also practiced expressing her needs to her son and sister in assertive ways during the therapy session, and was given homework to use this skill in actual situations. These increases in assertion were accompanied by other self-improvement activities, including dieting and taking classes. Despite a couple of setbacks, she gradually felt more in control and more satisfied with her handling of these relationships.

Cognitive Approaches to Treatment. The development of behavioral approaches to treatment in the last decade has led to increased attention to the environmental context of maladaptive behaviors. At the same time, there has been a growing awareness that attention only to overt actions was not sufficient for a comprehensive treatment approach. Thoughts have a major role in the appraisal, control, and reinforcement of behavior. To give an example of how cognitive appraisal can influence behavior and emotions, 2 persons may be giving speeches before similar audiences. In both situations some individuals walk out of the meeting room during the talk. One speaker will interpret this action as a normal part of audience behavior that does not reflect on his speech. The other speaker, however, might appraise the audience's inattention as due to his deficiencies as a speaker, or as a person (Mahoney 1974). Behavioral approaches to difficulties in public speaking have focused on the person's anxiety, or on helping him be more effective in presentations before an audience. If, however, his performance as a speaker is adequate, then the problem is not one of altering his behavior, but of changing how he evaluates and covertly rewards or punishes his own actions. Many times persons function competently in a situation, but feel bad, guilty, or upset over their performances because they have evaluated themselves or their actions negatively.

In contrast to traditional psychotherapies that looked exclusively at the content of thoughts, cognitive approaches have also considered the role of thoughts in cuing, mediating, or reinforcing other thoughts or behaviors (Mahoney 1974). Thoughts may function as stimuli that lead to depression, anxiety, or other covert or overt events. Images or thoughts can be associated with anxiety, tranquility, or other emotions. Thoughts can also act as mediators in a chain of events between stimulation and overt or covert actions. As in the example above, the persons who were giving speeches evaluated their performances either in a positive or negative way, depending on their cognitive set toward their own actions. Similarly, thoughts can be reinforcing or punishing. Positive or pleasing thoughts can increase the frequency either of overt or covert events, while unpleasant or painful thoughts can reduce the occurrence of other thoughts or actions. These self-monitoring capacities of humans to instruct and evaluate ourselves constitute an integral part of guiding actions, and can be used to help persons function more competently (Meichenbaum, Gilmore, and Fedoravicius 1971; Meichenbaum 1976; Meichenbaum and Cameron 1973).

Cognitive psychotherapies can be traced to the work of George Kelly (1955) and have been developed by Ellis (1962) and Beck (1976). Recently Meichenbaum (1977), Mahoney (1974), Thoresen (1977), and others have articulated a cognitive-behavioral therapy that integrates elements of each approach.

Ellis's method is to identify thoughts associated with disturbing emotions and demonstrate to clients that these thoughts are irrational. He presents to clients a paradigm of thoughts and feelings called the "A-B-C's of personality formation and disturbance-creation" (Ellis 1962; 1970). According to this model, the various events (at point A) activate belief systems (B) that the person has previously learned. If these belief systems are rational and empirically based, they will enable the person to make an appropriate and adaptive response (C) to the activating event. If A involves some successful action, the person would consequently feel proud and positive. If, on the other hand, he has made an error or mistake at A, he would be appropriately sorry or regretful at point C, but would not feel emotionally upset, depressed, or destroyed. A person with an irrational belief system, that is, one in which he distorts or misperceives events in some important ways, might feel he has failed even when he has been successful. Similarly, if one has not done well, Ellis maintains it is appropriate to feel regret or irritation, but irrational to take instances of failure as indicating that one is a worthless or terrible person. Ellis proposes that many distressing emotional reactions are the result of not appraising one's actions correctly or of overgeneralizing the impact of failures or disappointments.

Ellis (1970) has developed a list of 12 irrational ideas or belief systems (part B of his A-B-C paradigm) that cause emotional disturbances. These beliefs are shown in Table 11.4. As an example, one irrational belief is the idea that it is necessary to be loved by everyone for everything one does. The consequences of this belief are, first, to make a person feel unloved and worthless whenever anyone disapproves of anything he does, and, second, to motivate the person to try very hard to please everyone. Ellis would maintain, however, that an empirically based belief system acknowledges that it is unlikely that a person will be appreciated by everyone or for all his actions. Moreover, the fact of not being appreciated by some persons does not mean that one is worthless or terrible; it only indicates that some persons hold different values than oneself.

Another irrational belief Ellis identifies is the idea that it is horrible when things are not the way one would like them to be. A person who is eating at an expensive restaurant may feel that the whole meal is ruined because one dish is not perfect. This idea is irrational because, in the course of everyday events, things will go wrong. A person who maintains that it is necessary for everything to be perfect will find few opportunities to feel happy or satisfied. While it is unfortunate that things do not go as one would like, and it is important to try to change conditions so that they become more satisfactory, it is irrational to have a catastrophic reaction when events do not turn out as one expected.

Working in a similar vein, Beck (1967; 1976) has identified 4 broad patterns of dysfunctional or irrational thoughts: (1) arbitrary inference; (2) overgeneralization; (3) catastrophizing; and (4) selective abstraction. Arbitrary inference involves drawing a conclusion when the evidence for that conclusion is minimal or actually contrary to the evidence. A person may decide, for example, that the host at a party is mad at her because he spent only a brief time talking with her. Yet there may be no

TABLE 11.4 Summary of irrational thoughts associated with emotional disturbances

1. The idea that you must—yes, *must*—have sincere love and approval almost all the time from all the people you find significant.
2. The idea that you must prove yourself thoroughly competent, adequate, and achieving; or that you must at least have real competence or talent at something important.
3. The idea that people who harm you or commit misdeeds rate as generally bad, wicked, or villainous individuals and that you should severely blame, damn, and punish them for their sins.
4. The idea that life proves awful, terrible, horrible, or castastrophic when things do not go the way you would like them to go.
5. The idea that emotional misery comes from external pressures and that you have little ability to control your feelings or rid yourself of depression and hostility.
6. The idea that if something seems dangerous or fearsome, you must become terribly occupied with and upset about it.
7. The idea that you will find it easier to avoid facing many of life's difficulties and self-responsibilities than to undertake more rewarding forms of self-discipline.
8. The idea that your past remains all-important and that because something once strongly influenced your life, it has to keep determining your feelings and behavior today.
9. The idea that people and things should turn out better than they do, and than you have to view it as awful and horrible if you do not quickly find good solutions to life's hassles.
10. The idea that you can achieve happiness by inertia and inaction or by passively and uncommittedly "enjoying yourself."
11. The idea that you must have a high degree of order or certainty to feel comfortable, or that you need some supernatural power on which to rely.
12. The idea that you can give yourself a global rating as a human and that your general worth and self-acceptance depend upon the goodness of your performances and the degree that people approve of you.

Source: A. Ellis and R. A. Harper, *A New Guide to Rational Living* (Englewood Cliffs, N.J.: Prentice-Hall, and Hollywood, Calif.: Wilshire Books, 1975). Reprinted by permission of the authors.

direct evidence of anger or indifference; the host may have spent his time briefly with all the guests. Overgeneralization involves drawing a conclusion about something based on a single incident. An example of overgeneralization would be if a person who is turned down by a friend when he asks a favor concludes that no one can be trusted or that he has no real friends. Catastrophizing involves expecting the worst to happen in a given situation. Selective abstraction refers to taking a detail out of context, so that the person misses its actual significance.

A cognitive treatment program involves identifying these self-defeating and irrational thoughts and gradually replacing them with a more adaptive belief system. The first aspect of treatment is to make the client aware of self-defeating thoughts and to share with the therapist the idea that some of his problems are related to them. At these initial stages the therapist will give assignments to clients to monitor their thoughts in situations where they make negative self-evaluations. In this way they may begin to recognize the emotional consequences of these thoughts. As these irrational beliefs are identified, the therapist then provides alternative statements to take the place of the negative self-evaluations. A woman who reported feeling depressed when her daughter turned down a dinner invitation learned to express disappointment rather than despair or worthlessness. To cite another example, a 65-year-old woman felt worthless because she was not given much time to work in a hospital at which she was a volunteer. This hospital, however, had a surfeit of volunteers, and this client's experience was a common one. The therapist pointed this out and helped the client generate self-statements that indicated her disappointment at not having more involvement. Rather than telling herself she was worthless, she substituted this more accurate thought. These positive self-statements would be practiced during sessions through rational analysis and modeling. The client would then be given homework tasks to use the new self-statements.

Cognitive therapists also use behavioral assignments. Beck (1976), for example, assigns tasks that involve mastery or pleasure. The behavior therapist uses these activities for their reinforcing value. In a cognitive approach, the therapist employs assignments to provide evidence to clients that they have positive abilities or that they can enjoy themselves. Similarly, other adaptive behaviors may be taught in therapy sessions using behavioral and covert rehearsals, modeling, attention, and reinforcements by the therapist (Meichenbaum 1976). Homework assignments involving these tasks would also be given.

Donald Meichenbaum (1977) has introduced an important concept in cognitive therapy: the way we talk to ourselves, our private speech, has an impact on behavior and emotions. Working with school-age children, he and his associates demonstrated that children judged to be hyperactive talked to themselves in different ways when approaching a task than children who performed well in school. In particular, the hyperactive child did not think about the goal, did not plan out his actions, failed to monitor his progress as he worked, and made negative self-statements, such as "I can't do this." In several studies the hyperactive children were taught to talk to themselves in ways that would improve their performance. This was first modeled by an adult, then practiced aloud by the child while doing a task, and then practiced subvocally. The training resulted in improved school performance and reduced behavioral problems (see Meichenbaum 1977, for a review).

Because the concept of inner speech can readily be grasped by most older people, this procedure appears to have potential for use in many situations. Inner speech can help older persons perform particular tasks better. Someone concerned about poor memory, for example, can tell himself appropriate strategies for learning and remembering that improve memory (Zarit et al. 1978). He could also decrease the number of negative self-statements about his ability. Another use for this approach is in controlling excessive feelings of distress. Meichenbaum and Cameron (1973) have trained schizophrenics to make new self-statements, telling themselves to be "relevant and coherent, to make myself understood" (p. 70). Training in this and similar self-statements was found to be related to improved behavior and better performance on projective psychological tests. It is likely that this training has applications for other clinical groups, including such hard-to-treat clients as hypochondriacs or chronic pain patients.

Homework Tasks. In all the therapies discussed above, there has been an emphasis on utilizing what has been learned in the counseling session in those situations in which the person has difficulties or feels distressed. The therapist facilitates this generalizing through the use of graduated homework tasks. Gaining compliance with those tasks often becomes a major issue between client and therapist, on which the success or failure of treatment hinges. There are a number of ways of increasing compliance. If someone does not follow through on a task, some consideration should be given as to whether the assignment was appropriate, and perceived by the client as relevant. Sometimes the therapist must explain the rationale of this approach again, stressing the importance of taking small steps, and how each task will eventually contribute to solving the person's major difficulty. It should also be considered whether there are any positive consequences contingent on the client's inaction, or negative consequences if the client complies. Often clients fail to carry out tasks, but divert the therapist in sessions by bringing up interesting issues to discuss. The therapist can sometimes make it significantly more rewarding to the client to comply with subsequent tasks. In their treatment program for depressed individuals, Lewinsohn and his associates (Lewinsohn, Biglan, and Zeiss 1976) reduce the fees clients pay when they follow through successfully on assigned tasks.

Another approach to gaining compliance is the use of paradoxical directives (Haley 1976). One gets compliance by first directing the client to resist the assignments. This type of double-bind communication can be successful for 2 reasons. If the client resists this directive, it means he will begin undertaking those tasks that were previously assigned. On the other hand, if the client follows this directive, his resistance is now under the therapist's control and he can be gradually influenced to attempt new behaviors.

Haley (1976) suggests a related way of increasing a client's motivation to comply with tasks. If a client does not carry out a particular assignment, the therapist can state that he missed an important opportunity. The client may then request another chance to do that task, but the therapist should insist that the opportunity has passed. The therapist can then give another task for homework. By stressing that it is the client's loss in not complying, the therapist is likely to ensure compliance with the next task.

Another possibility with a resistant client is to discontinue treatment. This step is particularly appropriate in ongoing cases if the client has already met his initial goals for coming into treatment. It often happens, however, that clients with the most extensive behavioral deficits are not compliant. Their difficulties may be due in part to the fact that they are not highly suggestible and have a great deal of difficulty in carrying out any actions. In that case, every effort that is possible to gain compliance should be attempted for as long as the individual wants to continue in treatment. All too often this type of person makes the rounds of community agencies, with each agency offering services for a while and then becoming frustrated at the lack of progress. By placing this individual back on the circuit of service agencies, one inadvertently reinforces his problems with attention and stimulation. Some older clients will have a long history of involvements with social agencies, and it is crucial not to refer these individuals someplace else or, if at all possible, not to terminate treatment before some minimal goals are reached. Like hypochondriacs whose symptoms are reinforced by continued medical attention, these individuals have developed patterns of complaining that have been reinforced, but their more pressing problems have not been treated.

It is not known if older clients are more or less likely to comply with tasks. Based on clinical experience, however, a reasonably high percentage of aged persons are able to follow through on assignments when they are given adequate explanations about the importance of doing so.

Further Issues in Treatment

ETHICAL ISSUES

Concern about the ethics of treatment should be foremost in the mind of the therapist for each individual he or she sees. The history of the development of psychotherapy contains numerous examples of therapists' imposing their values and preferences on clients. This has been particularly the case when differences have existed in the social or cultural background or status of the therapist and client. Thus, in the treatment of women by male therapists, female sexual responses were for a long time misunderstood, and it was prescribed in pseudoscientific language that women ought to stay home and have children. Ethnic minorities and homosexuals also have been subjected to value indoctrination that was presented in the guise of treatment. The aged as a group are likely to have some values different from those of a younger therapist, because of generational and educational differences. Moreover, since old age carries with it a negative stigma, there will also be a difference in status between therapist and client. For those reasons it is critical for a therapist to develop treatment plans that are reflective of the goals and objectives of one's clients.

Behavioral and cognitive approaches to treatment, such as have been presented in this chapter, have sometimes been criticized as manipulative of clients or as being employed to make a person adjust to a bad situation. While these criticisms are undoubtedly true concerning specific therapists who have used these techniques, behavioral and cognitive approaches should be employed to facilitate clients to state goals and to develop actions to enable them to reach those goals. The therapist also needs to have limited objectives. A person's life style may include many features that the therapist finds disagreeable, but these behaviors should be part of treatment only when related to the person's problems in functioning.

An example of how the therapist's values might distort a situation is in the area of marital relationships, where beliefs about the proper roles of husband and wife have been changing. Older couples who have been married for 30, 40, or even 50 years may prevent styles of relationship that are not currently in vogue, such as the wife's doing virtually all the household tasks. Changing the balance of power or the beliefs underlying the relationship should only be undertaken when it is the expressed goal of the couple, or is clearly related to the problems they are having, and not on the therapist's initiative. This distinction between values and treatment is one of the most difficult to maintain.

Use of Psychoactive Medications

Psychoactive medications can play a major part in the treatment of behavioral problems in older persons. The effects of drugs, however, must be assessed cautiously in any patient, and especially in older persons. Many people assume that medications are targeted to particular symptoms, but the effects are not that specific and are usually accompanied by side effects. Highly potent drugs such as the tricyclic antidepressants and major tranquilizers, the phenothiazines, have ramifications throughout the body. The presence of side effects may be so disturbing to some people as to offset the therapeutic gains of the medication. These side effects and other adverse reactions are heightened in the aged. Older persons have been found to absorb drugs more slowly, to distribute them somewhat differently through their bodies, and to metabolize and excrete them from their systems more slowly than the young (Kapnick 1978). As a result, high levels of medication can build up in their systems in a relatively brief period of time. Recommended therapeutic doses of drugs are generally lower for the aged, but even in small amounts they can build up to toxic levels. Another common problem is polypharmacy—the tendency of older persons to take several prescriptions and over-the-counter medications at once. Because medications can interact with one another to create adverse and sometimes dangerous effects, persons taking many drugs run an increased risk.

The effects of medications may also vary somewhat in older persons, and paradoxical reactions have sometimes been observed, in which a drug has an impact opposite to that usually found in the young. Just as stimulants have a calming effect on hyperactive children, tranquilizing medications given to older persons sometimes produce more anxiety.

Psychoactive medications and their uses with the aged have been reviewed by Salzman and Shader (1975) and by Kapnick (1978). A summary of research on antidepressant medications, which are widely given to older patients, has been made by Morris and Beck (1974). Table 11.5 lists the major psychoactive drugs and their effects.

Professionals working with the elderly need a familiarity with these medications, and with the effects of other commonly prescribed drugs. Perhaps the most important skill for nonmedical personnel is to be a good observer of patients after medications are introduced or changed, in order to identify any adverse consequences. The potential benefits of drug therapy in the psychiatric problems of the aged can be increased if there is more attention to controlling adverse reactions.

Terminating Treatment

Setting objective goals for patients in psychotherapy helps in reaching the decision to terminate treatment. Many older persons have been observed to progress rapidly, so that they judge themselves improved after a few counseling sessions. This rapid improvement should not be conceptualized in a pathological way, such as implied by the idea of "flight into health." Rather, observations of human behavior reveal that minimal contact between a client and a concerned counselor is often sufficient to give the client a sense that he can now deal with those situations that had seemed overwhelming.

When someone terminates treatment, the opportunity to return for further sessions should be left open. This open-ended contract should be phrased in a positive way, so that if the individual has problems in the future, he or she does not experience them as a failure. Clients can be told, for example, that maladaptive habits sometimes recur spontaneously, but will respond again to treatment.

A more common problem with older clients is that they do not want to stop treatment. The counseling session may be a person's one significant social interaction. It is sometimes possible to involve someone who is socially isolated in other social activities that will take the place of the therapy. For persons with good social skills, that can take place readily.

TABLE 11.5. Generic drugs with their most commonly used trade names

Generic	Trade	Generic	Trade
Major Tranquilizers		*Antidepressants* (cont.)	
		MAO inhibitors	
Chlorpromazine	Thorazine		
Fluphenazine	Prolixin	Isocarboxazid	Marplan
Haloperidol	Haldol	Phenelzine	Nardil
Loxapine	Loxitane	Tranylcypromine	Parnate
Mesoridazine	Serentil		
Molindone	Moban	*Antimanics*	
Perphenazine	Trilafon		
		Lithium Carbonate	Eskalith
Prochlorperazine	Compazine		
Thioridazine	Mellaril	*Stimulants*	
Thiothixene	Navane		
		Amphetamine	Benzedrine
Trifluoperazine	Stelazine	Dextroamphetamine	Dexedrine
		Methylphenidate	Ritalin
Minor Tranquilizers			
		Sedatives and Hypnotics	
Benzodiazepines (Antianxiety)		*Nonbarbiturate*	
Chlordiazepoxide	Librium		
Clorazepate	Tranxene	Chloral Hydrate	Noctec
Diazepam	Valium	Ethchlorvynol	Placidyl
Oxazepam	Serax	Flurazepam	Dalmane
		Gluthethimide	Doriden
Mephesine-like compounds		Methaqualone	Quaalude
			Sopor
Meprobamate	Equanil	Methyprylon	Noludar
	Miltown		
		Barbiturate	
Sedating antihistamines			
		Amobarbital	Amytal
Hydroxyzine	Atarax	Amobarbital and	Tuinal
	Vistaril	Secobarbital	
Promethazine	Phenergan	Pentobarbital	Nembutal
		Phenobarbital	Luminal
Antidepressants		Secobarbital	Seconal
Tricyclics		*Anti-Parkinsonism Agents*	
Amitriptyline	Elavil		
Desipramine	Norpramin	Amantadine	Symmetrel
Doxepin	Adapin	Benztropine	Cogentin
	Sinequan	Carbidopa and	Sinemet
Imipramine	Tofranil	Levodopa	
Nortriptyline	Aventyl	Levodopa	Dopar
Perphenazine and	Triavil		Larodopa
Amitriptyline	Etrafon	Trihexyphenidyl	Artane
Protriptyline	Vivactil		

Source: P. L. Kapnick, "Organic Treatment of the Elderly," in M. Storandt, I. C. Siegler, and M. F. Elias, eds., *Clinical Psychology of Aging* (New York: Plenum, 1978). Copyright © 1978 by the Plenum Publishing Corporation. Reprinted by permission.

Other inviduals, however, might first have to be trained in the requisite skills for developing friendships. There will also be clients who, because of physical limitations, have few other options available to them. In these cases therapy may indeed be a substitution for friendship. Trained volunteers may be useful in meeting the social needs of these individuals. Some recent projects have demonstrated that older persons can acquire the communication skills that enable them to serve in the role of peer counselor (Becker and Zarit 1978; Alpaugh and Hickey-Haney 1978). These trained volunteers can be used effectively with many isolated and lonely older persons.

Summary

Individual psychotherapy with older clients involves knowledge about the aging process and basic treatment skills. The clinician needs to be able to be both an advocate and a therapist. A problem-oriented approach is recommended that provides support to clients and generates specific behavioral objectives for treatment. Behavioral methods can be used to increase the occurrence of desirable actions and to decrease unwanted behaviors and feelings of distress. Cognitive therapies are effective in modifying thoughts that are associated with dysfunctional behaviors or emotions. There has been no research on the effectiveness of these treatments with the aged, but their emphasis on specific goals, time-limited treatment, and the active participation of clients are important features of any therapy program with older persons.

CHAPTER 12

Group and Family Intervention

THE PAST 30 YEARS in the mental health field have been marked by a major extension of therapeutic approaches from the one-to-one doctor-patient interaction into modalities that more closely approximate the conditions in which the person has difficulty functioning. Group therapy had its initial impetus during World War II as a method of reaching more persons with a limited number of trained therapists, but the curative properties of the group experience itself soon became recognized, and group treatment became a method of intervention in its own right. Current group therapies encompass a broad theoretical spectrum of approaches, from traditional analytic to those stressing the immediate here-and-now of the group experience to the exclusion of any past or future actions. Family therapy, on the other hand, was born from the clinical observations of many therapists that the treatment of one member of a married couple or family was often frustrated or blocked by other members. In some instances if the "patient" began to show improvements, then another family member manifested increasing problems. By bringing the whole family together for treatment, the system of communications among family members that leads to the dysfunctional behavior of one person can be modified. Both these approaches, then, share in having treatment occur in contexts that more closely resemble the situations in which the person has difficulty—in the case of groups, in a social setting where one can receive training in and understanding of problems in human relationships, and for family treatment, with other significant family members actually present and participating in the therapy.

Despite their potential with older clients, neither group nor family treatment approaches have been used extensively. Group work has been a fixture in many institutional settings, but the potential for outpatient treatment has not been sufficiently explored. Similarly, despite the frequent concerns of older persons and of their children about family relationships, there is only a minuscule literature on family and marital treatment with aged persons (Herr and Weakland 1979 is a noteworthy exception). Most research in these fields has not systematically explored theoretical approaches developed with younger populations, nor has there been any consistent attempt to measure outcome under controlled conditions. As Hartford (1978) has observed of group work, many people seem to think that all that is necessary for something positive to happen is just to get some clients together. There is, however, a potential for harm as well as improvement in these treatment approaches (see Lieberman, Yalom, and Miles 1973). An atheoretical approach may fail to incorporate important aspects of the treatment modality and may be more likely to expose clients to the dangers involved in using these techniques.

This chapter will review major approaches to group and family treatment and suggest applications for older persons. Concepts of group therapy, including a behavioral approach to group work, will be presented, and there will be discussion of the use of groups formed around specific problems of elderly clients. Family therapy will be reviewed from the perspectives of a systems approach to interpersonal communications and other types of behavioral intervention that are appropriate for older clients.

Group Treatment

GROUP WORK WITH THE AGED: THE STATE OF THE ART

Group treatment of older persons has great potential for offering supportive and socializing experiences, and for leading to new learning to overcome specific difficulties. The prevalence of social isolation among the elderly and the lack of trained personnel to work with older persons have made group work seem a desirable technique.

Groups having many different goals have been described, including remotivation, socialization, adjustment, psychotherapy, and reorientation. Procedures have focused on feelings, interpersonal behaviors, reminiscences, objective goals for personal care, and adjustment to institutional life. Despite the interest in group approaches, however, there are 3 major deficiencies in the existing literature: (1) the preponderant focus is on adjustment to institutions; (2) there is a lack of clear objectives for treatment; and (3) there have been few controlled studies to evaluate outcome.

As reviews of group programs for older persons indicate, nearly all examples of group treatment in the literature involve samples of institutionalized persons in nursing homes, old age homes, or state mental hospitals (see Burnside 1970; Eisdorfer and Stotsky 1977). Generalizing these experiences to noninstitutionalized populations offers serious problems. Since total care institutions can have profound effects on behavior (see Chapter 10), it is not clear if these group programs treat behavior problems presented by residents before entering that setting, or if the focus is on the consequences of institutionalization. While behaviors such as apathy, withdrawal, and other depressive symptoms are likely to be found among community elderly, their treatment may proceed quite differently in institutional settings, as residents react to a lack of privacy, limited environmental stimulation, and a regimented daily routine. Most papers on group work point out its rehabilitation potential but there are few examples of programs that resulted in the discharge of patients to less restrictive settings. Patient groups in truly rehabilitative settings, such as a physical rehabilitation program, appear to provide the opportunity for mutual support and sharing of experiences, but most other institutional programs do not have this goal of returning the individual to his prior level of functioning.

A second problem with the existing group literature, specifically those studies carried out in institutional settings, is the lack of controlled research on outcomes. While virtually all studies report positive findings, these are typically stated in vague ways or reflect measures of dubious validity, such as ratings made by ward personnel (Kahn and Zarit 1974). Compounding this problem is the lack of suitable comparison groups. While the majority of reports in the literature are case studies, the few attempts at more systematic research on outcome contrast the treatment group with an untreated sample of residents. A more appropriate comparison would be between 2 types of group interaction. That design would allow for an assessment of whether a treatment procedure had greater impact than any other type of increased stimulation.

The third problem with the existing studies is the lack of clarity of goals. The term "group" is typically used in a way to imply a specific therapeutic process, but the helping properties of specific treatment programs are usually not spelled out in detail and not measured. Most groups reported in the literature emphasize the socializing of institutionalized patients, while there are few examples of the systematic use of groups for psychotherapy or behavior change. It is critical to distinguish clearly one's goals. While getting people together and providing some interesting focus for a discussion may be sufficient for a socializing experience, treatment of specific behavioral problems requires something more than just joining a group.

An appropriate objective of psychotherapy groups is to effect some change in behavior, feelings, or attitudes of group members. These groups will both provide the stimulation or socializing experiences of unfocused groups, and intervene in specific problems of clients in the group. The difference between individual psychotherapy and group treatment is that the latter uses specific properties of the group experience to effect changes (Yalom 1975; Hartford 1978). An understanding of how groups function is necessary for setting goals that are appropriate for group treatment.

Treatment Properties of Group Experiences

In his valuable work on group psychotherapy, Yalom (1975) identifies what he calls the 11 curative factors of groups. These 11 dimensions are summarized in Table 12.1. According to Yalom, the difference between individual and group psychotherapy is that in the former the therapist takes actions that lead to changes, while in the group situation the leader facilitates features of the group that have positive effects.

The first curative factor is that the group is useful for imparting information. Issues such as what the process of "getting better" involves, the effects of various medications, or other treatment concerns can be dealt with during group discussions. As noted in Chapter 11, it is often valuable to provide clients with an understanding of how therapy works in order to gain their cooperation, and in a group this type of information can be imparted both from therapist to patients and among the group members themselves.

The second factor in group psychotherapy is that the experience can instill hope in clients. Seeing other persons coping well with similar problems, or observing them improve over the course of several sessions, can give someone the assurance that change is possible. In a group of

---

TABLE 12.1   The 11 curative factors in groups

Imparting of information
Instillation of hope
Universality
Altruism
Imitative behaviors
Development of socializing techniques
Corrective recapitulation of the primary family group
Catharsis
Existential factors
Interpersonal learning
Group cohesiveness

Source: I. D. Yalom, *Theory and Practice of Group Psychotherapy* (New York: Basic Books, 1975). Copyright © 1975 by Basic Books, Inc., Publishers. Reprinted by permission.

older persons with various visual problems, one participant announced she had been able to take the bus that day for the first time in 2 years, after working with a mobility specialist to improve her skills and confidence. This disclosure provided the incentive to other persons in the group, who were also struggling with trying to maintain their independence.

A third feature of groups is that they can lead to a sense of universality. Participants discover they are not unique in their situations. Persons having psychological difficulties often feel isolated from others. The group experience serves to help establish ties to other people, in spite of the individual's difficulties.

Another curative factor is what Yalom calls altruism. Having the opportunity to assist others with their problems can help raise the person's own estimation of himself. Furthermore, by helping other individuals in the group through questioning, modeling, or role-playing, the person giving the assistance, as well as the individual being helped, may actually learn the new behaviors.

A similar feature of groups is that they facilitate modeling. Although modeling is a powerful tool for learning new behavior (see Bandura 1971), it is seldom used systematically in treatment settings. A group maximizes the potential for learning by observing others. Because of the presence in any group of persons with a variety of behavioral skills, there is an opportunity to acquire many new actions. In one-to-one treatment, differences between therapist and client in social class, background, interests, or age may limit the effectiveness of modeling, while in a group there is more likely to be someone similar to oneself who can be an appropriate role model.

The group setting makes other types of learning possible. Yalom (1975) suggests that groups offer the possibility of learning social skills through observing and modifying the communications among group members. He also feels that groups afford the opportunity for learning about unsatisfactory family relationships in one's past and correcting some unresolved family conflicts. While Yalom emphasizes correcting emotional experiences from one's family of origin, the focus in a group of older persons may more likely be on their relationships with their own children. It is typically assumed that psychological growth occurs when persons clarify and transcend problems with their parents, but a similar growth may also be possible for parents in relation to their children.

Another factor that Yalom considers important in groups is the opportunity for emotional catharsis, or the expression of strong emotions. Leaders of the encounter group movement have sometimes considered emotional release to be the most vital ingredient leading to change. Research on encounter groups, however, has suggested that leaders who overemphasize confrontation and emotional release are likely to cause harm to some participants. Groups in which the most positive changes were found were those in which there was both new learning and emotional expression (Lieberman, Yalom, and Miles 1973).

One curative dimension that may have important significance in some groups of the elderly is that of existential factors. These include dealing with the inevitability of death, the fact that people are basically alone in encountering the major issues in their lives, and the necessity of assuming responsibility for one's life.

Yalom considers the 2 most important curative factors in groups to be the opportunities for interpersonal learning, and group cohesion. In his discussions of these dimensions he gives examples of how group leaders can manipulate these properties of a group for particular goals.

Interpersonal learning takes place because the group setting offers the opportunity for the individual to observe and receive feedback about his own interpersonal behavior. People typically overemphasize their own faults and have a limited appraisal of their strengths. They are also unaware of some of the effects of their behaviors on others, and of ways in which persons distort their perceptions of others' actions. In everyday life we have few opportunities to learn about these idiosyncrasies. Other people are typically too polite to tell us about behaviors that annoy them, or they may begin to avoid us rather than confront us about certain unpleasant habits. In a group, however, it is possible to create the climate in which one can learn more about one's own interpersonal behaviors.

The ways in which groups approach this learning varies, depending on the style of leadership. Some groups are based on the model of individual therapy and conduct treatment between the leader and individual members of the group. In that type of setting the opportunity for interpersonal learning is mainly through observation. In contrast, Yalom (1975) emphasizes focusing on the here-and-now of the group experience, using the immediate interactions of participants to increase their awareness about their own behaviors. Stress is on how the person feels or acts at that moment, and not how his problems originated in the past or what he will do in the future. It is also possible to use groups to teach new behaviors and perceptions specifically for situations outside the group setting. The focus in that type of behaviorally oriented group is on the goals individuals have set for themselves, rather than solely on the here-and-now interactions (Rose 1977). The opportunities for learning about interpersonal behaviors occur principally in role-playing particular situations and through modeling and shaping new behaviors.

Yalom identifies group cohesiveness as an absolutely necessary condition for effective treatment. Group cohesiveness can be defined as the attractiveness of a group for its members, the strength of the emotional tie one has to the group and the other individuals in it. Cohesiveness facilitates change because having positive feelings toward the group makes it more likely that one will learn from the comments of others and will model new behaviors.

It is important to build up group cohesiveness in early stages of a group. In the reports on group work with the elderly, however, little attention has been paid to this factor. Several ways of increasing the attractiveness of a group in the early meetings may add to the cohesion in groups of older persons. Initially most persons are apprehensive about what will happen in the group and how others will perceive them. Activities that reduce this anxiety will make the group more attractive to participants. Introductions, for example, often make people anxious. Instead of going around the room and having everyone introduce him- or herself to the group, one can instead have people make the introductions to one another in pairs. Individuals can then be introduced to the whole group by someone else, and they will also have made the acquaintance of one other group member in the process. Other procedures that can reduce anxiety in early stages are the use of deep-muscle relaxation exercises (see Chapter 11) and role-playing, both of which are generally enjoyed (Rose 1977). Serving food after the initial sessions may also facilitate cohesiveness. One factor that has not been used in treatment groups but that has been found in various studies of small group behavior to increase cohesion is the creation of a sense of competition with some other group. By striving to make one's own group better, stronger emotional ties to the group will develop (Yalom 1975). It is sometimes assumed that older patients do not have much that they can give to each other, and that the group leaders have to be more active than with younger clients in order to build up cohesion. The experience of group leaders is, however, that participants have more resources than they expected, and they do not have to spend as much time as they anticipated stimulating or protecting their older clients (Finkel and Fillmore 1971). Encouraging mutual support and understanding among group members early in the life of the group can help increase the attractiveness and cohesion of the group.

These 11 curative properties of therapy groups can be brought into play through the direction of the group leader. These qualities, however, are not goals in themselves, but means to accomplish the specific goals for that group. With interpersonal learning, for example, some learning is bound to occur in all but the most fragmented groups, but what type of learning and how it is fostered depend on what the clients and therapist want to get out of the group. The clearer one's goals for the group, the more appropriately can specific interventions be made that maximize learning through the use of the inherent properties of group interaction.

Many of these features of groups can be seen in reports of successful psychotherapy groups. In a description of a program for older persons run in a private psychiatric hospital, Finkel and Fillmore (1971) observed that the group served as a socializing agent for persons who had previously been socially isolated, provided a forum for the discussion of problems on the ward and for the dissemination of information about treatment and hospital policies, taught appropriate social behaviors, and increased the motivation of patients. The group also gave a role to patients, who were able to help one another within the group. Finkel and Fillmore reported that those patients who showed the most improvement were more likely to have assumed a constructive, helping role within the group. In the main, however, reports on group work with the elderly do not specify how these properties of group experience were employed (Lowy 1967; Hartford 1978). All too often it is assumed that just being in a group is somehow curative, or the major emphasis is on the socializing component, but not on other features of the experience.

Other important aspects of groups are the process of group formation and how group norms are established. Most of the research on groups indicates that there are distinct stages of development (Yalom 1975; Hartford 1971). In psychotherapy groups in particular one can identify 3 stages during formation: (1) a period of tentative participation: (2) a rebellion or storming phase; and (3) the development of group cohesion. Underlying these stages is the establishment of group norms that influence what topics are discussed, how members interact with one another, and what are appropriate emotional expressions. Group leaders need to be aware of the norms being established in the early stages of a group, in order to ensure that they facilitate therapeutic changes.

The process of developing group norms begins with the instructions that the group leader gives participants, either before the group meets or during the first meeting. These instructions convey what it is the leader expects both for the individual client and for behaviors during the sessions. Preparation of participants for the start of a group has been found to be related to better outcomes than when persons receive no preparation (Yalom et al. 1967). In early group sessions this preparation can take the form of teaching clients how to set goals for themselves and to observe their own actions (Rose 1977).

Norms in a group develop from the actions of participants as well as from statements by the therapist. In an early session, for example, a few clients may change the subject whenever an emotion-laden issue begins to make them uncomfortable. By doing so, they are creating an expectation that it is inappropriate to bring up these issues. Similarly, how members respond to one another leads to a sense of whether one can bring up difficult personal issues. If someone who has discussed personal material is criticized or put down in some other way, the climate of the group will not foster work on sensitive materials. On the other hand, responses that encourage, support, and show understanding of one's problems lead to norms where one can feel safe in bringing up even the most painful or embarrassing experiences.

The intervention of the group leader can be critical in helping to establish therapeutic norms, that is, norms that facilitate reaching the goals set for group members. In actual practice group leaders vary considerably in the attention they pay to this facet of group process. Some leaders virtually ignore group process, focusing only on the interactions between themselves and individual group members. Other leaders comment *only* on process, that is, on the attempt of the group to formulate its own goals and norms.

Statements by the leader on group process can be used to break down antitherapeutic norms and to establish facilitative ones (Yalom 1975). Examples of untherapeutic norms would be such things as interrupting people while they talk, excessive intellectualizing, letting one person dominate the sessions, and scapegoating one member. Similarly, coming late or missing sessions can have an adverse impact on the emotional climate of the group.

The types of problem encountered in establishing therapeutic norms vary with the stage of group formation. Early in therapy groups one often observes the person with the most obvious problem monopolizing the discussions. Other members encourage keeping the focus on this individual, since that relieves their anxiety about discussing their own problems. When too much encouragement is given to this type of individual, either by the leader or other group members, the group can have an unfavorable outcome, including substantial harm to this person (Yalom 1975). Similarly, during any period of storming against the therapist, it is important to deal in an open but also calming way with the criticism. Therapists who ignore or stifle criticism or attacks on themselves limit the extent of openness in the group. At the other extreme, a leader who encourages an excessive display of combativeness or aggression among members runs the risk of harming psychologically vulnerable participants (Lieberman, Yalom, and Miles 1973). Untherapeutic norms can also develop after these initial phases of group formation, and may inhibit further progress. The group leader must therefore pay attention to members' assumptions about group norms throughout the life of the group.

The literature on groups with older persons has paid scant attention to these factors of group formation and group norms. Several basic questions remain to be answered, such as whether group formation proceeds in a similar fashion and rate as among younger persons, whether older members tend to set types of norm different from those set by younger members, and what types of norm lead to positive changes. Based on research with young participants, several suggestions can be made for improving outcome, including paying attention to any person in the group with low approval and low acceptance from other participants and, if necessary, making the group aware of their behavior toward this individual; increasing the group's tolerance of individual differences manifested by participants; understanding the experience of individual members by placing oneself in their situation during group discussions; getting feedback on leadership from the group; and providing a conceptual framework for group members to help them understand their experiences (Lieberman, Yalom, and Miles 1973). Another factor to consider is screening persons before the group is formed to exclude individuals who have strong ideas that would lead to untherapeutic group norms. An individual who feels that people really do not change or is convinced that most other persons are foolish or stupid would have an adverse effect on any group, and should be dealt with individually. Among the older population there are fewer individuals who are psychologically sophisticated, so that one is more likely to find persons who are convinced that this type of experience will not work for them, or who have other strong biases that would create serious problems in a group. In selecting for a group, however, one should not exclude persons who are unattractive or whose manner of relating is offensive, such as someone who complains about everything. Similarly, an older person who is not sophisticated about psychological matters or who is not highly verbal can still benefit from the group relationship.

The above comments suggest the issue of group composition. There has been much discussion in the literature of whether persons with similar or different problems should be included in a group. Another consideration in forming groups is the behavioral characteristics of participants, such as whether there should be a balance between talkative and quiet members. Aside from excluding persons who are currently having psychotic episodes, there is little research to suggest the proper balance of participant characteristics. Furthermore, a successful balance may vary depending on the goals of the group. There are, however, some general criteria that can be applied to groups of older persons. A person with severe cognitive deficits that are associated with senile dementia is not likely to benefit from inclusion in a group of persons with normal intellectual function, and may be a disrupting influence on other members. Individuals with mild cognitive deficits, however, appear to benefit from group treatment. While it is sometimes considered that paranoid persons are poor risks for therapy groups, there are case examples of older persons with mild paranoid ideation who improve in group treatment (Finkel and Fillmore 1971). The presence in a group of persons with severe hearing loss is likely to be disruptive. Because of the prevalence of depressed persons among aged patients, it is probable that a treatment group will include several who are depressed. Whether one can have too many depressed persons in a group is not known. Treatment groups have been developed specifically for depressed older persons, but research on their effectiveness remains to be performed. Based on clinical experience, the presence of several depressed persons can have a depressing effect on everyone in the group, including the leader, unless certain steps are taken to counter the low mood and energy level of the participants. These steps include maintaining a high level of energy, using colorful, dramatic, and forceful language, and giving a lot of structure to the group. Because it can be an emotionally draining experience to work simultaneously with several persons who are depressed, it may be beneficial to use cotherapists who can support one another and keep the interactions lively.

An understanding and awareness of group process and development gives a group leader the tools to establish and maintain a therapeutic environment. Specific interventions, however, can go beyond the immediate here-and-now of group interactions. Since a person's problems in functioning are rooted in the contexts in which they occur, as well as in personal habits and characteristics, a focus on these actual situations is desirable. There is some indication that groups too far removed from everyday concerns are not appealing to many older persons. Lowy (1967), for example, notes that "reality needs" such as income, health, and family relationships are very important to older participants, and that good group experiences include attention to these issues.

A treatment group can be used for cognitive and behavioral change by applying many of the procedures of individual treatment. One must, however, always be aware of the group context of the treatment and of the influence of group norms. At the same time, the group offers major advantages for this style of treatment, including immediate reinforcement of clients by peers, opportunity for modeling the behaviors of several persons, and more effective use of role-playing than in individual therapy. Rose (1977), describing a behaviorally oriented group, stresses first helping clients to formulate specific goals. He notes that the therapist may initially have to be relatively active in setting these goals, but then can let participants take more responsibility. Older persons in particular may need more assistance in the initial stages of treatment in establishing specific goals. As an example, a person who is depressed and who has trouble making requests of or refusing requests from other people may not see how learning to make a request in a particular situation is going to make him or her feel better. It must be stressed that these small steps will gradually help the person to become effective in everyday life and to feel less depressed. The leader, then, must be able to reformulate the general complaints of group participants into specific behaviors, and to set goals for the learning and mastery of these behaviors.

Once some specific goals have been set for clients, several procedures can be used to facilitate learning. Problems can be dealt with through the

reinforcement, shaping, or modeling of behaviors. Persons can obtain reinforcements from other group members or can administer reinforcements
to themselves by setting contingency contracts to receive something
desirable when they reach a goal, or they may learn to provide self-
reinforcements by appraising their own actions favorably when they
move toward a goal (Rose 1977). Other procedures that can be used in a
group setting include extinction schedules, relaxation training, desensitization, and cognitive interventions. Clear homework assignments are useful,
in order for clients to generalize new behaviors from the therapy session
to everyday situations. Successes in these homework assignments can be
used as evidence of the person's improvement. This is especially important
early in treatment, when many clients do not see the relation between
specific actions and their presenting problem.

USES OF GROUPS WITH OLDER PERSONS

These comments on groups have been made with a general type of
psychotherapy group in mind. As noted at the start of the chapter, however, the broad term "group" has been used to include everything from
psychotherapy to everyday socializing. In addition to psychotherapy
groups, one can identify 2 other major types of group that have been
used with the elderly: those organized around a specific problem or goal,
and socialization groups.

Groups with specific goals have potentially wide appeal to the community elderly and can have beneficial effects. These groups are formed
around such specific themes as memory concerns (Zarit, Gallagher,
and Kramer 1980), life review (Butler and Lewis 1977), or increasing
personal effectiveness or assertion (Corby 1975). The use of groups for
weight loss has been effective, and such programs for older persons may
contribute to their overall health and well-being. In an early study of the
use of groups with the elderly, Schwartz and Goodman (1952) found
that 13 of 19 diabetics lost significant amounts of weight during a group
therapy program, and 2 were sufficiently improved to discontinue insulin.
Groups can also be used for particular problems in family relationships,
including those faced by spouses of persons with senile dementia,
bereavement counseling for widows and widowers, the relationship issues
that arise between middle-aged children and their parents, and marital
concerns. Groups in specific settings, such as in a rehabilitation hospital,
appear to have a beneficial effect for both patient and family members.
In all cases these groups have specific goals around which the group
interactions can be organized.

Socialization groups, which may actually be the most frequent type,
are the most difficult to conceptualize. It is often stated that the groups
are intended to deal with such issues as loneliness and increasing contact

with other persons, although some implicit or explicit psychotherapy goals are usually included. Many community socialization groups have a hidden agenda for providing corrective psychotherapy experiences to the group participants. There are 2 major problems with this approach. First, it is important for ethical reasons to represent a group experience as accurately as possible to potential participants. Second, it is likely that many people who would be drawn to some sort of discussion or socializing group do not actually need psychotherapy. Persons who join group programs for senior citizens are often among the best-functioning persons in the community (Hanssen et al. 1978), and they may want to join a group for socializing and discussion, rather than for behavioral or emotional change.

Based on the experience of a 2-year group run in a multiservice center and supervised by the author, persons who are drawn to a rap group have included both those with specific problems and well-functioning individuals. Because of the group's connection to a counseling program, those with major difficulties are typically seen in individual therapy, at least for a brief period of time. Rather than attempt group psychotherapy, the group leaders, who themselves are 2 older persons trained as peer counselors, choose a topic for discussion each week and guide the group interactions around that topic. Issues that the group has considered include: relationships with children and friends, making new friends, relating to younger persons, activities for older persons, self-esteem, fears, problems with sleep, wishes, preparing for the rest of one's life, maintaining health and vigor, assertion, and dealing with physicians. Overall, this group has a nonspecific impact. There are lively discussions and a lot of support given mutually among group members. There is also a certain amount of socializing of unpleasant habits, as the group redirects persons who try to dominate the discussion or do not listen to others. Because of the supportive and cohesive atmosphere that has developed, some of the persons with specific problems who joined the group have been helped. One man, for example, who was angry and depressed after a severe stroke forced him to retire, joined the rap group after several sessions of individual treatment. Over the course of time he has steadily increased his participation and has become one of the most active and best-liked participants. Similarly, a man with Parkinson's Disease who initially was somewhat depressed and withdrawn because he was concerned that other people would be upset with his slow and halting speech has become more active and outgoing. For other members, however, the group is principally a stimulating place to get together with others. The important distinction is that while a supportive group experience may have a beneficial impact on some persons with major problems, this can be accomplished without a hidden agenda for turning it into a psychotherapy group. Furthermore, when dealing with major problems, a socializing group probably should not be the only mode of treatment.

As was noted earlier, this distinction between socializing and psychotherapy groups is often blurred in institutional settings. Because residents of a nursing home constitute a captive audience for a group leader, it is all the more important to clarify and state openly what the objectives of a group are. If one wants to organize a socializing group, it should not be vaguely psychotherapeutic. With relatively active and alert residents, one can also organize groups around specific topics, such as life review or family relationships. Another group that can be run in institutional settings is a drop-in group for family members. Families who place an older person in a facility could be invited to join immediately after the placement and, after a few sessions, could come back as they feel the need. This type of group could reduce the tendency of families to decrease their visits to aged relatives in nursing homes by providing a supportive place for them to discuss feelings of guilt and depression, as well as specific relationship issues. Some types of group, however, are not appropriate for institutional settings. Assertion training, for example, may place residents in a double-bind situation. While trained to be assertive in the group, they may actually be punished by the nursing home staff for acting assertively.

Groups have also been used for severely impaired persons in nursing homes, such as those with senile dementia (see Chapter 13). Although it is often claimed that these treatments have a therapeutic effect, research studies have indicated that their gains are limited and they might more properly be conceived of as maintenance groups (see Kahn and Zarit 1974 for a review). Since an institutional setting typically offers little stimulation, groups are a means of providing an opportunity for interaction and activity to several people at one time, utilizing staff involvement in an efficient way. Thus groups can be used to establish a pattern of daily activity that takes the place of what one would do if living in one's own home. Rather than conceptualizing these groups as therapeutic, it is more appropriate to view the creation of daily group activities as necessary to maintain whatever capacities for functioning the residents have. Opportunities for activities and interaction are not a treatment, but should be a basic, minimum requirement for good care.

THE PROBLEM-ORIENTED GROUP: MEMORY CONCERNS AS AN EXAMPLE

Because of the interest and concern of older persons regarding memory problems, groups that offer memory training have a wide appeal for the community elderly. The effects of these groups, though not straight-forward, offer an example of both the problems and potential for prob-lem-oriented groups.

Since several research studies have indicated that memory complaints are associated with depression and not actual memory loss (see Chapter 2), a project was established to determine the most effective way of re-ducing concerns about memory among older community residents: by improving memory functioning or improving morale (Zarit, Gallagher, and Kramer 1980). Memory training consisted of the use of age-old techniques for improving memory, such as organizing strategies and visual imagery to facilitate learning and recall (see Cermak 1976 and Lorayne and Lucas 1974 for discussions of various memory strategies). Many of these procedures had been used in prior research on memory with older persons and were found to be somewhat effective in improving recall. The treatment for depression consisted of helping to make persons more effective in their everyday lives and teaching them strategies to overcome specific problems. Community volunteers were randomly as-signed into one of these 2 treatment programs. Persons with evidence of the severe cognitive deficits associated with senile dementia were not included in the training, though surprisingly few impaired persons (or their relatives) requested to participate.

The results of this study indicated that persons in both groups im-proved in memory function and reported fewer complaints about memory. Changes in memory complaints, however, were correlated with lower de-pression scores, and not with improved memory. This relation between depression and memory complaints was confirmed in 2 subsequent mem-ory-training studies. Memory training was contrasted, respectively, with a current events discussion group and a waiting list. The current events discussions were explained to participants as a way of stimulating their minds to facilitate memory. They were also assured they were not senile and could improve. Compared with the current events group, persons receiving memory training showed improved memory, but complaints went down in both groups. As in the previous study, persons who com-plained less about memory were also those who were less depressed at the completion of the group. When contrasted with a waiting list, how-ever, memory training resulted in both improved memory and fewer complaints (Zarit et al. 1978).

The group setting was thus an effective way of responding to the concerns of older people about memory. Persons in all the groups had an opportunity to observe that others had similar memory concerns. They also shared mutual worries that occasional absentmindedness was an early sign of senility, and were given assurances by the group leaders in all training conditions that they were not senile. This combination of reassurances and positive group experiences probably accounted for the diminished memory complaints in all the groups. These studies suggest that memory training with groups can be effective in addressing concerns of the elderly about memory. Actual memory performance, however, is less important for an older person with no apparent signs of senility than is restoring feelings of confidence in one's abilities.

Family and Marital Therapy

There is a widespread acceptance of the notion that older families have problems, such as the tensions that occur with a couple who have been married for 40 years, or the disagreements that can arise between aged parents and their adult children. In contrast to group therapy, however, which has been used extensively with older persons, family treatment approaches have not generally been applied.

There has been a vast amount of research and publication on family therapy over the past 20 years, but few articles deal with problems of the aged. In using the techniques of family therapy with older clients and their families, one must be careful not to view the treatment procedures as a methodology that can be applied in toto, but rather as procedures to be brought into therapy in an experimental way, with their utility evaluated at each step.

Family and group therapy developed for similar reasons. While group approaches made it possible to observe and retrain the individual in actual interpersonal situations, marital therapy with a husband and wife allowed the therapist to work directly with the problems that affected the relationship, rather than trying to treat each person individually. In contrast to individual therapy, the persons involved in the family problem interact with one another in front of an observer, who can then intervene to change the sequences of behavior leading to dysfunctional behavior (Haley 1963).

Family treatment approaches were also developed in response to a common clinical observation that when a therapist worked individually with one member of a family system and that person improved, another person in the family often began manifesting symptoms (Haley 1963; 1971). The problems of one person in a family can represent a way of dealing with other family members, and may also be related to problems shared by the whole family. In cases of families with a disturbed child, for example, the child's problem behavior may be part of other sequences of actions, such as the parents' inability to communicate with each other on certain issues. If the child were to improve, parents' difficulties in dealing with one another would become more obvious and more distressing to family members. At the same time, working only with an individual in that kind of situation means that advances made in therapy could be undermined by other family members whose behaviors have not changed.

Types of Family Problem of the Aged

As with groups, family treatment refers to several different kinds of therapy situation, each having different goals and requiring perhaps somewhat different approaches. In working with the aged there are circumstances in which one will work with husband and wife, and other times where involvement of adult children with their aged parents would be appropriate.

Marital problems of older persons fall into at least 2 types. The first is when one's clients express concern about marital discord and increasing the satisfaction one or both partners get from the relationship. The treatment issues involved in this type of marital therapy are probably not different from cases of younger couples. The difficulties presented by some couples may be of long standing, perhaps going back to the start of the relationship. In other instances the problems may be of recent origin, such as following the husband's retirement or some other change in the couple's situation. There is no research to indicate whether the response to treatment in cases of long-term marital discord will be as positive as when dealing with problems with a shorter history. A longer duration of marital difficulties may increase feelings of hopelessness. The couple may also be more resistant to change, with both husband and wife feeling that the other must first demonstrate his or her willingness to make changes and to pay the other back for the many years of past discord. As a result, neither person is willing to make simple changes. On the other hand, an aged couple faces none of the problems associated with raising small children that can interfere in their relationship with one another. Many couples report increased happiness with their marriages after their children are on their own (Blood and Wolfe 1960; Troll 1971; Kimmel 1974). It may be possible in therapy to take advantage of this situation, which offers several potential sources of satisfaction for a couple, including privacy, greater opportunities for spontaneous actions, and often a better financial condition when one no longer supports one's children.

The other major situation in which marital therapy may be undertaken is where one spouse has become impaired due to a chronic ailment. The effects of senile dementia on marital relationships are discussed in Chapter 13. Other health problems, of course, can alter a person's capacities for self-care and for providing physical and emotional support for his or her spouse. The presence of an incapacitating illness can also lead to depression in the affected individual. As a consequence, the whole balance in a relationship can be upset. The focus of treatment is on adapting to the changed capacities of the impaired person (Grauer, Betts, and Birnbom 1973). As in many relationships, the couple may also present some dysfunctional patterns of behavior that existed before the development of physical impairments in one of them. In that event it is preferable to respond principally to the couple's altered circumstances, and to treat long-standing problems only when they markedly interfere with adapting to present conditions, or when the couple expresses interest in pursuing wider goals. Because of the difficulties in dealing with the incapacity of a husband or wife, the therapy could easily overwhelm a couple by stressing that they must also undertake other tasks. Whenever possible, it is better to work out a solution to the problems of physical infirmity within the existing structure of the marriage.

Problems in relationships between aged parents and adult children are also likely to fall into several patterns. The most obvious is when a parent develops an incapacity that limits his or her functioning, and must rely increasingly on one or more children for support. In a study of 50 cases of middle-aged children who came to a family service agency for help with an aged parent, Simos (1973) reports that almost all the parents had physical problems that either caused a disability or were life-threatening. Children were involved in managing the consequences of their parents' physical problems, such as finding medical care, making appointments with doctors, taking them to doctors' appointments, monitoring medications, and filling prescriptions. Another problem that the children face is that parents suffering from physical problems are also likely to have psychological difficulties, especially depression (Simos 1973).

One conflict that can occur when children must assume some responsibility for a parent is that the parent resists their attempts to monitor the care. The children may provoke their parents' resistance by an excessive concern, trying to overprotect the parent at every step; for example, telling one's mother and father not to go out because he or she might fall, even though this has never happened. The parent may complain about the care being provided by medical personnel and children alike, or may make requests for even greater involvement from the children. When faced with these demands, the children will feel guilty at not being able to do more and angry at the demands made upon them.

A treatment plan for a family that has had to assume responsibility for an ailing parent includes helping them decide what type of care and involvement they want. Family members are often uncertain about what their responsibilities are, and how much time and effort they should put into caring for a parent. They need to clarify what they feel they can do, while at the same time the counselor provides a professional judgment of how much and what kind of care is needed. Most often families assume that their parent needs far more help than is actually necessary, and thus feel overwhelmed by the prospect of giving assistance. If the counselor can help them formulate limited and specific goals, their ability to provide care will be enhanced.

Family members are also often unaware of other resources that are available to help them provide home care. The therapist may need to assist them in arranging for supportive services, such as home health aides or homemakers.

Other goals include helping the parent adapt to the incapacity and, when possible, facilitating a better understanding between parent and child. The latter can be achieved by helping the parent express more clearly what it is he wants from his children and by helping children to respond in new ways to their parent. When parents, for example, complain excessively about physical problems or aspects of their care, the most common response is for their children to argue with them. The children usually feel that their parents want them to do more, and feel angry, guilty, or resentful about this implicit demand. In arguing with a parent over whether pains are real or whether a doctor is doing a good job, the children are attempting both to make their parent better through the force of their arguments and to deny the implicit request to increase their own involvement. These arguments often leave both parent and child feeling upset and misunderstood. An alternative approach is to instruct children to agree with their parents' complaints. A person who complains of pains, for example, is feeling distressed whether the pain is exaggerated or not. By agreeing with the complaints, children can begin to convey that they have some understanding of their parents' dilemma, without feeling an obligation to do something to alleviate the distress. Since there are no easy solutions to many chronic problems, including psychosocial dilemmas such as loneliness, the child who is otherwise involved and attentive to his parent's needs is not doing any disservice by failing to act upon certain complaints.

Children also frequently report that they are angry because their parents do little to keep themselves active or to develop a social life independent of their children (Simos 1973). This problem can be especially acute after a parent has moved in with children, leaving behind whatever friends or activities he or she had. Children react to this situation by feeling they have to provide a stimulating social life for their parent. They fear they will have to spend all their free time with their mother or father and involve the parent in all their activities. In some instances they may even be afraid to leave an otherwise competent parent at home alone while they go out. As a consequence, they insist their parent get involved on his or her own, even when the opportunities for activities are limited.

When an older person is inactive, there are occasions when increasing the level of activities is useful, but at other times few appropriate involvements are available. In the latter case families need to be counseled to decide how much time they can and want to give to their parent, and then to react sympathetically but nondefensively when their father or mother makes additional demands. If a parent complains of being left out of a social activity, they can respond that they know he or she is bored or lonely, but they cannot involve the parent in all their activities. It is the expectation of such a responsibility that leads to arguments and guilt feelings on their part; by changing that expectation, the children can respond to parents without anger or resentment and limit their involvement to what they have decided is necessary and appropriate.

Throughout the counseling with children of ailing parents, it is important to stress that the children also have to meet their own needs. One can emphasize, for example, that the child who does not take time off from caring for a parent and for meeting other responsibilities will gradually become exhausted or resentful, or both, and will then be unable to continue the kind of care that he or she wants to provide. Perhaps the most important step is to help children and, if possible, parents as well, to realize that while they have responsibilities toward their parents, they will at some point reach their limit in being able to provide assistance. That limit varies considerably among families, depending on the material resources available and the willingness of the children to provide care. Rather than automatically assuming that families will want to place a parent in an institution, however, one needs to explore with the children what alternatives are available. Furthermore, by assuring children that supportive services including institutionalization will be made available if needed, there may be the paradoxical effect of reducing the need for such services (Kahn 1975).

While there is considerable awareness of the problems faced by middle-aged children when an aged parent is incapacitated, it is often overlooked that parents continue to provide material and emotional support to their children, and may seek assistance in dealing with serious problems of their children. People recognize the need to work with families when there is a problem child, but the potential gains of family treatment are frequently ignored when the problem child is an adult. This is the case even when parents are very much involved in their child's life and may be contributing to some of the disturbed behavior patterns.

Aged parents of adult schizophrenic children are a specific example. The most frequent situation encountered is where parents do not allow their children to assume any responsibility for their actions. Although some schizophrenic adults are able to maintain stable work habits and relationships, others find it hard to live an independent life. When they get into difficulty, they turn to their parents to support them. Even in cases where children have repeatedly abused their parents verbally and physically, some parents will readily give them money or take them back into their homes. As one 77-year-old man stated about his schizophrenic son, he was fearful that the son would end up in the gutter like a bum. Because of his fear of harming the son, he would set no standards of behavior for him. At the time the father came for help at a counseling center, the son would only enter his house through a window, was verbally abusive to his father, and would not leave his own room while in the house, even to eat. But the father felt he could not demand that his son behave appropriately or seek treatment, because he was afraid the son would go off on his own. In several families seen by the author, parents gave their adult children a similar double message: "I don't want you to act this way, but I will not do anything if you do."

Even though parents were contributing in various ways to their children's ongoing problems, the treatment that had typically been given in these cases was a combination of drugs and psychotherapy for the children, with no attention to the family situation.

When children are in individual treatment, some gains can be made through counseling of the parents. The parents of schizophrenic children are often in need of support. They have sometimes been blamed by others and often blame themselves for their children's condition. Furthermore, their children's current behavior may be creating a crisis in the household, which needs attention. When there is no crisis, parents can be helped to decide how much involvement they want with their children. If, for example, their child repeatedly moves back into their house, upsetting them with disturbed behavior, they can decide whether to take the child back in, or to tell him to return to the center or hospital where he has been receiving treatment. In setting limits of this kind, they can also develop new behaviors toward their children, particularly in treating them as adults. One mother, for example, provoked angry outbursts from her 30-year-old son by insisting he get a haircut. The son refused to yield, resorting to bizarre behavior to win his point. Through counseling the mother was helped to diminish her excessive concern and involvement with her son. Finally, counseling the parents can help the father and mother of these children develop new patterns of behavior toward one another. As Haley (1963) observed, the disturbed behavior of children is often reinforced because it takes attention away from problems in the parents' relationship with one another. This has been observed to be the case even when the children are grown. The focus of treatment in many cases becomes improvement of the parents' relationship.

The last type of family problem that is commonly encountered among the aged is where parent or adult child wants to improve the relationship with the other. The type of concern may involve increasing understanding in a difficult but otherwise stable relationship, or healing what may have been a long-standing breach between parent and child. In the latter instances there is often much blame and guilt on both sides, and it is sometimes difficult to rekindle positive feelings between parent and child.

In one example, a 74-year-old woman wanted to reestablish her relationship with her 50-year-old son. After having been relatively close for a long time, the son had broken off from his mother about 10 years earlier. At that time he had joined Alcoholics Anonymous because of a drinking problem. After overcoming this problem he began to blame his mother for his drinking, saying that she preferred it when he was drunk, because then he needed her and she could take care of him. He called his mother occasionally, but visited only a few times a year. His mother stated she wanted him to come over on a regular basis of perhaps once a week, and to take her out occasionally. He would agree during counseling sessions that he wanted to do that, but then would not follow through on any plans they made. He felt throughout that she wanted more than an occasional visit and would try again to interfere in his life and to dominate him. As a consequence, it was not possible to effect much improvement in their relationship.

FAMILY TREATMENT TECHNIQUES

As in the case of group therapy, family treatment involves more than applying techniques of individual psychotherapy with all family members present. There are unique aspects of the family situation and of the therapist's relationship to family members that can be capitalized on to further treatment goals.

When starting family or marital therapy it is important to give clients a clear rationale for why they have all been asked to come. Initially some family members will be reluctant about attending, insisting it is "Mother's problem," or "Bill's problem," or someone else's problem. A statement can be made to the family that it is useful to meet with the whole family first, or that it is important for all of them to work together to understand one another (Jackson and Weakland 1971). During a first interview family members will be anxious about what will happen, fearing particularly that they might get blamed for the problem. The therapist should shift the focus gradually from the person with the presenting problem to the group, and keep them from drawing conclusions such as "Nothing is wrong with me; it is my wife's problem."

The initial family interviews are major sources of information about the nature of the problem. One can get everyone's view, as well as how each may contribute to dysfunctional patterns of behavior. It is important to note such factors as how people interact with one another, their predominant mood, and what alliances there seem to be. When making these observations, however, Haley (1976) cautions that the therapist keep them to himself for later use. If the therapist were to comment, for example, that 2 family members sitting close to one another seem to be supporting each other, he is telling them either something they already know, or something they do not want to acknowledge to the therapist. In either case, that kind of insight will not have any therapeutic benefits and is likely to make the family apprehensive about treatment.

A SYSTEMS APPROACH TO FAMILY THERAPY

According to Haley (1963), marital and family conflicts often center on the process of defining the relationships among family members. He writes:

> When one person communicates a message to the other, he is by that act making a maneuver to define the relationship. By what he says and the way he says it he is indicating, "This is the sort of relationship we have with each other." The other person is thereby posed the problem of either accepting or rejecting that person's maneuver. He has a choice of letting the message stand, and thereby accepting the other person's definition of the relationship, or countering with a maneuver of his own to define it differently. He may also accept the other person's maneuver but qualify his acceptance with a message that indicates he is *letting* the other person get by with the maneuver. (pp. 8–9)

Through this kind of interchange family members work out sets of implicit and explicit rules governing their interactions and defining what types of relationship there will be among them. Rules may involve such things as a husband comforting his wife when she is distressed, or parents helping their children when they are having problems. Conflicts arise over this process of defining the relationship. Haley (1963) notes 4 sources of marital conflict: (1) disagreement over the implicit and explicit rules governing the relationship; (2) disagreement over who sets the rules; (3) attempts to enforce rules that are incompatible with each other, or "paradoxical communications"; and (4) rules for setting conflicts that are incompatible with other rules.

Haley (1963) argues that symptomatic behavior arises from the third and fourth types of marital conflict, that is, when there are incompatible or paradoxical rules defining the couple's relationship. As an example, a wife may tell the husband, "You make the decisions." This statement is paradoxical because the wife has actually taken control of the situation. Her directive that her husband make decisions is incompatible with the fact that she decided to let him decide. It is, in effect, still her decision. Similarly, a couple may define their relationship as a partnership between equals, but when settling conflicts, one person retains control over their resolution.

When given a paradoxical message, a person can respond in several ways, such as leaving the relationship, commenting on the difficult position the communication puts him in, or responding in turn with another paradoxical communication (Haley 1963). If a husband, for example, insists that his wife should show an interest in sex, but then is unresponsive when she does, she may suddenly have headaches or some other symptom that interferes with sexual functioning. Similarly, if a wife tells a husband to make the decisions, but criticizes him when he does, he may become obsessive about even the smallest decisions. In both of these examples the symptoms are responses to a paradoxical aspect of the relationship, and themselves pose a further paradox. The symptomatic behavior has the effect of allowing the person to gain control over the relationship but, because the individual is responding to paradoxical communications, he or she will report that these actions are involuntary. Like hypnotism, which has similar features, paradoxical communications have the effect of making people respond while feeling they have no control over what they are doing. From this perspective, symptoms are an attempt to respond to incompatible messages, while at the same time the person denies doing so.

Haley's (1963; 1976) approach to working with families involves 2 major steps: (1) relabeling the problems that families present in ways to facilitate their solution; and (2) using specific directives to resolve the conflict over the rules governing the relationship. In relabeling the problems, Haley emphasizes several features. First, he stresses that the therapist should bring out positive aspects of a relationship, especially early in treatment when family members are likely to be more distressed. As an example he cites the relabeling of nagging by a wife as her attempts to communicate with her husband. Similarly, if a husband withdraws whenever a conflict with his wife arises, it can be said that he wants to avoid conflict and to make the relationship work, but that he goes about it in the wrong way. Haley also stresses that it is not productive to bring out how much family members dislike one another, which only makes each person feel despondent. Rather, relabling some of these destructive behaviors in a positive way can lead to spontaneous changes by family members.

In working with families of aged persons with physical infirmities, Grauer, Betts, and Birnbom (1973) advocate a similar technique. They ask that the children share experiences of love, happiness, pride, or other positive emotions from their family life, even if these feelings occurred only in the past. These types of statement can help place the current problem in a broader perspective and, by bringing about more positive feelings, lead to better interactions. In general, it is useful in initial sessions to have a couple or family state some positive things about the others, even if they can only acknowledge some small feature.

Another important aspect of relabeling for Haley (1976) is to be able to formulate the presenting problem in terms of more than one person. He notes that while the therapist should work on the problem that a family brings in, the ways in which the family members have looked at that problem have not led to a solution. It is thereby up to the therapist to restate the problem in a solvable way. In particular, it has done no good to see the problem as being inside one of them. By phrasing it in terms of the relationship, the therapist identifies how all the family members contribute to the problem, and thus can make appropriate interventions that in some way change the sequence of behaviors that led to it. A couple may come in concerning the wife's depression but, rather than looking at the problem as something internal to her, the therapist can observe the patterns of interaction between the couple. Even when there is something literally "inside" the person, such as a physical illness, this approach is useful. If children come to counseling because of difficulty in dealing with an aged parent who has become ill, it is important to keep in mind that there are families who cope well in this kind of situation, and that it is the pattern of interactions in this particular family that have led to difficulties. When a problem is stated in terms of something inside a person, others are left angry and frustrated in their interactions with that person. By rephrasing it in terms of 2 or more people, there is more likely to be a change in behavior (Haley 1976).

The second major aspect of Haley's approach is to give directives to families to change certain behaviors. These directives can be straightforward or paradoxical. A straightforward directive would involve changing some aspect in the sequence of behavior associated with the presenting problem. If a mother and daughter always fight over taking medications, for example, the therapist might direct someone else in the family, such as the daughter's husband, to assume the responsibility of checking if the mother has had the appropriate drugs. The directives can also be paradoxical, such as telling a couple to go home and continue the behavior that brought them into therapy in the first place. This communication is paradoxical if the therapist has been able to indicate that he is concerned with helping the couple. A therapist can, for example, give a couple the directive to go home and fight with one another as they have been doing, but to do so at a specific time. This directive may accomplish several things. First, by telling a couple to go home to fight, one takes the spontaneity out of the encounters. Since people do not like being told what to do, particularly when it is not pleasant, they may resist the directive. Rather than fighting, they may spend the time talking to one another. Second, the couple have been fighting over control in the relationship. By giving them directives, the therapist is trying to assume control over them, thereby influencing them to shift their relationship with one another in response to his efforts to take control.

The use of paradoxical directives is not a simple process. Their success depends on a careful understanding of the patterns of behavior as well as an assessment of the clients' strengths, weaknesses, and perceptions of the therapist. Like other therapeutic techniques, there is also the potential for harm when used inappropriately. Because of their usefulness in dealing with issues of control that are often central in relationship problems, and in mobilizing the resistances of clients in positive ways, paradoxical communications warrant further development and evaluation.

Behavioral Family Therapy

A straightforward approach to marital therapy is offered by Hops (1976), who suggests a behavioral treatment plan for marital problems. Many of the procedures that he proposes can be extended to include treatment of other family problems presented by older persons.

Hops views a successful marriage as one in which there is a reciprocal exchange of reinforcers that is satisfactory to both husband and wife. In contrast to Haley, who focuses on issues of control, Hops feels marital problems arise when a person does not receive sufficient positive gratification from his or her spouse, when the person misperceives the spouse's positive or neutral behavior as aversive, or when the individual receives too much aversive stimulation. His approach in therapy is to increase the amount of satisfying interactions that occur.

There are 4 procedures that Hops uses to increase the amount of reinforcement received by each spouse. First, he teaches the couple to break down their general complaints about one another into specific examples, or what he calls "pinpointing." If a wife, for example, states that she leads a dull life, the therapist asks her to indicate specifically what makes it dull and what things would make her life more interesting. Related to pinpointing, couples are taught to be more specific about what they like and dislike about one another. They are encouraged to enumerate specific actions of the other that please or displease them, and to chart the amount of pleases and displeases they receive. Sometimes a couple will be so angry with one another that they report that nothing the other person does pleases them. In those situations the therapist must improve their skills at discriminating positive from negative behaviors. Hops (1976) suggests the use of videotapes of the couple's interactions to facilitate this process. Because of problems of body image and the lack of sophistication about psychological techniques of many older persons, taping should be done cautiously.

Once behaviors that please and displease each spouse are identified, Hops gives instructions to them to increase at specific times the amount of pleasing behaviors directed toward the other person. Underlying this procedure, he is teaching a model of a relationship as based on give-and-take. Many persons experiencing marital problems insist they will not make changes until their spouse does. While Haley intervenes directly around these issues of control, Hops uses the experience of receiving positive reinforcements from one's spouse to alter the struggle for control, and to create a more mutually satisfying balance.

Another way that he facilitates this give-and-take process is to teach couples directly how to problem solve and negotiate their differences. They are encouraged to negotiate in a straightforward way with one another over differences, rather than to use indirect or paradoxical approaches. They are also taught how to compromise their demands. In making various decisions, ranging from simple things like what restaurant to go to during an evening out, to important issues such as where to live, couples have had little training in how to reach joint decisions and how to compromise. Hops instructs them how to state in nondefensive and nonaggressive ways what it is they each want, and then how to work out compromises that do not leave them feeling they have to get back at the other in return for having given up something.

An important feature of Hops's therapy program is to instruct couples in communications skills. One frequent complaint is that a spouse has not listened to what the other has said. Where that happens, Hops teaches the couple to paraphrase each other's statements as a way of ensuring they have actually listened. Another common problem is when one partner talks excessively and completely dominates the conversation. Training to share the conversation equally consists in allowing each person to speak for a designated period of time, for example, for one or two minutes. Other training in communications skills reduces aversive exchanges, such as when one person uses sarcasm or ridicule, and decreases the extent to which spouses change the subject or in other ways sidetrack important conversations.

Summary

Groups of older persons can have several different objectives, including socializing, psychotherapy, and dealing with a specific problem, such as memory or caring for impaired relatives. The leaders should be clear about the goals and not have a hidden agenda for participants. The unique properties of the group can be used to facilitate goals. Problems that involve interpersonal relationships or that can be helped through positive feedback from others are probably dealt with best in a group setting. Though groups have been widely used with the aged in the past, there is considerable potential for expanding the scope of group work, particularly for psychotherapy groups and those organized around specific problems or tasks.

Marital and family treatment techniques offer some direct and potentially beneficial ways of intervening in various problem situations. Rather than being an end in themselves, however, these interventions need to be used carefully in the service of specific goals that have been arrived at jointly by the therapist and the family. Because of the importance of family ties to one's sense of well-being, there must be particular care taken that one's intervention is not harmful or stressful. At the same time the therapist should encourage the development of positive behaviors. The extent to which older persons can benefit from marital and family therapy remains to be determined, but from clinical experiences there appear to be at least some situations where the personal happiness and understanding of family members can be increased and where each can be helped to lead a more satisfying life, even under unfavorable circumstances.

CHAPTER 13

Treatment of Brain Disorders

THE BRAIN DISORDERS OF THE ELDERLY present difficult and persistent problems for treatment. The general therapeutic nihilism toward the aged is even stronger when dealing with persons with suspected brain damage. This pessimism, however, is not warranted on 2 counts. First, acute reactions, which are typically characterized by delirium, are often reversible. Persons with delirium can show dramatic improvements with appropriate treatment. Even those individuals who have senile dementia and who develop an acute dysfunction can make major gains in functioning with proper treatment of the reversible portion of their disorder. Second, while there are no procedures that effectively reverse the course of dementia or overcome the major intellectual impairments that result, there are therapeutic goals that can be achieved to reduce the disruption within the family caused by the brain impairment and to help the affected person function as well as possible, despite the illness.

It is in this area of treatment of persons with brain disorders that mental health professionals with training in aging can have the most impact. The level of knowledge about these problems in both the lay population and among professionals is limited. There are many myths and fears about senility. Providing information in itself often leads to improvements in the situation. As an example, many families do not know what is happening to a relative who is suddenly experiencing major memory losses. They may have been told it is hardening of the arteries, or that the person is just depressed, or that it is age. They are troubled, and the explanations offered to them are inadequate. If they are given an accurate description of what is occurring and what they can expect, they will be able to make more planned responses to the affected person, as well as to begin to think of long-range plans for care. In cases of delirium a rapid identification and intervention can save the person's life and prevent irreversible brain damage.▸

In this chapter treatment approaches for brain impairments will be presented, with case examples. Because the major intervention in cases of acute reaction is medical, their treatment will be described briefly. Some current therapeutic approaches for senile dementia will be reviewed, and an alternative program of counseling families of the organically impaired will be presented.

Reversible Brain Disorders

As discussed in Chapter 6, there are several possible physiological causes of reversible brain disorders. These include such factors as toxic drug reactions, somatic infections, electrolyte imbalances, malnutrition, alcoholic intoxication, and fractures. When an older person manifests sudden changes in behavior and any of the signs of delirium, including such things as hallucinations and delusions, disorientation, restlessness, or agitation, a thorough medical examination is warranted. It is unfortunate that some physicians are not aware of the reversibility of these states and are not interested in making this type of evaluation. For the nonphysician working with the aged, it is imperative to locate adequate medical backup services, to ensure proper evaluation for and treatment of reversible brain syndromes.

To cite an example of this type of problem, a consultant to a nursing home identified a recent admission as possibly having an acute disorder. On a mental status examination the patient gave several symbolic answers, including that she was in a hotel and locating it across town closer to her own home. She also presented a typical history of persons with delirium. She had been described by friends as being depressed and gradually withdrawing from activities. Before she was relocated, she was found in a filthy apartment with no food. It was not known if she had been eating. Because of the history, the consultant felt it was possible the patient was malnourished, and asked the attending physician to make an evaluation. His opinion was that the woman was senile and that further medical evaluation was not needed. After a month of prompting by the consultant, however, another evaluation found the woman to have deficiencies in important nutrients. With treatment her mental status and ability for self-care activities improved and she was discharged to her home.

This case example points out many of the problems as well as the potential for identification of delirium. The physician was reluctant to make any assessment, and only did so because of repeated requests. It cannot be estimated how many other persons with reversible conditions never receive proper evaluations. In this example the cause of relocation was the behavioral disturbance associated with the malnutrition, but no systematic assessment was made before placing her into a long-term care facility. When persons in the community are unable to care for themselves, it is routinely assumed that they are suffering from senility and can only be dealt with in a custodial setting. While that is sometimes the case, evaluations are warranted to identify those persons with reversible problems.

As in the example, the histories of many persons with reversible conditions include a period of withdrawal and depression, often following some losses. As a consequence of the depression, they no longer eat adequately. The resultant malnutrition then brings on the brain impairment and the concomitant problems of self-care. In other cases such common occurrences as influenza or reactions to medications are the precipitants but, if not properly identified, the person may be inappropriately placed.

A third feature of the case discussed above is the improvement that results from proper treatment. In discussing outcomes of persons with acute organic brain syndromes, Simon and Cahan (1963) report on patients seen in a comprehensive geriatric screening ward. In over half the geriatric admissions the diagnosis was either acute organic syndrome or an acute syndrome in a person with chronic brain syndrome. In both of these clinical groups there was a high mortality (approximately 17 percent) in the first month after admission. The authors felt that the brain impairment in these cases was likely to be the result of a terminal disease process. For survivors, however, the prognosis was quite good. Despite the presence of physical limitations in many persons, the majority were able to return to the community after brief hospitalizations. At a one-year follow-up, only 13 percent of the acute group and 36 percent of persons with a mixed acute and chronic diagnosis were still institutionalized, compared to 51 percent of persons with senile dementia and no reversible disorder. Both acute groups also improved in intellectual performance, as measured by the WAIS verbal IQ.

This potential for gains in self-care and intellectual functioning is sometimes not understood by professionals. Even when appropriate treatment for reversible brain disorders is given, discharge planning is based on the person's condition prior to admission. The following example illustrates this point. A county caseworker was called in to visit an 82-year-old man. The man was bedridden, incontinent, and spoke only garbled words. The apartment was dirty and there was no food in the house. Neighbors said they found the man that way the day before and took him to the hospital. They were told in the emergency room, however, that his problem was old age, and he was sent home. The caseworker returned him to the hospital and secured an admission. Medical evaluation revealed that the man was suffering from acute malnutrition, a bladder infection, and pneumonia in one lung, any of which could contribute to acute brain dysfunction. With treatment the man began regaining his strength. He was able to walk, to express himself well, and to perform self-care activities. Despite the dramatic improvements, the caseworker began arranging for placement in a protected setting, possibly board and care or a health-related facility. Not knowing about reversible brain syndromes, he continued to see this man's problems as signs of senility. It is more likely, however, that the man's illnesses had brought about the problems in self-care. Because he now appeared capable of living independently again, the best plan would be to return him to his own apartment. The worker could then follow him up to ensure that there were no lingering problems in self-care, and to try to arrange for community-based services if some problems arose.

Working with families to educate them about the reversible nature of the condition can be critical. The family may interpret the onset of disturbed behavior as senility or, if the person has a history of cognitive decrements, the next stage of senility. The types of behavioral disturbance encountered by the family or other supporting persons are likely to be highly troubling. In the sample of persons with acute or acute and chronic organic brain syndromes studied by Simon and Cahan (1963), the following symptoms were most common: confusion, memory loss, suspicions, delusions, hallucinations, depression, losing things, getting lost, committing hazardous acts, disturbed behavior in the night, threats of suicide, and threats to others. Because these are upsetting behaviors, family members may have been frightened or fearful that they could no longer manage the person. Telling them the symptoms will gradually abate, and providing assurance that they will be helped in the event they feel overwhelmed with the care of the person during the recovery period, can help the future adjustment.

There are 2 situations in particular in which family members are likely to come for counsel. In the first, a person who is being cared for in the home has an acute disturbance, precipitating a crisis in the family. As an example, a woman came to a gerontology counseling service because of a worsening in her father's condition. She had been caring for him for 2 years following a series of strokes that limited his physical activities, and possibly caused some degree of cognitive impairment. Three weeks before her visit, he developed the flu and ran a fever for several days. During that period he became delusional, became more dependent and demanding of her attention, and sometimes misidentified her as another person. Even though these behavior problems had already begun to subside, she saw this as a worsening of his condition, and not as temporary. In other cases commonly encountered in the community, the introduction of new medications or the increase to toxic levels of old medications can lead to similar disturbances.

A second situation in which families are likely to benefit from counseling focuses on hospitalizations, especially involving surgical procedures and the use of anesthetics. Relocation into the hospital is stressful of itself, and the various tests, treatments, and medications given to patients induce further stress. In any hospital ward with older patients, at least some persons can be observed to be wandering around, uncertain of where they are and manifesting other disturbed behaviors. These can range from irritability and restlessness to inappropriate sexual behavior or even delusions or hallucinations. This behavior has been observed to be especially pronounced at dusk, and has been described as "sundowner's syndrome." The incidence of altered behavior in older persons is especially high following surgical procedures. In one sample of 21 persons with a median age of 75 who had cataract surgery on one eye, 18 manifested behavioral disturbances consistent with an acute organic brain syndrome during the week following the surgery. These problems included denial that the surgery had occurred, paranoid accusations, and other delusions and hallucinations (Linn et al. 1953). After a week, however, these problems subsided in 14 of the 18 patients. In the remaining 4, medical complications had developed. Thus the manifestation of disturbed behavior for a longer period of time was associated with continuing medical problems.

The importance of identifying these changes as acute and reversible is particularly applicable to discharge planning and the counseling of family members. The presence of delirium in a hospitalized patient does not indicate in most cases that protective services are required upon discharge. A supportive home environment would be most conducive to recovery. It has been widely observed that persons with both acute and chronic brain syndromes perform better in familiar settings. If the person does need some monitoring that is not available at home, a short stay in a convalescent facility may be necessary. In that instance, it is vital that no new stresses be introduced, such as might occur if the person is heavily sedated. Throughout this period, counseling with family members or other community supports is critical, so that they do not despair over the behavioral problems being manifested, or come to see those changes as irreversible. The counselor's role in that situation is to provide education, support, and follow-up. If family members are assured that there will be effective follow-up, they will be less apprehensive about taking the patient home. If their management skills are strained, they should be confident that assistance will be available, including temporary hospitalization or other community-based help.

Once effective treatment for delirium is begun, or following the removal of a stressor such as a medication, there can be considerable variability in the length of time for recovery. No figures are available on the rate at which the behavioral disturbances diminish. Based on clinical experiences, acute brain impairments have been observed to vanish dramatically in a few days or to take as long as one month before symptoms are no longer present.

The care for someone manifesting symptoms of delirium involves patience and support, whether the person is at home or in the hospital. If the person continually repeats the same question, such as asking when he will be able to go home, staff should be instructed to answer patiently each time. For more disturbing behavioral problems, such as paranoid accusations, wandering, or sexual advances, a firm but reassuring intervention is often effective. One can address the concern implicit in the patient's behavior, while also limiting it. Someone who complains that the staff is stealing things, for example, can be assured that the hospital is an upsetting place. Some authors recommend the use of mild sedatives for persons with acute brain syndrome (Snyder and Harris 1976). Any tranquilizing medication should be monitored closely, however, as these have been observed in some instances to result in increased behavioral problems, including restlessness, agitation, and hallucinations.

Taking a reality orientation approach, that is, repeatedly giving patients information about where they are and what the date is, is irrevelant in cases of delirium. Disorientation in these cases is due to an underlying cerebral disturbance. A person who wants to know the name of the hospital or the date would, of course, be told, but a patient's improvement is not likely to be hastened by constant bombardment with this information. The following example illustrates this point. A 55-year-old-man suffered a mild heart attack while intoxicated by alcohol. He was hospitalized in a coronary care unit for 4 days. When discharged to a medical ward he exhibited disturbed behavior, including restlessness, agitation, and making inappropriate sexual advances toward female patients. He also had some paranoid delusions. A consulting psychiatrist placed him on Thorazine and then increased the dosage after the patient displayed no initial response. After one week his behavioral problems had worsened and he was transferred to the psychiatric inpatient unit. At that point he was gradually withdrawn from the Thorazine, and no other active treatment was begun. A mental status examination indicated he thought he was either at work or in the county jail. He was preoccupied with getting back to work, and would stand at the door of the unit, asking to be allowed to return to work. Some staff members began a program of informing him of the name of the hospital, in the expectation that once he learned that, he would be better. After 2 weeks he did learn to state the hospital name during a mental status examination, but gave his work address as the address of the hospital. His altered responses gradually diminished as the medication was removed from his system.

In this case the acute reaction could have been caused by several factors, including alcoholic intoxication, the myocardial infarction, or the restricted sensory stimulation of the coronary care unit. Medication was associated with increasing symptomatology. Trying to teach him to say the name of the hospital only shifted the basis of his delusions somewhat. It should be noted, as in many instances of both delirium and dementia, that this man's preoccupation with work represented a denial of illness and assertion of health. This type of adaptation is very common (Weinstein and Kahn 1955). Because it involves the person's attempt to cope with his situation, a reality orientation program to combat these misrepresentations could have the effect of further undermining the person's coping ability. In other words, denial and, to some extent, disorientation appear to function to maintain a sense of personal adequacy in the face of cerebral dysfunction.

In summary, the effective treatment of reversible brain disorders involves, first, medical evaluation that identifies and, when appropriate, treats the cause of the problem. In addition, however, psychosocial services are often effective in minimizing the disruption that the delirium causes for the person and his family. Providing information about the nature of the disorder, assurances of further assistance after discharge, and simple management skills also have beneficial effect.

Senile Dementia

The treatment of persons with senile dementia is basically supportive both of affected individuals and of their social networks. The source of the behavioral and cognitive problems is the underlying cerebral damage. At present there are no methods that effectively restore intellectual function or prevent further deterioration in cases of senile brain disease. Treatment involves minimizing the disruption caused by the disorder. Goals for treatment include: maintaining the person in a community setting; allowing affected persons the opportunity of discussing their illness and its consequences; giving information to family members and other concerned persons about the nature of this disorder; supporting family members so that they can continue to provide assistance to the affected person; and using behavioral and problem-solving methods to deal with specific issues that arise as the result of the brain disorder.

The benefits of supporting older persons with behavioral impairments in community, rather than institutional, settings were discussed in Chapter 10. The treatment described in this section is based on maintaining persons in their own homes. The usual treatment for persons with senile dementia, however, is placement in a long-term care setting. According to Pfeiffer (1977), over 50 percent of patients in nursing homes and other long-term care settings have impairments associated with dementia. The need for long-term care, however, is not an inevitable consequence of dementia. It has been found, for example, that persons with brain syndrome exist in community settings, although their intellectual impairment is as great as that in persons in total care institutions (Lowenthal, Berkman, and associates 1967). Where there is an emphasis on home care, persons having brain impairments can be served effectively in community settings without undue stress on family members or other supporting persons (Glasscote, Gudeman, and Miles 1977).

Because of the current emphasis on institutional care for brain-impaired individuals, the majority of studies on this problem have taken place in nursing homes or the geriatric wards of mental hospitals. These studies, unfortunately, offer few guidelines for community care, since most descriptions of problems encountered in brain syndrome patients include behavioral patterns brought about in response to an unfamiliar and regimented environment. There is some indication that persons with altered brain function have the greatest difficulty in adjusting to new environments (Blenkner 1967). This difficulty follows from the fact that new learning is only partly retained or not remembered at all by the dementia patient. Persons with severe intellectual deficits can sometimes function well in restricted, but familiar, settings, but they manifest severe disturbances if moved to a new place. There is also a tendency to overmedicate persons in some long-term care settings, raising the possibility that behavioral disturbances are the result of toxic reactions to medication.

On the other hand, it is not possible to generalize to the community from intervention studies conducted in long-term care facilities. These treatment programs often respond to the problems created by institutional life, and not to disabilities caused by the brain disorder. Furthermore, treatment in an institutional setting can be successful because of its novelty in an otherwise boring environment (Kahn and Zarit 1974). This type of serendipitous change is often unrelated to long-term improvements. Despite the large number of community persons with senile dementia, there has been little attention to their care. The treatment proposed in this chapter is based on clinical experience, and more objective evaluations remain to be made. Aspects of this approach would be applicable to long-term care, but the general focus is on supporting individuals and their families so that they can remain in familiar surroundings for as long as possible.

Some older persons with senile dementia have either no close relatives or none who are available to offer supportive services. No estimates are available on the percentage of persons in that situation. Supporting these individuals in a community setting is, of course, considerably more difficult. In some instances friends or neighbors will take on some tasks, such as checking in regularly to make sure the person is all right, or taking the person shopping. Community agencies, such as meals-on-wheels, may be able to provide sufficient assistance in some cases. When neighbors are involved they can be brought into the treatment, even for only one or two sessions, and supported in the same ways as family members. If this support system breaks down, however, institutionalization may become necessary.

Working with Families

The proposed treatment regimen is designed to support family members or other involved caregivers in their efforts to provide assistance. As noted in earlier chapters, institutionalization of the impaired elderly occurs when there is a breakdown in the family support system (Lowenthal, Berkman, and associates 1967). Giving relief to family members has been found to reduce the rate of institutionalization (Bergman et al. 1979).

The symptoms that can be manifested by a dementia patient vary in the degree of difficulty they cause caregivers. Sanford (1975) reports that the problems tolerated least by family members were sleep disturbances, incontinence, and not walking. A majority of caregivers, however, stated they could accept the limits that providing assistance placed on their social life. In a recent study, the caregiver's support system was found to be more important than the presence of any particular symptoms. Caregivers' feelings of burden were explored in relation to several factors, including the degree of impairment of the patient's intellectual and self-care abilities, the amount of memory and behavioral problems, the presence of formal or informal assistance to the caregiver, and the frequency with which other persons visited the household. Subjects were 29 community-living older persons with definite signs and history of senile dementia, and their caregivers, 18 spouses and 11 daughters. It was found that only the frequency of visits to the household by other people was significantly associated with the caregiver's feelings of burden (Reever, Bach-Peterson, and Zarit 1979). These results reaffirm that the critical factor in working with dementia patients is the family support system, and not the severity of symptoms. While particular factors such as incontinence are more troubling, they are not consistently related to feelings of burden and can apparently be tolerated where other aspects of the family situation are positive. A counseling program that helps bolster the caregiver in the face of increasing demands of time and energy will have the best outcome for both the impaired older person and the caregiver.

Counseling families of a senile dementia patient involves several aspects. First, it must be assessed if dementia is actually present. Second, the family often needs information about the types of problem the person is having and help in solving some of those problems. Third, the principal caregiver often needs support and encouragement. Fourth, the person affected by the brain disease may also engage, at least briefly, in a therapeutic relationship. Finally, there is often the need to help the caregiver arrange for supportive services, such as homemakers or other kinds of assistance. Both family and individual counseling sessions can be used to facilitate these goals. Wherever possible, joint problems should be dealt with in family sessions, bringing into the sessions any persons who are likely to play an important role in the situation. Individual sessions are also important at times, both for the principal caretaker and for the person with the dementia, to provide support and encouragement to them, as well as an opportunity to express their concerns to an objective, non-judgmental counselor.

INITIAL PHASE OF TREATMENT

When a person is brought in with a suspected brain impairment, the first step is to determine if there actually is a problem. In some situations families will report that the patient has an organic deficit when none is present. In one case, for example, a daughter arranged for her 78-year-old mother to visit a gerontology clinic. The daughter was concerned that her mother had decreased her activities somewhat during the past 3 years and that she was getting forgetful. Following gall bladder surgery 3 years earlier, there had been an acute period of disturbed memory, but the daughter felt her mother never regained her prior level of functioning. The daughter had a strong belief in health foods and felt some nutritional deficit might be the cause of the forgetfulness. Another daughter who accompanied the mother on the interview said the relationship between the concerned daughter and her mother had always been difficult, and the mother said that the first daughter worried about her because she did not have enough to do in her own life. On examination the client revealed no apparent intellectual impairment. She stated that she felt like taking things easier, and was satisfied with her way of life. Follow-up indicated no evidence of a gradual deterioration. Thus an apparent delirium reaction following surgery led one daughter to think that her mother might be senile. Whether the mother was actually more forgetful could not be determined, but there was no gross intellectual deficit. It is more likely that the acute disturbance sensitized the family to the issue of memory loss. The complaints seemed to reflect differences between mother and daughter, and not a brain disease.

While verifying the diagnosis of dementia is critical when the presenting problems involve memory loss, there will be some instances when a family will bring a person in for another problem, but on examination an organic deficit will be discovered. In one case a daughter was concerned because her mother had been withdrawing from activities and having increasing problems maintaining her apartment. The daughter thought this was the recurrence of depression, which had affected her mother a few years prior to this visit. On examination, however, the mother did not show any depressed affect, but testing indicated a moderate degree of cognitive impairment. Since the mother was not depressed and not dissatisfied with her inactivity, no major intervention to increase her activity level was planned. Instead, a counselor was assigned to visit the woman occasionally and to maintain contact with her daughter. This plan was designed principally to reassure the daughter that her mother was being cared for and to maintain contact with the family in the event more intensive services would be needed in the future. A crisis did arise at a later point, and a counseling session with the family helped to develop a successful treatment plan.

When it has been adequately determined that the person has a dementia, there should be an evaluation of the specific types of problem that have resulted. The major symptoms associated with dementia involve intellectual impairment, particularly affecting memory. Principally, there is decreased ability to process new information in long-term or secondary memory. Primary memory, such as involved in the ability to repeat a phone number or a brief instruction, will not be impaired (Talland 1965; Zarit, Miller, and Kahn 1978). A person may thus be able to engage in a conversation, showing all the social signs of interest and comprehension, but 5 minutes later will not recall what was discussed. While that type of forgetfulness can occur occasionally in persons with normal brain function, especially when they are not paying attention to a conversation, it is more frequent and persistent when there is diffuse brain damage.

Intellectual impairment is the one consistent effect of the senile brain disorders. What other problems are manifested depend on the person's style of adaptation to the illness, the reactions of others, such as spouse or children, who are immediately involved with the patient, and the personal and economic resources available in dealing with the situation (Kahn and Miller 1978; Kahn and Zarit 1974; Zarit and Kahn 1975). The severity of the cognitive deficits does not necessarily correlate with the presence of other difficulties. Some persons with severe intellectual impairment have been observed to function adequately in their daily routines. Others, with only minimal cognitive decline, will present major behavioral problems (Reever, Bach-Peterson, and Zarit 1979). Thus it is important to consider that an evaluation of intellectual functioning only indicates whether a dementia is likely to be present. It does not measure the adequacy of psychosocial functioning or the capacity of supporting persons to respond to the problem. These critical dimensions must also be assessed to determine how the person is actually functioning, what specific problems are present, whether supportive services are needed, and, if all resources have been exhausted, whether relocation should be considered.

Because intellectual and self-care abilities are independent in many cases, some persons with moderate or even severe memory losses can function at surprising levels of effectiveness. In one case a woman came to a counseling program concerning her husband, who had had deteriorating mental functioning for about 4 years and now had a minimal to moderate degree of cognitive impairment. His wife was concerned about several management issues, such as how much activity to encourage, and how to respond to her husband's feelings of despair over his condition. After a few counseling sessions she felt more adequate in her own responses to him, and the counseling was discontinued. Within a week, however, she was in the hospital with head injuries and a broken hip, following a beating during a robbery attempt. Her husband managed all the necessary self-care activities during the month of her hospitalization, with only a small amount of assistance from one child and from the counselor. This was a particularly remarkable feat, since he had not done these tasks for himself in their 55 years of marriage. Thus, despite his cognitive impairment, he managed adequately under stressful circumstances.

INFORMATION AND PROBLEM SOLVING

Families often have misconceptions about the effects of brain damage and of how to respond to the patient's altered behavior. Family members may deny that any changes in the person's functioning have taken place. In particular, they may feel that the person could remember effectively again if he only tried. In some instances they ascribe the memory loss to depression, vitamin deficiencies, or a lack of interest or activity. Sometimes family members have not been given information as to their relative's actual condition. Physicians may have termed the memory loss as due to age, hardening of the arteries, or some other nonspecific cause. The family often has not been told that the intellectual deficits are brought about by structural damage to the brain. Giving the family this information often has a positive effect. It increases their understanding of the affected person's behavior and, consequently, they do not make excessive demands on the person to try harder to remember. Some persons, however, may persist in denying that there is anything organically wrong with their relatives. In those cases it is important to challenge their denial if they are behaving toward the affected person in ways that are harmful. The most common problem is where the family members insist relentlessly that the brain-damaged person try harder to remember, or set up memory tasks for the person, or in some other ways make demands for competence that the person cannot meet.

Family members often believe that by exercising one's memory, specific deficits will be overcome. Rote practice, however, usually has little impact, so the family needs to be advised not to persist in their efforts. It is all right, for example, to see if the affected person can remember someone's name, but this encounter should not be turned into a quiz, with various family members trying to draw out the correct answer.

In the following example, the spouse of a man with an Alzheimer's-type degenerative disease continued to manifest denial of the problem, though with no harmful consequences. Mr. G. was 66 and recently retired. While the onset of his memory difficulties preceded his retirement, his wife saw them as an adjustment reaction to retirement. She was concerned because Mr. G. was apparently content to spend long periods of time inactive. Their family physician had not pursued her concerns, saying he was forgetful, too. Mental status testing indicated a moderate degree of intellectual impairment. It was explained to Mrs. G. that there was an organic basis to her husband's problem. At first she was upset, and then began making some plans for daily activities that she and her husband would enjoy. In particular, they began taking long daily walks together. After a few weeks she reported improvements in her husband's mood and other behaviors, as well as in her own outlook. At this time, however, she ascribed his memory problem to a lack of activity, even though he continued to manifest intellectual deficits. As her behaviors toward her husband were very supportive, this denial was not considered harmful.

While some family members deny the presence of an organic illness, others react strongly to the denial or unawareness of the affected individual. They maintain that their problems in coping with the person's memory loss will be lessened if the affected individual would simply admit that he or she has a problem. One common complaint is that the person asks the same question repeatedly, such as inquiring every 5 minutes when dinner will be ready. The spouse or other family member quickly becomes exasperated by this behavior and cannot understand why the person does not acknowledge that he is forgetting. They feel that if he would admit to the problem, he would not engage in these repetitive behaviors. But the patient often cannot acknowledge the memory loss, especially when the extent of cognitive impairment is great. He often cannot remember that he cannot remember, and it is crucial to inform the family of that. Even if some denial is involved in the patient's response, confronting him is not likely to result in any changes in behavior. The best response is for the family member to give the same answer to the person each time the question is asked, and to try patiently to orient him to the situation. Family members should also know that no malicious intent is involved in asking repetitive questions.

The practitioner should also evaluate these types of repetitive situations for their consequences. The annoying behavior may in some cases be rewarded. For example, the major problem reported by a wife was that her husband would ask frequently if it was time to eat, even if they had just eaten 5 minutes earlier. This was, however, the principal interaction that took place between them all day. The wife had taken away many of the husband's activities, including such things as dressing, because it was easier for her to do them. She also regarded him as if he were a child, capable of no activities or conversation. As a result, she did not interact with him except on those occasions when he asked about meals. The frequency of his behavior appeared to be a substitute for other types of interaction. While repetitive behavior does not always function as clearly as in this example, the possibility that it is being reinforced should be explored. Under the circumstances, an intervention to create more positive interactions is appropriate.

A related issue is that families often want the affected persons to be able to limit themselves, that is, to know when they can no longer adequately complete an activity that they had formerly done. In one case a woman with Alzheimer's-type dementia could no longer manage paying the bills. She was not able to keep track of whether she had paid a bill, and sometimes paid twice. Her husband, however, disliked managing the family finances, and insisted that she continue taking care of the bills, although he wanted her to come to him when she was uncertain about what she was doing. One common aspect of dementia is that persons have a limited awareness of their own difficulties. Because of her intellectual impairment, this woman was not capable of monitoring herself sufficiently to know when she was making an error and needed help. It is usually not possible for persons with brain disorders to be aware of their problems so that they can limit themselves. The focus of treatment in this case became helping the husband assume responsibilities in areas where his wife clearly could not manage.

As this last example shows, it becomes necessary for other persons gradually to assume some of the responsibilities of the affected person. There is a danger, however, that the family will take away too much independence, and do too many things for the affected person. Based on observation of clinical cases, loss of ability to perform certain activities does not mean that the person is incompetent in all areas of functioning. The fact that someone can no longer write checks, for example, does not indicate he cannot garden, cook, or engage in other activities. Sometimes the affected person can carry out an activity, but in a less than optimal way. One woman with a severe intellectual deficit was able to dress herself, but would choose clothes that clashed and that offended the taste of the nurse who was caring for her. The nurse attempted to pin together outfits that matched but the woman would still take part from one outfit and part from another to make an unlikely combination. Because this behavior was causing no negative consequences for the woman, it was important that the nurse not begin dressing her. Doing so would have removed one more activity that she was capable of, and increased her dependence. In situations such as this, family members have to be counseled to be tolerant of the person's inadequate performance. When this type of problem has no major impact, they should not intervene. Overprotection and overcaring for the cognitively impaired patient often leads to excess disabilities, and to a situation where the family then *must* provide a lot of assistance.

Families and practitioners often have a difficult time distinguishing between those activities where there is a high risk of danger, and those in which the person's dysfunction will have little consequence. If someone persistently leaves the burners of a stove lighted, that clearly constitutes a major risk. On the other hand, some inadequacy in self-care may be annoying to the spouse or family but presents no real danger. These two types of situation must be clearly differentiated so as to avoid increasing the person's dependencies. Family members sometimes insist that the person's performance of a particular activity is so annoying that they have to take it over. But in that situation their annoyance is the real problem, not the person's inadequacy in dressing or shaving. By explaining the consequences of their assuming too much care for the affected person and by expressing empathy for their annoyance, the counselor can help them to tolerate some unattractive habits.

The bad habits that are annoying to a spouse or child are sometimes behaviors that the person manifested long before the onset of the brain disease. In one case a husband was annoyed with his wife's habit of writing away for mail-order bargains. She had always done this, however, and she was not presently buying to excess. In fact, her behavior in this area was described by her husband as being the same as before her illness. He wanted her to stop, however, and used the fact of her incompetence in other areas to justify his demand. The counselor encouraged him instead to allow his wife to continue sending off for bargains.

As this example suggests, the intact spouse will sometimes seek the resolution of long-standing marital problems, using the illness as a way of justifying his or her demands. Because of changes of power in the relationship, the intact spouse now feels that his or her wishes should be enforced in all areas. Thus, before making an intervention, the therapist should consider how long the problem behavior has been present. In general, one should try to change the affected person's behavior only when necessary, that is, when specific habits or behaviors have potentially harmful consequences. Otherwise, by siding with a spouse in a long-standing marital conflict, there is the risk of taking away too much of the person's independence, or of undermining the affected person's self-esteem.

One issue that creates serious problems for a family is whether the affected person can continue to drive. This is particularly important in areas with inadequate public transportation and where the person with the brain impairment is the only driver in the household. There are no clear guidelines to indicate when the person with senile dementia is no longer competent to drive. In several cases seen by the author, affected persons continued to drive for a long period of time with no accidents. As a result, they remained independent in certain important activities. With severe impairment, however, continuing to drive would no longer be possible. Determining when that point is reached is a difficult process, both as an assessment problem and in terms of the emotional investment persons often place in driving.

Another issue often raised by family members is how much activity is appropriate for the person or what kinds of activity are best. In some instances the patient may voluntarily withdraw from various activities, and will state he has little interest in doing anything. Family members will want the affected person to resume old activities or do something that would be therapeutic. In encouraging persons to resume old activities that were given up voluntarily, one runs the risk of increasing their frustration if they can no longer perform as in the past. In the same way, new activities may be more than some brain-damaged persons can handle. There must be caution, therefore, in encouraging activities. As a general rule, most impaired persons could be challenged a little more than they already are. If their responses are positive, then the activity level can be increased even further. If, however, persons resist these attempts to involve them in programs or activities, the family should be helped to tolerate long periods of apparent inactivity. The value of activity in the treatment of senile dementia is unknown. While engaging in vigorous activity is related to overall physical fitness, it has not been shown to restore intellectual functioning in brain-damaged persons. Long periods of inactivity seem to be the preference of some brain-impaired older persons, and may actually be adaptive.

A related issue arises when affected persons engage in meaningless repetitive activities. One client with severe cognitive impairment, for example, would fold and refold towels for a long period. The family was concerned that this was demeaning. The affected person, however, had initiated the activity and expressed no displeasure in it. Thus, in some instances, the family needs to view the person's activities with values other than their own. What they feel is meaningless may actually be providing some important stimulation for the impaired person.

Perhaps the activity of major importance to families is memory. As discussed earlier, many families develop their own system of rote memory training to try to help the person remember more effectively. There is, at present, no effective training system for helping persons with senile dementia to remember better. Procedures that have worked with normal aged populations, such as the use of visual imagery, have not had much impact on persons with a severe memory loss (Lewinsohn, Danaher, and Kikel 1977). On the other hand, organizational strategies sometimes are effective. These include writing down appointments in a central place, developing the habit of checking the appointments before going out, keeping keys or other potentially elusive possessions in one place, developing a routine before leaving the house to check the gas or any other appliance the person is concerned with, and other ways of developing organized habits for areas affected by the memory loss. The major reason for forgetting these types of task is a lack of organization. In many families, either the affected person or other family members had inefficient methods of organizing even before the onset of the brain disease. In one family, for example, the wife kept appointments and social engagements on scraps of paper that were scattered throughout the house. This system was effective for her before the onset of the illness. When she was affected by Alzheimer's type dementia she was no longer able to keep track of appointments in this way, and her system was too idiosyncratic for her husband to use. He was even less organized in keeping track of engagements and, though his functioning was normal, he was responsible for their forgetting several counseling appointments. In contrast, one man who had been a writer kept a very effective pocket diary that contained information on appointments and other things that were useful. He would jot down reminders to himself as well and would later utilize that information. He had used this type of organizing strategy before the onset of the illness and was able to continue it, with the effect that he was able to compensate well for his memory loss.

In trying to train persons in the use of organizing strategies, 2 considerations must be made. First, improving the organization of information should not be regarded either by the counselor or the family as a panacea for memory loss. In most cases the extent of improvement that will result will be small. There will still be instances of forgetting and of breakdowns in this organizing system, especially during the period when the person tries to learn it. Better organization is also not likely to help the individual with severe cognitive impairment. Second, if the affected person is unwilling to try these organizational strategies, the issue should not be pressed. Since this training will have only limited benefits, there is no need to force the person who does not want it.

As the last point implies, a major focus of the counseling is to help family members understand and respond empathically to the ways in which the affected person is adapting to his impairments. This is often a difficult step for the family, who would like to see the person functioning again as he did in the past. By helping families to respond in an accepting way, however, more harmonious relationships have been observed to occur.

COUNSELING THE ORGANICALLY IMPAIRED PERSON

The most common reactions of persons with organic brain syndrome to their deficits are denial, withdrawal, depression, paranoid thoughts, and dependency. Hypochondriasis and obsessional behavior have also been observed (Walsh 1976). These adaptational patterns can overlap with one another. Persons' behaviors may shift from day to day, or include aspects of each of these patterns. Denial is the most common adaptation, and becomes more prominent as the severity of the brain impairment increases (Zarit and Kahn 1974). Affected persons may minimize their difficulties or deny them outright. They may say, for example, that they have always been forgetful. In mental status examinations some persons will give rationalizations for why they forget certain items, such as not liking the current president and therefore being unable to recall his name. Some persons who are adept at social skills may be able to cover up their deficit by guiding the conversation away from areas that give them problems. They will seem to be functioning well, and can maintain that facade unless their memory is directly tested. Withdrawal is also quite common. The person stops engaging in activities, and may avoid social situations altogether. One woman, for whom an active social life had always been an important activity, would complain of headaches or other ailments just before she and her husband were about to go out. She seemed to want to avoid those situations where others would take notice of her deficit. Depression is more common when the cause of the dementia is vascular disease, although it can be manifested by persons with brain damage of other origins, particularly in the early stages of brain disease. As discussed in Chapter 9, there is an increased risk of suicide in these individuals.

Paranoid reactions in dementia patients can range from transitory accusations to full delusions. As an example of the former, one woman would periodically blame her husband for causing her memory problems. She said that she became forgetful only when he yelled at her. Paranoid delusions usually involve stealing—the accusation that someone has taken things from the person, or has rearranged his possessions so that he cannot find them. Occasionally these are persistent and can be very upsetting to caregivers.

Increased dependency behaviors involve wanting spouses or children to stay constantly with the affected persons, or wanting to have done for them tasks of which they are still capable. The dependency may occur in specific contexts. In one case a woman with severe cognitive impairment made no objection when her husband went to work during the day, but would be upset if he went out in the evening. Before the onset of her illness, however, she had not objected to his taking an occasional evening out.

The counselor should also attempt to build up a supportive relationship with the dementia patient. The major goal is to allow him the opportunity to discuss his loss and other relevant experiences. Persons who are depressed are the most likely to want to engage in this process. In some instances the conversation may be intense but concern issues in the past. One man, for example, with a moderate degree of cognitive loss, spent an hour with his counselor vividly discussing his relationship with his mother, particularly his long-standing resentments toward her. While not related to his current concerns, and not initiated by the counselor, the process appeared beneficial to him. In subsequent sessions he did not bring up this topic. In the majority of cases, counseling the affected person will be brief, that is, comprising a few sessions. Many persons with brain syndrome will be reluctant to engage in counseling. They will state overtly they have no problems, or will withdraw passively during the session. They should not be coerced into counseling, but instead be informed that counseling will be available if they want it. If their behaviors are creating problems in the household, that should be discussed in a family session with all the relevant persons present. Even if affected persons are reluctant to come for counseling, they can often be involved in the problem-solving process when their behaviors are causing difficulties.

In counseling organically impaired persons, there is some temptation to try to shift their pattern of adaptation, for example to help a withdrawn individual to explore more openly his feelings about his disability. This type of awareness may not be possible because of the cognitive limitations that resulted from the brain disease, or because the psychological impact is too great. Furthermore, denial in some circumstances may be the most effective coping strategy for an individual. Counseling, then, can create the opportunity for the affected person to talk about issues concerning him, but should not impose the therapist's goals.

COUNSELING SPOUSES AND CHILDREN

Working with the principal caregiver is probably the most important aspect of counseling families of organically impaired individuals. By supporting that person, the counselor helps him or her to continue to provide for the increasing needs of the affected individual. In addition to the types of information and problem-solving described earlier in this chapter, some specific concerns of the caregiver are likely to arise. These include: how much assistance to give, feelings of guilt, anger, or depression over the spouse's or parent's illness, the need for outside, supportive services, and how to respond to the most persistent behavioral problems of the impaired person.

The first issue that usually arises, especially in cases where the organic deficit is severe, is the amount of assistance the caregiver is providing to the impaired person. Often the spouse or child gives up many activities and interests in order to be present or available whenever the affected individual might need help. In some cases caregivers are hesitant to leave the house, out of fear that the impaired person will do something dangerous in their absence. In other instances the person with dementia will complain about being left alone when the caregiver returns home. As a result, many caregivers are feeling either resentment or exhaustion from providing virtual 24-hour care when they first seek counseling.

When this situation exists, one can give caregivers permission to engage in activities that are satisfying to themselves. It can be stressed to them that they will not be able to provide help unless they take breaks and arrange for activities for themselves. In some instances the caregiver will respond quickly to this suggestion. In other cases, however, the caregiver will at first feel too guilty or responsible to take this step, and will need encouragement over several sessions before being able to meet some personal needs. When a spouse or child states that the impaired person cannot safely stay at home alone, that situation should be evaluated. If it is actually the case, the counselor should try to arrange for someone to come into the home for periods of time to give the caregiver some relief. If day care is available, that might also be considered. Unfortunately, there are few persons who are trained or willing to provide this important type of assistance. Families thus often face the dilemma of not being able to arrange for any competent, in-home assistance. When the impaired person can be left alone, but gets angry or upset, he or she can be involved in the counseling. Through exploring the problem, the impaired person may see the need for the caregiver's having some free time. Many times, however, the affected person cannot be involved in this decision-making process, or his understanding is short-lived, perhaps forgotten because of the memory problems. The primary focus would then be to help caregivers respond to accusations in ways that do not increase their guilt. Often the first response of the spouse or child is to argue with the impaired person, especially if the accusations are exaggerated, such as the patient's saying that his wife is always leaving him alone. Rather than disputing what has or has not happened, caregivers should respond to the feelings expressed in the impaired person's complaints. Statements such as "I know it is hard for you when I'm gone" will acknowledge the impaired person's feelings, but without undercutting the importance of the spouse's independent activities. In other words, caregivers can accept the feelings of abandonment, anger, or dependency without giving up the time they require for their own pursuits. Through this approach, it is possible for the impaired person to gain some tolerance of being left alone. More centrally, however, it provides a way for the caregiver to respond in an understanding way, without feeling unnecessarily guilty for having the free time.

After the caregiver's role and responsibilities have been clarified, more general concerns often arise, including feelings of depression, guilt, anger, or embarrassment that are related directly to the patient's illness or to more long-standing issues in the marital or parent-child relationship. A supportive counseling relationship can help resolve some of these feelings.

One important step is to ask caregivers to envision how they would like events to turn out. While the brain disease often prevents the family from doing some of the things they might have done otherwise, or from resolving long-standing conflicts, some planning might actually enable them to live more in the way they would like.

Another behavioral step is to explore those activities that the couple (or parent and child) enjoyed doing together in the past. If the affected person can still engage in an activity that both had previously enjoyed, such as going out to dinner, this can be encouraged. Often, too, a caregiver will report that the impaired person's behavior or mental functioning fluctuates somewhat from day to day. This type of fluctuation appears to be present in most cases of dementia, whether the cause is principally vascular or due to a degenerative illness. When there is fluctuation, the caregiver can be encouraged to initiate interactions and activities with the impaired person at those times when the mental impairment seems less. This step can increase the amount of time the couple spends together in mutually satisfying activities, and can also give caregivers a sense of accomplishment in their efforts.

One problem that frequently arises is that the caregiver feels embarrassed in social situations for the impaired person's memory lapses. This is particularly the case for spouses, rather than when a child is providing the care, because husband and wife interact more together in the same social circle. Sometimes old friends are not recognized, or the affected person repeats the same stories or questions. Occasionally the person's social behavior will be impaired, such as in developing sloppy eating habits. The caregiver may also not know what to tell friends or relatives about the impaired person's problems. Friends, however, are likely to be supportive, and a caregiver needs to elicit that help. Where it is appropriate the spouse can initiate discussions with friends over the difficulties that are occurring. In talking about the impaired person's problems, the spouse usually will want to avoid the disparaging term "senility." A better way of labeling the problem can be explored during counseling. In some cases caregivers have been comfortable telling others that the problem is "Alzheimer's Disease," a term that is approximately correct but carries no negative connotations. They can also explain to friends that the affected person cannot help his forgetfulness, and that it is not a mental disease, which also carries negative connotations. The counselor needs to be sensitive to these feelings of embarrassment because, if they are not dealt with adequately, they can lead to the increasing social isolation of the caregivers.

A third important feature of the counseling relationship with the caregivers is to help arrange for supportive services when these are appropriate. Most persons are capable of making their own arrangements for assistance, but are not likely to be aware of what services are available or able to make their way through the maze of regulations and varying eligibility requirements. It is critical that the counselor help families with these tasks. Referring them to an information and referral specialist is, unfortunately, usually not sufficient. Moreover, the more persons the caregiver has to deal with, the more frustrated he or she is likely to become. In order to make sure that available services are actually being provided, the counselor should play the role of advocate.

A fourth aspect of the counseling relationship is to help the spouse cope with the more persistent, disturbing, or potentially dangerous behavioral problems of the impaired person. These include such things as leaving the gas on, wandering off, incontinence, and paranoid reactions. The counselor should investigate each problem carefully, helping the spouse to determine when an activity should be limited, for example, when the impaired person should no longer cook or drive, and also developing more intensive behavioral interventions, if that is appropriate. Problems such as wandering or incontinence may respond to simple management approaches, or to a program of operant conditioning.

In cases of paranoid delusions, 3 steps should be undertaken. First, the caregiver should be instructed to respond to the delusions with concern, rather than trying to argue about whether something has actually been stolen. Second, the caregiver should develop a plan for responding to the impaired person around topics and issues other than the delusions, in order to reinforce more appropriate behaviors. Third, it should be pointed out to the caregiver that these paranoid delusions are likely to be transitory. The paranoid delusions of dementia patients usually diminish over time, as the person's memory loss becomes worse. A caregiver who is particularly troubled by the paranoid behaviors may feel encouraged in knowing that this is a temporary aspect of the illness. Where a person manifests severe behavioral problems and has not been followed medically, an evaluation should be arranged for possible acute factors contributing to the problem, especially drug reactions, previously undiagnosed somatic ailments, and malnutrition. This type of evaluation is also particularly important where there is a sudden deterioration in behavior. While tranquilizing medications are sometimes prescribed for such problems as wandering, agitation, or restlessness, these have been observed clinically to exacerbate the behavioral disturbance in some persons with senile dementia. Thus, if a new medication is prescribed in an attempt to alter a dangerous behavioral pattern, the patient's reaction should be closely observed. If there is further deterioration or no effect, consideration should be given to removing the medication. When a person is on multiple medications, the possibility of toxic reaction of the drugs either individually or in combination is high, perhaps contributing to the behavioral problems. This possibility should be carefully pursued. Reductions in medication have sometimes been observed to result in considerable functional improvement in persons with senile dementia.

Another time when behavioral disturbances have been observed in persons with senile dementia is during stressful situations. These may involve unpleasant circumstances, such as the death of someone close to the impaired person, or stimulating activities, such as taking a trip. Family members should be helped to identify these problems as transient, and not as a worsening of the person's condition. Particularly where relocations are involved, such as a vacation, or moving an impaired person to stay briefly with another relative, families should be told of the possibility of temporary behavioral disturbances. They can be advised that if there is a problem, they should offer the impaired person calm reassurances until the behavioral disturbance subsides. The impaired person's disorientation or other difficulties can persist for a few days, so families should not become anxious if there is no sudden improvement.

One final issue involves the decision to relocate the impaired person. This concern is likely to arise in 2 ways: when initiated by others or when the caregiver is considering institutionalization. When behavioral problems are first manifested to a serious degree by the impaired person, the caregiver may receive advice from a variety of persons that the best course is placement in a convalescent facility. This advice may come from physicians, friends, children, or other relatives. Caregivers are often not ready to take that step, but feel they may not be doing the best thing for the impaired person by keeping him or her at home. If that is the case, the counselor should stress that it is probably better for the spouse to continue to provide care in the home for as long as that is possible. It should also be explained that it may not be necessary to institutionalize the person at any point. If the problems become worse, supportive services can often be brought into the home. Institutional care might become necessary in the future, but families should not be told that it is inevitable. If other family members are pressuring the caregiver to institutionalize the impaired person, they should be contacted and, if possible, involved to some extent in the counseling process, so that they can understand the caregiver's decision and the alternatives available in this situation.

When a caregiver makes a decision to institutionalize the person with dementia after having had the opportunity to explore the available alternatives, this decision should be supported. Caregivers should be helped to see that they have done the best that is possible. They should also be given assistance in choosing a facility, taking into account issues such as finding a place that will be convenient for them to visit after the placement is made.

Two other possibilities are likely to arise involving institutionalization: first, when in the judgment of the counselor it is premature, and second, when the counselor feels that placement is actually overdue, given the amount of strain experienced by the caregiver. The counselor can offer alternatives in both situations, but the decision ultimately has to be made by the family members themselves. Even when demonstrable pain is involved in continuing to maintain the affected person at home, some families may still find that preferable to a permanent separation. Thus it is important only to suggest, and not to direct or pressure families into making this decision.

One promising approach for working with caregivers is in a group setting. By coming together with people in similar circumstances, spouses or children can get support from one another, and exchange information on successful management procedures. The group can also serve to reduce their feelings of isolation by showing them that they are not alone in their situation. Caregivers who feel guilt, resentment, or some other strong emotion will realize that these are normal, even appropriate reactions when they observe the same feelings in others.

OTHER TREATMENTS FOR SENILE DEMENTIA

The approach to the treatment of senile dementia described in this chapter has emphasized management of the behavioral and relationship problems that have been observed to emerge. In recent years there has also been a search for procedures that would offer more basic treatments. Two approaches are possible. First, research that unravels the mechanisms that lead to cerebral degeneration in brain syndrome patients may lead to the development of therapeutic regimens that prevent or arrest the brain disorder at an early stage. This type of preventive approach would minimize the extent of cognitive and behavioral impairments. A second approach is to find procedures for increasing the functional efficiency of undamaged brain cells, thus improving intellectual performance. Several interventions that purport to increase cognitive functioning have become available, including various medications and the use of hyperbaric oxygenation. While initially promising, these approaches have usually not resulted in significant gains for most patients.

Medications. In a recent review of medications for the treatment of cognitive impairments associated with senile dementia, Eisdorfer and Stotsky (1977) conclude that no substance has been found that produces long-term gains in intellectual functioning. While various medications are associated with other types of behavioral improvement, for example, in carrying out activities of daily living, intellectual performance has been found to change little or not at all under controlled experimental conditions.

Among the substances most commonly used in attempts to improve intellectual functioning have been stimulants, analeptics, and vasodilators.

Vasodilators, which have received considerable attention, have the effect of relaxing the smooth muscles in the walls of blood vessels, thereby increasing blood flow to the brain and increasing the level of oxygen available to brain cells. Controlled studies of these medications indicate their use is associated with general improvements in behavior but not with intellectual improvement (Eisdorfer and Stotsky 1977). It should be noted that at one time all cases of senile dementia were thought to involve reduced oxygen flow to the brain. Research has indicated, however, that the availability of oxygen is only a problem in persons with vascular diseases. While there is some reduced cerebral blood flow in cases of Alzheimer's-type dementia, this appears secondary to the brain atrophy that takes place, rather than a cause of it (Meier-Ruge et al. 1975). Increased oxygen would not, in theory, be related to improved functioning, because an oxygen deficiency is not a problem in the first place. Thus the potential value of vasodilators in cases of degenerative illness is limited. Another medication, Hydergine (a dehydrogenated ergot alkaloid), which may act directly on cerebral metabolism, has also not been shown to have any long-term benefits for intellectual functioning (Eisdorfer and Stotsky 1977). Though some studies report positive changes, their measures have been based on global clinical impressions, not objective testing of cognitive performance.

One medication that has been reported to have positive effects on intellectual functioning is bishydroxycoumarin, an anticoagulant (Walsh 1969; Walsh and Walsh 1974). The practical use of this drug may be limited, however, because of the high risk of adverse reactions (Eisdorfer and Stotsky 1977). Other medications that have been used in attempts to reverse the intellectual impairments associated with chronic organic brain syndrome include antidepressants, vitamins, antioxidants, hormones, and antipsychotic drugs. These have also been found not to have any significant effect (Eisdorfer and Stotsky 1977). It should be noted that a person with specific deficits in important substances like vitamins or hormones can manifest severe behavioral disturbances. Nutritional deficiencies are a cause of delirium. When there are such deficiencies, treatment does result in improved behavior and intellectual performance. If there are no deficiencies, however, additional amounts of substances such as vitamins have not been found to be related to intellectual improvements.

Hyperbaric Oxygenation. Reports have been made of improved intellectual functioning in persons with senile dementia through the breathing of pure oxygen that is delivered under high pressure (Jacobs et al. 1969) Attempts to replicate these findings under controlled conditions have been unsuccessful (Goldfarb et al. 1972; Thompson et al. 1976). In a carefully controlled study, Thompson and his associates administered hyperbaric oxygen to 2 patient groups, one with cerebrovascular disorders and the other with an Alzheimer's-type brain disease. Neither group improved on a battery of cognitive tests, compared to each other or to a control group. There were also no changes in electrical activity in the brain as measured by EEGs. As in the case of the vasodilators, the principal effect of hyperbaric oxygenation would be to increase the amount of oxygen available to brain cells. This would appear to be most critical where the intellectual deficits are due to vascular problems that restrict oxygen flow. But as Thompson and his associates failed to find improvement in either group of patients through the use of hyperbaric oxygen, this treatment would appear to have limited value.

Reality Orientation. A nonmedical technique that has come into extensive use in the treatment of persons with senile dementia is reality orientation (Folsom 1968). While this procedure has many variations, the core idea is that there will be gains if persons with intellectual impairments are provided reminders of such orienting information as date and place. This information is often given in 2 ways: through the prominent placing of calendars in wards or floors of long-term care facilities, and through conducting orienting classes in which persons with dementia are instructed in orientation information.

Claims of improvements in intellectual and other behavioral areas have been made for reality orientation, but unequivocal evidence is lacking. In particular, there are 2 critical factors that prior reports have not taken into account. First, all studies of reality orientation have been made in chronic care facilities. As noted in Chapter 10, these are usually boring and unstimulating environments. Thus it cannot be determined if gains associated with a reality orientation program are due to the program itself or would have occurred with any change in the environment. Second, the theoretical underpinnings of reality orientation are unclear. Not knowing where one is, or the date, is a symptom of significant degrees of brain dysfunction. Helping someone to learn the date does not seem likely to signify any corresponding improvement in the brain pathology that led to the orientation problem in the first place. In the same way, it is not apparent why learning what the date is would be related to behavioral improvement in other areas. Finally, as in the case of vasodilators and hyperbaric oxygenation, long-term improvements in intellectual functioning have not been demonstrated.

One defense of reality orientation is that it gives staff a way of interacting with severely disturbed and disoriented patients. But even if presented as a way of upgrading staff, reality orientation is a limited strategy. First, when it comes to truly disoriented patients who symbolically place themselves in different settings and times, there is usually not sufficient medical screening in long-term care facilities for potentially reversible acute brain conditions that are associated in many instances with these types of symptom. Rather than treating the disoriented patient by telling him where he is, there should be training to recognize signs of possible acute problems, and more vigorous treatment of them. Second, patients who are concerned about not knowing the date or where they are should be given explanations and reassurances. This problem often arises in persons with delirium, especially as they begin to improve, and in these instances some amount of reality orientation can have a calming effect. Most persons with senile dementia, however, are neither concerned about nor aware of their lack of orientation. Thus the number of persons in long-term care who view orientation as a problem or concern is small. Rather than training a staff to interact with them around orientation issues, it should be possible to instill a broader, structured approach to care. All too often, however, staff training is inadequate, or the staff is constantly changing because of the low pay and lack of other incentives. Reality orientation can only be viewed as an inadequate panacea for these more basic problems of long-term care facilities.

Summary

Approaches to the treatment of the brain disorders delirium and senile dementia have been reviewed. In cases of delirium, the importance of effective medical diagnosis has been stressed. With proper identification and treatment of the factors that have led to the acute disturbance, there is often dramatic improvement. In many cases of delirium, persons' functioning will return to levels found before the onset of the brain disorder. In senile dementia, no medical approaches have been found that effectively reverse or slow the deterioration. Neither medications that are currently available nor hyperbaric oxygenation have been found to result in long-term improvements in intellectual functioning. Treatment of persons with senile dementia can be successful, however, if it is focused on minimizing the behavioral disturbances associated with brain dysfunction. This can be done through a program of educating and supporting family members or others who are providing care for the impaired person, through the development of a therapeutic relationship with the impaired person when that is possible, and by helping family members to become aware of and to find community services that relieve them of some of the burden of care. This approach is often helpful in allowing the impaired person to remain in a familiar setting and in providing support to family members.

CHAPTER 14

Sexuality and Aging

THE SEXUAL FUNCTIONING of aging persons has been shrouded with fears, myths, and misunderstandings. From the studies that have been conducted on sexuality and aging, however, one fact has clearly emerged—healthy older persons who want to maintain their sexual activity into their 80s and possibly beyond are able to do so. Persons cease engaging in sex not because of age, although old age may be an excuse to do so. The major reasons are negative attitudes and expectations about sexuality in old age, low personal concern about sexual activity, illness, misunderstanding of age changes in sexual functioning, the illness or loss of one's sexual partner, and specific dysfunctions that inhibit sexual expression but that potentially respond to treatment. When sexual problems develop in old age, interventions are often successful in restoring the person to good functioning.

In his review of changes in sexual activities with age, Botwinick (1978) points out that declines in other abilities such as the senses or psychomotor skills are more important for day-to-day functioning, but because they are stressed highly by society and are taken as a sign of one's self-worth, sexual changes arouse considerable anxiety. In our sexually oriented society, persons with no or low sexual interest are often made fun of. Despite some speculations to the contrary, however, persons with little interest in sex or with a low level of sexual activity are not necessarily more neurotic, frustrated, or restricted in other areas of life than are other individuals. Sexual abstinence at any age is a matter of life style and personal values. Certainly in old age, when there are no longer pressures for individuals to pair off and to maintain sexual relationships, refraining from sex is not likely to be associated with either better or worse adaptation in other areas of one's life. On the other hand, for individuals who desire to remain active, the contribution of continued sexual relations to their vigor and sense of well-being is considerable. As one 74-year-old woman reports: "Sex isn't as powerful a need as when you're young, but the whole feeling is there; it's as nice as it ever was. He puts his arms around you, kisses you and it comes to you—satisfaction and orgasm—just like it always did . . . don't let anybody tell you different" (Wax 1977, p. 150).

Sexual functioning in older persons will be reviewed from 3 perspectives. First, differences in frequency of sexual activities and some determinants of continued sexual functioning in old age will be considered. Second, there will be a review of changes in the physical aspects of sexual arousal in later life and their implications for understanding sexual behavior in older persons. Third, attitudes about sexuality and aging and their impact on sexual functioning will be evaluated. The final sections of this chapter will present a program of sex therapy for specific sexual dysfunctions of older persons.

Frequency of Sexual Activities

Information on the frequency of sexual activity among older persons and on changes in frequency with aging is drawn principally from 2 community surveys. The first is the famous Kinsey study of the 1940s and 1950s, which examined sexual attitudes and behaviors in a national survey (Kinsey, Pomeroy, and Martin 1948; Kinsey et al. 1953). While sexual behaviors are presumed to have changed rapidly since the publication of these studies, they remain the most comprehensive data available on sexuality. The second survey is the Duke Longitudinal Study, which, beginning in 1954, followed a community sample of older persons in the Durham, North Carolina, area for a period of approximately 10 years (Pfeiffer, Verwoerdt, and Wang 1968; 1969; Pfeiffer and Davis 1972). Although the dropout rate was high for various reasons, including the deaths of subjects and refusals to be reinterviewed, this survey provides the best source of longitudinal data on sexual functioning.

In their reports on human sexuality, Kinsey and his associates (Kinsey, Pomeroy, and Martin 1948; Kinsey et al. 1953) focused principally on the number and sources of orgasms in men and women. For men, 6 possible sources of orgasm were considered: masturbation, nocturnal emission, orgasm during heterosexual petting, heterosexual intercourse, homosexual relationships, and intercourse with animals. Based on their findings on the frequency of orgasm over the life span, Kinsey, Pomeroy, and Martin report more variation in behavior than for any other known characteristic in human or animal biology. Men ranged from negligible numbers of orgasms over a period of several years to as many as 30 or more per week. Three-quarters of their subjects reported between 1 and 6.5 orgasms per week, but they also point out that 22.3 percent of the sample fell in the more extreme ranges, either higher or lower than those typical amounts. These variations, however, did not correlate with other observations. In contrast to cases in the clinical literature, they reported that persons in their community samples with either high or low sexual activity were functioning adequately in other aspects of their lives. Thus, extremes of sexual activity generally represent normal variations of a behavior that is highly variable from one person to another.

Despite this variability, Kinsey, Pomeroy, and Martin report that older male subjects had less frequent sexual activity. As shown in Figure 14.1, there was a general decrease in the average number of orgasms per week for all sources, from a high of 2.87 in late adolescence to 0.84 among men 60 to 65. While the number of subjects past 65 who were surveyed was quite small, a continued diminishing of sexual output could be seen. The frequency of sexual inactivity also rose dramatically with age. Among 60 year olds, 5 percent of the men surveyed were completely inactive; at age 70, 30 percent were inactive. Even among the oldest persons, however,

FIGURE 14.1. Frequency of total outlet in relation to age. Based on total population, including single, married, and previously married groups. Broken lines represent raw data; the solid black line represents the mean corrected for the U.S. Census distribution.

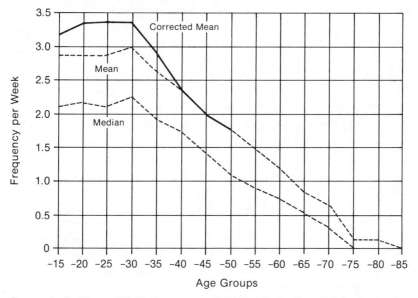

Source: A. C. Kinsey, W. B. Pomeroy, and C. E. Martin, *Sexual Behavior in the Human Male* (Philadelphia: W. B. Saunders, 1948). Copyright © 1948 by the Institute for Sex Research, Inc. Reproduced by permission.

there was some variation in the total amount of sexual activity, including evidence of men in their late 80s who still had regular intercourse. The figures on inability to obtain an erection parallel these on the total number of orgasms (although it should be noted that it is possible to have an orgasm without an erection). The prevalence of erectile incapacity begins to rise between ages 45 and 50 to a rate of 27 percent among men who are 70 years of age, and 55 percent at age 75. Thus, these cross-sectional findings suggest a gradual diminishing of sexual activity in men over the life cycle and increasing numbers of sexually inactive men in the later years past 60.

Estimates on women's sexual activity in the Kinsey studies were more problematic. While the frequency of orgasm was used as an index for men, men almost always reach orgasm during intercourse and other sexual activities. For women, however, orgasm does not necessarily occur during intercourse.

Focusing instead on the frequency of masturbation, Kinsey et al. (1953) reported little change over the life span. Two subsequent re-analyses of these data, however, suggested some decline in sexual activity past age 60. In the first study (Christenson and Gagnon 1965) the sexual activities of married and postmarried (divorced or widowed) women were contrasted. For married women, the frequency of intercourse dropped be-tween ages 50 and 79, while the rate of masturbation stayed about the same. Among postmarried women, the amount of sexual activity from all sources was typically lower than for married women. Focusing only on masturbation, a much lower rate was found among the oldest (age 70) group than among the 50 year olds. Thus, in both married and postmarried women, sexual activity was lower in the 70 year olds, suggesting that the drop is independent of a husband's ability to sustain regular intercourse. In a second study of respondents to the earlier projects, Christenson and Johnson (1973) found a consistent drop between the ages of 45 and 60 in sexual activity of women who never married, including masturbation and dreams that led to orgasm. Among both women and men, then, there is a lower frequency of sexual activity at later ages, with a more marked de-crease in men.

Reports from the Duke Longitudinal Study present a somewhat different and more distinct view of sexual behavior and interests in old age (Pfeiffer, Verwoerdt, and Wang, 1968; 1969). Looking first at sexual behavior in men, they found that two-thirds of men in their 60s were sexually active, but only 1 in 5 in their 80s indicated continuing activity. A longitudinal analysis of 39 persons on whom data on sexual behavior and attitudes were available for the whole 10-year period confirms the general finding that more men become sexually inactive with advancing age. Persons in this small sample had an average age of 67 years at the start of the study and 76 at completion. As shown in Figure 14.2, the men in this sample showed a decline over the 10-year period in the num-

FIGURE 14.2.   Raw score totals of male Ss on interest and activity levels.

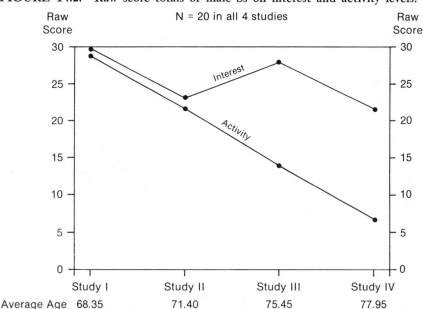

Source: E. Pfeiffer, A. Verwoerdt, and H. S. Wang, "The Natural History of Sexual Behavior in a Biologically Advantaged Group of Aged Individuals," *Journal of Gerontology* 24 (1969): 193–198. Copyright © 1969 by the Gerontological Society. Reprinted by permission.

bers reporting continuing sexual activity. While at the start of the study 44 percent were active, only 20 percent indicated continued activity at its completion. Interest in sexual activity, however, showed little change over the 10-year period. In fact, sexual interest among men in the whole sample was high. Based on these findings, the authors suggest there is an interest-activity gap among older men that increases with age (Pfeiffer, Verwoerdt, and Wang, 1969). It should also be noted that some men reported increased sexual activity over time, despite the average decline.

Among women in this study, the levels of sexual activity and interest were lower than in men at all ages. Overall, approximately one-third of women in the total community sample reported interest in sex, and one-fifth were sexually active. Among the smaller group of 39 who were followed for a 10-year period, there was little change in either sexual interest or activity, as shown in Figure 14.3. At the start of the study, 16 percent were sexually active, and a similar proportion reported activity after 10 years (Pfeiffer, Verwoerdt, and Wang, 1969). As with the men, some women in the larger sample also reported increased sexual activity at repeated testings.

The lower interest and sexual activity reported by women can be accounted for by 2 factors. First, their lower level of activity may be

FIGURE 14.3.   Raw score totals of female Ss on interest and activity levels.

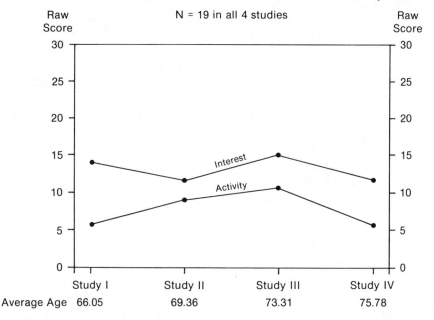

Source: E. Pfeiffer, A. Verwoerdt, and H. S. Wang, "The Natural History of Sexual Behavior in a Biologically Advantaged Group of Aged Individuals," *Journal of Gerontology* 24 (1969): 193–198. Copyright © 1969 by the Gerontological Society. Reprinted by permission.

related to changes in their husbands. The major reason women gave for ceasing sexual activity was the death or illness of their husband, or because he lost either interest or potency (Pfeiffer, Verwoerdt, and Wang, 1968). When men who died were excluded from the analysis, there was a general agreement among husbands and wives that husbands were responsible for ceasing sexual activity. Husbands were on the average 4 years older than their wives in this sample, and their greater age may have made them more likely to develop illnesses or experience other changes that led to decreased sexual activity. Second, based on retrospective reports, women stated they had lower sexual interest when they were younger than did men. Only 32 percent of women reported high sexual interest when young, as opposed to 80 percent of men (Pfeiffer, Verwoerdt, and Wang 1969).

Another study of men and women between the ages of 46 and 71 confirmed these findings on the importance of marital status for the continued sexual functioning of older women. Using a regression analysis, Pfeiffer and Davis (1972) looked at factors related to continued sexual activity, interest, and enjoyment. Among women, the presence of a husband and the past enjoyment of sexual relations were the principal factors related to continued sexual activity. Among men, in contrast, age, the past frequency of sexual activity, current health, and predicted future life satisfaction were related to sexual activity.

While the Kinsey and Duke studies constitute a beginning in understanding how sexual activity changes over the life span, some consistent patterns emerge from these findings. First, at all ages men report more interest and higher activity, especially when young, than do women. Second, the change in sexual activity is somewhat greater in men, although their interest in sex remains higher than women's throughout the life span. Third, the major reasons for a married woman's ceasing sexual activity in old age involve her husband's status: if he dies, becomes ill, or loses interest in sex. These differences in sexual activity and interest between men and women are, of course, affected by cultural factors that limit the number of socially sanctioned sexual partners for older women, and caused different socialization of sexual attitudes and feelings in the first place. Finally, these findings suggest the potential for continued sexual activity to advanced ages for at least some persons.

Changes in Sexual Response

Differences in the sexual responses of older men and women have been studied by Masters and Johnson (1966; 1970). Although based on small and select samples, these findings provide some preliminary evidence on sexual functioning of the aged. As with the survey findings above, these data also suggest the capacity for continued sexual activity into the later years.

In studying the sexual behavior of men and women, Masters and Johnson (1966) have described a sexual response cycle consisting of 4 phases: excitement, plateau, orgasm, and refractory period. The purpose of this division into phases is for observation and description. In actual observations, of course, sexual activity proceeds continuously and not by stages, and the 4 phases overlap with one another (Katchadourian and Lunde 1972). For studying age changes, the division of sexual response into 4 phases helps clarify differences between young and old.

Age Differences in Men

For older men and women there is generally a slowing of all phases of the sexual response cycle. Among men the excitement phase, or the time needed to attain an erection, takes longer. While a young man might have an erection in a few seconds, it may require several minutes for older men. Direct manual stimulation is often required to produce an erection, in contrast to the young, who often respond to visual stimulation. These changes can cause considerable anxiety in men who interpret them as early signs of impotency. If they respond by trying to force an erection, they may find they are unable to do so and their panic increases. This slowing is, however, a normal change and does not foretell an end to one's sexual life.

The next phase of the sexual response cycle, plateau, also has a longer duration in older men. There is less drive for immediate ejaculatory release than in younger men and, as a result, older men can maintain this plateau phase longer for their own pleasure or that of their partners.

Somewhat greater changes are found in the orgasmic phases. In the young the orgasmic phase has 2 distinct stages: ejaculatory inevitability, a brief period during which there is pressure to ejaculate, and then the actual ejaculation. Older men have been observed to display several variations of this process. There may either be no first stage or a somewhat prolonged first stage (5 to 7 seconds, as opposed to 2 to 4). In the second stage there is less expulsive force delivering the seminal fluid, and the volume of fluid is less. These changes, however, do not appear to be related to decreased sensual pleasure, except when men misinterpret them as signs of dysfunction (Masters and Johnson 1970). There is also less pressure to ejaculate during every sexual encounter. If the older man does not ejaculate, he can more rapidly achieve another erection.

The refractory period following ejaculation is also longer in older men. While a young man can achieve an erection in sometimes as little as a few minutes following ejaculation, older men require several hours. In addition, the loss of the erection following ejaculation may be more sudden.

In reviewing these changes in the sexual responses of men, Comfort (1980) suggests that age alone never brings about erectile failure (impotency). He identifies several distinct causes of erectile dysfunction. First, as noted above, older men who misidentify the signs of aging as symptoms of oncoming impotency can become overly anxious about their sexual performance, thereby inhibiting their functioning. Performance anxiety at all ages is a major cause of impotency. Second, Comfort suggests that some men have always had a low interest in sexual activity, perhaps because of feelings of guilt or other psychological conflicts, and they use old age as an excuse to stop functioning. In the findings of Kinsey, Pomeroy, and Martin (1948), men with an earlier onset of sexual activity reported higher levels of activity at all ages. Their data suggested that highly active men continued to function at higher levels past age 50, while less active men were more likely in later life to report no current sexual activity. Similar findings are reported by Pfeiffer and Davis (1972).

Another major cause of erectile dysfunction in older men are illnesses and the medications used to treat them. In particular, diabetes and vascular insufficiencies are associated with higher rates of impotency. Estimates of erectile dysfunction in diabetic men range from 7 to 50 percent (Shearer and Shearer 1977; Ellenberg 1978). When caused by poorly controlled diet, the problem can often be treated by restoring proper nutrition. Ellenberg, however, reports that the majority of cases of impotency in diabetic men are caused by peripheral diabetic neuropathy, for which no treatment is effective. Among medications that affect potency are those used for hypertension, particularly reserpine, antidepressants, some ganglion-blocking agents, alcohol, and other tranquilizing medications.

Illnesses that are commonly thought to affect sexual performance are heart disease and prostate disease, but neither necessarily has adverse effects on sexual functioning. Reviewing studies of sexual activities of men having suffered a coronary episode, Friedman (1978) concludes that there is a major drop in sexual activity and interest in the year following a heart attack, ranging from decreased activity to total inactivity. This decline can be observed even when other life activities, including work, have been resumed. Major causes of this decline appear to be 2 related factors: lack of information provided by physicians about sexual activity following a coronary, and fears that sexual activity will provoke another episode or cause death. Physicians typically provide little or no information to the heart attack patient, with two-thirds of patients reporting they received no advice from their doctor about sex. Recent evidence, however, suggests that fears of provoking further heart problems during sex appear unjustified. In a study of postmyocardial patients, Hellerstein and Friedman (1970) found that heart rate was slightly lower during orgasm than when the person engaged in everyday activities, such as walking, climbing stairs, or doing sedentary work (117.4 beats per minute, compared to 120.1). Glover (1975) also notes that the rate of heart attacks during the treadmill test, which involves more stress than sexual intercourse, is only 1 in 10,000. There are reports in the medical literature of sudden deaths following intercourse, but these typically have involved situations in which men had sex with a new sexual partner and in an unfamiliar setting (Friedman 1978), frequently following food and alcohol ingestion. Pain caused by angina can inhibit sexual functioning in the myocardial patient, but the use of nitroglycerin and physical conditioning is often effective in reducing this distress (Friedman 1978). Friedman reports other causes of sexual problems in the postcoronary patient, including depression, incorrect interpretations of age changes in sexual response, the use of inhibiting medications, especially antihypertensive drugs, and the fears of the person's sexual partner.

It can be concluded from these findings that myocardial patients can resume sexual activities as soon as their physical condition permits engaging in other life activities. The occurrence of symptoms during or following sexual intercourse, however, such as angina, palpitations lasting

for more than 15 minutes after intercourse, sleeplessness following intercourse, or unusual fatigue, require medical attention (Friedman 1978).

In contrast to the coronary patients, persons suffering from congestive
heart failure are generally limited in all activities and should not resume
sexual intercourse until their functioning is controlled (Glover 1975;
Friedman 1978). These persons can, however, engage in other sexual
activities, such as stroking, touching, or embracing.

Following prostate surgery there will be some altered sensation during
orgasm and ejaculation. Unless a radical prostatectomy is necessary, however, competently performed prostate surgery does not affect potency
(Comfort 1980).

Two psychological problems are often related to erectile failure. The
first is depression, where complaints of sexual dysfunction can be both
a presenting sign and one consequence of antidepressive medications.
Second, older men who have not engaged in sexual activity for a period
of time may find they are impotent when they try to resume sexual
relations. Comfort (1980) calls this phenomenon "widower's syndrome"
and states that it occurs frequently in men whose wives have had incapacitating and terminal diseases. These men are likely to have abstained
from sexual activity during their wife's illness. Because of anxiety about
their performance and atrophy brought about by disease, they have difficulty starting a new sexual relationship. In general, any long period of
disease may be followed by erectile failure, although sexual functioning
can usually gradually be restored. Thus, following an illness, it is important
to resume sexual activity as soon as possible (Comfort 1980).

Although the male sex-steroid, testosterone, declines with age, its
relation to sexual interest and potency is not a straightforward one.
Masters and Johnson (1970) suggest sex-steroid replacement only for
specific problems, such as prostatic pain during and following ejaculation.
Androgen deficits and supplements, however, have not typically been
found to be related to potency, except where the adminstration of
hormones has a placebo effect (Comfort 1980). Comfort, in fact, suggests
that high levels of testosterone may be the result, rather than the cause, of
high levels of sexual activity. Although many writers have speculated on
the existence of a male climacteric in late middle age, with shifts in
hormone levels leading to altered behavior and sexual functioning, there
is little evidence at this time of direct relations between hormone levels
and behaviors in men.

Age Differences in Women

Among women the findings on changes in sexual response are even
more strongly suggestive of the potential for continued sexual functioning
to advanced ages. Comfort (1980) states there is no evidence that the

capacity for orgasm in women declines at any age. In their review of physiological changes in women in the later years, Masters and Johnson (1966) conclude: "In short, there is no time limit drawn by the advancing years to female sexuality" (p. 247).

As with men, there are some differences in the sexual response cycle of older women. Parallel to the changes in men, the excitement phase, particularly the time for lubrication to develop, takes longer in post-menopausal women. While in a younger woman lubrication often appears in 15 to 30 seconds following sexual stimulation, an older women may need 1 to 5 minutes of sexual play for a similar effect. During the excitement and plateau phases there is often a delay in expansion of the length and depth of the vagina. While the elasticity of the vaginal barrel in younger women is lost, sexual stimulation usually produces some expansion (Masters and Johnson 1970). The orgasmic phase of the sexual response cycle may be briefer in older women, with 4 or 5 contractions, in contrast to 8 to 12 in younger women. The resolution or refractory stage during which the woman returns to an unstimulated condition is also briefer in older women. During this period, spastic rather than rhythmic contraction of the uterus can occur. These contractions are usually experienced as pain in the lower abdomen, in the vaginal barrel, or in the legs.

Intercourse and other sexual activities may become uncomfortable due to several factors, including diminished lubrication, atrophy of vaginal walls, and the spastic uterine contractions described above. Many women experience pain during and following intercourse because of thinning of the vaginal walls. Irritation to the bladder and urethra in postmenopausal women can also occur during intercourse, and there is often an urge to urinate following coitus. In addition, the clitoris is more easily irritated, and direct stimulation that would be pleasurable to a younger women can be painful for someone older (Masters and Johnson 1970).

In their discussion of these problems, Masters and Johnson (1970) suggest that they arise as the consequence of hormone changes in menopause, and recommend sex-steroid replacement as an effective treatment. More recently, however, the use of estrogen in postmenopausal women has been linked to a higher risk of endometrial cancer. For problems such as vaginal atrophy, topical applications of estrogen creams may be a safer procedure (Estrogen Therapy 1976). Estrogen therapy has generally been promoted for a variety of purposes, including as a general retardant of aging in women. Its effects, however, are limited to treating vaginal atrophy and vasomotor symptoms, such as hot flashes and sweats that are experienced by about 50 percent of menopausal women. Its use as a general cure-all for the effects of aging does not seem warranted (Estrogen Therapy 1976).

Despite the commonly held assumptions about hormones and sexuality, the impact of menopause and hormone levels on sexual interest and sexual functioning is limited. While on rare occasions menopause is experienced psychologically by a woman as the end of her femininity, many women report increased sexual interest after menopause, usually because they no longer fear pregnancy (Masters and Johnson 1966; Neugarten et al. 1968). Furthemore, problems such as vaginal atrophy and diminished lubrication are not experienced by all postmenopausal women. Based on clinical experience, there is some indication that women who have regular intercourse once or twice a week have fewer physical changes following menopause (Masters and Johnson 1970; Comfort 1980). There is less contraction of the vaginal barrel and less decrease of lubrication. Spastic contractions of the uterus have not been found in older women having regular intercourse. As the survey results discussed earlier indicate, however, few older women have regular and frequent sexual intercourse.

According to Comfort (1980), the major reasons for sexual inactivity among older women are social conventions and the lack of a partner. Because of the greater longevity of women and the tendency for men to seek out sexual partners younger than themselves, few men are available for sexual relationships with older women. Moreover, there are strong cultural proscriptions against sexual activity in older women. As has been noted previously, women over the life cycle have less interest and less sexual activity than men. For women who experienced conflict over sexual activity or who never had satisfying sexual relationships, age stereotypes provide a reason to give up sexuality altogether. Masters and Johnson (1970) report that of the older couples they have treated, the husband almost always initiates the referral, even when the problem in functioning is his.

There are several reasons why sexual relations may not be satisfying to an older woman. In many marriages, the focus in sexual encounters has been on the husband's pleasure, with little attention to women's sexual satisfaction. Some women, especially among the older population, hold the Victorian attitude that sexual pleasure is base and only appropriate for men. They submitted to their husbands, but derived little pleasure from sexual activity. Another problem is a couple's understanding of women's sexual responses. Many people assume that women's orgasms occur naturally with intercourse. Women are often reluctant to admit when they did not have an orgasm for fear of hurting their husband's pride, or because of prior training that says that direct stimulation other than through intercourse is improper or damaging to a healthy sexual response. For a long time sex therapists and psychotherapists stressed that there were 2 kinds of orgasm: vaginal and clitoral. It was wrongly asserted that vaginal orgasms (which supposedly occurred only during intercourse) represented the true form of adult female sexuality. There is, however, only one type of female orgasm, focused in the clitoral area, and similar physiologically whatever the source of sexual stimulation (Masters and Johnson 1966). Furthermore, there are some women who require a high level of stimulation to reach orgasm and probably never can have regular orgasms during intercourse (Kaplan 1974). Because of beliefs that it is not proper for women to seek direct stimulation from their sexual partners, many older women have had less than satisfying sexual relationships over their lives, and have not experienced sex activity that is focused on their pleasure.

Implications of Changes in Sexual Responses

The effects of these changes in sexual response can have a positive or negative impact on one's subjective pleasure in lovemaking, depending on how they are perceived. If persons view these differences only as signs of a decline, then their subjective enjoyment of sex will be impaired by constant comparison with how it was when they were younger. On the other hand, these changes can actually have a beneficial effect on lovemaking and can help persons achieve a more tender and sensual relationship. Among older men, the need for more stimulation to reach an erection can lead to greater attention to touch and to other sensual activities. Women sometimes complain that men hurry their lovemaking and do not allow women sufficient time to become aroused or to enjoy the pleasurable feelings associated with sexual excitement. The older man who perceives the positive side of his slowed sexual response can approach lovemaking in a more relaxed and leisurely way than he did when younger. He may, therefore, become a better sexual partner. Similarly, since the plateau phase is longer, the older man will have more ejaculatory control, and is less likely to reach orgasm before his partner is satisfied. The misunderstandings and hurt feelings in younger couples where the man has little ejaculatory control need not exist among older persons.

For women, too, the longer time required to become sexually aroused creates the opportunity to explore more fully various forms of sensual stimulation and to take a leisurely and unhurried approach to lovemaking. In addition, the need of both men and women for greater-stimulation opens the possibility that each will play somewhat different roles and have new experiences sexually. Men have typically been active in a sexual relationship, both in initiating contact and setting the pace. To offset the somewhat greater rate of change that occurs in men, women could assume a more active role, both in starting sexual activity and in directly stimulating the man. Similarly, because older women also need somewhat more stimulation, they could take a more active role in guiding their partner in actions that they find pleasurable. Thus, unlike sexual relationships that function in a stereotyped way, an older man and woman could have the experience of both giving and receiving. The importance for sexual satisfaction of each person's assuming both active and passive roles is discussed more fully in the subsequent sections on sexual therapy.

Social Attitudes and Sex in the Aged

It has been alluded to at several points in the preceding discussion that sexual activity in the aged is generally discouraged. Sexual activity that is considered appropriate or at least tolerated in a young man or woman is often ridiculed in an old one. A man who has liaisons with young women may be called an old goat or a dirty old man. Aging homosexuals are said to prey upon young boys, although limited studies suggest they actually form relationships with men their own age (Kelly 1977). Older women are typically not perceived by others as sexually attractive, and have few socially approved outlets for sexual activity if they do not have a husband.

In institutions for the aged, prohibitions against sexual activity are strong. Husbands and wives who enter the same facility are sometimes made to reside in separate rooms. Often patients are not allowed to close their doors or to have any privacy for intimate and sexual relationships. Any heterosexual and homosexual liaisons that develop are ridiculed by staff members and residents.

The low tolerance of sexual activity by staffs in nursing homes is often taken as a sign of an age bias, but it may have more to do with a generally negative view of sexual behavior, irrespective of age. In a study that compared responses by nursing home staffs and a student sample to stories involving sexual activities of older and younger persons, LaTorre and Kear (1977) report that there were few differences in ratings of the stories when the characters involved were young or old, but that staffs of nursing homes consistently made more negative statements about sex than did students. Since sexual activities are typically punished by staffs of institutions, whatever the age of the inmates, the reactions of nursing home personnel may reflect this general tendency to control and repress the actions of inmates. Gerontologists have frequently stressed the need to educate staffs about sexuality and aging, but the implication of this study is that changing their attitudes about old age may not be sufficient, because of their negative beliefs about sexuality in general.

Among noninstitutional aged, many undoubtedly experience disapproval from others for sexual activity. Masters and Johnson (1970) cite cases in which older persons were told by physicians or clergymen that one's sex life should be over in later life, or that it was improper to continue sex past childbearing years. They also report that some of these patients had previously been told by physicians that their sexual problems were due to aging. The ages of patients receiving this information ranged from 42 to 68. In this author's experience, clients who want help with sexual problems have all previously been told by physicians that they are too old to worry about that. Berezin (1976) cites one survey of physicians that indicates about one-third exhibited serious discomfort when discussing sexual issues with interviewers, including blushing, fidgeting, and looking away. Almost all the physicians surveyed stated they had no training in human sexuality either in medical school or in postgraduate education, but almost all dealt at times with the sexual problems of their patients. This discomfort and lack of information about sexuality certainly is magnified when dealing with an area in which even less is known—sex in old age.

When an older person is sexually active, other family members, particularly adult children, may disapprove. Older couples who decide to live together rather than marry are often chastised by middle-aged children (Wax 1977). Even older persons who remarry may face the disapproval of their children (McKain 1972).

The attitudes of older persons themselves about sexual activities are somewhat more conservative than are the attitudes of the young. In one survey, older persons were generally more disapproving of premarital, extramarital, and homosexual relationships than were young persons (Snyder and Spreitzer 1976). Other factors that were related to more negative attitudes were less education, higher church attendance, being married, and having children. Attitudes of older persons toward pornography and erotic material are also more negative than those seen in the young (Merritt, Gerstl, and LoSciuto 1975).

The sex education that many older persons received was often limited or contained many misconceptions. Among the more common myths are that masturbation is harmful, that too much sex when one is young will lead to a burning out and to impotency, and that oral sex is dangerous, unhealthful, or unnatural. There has also been, as discussed above, considerable misunderstanding of female sexuality both by men and women. Being aware of an older person's assumptions about sexuality is an important prerequisite to developing the trust necessary for therapy of sexual problems.

Treatment of Sexual Dysfunction

BASIC CONCEPTS

While the sexual disorders of the aging often have their roots in misunderstandings of age changes and in negative expectations and sanctions for continued sexuality, direct treatment approaches for these problems offer a way of restoring sexual functioning in many affected persons.

Before the 1970s the dominant theme in psychotherapy was that sexual problems were the manifestation of deep-seated personality disorders that went back to childhood traumas or conflicts. The sexual problems of the aging were largely unmentioned, and one can assume that older persons were regarded as having lost their sexual capacity. Early direct approaches to treatment were developed by Semans (1956), for the control of premature ejaculation, and by Wolpe (1958), who used relaxation and desensitization for a variety of sexual disorders (see LoPiccolo 1978 for a review). Publication of the Masters and Johnson book, *Human Sexual Inadequacy* (1970), which presented a comprehensive treatment plan, thorough case histories, and impressive outcome data, led to the widespread acceptance of direct approaches. As in their earlier work, *Human Sexual Response* (1966), they devote attention to the problems of older persons, and report using similar therapeutic procedures with the old as the young, with little or no difference in outcome. Since the publication of *Human Sexual Inadequacy*, a number of researchers and clinicians have elaborated on methods of direct treatment of sexual disorders. Among the most noted are works by Hartman and Fithian (1972), Kaplan (1974), Annon (1976), Caird and Wincze (1977), and a recent collection of writings edited by LoPiccolo and LoPiccolo (1978). These works have provided further information on treatment approaches for and on the positive response of older persons.

In a review of several approaches to sex therapy, LoPiccolo (1978) identifies several features common to most approaches. Included among these are: (1) the mutual responsibility of both sexual partners for the sexual problem; (2) providing information and education about human sexuality; (3) changing negative attitudes about sex; (4) eliminating performance anxiety; (5) increasing communication; (6) improving sexual techniques; (7) changing other problem interactions of the couple that affect sexual feelings and expression; and (8) the use of a series of behavioral steps for inducing changes in performance. Annon (1976; Annon and Robinson 1978) proposes a hierarchical model of sex therapy that incorporates many of these features. Called the P-LI-SS-IT model, it has 4 steps: (1) giving people permission to engage in sexual behaviors; (2) providing limited information about sexual functioning; (3) giving specific suggestions for improving sexual behavior; and (4) intensive therapy. Annon indicates that most clients do not require all aspects of this program, but can be provided those features that are suited to their situations. Sometimes giving permission to persons to continue doing whatever they are already doing, and reassuring them that their behaviors are normal and not perverted or pathological, is sufficient to resolve a sexual problem. Presenting limited information about the client's problem can also be beneficial. In the aged in particular, knowledge about the slowing of the sexual response cycle and other age changes can alleviate concerns over the adequacy of one's functioning. According to Annon, specific directions for sexual behaviors and intensive therapy need be given only when it is assessed that the less intensive procedures are not adequate to deal with the problem.

The treatment plan of Masters and Johnson (1970) includes both specific procedures for inducing cognitive and behavioral changes in clients and a structure in which therapy is facilitated. Among the major structural features of their therapy are the isolation of couples at the Reproductive Biology Research Foundation in St. Louis for 2 weeks of treatment; emphasis on treating couples; and use of male and female co-therapists.

Rather than using the usual outpatient treatment model of weekly visits, Masters and Johnson developed a 2-week, 7-days-a-week, intensive training program. They feel the advantages of this approach are to isolate persons from their usual routines and social demands so that there are no distractions from the therapy assignments, and to increase the interaction of the couple. Unlike many institutional programs where behavioral changes within the setting do not generalize to everyday life, their follow-up data indicate that improvements are maintained. A limitation of this model is that many people are not willing to take a 2-week intensive training program. While many aspects of the Masters and Johnson approach have been used in more typical outpatient settings, there is no systematic research on how the setting affects length of treatment. Rates of improvement from various settings, however, appear comparable.

Of major importance to Masters and Johnson is the concept of sex therapy as conjoint treatment. While couples often enter treatment blaming one or the other for the sexual problem, Masters and Johnson (1970) maintain that both partners are involved in the problem and must make changes in order to resolve it. They emphasize that unless both partners are included, the supposedly "well" spouse may undermine or frustrate many of the gains made in treatment, and isolation of the partners from one another will further weaken their communication in sexual matters. As examples, they cite that the wife of a man with erectile failure who is not involved in treatment may wonder what role to play during sexual encounters: active, passive, or some other. Similarly, the husband of a nonorgasmic woman would not know when and in what ways to approach her sexually, unless he is made part of the treatment. Furthermore, based on their case examples, they assert that even in those couples where one person had the sexual dysfunction before entering this relationship, the other contributes in some ways to maintaining the problem behavior out of frustration, ignorance, or because the couple cannot communicate their sexual needs to one another.

This emphasis on conjoint therapy means that persons without a sexual partner typically do not receive treatment. Because many aged persons, especially older women, do not have sexual partners, the applicability of the Masters and Johnson program to them is limited. Masters and Johnson (1970) and other sex therapists have at times used surrogate partners for those individuals who are not currently in a relationship. While proponents of surrogate therapy emphasize that the surrogates are highly trained and are not prostitutes, this form of treatment remains controversial (Wolfe 1978). Alternative treatment approaches for single persons are presented later in this chapter.

A third feature of the Masters and Johnson program is the use of a male and female team of therapists. They suggest a number of reasons for using a team. First, it prevents the development of alliances of the therapist and one client against the other client. Alliances of that nature would undermine a central tenet of their program, that both persons in the couple have a responsibility for the sexual problem. These alliances can also direct energy and sexual interest away from one's partner and toward the therapist. When a client begins directing attention principally to the opposite-sexed member of the team, it is the practice of the teams to redirect this alliance and to involve the person's partner more centrally. Masters and Johnson (1970) further caution: "To create further emotional trauma for either sexually insecure marital partner by encouraging or accepting such alignment, however deliberately or naively proffered, is not only professionally irresponsible, but can also be devastating to therapeutic results" (p. 8). Another reason for the use of a male and female team is that it affords the possibility of each person's sexual experiences being interpreted by a therapist of the same sex. The problems that arose in the past, when female sexuality was largely explained by male psychotherapists, are thereby avoided. It is also easier to overcome inhibitions of clients when obtaining a sexual history if the interviewer is of the same sex.

Other sex therapists have suggested that cotherapists are not an essential part of the treatment program, so long as each therapist is trained to understand the viewpoint of persons of the opposite sex. In a review of the few research studies on this point, Hogan (1978) finds no evidence that male-female teams are more effective than single therapists. It is possible, nonetheless, that particular individuals will react unfavorably to sex therapy unless there is a person of the same sex as therapist or cotherapist. It is also noted by Kaplan (1974) that the team approach is useful for training inexperienced therapists by pairing them with someone having more experience.

Treatment Program: Initial Phase

The initial phases of treatment involve orienting patients to the therapy program and assessing their behaviors. Masters and Johnson

(1970) introduce 2 important features of treatment at this initial point. First, patients are told to refrain from sexual activity until specifically directed by the staff. This instruction brings sexual behavior under the control of therapists so that dysfunctional actions can be retrained, and lowers fears concerning performance, which Masters and Johnson consider central to most sexual dysfunctions. A second feature at this point in treatment is to emphasize to couples that both are involved in the sexual problem and must be committed to the treatment.

In conducting an initial evaluation, it is critical to identify the relevant causal factors for the sexual problems that a couple present. According to Hogan (1978), 6 factors have been linked in varying degrees to the etiology of sexual dysfunction, and therefore should be evaluated during initial sessions: (1) physical illnesses and medications; (2) early life influences on sexual attitudes and early sexual experiences; (3) misinformation and lack of information about sex; (4) a lack of skill in one's partner; (5) psychological factors such as anxiety, depression, and the fear of losing control of one's self; and (6) relationship problems. Other factors to take into account include a description of the current sex problem and its development over time, current and past sex attitudes and behavior, and each person's motivation for treatment (Lobitz and Lobitz 1978). A client's willingness to cooperate with a treatment program can critically affect its outcome.

In a discussion of assessment, Lobitz and Lobitz (1978) suggest focusing on behavioral, cognitive, and affective components of the sexual problem. Behavioral aspects include inappropriate or ineffective sexual behaviors. In the cognitive sphere, some common dysfunctional ideas include ignorance about sexual functioning, destructive attitudes about sexuality, such as the good-girl—bad-girl dichotomy that is still prevalent in concepts of female sexuality, and self-defeating thoughts. Masters and Johnson (1970) emphasize two self-defeating thoughts that are related to sexual problems: concern over one's performance and playing a spectator role during the sexual encounter. They advise constant monitoring during therapy of these thoughts and the corresponding anxiety that concern over performance usually engenders. Affective behaviors include the predominant feelings of the person while engaging in sex. While most persons with sexual problems report feeling anxiety, depression is sometimes present. Lobitz and Lobitz also suggest finding out what is arousing to the person, including sensory stimulations and fantasies.

Certain findings during this initial assessment may indicate that sex therapy should not be started. Illnesses or medications that inhibit sexual responses should be treated before attempting a behavioral approach. The prevalence among the aged of diseases such as hypertension and diabetes, and of medications affecting sexual functioning, means that an initial physical examination is a critical step. Among nonprescription drugs, alcohol inhibits sexual functioning. Lobitz and Lobitz caution against treating alcoholics in sex therapy unless the drinking has been controlled for 6 months or longer.

Depression among persons seeking treatment is sometimes secondary and brought about by the sexual difficulties the person is experiencing. If the sexual difficulties appear to be the consequences of depression, however, treatment for depression is recommended first, because the depressed person will not have much enthusiasm for sexual activity and generally is not a very appealing sex partner (Kaplan 1974). The presence of other types of psychopathology may also be reason for not beginning treatment. Masters and Johnson (1970) emphasize that sexual problems are not necessarily a sign of psychopathology, and are manifested by many persons who otherwise are functioning adequately. Among persons with neurotic personality styles, Kaplan indicates that sex therapy can often be successful in relieving sexual difficulties, but treatment often proceeds more slowly, since the person puts up more roadblocks against it. One criterion is to accept persons for sex therapy if their other problems do not interfere greatly with daily functioning and are not likely to impede the treatment (Lobitz and Lobitz 1978). Kaplan also recommends caution in the treatment of schizophrenics, noting that therapy is not to be undertaken during an acute episode or when the sexual problem has a special significance to the client.

Another factor to be evaluated before initiating treatment is the adequacy of a couple's relationship. Almost all writers in this area suggest that therapy cannot be successful unless there is a commitment to the relationship by both persons, but the degree of marital difficulty that inhibits treatment progress has not been operationally defined. Masters and Johnson (1970) focus their treatment on both sexual and nonsexual aspects of the relationship, and see the good feelings that develop between the couple during sex therapy as radiating out to other aspects of the relationship. They note, however, that in a severely disturbed marriage, sexual acts can be used as a weapon or punishment by one spouse against the other. Both Kaplan (1974) and Annon (1976) recommend marital therapy first if the relationship problems appear severe. Lobitz and Lobitz (1978) suggest evaluating whether the relationship problems are so salient they are likely to interfere with the sex therapy. In particular, the presence of severe discord and hostility indicate that marital therapy should be attempted first. They also recommend that observations of the couple during interviews provides useful information about whether to treat the sexual or marital problems. Excessive blaming of one another, derogatory remarks, and a high level of discord all indicate that marital therapy is more appropriate. Hence, there is agreement that persons experiencing severe marital discord are not good candidates for sex therapy, but since most couples having sexual problems also have other areas of disagreement, it remains to be clarified as to what severity of marital strife contraindicates direct sexual treatment.

The degree of marital distress may also vary according to the type of sexual problem. In one study that compared couples where the woman had a primary orgasmic dysfunction against those where the problem was secondary or situational orgasmic dysfunction, marital adjustment was better among the former (McGovern, McMullen, and LoPiccolo 1978). This finding probably reflects different histories of the problem. Primary orgasmic dysfunction, in all likelihood, preceded the marital relationship, while secondary dysfunction often develops during the marriage.

Among older couples who have been married for a long period of time, some will undoubtedly present histories of chronic and interrelated sexual and relationship difficulties. In some instances one or both spouses may have already given up on having a more satisfying relationship. Until positive feelings have been reestablished, there is likely to be little commitment to sex therapy by one or both partners. A less severe problem among older couples is boredom in the relationship. It may be necessary as part of the therapy to rekindle romantic feelings by directing the couple to engage in activities such as candlelight dinners and other courtship behaviors (Sviland 1975). Encouraging erotic feelings and sexual fantasies may also increase sexual interest in one another in a long-standing marriage.

In conducting an evaluation it is important for the interviewer to be comfortable in discussing sexual matters. Two other qualities are stressed by Masters and Johnson (1970). They feel the interviewer should be able to provide factual information about human sexuality, if it becomes appropriate to do so during the evaluation. They also note that the interviewer should maintain an attitude of acceptance rather than prejudice toward the sexual values, ideas, and practices of the client.

Even when the interviewer is at ease, many clients will feel some degree of embarrassment or other emotions when discussing their sexual problems. The therapist should be careful not to dismiss too quickly clients' fears or embarrassment. The belief that sexuality is normal and all right to discuss is not likely to be shared by many clients, so it is necessary to assess continually whether one's clients are becoming too upset or embarrassed, and to be patient until they are able to relate more openly on sexual matters.

It is often desirable during the initial evaluation to elicit simultaneously specific information about a person's sexual behavior and about attitudes and beliefs concerning sexuality. Lobitz and Lobitz (1978) suggest the use of a ubiquity statement to elicit information. As an example of such a statement, they ask: "People sometimes hear strange stories about masturbation, as they grow up. How did you first learn about it?" (p. 93). This approach indicates in advance an acceptance of whatever the client might say, and can identify attitudes that interfere with adequate sexual functioning.

Treatment Program: Sensate Focus

A major innovation in the treatment of sexual dysfunction has been the development of sensate focus exercises by Masters and Johnson (1970). These exercises are used by them as the starting point for the treatment of most sexual problems. Sensate focus exercises involve a guided series of steps of massage, caressing, and touching that are practiced in privacy by the couple. Clients are told that touch and stimulation of the other senses is a medium of social exchange and communication that is vital for sexual response. The sensate focus exercises are paired with round-table discussions that include the couple and the cotherapists. These discussions are used to evaluate how the exercises have proceeded, and to provide specific instruction and therapy.

For the sensate focus exercises, clients are instructed to be relaxed and not overly weary. They are also to remove all their clothes before the exercise begins. One person in the couple has been previously selected arbitrarily by the therapists to begin. That person initiates manual touch, which may be massage, tracing, or fondling. Usually specific suggestions for what is pleasing to the other person are made during roundtable discussions, but if one or both partners do not know, they are advised to discover, through a process of trial and error, what sensations are preferred. Before the first exercise couples are directed not to touch the genital areas or the woman's breasts, and told that the exercises are not to terminate in any specific sexual activity. In particular, couples are not to attempt intercourse. When the touching is completed by one partner, the other then takes a turn giving while the first person has the experience of receiving sensual pleasure. In addition to touch, these exercises are used to discover what is pleasing to the couple's other senses, especially olfactory and visual. The use of body lotions has been found enjoyable to many persons, some of whom do not respond to massage without the use of a lotion (Masters and Johnson 1970).

The sensate focus exercises have several different functions. First, the directive not to engage in sexual behavior unless expressly told by the therapist serves to bring the problem behavior under the control of the therapist. The use of this type of paradoxical instruction (Haley 1976) has 3 major consequences. First, by eliminating all sexual responses, the therapist helps the clients avoid making the mistakes that brought about sexual dysfunction. The process of therapy involves a gradual retraining of sexual habits. By making a completely fresh start with these new behaviors, the person is less likely to engage in old dysfunctional habits. Second, the instruction not to engage in sexual behavior helps relieve much of the performance fear of persons with sexual dysfunction. Masters and Johnson (1970) consider performance fears as one of the central features of sexual dysfunction, and emphasize a goalless approach throughout their therapy. Their objective is for clients to learn to appreciate sensual responses but not to measure their behavior against an arbitrary performance standard. Third, this type of paradoxical instruction helps bring clients under the influence of the therapist and heightens their degree of suggestibility.

A second function of the sensate focus exercises is to train clients in an increased awareness of their sensuality. Masters and Johnson (1970) assert that normal sexual responses develop naturally as persons learn to focus uncritically on sensual experiences. Often these responses have been inhibited because of the high degree of anxiety that has come to be associated with sexual activity and/or because of poorly learned sexual habits. Persons who are worried about sexual performance, for example, do not pay attention to the stimulation of touch and of the other senses, while at the same time their anxiety affects performance. Similarly, many persons play a spectator's role during sexual activity, observing but never allowing the sensual feelings to be perceived. These exercises also inhibit anxiety because of their calming effect. They probably function in a similar way to the use of relaxation during systematic desensitization. Similar to Wolpe's (1958) theory of reciprocal inhibition, Masters and Johnson (1970) note that the pleasurable state induced by sensate focus prevents the person from feeling anxieties or fears that were previously associated with sexual behavior.

A third feature of these exercises lies in facilitating sexual communication between sexual partners. The instructions include developing positive ways of guiding the other person's behavior so that it is pleasurable. Rather than waiting for one's sexual partner to discover by chance what the person experiences as exciting, each person instructs the other in what each finds pleasing through verbal statements or actions. Destructive feedback, such as "Stop, I don't like that," is discouraged. Clients are instead helped to provide positive communication, like "It feels better if you rub a little hard and more over here" (LoPiccolo 1978).

Concerning communication during lovemaking, Masters and Johnson (1970) note that one of the more dangerous myths about sexuality is that the good male lover is supposed to be able to tell instinctively what is pleasing to a woman. He is also held responsible for making the sexual experience satisfying for both of them. Education of couples about the fallacy of this myth takes place in roundtable discussions. Their therapists point out that it is often impossible to tell what will be pleasing without specific communication, because the sexual stimulation that women will respond to changes from situation to situation. Furthermore, these expectations of male clairvoyance can lead to excessive concerns about performance.

Related to this point, the sensate focus exercises teach a model of sexual behavior involving give and take. Rather than one person always initiating sexual behavior and the other generally receiving, both persons are expected at times to give and at other points to receive. Many couples with sexual dysfunction are in conflict over whose needs are to be satisfied during sex, and each thinks the other is selfish about his or her own personal needs. The sensate focus exercises help establish a different basis of sexual exchange whereby the mutuality of giving and receiving is stressed. These exercises can thereby create a sense of trust that each person will respond in time to the other person's needs. The alternation of roles also helps overcome previously socialized sex-role expectations. In particular, men typically have little experience receiving pleasure, and women often have not taken an active, initiating role in sexual matters.

This stress on mutuality also sets some expectations for the couple's nonsexual exchanges. Masters and Johnson (1970) note that they often try to correct what they feel are destructive sex-role patterns in the relationship. A couple with no mutual tasks or interests is not likely to find in one another a sexually interesting partner (LoPiccolo 1978). The experience of pleasurable contacts during the sensate focus and alternation of roles undoubtedly creates positive feelings in a couple that facilitate better communication in other areas.

A key feature of the sensate focus exercises used by Masters and Johnson (1970) is the roundtable discussion of the couple's experiences engaging in the exercises. It is important during these discussions to ascertain if each person is beginning to feel a new sensual awareness. At the same time, one must take care not to introduce performance expectations. Instances of failure can be put in a positive light by showing the couple amicable ways of overcoming breakdowns in communication and other problems. Masters and Johnson even suggest inducing some failure during the treatment, if none occurs spontaneously, in order to give the couple the experience of overcoming difficulties in a positive manner.

Specific problems that may be inhibiting persons' responses to the exercises will be brought up and discussed. Among the more common difficulties are the rejection of sexual and sensual feelings, concern about one's appearance, or other negative attitudes about sexual behavior. Tendencies for the couple to enter a spectator role or to be concerned over performance are also discussed, and they are instructed in how they might more fully experience the giving and receiving in the sensate exercises. There is also education about sexual functioning during the roundtable discussions, including, if necessary, instruction in anatomy. The goals of these discussions are summarized in Table 14.1.

When the initial sensate focus exercises have had a pleasurable effect for both persons, new instructions are given to include the genital areas and the woman's breasts. Clients are reminded, however, not to proceed to any other sexual activities. Care is taken again not to introduce any

TABLE 14.1. Summary of roundtable goals

1. Reflect from the patient's own accounts of personal and marital histories (Day 1 and Day 2) those attitudes, beliefs or misbeliefs, sexual practices, and factors of background and environment seen as probable correlates to the presenting distress of the specific sexual dysfunction.
2. Employ the "mirror" of professional objectivity and knowledge of sexual function and dysfunction to indicate the personal behavior patterns of each partner that have contributed specifically to loss of sexual understanding and generally to loss of unit communication.
3. Initiate an education process describing the nature of effective sexual functioning by emphasizing and explaining:
   (a) That sexual functioning is a natural physiological process.
   (b) The impossibility of employing the goal of end-point release in sexual expression as a means to overcome basic sexual dysfunction.
   (c) That sexuality is a dimension of personality (being male or female) expressed in every human act.
   (d) That sex or sexual functioning is specific sexual activity (masturbation, intercourse, partner genital manipulation, etc.).
   (e) The profound role played by fears of performance (felt by either sex) which specifically grow from lack of knowledge of effective sexual performance and lead to a spectator's role.
   (f) The sexual myths, misconceptions, and prejudices that have been defined in the material shared by the marital unit with the cotherapists.
   (g) The fact that individual sexual preferences may differ because marital partners are two different personalities, have two different sets of attitudes, and often bring two different social, ethnic, and religious backgrounds to the relationship.
   (h) That sexual patterns, habits, and values desirable to both partners usually have to be developed or identified by mutual effort.
   (i) That cotherapists' interest will be focused upon gradual development of pleasurable sexual interaction by means of those elements of sensate focus meaningful to and understood by both sexual partners.
   (j) That sexual effectiveness will be evolved from this gradual sensory appreciation and not from goal-oriented sexual performance.
   (k) That "mistakes" generally are even more contributory to progress of therapy than successes during the marital unit's attempts to follow the Foundation's authoritative directions.
   (l) That the marital relationship remains the focus for therapeutic attention during the rapid-treatment program rather than either of the marital partners.

Source: W. M. Masters and V. E. Johnson, *Human Sexual Inadequacy* (Boston: Little, Brown, 1970). Copyright © 1970 by Little, Brown and Company, Inc. Reprinted by permission.

goal at this point, but for each couple to focus on what is stimulating and pleasing to them, and to communicate that to the other person.

The results of these exercises are reviewed during roundtable discussions. Masters and Johnson (1970) emphasize inquiring about sexual response in a way that does not require a positive answer or in other ways arouse performance fears. As an example, they suggest asking, "What, if any, degree of erection (husband) or lubrication (wife) did you notice while you were pleasuring one another yesterday? " (p. 89). Completion of this phase of sensate focus exercises leads to the treatment of specific sexual problems.

Other types of guided exercises have been used in the treatment of sexual dysfunction, including systematic desensitization, guided imagining, and vicarious experiences (see Hogan 1978 for a review). There are, as yet, few empirical studies that compare the effectiveness of these approaches, although some evidence suggests that a graded approach such as used in desensitization or in the sensate focus exercises has better results than nongraded tasks (Hogan 1978).

TREATMENT OF SPECIFIC SEXUAL DYSFUNCTIONS

Among the sexual problems that occur most frequently among older persons are orgasmic dysfunctions in women and erectile dysfunction in men. Other difficulties such as vaginismus, dyspareunia, premature ejaculation, and ejaculatory incompetence are encountered less frequently and will not be dealt with in this chapter. For treatment procedures for those problems, the reader is referred to any of the texts on sexual behavior cited earlier.

Orgasmic Dysfunction. The rate among women of problems in attaining an orgasm is relatively high. According to the data from the Kinsey studies of women married for 10 years, 11 percent were nonorgasmic (Kinsey et al. 1953). An important distinction is between primary and secondary orgasmic dysfunction. Primary dysfunction refers to a woman who has never had an orgasm under any circumstances, whereas a woman with secondary dysfunction can reach orgasm but not with the frequency she desires or not in particular situations. Women with situational problems may, for example, be able to masturbate to produce an orgasm, but do not have one during intercourse.

There is an indication that the origins of primary and secondary orgasmic dysfunction may be somewhat different. Women with primary dysfunction are typically described as having no or negative sex training. Because of strict religious or parental education, they are inhibited in their sexual responses and consequently do not find sexual stimulation arousing (LoPiccolo 1978). Situational or secondary dysfunctions appear to involve specific rather than global inhibitions about sexual expression, such as caused by inadequate lovemaking procedures, especially a partner who ejaculates prematurely, and marital problems. In addition, some women apparently have thresholds requiring very high degrees of stimulation to achieve an orgasm (Kaplan 1974).

LoPiccolo (1978) suggests somewhat different approaches for women with primary and secondary orgasmic dysfunctions. For the former he recommends an emphasis on training in positive attitudes and providing information about sexual functioning. He also proposes beginning with a program of masturbation involving the woman alone, without a partner. Since the rate of achieving orgasm in women is higher with direct manipulation, this method is more likely to be successful. For the women with secondary dysfunction, he recommends more attention to fears about performance and to improving communications between the partners. While reporting differences in the history and backgrounds of women with primary and secondary dysfunctions, Masters and Johnson (1970) use the same treatment approach for both, involving the husband throughout.

In the treatment of secondary or situational dysfunction, there is some controversy over whether it is appropriate to attempt to achieve orgasm during intercourse. Because of the low level of stimulation to responsive areas of the woman's genitals during intercourse, it has been suggested that situational disturbances are not a problem at all. Kaplan (1974) makes a distinction between women with situational difficulties because of a high stimulation threshold and those who are not orgasmic during intercourse for other reasons. She suggests that it is among the former that treatment for situational dysfunction is often not successful, and recommends teaching the woman and her partner either how to engage in direct manipulation of the genital area during intercourse, or to accept other methods of achieving orgasm as her primary and preferred outlet.

Masters and Johnson (1970) treat orgasmic dysfunction by adding new steps during the sensate focus exercises and the roundtable discussions. When genital play is introduced, the woman is given permission to enjoy it. She is also urged to guide her partner in stimulating her by placing her hand on his and indicating the movement or amount of pressure she wants. The man is discouraged from trying to anticipate her desires or from doing what he feels she will enjoy. Masters and Johnson feel it is more likely that the woman will find pleasing stimulation by guiding the movement herself than through a trial-and-error method introduced by her partner. In particular, the man is discouraged from making a direct attack upon the clitoris, which sometimes causes irritation or pain. It is recommended to the couple, instead, that they explore what areas are pleasurable, especially the general mons area and either side of the clitoral shaft.

At this point it is restated by the therapists that there is no specific goal to the exercise other than increasing one's sensual pleasure. The man is discouraged from placing any performance pressure on the woman. It is repeatedly emphasized that sexual responsiveness is not under voluntary control, but occurs through sensual pleasure.

These genital manipulative sessions are continued until they produce obvious physical arousal in the woman. At that time the couple is instructed to engage in intercourse in the female superior position. After intromission, both man and woman are to remain still while the woman focuses on the sensations that the penis produces. When she feels the desire for more stimulation, she can engage in slow, pelvic thrusting for brief periods. After several trials these activities should become pleasurable to her. Once that occurs the man is instructed to begin moving in a slow, nondemanding way, with the pace guided by his partner. Finally, when the levels of sexual pleasure and excitement from this approach are high, the couple is taught the use of the lateral coital position. This position is recommended because it allows both persons considerable freedom of movement. After the couple takes these steps, they review their experiences in discussions with the therapists, and further instruction is given to both persons as needed.

In addition to the use of sensate focus exercises for treating orgasmic dysfunction, LoPiccolo (1978) notes that some women fear or are embarrassed by the loss of control during orgasm. He has employed a method of having the woman role-play an orgasm as a means of reducing her fears.

While controlled studies of treatment of sexual dysfunction have not been made, Masters and Johnson (1970) report high rates of success. For women with orgasmic dysfunction they had an overall failure rate of 19 percent, with approximately similar rates for women with primary and secondary dysfunction. Kaplan (1974) reports higher success than found by Masters and Johnson in treating primary orgasmic dysfunction, but a lower rate of achieving orgasm during intercourse. Among older clients (aged 50–79), Masters and Johnson report a failure rate of 40 percent for both types of disorder, or twice the amount as in the young.

Erectile Failure. As with orgasmic dysfunction, erectile failure is classified as primary or secondary, the former indicating men who have never had an erection, the latter referring to men who at one time functioned adequately. Masters and Johnson (1970) report that a history of premature ejaculation and excessive use of alcohol are the principal reasons for secondary erectile failure. In older men, fears about reductions in potency with age, especially when coupled with the use of alcohol, often result in erectile failure. As discussed earlier, erectile dysfunction can also be caused by a variety of illnesses and medications, so a thorough physical evaluation should take place before treatment begins.

LoPiccolo (1978) proposes that treatment of erectile failure involves 2 simultaneous processes: (1) ensuring a high level of physical and psychological sexual stimulation by the man's partner; and (2) eliminating anxiety and performance demands. These processes can be seen in many aspects of the Masters and Johnson treatment approach. As with the treatment of orgasmic dysfunction, sensate focus exercises and roundtable discussions are used. The couple is instructed not to attempt intercourse or any other sexual activity unless specifically told to do so by the therapists. Considerable attention is paid to the man's performance fears. It is explained carefully, and repeatedly, that a man cannot control or will an erection, nor can he be taught to have one. He can, however, become an active participant in sexual behavior, so that the natural processes that lead to an erection take over.

The sensate focus exercises begin with nongenital stimulation; after a couple of sessions genital touch is added. The therapist does not express concern for the effectiveness of this procedure either in producing an erection or in the amount of vaginal lubrication. During the sensate focus, the man guides the woman in what types of touching are more pleasant and stimulating. It is under this nondemand approach that erectile function is reestablished.

When the man achieves an erection, the couple is then taught a teasing technique, which Masters and Johnson (1970) regard as the most important aspect of their treatment. The couple is encouraged to continue the direct manipulation until an erection occurs, to rest while the erection is lost, and then to resume the activity to cause a return of the erection. This teasing probably has the effect of producing confidence in the man that he can achieve an erection, without excessive concern or anxiety over performance.

Following the success of this teasing technique, intercourse is attempted in the female superior position. It is emphasized to the couple that they attempt intromission in an unhurried way. If the man loses the erection, they can return to the manipulative play. The woman is instructed to control the insertion of the penis, since she will be able to do this more easily than the man. Once intromission occurs, the couple engages in a teasing exercise like the earlier one, with repeated intromissions, so that the man loses his fears over performance.

Some men are concerned that they will lose their erection during intercourse and fail to satisfy their partner. To deal with that fear, a couple is taught that if an erection is not satisfactory they can resume their sex play. They are strongly advised against placing time pressure on the activity or trying willfully to produce the erection.

One other feature of the treatment is concern over the woman's responses. Following a long history of sexual dysfunction in a marriage, the woman is often angry, resentful, or indifferent to the man's situation. If she is an unresponsive partner during the sensate focus, the exercises will not be stimulating. It is important, therefore, to involve her at the start of treatment and to be concerned throughout with whatever reservations, demands for performance, or anxieties that she may have about the retraining process. Her own enjoyment should also be part of the therapy.

The rates of improvement for erectile failure reported by Masters and

Johnson (1970) are somewhat lower than for orgasmic dysfunction. For all cases, the failure rate in the treatment of primary impotence was 40 percent, while for secondary impotence it was 31 percent. Among older men with secondary erectile dysfunction, the failure rate was similar to that of all cases, 36 percent. Masters and Johnson treated only one older man for primary impotence and were not successful.

Treatment of Persons without Partners

Individuals rather than couples have been treated for sexual dysfunction in 2 circumstances: (1) when the person has no current sexual relationship; or (2) when the person's spouse is not willing to come for treatment. In the latter instance, some therapists have reported successful treatment when the major responsibility for the sexual problem lies with the client (Husted 1978; LoPiccolo and Lobitz 1978). A woman with primary orgasmic dysfunction or a man with primary impotence are examples in which the dysfunction usually precedes the relationship. There is only limited and inconclusive evidence concerning the relative effectiveness of conjoint versus individual treatment (see Hogan 1978 for a review).

A number of procedures have been used for persons without partners, including systematic desensitization, rational emotive therapy, and exercises involving masturbation (Annon 1976; Hogan 1978). For women with orgasmic dysfunction, primary dysfunction cases (that is, who have never had an orgasm) appear to respond best to a series of exercises that first identify pleasure-sensitive areas and then use masturbation to achieve orgasm (LoPiccolo and Lobitz 1978). Since these techniques do not depend on the presence of a partner, they can be adapted to single persons.

Before starting treatment, the woman's acceptance of masturbation as an appropriate sexual behavior should be assessed. LoPiccolo and Lobitz (1978) suggest overcoming negative attitudes about masturbation by discussing with clients the large numbers of persons who do masturbate, and through self-disclosure of the therapist's own masturbatory experience. Specific fears—that masturbation damages one's sex organs or impairs normal sexual responsiveness, or that old bugaboo that it leads to mental illness—should, of course, be dealt with. In addition, if the woman has a partner, his involvement and feelings about masturbation should be elicited from the outset.

The treatment program developed by LoPiccolo and Lobitz is comprised of 9 steps, with the last 3 involving the woman's sexual partner, if one is present. In step 1 the woman explores her nude body, including use of a mirror to identify parts of the genital area. This is done following a bath, both for cleanliness and because of its relaxing properties. A diagram is used to facilitate the identification of various areas. Step 2 involves exploring her genitals tactually as well as visually. No instruction or suggestion is made about feeling sexually aroused at this time, so that performance anxiety is not increased. In step 3 the tactual and visual exploring is continued, with instructions to locate sensitive areas that produce pleasurable feelings. The woman is directed to explore thoroughly the area of the clitoral shaft and hood, the major and minor labia, the vaginal opening, and the perineum, but not to concentrate on one particular area. Step 4 involves concentrating tactual stimulation on the pleasure-producing areas identified during the previous stage. No specific instruction about reaching orgasm is given, although many women do achieve an orgasm at this stage. If that does not happen, the woman is instructed in Step 5 to increase the intensity and duration of the masturbation until either "something happens" or she becomes tired or sore. The use of pornographic material or fantasies to increase arousal is suggested. If manual stimulation does not result in an orgasm, the woman is instructed in Step 6 in the use of a vibrator.

Though used so far only in a small number of cases of primary orgasmic dysfunction, this procedure has produced orgasms in 100 percent of the persons treated (LoPiccolo and Lobitz 1978). Extension of these techniques after step 6 to include the woman's partner has resulted in orgasm during intercourse for 75 percent of the women treated.

Masturbation for the treatment of premature ejaculation and erectile failure has been described by Annon (1976).

Sexual Dysfunction in Aging Homosexuals

There is little information on the sexual problems of aging homosexuals, or, indeed, on other changes they experience. Sex therapists have for the most part given their attention to heterosexual couples. Except for the focus on techniques of intercourse, however, there is no reason why similar approaches should not be equally effective for improving sexual relationships between homosexual couples.

Despite some expectations that aging homosexuals experience increasing problems and distress, the limited studies available suggest that their adaptation is not worse than that of other older persons (Kelly 1977). Homosexuality among older women has been proposed as an adaptive life style. Because of the limited number of older men available as potential sexual partners, some aging women may be better able to find continuing intimate and sexual relationships by turning to one another. As noted earlier, however, sexual attitudes of today's aged population are somewhat more conservative than those of the young, so this alternative may not be appropriate for many older women. Clearly, there needs to be more attention to the sizable number of older persons with a homosexual preference, both with respect to sexual functioning and for other facets of their aging.

Summary

Aging is associated with a diminishing of sexual activity and responsiveness, but there is evidence that a significant minority of older persons remain sexually interested and sexually active until advanced ages. Major reasons for ceasing sexual activity include lifelong low interest in sex, illness, and negative social expectations for continued sexual functioning in old age. For married women, cessation of sexual activity is usually related to changes in their husbands due to illness, loss of interest in sex, or death. The direct treatment of sexual dysfunctions in persons of any age has provided brief and effective therapeutic procedures for many common types of problem. There is limited evidence that the 2 most common sexual problems in the aged, orgasmic dysfunction in women and erectile failure in men, respond adequately to treatment, although the failure rates are somewhat higher than among younger persons. Continuing sexual activity into later life offers the older person opportunities for closeness to another person, and for pleasurable, stimulating experiences. While successful aging does not depend on being sexually active, a pleasurable sex life undoubtedly contributes a lot to the overall well-being and zest for life of older persons who choose to remain active.

References

Agnew, H. W.; Webb, W. B.; and Williams, R. L. Sleep patterns in late middle aged males: An EEG study. *Electroencephalography and Clinical Neurophysiology* 1967, 23: 168–71.

Aita, J. F. Computerized tomography of the head. Part I. Introduction. *Nebraska Medical Journal* 1977a, 62: 349–54.

Aita, J. F. Computerized tomography of the head. Part II. Mechanics. *Nebraska Medical Journal* 1977b, 62: 383–87.

Akiskal, H. S., and McKinney, W. T. Depressive disorders: Toward a unified hypothesis. *Science* 1973, 182: 20–29.

Akpom, C. A., and Mayer, S. A survey of geriatric education in U.S. medical schools. *Journal of Medical Education* 1978, 53: 66–67.

Alarcón, R. de. Hypochondriasis and depression in the aged. *Gerontologica Clinica* 1964, 6: 266–77.

Albert, W. C., and Zarit, S. H. Income and health care of the aging. In S. H. Zarit, ed., *Readings in aging and death: Contemporary perspectives.* New York: Harper & Row, 1977.

Alberti, R. E., and Emmons, M. L. *Your perfect right: A guide to assertive behavior.* 2d ed. San Luis Obispo, Calif.: Impact, 1974.

Alberts, R. C. Report from the twilight years. In S. H. Zarit, ed., *Readings in aging and death: Contemporary perspectives.* New York: Harper & Row, 1977.

Aldrich, C. K., and Mendkoff, E. Relocation of the aged and disabled: A mortality study. *Journal of the American Geriatrics Society* 1963, 11: 185–94.

Alexander, F. Evaluation of psychotherapy. In P. Hoch and J. Zubin, eds., *The evaluation of psychiatric treatment.* New York: Grune & Stratton, 1964.

Alpaugh, P., and Hickey-Haney, M. *Counseling older adults: A training*

409

manual for beginning counselors and paraprofessionals. Los Angeles: Andrus Gerontology Center, 1978.

AMIN, M. M. Drug treatment of insomnia in old age. *Psychopharmacology Bulletin* 1976, 12: 52–55.

ANDERSON, T. P. Stroke rehabilitation: Evaluation of its quality by assessing patient outcomes. *Archives of Physical Medicine and Rehabilitation* 1978, 59: 170–75.

ANDERSON, W. F. The clinical assessment of aging and problems of diagnosis in the elderly. *South African Medical Journal* 1976, 50: 1257–59.

ANNON, J. S. *The behavioral treatment of sexual problems: Brief therapy.* New York: Harper & Row, 1976.

ANNON, J. S., AND ROBINSON, C. H. The use of vicarious learning in the treatment of sexual concerns. In J. LoPiccolo and L. LoPiccolo, eds., *Handbook of sex therapy.* New York: Plenum, 1978.

ANTUNES, G. E.; COOK, F. L.; COOK, T. D.; AND SKOGAN, W. G. Patterns of personal crime against the elderly: Findings from a national survey. *Gerontologist* 1977, 17: 321–27.

ATCHLEY, R. A. *The social forces in later life: An introduction to social gerontology.* 2d ed. Belmont, Calif.: Wadsworth, 1977.

AYLLON, T., AND AZRIN, N. *The token economy: A motivational system for therapy and rehabilitation.* New York: Appleton-Century-Crofts, 1968.

BAFFA, G. A., AND ZARIT, S. H. Age differences in the perception of assertive behavior. Paper presented at the meetings of the Gerontological Society, San Francisco, 1977.

BAILEY, M. B.; HABERMAN, P. W.; AND ALKSNE, H. The epidemiology of alcoholism in an urban residential area. *Quarterly Journal of Studies on Alcohol* 1965, 26: 19–40.

BALDESSARINI, R. J. Psychopharmacology of the amphetamines. *Pediatrics* 1972, 49: 694–701.

BALDESSARINI, R. J. Biogenic amine hypothesis in affective disorders. In F. F. Flach and S. C. Draghi, eds., *The nature and treatment of depression.* New York: Wiley, 1975.

BANDURA, A. Psychotherapy based upon modeling principles. In A. E. Bergin and S. Garfield, eds., *Handbook of psychotherapy and behavior change.* New York: Wiley, 1971.

BARKER, R. G., AND BARKER, L. S. The psychological ecology of old people in Midwest, Kansas, and Yoredale, Yorkshire. In B. L. Neugarten, ed., *Middle age and aging: A reader in social psychology.* Chicago: University of Chicago Press, 1968.

BARRETT, C. J. Effectiveness of widows' groups in facilitating change. *Journal of Consulting and Clinical Psychology* 1978, 46: 20–31.

BARROWS, C. H. The challenge—Mechanisms of biological aging. *Gerontologist* 1971, 11: 5–11.

BECK, A. T. *Depression: Clinical, experimental and theoretical aspects.* New York: Harper & Row, 1967.

BECK, A. T. *Cognitive therapy and the emotional disorders.* New York: International Universities Press, 1976.

BECK, A. T.; LESTER, D.; AND KOVACS, M. Attempted suicide by males and females. *Psychological Reports* 1973, *33:* 965–66.

BECK, A. T.; KOVACS, M.; AND WEISSMAN, A. Hopelessness and suicidal behavior: An overview. *Journal of the American Medical Association* 1975, *234:* 1146–49.

BECK, A. T.; RUSH, J.; AND KOVACS, M. Individual treatment manual for cognitive/behavioral psychotherapy of depression. Unpublished manuscript.

BECKER, F., AND ZARIT, S. H. Training older adults as peer counselors. *Educational Gerontology* 1978, *3:* 241–50.

BEERS, T. M., JR., AND KAROLY, P. Cognitive strategies, expectancy and coping style in the control of pain. *Journal of Consulting and Clinical Psychology* 1979, *47:* 179–82.

BEM, D., AND ALLEN, A. On predicting some of the people some of the time: The search for cross-situational consistencies in behavior. *Psychological Review* 1974, *81:* 506–20.

BEM, S. L. Sex role adaptability: One consequence of psychological androgyny. *Journal of Personality and Social Psychology* 1975, *31:* 634–43.

BENDER, M. B. *Disorders in perception, with particular reference to the phenomena of extinction and displacement.* Springfield, Ill.: Thomas, 1952.

BENGSTON, V. L., AND CUTLER, N. E. Generations and intergenerational relations: Perspectives on age groups and social change. In R. H. Binstock and E. Shanas, eds., *Handbook of aging and the social sciences.* New York: Van Nostrand Reinhold, 1976.

BERARDO, F. M. Survivorship and social isolation: The case of the aged widower. *Family Coordinator* 1970, *19:* 11–25.

BEREZIN, M. A. Sex and old age: A further review of the literature. *Journal of Geriatric Psychiatry* 1976, *9:* 189–209.

BERGER, K. S., AND ZARIT, S. H. Late life paranoid states: Assessment and treatment. *American Journal of Orthopsychiatry* 1978, *48:* 528–37.

BERGMAN, M.; BLUMENFELD, V. G.; CASCARDO, D.; DASH, B.; LEVITT, H.; AND MARGULIES, M. K. Age-related decrement in hearing for speech: Sampling and longitudinal studies. *Journal of Gerontology* 1976, *31:* 533–38.

BERGMANN, K.; FOSTER, E. M.; JUSTICE, A. W.; AND MATHEWS, V. Management of the demented elderly patient in the community. *British Journal of Psychiatry* 1979, *132:* 441–49.

BERSANI, M. Services for older adults: A study of availability and satisfaction. Master's thesis, University of Southern California, 1978.

BERSOFF, D. G. Silk purses into sow's ears: The decline of psychological testing and a suggestion for its redemption. *American Psychologist* 1973, *28:* 892–99.

BIDWELL, G.; BERNER, B.; AND MEIER, R. D. Chronic disability post-hospital survey: A focus on ancillary service needs. *Rehabilitation Psychology* 1972, *19:* 80–84.

BILD, B. R., AND HAVIGHURST, R. J. Senior citizens in great cities: The case of Chicago. *Gerontologist* 1976, *16* (1, pt. 2); whole issue.

BIRKHILL, W. R., AND SCHAIE, K. W. The effect of differential reinforcement of cautiousness in intellectual performance among the elderly. *Journal of Gerontology* 1975, *30*: 578–83.

BIRREN, J. E. Principles of research on aging. In J. E. Birren, ed., *Handbook of aging and the individual: Psychological and biological aspects.* Chicago: University of Chicago Press, 1959.

BIRREN, J. E. Translations in gerontology—From lab to life: Psychophysiology and speed of response. *American Psychologist* 1974, *11*: 808–15.

BIRREN, J. E., AND BOTWINICK, J. Age differences in finger, jaw, and foot reaction time to auditory stimuli. *Journal of Gerontology* 1955, *10*: 429–32.

BIRREN, J. E.; BUTLER, R. N.; GREENHOUSE, S. W.; SOKOLOFF, L.; AND YARROW, M. R., eds. *Human aging: A biological and behavioral study.* Washington: U.S. Department of Health, Education, and Welfare, 1963.

BIRREN, J. E., AND CLAYTON, V. History of gerontology. In D. S. Woodruff and J. E. Birren, eds., *Aging: Scientific perspectives and social issues.* New York: Van Nostrand, 1975.

BIRREN, J. E., AND HIRSCHFIELD, I. S. *An analysis of professional education in the State of California for services to retired and aged.* Los Angeles: Andrus Gerontology Center, 1977.

BIRREN, J. E., AND RENNER, V. J. Research on the psychology of aging: Principles and experimentation. In J. E. Birren and K. W. Schaie, eds., *Handbook of the psychology of aging.* New York: Van Nostrand Reinhold, 1977.

BIRREN, J. E., AND SLOANE, R. B. *Manpower and training needs in mental health and illness of the aging.* Los Angeles: Andrus Gerontology Center, 1977.

BIRREN, J. E., AND RENNER, V. J. Notes on the history of training in mental health and aging. In J. E. Birren and R. B. Sloane, *Handbook of mental health and aging.* Englewood Cliffs, N.J.: Prentice-Hall, 1980.

BLENKNER, M. Environmental change and the aging individual. *Gerontologist* 1967, *7*: 101–105.

BLENKNER, M.; BLOOM, M.; AND NIELSON, M. A. A research and demonstration project of protective services. *Social Casework* 1971, *52*: 483–99.

BLESSED, G.; TOMLINSON, B. E.; AND ROTH, M. The association between quantitative measures of dementia and of senile change in the cerebral gray matter of elderly subjects. *British Journal of Psychiatry* 1968, *114*: 797–811.

BLOOD, R. O., AND WOLFE, D. M. *Husbands and wives.* New York: Free Press, 1960.

BLUM, J. E.; CLARK, E. T.; AND JARVIK, L. F. The New York State Psychiatric Institute study of aging twins. In L. F. Jarvik, C. Eisdorfer, and J. E. Blum, eds., *Intellectual functioning in adults: Psychological and biological influences.* New York: Springer, 1973.

BLUMENTHAL, M. D. Measuring depressive symptomatology in a general population. *Archives of General Psychiatry* 1975, *32*: 971–78.

BORKOVEC, T. D. Relaxation treatment of sleep disorders. Paper presented at the meetings of the American Psychological Association, San Francisco, 1977.

BORUP, J. H.; GALLEGO, D. T.; AND HEFFERNAN, P. G. Relocation and its effect on mortality. *Gerontologist* 1979, *19*: 135–40.

BOTWINICK, J. *Cognitive processes in maturity and old age.* New York: Springer, 1967.

BOTWINICK, J. Intellectual abilities. In J. E. Birren and K. W. Schaie, eds., *Handbook of the psychology of aging.* New York: Van Nostrand Reinhold, 1977.

BOTWINICK, J. *Aging and behavior.* 2d ed. New York: Springer, 1978.

BOTWINICK, J., AND BIRREN, J. E. Differential decline in the Wechsler-Bellevue subtest in the senile psychoses. *Journal of Gerontology* 1951, *6*: 365–68.

BOTWINICK, J., AND THOMPSON, L. W. Age differences in reaction time: An artifact? *Gerontologist* 1968, *8*: 25–28.

BOUVIER, L.; ATLEE, E.; AND McVEIGH, F. The elderly in America. *Population Bulletin* 1975.

BOWLBY, J. *Attachment and loss.* Vol. 2. *Separation: Anxiety and anger.* New York: Basic Books, 1973.

BRECKENRIDGE, K. Medical rehabilitation program evaluation. *Archives of Physical Medicine and Rehabilitation* 1978, *59*: 419–23.

BROCKLEHURST, J. C., ed., *Textbook of geriatric medicine and gerontology.* London: Churchill Livingstone, 1973.

BRODY, E. M., AND COLE, C. Deferred status: Applicants to a voluntary home for the aged. *Gerontologist* 1971, *11*: 219–25.

BRODY, E. M.; KLEBAN, M. M.; LAWTON, M. P.; AND SILVERMAN, H. A. Excess disabilities of mentally impaired aged: Impact of individualized treatment. *Gerontologist* 1971, *11*: 124–32.

BRODY, H., AND VIJAYASHANKAR, N. Anatomical changes in the nervous system. In C. E. Finch and L. Hayflick, eds., *Handbook of the biology of aging.* New York: Van Nostrand Reinhold, 1977.

BROVERMAN, I. K.; VOGEL, S. R.; BROVERMAN, D. M.; CLARKSON, F. E.; AND ROSENKRANTZ, P. S. Sex-role stereotypes: A current appraisal. *Journal of Social Issues* 1972, *28*: 59–78.

BROWN, G. W.; SKLAIR, F.; HARRIS, T. O.; AND BIRLEY, J. L. T. Life events and psychiatric disorders. Part I: Some methodological issues. *Psychological Medicine* 1973, *3*: 74–87.

BROWN, R., AND McNEILL, D. The "tip of the tongue" phenomenon. *Journal of Verbal Learning and Verbal Behavior* 1966, *5*: 325–37.

BUHLER, C. Meaningful life in the mature years. In R. W. Kleemeier, ed., *Aging and leisure.* New York: Oxford University Press, 1961.

BURNSIDE, I. M. Group work with the aged: Selected literature. *Gerontologist* 1970, *10*: 241–46.

BURNSIDE, I. M. Sexuality and aging. In I. M. Burnside, ed., *Sexuality and aging.* Los Angeles: Andrus Gerontology Center, 1975.

Busse, E. W. Psychoneurotic reactions and defense mechanisms in the aged. In E. Palmore, ed., *Normal aging: Reports from the Duke Longitudinal Study.* Durham, N.C.: Duke University Press, 1970.

Busse, E. W. Mental disorders in later life—organic brain syndromes. In E. W. Busse and E. Pfeiffer, eds., *Mental illness in later life.* Washington: American Psychiatric Association, 1973.

Busse, E. W. Hypochondriasis in the elderly: A reaction to social stress. *Journal of the American Geriatrics Society* 1976, 4: 145–49.

Butler, R. N. The life review: An interpretation of reminiscence in the aged. *Psychiatry* 1963, 26: 65–76.

Butler, R. N. Age-ism: Another form of bigotry. *Gerontologist* 1969, 9: 243–46.

Butler, R. N. *Why survive: Being old in America.* New York: Harper & Row, 1975.

Butler, R. N. Toward a psychiatry of the life cycle: Implications of socio-psychologic studies of the aging process for the psychotherapeutic situation. In S. H. Zarit, ed., *Readings in aging and death: Contemporary perspectives.* New York: Harper & Row, 1977.

Butler, R. N., and Sulliman, L. C. Psychiatric contact with the community resident, emotionally disturbed elderly. *Journal of Nervous and Mental Diseases* 1963, 137: 180–86.

Butler, R. N., and Lewis, M. *Aging and mental health.* 2d ed. St. Louis: Mosby, 1977.

Cadoret, R., and Winokur, G. Genetic studies of affective disorders. In F. F. Flach and S. C. Draghi, eds., *The nature and treatment of depression.* New York: Wiley, 1975.

Caird, F. I. Computerized tomography (Emiscan) in brain failure in old age. *Age and Ageing* 1977, 6 (supp.): 50–51.

Caird, W., and Wincze, J. P. *Sex therapy: A behavioral approach.* New York: Harper & Row, 1977.

Caird, W. K.; Sanderson, R. E.; and Inglis, J. Cross-validation of a learning test for use with elderly psychiatric patients. *Journal of Mental Science* 1962, 108: 368–70.

Camp, C.; Lachman, R.; and Lachman, J. Age and the retrievability of world knowledge. Paper presented at the annual meetings of the Gerontological Society, San Francisco, 1977.

Canestrari, R. E., Jr. Paced and self-paced learning in young and elderly adults. *Journal of Gerontology* 1963, 18: 165–68.

Canestrari, R. E., Jr. Age changes in acquisition. In G. A. Talland, ed., *Human aging and behavior.* New York: Academic Press, 1968.

Carey, R. G., and Posavac, E. J. Program evaluation of a physical medicine and rehabilitation unit: A new approach. *Archives of Physical Medicine and Rehabilitation* 1978, 59: 330–37.

Carp, F. M. *A future for the aged: The residents of Victoria Plaza.* Austin: University of Texas Press, 1966.

CARP, F. M. Differences among older workers, volunteers, and persons who are neither. *Journal of Gerontology* 1968a, *23*: 497–501.

CARP, F. M. Impact of improved housing on morale and life satisfaction. *Gerontologist* 1975, *15*: 511–15.

CARSKADON, M.; DEMENT, W. C.; MITLER, M. M.; GUILLEMINAULT, C.; ZARCONE, J. P.; AND SPIEGEL, R. Self-reports versus sleep laboratory findings in 122 drug-free subjects with complaints of chronic insomnia. *American Journal of Psychiatry* 1976, *133*: 1382–88.

CATTELL, R. B. *Personality and motivation structure and measurement*. New York: World Book, 1957.

CERMAK, L. S. *Improving your memory*. New York: Norton, 1976.

CHERRY, D. L., AND ZARIT, S. H. Sex-role and age differences in competency, flexibility and affective status of women. Paper presented at the meetings of the Gerontological Society, Dallas, Texas, 1978.

CHEUNG, A. Personal communication, 1977.

CHOWN, S. M. Age and the rigidities. *Journal of Gerontology* 1961, *16*: 353–62.

CHRISTENSON, C. V., AND GAGNON, J. H. Sexual behavior in groups of older women. *Journal of Gerontology* 1965, *20*: 351–56.

CHRISTENSON, C. V., AND JOHNSON, A. B. Sexual patterns in a group of older never-married women. *Journal of Geriatric Psychiatry* 1973, *6*: 80–98.

CLAYTON, P. J.; HALIKES, J. A.; AND MAURICE, W. L. The bereavement of the widowed. *Diseases of the Nervous System* 1971, *32*: 597–604.

CLAYTON, V., AND BIRREN, J. E. The development of wisdom across the life-span: A re-examination of an ancient topic. In P. B. Baltes and O. G. Brim, Jr., eds., *Life-span development and behavior*. Vol. 3. New York: Academic Press, in press.

COATES, T. J., AND THORESEN, C. E. *How to sleep better: A drug-free program for overcoming insomnia*. Englewood Cliffs, N.J.: Prentice-Hall, 1977.

COHEN, E. S., AND KRAFT, A. C. The restorative potential of elderly long-term residents of mental hospitals. *Gerontologist* 1968, *8*: 264–68.

COLE, P. Morbidity in the United States. In C. L. Erhardt and J. E. Berlin, eds., *Mortality and morbidity in the United States*. Cambridge, Mass.: Harvard University Press, 1974.

COMFORT, A. Biological theories of aging. *Human Development* 1970, *13*: 127–39.

COMFORT, A. Sexuality in later life. In J. E. Birren and R. B. Sloane, eds., *Handbook of mental health and aging*. Englewood Cliffs, N.J.: Prentice-Hall, 1980.

COOPER, A. F.; KAY, D. W. K.; CURRY, A. R.; GARSIDE, R. F.; AND ROTH, M. Hearing loss in paranoid and affective psychoses of the elderly. *Lancet* 1974, *2*: 851–54.

COOPER, A. F.; GARSIDE, R. F.; AND KAY, D. W. K. A comparison of deaf and non-deaf patients with paranoid and affective psychoses. *British Journal of Psychiatry* 1976, *129*: 532–38.

COOPER, A. F., AND PORTER, R. Visual acuity and ocular pathology in the paranoid and affective psychoses of later life. *Journal of Psychosomatic Research* 1976, 20: 107–14.

COPELAND, J. R. M.; KELLEHER, M. J.; KELLETT, J. M.; FOUNTAIN-GOURLAY, A. J.; COWAN, D. W.; BARRON, G.; AND DeGRUCHY, J. (U. K.), with GURLAND, B. J.; SHARPE, L.; SIMON, R. J.; KURIANSKY, J. B.; AND STILLER, P. (U.S.). Diagnostic differences in psychogeriatric patients in New York and London. *Canadian Psychiatric Association Journal* 1974, 19: 267–71.

CORBY, N. H. Assertion training with aged populations. *Counseling Psychologist* 1975, 5(4): 69–73.

CORSELLIS, J. A. N. *Mental illness and the aging brain.* London: Oxford University Press, 1962.

CORSO, J. F. Auditory perception and communication. In J. E. Birren and K. W. Schaie, eds., *Handbook of the psychology of aging.* New York: Van Nostrand Reinhold, 1977.

COSIN, L. Z.; MORT, M.; POST, F.; WESTRUPP, C.; AND WILLIAMS, M. Experimental treatment of persistent senile confusion. *International Journal of Social Psychiatry* 1958, 4: 24–42.

CRAIK, F. I. M. Age differences in human memory. In J. E. Birren and K. W. Schaie, eds., *Handbook of the psychology of aging.* New York: Van Nostrand Reinhold, 1977.

CRAIK, F. I. M., AND MASANI, P. A. Age differences in the temporal integration of language. *British Journal of Psychology* 1967, 58: 291–99.

CRAPPER, D. R., AND DE BONI, U. Alzheimer's senile dementia: Virus or mental? Paper presented at the 11th International Congress of Gerontology, Tokyo, 1978.

CUMMING, E., AND HENRY, W. R. *Growing old: The process of disengagement.* New York: Basic Books, 1961.

CURTIN, S. R. *Nobody ever died of old age.* Boston: Little, Brown, 1972.

DANIEL, C. W. Aging of cells during serial propagation *in vivo. Advances in Gerontological Research* 1972, 4: 167–98.

DANIEL, C. W. Cell longevity: *In vivo.* In C. E. Finch and L. Hayflick, eds., *Handbook of the biology of aging.* New York: Van Nostrand Reinhold, 1977.

DAVIS, M. S. Variations in patients' compliance with doctors' advice: An empirical analysis of patterns of communication. *American Journal of Public Health* 1968, 58: 274–88.

DAVIS, R. W. Activity therapy in a geriatric setting. *Journal of the American Geriatric Society* 1967, 15: 1144–52.

DAVISON, G. C. Appraisal of behavior modification techniques with adults in institutional settings. In C. M. Franks, ed., *Behavior therapy.* New York: McGraw-Hill, 1969.

DENNY, P. Cellular biology of aging. In D. S. Woodruff and J. E. Birren, eds., *Aging: Scientific perspectives and social issues.* New York: Van Nostrand, 1975.

DEPARTMENT OF HEALTH, EDUCATION, AND WELFARE. *Medical care, expendi-*

tures, prices and costs: Background book. Washington: Government Printing Office, 1975.

DE VRIES, H. A. Physiological effects of an exercise training regimen upon men aged 52–88. *Journal of Gerontology* 1970, 25: 325–36.

DE VRIES, H. A. Physiology of exercise and aging. In D. S. Woodruff and J. E. Birren, eds., *Aging: Scientific perspectives and social issues.* New York: Van Nostrand, 1975.

Diagnostic and statistical manual of mental disorders. Draft of third edition. Washington: American Psychiatric Association, 1978.

DIETHELM, O. The evolution of the concept of depression. In F. F. Flach and S. C. Draghi, eds., *The nature and treatment of depression.* New York: Wiley, 1975.

DOHRENWEND, B. P., AND DOHRENWEND, B. S. *Social status and psychological disorder: A causal inquiry.* New York: Wiley Interscience, 1969.

DORPAT, T. L., AND BOSWELL, J. W. An evaluation of suicidal intent and suicidal attempts. *Comprehensive Psychiatry* 1963, 4: 114–25.

DOVENMUEHLE, R. H., AND VERWOERDT, A. Physical illness and depressive symptomatology. *Journal of the American Geriatrics Society* 1962, 10: 932–47.

EARLEY, L. W., AND VON MERING, O. Growing old the out-patient way. *American Journal of Psychiatry* 1969, 125: 963–67.

EISDORFER, C., AND WILKIE, F. Intellectual changes with advancing age. In L. Jarvik, C. Eisdorfer, and J. E. Blum, eds., *Intellectual functioning in adults: Psychological and biological influences.* New York: Springer, 1973.

EISDORFER, C., AND STOTSKY, B. A. Intervention, treatment and rehabilitation of psychiatric disorders. In J. E. Birren and K. W. Schaie, eds., *Handbook of the psychology of aging.* New York: Van Nostrand Reinhold, 1977.

ELLENBERG, M. Impotence in diabetes: The neurologic factor. In J. LoPiccolo and L. LoPiccolo, eds., *Handbook of sex therapy.* New York: Plenum, 1978.

ELLIS, A. *Reason and emotion in psychotherapy.* Seacaucus, N.J.: Stuart, 1962.

ELLIS, A. *The essence of rational psychotherapy: A comprehensive approach to treatment.* New York: Institute for Rational Living, 1970.

ELLIS, A., AND HARPER, R. A. *A new guide to rational living.* Englewood Cliffs, N.J.: Prentice-Hall, and Hollywood, Calif.: Wilshire Books, 1975.

ELLWELL, C. C., II. The sage spirit. In S. H. Zarit, ed., *Readings in aging and death: Contemporary perspectives.* New York: Harper & Row, 1977.

ENGEL, G. L., AND ROMANO, J. Delirium, a syndrome of cerebral insufficiency. *Journal of Chronic Diseases* 1959, 9: 260–77.

ENGEN, T. Taste and smell. In J. E. Birren and K. W. Schaie, eds., *Handbook of the psychology of aging.* New York: Van Nostrand Reinhold, 1977.

EPSTEIN, L. J. Depression in the elderly. *Journal of Gerontology* 1976, 31: 278–82.

EPSTEIN, L. J., AND SIMON, A. Alternatives to state hospitalization for the geriatric mentally ill. *American Journal of Psychiatry* 1968, 124: 955–61.

ERIKSON, E. H. *Childhood and society*. 2d ed. New York: Norton, 1963.

Estrogen therapy: The dangerous road to Shangri-La. *Consumer Reports* 1976, *41*: 642–45.

EYSENCK, M. Age differences in incidental learning. *Developmental Psychology* 1974, *10*: 936–41.

FAIRWEATHER, G. W.; SANDERS, D. H.; CRESSLER, D. L.; AND MAYNARD, H. *Community life for the mentally ill: An alternative to institutional care*. Chicago: Aldine, 1969.

FARBEROW, N. L. Group psychotherapy with suicidal persons. In H. L. P. Resnik, ed., *Suicidal behavior: Diagnosis and management*. Boston: Little, Brown, 1968.

FEDERAL COUNCIL ON AGING. *The interrelationships of benefit programs for the elderly*. Appendix II: Programs for older Americans in four states: A case study of federal, state, and local benefit programs. Washington: Government Printing Office, 1975.

FEDORAVICIUS, A. S. When relaxation treatment fails. . . . Paper presented at the meetings of the American Psychological Association, San Francisco, 1977.

FEINBERG, I. Functional implications of changes in sleep physiology with age. In R. D. Terry and S. Gershon, eds., *Neurobiology of aging*. New York: Raven Press, 1976.

FEINBERG, I.; KORESKO, R. L.; AND HELLER, N. EEG sleep patterns as a function of normal and pathological aging in man. *Journal of Psychiatric Research* 1967, *5*: 107–144.

FEINBERG, I., AND CARLSON, V. R. Sleep variations as a function of age in man. *Archives of General Psychiatry* 1968, *18*: 239–50.

FELDMAN, M. G., AND DiSCIPIO, W. J. Integrating physical therapy with behavior therapy. *Physical Therapy* 1972, *52*: 1283–85.

FERSTER, C. B. A functional analysis of depression. *American Psychologist* 1973, *28*: 857–70.

FIEVE, R. R., AND DUNNER, D. L. Unipolar and bipolar affective states. In F. F. Flach and S. C. Draghi, eds., *The nature and treatment of depression*. New York: Wiley, 1975.

FILER, R. N., AND O'CONNEL, D. D. Motivation of aged persons in an institutional setting. *Journal of Gerontology* 1964, *19*: 15–22.

FINCH, C. E. Neuroendocrine and autonomic aspects of aging. In C. E. Finch and L. Hayflick, eds., *Handbook of the biology of aging*. New York: Van Nostrand Reinhold, 1977.

FINCH, C. E.; FOSTER, J. R.; AND MIRSKY, A. E. Ageing and the regulation of cell activities during exposure to cold. *Journal of General Physiology* 1969, *54*: 690–712.

FINK, M.; GREEN, M. A.; AND BENDER, M. B. The face-hand test as a diagnostic sign of organic mental syndrome. *Neurology* 1952, *2*: 48–56.

FINKEL, S., AND FILLMORE, W. Experiences with an older adult group at a private psychiatric hospital. *J. Geriatric Psychiatry* 1971, *4*: 188–99.

Fish, F. Senile schizophrenia. *Journal of Mental Science* 1960, *106*: 938–46.

Flanagan, J. C. A research approach to improving our quality of life. *American Psychologist* 1978, *33*: 138–47.

Flanagan, J. C. *Identifying opportunities for improving the quality of life of older age groups.* Palo Alto, Calif.: American Institutes for Research, 1979.

Folsom, J. C. Reality orientation for the elderly patient. *Journal of Geriatric Psychiatry* 1968, *1*: 291–307.

Folstein, M. F.; Folstein, S. E.; and McHugh, P. R. "Mini-mental state": A practical method for grading the cognitive state of patients for the clinician. *Journal of Psychiatric Research* 1975, *12*: 189–98.

Fordyce, W. E.; Fowler, R. S.; Lehman, J. F.; and DeLateur, B. Operant conditioning in the treatment of chronic pain. *Archives of Physical Medicine and Rehabilitation* 1973, *54*: 399–408.

Forsyth, R. P., and Fairweather, G. W. Psychotherapeutic and other hospital treatment criteria. *Journal of Abnormal and Social Psychology* 1961, *62*: 598–604.

Foster, J. R.; Gershell, W. J.; and Goldfarb, A. I. Lithium treatment in the elderly. I. Clinical usage. *Journal of Gerontology* 1977, *32*: 299–302.

Fox, J. H.; Topel, J. L.; and Huckman, M. S. Use of computerized tomography in senile dementia. *Journal of Neurology, Neurosurgery and Psychiatry* 1975, *38*: 948–53.

Fozard, J. L.; Wolf, E.; Bell, B.; McFarland, R. A.; and Podolsky, S. Visual perception and communication. In J. E. Birren and K. W. Schaie, eds., *Handbook of the psychology of aging.* New York: Van Nostrand Reinhold, 1977.

Fracchia, J.; Sheppard, C.; and Merlis, S. Treatment patterns in psychiatry: Relationships to system features and aging. *Journal of the American Geriatrics Society* 1973, *21*: 134–38.

Frenkel-Brunswick, E. Adjustments and reorientation in the course of the life span. In B. L. Neugarten, ed., *Middle age and aging: A reader in social psychology.* Chicago: University of Chicago Press, 1968.

Freud, S. Mourning and melancholia. In *Collected Papers.* Vol. 4. London: Hogarth Press, 1950.

Freymann, J. C. *The American health care delivery system: Its genesis and trajectory.* New York: Med Com Inc., 1974.

Friedman, A. S. Minimal effects of severe depression on cognitive functioning. *Journal of Abnormal and Social Psychology* 1964, *69*: 237–43.

Friedman, E. P. Spatial proximity and social interaction in a home for the aged. *Journal of Gerontology* 1966, *21*: 566–70.

Friedman, J. M. Sexual adjustment of the postcoronary male. In J. LoPiccolo and L. LoPiccolo, eds., *Handbook of sex therapy.* New York: Plenum, 1978.

Gaitz, C. M., and Hacker, S. Obstacles in coordinating services for the care of the psychiatrically ill aged. *Journal of the American Geriatrics Society* 1970, *18*: 172–82.

GAITZ, C. M., AND BAER, D. E. Characteristics of elderly patients with alcoholism. *Archives of General Psychiatry* 1971, *24*: 372–78.

GAMBRILL, E. D., AND RICHEY, C. A. *It's up to you: Developing assertive social skills.* Millbrae, Calif.: Les Femmes, 1976.

GARDNER, E. A.; BAHN, A. K.; AND MACK, M. Suicide and psychiatric care in the aging. *Archives of General Psychiatry* 1964, *10*: 547–53.

GAUGER, A. B.; BROWNWELL, M. W.; RUSSELL, W. W.; AND RETTER, R. W. Evaluation of levels of subsistence. *Archives of Physical Medicine and Rehabilitation* 1964, *45*: 286–92.

GELBA, B. *Vitality training for older adults.* New York: Random House, 1976.

GENDLIN, E. T. Focusing. *Psychotherapy: Theory, research, and practice* 1969, *6*: 4–15.

GENDLIN, E. T. *Focusing.* New York: Everest House, 1978.

GENDLIN, E. T.; BEEBE, J., III; CASSENS, J.; KLEIN, M.; AND OBERLANDER, M. Focusing ability in psychotherapy, personality, and creativity. In J. Shlien, ed., *Research in psychotherapy III.* Washington: American Psychological Association, 1968.

GILBERSTADT, H., AND SAKO, Y. Intellectual and personality changes following open-heart surgery. *Archives of General Psychiatry* 1967, *16*: 210–14.

GLASER, B. G., AND STRAUSS, A. L. *Awareness of dying.* Chicago: Aldine, 1965.

GLASSCOTE, R.; BIEGEL, A., BUTTERFIELD, A., JR.; CLARK, E.; COX, B.; ELPERS, K.; GUDEMAN, J. E.; GUREL, L.; LEWIS, R.; MILES, D.; RAYBIN, J.; REIFLER, C.; AND VITO, E. *Old folks at home: A field study of nursing and board and care homes.* Washington: American Psychiatric Association, 1976.

GLASSCOTE, R.; GUDEMAN, J. E.; AND MILES, C. D. *Creative mental health services for the elderly.* Washington: American Psychiatric Association, 1977.

GLOVER, B. H. Sex in the aging. *Postgraduate Medicine* 1975, *57*: 165–69.

GOFFMAN, E. *Asylums: Essays on the social situation of mental patients and other inmates.* Garden City, N.Y.: Doubleday, 1961.

GOLDFARB, A. I. The psychodynamics of dependency and the search for aid. In R. Kalish, ed., *The dependencies of old people.* Ann Arbor, Mich.: Institute of Gerontology, 1969.

GOLDFARB, A. I., AND TURNER, H. Psychotherapy of the aged: II. Utilization and effectiveness of "brief" therapy. *American Journal of Psychiatry* 1953, *109*: 916–21.

GOLDFARB, A. I., AND SHEPS, J. Psychotherapy of the aged: III. Brief therapy of interrelated psychological and somatic disorders. *Psychosomatic Medicine* 1954, *16*: 209–18.

GOLDFARB, A. I.; FISCH, M.; AND GERBER, I. Predictors of mortality in the institutionalized aged. *Diseases of the Nervous System* 1966, *27*: 21–29.

GOLDFARB, A. I.; HOCHSTADT, N.; JACOBSON, J. H.; AND WEINSTEIN, E. A. Hyperbaric oxygen treatment of organic mental syndrome in aged persons. *Journal of Gerontology* 1972, *27*: 212–17.

GOLDFRIED, M. R., AND KENT, R. N. Traditional versus behavioral personality assessment: A comparison of methodological and theoretical assumptions. *Psychological Bulletin* 1972, 77: 409–20.

GOLDSTEIN, S. E., AND BIRNBOM, F. Hypochondriasis and the elderly. *Journal of the American Geriatrics Society* 1976, 24: 150–54.

GOODMAN, M. N. Age and adaptation to acute illness (myocardial infarction). *Proceedings*, 80th Annual Convention, American Psychological Association, 1972.

GOODWIN, F. K., AND BUNNEY, W. E., JR. Psychobiological aspects of stress and affective illness. In J. P. Scott and E. C. Senay, eds., *Separation and depression: Clinical and research aspects*. Washington: American Association for the Advancement of Science, 1973.

GORDON, S. K., AND CLARK, W. C. Application of signal detection theory to prose recall and recognition in elderly and young adults. *Journal of Gerontology* 1974, 29: 64–72.

GOTTESMAN, L. E. Resocialization of the geriatric mental patient. *American Journal of Public Health* 1965, 55: 1964–70.

GOTTESMAN, L. E. Milieu treatment of the aged in institutions. *Gerontologist* 1973, 13: 23–26.

GOTTESMAN, L. E., AND BOURESTOM, N. C. Why nursing homes do what they do. *Gerontologist* 1974, 14: 501–506.

GOULD, R. Adult life stages: Growth toward self-tolerance. *Psychology Today* 1975, 8 (Sep.): 74–78.

GRANGER, C. V., AND GREER, D. S. Functional status measurement and medical rehabilitation outcomes. *Archives of Physical Medicine and Rehabilitation* 1976, 57: 103–109.

GRANICK, S., AND PATTERSON, R. D. *Human aging II: An eleven-year follow-up biomedical and behavioral study*. Washington: Government Printing Office, 1972.

GRAUER, H.; BETTS, D.; AND BIRNBOM, F. Welfare emotions and family therapy in geriatrics. *Journal of the American Geriatrics Society* 1973, 21: 21–24.

GUREL, L.; LINN, M. W.; AND LINN, B. S. Physical and mental impairment-of-function evaluation in the aged: The PAMIE scale. *Journal of Gerontology* 1972, 27: 83–90.

GURLAND, B. J. A broad clinical assessment of psychopathology in the aged. In C. Eisdorfer and M. P. Lawton, eds., *The psychology of adult development and aging*. Washington: American Psychological Association, 1973.

GURLAND, B. J. The comparative frequency of depression in various adult age groups. *Journal of Gerontology* 1976, 31: 283–92.

GURLAND, B. J. The assessment of the mental status of older adults. In J. E. Birren and R. B. Sloane, eds., *Handbook of mental health and aging*. Englewood Cliffs, N.J.: Prentice-Hall, 1980.

GURLAND, B. J.; FLEISS, J. L.; GOLDBERG, K.; SHARPE, L.; COPELAND, J. R. M.; KELLEHER, M. J.; and KELLETT, J. The geriatric mental state schedule: A factor analysis. *International Journal of Aging and Human Development* 1976, 7: 303–11.

HALEY, J. *Strategies of psychotherapy.* New York: Grune & Stratton, 1963.

HALEY, J. A review of the family therapy field. In J. Haley, ed., *Changing families: A family therapy reader.* New York: Grune & Stratton, 1971.

HALEY, J. *Uncommon therapy: The psychiatric techniques of Milton H. Erickson.* New York: Ballantine Books, 1974.

HALEY, J. *Problem solving therapy.* San Francisco: Jossey-Bass, 1976.

HANEY, C.; BANKS, C.; AND ZIMBARDO, P. Interpersonal dynamics in a simulated prison. *International Journal of Criminology and Penology* 1973, 1: 69–97.

HANSSEN, A.; MEIMA, N.; BUCKSPAN, L.; HELBIG, T.; HENDERSON, B.; AND ZARIT, S. H. Correlates of senior center participation. *Gerontologist* 1978, 18: 193–200.

HARRIS, L., AND ASSOCIATES. *The myth and reality of aging in America.* Washington: National Council on Aging, 1975.

HARTFORD, M. E. *Groups in social work: Applications of small group research to social work practice.* New York: Columbia University Press, 1971.

HARTFORD, M. E. Groups in the human services: Some facts and fancies. *Social Work with Groups* 1978, 1: 7–13.

HARTMAN, W. E., AND FITHIAN, M. A. *Treatment of sexual dysfunction.* Long Beach, Calif.: California Center of Psychiatry, 1972.

HARTSHORNE, H., AND MAY, M. A. *Studies in deceit.* New York: Macmillan, 1928.

HAWKINS, D., AND MENDELS, J. Sleep disturbance in depressive syndromes. *American Journal of Psychiatry* 1966, 123: 6.

HAYFLICK, L. The biology of aging. *Natural History* 1977a (Sep.): 22–30.

HAYFLICK, L. The cellular basis for biological aging. In C. E. Finch and L. Hayflick, eds., *Handbook of the biology of aging.* New York: Van Nostrand Reinhold, 1977b.

HEINICKE, M. Parental deprivation in early childhood: A predisposition to later depression. In J. P. Scott and E. C. Senay, eds., *Separation and depression: Clinical and research aspects.* Washington: American Association for the Advancement of Science, 1973.

HELLERSTEIN, H. K., AND FRIEDMAN, E. H. Sexual activity and the post-coronary patient. *Archives of Internal Medicine* 1970, 125: 987–99.

HENDRICKS, J., AND HENDRICKS, C. D. *Aging in mass society: Myths and realities.* Cambridge, Mass.: Winthrop, 1977.

HERMAN, M. Activity programs in personal care homes. *Canadian Journal of Occupational Therapy* 1968, 35: 98–100.

HERON, A., AND CRAIK, F. I. M. Age differences in cumulative learning of meaningful and meaningless material. *Scandinavian Journal of Psychology* 1964, 5: 209–17.

HERR, J. J., AND WEAKLAND, J. H. *Counseling elders and their families.* New York: Springer, 1979.

HEYMANN, D. S., AND SABOL, S. M. A comparison of life satisfaction among three groups of older persons: Workers, volunteers, and those doing neither. Master's thesis, University of Southern California, 1977.

HILBERT, N. M.; NEIDEREHE, G.; AND KAHN, R. L. Accuracy and speed of memory in depressed and organic aged. *Educational Gerontology* 1976, 1: 131–46.

HOEHN-SARIC, R.; FRANK, J. D.; IMBER, S. D.; NASH, E. H.; STONE, A. R.; AND BATTLE, C. C. Systematic preparation of patients for psychotherapy: I. Effects on therapy behavior and outcome. *Journal of Psychiatric Research* 1964, 2: 267–81.

HOGAN, D. R. The effectiveness of sex therapy: A review of the literature. In J. LoPiccolo and L. LoPiccolo, eds., *Handbook of sex therapy*. New York: Plenum, 1978.

HOLLINGSHEAD, A. D., AND REDLICH, F. C. *Social class and mental illness.* New York: Wiley, 1958.

HOLMES, T., AND RAHE, R. H. The social readjustment scale. *Journal of Psychosomatic Research* 1967, 2: 213–17.

HOMBURGER, F., AND BONNER, C. D. *Medical care and rehabilitation of the aged and chronically ill.* 2d ed. Boston: Little, Brown, 1964.

HONZIK, M. P., AND MACFARLANE, J. W. Personality development and intellectual functioning from 21 months to 40 years. In L. F. Jarvik, C. Eisdorfer, and J. E. Blum, eds., *Intellectual functioning in adults: Psychological and biological influences.* New York: Springer, 1973.

HOPS, H. Behavioral treatment of marital problems. In W. E. Craighead, A. E. Kazdin, and M. J. Mahoney, eds., *Behavior modification.* Boston: Houghton Mifflin, 1976.

HORN, J. L., AND DONALDSON, G. On the myth of intellectual decline in adulthood. *American Psychologist* 1976, 31: 701–19.

How to buy a hearing aid. *Consumer Reports* 1976, 41: 345–51.

HOYER, W. J. Application of operant techniques to the modification of elderly behavior. *Gerontologist* 1973, 13: 18–22.

HULICKA, I. M. Age differences in retention as a function of interference. *Journal of Gerontology* 1967, 22: 180–84.

HULICKA, I. M., AND GROSSMAN, J. L. Age-group comparisons for the use of mediators in paired-associate learning. *Journal of Gerontology* 1967, 22: 46–51.

HULTSCH, D. Adult age differences in the organization of free recall. *Developmental Psychology* 1969, 1: 673–78.

HULTSCH, D. Adult age differences in free classification and free recall. *Developmental Psychology* 1971, 4: 338–42.

HUSTED, J. R. Desensitization procedures in dealing with female sexual dysfunction. In J. LoPiccolo and L. LoPiccolo, eds., *Handbook of sex therapy.* New York: Plenum, 1978.

INGLIS, J. Memory disorder. In C. G. Costello, ed., *Symptoms of psychopathology.* New York: Wiley, 1970.

IRVING, G.; ROBINSON, R.; AND McADAM, W. The validity of some cognitive tests in the diagnosis of dementia. *British Journal of Psychiatry* 1970, *117*: 149–56.

JACKSON, D. D., AND WEAKLAND, J. H. Conjoint family therapy: Some considerations on theory, technique and results. In J. Haley, ed., *Changing families: A family therapy reader*. New York: Grune & Stratton, 1971.

JACOBS, E. A.; WINTER, P. M.; ALVIS, H. J.; AND SMALL, S. M. Hyperoxygenation effects on cognitive functioning in the aged. *New England Journal of Medicine* 1969, *281*: 753–57.

JACOBS, J. *Fun city: An ethnographic study of a retirement community*. New York: Holt, Rinehart and Winston, 1974.

JACOBS, J. W.; BERNHARD, M. R.; DELGADO, A., AND STRAIN, J. J. Screening for organic mental syndromes in the medically ill. *Annals of Internal Medicine* 1977, *86*: 40–46.

JACOBS, S. C.; PRUSOFF, B. A.; AND PAYKEL, E. S. Recent life events in schizophrenia and depression. *Psychological Medicine* 1974, *4*: 444–53.

JARVIK, L. F. Thoughts on the psychobiology of aging. *American Psychologist* 1975, *30*: 567–83.

JEFFREY, D., AND KATZ, R. C. *Take it off and keep it off: A behavioral program for weight loss and exercise*. Englewood Cliffs, N.J.: Prentice-Hall, 1977.

JONES, D. C. Social isolation, interaction and conflict in two nursing homes. *Gerontologist* 1972, *12*: 230–34.

JUNG, C. G. *Modern man in search of a soul*. New York: Harcourt Brace Jovanovich, 1933.

KAHANA, B., AND KAHANA, E. Changes in mental status of elderly patients in age-integrated and age-segregated hospital milieus. *Journal of Abnormal Psychology* 1970, *75*: 177–81.

KAHN, E., AND FISHER, C. The sleep characteristics of the normal aged male. *Journal of Nervous and Mental Disease* 1969, *148*: 477–94.

KAHN, R. L. The mental health system and the future aged. *Gerontologist* 1975, *15* (1, pt. 2): 24–31.

KAHN, R. L. Excess disabilities. In S. H. Zarit, ed., *Readings in aging and death: Contemporary perspectives*. New York: Harper & Row, 1977.

KAHN, R. L., AND SCHLESINGER, B. Preoperative and postoperative personality changes accompanying frontal lobe meningioma. *Journal of Nervous and Mental Disease* 1951, *114*: 492–510.

KAHN, R. L., AND FINK, M. Changes in language during electroshock therapy. In P. H. Hoch and J. Zubin, eds., *Psychopathology of communication*. New York: Grune & Stratton, 1958.

KAHN, R. L.; GOLDFARB, A. I.; POLLACK, M.; AND PECK, R. Brief objective measures for the determination of mental status in the aged. *American Journal of Psychiatry* 1960, *117*: 326–28.

KAHN, R. L., AND ZARIT, S. H. Evaluation of mental health programs for the aged. In P. O. Davidson, F. W. Clark, and L. A. Hamerlynck, eds., *Evalua-

tion of behavioral programs: In community, residential and school settings. Champaign, Ill.: Research Press, 1974.

KAHN, R. L.; ZARIT, S. H.; HILBERT, N. M.; AND NIEDEREHE, G. Memory complaint and impairment in the aged. *Archives of General Psychiatry* 1975, *32:* 1569–73.

KAHN, R. L., AND MILLER, N. E. Assessment of altered brain function in the aged. In M. Storandt, I. C. Siegler, and M. F. Elias, eds., *The clinical psychology of aging.* New York: Plenum, 1978.

KALES, A., AND KALES, J. D. Evaluation, diagnosis and treatment of clinical conditions related to sleep. *Journal of the American Medical Association* 1970, *213:* 2229–34.

KALES, A.; BIXLER, E. O.; TAN, T. L.; SCHARF, M. B.; AND KALES, J. Chronic hypnotic use: Ineffectiveness, drug withdrawal and hypnotic drug dependence. *Journal of the American Medical Association* 1974, *227:* 513–17.

KANFER, F. H., AND SASLOW, G. Behavioral analysis: An alternative to diagnostic classification. *Archives of General Psychiatry* 1965, *12:* 529–38.

KANFER, F. H., AND SASLOW, G. Behavior diagnosis. In L. R. Allman and D. T. Jaffe, eds., *Readings in abnormal psychology: Contemporary perspectives.* New York: Harper & Row, 1976.

KAPLAN, H. S. *The new sex therapy: Active treatment of sexual dysfunctions.* New York: Brunner/Mazel, 1974.

KAPNICK, P. L. Organic treatment of the elderly. In M. Storandt, I. C. Siegler, and M. F. Elias, eds., *The clinical psychology of aging.* New York: Plenum, 1978.

KARACAN, I.; WILLIAMS, R. L.; LITTELL, R. C.; AND SALIS, P. J. Insomniacs: Unpredictable and idiosyncratic sleepers. In W. P. Koella and P. Levin, eds., *Sleep: Physiology, biochemistry, psychology, pharmacology—clinical implications.* Basel, Switzerland: Karger, 1973.

KASNIAK, A. W.; GARRON, D. C.; AND FOX, J. H. Mental status questionnaire scores, short-term memory and cerebral atrophy as measured by computerized tomography. Paper presented at the meetings of the Gerontological Society, Louisville, Ky., 1975.

KASTENBAUM, R. J. Loving, dying and other gerontologic addenda. In C. Eisdorfer and M. P. Lawton, eds., *The psychology of adult development and aging.* Washington: American Psychological Association, 1973.

KATCHADOURIAN, H. A., AND LUNDE, D. T. *Fundamentals of human sexuality.* New York: Holt, Rinehart and Winston, 1972.

KATZ, S.; FORD, A. B.; MOSKOWITZ, R. W.; JACKSON, B. S.; AND JAFFE, M. W. Studies of illness in the aged. The index of ADL: A standardized measure of biological and psychosocial function. *Journal of the American Medical Association* 1963, *185:* 914–19.

KAY, D. W. K. Late paraphrenia and its bearing on the etiology of schizophrenia. *Acta Psychiatrica Scandinavia* 1963, *39:* 159–69.

KAY, D. W. K. Epidemiological aspects of organic brain disease in the aged. In C. M. Gaitz, ed., *Aging and the brain.* New York: Plenum, 1972.

KAY, D. W. K. The epidemiology and identification of brain deficit in the elderly. In C. Eisdorfer and R. O. Friedel, eds., *Cognitive and emotional disturbances in the elderly*. Chicago: Year Book Medical Publishers, 1977.

KAY, D. W. K.; ROTH, M.; AND HOPKINS, B. Affective disorders arising in the senium: I. Their association with organic cerebral degeneration. *Journal of Mental Science* 1955, 101: 302–14.

KAY, D. W. K., AND ROTH, M. Environmental and hereditary factors in the schizophrenia of old age ("late paraphrenia") and their bearing on the general problem of causation in schizophrenia. *Journal of Mental Science* 1961, 107: 649–86.

KAY, D. W. K.; BEAMISH, P.; AND ROTH, M. Old age mental disorders in Newcastle upon Tyne. Part I. A study of prevalence. *British Journal of Psychiatry* 1964a, 10: 146–58.

KAY, D. W. K.; BEAMISH, P.; AND ROTH, M. Old age mental disorders in Newcastle upon Tyne. Part II. A study of possible social and medical causes. *British Journal of Psychiatry* 1964b, 110: 668–82.

KAY, D. W. K.; COOPER, A. F.; GARSIDE, R. F.; AND ROTH, M. The differentiation of paranoid from affective psychoses by patients' premorbid characteristics. *British Journal of Psychiatry* 1976, 129: 207–15.

KELLER, M. D. Living with pathology: The one-horse shay syndrome. In L. E. Brown and E. O. Ellis, eds., *Quality of life: The later years*. Acton, Mass.: Publishing Sciences Group, 1975.

KELLY, G. *The psychology of personal constructs*. 2 vols. New York: Norton, 1955.

KELLY, J. The aging male homosexual: Myth and reality. *Gerontologist* 1977, 17: 328–32.

KELMAN, H. R. An experiment in rehabilitation using nursing home patients. *Public Health Reports*. Public Health Service, U.S. Department of Health, Education, and Welfare, 1962, 77: 356–66.

KENNEDY, P. F. Schizophrenia and related paranoid states. *British Medical Journal* 1975, 2: 257–60.

KENSHALO, D. R. Age changes in touch, vibration, temperature, kinesthesis, and pain sensitivity. In J. E. Birren and K. W. Schaie, eds., *Handbook of the psychology of aging*. New York: Van Nostrand Reinhold, 1977.

KILLIAN, E. Effects of geriatric transfers on mortality rates. *Social Work* 1970, 15: 19–26.

KILOH, L. G. Pseudo-dementia. *Acta Psychiatria Scandinavia* 1961, 37: 336–51.

KIMMEL, D. C. *Adulthood and aging: An interdisciplinary, developmental view*. New York: Wiley, 1974.

KINSEY, A. C.; POMEROY, W. B.; AND MARTIN, C. E. *Sexual behavior in the human male*. Philadelphia: Saunders, 1948.

KINSEY, A. C.; POMEROY, W. B.; MARTIN, C. E.; AND GEBHARD, P. H. *Sexual behavior in the human female*. Philadelphia: Saunders, 1953.

KISTIN, H., AND MORRIS, R. Alternatives to institutional care for the elderly and disabled. *Gerontologist* 1972, *12*: 139–42.

KLEBAN, M. M., AND BRODY, E. M., Prediction of improvement in mentally impaired aged: Personality ratings by social workers. *Journal of Gerontology* 1972, *27*: 69–76.

KLEBAN, M. M.; BRODY, E. M.; AND LAWTON, M. P. Personality traits in the mentally impaired aged and their relationship to improvements in current functioning. *Gerontologist* 1971, *11*: 134–40.

KLERMAN, G. L. Clinical research in depression. *Archives of General Psychiatry* 1971, *24*: 305–19.

KOVACS, M., BECK, A. T., AND WEISMAN, A. The use of suicidal motives in the psychotherapy of attempted suicides. *American Journal of Psychotherapy* 1975, *29*: 363–68.

KRAL, V. A. Confusional states: Description and management. In J. G. Howells, ed., *Modern perspectives in the psychiatry of old age*. New York: Brunner/Mazel, 1975.

KRAMER, M.; TAUBE, A.; AND REDICK, R. W. Patterns of use of psychiatric facilities by the aged: Past, present and future. In C. Eisdorfer and M. Lawton, eds., *The psychology of adult development and aging*. Washington: American Psychological Association, 1973.

KRASNER, L. The operant approch in behavior modification. In J. T. Spence, R. C. Carson, and J. W. Thibaut, eds., *Behavioral approaches to therapy*. Morristown, N.J.: General Learning Press, 1974.

KÜBLER-ROSS, E. *On death and dying*. New York: Macmillan, 1968.

KÜBLER-ROSS, E. *Death: The final stage of growth*. Englewood Cliffs, N.J.: Prentice-Hall, 1975.

KUHLEN, R. G. Developmental changes in motivation during the adult years. In B. L. Neugarten, ed., *Middle age and aging: A reader in social psychology*. Chicago: University of Chicago Press, 1968.

KUYPERS, J. A. Internal-external locus of control, ego functioning and personality characteristics in old age. *Gerontologist* 1972, *12*: 168–73.

LABOUVIE-VIEF, G. Toward optimizing cognitive competence in later life. *Educational Gerontology* 1976, *1*: 75–92.

LANGE, A. J., AND JAKUBOWSKI, P. *Responsible assertive behavior*. Champaign, Ill.: Research Press, 1976.

LARSON, R. Thirty years of research on the subjective well-being of older Americans. *Journal of Gerontology* 1978, *33*: 109–29.

LATORRE, R. A., AND KEAR, K. Attitudes toward sex in the aged. *Archives of Sexual Behavior* 1977, *6*: 203–13.

LAWTON, M. P. The functional assessment of elderly people. *Journal of the American Geriatrics Society* 1971, *19*: 465–81.

LAWTON, M. P., AND SIMON, B. B. The ecology of social relationships in housing for the elderly. *Gerontologist* 1968, *8*: 108–15.

LAWTON, M. P.; LIEBOWITZ, B.; AND CHARON, H. Physical structure and the behavior of senile patients following ward remodeling. *Aging and Human Development* 1970, *1*: 231–39.

LAWTON, M. P., AND NAHEMOW, L. Ecology and the aging process. In C. Eisdorfer and M. P. Lawton, eds., *The psychology of adult development and aging.* Washington: American Psychological Association, 1973.

LAWTON, M. P., AND GOTTESMAN, L. E. Psychological services to the elderly. *American Psychologist* 1974, *29*: 689–93.

LEFF, M. J.; ROATCH, J. F.; AND BUNNEY, W. E. Environmental factors preceding the onset of severe depressions. *Psychiatry* 1970, *33*: 293–311.

LEIGHTON, D. C.; HARDING, J. S.; MACKLIN, D. B.; MACMILLAN, A. M.; AND LEIGHTON, A. H. *The character of danger: Psychiatric symptoms in selected communities.* New York: Basic Books, 1963.

LEVI, L. D.; FALES, C. G.; STEIN, M.; AND SHARP, V. H. Separation and attempted suicide. *Archives of General Psychiatry* 1966, *15*: 158–65.

LEVINSON, D. J.; DARROW, C. M.; KLEIN, E. B.; LEVINSON, M. H.; AND McKEE, B. The psychosocial development of men in early adulthood and the mid-life transition. In D. F. Ricks, A. Thomas, and M. Roff, eds., *Life history research in psychopathology.* Vol. 3. Minneapolis: University of Minnesota Press, 1973.

LEWINSOHN, P. M. *Manual for decreasing unpleasant activities and increasing pleasant activities.* Unpublished manuscript.

LEWINSOHN, P. M., AND LIBET, J. Pleasant events, activity schedules, and depression. *Journal of Abnormal Psychology* 1972, *79*: 291–95.

LEWINSOHN, P. M., AND MACPHILLAMY, D. The relationship between age and engagement in pleasant activities. *Journal of Gerontology* 1974, *29*: 290–94.

LEWINSOHN, P. M.; BIGLAN, A.; AND ZEISS, A. M. Behavioral treatment of depression. In P. O. Davidson, ed., *The behavioral management of anxiety, depression and pain.* New York: Brunner/Mazel, 1976.

LEWINSOHN, P. M.; DANAHER, B. G.; AND KIKEL, S. Visual imagery as a mnemonic aid for brain-injured persons. *Journal of Consulting and Clinical Psychology* 1977, *45*: 717–23.

LEWINSOHN, P. M.; MUNOZ, R. F.; YOUNGREN, M. A.; AND ZEISS, A. M. *Control your depression.* Englewood Cliffs, N.J.: Prentice-Hall, 1978.

LIBB, J. W., AND CLEMENTS, C. B. Token reinforcement in an exercise program for hospitalized geriatric patients. *Perception and Motor Skills* 1969, *28*: 9–17.

LIBOW, L. S. Senile dementia and "pseudosenility": Clinical diagnosis. In C. Eisdorfer and R. O. Friedel, eds., *Cognitive and emotional disturbances in the elderly.* Chicago: Year Book Medical Publishers, 1977.

LIEBERMAN, M. A. Psychological correlates of impending death: Some preliminary observations. In B. L. Neugarten, ed., *Middle age and aging: A reader in social psychology.* Chicago: University of Chicago Press, 1968.

LIEBERMAN, M. A. Institutionalization of the aged: Effects on behavior. *Journal of Gerontology* 1969, *24*: 330–40.

LIEBERMAN, M. A. Relocation research and social policy. *Gerontologist* 1974, *14*: 494–501.

LIEBERMAN, M. A.; YALOM, I. D.; AND MILES, M. B. *Encounter groups: First facts.* New York: Basic Books, 1973.

LINN, L.; KAHN, R. L.; COLES, R.; COHEN, J.; MARSHALL, D.; AND WEINSTEIN, E. A. Patterns of behavior disturbance following cataract extraction. *American Journal of Psychiatry* 1953, *110*: 281–89.

LINN, M. W. Studies in rating the physical, mental and social dysfunction of the chronically ill aged. *Medical Care* 1976, *14* (5, supp.): 119–25.

LIPOWSKI, Z. J. Delirium, clouding of consciousness and confusion. *Journal of Nervous and Mental Disease* 1967, *145*: 227–55.

LIPTON, M. A. Age differentiation in depression: Biochemical aspects. *Journal of Gerontology* 1976, *31*: 293–99.

LOBITZ, W. C., AND LOBITZ, G. K. Clinical assessment in the treatment of sexual dysfunction. In J. LoPiccolo and L. LoPiccolo, eds., *Handbook of sex therapy.* New York: Plenum, 1978.

LOPATA, H. Z. *Widowhood in an American city.* Cambridge, Mass.: Schenkman, 1973.

LOPICCOLO, J. Direct treatment of sexual dysfunction. In J. LoPiccolo and L. LoPiccolo, eds., *Handbook of sex therapy.* New York: Plenum, 1978.

LOPICCOLO, J., AND LOBITZ, W. C. The role of masturbation in the treatment of orgasmic dysfunction. In J. LoPiccolo and L. LoPiccolo, eds., *Handbook of sex therapy.* New York: Plenum, 1978.

LOPICCOLO, J., AND LOPICCOLO, L., eds. *Handbook of sex therapy.* New York: Plenum, 1978.

LORAYNE, H., AND LUCAS, J. *The memory book.* New York: Ballantine Books, 1974.

LOWENTHAL, M. F. Social isolation and mental illness in old age. *American Sociological Review* 1964, *29*: 54–70.

LOWENTHAL, M. F. Antecedents of isolation and mental illness in old age. *Archives of General Psychiatry* 1965, *12*: 245–54.

LOWENTHAL, M. F. Social isolation and mental illness in old age. In B. L. Neugarten, ed., *Middle age and aging: A reader in social psychology.* Chicago: University of Chicago Press, 1968.

LOWENTHAL, M. F., AND BOLER, D. Voluntary versus involuntary withdrawal. *Journal of Gerontology* 1965, *20*: 363–71.

LOWENTHAL, M. F.; BERKMAN, P.; AND ASSOCIATES. *Aging and mental disorder in San Francisco.* San Francisco: Jossey-Bass, 1967.

LOWENTHAL, M. F., AND HAVEN, C. Interaction and adaptation: Intimacy as a critical variable. *American Sociological Review* 1968, *33*: 20–30.

LOWENTHAL, M. F., AND CHIRIBOGA, D. Transition to the empty nest. *Archives of General Psychiatry* 1972, *26*: 8–14.

LOWENTHAL, M. F., AND CHIRIBOGA, D. Social stress and adaptation: Toward a life course perspective. In C. Eisdorfer and M. P. Lawton, eds., *The psychology of adult development and aging.* Washington: American Psychological Association, 1973.

LOWENTHAL, M. F.; THURNHER, M.; AND CHIRIBOGA, D. *Four stages of life.* San Francisco: Jossey-Bass, 1975.

LOWENTHAL, M. F., AND ROBINSON, B. Social networks and isolation. In R. H. Binstock and E. Shanas, eds., *Handbook of aging and the social sciences.* New York: Van Nostrand Reinhold, 1976.

LOWY, L. Roadblocks in group work practice with older people: A framework for analysis. *Gerontologist* 1967, *2*: 109–13.

LUCE, G. G., AND SEGAL, J. *Insomnia: The guide for troubled sleepers.* Garden City, N.Y.: Doubleday, 1969.

MAAS, H. S., AND KUYPERS, J. A. *From thirty to seventy.* San Francisco: Jossey-Bass, 1974.

MACDONNELL, J. A.; MCKENZIE, D. A.; AND CHEETHAM, E. Social effects of intermittent readmission. *Gerontologist* 1968, *8*: 38–42.

MACMILLAN, D. Hospital-community relationships. In *An approach to the prevention of disability from chronic psychoses: The open mental hospital within the community.* New York: Millbank Memorial Fund, 1958.

MACMILLAN, D. Problems of a geriatric mental health service. *British Journal of Psychiatry* 1967, *113*: 175–81.

MADDISON, D., AND VIOLA, A. The health of widows in the year following bereavement. *Journal of Psychosomatic Research* 1968, *12*: 297–306.

MADDOX, G. L. Self-assessment of health status: A longitudinal study of selected elderly subjects. *Journal of Chronic Diseases* 1964, *17*: 449–60.

MADDOX, G. L. Persistence of life style among the elderly: A longitudinal study of patterns of social activity in relation to life satisfaction. In B. L. Neugarten, ed., *Middle age and aging: A reader in social psychology.* Chicago: University of Chicago Press, 1968.

MAHONEY, F. I., AND BARTHEL, B. W. Functional evaluation: The Barthel index. *Maryland State Medical Journal* 1965, *14*: 61–65.

MAHONEY, M. J. *Cognition and behavior modification.* Cambridge, Mass.: Ballinger, 1974.

MANDLER, G. Organization and memory. In K. W. Spence and J. T. Spence, eds., *The psychology of learning and motivation: Advances in research and theory.* Vol. 1. New York: Academic Press, 1967.

MARMOR, J. *Psychiatrists and their patients: A national study of private practice psychiatrists.* Washington: American Psychiatric Association, 1975.

MARSH, G. R., AND THOMPSON, L. W. Psychophysiology of aging. In J. E. Birren and K. W. Schaie, eds., *Handbook of the psychology of aging.* New York: Van Nostrand Reinhold, 1977.

MARX, J. L. Aging research (I): Cellular theories of senescence. *Science* 1974a, *186*: 1105–1107.

MARX, J. L. Aging research (II): Pacemakers for aging. *Science* 1974b, *186*: 1196–97.

Maslow, A. H. *Toward a psychology of being.* 2d ed. New York: Van Nostrand Reinhold, 1968.

Masters, W. H., and Johnson, V. E. *Human sexual response.* Boston: Little, Brown, 1966.

Masters, W. H., and Johnson, V. E. *Human sexual inadequacy.* Boston: Little, Brown, 1970.

McGinity, P. J., and Stotsky, B. A. The patient in the nursing home. *Nursing Forum* 1967, 6: 238–61.

McGovern, K. B.; McMullen, R. S.; and LoPiccolo, J. Secondary orgasmic dysfunction. I. Analysis and strategies for treatment. In J. LoPiccolo and L. LoPiccolo, eds., *Handbook of sex therapy.* New York: Plenum, 1978.

McKain, W. C., Jr. A new look at older marriages. *Family Coordinator* 1972, 21: 61–70.

McLemore, C. W., and Benjamin, L. S. What ever happened to interpersonal diagnosis? A psychosocial alternative to DSM III. *American Psychologist* 1979, 34: 17–34.

McNulty, J. A., and Caird, W. K. Memory loss with age: Retrieval or storage. *Psychological Reports* 1966, 19: 229–30.

Mechanic, D. Social factors affecting the presentation of bodily complaints. *New England Journal of Medicine* 1972, 286: 1132–39.

Mechanic, D. *Medical sociology.* 2d ed. New York: Free Press, 1978.

Meichenbaum, D. Cognitive behavior modification. In J. T. Spence, R. C. Carson, and J. W. Thibaut, eds., *Behavioral approaches to therapy.* Morristown, N.J.: General Learning Press, 1976.

Meichenbaum, D. *Cognitive-behavior modification.* New York: Plenum, 1977.

Meichenbaum, D.; Gilmore, B.; and Fedoravicius, A. Group insight versus group desensitization in treating speech anxiety. *Journal of Consulting and Clinical Psychology* 1971, 36: 410–21.

Meichenbaum, D., and Cameron, R. Training schizophrenics to talk to themselves: A means of developing attentional controls. *Behavior Therapy* 1973, 4: 515–34.

Meier-Ruge, W.; Enz, A.; Gygas, P.; Hunziker, O.; Iwangoff, P.; and Reichlmeier, K. Experimental pathology in basic research of the aging brain. In S. Gershon and A. Raskin, eds., *Aging: Volume 2. Genesis and treatment of psychologic disorders in the elderly.* New York: Raven Press, 1975.

Mendels, J., and Chernik, D. A. Sleep changes and affective illness. In F. F. Flach and S. C. Draghi, eds., *The nature and treatment of depression.* New York: Wiley, 1975.

Mendelson, M. A. *Tender loving greed: How the incredibly lucrative nursing home industry is exploiting America's old.* New York: Knopf, 1974.

Mendlewicz, J. The age factor in depressive illness: Some genetic considerations. *Journal of Gerontology* 1976, 31: 300–303.

Merritt, C. G.; Gerstl, J. E.; and LoSciuto, L. A. Age and perceived effects

432   References

of erotica-pornography. A national sample study. *Archives of Sexual Behavior* 1975, 4: 605–21.

MEYER, J. E. Psychoneuroses and neurotic reactions in old age. *Journal of the American Geriatrics Society* 1974, 22: 254–57.

MINTZ, R. S. Psychotherapy of the suicidal patient. In H. L. P. Resnik, ed., *Suicidal behavior: Diagnosis and management.* Boston: Little, Brown, 1968.

MISCHEL, W. *Personality and assessment.* New York: Wiley, 1968.

MISCHEL, W. *Introduction to personality.* 2d ed. New York: Holt, Rinehart and Winston, 1976.

MISCHEL, W. On the future of personality measurement. *American Psychologist* 1977, 32: 246–54.

MONROE, J. L. Psychological and physiological differences between good and poor sleepers. *Journal of Abnormal Psychology* 1968, 72: 255–64.

MONTGOMERY, J. E. The housing patterns of older families. *Family Coordinator* 1972, 21: 37–46.

MORRIS, J. B., AND BECK, A. T. The efficiency of anti-depressant drugs: A review of research 1958–1972. *Archives of General Psychiatry* 1974, 30: 667–74.

MORRISON, M. Rehabilitation of the elderly patient. *Physiotherapy* 1969, 55: 190–97.

MOUSTAKAS, C. Communal loneliness. In S. H. Zarit, ed., *Readings in aging and death: Contemporary perspectives.* New York: Harper & Row, 1977.

MURPHY, G. E., AND ROBINS, E. The communication of suicidal ideas. In H. L. P. Resnik, ed., *Suicidal behaviors: Diagnosis and management.* Boston: Little, Brown, 1968.

NASH, B. E. Foster grandparents in child care settings. *Public Welfare* 1968, 26: 272–80.

NATHAN, P. E., AND HARRIS, S. L. *Psychopathology and society.* New York: McGraw-Hill, 1975.

NEUGARTEN, B. L. Personality and the aging process. *Gerontologist* 1972, 12: 9–15.

NEUGARTEN, B. L. Personality change in late life: A developmental perspective. In C. Eisdorfer and M. P. Lawton, eds., *The psychology of adult development and aging.* Washington: American Psychological Association, 1973.

NEUGARTEN, B. L. The future and the young-old. *Gerontologist* 1975, 15 (1, pt. 2): 4–9.

NEUGARTEN, B. L. Personality and aging. In J. E. Birren and K. W. Schaie, eds., *Handbook of the psychology of aging.* New York: Van Nostrand Reinhold, 1977.

NEUGARTEN, B. L., AND ASSOCIATES. *Personality in middle and late life.* New York: Atherton, 1964.

NEUGARTEN, B. L., AND GUTMANN, D. L. Age-sex roles and personality in middle age: A thematic apperception study. In B. L. Neugarten, ed., *Middle age and aging: A reader in social psychology.* Chicago: University of Chicago Press, 1968.

NEUGARTEN, B. L.; HAVIGHURST, R. J.; AND TOBIN, S. S. Personality and patterns of aging. In B. L. Neugarten, ed., *Middle age and aging: A reader in social psychology.* Chicago: University of Chicago Press, 1968.

NEUGARTEN, B. L., AND WEINSTEIN, K. K. The changing American grandparent. In B. L. Neugarten, ed., *Middle age and aging: A reader in social psychology.* Chicago: University of Chicago Press, 1968.

NEUGARTEN, B. L.; WOOD, V.; KRAINES, R. J.; AND LOOMIS, B. Women's attitudes toward the menopause. In B. L. Neugarten, ed., *Middle age and aging: A reader in social psychology.* Chicago: University of Chicago Press, 1968.

NEUGARTEN, B. L., AND HAGESTAD, G. O. Age and the life course. In R. H. Binstock and E. Shanas, eds., *Handbook of aging and the social sciences.* New York: Van Nostrand Reinhold, 1976.

OCHBERG, F. M.; ZARCONE, V.; AND HAMBURG, D. A. Symposium on institutionalism. *Comprehensive Psychiatry* 1972, *13*: 91–104.

ORNE, M. T., AND WENDER, P. H. Anticipatory socialization for psychotherapy: Method and rationale. *American Journal of Psychiatry* 1968, *124*: 1202–12.

PALMORE, E. B., AND WHITTINGTON, F. Trends in the relative status of the aged. *Social Forces* 1971, *50* (Sep.): 84–91.

PAPPAS, W.; PAGE, C. W.; AND BAKER, J. A controlled study of an intensive treatment program for hospitalized geriatric patients. *Geriatrics* 1958, *6*: 17–26.

PARKES, C. M. The effects of bereavement on physical and mental health: A case study. *British Medical Journal* 1964, *2*: 274.

PARKES, C. M. The first year of bereavement: A longitudinal study of the reaction of London widows to the death of their husbands. *Psychiatry* 1970, *33*: 444–67.

PARSONS, T. *The social system.* New York: Free Press, 1951.

PASTALAN, L. A.; MAUTZ, R. K.; AND MERRILL, J. The simulation of age-related losses: A new approach to the study of environmental barriers. In W. F. E. Preiser, ed., *Environmental design research.* Vol. 1. Stroudsberg, Penna.: Powden, Hutchinson and Ross, 1973.

PAUL, G. L., AND BERNSTEIN, D. A. Anxiety and clinical problems: Systematic desensitization and related techniques. In J. T. Spence, R. C. Carson, and J. W. Thibaut, eds., *Behavioral approaches to therapy.* Morristown, N.J.: General Learning Press, 1976.

PAYKEL, E. S. Recent life events and clinical depression. In E. K. E. Gunderson and R. H. Rahe, eds., *Life stress and illness.* Springfield, Ill.: Thomas, 1974.

PAYKEL, E. S. Environmental variables in the etiology of depression. In F. F. Flach and S. C. Draghi, eds., *The Nature and Treatment of Depression.* New York: Wiley, 1975.

PAYKEL, E. S.; MYERS, J. K.; DIENELT, M. N.; KLERMAN, G. L.; LINDENTHAL, J. J.; AND PEPPER, M. P. Life events and depression: A controlled study. *Archives of General Psychiatry* 1969, *21*: 753–60.

PEAK, D. Psychiatric problems of the elderly seen in an outpatient clinic. In E. Pfeiffer, ed., *Alternatives to institutional care for older Americans: Practice and planning.* Durham, N.C.: Center for the Study of Aging and Human Development, 1973.

PECK, R. C. Psychological developments in the second half of life. In B. L. Neugarten, ed., *Middle age and aging: A reader in social psychology.* Chicago: University of Chicago Press, 1968.

PENCHANSKY, R., AND TAUBENHAUS, L. J. Institutional factors affecting the quality of care in nursing homes. *Geriatrics* 1965, 20: 591–98.

PEREZ, F. I.; GAY, J. R. A.; TAYLOR, R. L.; AND RIVERA, V. M. Patterns of memory performance in the neurologically impaired aged. *Canadian Journal of Neurological Sciences* 1975, 2: 340–55.

PERLIN, S., AND BUTLER, R. N. Psychiatric aspects of adaptation to the aging experience. In J. E. Birren, R. N. Butler, S. W. Greenhouse, L. Sokoloff, and M. R. Yarrow, eds., *Human aging: A biological and behavioral study.* Washington: U.S. Department of Health, Education, and Welfare, 1963.

PERLIN, S., AND KAHN, R. L. A mental health center in a general hospital. In L. J. Duhl and R. L. Leopold, eds., *Mental health and urban social policy: A casebook of community actions.* San Francisco: Jossey-Bass, 1968.

PERLMUTTER, M. What is memory aging the aging of? *Developmental Psychology* 1978, 14: 330–45.

PETERSON, J. A. Death and dying and mental health. In J. E. Birren and R. B. Sloane, eds., *Handbook of mental health and aging.* Englewood Cliffs, N.J.: Prentice-Hall, 1980.

PFEIFFER, E. A short portable mental status questionnaire for the assessment of organic brain deficit in elderly patients. *Journal of the American Geriatrics Society* 1975a, 23: 433–39.

PFEIFFER, E. *Functional assessment: The OARS multidimensional functional assessment questionnaire.* Durham, N.C.: Duke University Center for the Study of Aging and Human Development, 1975b.

PFEIFFER, E. Psychopathology and social pathology. In J. E. Birren and K. W. Schaie, eds., *Handbook of psychology and aging.* New York: Van Nostrand Reinhold, 1977.

PFEIFFER, E.; VERWOERDT, A.; AND WANG, H.-S. Sexual behavior in aged men and women. I. Observations on 254 community volunteers. *Archives of General Psychiatry* 1968, 19: 753–58.

PFEIFFER, E.; VERWOERDT, A.; AND WANG, H.-S. The natural history of sexual behavior in a biologically advantaged group of aged individuals. *Journal of Gerontology* 1969, 24: 193–98.

PFEIFFER, E.; AND DAVIS, G. C. Determinants of sexual behavior in middle and old age. *Journal of the American Geriatrics Society* 1972, 20: 151–58.

PFEIFFER, E., AND BUSSE, E. W. Mental disorders in later life—affective disorders: Paranoid, neurotic and situational reactions. In E. W. Busse and E. Pfeiffer, eds., *Mental illness in later life.* Washington: American Psychiatric Association, 1973.

PILOWSKY, I. Primary and secondary hypochondriasis. *Acta Psychiatrica Scandinavica* 1970, *46*: 273–85.

POKORNY, A. D. Myths about suicide. In H. L. P. Resnik, ed., *Suicidal behaviors: Diagnosis and management.* Boston: Little, Brown, 1968.

POST, F. *The significance of affective symptoms in old age.* London: Oxford University Press, 1962.

POST, F. *Persistent persecutory states in the elderly.* New York: Pergamon Press, 1966.

POST, F. Psychological aspects of geriatrics. *Postgraduate Medicine* 1968, *4*: 307–18.

POST, F. Paranoid disorders in the elderly. *Postgraduate Medicine* 1973, *53*: 52–56.

POST, F. Dementia, depression, and pseudodementia. In D. F. Benson and D. Blumer, eds., *Psychiatric aspects of neurologic disease.* New York: Grune & Stratton, 1975.

POST, F. Paranoid, schizophrenia-like and schizophrenic states in the aged. In J. E. Birren and R. B. Sloane, eds., *Handbook of mental health and aging.* Englewood Cliffs, N.J.: Prentice-Hall, 1980.

PRANGE, A. J. Pharmacotherapy of depression. In F. F. Flach and S. C. Draghi, eds., *The nature and treatment of depression.* New York: Wiley, 1975.

PUNER, M. *To the good long life: What we know about growing old.* New York: Universe Books, 1974.

RAHE, R. H. Subjects' recent life changes and their near-future illness reports. *Annals of Clinical Research* 1972, *4*: 250–65.

RAHE, R. H. Life change and subsequent illness reports. In E. K. E. Gunderson and R. H. Rahe, eds., *Life stress and illness.* Springfield, Ill.: Thomas, 1974.

REDICK, R. W. Patterns in use of nursing homes by the aged mentally ill. *Statistical Note 107.* Rockville, Md.: Biometry Branch, N.I.M.H., 1974.

REEDY, M. N., AND BIRREN, J. E. How do lovers grow old together? Types of lovers and age. Paper presented at the meetings of the Gerontological Society, Dallas, 1978.

REES, J., AND BOTWINICK, J. Detection and decision factors in auditory behavior of the elderly. *Journal of Gerontology* 1971, *26*: 133–36.

REES, W. D., AND LUTKINS, S. G. Mortality of bereavement. *British Medical Journal* 1967, *4*: 13–16.

REEVER, K.; BACH-PETERSON, J. M.; AND ZARIT, S. H. Relatives of the impaired elderly: Correlates of feelings of burden. Presented at the meetings of the Gerontological Society, Washington, 1979.

REICHARD, S.; LIVSON, F.; AND PETERSON, P. G. *Aging and personality: A study of 87 older men.* New York: Wiley, 1962.

RESNIK, H. L. P., AND CANTOR, J. M. Suicide and aging. *Journal of the American Geriatrics Society* 1970, *18*: 152–58.

RETTERSTÖL, N. Paranoid psychoses. *British Journal of Psychiatry* 1968, *114*: 553–62.

RICHARDS, W. S., AND THORPE, G. L. Behavioral approaches to the problems of later life. In M. Storandt, I. C. Siegler, and M. F. Elias, eds., *The clinical psychology of aging*. New York: Plenum, 1978.

RIDING, J., AND MUNRO, A. Pimozide in the treatment of monosymptomatic hypochondriacal psychosis. *Acta Psychiatrica Scandinavica* 1975, 52: 23–30.

RIEGEL, K. F., AND RIEGEL, R. M. Development, drop and death. *Developmental Psychology* 1972, 6: 309–19.

RILEY, M. W.; FONER, A.; MOORE, M. E.; HESS, B.; AND ROTH, B. K. *Aging and society: Vol. 1. An inventory of research findings*. New York: Russell Sage Foundation, 1968.

RILEY, M. W.; FONER, A.; HESS, B.; AND TOBY, M. Socialization for the middle and later years. In D. Goslin, ed., *Handbook of socialization theory and research*. Chicago: Rand McNally, 1969.

RIMM, D. C., AND MASTERS, J. C. *Behavior therapy: Techniques and empirical findings*. New York: Academic Press, 1974.

ROBERTSON, D.; GRIFFITHS, A.; AND COSIN, L. Z. A community-based continuing care program for the elderly disabled: An evaluation of planned intermittent hospital readmission. *Gerontologist* 1977, 32: 334–39.

ROGERS, C. R. *Client-centered therapy*. Boston: Houghton Mifflin, 1951.

ROGERS, C. R., AND DYMOND, R. F., eds. *Psychotherapy and personality change; Co-ordinated studies in the client-centered approach*. Chicago: University of Chicago Press, 1954.

ROSE, S. D. *Group therapy: A behavioral approach*. Englewood Cliffs, N.J.: Prentice-Hall, 1977.

ROSENHAN, D. L. On being sane in insane places. *Science* 1972, 179: 250–58.

ROSIN, A. J., AND GLATT, M. M. Alcohol excess in the elderly. *Quarterly Journal of Studies on Alcohol* 1971, 32: 53–59.

Rosow, I. *Social integration of the aged*. New York: Free Press, 1967.

Rosow, I. *Socialization to old age*. Berkeley: University of California Press, 1974.

ROSSMAN, I., ed. *Clinical geriatrics*. Philadelphia: Lippincott, 1971.

ROTH, M. The natural history of mental disorder in old age. *Journal of Mental Science* 1955, 101: 281–89.

ROTH, M., AND HOPKINS, B. Psychological test performance in patients over sixty. I. Senile psychosis and the affective disorders of old age. *Journal of Mental Science* 1953, 99: 439–50.

ROTH, M.; TOMLINSON, B. E.; AND BLESSED, G. The relationship between quantitative measures of dementia and of degenerative changes in cerebral gray matter of elderly subjects. *Proceedings of the Royal Society of Medicine* 1967, 60: 254.

ROTHSCHILD, D. Pathological changes in senile psychosis and their psychiatric significance. *American Journal of Psychiatry* 1937, 93: 757–88.

ROTHSCHILD, D. Neuropathological changes in arteriosclerotic psychosis and their psychological significance. *Archives of Neurology and Psychiatry* 1942, 48: 417–36.

ROTTER, J. B. Generalized expectancies for internal versus external control of reinforcement. *Psychological Monographs* 1966, *80* (1, Whole No. 609).

RUBENSTEIN, B.; ZAIDI, Q.; AND KAHN, R. L. Factors affecting the relationship of stress and depression in older persons. Paper presented at the 29th Annual Meeting of the Gerontological Society, New York, 1976.

RUBENSTEIN, R.; MOSES, B.; AND LIDZ, T. On attempted suicide. *Archives of Neurology and Psychiatry* 1958, *79:* 103–12.

SAINSBURY, P. Suicide in later life. *Gerontologica Clinica* 1962, *4:* 161–70.

SALTZ, S. Aging persons as child-care workers in a foster grandparent program: Psychosocial effects and work performance. *Aging and Human Development* 1971, *2:* 314–40.

SALZMAN, C., AND SHADER, R. I. Response to psychotropic drugs in the normal elderly. In C. Eisdorfer and W. E. Fann, eds., *Psychopharmacology and aging.* New York: Plenum, 1975.

SANFORD, J. R. A. Tolerance of debility in elderly dependents by supports at home: Its significance for hospital practice. *British Medical Journal* 1975, *3:* 471–73.

SATHANANTHAN, G. L., AND GERSHON, S. Cerebral vasodilators: A review. In S. Gershon and A. Raskin, eds., *Aging: Vol. 2. Genesis and treatment of psychologic disorders in the elderly.* New York: Raven Press, 1975.

SAUL, S. R., AND SAUL, S. Group psychotherapy in a proprietary nursing home. *Gerontologist* 1974, *14:* 446–50.

SCHAIE, K. W. Age changes and age differences. *Gerontologist* 1967, *7:* 128–32.

SCHAIE, K. W. Age changes in adult intelligence. In D. S. Woodruff & J. E. Birren, eds., *Aging: Scientific perspectives and social issues.* New York: D. Van Nostrand, 1975.

SCHAIE, K. W., AND MARQUETTE, B. Personality in maturity and old age. In R. M. Dreger, ed., *Multivariate personality: Contributions to the under-standing of personality in honor of Raymond B. Cattell.* Baton Rouge, La.: Claitor, 1972.

SCHAIE, K. W., AND LABOUVIE-VIEF, G. Generational versus ontogenetic components of change in adult cognitive behavior: A fourteen-year cross-sequential study. *Developmental Psychology* 1974, *10:* 305–20.

SCHAIE, K. W., AND PARHAM, I. A. Stability of adult personality: Fact or fable? *Journal of Personality and Social Psychology* 1974, *34:* 146–58.

SCHAIE, K. W., AND GRIBBIN, K. Adult development and aging. *Annual Review of Psychology* 1975a, *26:* 65–96.

SCHAIE, K. W., AND GRIBBIN, K. The impact of environmental complexity upon adult cognitive development. *Proceedings of the 3rd Biennial Meeting of the International Society for the Study of Behavioral Development,* Guilsford, England, 1975b.

SCHAIE, K. W., AND SCHAIE, J. P. Clinical assessment and aging. In J. E. Birren and K. W. Schaie, eds., *Handbook of the psychology of aging.* New York: Van Nostrand Reinhold, 1977.

SCHEIN, V. E. Personality dimensions and needs. In M. W. Riley and A.

Foner, eds., *Aging and society. Vol. 1. An inventory of research findings.* New York: Russell Sage Foundation, 1968.

SCHIFFMAN, S. Food recognition by the elderly. *Journal of Gerontology* 1977, 32: 586–92.

SCHLESS, A. P.; SCHWARTZ, L.; GOETZ, C.; AND MENDELS, J. How depressives view the significance of life events. *British Journal of Psychiatry* 1974, 125: 406–10.

SCHONFIELD, D. Memory changes with age. *Nature* 1965, 28: 918.

SCHONFIELD, D. Translations in gerontology—From lab to life: Utilizing information. *American Psychologist* 1974, 29: 796–801.

SCHUCKIT, M. A. Geriatric alcoholism and drug abuse. *Gerontologist* 1977, 17: 168–74.

SCHULZ, J. H. Income distribution and the aging. In R. H. Binstock and E. Shanas, eds., *Handbook of aging and the social sciences.* New York: Van Nostrand Reinhold, 1976.

SCHULZ, R., AND BRENNER, G. Relocation of the aged: A review and theoretical analysis. *Journal of Gerontology* 1977, 32: 323–32.

SCHWARTZ, A. N., AND KLEEMEIER, R. W. The effects of illness and age upon some aspects of personality. *Journal of Gerontology* 1965, 20: 85–91.

SCHWARTZ, E., AND GOODMAN, J. Group therapy of obesity in elderly diabetics. *Geriatrics* 1952, 7: 280–83.

SELIGMAN, M. E. P. *Helplessness.* San Francisco: Freeman, 1975.

SELYE, H. *Stress without distress.* Philadelphia: Lippincott, 1974.

SEMANS, J. H. Pre-mature ejaculation: A new approach. *Southern Medical Journal* 1956, 49: 353–61.

SETHI, B. B. Relationship of separation to depression. *Archives of General Psychiatry* 1964, 10: 486–95.

SHANAS, E.; TOWNSEND, P.; WEDDERBURN, D.; FRIIS, H.; MILHØJ, P.; AND STEHOUWER, J. *Old people in three industrial societies.* New York: Atherton, 1968.

SHAPIRO, A. A pilot program in music therapy with residents of a home for the aged. *Gerontologist* 1969, 9: 128–33.

SHEARER, M. R., AND SHEARER, M. L. Sexuality and sexual counseling in the elderly. *Clinical Obstetrics and Gynecology* 1977, 20: 197–208.

SHEPPARD, H. L. Work and retirement. In R. H. Binstock and E. Shanas, eds., *Handbook of aging and the social sciences.* New York: Van Nostrand Reinhold, 1976.

SHNEIDMAN, E. S. Postvention and the survivor-victim. In E. S. Shneidman, ed., *Death: Current perspectives.* Palo Alto, Calif.: Mayfield, 1976.

SHNEIDMAN, E. S., AND FARBEROW, N. L. The suicide prevention center of Los Angeles. In H. L. P. Resnik, ed., *Suicidal behavior: Diagnosis and management.* Boston: Little, Brown, 1968.

SHOCK, N. W. Biologic concepts of aging. In A. Simon and L. J. Epstein, eds., *Aging in modern society.* Washington: American Psychiatric Association (Psychiatric Research Report #23), 1968.

SHOCK, N. W. Systems integration. In C. E. Finch and L. Hayflick, eds., *Handbook of the biology of aging.* New York: Van Nostrand Reinhold, 1977.

SILVERMAN, P. Widowhood and preventive intervention. In S. H. Zarit, ed., *Readings in aging and death: Contemporary perspectives.* New York: Harper & Row, 1977.

SIMON, A., AND CAHAN, R. The acute brain syndrome in geriatric patients. In W. M. Mendel and L. J. Epstein, eds., *Acute psychotic reaction.* Washington: American Psychiatric Association, 1963.

SIMON, A.; EPSTEIN, L. J.; AND REYNOLDS, L. Alcoholism in the geriatric mentally ill. *Geriatrics* 1968, 23: 125–31.

SIMOS, B. G. Adult children and their aging parents. *Social Work* 1973, 18: 78–85.

SMITH, M. J. *When I say no, I feel guilty.* New York: Bantam Books, 1975.

SNYDER, B. D., AND HARRIS, S. Treatable aspects of the dementia syndrome. *Journal of the American Geriatrics Society* 1976, 24: 179–84.

SNYDER, E. E., AND SPREITZER, E. Attitudes of the aged toward nontraditional sexual behavior. *Archives of Sexual Behavior* 1976, 5: 249–54.

SOKOLOFF, L. Cerebral circulation and metabolism in the aged. In S. Gershon and A. Raskin, eds., *Aging: Vol. 2. Genesis and treatment of psychologic disorders in the elderly.* New York: Raven Press, 1975.

SROLE, L.; LANGNER, T. S.; MICHAEL, S. T.; KIRKPATRICK, P.; OPLER, M. K.; and RENNIE, T. A. C. *Mental health in the metropolis: The midtown Manhattan study.* Rev. ed. New York: Harper & Row, 1975.

SROUR, G. M.; FINNEGAN, R. J.; AND DELCIOPPO, C. A. A new approach to recreational therapy with older chronically hospitalized patients. *Psychiatric Quarterly Supplement* 1966, 40: 10–16.

STEICHEN, E. *The family of man.* New York: Maco Magazine Corporation, 1955.

STENGEL, E. Attempted suicides. In H. L. P. Resnik, ed., *Suicidal behavior: Diagnosis and management.* Boston: Little, Brown, 1968.

STINNETT, N.; CARTER, L. M.; AND MONTGOMERY, J. E. Older persons' perceptions of their marriages. *Journal of Marriage and the Family* 1972, 34: 665–70.

STORANDT, M. Graduate education in gerontological psychology: Results of a survey. *Educational Gerontology* 1977, 2: 141–45.

STOTSKY, B. A. A systematic study of therapeutic interventions in nursing homes. *Geriatric Psychology Monographs* 1967, 76: 257–320.

STREHLER, B. L. *Time, cells and aging.* 2d ed. New York: Academic Press, 1977.

STREIB, G. F. Social stratification and aging. In R. H. Binstock and E. Shanas, eds., *Handbook of aging and the social sciences.* New York: Van Nostrand Reinhold, 1976.

STREIB, G. F., AND SCHNEIDER, C. J. *Retirement in American society: Impact and process.* Ithaca, N.Y.: Cornell University Press, 1971.

SUBCOMMITTEE ON LONG-TERM CARE, SPECIAL COMMITTEE ON AGING, U.S. SENATE. *Nursing home care in the U.S.: Failure in public policy.* Supporting Paper No. 1. Washington: Government Printing Office, 1974.

SUSSMAN, R. B., AND STEINBERG, F. The aged in public housing. Unpublished paper, 1970.

SVARSTAD, B. L. Physician-patient communication and patient conformity with medical advice. In D. Mechanic, ed., *The growth of bureaucratic medicine: An inquiry into the dynamics of patient behavior and the organization of medical care.* New York: Wiley, 1976.

SVILAND, M. A. P. Helping elderly couples become sexually liberated: Psychosocial issues. *Counseling Psychologist* 1975, 5: 41–45.

TALLAND, G. S. *Deranged memory: A psychonomic study of the amnesiac syndrome.* New York: Academic Press, 1965.

TANNA, V. Paranoid states: A selected review. *Comprehensive Psychiatry* 1974, 15: 453–70.

TAUB, H. A. Age differences in memory as a function of rate of presentation, order of report, and stimulus organization. *Journal of Gerontology* 1968, 23: 159–64.

TERRY, R. D., AND WIŚNIEWSKI, H. M. Structural and chemical changes of the aged human brain. In S. Gershon and A. Raskin, eds., *Aging: Vol. 2. Genesis and treatment of psychologic disorders in the elderly.* New York: Raven Press, 1975.

TERRY, R. D., AND WIŚNIEWSKI, H. M. Structural aspects of aging of the brain. In C. Eisdorfer and R. O. Friedel, eds., *Cognitive and emotional disturbances in the elderly.* Chicago: Year Book Medical Publishers, 1977.

THOMPSON, L. W., AND MARSH, G. Psychophysiological studies of aging. In C. Eisdorfer and M. P. Lawton, eds., *The psychology of adult development and aging.* Washington: American Psychological Association, 1973.

THOMPSON, L. W.; DAVIS, G. C.; OBRIST, W. D.; AND HEYMAN, A. Effects of hyperbaric oxygen on behavioral and physiological measures in elderly demented patients. *Journal of Gerontology* 1976, 31: 23–28.

THORESEN, C. E. *How to become an ex-smoker.* Englewood Cliffs, N.J.: Prentice-Hall, 1977.

THORESEN, C. E.; COATES, T. J.; ZARCONE, V. P.; KIRMIL-GRAY, K.; AND ROSEKIND, M. R. Treating the complaint of insomnia: Self-management perspectives. In J. M. Ferguson and C. B. Taylor, eds., *Advances in behavioral medicine.* Englewood Cliffs, N.J.: Prentice-Hall, in press.

THRONEBERRY, C.; LACHMAN, J.; AND LACHMAN, R. Age and the feeling-of-knowing phenomenon. Paper presented at the annual meetings of the Gerontological Society, San Francisco, 1977.

TIMIRAS, P. S. *Developmental physiology and aging.* New York: Macmillan, 1972.

TOBIN, J. B. Normal aging: The inevitability syndrome. In S. H. Zarit, ed., *Readings in aging and death: Contemporary perspectives.* New York: Harper & Row, 1977.

TOBIN, S. S.; HAMMERMAN, J.; AND RECTOR, V. Preferred disposition of institutionalized aged. *Gerontologist* 1972, 12: 129–33.

TOMLINSON, B. E., AND HENDERSON, G. Some quantitative findings in normal and demented old people. In R. D. Terry and S. Gershon, eds., *Neurobiology of aging*. New York: Raven Press, 1976.

TOWNSEND, C. *Old age: The last segregation*. New York: Grossman, 1971.

TROLL, L. E. The family of later life: A decade review. *Journal of Marriage and the Family* 1971, 33: 263–90.

TROLL, L. E.; MILLER, S. J.; AND ATCHLEY, R. C. *Families in later life*. Belmont, Calif.: Wadsworth, 1979.

TRUAX, C. B., AND CARKHUFF, R. R. *Toward effective counseling and psychotherapy: Training and practice*. Chicago: Aldine, 1967.

TUCKMAN, J., AND YOUNGMAN, W. F. Assessment of suicide risk in attempted suicides. In H. L. P. Resnik, ed., *Suicidal behavior: Diagnosis and management*. Boston: Little Brown, 1968.

TURNER, B. F.; TOBIN, S. S.; AND LIEBERMAN, M. A. Personality traits as predictors of institutional adaptation among the aged. *Journal of Gerontology* 1972, 27: 61–68.

UPTON, A. C. Pathobiology. In C. E. Finch and L. Hayflick, eds., *Handbook of the biology of aging*. New York: Van Nostrand Reinhold, 1977.

U.S. BUREAU OF THE CENSUS, CONSUMER INCOME. Current Population Reports, Series P-60, No. 97. Washington: Government Printing Office, 1975.

VICKERS, R. V. The therapeutic milieu and the older depressed patient. *Journal of Gerontology* 1976, 31: 314–17.

Vital statistics of the United States, 1970. Vol. 2. Mortality. Rockville, Md.: U.S. Public Health Service, 1974.

WAGNER, A., AND LERNER, J. Art therapy in the psychiatric hospital. *Journal of the American Geriatrics Society* 1968, 16: 867–73.

WALLACH, M. A., AND KOGAN, N. Aspects of judgment and decision making: Interrelationships and changes with age. *Behavioral Science* 1961, 6: 23–26.

WALSH, A. C. Prevention of senile and presenile dementia by bishydroxycoumarin (Dicumarol) therapy. *Journal of the American Geriatrics Society* 1969, 17: 477–87.

WALSH, A. C. Hypochondriasis associated with organic brain syndrome: A new approach to therapy. *Journal of the American Geriatrics Society* 1976, 9: 430–31.

WALSH, A. C., AND WALSH, B. H. Presenile dementia: Further experience with an anticoagulant psychotherapy regimen. *Journal of the American Geriatrics Society* 1974, 22: 467–72.

WALSH, D. A. Age differences in learning and memory. In D. S. Woodruff and J. E. Birren, eds., *Aging: Scientific perspectives and social issues*. New York: D. Van Nostrand, 1975.

WANG, H.-S. Organic brain syndromes. In E. W. Busse and E. Pfeiffer, eds., *Behavior and adaptation in late life*. Boston: Little, Brown, 1969.

Wax, J. Sex and the single grandparent. In S. H. Zarit, ed., *Readings in aging and death: Contemporary perspectives.* New York: Harper & Row, 1977.

Wechsler, D. A standardized memory scale for clinical use. *Journal of Psychology* 1945, *19*: 87–95.

Weinstein, E. A., and Kahn, R. L. *Denial of illness.* Springfield, Ill.: Thomas, 1955.

Weinstein, E. A.; Kahn, R. L.; and Slote, W. Withdrawal, inattention and pain asymbolia. *Archives of Neurology and Psychiatry* 1955, *74*: 235–48.

Weisman, A. *On dying and denying.* New York: Behavioral Publications, 1972.

Weiss, J. M. A. Suicide in the aged. In H. L. P. Resnik, ed., *Suicidal behavior: Diagnosis and management.* Boston: Little, Brown, 1968.

Weiss, J. M.; Glazer, H. I.; and Pohorecky, L. A. Neurotransmitters and helplessness: A chemical bridge to depression? *Psychology Today* 1974 (Dec.), pp. 59–64.

Wells, C. E., and Duncan, G. W. Danger of overreliance on computerized cranial tomography. *American Journal of Psychiatry* 1977, *134*: 811–13.

White, B. L. Child development research: An edifice without a foundation. *Merrill-Palmer Quarterly* 1969, *15*: 47–78.

Whitehead, A. *In the service of old age: The welfare of psychogeriatric patients.* Baltimore: Penguin Books, 1970.

Whitehead, T. Long-acting phenothiazines. *British Medical Journal* 1975, *2*: 502.

Wilder, C. S. *Chronic conditions and limitations of activity and mobility: United States, July 1965 to June 1967.* Vital and Health Statistics, 1971. Series 10, no. 61, Department of Health, Education, and Welfare.

Wilder, C. S. *Limitations of activity due to chronic conditions: United States, 1969 to 1970.* Vital and Health Statistics, 1973. Series 10, no. 80, Department of Health, Education, and Welfare.

Wilkie, F. L., and Eisdorfer, C. Intelligence and blood pressure in the aged. *Science* 1971, *172*: 959–62.

Wilkie, F. L., and Eisdorfer, C. Systemic disease and behavioral correlates. In L. F. Jarvik, C. Eisdorfer, and J. E. Blum, eds., *Intellectual functioning in adults: Psychological and biological influences.* New York: Springer, 1973.

Wing, J. K., and Brown, G. W. *Institutionalism and schizophrenia.* Cambridge, England: Cambridge University Press, 1970.

Witkin, H. A.; Dyk, R. B.; Faterson, H. F.; Goodenough, D. R.; and Karp, S. A. *Psychological differentiation.* New York: Wiley, 1962.

Wittels, I., and Botwinick, J. Survival in relocation. *Journal of Gerontology* 1974, *29*: 440–43.

Wolfe, L. The question of surrogates in sex therapy. In J. LoPiccolo and L. LoPiccolo, eds., *Handbook of sex therapy.* New York: Plenum, 1978.

Wolff, K. Depression and suicide in the geriatric patient. *Journal of the American Geriatrics Society* 1969, *17*: 668–72.

Wolpe, J. *Psychotherapy by reciprocal inhibition.* Stanford, Calif.: Stanford University Press, 1958.

Wood, W. G. The elderly alcoholic: Some diagnostic problems and considerations. In M. Storandt, I. C. Siegler, and M. F. Elias, eds., *The clinical psychology of aging.* New York: Plenum, 1978.

Woodruff, D. S. A physiological perspective of the psychology of aging. In D. S. Woodruff and J. E. Birren, eds., *Aging: Scientific perspectives and social issues.* New York: D. Van Nostrand, 1975.

Woodruff, D. S., and Birren, J. E. Age changes and cohort differences in personality. *Developmental Psychology* 1972, 6: 252–59.

Woods, A. M.; Harootyan, R.; and Birren, J. E. The increasing sex differences in life expectancy: Trends and implications for society. Paper presented at the meetings of the Western Psychological Association, Los Angeles, 1976.

Woods, A. M.; Birren, J. E.; and Zarit, S. H. Vertebral-basilar arterial insufficiency and behavioral deficits in the aged. Paper presented at the 86th Annual Convention of the American Psychological Association, Toronto, 1978.

Yalom, I. D. *The theory and practice of group psychotherapy.* 2d ed. New York: Basic Books, 1975.

Yalom, I. D.; Houts, P. S.; Newell, G.; and Rand, K. H. Preparation of patients for group therapy. *Archives of General Psychiatry* 1967, 17: 416–27.

Young, J. Acute psychiatric disturbances in the elderly and their treatment. *Clinical Practice* 1972, 26: 513–16.

Young, M.; Benjamin, B.; and Wallis, C. Mortality of widowers. *Lancet* 1963, 2: 454.

Zarit, S. H. Predictors of outcome among day care participants. *Long Term Care and Health Services Administration Quarterly* 1978, 1: 150–62.

Zarit, S. H., and Kahn, R. L. Impairment and adaptation in chronic disabilities. *Journal of Nervous and Mental Disease* 1974, 159: 63–72.

Zarit, S. H., and Kahn, R. L. Aging and adaptation to illness. *Journal of Gerontology* 1975, 30: 67–72.

Zarit, S. H.; Miller, N. E.; and Kahn, R. L. Brain function, intellectual impairment and education in the aged. *Journal of the American Geriatrics Society* 1978, 26: 58–67.

Zarit, S. H.; Cole, K.; Gallagher, D.; Guider, R.; and Kramer, N. Memory concerns of the aging: Cognitive and affective interventions. Paper presented at the 11th International Congress of Gerontology, Tokyo, 1978.

Zarit, S. H.; Gallagher, D.; and Kramer, N. Memory training in the community aged: Effects on depression, memory complaint and memory performance. *Educational Gerontology* 1980, 5 (in press).

Zax, M., and Cowen, E. L. *Abnormal psychology: Changing conceptions.* 2d ed. New York: Holt, Rinehart and Winston, 1976.

Zelinski, E.; Walsh, D.; and Thompson, L. Level of information processing, effects of electrodermal responsivity and recall in the aged. Paper presented at Western Psychological Association, Los Angeles, April, 1976.

Zimberg, S. The elderly alcoholic. *Gerontologist* 1975, *14*: 221–24.

Zung, W. W. K. Depression in the normal aged. *Psychosomatics* 1967, *8*: 287–92.

Zung, W. W. K., and Green, R. L. Detection of affective disorders in the aged. In C. Eisdorfer and W. E. Fann, eds., *Psychopharmacology and aging*. New York: Plenum, 1972.

Indexes

Name Index

445

Subject Index

451